SOUTHERN RELIGION *and* CHRISTIAN DIVERSITY *in the* TWENTIETH CENTURY

SOUTHERN RELIGION *and* CHRISTIAN DIVERSITY *in the* TWENTIETH CENTURY

WAYNE FLYNT

Foreword by Charles A. Israel and John M. Giggie

PUBLISHED IN COOPERATION WITH THE
FRANCES S. SUMMERSELL CENTER FOR THE STUDY OF THE SOUTH

THE UNIVERSITY OF ALABAMA PRESS
Tuscaloosa

The University of Alabama Press
Tuscaloosa, Alabama 35487-0380
uapress.ua.edu

Hardcover edition published 2016
Paperback edition published 2021.
eBook edition published 2016.

Typeface: Garamond

Cover design: Todd Lape/Lape Designs

Paperback ISBN: 978-0-8173-6022-1

A previous edition of this book has been cataloged by the Library of Congress.
ISBN: 978-0-8173-1908-3 (cloth)
E-ISBN: 978-0-8173-8971-0

To Southern Believers
(even those who are not certain what to believe
and others who seem to know everything)

Contents

Foreword

Wayne Flynt is one of the original architects of the field of southern religious history. This was not his first or only field of interest: he began as a historian of southern politics and later focused on poverty and what he called the "forgotten people," or the South's poor whites. Over a career spanning five decades, he has authored or edited twelve books, published nearly thirty historical journal articles, written numerous newspaper and opinion pieces, and spoken to hundreds of audiences across multiple continents. Although he retired from Auburn University in 2005 as Distinguished University Professor Emeritus, he continues to publish and lecture on topics of enduring importance at an impressive pace. Dubbed the "conscience of Alabama" by local wags, Flynt still appears frequently in the state's editorial pages and public forums promoting improvements to education, more equitable taxation, a fair and balanced history of the South, and a clear-eyed view of what must be done to achieve a more democratic future.

While he was not present at the formal creation of the field of southern religious history—he offers that honor to Sam Hill and the 1966 publication of *Southern Churches in Crisis*—Flynt has been among its most important contributors. The best of his essays in southern religion are collected here along with some more recent pieces and talks; arranged chronologically, they allow us to glimpse the development of Flynt's scholarship and the unfolding of the field itself. Flynt has added introductions to each article, providing new insights even to readers who have previously read the pieces. Viewing the collection as a whole, one gains an appreciation for Flynt's historical skill, moral force, and impact on our understanding of southern religion. A few characteristics of the scholarship also jump out. First, these are the works of an author deeply immersed in the primary sources of history. Be they oral histories from church members in Leeds, Alabama; boxes of letters from rural southern ministers to President Franklin D. Roosevelt; or runs of denominational newspapers, these artifacts allow Flynt to ground his arguments in the lives of real people. Second, the works chronicle the making of a southern religious historian. Flynt came to love this field not through graduate school seminars on the subject (there were none when he was in school!) but through self-discovery, a voracious appetite for reading and writing in the field, and the distinctive arc of his professional life. As both a historian and Baptist minister committed to social and racial justice, he experienced the complexities of sacred life in the South every day. Because he has recently detailed much of his personal history in a book of memoirs—*Keeping the Faith: Ordinary People, Extraordinary Lives*—Flynt is sparing in the autobiographical details in this volume. Still, reading his introduction and the two volumes in tandem provides even greater depth of understanding and appreciation of just what he accomplished as a scholar and citizen. Through his writings, Flynt challenged smooth generalizations about southern religion and replaced them with complicated stories of southerners rich and poor, white and black for whom religion united or divided, depending on the issue and time period. For example, while other scholars might begrudgingly admit the existence of "clerical radicals" existing "on the very fringes of southern Protestantism," Flynt made them the very center of his investigations.[1] As a result, we come to see that if the religion of white southerners in general has been conservative, conversion focused, and not prone to challenging the social order, it was that way only in the face of the religious individuals and groups that Flynt demonstrates were quite clearly pushing in other directions. And this is the importance of Flynt's work: he both broadens popular understandings of the varieties of southern religious experience and forces scholars to grasp the power of white evangelical conservatism in maintaining a powerful hold upon the identity of southern religion even in the face of such diversity.

In addition to his publications, Flynt aided in the flowering of the field through his skillful mentoring of numerous students, first at Samford University and then at Auburn, and by coediting the Religion and American Culture book series for the University of Alabama Press. Along with David Edwin Harrell and Edith Blumhofer, he helped identify, improve, and publicize an impressive array of important books on the American religious experience, many of which share a particular affinity for southern religious topics. As the new editors of the series, we feel fortunate for the firm foundation bequeathed to us by our senior colleagues. And as historians working in southern religion, we are especially thankful for the vastly richer landscape of the field made possible in a large part by the scholarship of Wayne Flynt.

Charles A. Israel	John M. Giggie
Auburn University	University of Alabama

Preface

Book titles can be tricky business. Sometimes the qualifiers can be as complicated as the book. In the case of *Southern Religion and Christian Diversity in the Twentieth Century*, I am aware that a volume fully faithful to the title would be longer than the Bible Christians venerate and just as open to misinterpretation.

So let me note briefly what the book is NOT about: the African American church; feminism; pentecostalism; Orthodox Christianity; Judaism or Islam; colorful but marginal sects, cults, and charismatic personalities; or a systemic, linear treatment of any single denomination or church. Although I mention all of these, they are treated elsewhere in volumes superior to mine.

Rather, I have written vignettes mainly about white evangelical and main line denominations, churches, and believers between 1900 and 2015—how they disagreed, debated, divided, and changed. To explain how the essays—written across half a century beginning in 1969—fit into the larger story, I have written a long introduction to the book followed by a short preface for each essay describing issues on my mind at the time.

Not only the title but also the organization and transitions may trouble readers. Once upon a time as a young man, I imagined the gigantic mountain that is southern religion and vowed to conquer it. My last work, I promised myself, would be a magnum opus based on a lifetime of research augmented by the collective wisdom of my many excellent doctoral students who pitched base camps on the same high slopes. Alas, the mountain was too high and life too short.

As a compromise, I fall back on a less lofty ambition: to reprise the best of more than thirty essays, book chapters, and lectures within this anthology. Although I have grouped these pieces roughly according to the chronology in which I wrote them careful readers will detect changes in my writing style, a growing confidence in my central thesis of religious diversity embedded within seemingly impervious religious orthodoxy, movement away from my self-absorption with Baptists, evolving battles within churches and denominations across the century—I have occasionally violated that pattern for the sake of grouping related themes or regions of the South.

The dedication page puzzled me as much as the title and format. My wife,

Dartie, shared this long journey with me and occupies the center of my life. My sons, David and Sean, gave too much of their father's time to this obsession. My mother and father made the first choices that carried me into the Kingdom of God. A series of Baptist pastors and religion professors at Samford University—Charles R. Bell Jr., B. Locke Davis, Otis Brooks, W. Albert Smith, Fred Maxey, J. W. Lester, John Jeffers, W. T. Edwards, Mabry Lunceford, and Vernon Davidson—ranging theologically from fundamentalist to liberal and politically from conservative Republican to Socialist and perhaps even Communist, opened my mind to more options within southern religion than I had dreamed of as a teenage ministerial student.

Perhaps it makes sense, then, to dedicate this volume simply to southern believers in the Book, the Word, and the Way, however differently they interpret what all those words mean.

SOUTHERN RELIGION *and* CHRISTIAN DIVERSITY *in the* TWENTIETH CENTURY

Introduction
Southern Religion and Christian Diversity, 1890–2015

Within three years of each other in 2005 and 2008, two Christian leaders in Jefferson County, Alabama, died. Neither was Baptist, Methodist, Presbyterian, Episcopalian, or Catholic. Neither fit popular or scholarly stereotypes about southern evangelicals. Both emerged from the shadowy margins of class, gender, theology, and "denomination," if their early ministries could even be called that. They would be described by historians of American religion as "outsiders" and "fundamentalist-pentecostals." That both became subjects of extensive stories in the state's largest newspaper suggests not only their wide popular following but also how much southern religion has changed since I began writing about it five decades ago. The stories also demonstrated how astute journalists had become in covering complex religious landscapes.

John Lyles grew up poor during the 1920s in a North Carolina farm family of 14. They were not churchgoers, so it was not until he turned 18 that Lyles prayed for God to save his soul. Shortly thereafter, he departed home to proclaim the Gospel.

Although unable to read or write, Lyles memorized long passages of Scripture. He preached his first sermons in an independent church that he had established but soon connected it to the Church of God of Prophecy in which he ultimately rose to the rank of bishop. The six-foot three-inch, 200-pound preacher had a booming voice that could stir an entire community when he arrived in their midst with an old-fashioned canvas revival tent. Crowds overflowed the seats and spilled into adjacent parking lots. After surviving years of itinerancy, the family finally settled in the Birmingham industrial suburb of Bessemer in 1955.

Embarrassed by his lack of formal education, Lyles studied with a tutor during the 1970s but never mastered much more than basic literacy. Transforming weakness into strength, he relied on his memorization of Bible verses and a simple message to reach ordinary people like himself. He trusted "the power of the Holy Spirit" in order to handle coals from a heated potbelly stove that did not burn his hands, and he faced down an intruder armed with a shotgun who threatened to kill him during a revival. In old age he bequeathed his ministry to his preacher daughter-in-law, Judy Lyles, then drifted into a fog of dementia until even the memory of Scripture eluded him.[1]

Three years later the same newspaper described in an obituary the remarkable life of Rev. Dr. Ruby Kile, who was born in 1929 in Herbine, Arkansas. Kile claimed a variety of miraculous personal healings: of leukemia during the 1960s and breast cancer—although the latter was aided by chemotherapy—in the 1990s.

Ordained in the Full Gospel Fellowship of Churches and Ministries International in 1969, Kile worked as a traveling evangelist for three years before pastoring her first church in Shreveport, Louisiana. She arrived in Jefferson County in Alabama in 1972 to become pastor of the struggling Powderly Faith Deliverance center, which had declined to eight white worshipers. A former coal mining town near Bessemer hard hit by economic change, Powderly had little to offer whites fleeing racial integration.

A series of revival services in 1973 and a growing reputation as a woman anointed by God to work miracles attracted both the faithful and curious to Kile's church. She assumed control of a local Pentecostal healing radio program that had begun in 1929 and later added a cable television ministry. As Kile's reputation spread and her media presence expanded, standing-room-only crowds numbering 500 or more crowded into the small church. By the time she opened a new sanctuary in 1984 and renamed the church Faith Temple, her 700 member congregation was 80 percent black and 20 percent white. Kile's emphasis on miracles and healing transcended racial boundaries in her impoverished neighborhood. She adopted the simple motto "All God's people are welcome." One speaker at her funeral explained: "Dr. Kile had a true love for God's people of every color. She always said, 'God had a rainbow.' She stood for Holiness and Godly character and integrity." Longtime church member Joyce Dew added: "I don't think that people realize Pastor Kile brought integration to this area against threats from the Ku Klux Klan and others. She really was a pioneer for all women pastors. Her greatest desire was that more churches would become integrated."[2] Those were not the usual encomiums extended to white female pastors in Jefferson County during the 1970s.

Rev. Kile became Dr. Kile when the African American Pentecostal Bible College of Tuskegee awarded her a Doctor of Divinity degree in 1994. The more prestigious black AME church presented her its Outstanding Humanitarian Award in 1992. A half-decade later, her own Full Gospel Fellowship of Churches and Ministries International awarded Kile its 25-year Service Certificate. Although none of these awards merited newspaper mention at the time, Kile's congregation in the mid-1970s was probably the most integrated in the county—and that in a Ku Klux Klan stronghold. After 35 years as pastor of Faith Temple, she became presiding bishop of Faith Temple Church of Deliverance in nearby Alabaster, pastored by a male, and of Mission with a Vision in Columbiana, started by a female.

Missing from the obituary was any reference to Kile's formal education or to the name of her husband, despite a list of parents, siblings, children, grandchildren, and even nieces. Perhaps neither mattered much in her life.

Where such people—white and black, rich and poor, male and female—fit in the tapestry of southern religion is a matter of contention. That southern religion had always been a more complex landscape than academics once believed now seems axiomatic. As I noted in 1977, the 1906 Census of "Religious Bodies" recorded matter-of-factly that 29 percent of Birmingham's church members were Roman Catholic, followed by 15 percent National (Black) Baptists, 14 percent Methodist Episcopal Church (white southern Methodists), and 7.5 percent Southern Baptists in a distant 5th place.[3]

My initial interest in religion predated my formal study of history. As for so many other religious historians of my generation, intrigue about "ultimate reality" first appeared in personal religious experience, not in academic study or theological speculation. I can trace such interest mainly to my teenage years at Parker Memorial Baptist Church in Anniston, Alabama. That congregation always seemed more complicated than the generalizations I later read in scholarly accounts of what Southern Baptists believed and how they acted. Perhaps we were merely outliers, I initially concluded. But as I broadened my horizons at a provincial Baptist college in Birmingham, I encountered more and more anomalies. If scholarly stereotypes did not fit me, how many other southern evangelicals did the standard narrative omit? More importantly, every subtopic of southern history that I engaged during a half century of research and writing—political economy; poverty; education; social institutions; race relations; southern fiction, art, and music—seemed in some way to draw their rock-hard certainty, fierce energy, loud proclamation, and apocalyptic urgency from religion.

When as a boy I first began seriously reading, studying, even memorizing, portions of the Bible, I became a biblicist without understanding the concept. The intricacies of theological debate about the Book—inerrancy, plenary inspiration, fundamentalism, neo-orthodoxy, liberalism—were entirely lost on me. None of my pastors mentioned such concepts. I suppose they were servant men too busy proclaiming the Gospel and tending their flocks.

As time passed, the Bible's major effect was severing me from the social and racial views of my region, although that was a long time coming. Southern Baptist preacher, seminary professor, and ethicist T. B. Maston sped me on my way with his books about religion, race, and region. Gradually, the Bible made me an alien in my own land. As I slowly connected racism to its systemic causes—poverty, disfranchisement, unjust tax policy, horrifying inequities in education and health—the Bible transformed me into what many fellow white southerners considered a dangerous radical. I never considered myself anything other than an evangelical Christian—a follower of Christ, who was deeply respectful of the Bible and who slowly awakened to the social and economic implications of the path I had decided to follow.

Long discussions (sometimes degenerating into heated debates) with evangelicals who fiercely disagreed with me administered a jolt to my maturing consciousness. How could we all read the same Book and follow the same Lord yet reach such different conclusions? In my adolescence, I decided either they could not be serious Bible students or, less charitably, that they must be really blind and dumb. As I grew older and, I hope, wiser, another thought occurred to me: equally devout and thoughtful Christians could disagree about elemental doctrines, beliefs, and ethics, especially when they violated long-accepted social and political norms. Not only did my assumptions about Baptist homogeneity change (to be blown apart entirely by the Southern Baptist conservative/moderate conflict of the 1980s and 1990s), but also did my understanding of Baptist history, which both sides laid claim to during the so-called "conservative resurgence."

One positive consequence of my dawning awareness about the complexity of Baptist history came in the form of intellectual hibernation in archives. I became increasingly frustrated that both denominational right and scholarly left wrote history as if theological, political, and social consensus prevailed and with far too little attention to original sources. Both sides could find evidence to support their arguments. But the debates tended to follow parallel rather than intersecting ideological trajectories except on one issue: fundamentalist Baptists were quite content for scholars to depict their history as largely seamless, overwhelmingly conservative, and mostly uninterrupted by contending schools of thought.

My sources suggested a different interpretation. Class, race (southern African Americans tended to be the most theologically conservative evangelicals and the most politically/economically liberal voters by the 1970s), gender, education, urban-rural residence, the era under discussion—all affected narratives of homogeneity/heterogeneity.

At first I mainly sought in archives validation for my own rambling racial heresies. Content in time that I had not fallen far from the theological tree that begat me, I began to extrapolate a wider story of religious dissent. Although I never concluded that the past conformed to my ideological meanderings, I did become convinced that there were lots more people who thought and wrote and preached like me than either the religious right or the scholarly left understood. Even confining myself to the elite short list of Baptist dissenters— Charles R. Bell, Will Campbell, Jimmy Carter, W. O. Carver, Bill Clinton, Martin Luther King Jr., T. B. Maston, and Fred Shuttlesworth, among an endless genealogy of courageous local black and white pastors during the 1950s and 1960s—the cast of characters grew longer by the day. Gradually my personal religious memoir turned into a scholarly disquisition on southern religious diversity. As I branched from theology into the study of political and labor reform movements, poverty, class, race, gender, anthropology, and folk culture, I felt as if I had wandered into the largest and finest buffet without any gastronomical restraint whatsoever. Sometimes an intellectual tummy ache resulted.

My first glimpse of what stood before me occurred in the late 1950s at Howard College (now Samford University). At the time, denominationalism swept all before it like a giant religious tsunami, which suited me fine. As a teenage ministerial student in that somnolent decade, triumphalist Baptist is what I was and what I wanted to know more about. Ironically, decades later I would help dismantle what I had once been and believed in a contribution to an anthology on congregationism whose theme was the ebb tide of denominationalism in America. That essay also was an object lesson in how the consoling certainties of adolescence can become the disturbing paradoxes of middle age.

When I ponder my pilgrimage from childhood into the twenty-first century, I am amazed at how much more my generation valued spirituality (at least as measured by personal prayer, Bible reading and "witnessing," although not by contemplation/meditation, which seemed vaguely "papist") than religious symbols and icons. Buttressed by our overwhelming domination of southern culture, Baptists had little need for external fortifications. Attention to symbols and icons beyond such obvious things as church steeples and baptism by total immersion seemed unnecessary when we never met an atheist or a Muslim and infrequently a Jew.

The 1960s changed that. Persuaded that Christianity was being hijacked everywhere and was actively under siege outside the South, evangelicals selected symbols and icons every bit as sacred as medieval Catholic relics. Abortion (which did not appear as a topic in most Baptist newspapers until the 1960s and 1970s) suddenly assumed biblical proportions as a cardinal sin, pushing aside greed (which had never seemed a culturally convenient moral deviation in a materialistic society anyway). Ostentatious display of the American flag in churches (previously confined to summer Vacation Bible School) reminded the faithful that just as the King James version was the authoritative translation of the Bible, southern evangelicalism was the authentic expression of patriotism.

Protecting this endangered species of faith required unprecedented governmental action. Whereas early Baptists had depicted government as the major threat to religious liberty, in an increasingly pluralistic world of religious belief and secularism, they turned to government (the government closest to them, of course, and the one most completely under their control) to maintain traditional verities, whether ancient or of recent vintage. Family values, prayer in schools, the Ten Commandments in public spaces, political candidates proclaiming fidelity to some local evangelical congregation, and state tuition credits to children attending private Christian academies became routine aspects of southern political life. In 2014 the veto-proof and proudly evangelical Republican majority in the Alabama legislature passed a bill requiring public schools to teach students about Christian and Jewish holidays but rejected an attempt by the Black caucus to include the African American celebration of Kwanzaa in the legislation. The fact that federal courts routinely declared such laws unconstitutional unless they included all religions simply made defiance all the more appealing to conservative evangelical voters. Belief in separation of church and state, once a centerpiece of Baptist theology, came to be viewed as apostasy practiced by those deemed denominationally impure.

In the Deep South, few venues escaped the symbolic tidal wave of regional civil religion—not even the South's real object of ultimate concern: college football. On November 13, 2010, I found myself squeezed into a tiny space in Auburn University's Jordan-Hare Stadium among 87,000 boisterous fans gathered to watch the Southeastern Conference's western division championship game. The pageantry began with the introduction of Vincent "Bo" Jackson in the 25th anniversary of his Heisman Trophy year. Following that, a golden eagle soared from the stadium's upper concourse high above our heads and descended menacingly on a target at midfield. Next, the Auburn band sprinted to midfield and surrounded a huge US shield. The public address announcer then solemnly intoned, "Please stand, take off your hat, put your hand over your heart, and sing with the band 'God Bless America.'" The crowd was much more respectful of "God Bless America" than of the national anthem that followed. Anxious to get on with the smash mouth gladiatorial combat on the field, many spectators interrupted the last word of the "Star-Spangled Banner" with shouts of "War Eagle!"

I consider myself as patriotic—and as evangelical a Christian—as the next guy. But this blurred religious and (what I consider to be) idolatrous American exceptionalism rankled me.

More to the point, when I attend football games at Florida State University, my alma mater only four hours driving time down the road from where I live, there are no such quasi-religious rituals. Alabama is ranked in the top three most religious states by Gallup polling (based on residents' claims to be "very religious" and frequency of church attendance), and 9 of the top 10 such states are in the South or border South (only Utah being an outlier). Florida is not among them. It is—along with Virginia, which also missed the cut—the most ethnically diverse, religiously pluralistic, and politically contested southern state.

My decision not to take off my Auburn cap or place my hand over my heart while singing "God Bless America" derived from many sources. Alabama elementary schoolteachers taught me that those symbols of respect belonged exclusively to our national anthem. Perhaps deeper embedded in my consciousness was an oral history I had conducted with Charles Bell, former pastor of the Baptist church in Anniston where I grew up. He resigned rather than display the American flag beside his pulpit in June 1944 to celebrate not only the allied invasion of Europe but also what he considered to be the ghastly slaughter of lives about to occur that day.

As I surveyed the crowd in Jordan-Hare during this ritual that took place after the attack on the World Trade Center in 2001, I noted only a handful of people whose heads remained covered and whose hands hung by their sides. That probably resulted from forgetfulness, inattention, youthful obstinacy, or a "hell-of-a-good fellow" refusal to follow instructions, rather than from religious conviction. But then, who knows—the central thesis of this book is that southern religion is more complicated than it seems. Perhaps the rest of those attendees whose heads remained covered and arms folded were Jehovah's Witnesses.

One interpretation of the centrality of religious symbols and icons is that as the substance of religion recedes, symbols that replace it gain added significance. Southern religion (like all religions, I believe) carefully selects what it venerates and what it opposes. As religious historians have long emphasized, white southern evangelicals have historically extolled bibical belief and personal ethics, not racial justice and social ethics.

In my youth, for instance, observance of blue laws limited Sunday activities. Strictures against dancing, alcohol, and gambling filled teenage Sunday school literature. Admonitions against necking and petting, not to mention premarital sex, rang in our ears at summer youth retreats. Curiously, abortion and homosexuality were not mentioned. Neither were materialism, racism, sexism, capital punishment, war, poverty, regressive and unjust tax systems, payday loan businesses, barbaric prison conditions, or torture of foreign combatants by Americans.

Some historians noted these contradictions, but most generally refused to go beyond obligatory and perfunctory treatment of New England's Puritan oligarchy, a tip of the hat to denominationalism, and limited attention to separation of church and state. They reserved religion for denominational historians who taught in divinity schools.

The reasons for this neglect vary. Some historians no doubt recoiled from religious triumphalism (depictions of America as "the New Jerusalem," the "New Zion," or "the city set on a hill," definitions of American imperialism as our "manifest destiny" ordained by God). Others remembered unfavorably their strict and narrow religious upbringing. European-style skepticism also infiltrated universities along with the seminar system, reliance on primary documents, and "higher criticism" of the Bible. From Charles A. Beard and V. L. Parrington to Richard Hofstadter, Arthur M. Schlesinger Jr., and C. Vann Woodward, many of the nation's "progressive historians" dismissed Calvinist and conservative religion as opiate, palliative, barrier, or burden, as source of superstition, emotionalism, anti-intellectualism, racism, sexism, and political reaction. Perhaps they believed or even hoped that in a generation or two no one would notice their omissions or care.

That this should have happened on the two coasts or in elite universities is not surprising. As colleges once founded to educate ministers (Harvard, begun in 1636, adopted the motto "*Veritas Christo et Ecclesiae*"—"Truth for Christ and the Church"—before changing it in 1843 to simply "Veritas" or "Truth") turned secular, their faculties occasionally opposed even the presence of a religion department. Evolutionary psychologist Steven Pinker spoke for many faculty, arguing that the primary goal of a Harvard education was the pursuit of truth through rational inquiry, which was antithetical to religion.[4]

In the South, elite private universities—such as Duke, Emory, and Wake Forest—employed historians of religion in their divinity schools. Vanderbilt also had an influential mentor of doctoral students in its history department. But Vanderbilt was the exception.

This inattention seeped into the nascent history profession in the South. From the establishment of the Southern Historical Association (SHA) in November 1934, to January 2014, only two SHA presidential addresses focused on religion. Walter B. Posey's November 1958 address in Nashville derived from the older although venerable denominational histories of the early twentieth century. Posey, a native Tennessean and graduate of two prominent religiously founded institutions—the University of Chicago and Vanderbilt—chaired the History Department of Agnes Scott College and taught church history at Emory. He possessed superb credentials for his paper on "The Protestant Episcopal Church: An American Adaptation," having already authored a trilogy of excellent books on Methodists, Presbyterians, and Baptists in the lower Mississippi Valley and Old Southwest.[5]

My SHA presidential address in Memphis nearly a half century later ("Religion for the Blues: Evangelicalism, Poor Whites, and the Great Depression") differed markedly from Posey's. I focused on class, not denomination, limited my scope to a single tumultuous decade, wrote about religion bottom up rather than top down, and derived perspectives more from folkways, anthropology, psychology, and sociology than from theology, ecclesiastical structures, and denominational hierarchies.[6]

That so central a theme as religion should have attracted so little attention from SHA presidents between 1934 and 2014 resulted from many factors, among them the growing secularization of academic culture; historical disinterest in America's religious past; and rejection of southern religious excesses, which many intellectuals attributed to evangelicalism.

One might assume that a generation of southern historians writing about its region in 1935 would have devoted more attention to religion than a secular generation three quarters of a century later. If so, one would be wrong. The first four issues of the *Journal of Southern History* (JSH) contained only one article about religion of the 17 published within and only one book among 64 titles reviewed (which, critiqued Posey's history of Methodism in the Old Southwest).

Occasionally during the 1970s and 1980s I read a book by a southern historian with a background similar to mine who addressed the complexity that I was discovering. Walter B. Shurden penned a provocative book for general readers about Southern Baptist theological differences titled *Not A Silent People: Controversies That Have Shaped Southern Baptists* (1972). John Lee Eighmy applied complexity to the social order in *Churches in Cultural Captivity: A History of the Social Attitudes of Southern Baptists* (1972). John Patrick McDowell even used the controversial "Social Gospel" words in his study of *The Social Gospel in the South: The Woman's Home Mission Movement in the Methodist Episcopal Church, South, 1886–1939* (1982).

As I read each of these books, I was surprised to learn that other historians whose careers ran parallel to mine were discovering much the same thing I was, a fierce battle about the nature of God and the church. I was not, as I imagined, the only historical climber bent on hoisting the first banner on some remote historigraphical mountaintop.

As undergraduate interest in religion increased at secular universities, so did serious scholarship. Topics moved beyond conventional denominational studies as young scholars who often claimed no personal experience with evangelicalism or even religion in general wrote about the subject from far-flung outposts in elite Northeastern or Pacific Coast—or even European—universities. Their scholarship filled the JSH with perceptive research which eventuated in monographs discussed in the book review section. Although as late as November 1964, only one book of the 23 reviewed focused on religion, by 2009 nearly 10 percent of the 76 book titles reviewed dealt with the subject (from familiar topics such as the Episcopal Church in Virginia and North Carolina to studies of Southern Holiness and pentecostal people to gender/racial analysis of rural southern women belonging to the Church of God in Christ). In 2013, the JSH reviewed 23 books about southern religion, 7.5 percent of the total. Of 18 topical categories listed in "Southern History in Periodicals" for 2012, "religion" ranked 5th, ahead of "African Americans," "Military and Naval," "Politics and Government," and "Social, Cultural, and Intellectual." Articles in new journals such as *Southern Cultures* added to this production.

As homogenous denominations fractured into diverse ethnic and racial congregations, old approaches to the study of religion became obsolete. Attention shifted from bishops, ministers, elders, and deacons to ordinary lay people, including women. We also learned from the rise of the religious right that evangelicals were by no means as otherworldly as secular Americans had once believed and now hoped for. Southern white evangelicals threatened to split the Republican Party and became a disruptive force not only in denominational life but also in education and politics. Church disputes often arose from culture war issues, such as homosexuality and abortion, that did not even appear on the radar in the 1950s. It turned out that southern religious conservatism also traveled well, gaining footholds in places across America by way of Jerry Falwell and Pat Robertson, as well as their acolytes. Some cleavage from times past remained—biblical inerrancy, creationism, racism, sexism—but I am not convinced they controlled the emerging conservative religious agenda.

During these decades, other changes also occurred. Historians punctured the narrative of consensus in America and paved the way for a more complex understanding of southern religious history, one that contained countercultural trends, discontinuity, and radicalism, as well as discontented black people, Hispanics, and women. The Baptist-Methodist hegemony of earlier times as well as the lifelong loyalty of believers to the denomination into which they were born collapsed in some southern states and weakened in all. Never had it been clearer that although black and white southerners claimed common denominational titles and conservative theology they shared little else. How could we assume religious homogeneity when the South manifested few other kinds of uniformity?

In this book, I do not deny the hubris common to most scholars. In addition to having tried for 40 years to convince 6,000 students of the correctness of my historical views, I wrote hundreds of opinion columns in newspapers as well as essays for popular magazines and denominational journals. Each contained a viewpoint. I spoke about southern religion in churches, on college and university campuses (at megaliths like Baylor University as well as at Lee College, a Church of God school in Cleveland, Tennessee), and at other venues around the world (Queens University Belfast; International Baptist Theological Seminary, Prague; and Hong Kong Baptist University).

As I reread years of personal correspondence, I recalled how often and vigorously I had engaged issues included in this book. I tried desperately to keep one foot in the Southern Baptist Convention (SBC) while planting the other solidly in the academy. I chaired both the Alabama and Southern Baptist Historical Commissions. Within the SBC, I lent my endorsement to Women in Ministry, which supported female ordination as deacons and ministers.

I also sought out bivocational, fundamentalist, and conservative pastors for oral histories and inclusion in my book about Alabama Baptists. It was in that endeavor that I met Rev. J. W. Lester, who came from a tenant farm family. He had paid his way through conservative Moody Bible Institute during the 1930s by working shifts in an auto factory. He and I struck up a warm friendship, although we did not share a common theology. His amazing sense of community, lifelong commitment to rural churches, and cooperative work with Auburn University county agents on behalf of small farmers won my respect.

By this time I was confident enough in my findings to both encourage others to study southern religion and to critique my friends' views of the subject. As coeditor with Ed Harrell and Edith Blumhofer of a series on Religion in American Culture for the University of Alabama Press, I spent time chasing manuscripts from promising young scholars, such as Andrew Manis, Barry Hankins, Keith Harper, and J. Lawrence Brasher (whose Alabama grandfather had been a major participant in the Methodist Holiness movement).

More assertive by the late 1970s and 1980s, I began to insist that colleagues include a broader, richer, and more complex rendering of southern history than in the past, with religion in its proper place. When I read Dewey Grantham's masterful manuscript about southern progressivism ("Southern Progressivism: The Reconciliation of Progress and Tradition") for the University of Tennessee Press in 1981, I urged him to restructure the work by combining anecdotal strands about religion and reform into an interpretive central thesis, which he did with considerable skill.[7]

When friends David R. Goldfield and Paul Escott asked for suggestions for their book *Major Problems in the History of the American South*, I responded, "I certainly hope you will strive for balance. Often religion receives brief attention as does folk culture. And, of course, I offer a special plea for plain/poor whites. It is time historians dealt seriously with pentecostals, holy rollers, mill workers, coal miners, etc., and not just as helpless victims of a callous industrial process." I particularly suggested they read Ed Harrell's books.[8]

In 1979 the National Endowment for the Humanities sent me a proposal to evaluate, which concerned rural people organizing for change. I criticized the author's absence of any mention of religion, noting that it is "one of the most significant aspects of rural organization." I mentioned the central role that religion had played in the Populist, Country Life, and Southern Tenant Farmers' Union movements.[9]

After getting to know lots of J. W. Lesters and mining archives sufficiently well to realize that what I was finding deviated from the prevailing narrative about southern religion, I began to correspond with established scholars in the field, sharing insights and offering hypotheses. They were uniformly kind and helpful to a novice.

In 1972 I wrote to Donald G. Mathews at the University of North Carolina about my determination to analyze the religious life of people at the bottom of society rather than its leaders. Mathews liked the idea and thought that it might "provide a new perspective on not only the past but also the present." "I suspect," he added presciently, that "the first barrier to breach is the prejudice of historians who think all study of groups who identify themselves in religious terms is 'church history,'" and therefore reserved for divinity school faculties.[10]

When Martin Marty, one of the nation's premier religious historians, visited Auburn in 1978 to participate in a conference, we exchanged ideas. I found him insightful and also quite interested in what I was doing: "We must stay in touch," he wrote, "since we share so many common interests."[11] As a result, a decade later I became involved with the University of Chicago's Institute for the Advanced Study of Religion's "Congregational History Project."

Sam Hill—longtime chair of the Religion Department at the University of Florida and one of my dearest friends despite our interpretive differences—agreed to write a letter on my behalf when I applied for the chairmanship of Auburn's history department. Characteristically generous in his praise, he thanked me for helping him understand how "diverse, unpredictable, and rich the southern religious tradition is."[12]

I relished additional contact with Ed Harrell, my Auburn University colleague from the early 1990s until our joint retirement in 2005. His expertise in restoration and Pentecostal religious traditions expanded my vistas exponentially. So did Chuck Lippy's American Religion Colloquium, which met annually in a southern city to discuss the works of religion and history faculty as well as doctoral students from regional universities. All of these scholars challenged me, changing some of my ideas and confirming others.

Ironically, I believe I influenced my profession more than I did my denomination (which I regretfully left a quarter century ago, although I found a warm home in the newly formed Cooperative Baptist Fellowship). I conceded to friends and critics such as Sam Hill, John Boles, and Ed Harrell their conclusions about the power and endurance of the tough core of white, conservative evangelicalism. Some of them, in turn, agreed that perhaps there were more outliers within this seemingly homogeneous mass than they had realized.

Over the decades we sparred, argued, thrust, parried, extrapolated, analyzed, explained, refined, and rebutted, perhaps appearing to others like so many Greek sophists who had long ago lost the point of the argument but soldiered on anyway.

Together, I believe we pushed the boundaries of debate about southern religion in important new directions, and in time so did our doctoral students. They constitute part of the best and largest generation of scholars ever to engage southern religion, and they bring unprecedented diversity, sophistication, and skill to the subject. Perhaps the way we understood southern religion in 1950 compared with the way we understand it now changed too slowly to be called a revolution. But it certainly came close.

The confluence of my interest in religion and local history found one expression in university outreach. For all the joy of discussing the subject with undergraduate and graduate students, I found special delight in venturing off campus to small cities and towns across Alabama to talk with older, intellectually curious audiences.

A team of Auburn University faculty teaching a variety of subjects formed local committees who gave us feedback about what they wanted to talk about. Predictably, religion always ranked high. In fact, our sessions in synagogues and African American churches often constituted the first time white Protestants had been inside such buildings or experienced different religious folkways. So, some were astounded one evening when a female African American colleague who had been raised in a black Alabama Baptist congregation chose not to walk to the high pulpit in such a church as male speakers before her had done. She explained that she knew the congregation did not consider that "a woman's place." To us and to our audiences, a sense of community was inseparable from a sense of sacred identity and respect for every person in the Kingdom of God. Even some Auburn faculty learned a lesson that evening.

During 1983, our initial year of Alabama history and heritage festivals, I tried to capture the complexity of Alabama's religious culture by referencing a specific person and place. Drawing from my life, augmented by months of archival research and hours of oral histories, I told a story common to most southerners: where I came from, how I arrived there, and the central role religion played in my journey.

Chapter 1
Growing Up Baptist in Anniston, Alabama
The Legacy of the Reverend Charles R. Bell Jr.

Parker Memorial Baptist Church does not even look like a Baptist church. There are no Corinthian columns, red bricks, or broad porticoes. Dominating the important corner of Twelfth and Quintard in Anniston, Alabama, the church rises in majestic glory, a Victorian tribute to God's presence in a small southern industrial town. It was constructed in 1890–1891 of sandstone, now darkened by age, and is dominated by a bell tower, presently to become a roost for pigeons and a peril to worshipers.

Even the church's name seemed unbaptistic. Whoever heard of a Baptist church named in memory of a person? Calvary or Shiloh Baptist, or even some harmless numerical designation such as First or Second Baptist seemed entirely biblical (after all, there is a 1st and 2nd Samuel, 1st and 2nd Chronicles, and even 1st, 2nd, and 3rd John); but churches named for people seemed vaguely idolatrous or perhaps even papist.

When my family moved to Anniston in 1956, leaving an exuberant young congregation in Dothan, I was not about to exchange Calvary Baptist for Parker Memorial, the austere concrete block church with folding chairs for the somber beauty and padded pews of Parker's sanctuary. Calvary seemed the proper incubator for Baptist ministerial students; Parker the kind of place where they perished.

My parents, who received all these impressions with mature patience and some trepidation over what kind of religious home I might select for us, were therefore shocked when I announced after attending one service of a youth revival that I had moved my letter to Parker Memorial. They joined me the following Sunday, and we settled into a pattern of religious life common to many Baptist congregations: Sunday school and Training Union and Wednesday night suppers served by a friendly black woman who could cook our food and attend our weddings and funerals, but not participate in our preaching services. There were summer youth retreats in Panama City, fellowships following Anniston High School football games, rigorous choir practices under the intimidating but immensely competent choir leader/organist Griff Perry (who amazed us all by his capacity to drive the organ to thunderous crescendos). Bible sword drills, young people's speaker's tournaments, Vacation Bible School, and county-wide associational youth rallies made sure young people avoided most of the sins of dance and drink about which we were constantly warned. They needn't have worried; there was little time left for iniquities of the flesh. But casual friendships and serious dating naturally turned inward toward those we knew so well.

Because the congregation was affluent, at least by Anniston standards, it dominated much of the social and economic life of the city. Its rivals—the spectacular Church of St. Michael and All Angels, Grace Episcopal, or First Methodist—lacked either Parker Memorial's size and scope of programs, or its historic building and energy. From the ranks of its youth came a regular procession of appointees to the Naval Academy as well as students who distinguished themselves at fine colleges. Among its influential members was Harry M. Ayers, publisher of the *Anniston Star*. Ayers, an uncharacteristically liberal man for a small southern town, had been offered the ambassadorship to Sweden by Harry S. Truman and endorsed a Roman Catholic for the presidency in 1960. And then there was Charles R. Bell, president of Anniston National Bank.

Bell crossed my life more than once. A kindly, even godly man if bankers are allowed such exalted designations, he directed the bank that owned the land at Shady Glen where my grandfather was a sharecropper during the 1920s and 1930s. My grandfather had often praised Bell as the best and fairest of landlords, a man who had tried, to no avail, to persuade him to purchase the farm during the 1930s using as payment his share of the cotton crop. It was a measure of Bell's respect in the church and community that his son was called as pastor of Parker Memorial in the 1930s and that he lasted as long as he did. But that is getting ahead of the story.

Parker only barely became a church at all. The first Baptist church in the new industrial town of Anniston was as carefully planned as was the rest of the city. To the Tyler and Noble families that established the community, churches contributed stability, decorum, and a spiritual dimension to life. When some members of First Baptist decided to build a second Baptist church across town at Twelfth Street in 1887, the pastor of the older congregation so resented the missionary effort that he refused to deliver the invocation at the organization of the new church or to preach from its pulpit. Despite his recalcitrance, Twelfth Street enrolled as charter members many of the city's most prominent people, including Dr. and Mrs. T. W. Ayers.

A native of Georgia, Dr. Ayers purchased his first newspaper there at the age of eighteen. Later he established a paper in Jacksonville, Alabama, and then opened a drugstore in Anniston sometime during 1883. Using the earnings from his drugstore, he attended medical school in Baltimore, returning to Anniston in 1886 to practice medicine. He founded and edited the *Alabama Medical Journal*; edited Anniston's daily, *The Hot Blast*; established the local chamber of commerce; and became the first president of Alabama's Good Roads Association. Always interested in politics, he was also chairman of the fourth district Democratic Congressional Campaign Committee for six critical years during the Populist uprising of the 1890s.

He devoted the same energy to the new Baptist congregation that he lavished on secular affairs, serving as deacon, superintendent of the Sunday school, chairman of the building committee, and organizer and president of the first Baptist Young People's Union. A man who combined so many skills with such obvious spiritual devotion surprised few with his announcement in 1900 that he intended to embark on yet another career, that of Baptist missionary. According to Ayers's account, while on his knees praying one day, "there came as clear as if there had been an audible voice the command to go as a missionary doctor to China and I immediately wrote . . . offering my services as a foreign missionary."[1]

In 1901, Dr. Ayers, his wife, and three of their children booked passage for China. Applying his indefatigable energies to Shantung Province, Dr. Ayers built two hospitals and was twice decorated by the president of the People's Republic of China for work during plague and civil war. After he returned from China in 1926 because of his wife's failing health, the Chinese government constructed a monument in his honor. Ayers's grandson returned to China after the Second World War with a United Nations team and found the monument still standing amidst the rubble of the Baptist schools, church, and hospital. Japanese and Communist troops had left the statue, perhaps impressed with its simple inscription: "He treated the rich and poor alike."

In a sense, that classless inscription inspired a generation of urban middle-class church people devoted to moral uplift, and it also animated the Baptist congregation. Established during an era of shifting religious values, the church exhibited many aspects of new religious thought. The first pastor, Dr. G. A. Nunnally, was deeply committed to education and left the church in 1889 after a two-year pastorate to become president of Mercer University in Georgia.

The new pastor was chosen not in the conventional Baptist way, but by Duncan T. Parker who was not even a member of the congregation. Parker was president of the First National Bank of Anniston and husband of the church's first organist. He informed the pulpit committee that he would contribute $1,000 a year toward the pastor's salary if it would call Dr. George B. Eager from his pastorate in Danville, Virginia. Such an offer was too good to turn down, and the handsome, scholarly Eager preached his first sermon on October 20, 1889. His involvement in public issues was as intense as that of his parishioner Dr. Ayers. In later years, as pastor of First Baptist Church in Montgomery, Eager championed women's rights and other political and economic reforms. But Eager's courageous stand for moral principles at Parker led to his resignation in 1892. The occasion was a controversy with the Calhoun Club, a social organization to which several prominent Parker members belonged. The club served liquor and Eager scolded the members in a sermon so strong that the club threatened legal action. Club members retaliated in the press and demanded that he retract his charges. This Eager steadfastly refused to do. Although a majority of his congregation supported him, the division within his church convinced him that only his resignation could heal the wounds.

During Eager's pastorate, Duncan Parker lost both his eldest son and wife, and in memorial to them he offered to build the young church an imposing edifice. Although Duncan Parker died before the building was completed in 1891, his $85,000 constructed a worthy memorial, complete with magnificent stained glass windows, each memorializing a member of the Parker family. The name was changed from the pedestrian Twelfth Street to the imposing Parker Memorial (locals soon dropped the "Memorial" and "Baptist" as useless information; everyone knew what was meant by Parker Church).

Subsequent pastors maintained both the social involvement and the penchant for controversy that were characteristic of Eager's tenure. Dr. Samuel Clopton, of Richmond, Virginia, replaced Eager, but he had a short and stormy pastorate as well. He was married to a much younger, independent-minded woman who refused to hold church dinners in her home. Further, when the Ladies' Aid Society, which traditionally raised money to pay church debts by sponsoring a theatrical event, agreed to the suggestion of the wife of a wealthy deacon and Sunday school superintendent to perform a blackface minstrel show in the church auditorium, Clopton was appalled at such sacrilege. The woman's husband resigned as deacon, and Clopton resigned as pastor.

Joshua Hill Foster, formerly pastor of Birmingham's Ruhama Baptist Church, served a long pastorate from 1896 to 1909. Like his predecessors, he was a well-educated man from a prominent family, one that had furnished a president to the University of Alabama. Foster would himself serve as a college president after his tenure in Anniston. He brought a sensitive social consciousness to the industrial town. During a lengthy strike in Birmingham, he brooded about strikers who were literally starving. When his cow disappeared, he searched for it until told that some miners had been seen butchering the animal. Foster shrugged and said, "Well, they were starving. They're welcome to the cow."[2] Traditional in many ways—he persuaded Parker to avoid fund-raising festivals and continued the strong prohibitionist sentiment of the church's pastors—he began a mission at a local cotton mill to minister to poorer whites, and he also brought the Chautauqua to Anniston.

William F. Yarborough, a Mississippi native, succeeded Foster. The new pastor's social conscience matched Foster's. Parker was Alabama's sixth largest Baptist church in membership and third in contributions. But because it chiefly represented the privileged, Yarborough advocated the "abolition of class spirit in the church life, insisting that there was no distinction" between men in the sight of God. Animated by that theology, he persuaded the church to employ a social worker whose ministry was directed toward the city's mill families. Miss Linda Martin, of Springfield, Missouri, a trained social worker, conducted Sunday school on the Sabbath, but used Parker's building in the mill district for social ministries during the week.[3] Yarborough left Parker in 1916 to become executive secretary of the Alabama Baptist Executive Board, the highest office in the state Baptist hierarchy.

Dr. Leon Latimer, of Sylacauga, pastored Parker from 1916 until 1921. He was a strong advocate of the YMCA and of extending ministries to the thousands of soldiers being trained at the newly created Camp McClellan just north of town. When Latimer left to become pastor in Greenville, South Carolina, Parker Memorial called Dr. J. T. McGlothlin, a robust, aggressive pastor from Franklin, Kentucky, whose brother was the president of Furman University. McGlothlin continued both the church's rapid membership growth and its tradition of strong-minded and controversial pastors. In 1928 he divided the community by openly supporting Republican Herbert Hoover for president in opposition to the anti-prohibitionist Catholic Alfred E. Smith. When he left in 1932 to become business manager of the Southern Baptist Sunday School Board, Parker Memorial summoned one of its own as pastor: Charles R. Bell Jr.[4]

In my teenage years I noticed the downcast eyes and quick digressions when Bell's name was mentioned, which it seldom was despite his long tenure. The sense of unease fascinated and perplexed me. So it was with considerable interest that I anticipated his return during a church anniversary in the late 1950s. Although several former pastors were still alive, Bell was asked to preach. His sermon gave no clue to the disquietude of so many members; it was well conceived and brilliantly delivered. Even from the distance of twenty-five years I remembered that it concerned umbrellas and how the church should both shield people and radiate God's presence into the world. For me to remember a sermon for a quarter of a century, it had to be good. When a love affair with history interrupted my ministerial career, I finally got my chance to unravel the mysterious relationship between the Rev. Charles R. Bell Jr., and Parker Memorial Church.

Bell grew up in the affluence of a small-town banking family, wealthy compared to Anniston's pipe shop and textile mill workers or rural Calhoun County sharecroppers. Anniston was a town whose classes were separated both by race and by neighborhood. West of the main shopping district of Noble Street were the pipe shops, railroad yards, and textile mills with their adjacent neighborhoods of workers. They formed their own subcommunities, such as Glen Addie and Blue Mountain, complete with local grocery stores, playgrounds, and most certainly churches. Here and there black enclaves sprang up, even crossing Quintard Avenue in South Anniston to intrude on the perimeter of the Anniston Country Club. When we first lived in Anniston in the late 1940s, only a high fence and an alley separated our house from a black neighborhood. We lived in East Anniston and that was important. Living in East Anniston determined where you attended church, which group you ran with at Anniston High School, and gave you general standing in the community. True, there were areas where the two Annistons met—on high school athletic teams, at Baptist associational youth rallies, and especially dating—but all such occasions provided parents with opportunities for lectures on marrying people of similar backgrounds or how "old so-and-so" was really very nice but somehow not our kind of person. On Saturdays yet another stratum was added to the town's population as hundreds of country people descended on the stores. Old men whittled in front of the courthouse, and if you were not careful you discovered why signs dotted Noble Street forbidding spitting on the sidewalks.

Young Bell's house, not far from Parker, was accommodating although not ostentatious. In fact, that held true for the entire Bell family. They were well-to-do committed Baptists without being stuffy or calling attention to themselves. Parker was filled with that kind of Baptist. Set on a ministerial course by his devout family, a warm creative congregation, and a Baptist church that was unusually open and ecumenical, Bell enrolled at the denomination's Howard College. But he chafed under the constraints and parochialism of the place. He was a free-spirited young man with a residue of the world about him; he attended football games without paying and was not overly pious by Howard's standards.

After several years he transferred to a more challenging Baptist institution, Brown University in Rhode Island, which had lost its denominational distinctiveness while gaining a splendid faculty and a reputation for fine scholarship. From the scintillating world of Brown he pursued a safer course into the Baptist pulpit by taking his degree from Southern Baptist Theological Seminary in Louisville, Kentucky. There he came under the spell of W. O. Carver, beloved professor of Comparative Religion and Missions, and H. W. Tribble, who taught theology. Brown and Southern left their mark on him: "I had a whole new vista of life to open that I had just never known was there. It intrigued me, and it fascinated me; I began reading and I began reaching out for every possible source of information that I could get hold of."[5]

Bell returned in 1932 to the congregation where he was raised. It was a moment of rejoicing for the Bell and Ayers families in a world fast coming apart. The depression had hit Anniston hard, closing many of its shops and mills and bringing labor strife to those remaining open. In the rural districts of Calhoun County, where my grandfather sharecropped on "Captain Bell's place," poverty reigned. That perplexing world soon caught the attention of Parker's new preacher.

Actually, the Rev. Mr. Bell was rather traditional in many ways. He struggled over the ethics of performing marriages for the divorced, protested the use of rationed sugar for the production of liquor, and persuaded his church to sponsor its own missionary to Nigeria.[6] The generosity of the church toward unfortunates was broadened by Bell's international vision, but even that found precedent in Dr. T. W. Ayers's long sojourn in China and in the vigorous internationalism of his son, Harry, who made the *Anniston Star* one of the handful of consistently liberal newspapers in Alabama. Harry Ayers relished young Bell's vision and together they stimulated Parker Memorial to new heights. From his position of power as teacher of the quasi-independent Baraca Sunday school Class, Harry Ayers helped establish the International House at nearby Jacksonville State University for the exchange of international students and provided financial support for missionary Christie Poole.[7] The church sent money to India in 1937, to Lebanon for the purchase of free medicines for poverty-stricken patients of American University's hospital in 1938, and to China for war relief in 1941.[8]

But as Bell confessed, education had stretched his mind and opened new vistas. Perhaps because he was a bachelor until the late 1930s when he married Ann Cole, a wealthy young woman, he struggled particularly hard to deepen the quality of relationships within his congregation. The method he chose for this ministry of deepened spirituality was a strange one, which had first attracted him at Brown. The Oxford Group, or Buchmanite Movement, had been founded in England by Frank Buchman. Devoted to pure, simplified Christianity, it encouraged mutual confession and restitution. What often followed was release from guilt and an overwhelming sense of gratitude and happiness. As Bell described it, the Oxford Group "brought the most powerful influence into my life . . . for righteousness and goodness. It helped me to see myself as I had never seen myself before."

In addition to being a young, idealistic, and naive minister, Bell was a compelling pulpit orator, and members of his congregation were attracted by his obvious dedication to a more serious discipleship. Soon about fifty mostly young people were meeting regularly. They confessed sins, made restitution, shared testimonies, and developed a close fellowship. Bell had intended to expand the Oxford Group into a new kind of church fellowship, but the religious intimacy and self-revelation demanded by the group repelled many members and excited the jealousy of others. To Bell, the Oxford Group was a saving remnant that took the ethical and spiritual demands of the Bible seriously and could radiate this new discipleship throughout the church. To many members, it was Charlie's clique, a self-righteous, exclusive group that laid claim to a special holiness.

In the early days of his ministry, Bell's obvious sincerity provoked disbelief and comical dilemmas. He insisted on paying for football games he had attended without tickets while a student at Howard College. When officials praised his honesty and told him to forget it, he persisted until they accepted his checks. He insisted on paying more for his cabin on an around-the-world cruise because he was charged too little in a misunderstanding. He refused to sign the standard oath of allegiance to defend the United States when applying for a passport, creating a bureaucratic deadlock that finally forced the State Department to offer him not one but two alternative Christian oaths.[9] Bell himself conceded years later that his youthful immaturity and idealism caused much of the trouble at Parker. Some elements of the Oxford Group were faddish and he did not attempt to form such groups in subsequent parishes.[10]

But Bell brought a far deeper and more threatening vision of the gospel to Parker than the Oxford Group. The Buchmanite controversy might evoke vigorous debate within the church and frivolous gossip around town, but Bell's devotion to rural cooperatives, socialism, justice for workers and black citizens, and a host of other liberal causes seemed to threaten the entire underpinnings of southern society.

In 1936, while still a bachelor and after four years as pastor in Anniston, Bell requested a six-month leave of absence to travel and study. The trip was a turning point in his life. He traveled to Europe with a group, but then they parted ways. Bell sailed through the Suez to India where he talked with Mohandas Gandhi in his home and observed the wretched poverty of Indians under British colonial rule. He traveled to Singapore and China and then to Japan, where he stayed with a Mr. Hourinuchi, whom he had come to know through the Oxford Movement. He and his wife were enthusiastic Christians, and they remained close friends until Hourinuchi became Japanese ambassador to the United States and relations between the two countries worsened.

While in Japan, Bell met Toyohiko Kagawa, a celebrated Christian leader who had begun urban social ministries and cooperatives in Tokyo. Bell attended his revivals and an intensive training session for his followers and associates. He spent time in Kagawa's home and was obviously thoroughly converted to cooperative principles. Kagawa toured the United States in 1936 to mixed reactions, and Charles persuaded his younger brother, Tartt, then an impressionable student at Tulane University, to attend Kagawa's lectures in New Orleans; the Bell family had another convert to cooperatives.

During Kagawa's tour, a Baptist missionary friend in Japan who also was a Kagawa disciple, sent Bell a copy of a letter from the editor of the Texas *Baptist Standard*. The editor relayed the enormous interest in Kagawa's visit to Dallas, where the First Baptist Church could not accommodate all the requests for seats. But he inquired privately about rumors circulating through the South that the eminent Japanese Christian was also a socialist.[11] The letter must have amused Bell, who voted three times for Socialist Party presidential candidate Norman Thomas. Although Bell did not flaunt his socialism from the pulpit, he did make it clear that the existing distribution of goods in the 1930s was not consistent with Christian ethics.

When Bell came to Anniston, he vowed he could not share conditions there until he "moved across the railroad tracks," a goal he never achieved.[12] But as the Depression settled over the community, not even the tracks shielded his view. When President Roosevelt wrote clergymen in 1935 seeking reports on conditions in their communities, Bell minced no words. Conditions were wretched, especially housing for low-income black and white people: "Living in the most degrading circumstances, hounded by loan sharks and getting nothing for a crop is a fair description of the life so many of our people know. Our government should do something about it."[13]

But Bell was unwilling to wait for federal programs. When he returned from Japan, he launched a rigorous study of the cooperative movement. He wrote friends at Brown University for information as well as the Cooperative League of the United States. Bell gathered information about cooperative farms in Raleigh, North Carolina; Jacksonville, Florida; and elsewhere. In July 1937, he visited the Delta Cooperative Farm in Hillhouse, Mississippi. He also studied carefully Jim Perry's Sky Valley Farm at Zirconia, North Carolina, and another in Copiah County, Mississippi. Patterned after Kagawa's socialist spiritual community, the farms were designed as self-supporting economic units. He also developed a lifelong friendship with Clarence Jordan, a seminary classmate who founded Koinonia Farm in Georgia.[14]

Excited by what he saw and heard, Bell determined to establish his own cooperative outside Anniston. He intended to move there (at last, "across the tracks") and create a cooperative farm, working it in conjunction with his church. But Parker's leaders denied their support and the project never materialized. He actually planted and harvested crops himself and conducted a camp there for the black children, but the cooperative features were never implemented. Later attempts in Madison, Wisconsin, failed also, and he gave up that dream as he did the Oxford Group. The best he could do was persuade Parker to contribute to Sky Valley Farm.[15]

Bell's deepening involvement in the rural cooperative movement branched into many subsidiary relationships. Several liberal ministerial friends gave his name to Lucy Randolph Mason, a native Virginian who came to Atlanta in 1937 to help improve the image of the Congress of Industrial Organizations (CIO) in the South. She assisted the Textile Workers Organizing Committee, which was particularly active in the Anniston area. She used Bell as one of her Alabama contacts, and he sent her names of liberal ministers in the state who might be sympathetic to labor unionism. There weren't many names to send. But his respect within the community did allow him to mediate a textile strike at the Utica Mills, where he knew the manager well, and to advise on a later strike at the Lengel-Fencil Mill.[16] Later, the National Religion and Labor Foundation asked him to coordinate its work in Alabama, and William Mitch and other United Mine Workers–Congress of Industrial Organizations (UMW-CIO) leaders in Birmingham met with him to try to develop more community support for unions in the Anniston area.

Labor could not co-opt Bell into a narrowly partisan position. In fact he wrote UAW-CIO Vice President Walter Reuther that labor needed a broader vision than that of just another "narrow economic pressure group." Reuther agreed that the real hope of American labor was to advance democracy during peacetime with the same zeal with which the nation pursued victory in wartime.[17]

The preservation of caste was even more fundamental to the survival of Anniston's social mores than the maintenance of economic class boundaries. And once again Bell ran counter to the white community. From his earliest days in Anniston, he had crossed the color line. In fall 1932, shortly after arriving back home, he met with Dr. George Washington Carver at Tuskegee Institute. During subsequent years Bell attended meetings with Anniston's black leaders, ran camps for black children, corresponded with black college students, and finally, toward the end of his Anniston ministry, defied one of the most sacred racial taboos by entertaining black people at a Christmas party in his home.

That such racial iconoclasm was genuine is clearly shown in his correspondence. Robert Lee Moffett was a young black man from Anniston who knew Bell's family well. When Moffett departed for college in Philadelphia, Bell kept in touch, deepening the relationship with probing questions about Moffett's studies and philosophy of life. The younger man responded to Bell with frankness and candor. How could Congress speak seriously of equality for all people and reject anti-lynching and anti-poll tax bills? Did such action correspond to the notion that "all men are created equal"? Perhaps he told Bell more than the minister cared to know: "This is what life means to me: I cannot have a job equal to that of a white man with the same preparation and qualification; I cannot enjoy the things of nature as God put them here on earth because of some unscrupulous men; I am considered to be inferior to the white man because of my heritage and color; I am separated and discriminated against because I was born in an unfortunate position."

The church was far from the teachings of Christ, but Moffett harbored no hatred toward white people: "Of a truth I can say that some of my best friends are white [such] as you and many others. I write these things to you because you are broad minded and can understand my feelings."[18]

Whoever was to blame for Robert Lee Moffett's world, it certainly was not Charlie Bell. As he often did, Bell turned from the personal to the political realm for amelioration, lobbying Alabama's liberal congressional delegation for precisely the kind of changes Moffett sought. But he soon discovered that their liberalism did not extend quite so far. When he urged Senator Hugo Black, a fellow Alabama Baptist, to support the anti-lynching bill then before Congress, Black demurred: "It is a real pleasure for me to know that Parker Memorial Baptist Church has a Minister with the liberal views expressed by you in your communication. It is my earnest hope that our denomination may have more who are willing to view economic and social abuses with your own liberal vision." However, he wrote that the federal legislation would not prevent lynchings and might even encourage them.[19]

Bell next urged repeal of the poll tax, which disfranchised hundreds of thousands of poor Alabama citizens of both races. Black's successor, Senator Lister Hill, was a thoroughgoing liberal on most issues, but Bell had asked too much: "I regret that I do not find myself in accord with your views with reference to Federal action on the poll tax. You and I are so much in accord on so many other matters and seem to be fundamentally so much in agreement in the cause of human rights, human progress and human welfare that I particularly regret our difference of views in the poll tax matter." Senator John H. Bankhead also opposed federal action, worrying that it would further expand federal powers at the expense of state rights.[20]

Bell was a stubborn man, and he would not relent. He encouraged like-minded racial liberals across the South and began publicizing his own views.[21] His essay "Race in the Deep South" appeared in a 1944 issue of *Fellowship*, the publication of the Fellowship of Reconciliation. That same year he penned an essay entitled "A Southern Approach to the Color Issue" for *Christian Century*, suggesting prophetically that black southerners should adopt a strategy of peaceful noncooperation. Bell was intrigued by Gandhi's civil disobedience in India and believed it might work in American race relations.

Although he did not advertise his views in Anniston, word of Bell's biracial activities circulated through his congregation. One anonymous member wrote to him in January 1944:

> There is an ugly rumor going the rounds of town which I am sure must be untrue, namely what you did during the holidays, entertain a bunch of negroes in your home, that you and your wife sat at the table with them and entertained them in your living room.
>
> . . . I can hardly believe this rumor, but if it is true you ought to explain it to your congregation and explain why you lowered yourself lower than a negro.

If true, Bell should resign. In an ironic but revealing climax, the outraged parishioner concluded: "If you had gone down the streets of Anniston blind drunk, the people of Anniston might forgive that, but they will never forgive nor forget this evidence on your part that you feel that a negro is the equal of a white person."[22]

At least Bell got the outraged critic to church; he promised to attend Sunday to hear Bell defend himself.

That letter was subtle compared to another that featured four newspaper articles reporting black rapes and murders of whites. The gruesome montage had a cryptic message attached:

> Since the negro is the object of your particular fanaticism I am enclosing clippings which are evidences of their gentle, Christlike, un-brutal characters.
>
> . . . The next time you throw a nigger party you ought to give the item to the social editor of the paper. There are few people in town who have not heard of your former party in your home.
>
> . . . Many of the people who go to hear you do so from curiosity and not to hear the word of God.[23]

Bell tendered his resignation within months of these messages, but in retrospect he believed his racial views played little role in the denouement. Few Parker members shared his racial liberalism, but they were more tolerant of his eccentricities on the issue than were his anonymous critics.[24]

Perhaps his solace did not come from white liberals at all. During a 1939 resignation crisis, Bell received a letter from an Anniston black woman named Louise J. Moses. She had heard that he planned to leave Anniston and could not let him depart without letting him know how far-reaching had been his influence: "We, who represent the minor group of the population have appreciated every brave word spoken for us through Christ. A gradual change is taking place in the hearts of those you have touched. You have been a great inspiration to many of us directly and indirectly. The days of indecision, perhaps, to follow shall call for strength, but remember—the message you have been called to bear cannot die; for 'the seed has been sown' and 'the bread cast out upon the waters.'"[25]

It was his interest in racial justice and dignity for the poor that involved him in the Southern Conference of Human Welfare. Charles Dobbins, his Howard College classmate, had settled in Anniston during the 1930s where for some years he published the *Anniston Times*. Bell wrote a column for the *Times* each week. He and Dobbins attended the organizational meeting of the Southern Conference in Birmingham. His most vivid memories of the 1938 event were meeting Eleanor Roosevelt and Eugene "Bull" Connor's vigorous imposition of racial segregation on the delegates in the Municipal Audtorium.[26]

The American Civil Liberties Union tried to persuade Bell to become its Alabama state chairman in 1938, but Bell, deeply enmeshed in enough controversy already, declined. That did not keep him from bombarding Alabama's congressional delegation with protests against the red-baiting Dies Committee. That committee, better known in later years as the House Un-American Activities Committee, labeled as communist every liberal organization from the CIO to the World Council of Churches. Congressman William Bankhead seemed little interested, but Sam Hobbs of Alabama's Fourth Congressional District was inclined to terminate funding to the committee as Bell proposed.[27]

Despite his iconoclasm on a multitude of domestic issues, it was his vision of a Christian's responsibility in international relations that provoked the final split in his congregation. Bell was exceptionally well informed on international issues and, as usual, had strong opinions regarding proper moral conduct. Like many 1930s liberals, he vigorously opposed US involvement in the European war that began in 1939. Both he and his brother, Tartt, were greatly influenced by isolationist Senator Gerald Nye whose senate committee had concluded that international bankers had manipulated America into the First World War without strategic or ethical justification. Bell believed British imperialism in India was an issue as compelling as fascist aggression. He and Harry Ayers conducted a prolonged debate on the subject, with Ayers defending Winston Churchill's policies toward the Indian subcontinent and Bell pressing for immediate independence.[28]

He was equally prescient regarding China. In 1943 he championed repeal of the nativist Chinese Exclusion Act in order to open America's doors to Chinese displaced by the war. Regarding the postwar future of China, he and his brother speculated that the real struggle would be between communists and Kuomintang after the war with Japan had ended. In both China and India, America should oppose the reimposition of imperialistic and reactionary governments. She should be as thoroughly committed to the establishment of democracy in Asia as she was to winning the war. On this issue he received a sympathetic hearing from Senator Hill: "I am tremendously interested in what you write me about the situation in the Far East. Vice President Wallace has just left for China. Frankly, I took the liberty of letting him read your letter. I am sure he was as much impressed with what you said as I am. I do not believe that we can build a lasting peace unless we are true to Democracy and its ideals."[29]

Given his international and theological views, it was a short step to pacifism. Bell saw no justification for violence, whether in the realm of domestic labor relations or in politics between nations. With restraint and mutual forbearance, statesmen could resolve national differences. During the Second World War, Bell supported Christians who declared themselves conscientious objectors. He corresponded extensively with a young conscientious objector (CO) in Nashville who was sentenced to four years in prison for his beliefs. Bell was actively supportive of the Fellowship of Reconciliation, a national pacifist organization with deep Quaker roots. Brother Tartt worked for the fellowship designing strategy and training recruits. Charlie Bell contributed financially and helped organize a network of Southern Baptist COs, which included his friend Clarence Jordan, Dr. Frank Leavell, Charles Maddrey, and others. At the state level, Bell used his influence to lobby for the employment of conscientious objectors at the state mental hospital in Tuscaloosa. Many of the hospital's aides had been drafted, and the use of COs would fill a critical need. The Selective Service System rejected the proposal, however, bowing to intense pressure from the Veterans of Foreign Wars and the American Legion.[30]

As dear to his heart as was the plight of the nation as it drifted toward war was the position of his own denomination. He watched with horror and incomprehension as Southern Baptists were caught up in the rhetoric of violence. Blind to the domestic and racial injustice within the South, his colleagues seemed only too certain of how to restrain the international violence of a world gone mad. From the big limestone church on Quintard Avenue in Anniston, Bell launched his own offensive for restraint and sanity.

Choosing the most unlikely of settings, Bell proposed his alternative course at the May 1937 Southern Baptist Convention (SBC) meeting in New Orleans. Each year the Social Service Commission of the SBC presented a resolution on social concerns that was routinely adopted. Commission Director Arthur J. Barton thought of his agency as the conscience of Southern Baptists, but its positions tended to be more a reflection of consensus than prophetic proclamation. The report delivered in New Orleans was no exception. It condemned the use of alcohol, child marriages, large armaments programs, and the use of tobacco by women, preachers, and other church workers. Bell could hardly believe what he was hearing. When one Oklahoma minister charged that four babies had died in a hospital because their mothers used tobacco, Bell could sit quietly no longer. Addressing the six thousand "messengers," the twenty-eight-year-old minister suggested that perhaps the children died because their parents could not afford orange juice, fresh vegetables, and nutritious food. Restrained, but very much in earnest, he continued, "We must face the real issues of life. . . . I cannot adopt such a weak report in a day when we are faced with hunger throughout the land. . . . Why is there nothing in this report condemning conditions among the sharecroppers . . . ? Starvation wages . . . ? You talk about the brotherhood of man. Why, there are Negroes standing outside the door of your convention and you won't let them in! This convention ought to go on record favoring the anti-lynching bill."[31]

Throughout his speech the messengers became increasingly restive, but hearing his plea for racial equality was more than they would tolerate. They greeted his call for support of anti-lynching legislation with shouts of "no, no, no." Georgia's famed William David "Dry Willie" Upshaw rose to his feet and announced, "I am going to refute this young man. He is not an old-time Baptist." And with that he launched a vigorous rebuttal. Bell's alternate resolutions addressing the problems of economic and racial injustice drew surprisingly strong support but not enough to pass the convention.

Literally overnight Bell was transformed from an obscure Southern Baptist minister into a controversial denominational leader. Letters poured in from like-minded ministers who had labored in intellectual isolation, despairing at the conservatism and injustice of their communities and at the deadening and irrelevant pietism of their denomination. Suddenly they were aware that, although a distinct minority, there were dozens of them scattered across the South.[32]

Edward A. McDowell, an influential professor at Southern Baptist Seminary, revealed most fully their dilemma in a long, insightful letter to Bell: "I agree with you that something is wrong in our Southern Baptist life and that something needs to be done. I am thoroughly sympathetic with your views . . . and I wish there were more like you. I hope to do my part here at this strategic place by planting ideas in young preachers' heads."

McDowell suggested that a group of like-minded Southern Baptists should meet the following spring at the SBC meeting in Richmond to plan a retreat where they could talk about mutual concerns, pray, and enjoy fellowship. "And this piece of philosophy I pass on to you for what it is worth. I love Southern Baptists—they are *my* people, *my* brethren, and I am going to stay with them unless they run me out. Because I want to stay with them I shall not say all I would like to say all the time, neither will I permit the reactionaries to 'label' me. I shall engage in controversy as little as possible, and I shall strive always to let *love* be my dominating motive. If people criticize me, I shall love them; if they despise me, I shall love them."[33]

Lonnie W. Meachum, pastor of First Baptist Church in Virginia Beach, Virginia, struggled with similar emotions and contradictions. In 1935, full of idealism and confidence, he boldly preached a sermon on "The Meaning of Pacifism" to an uncomprehending congregation. By 1937 he was "so disgusted by organized religion that sometimes I am almost ready to have done with it." His beliefs about war, race, forgiveness, and the brotherhood of man had imperiled his ministry. And worse, his fear for the economic well-being of his wife and three children entrapped him in an awful triangle of family, religious system, and the ethical teachings of Jesus. By 1941 he had despaired. Some members were seeking to fire him, and he contemplated leaving the ministry.

Maxie Collins of Batesburg Baptist Church in South Carolina had given up even attending the SBC:

> It is too bad that even our leaders cannot see the truth or will not. With regard to the race question, economics, and education, not to mention war, I find that while millions of laymen are turning toward the Christian solution, relatively few religious leaders are willing to go all the way with Jesus. Possibly it is too much to expect all men to accept universal brotherhood in reality, but it is not too much to expect them to accept it in principle and do their best to act toward all men as tho all were brothers.
>
> . . . Charlie, what can we do? We have a few souls in S.C. who are laboring—and in every state it is the same. Is it too late to do anything through the church? I am beginning to wonder.[34]

Bell did not share this spirit of pessimism. Such sentiments only provided new urgency to his campaign to change the denomination. After the controversial New Orleans convention, he wrote Arthur Barton, assuring him of his personal respect and support of the Social Service Commission. But he did not waver in his determination to deflect the course of Baptist thought. No sooner had he lost at New Orleans than he was mapping a new strategy for the next convention at Richmond. Two friends at Southern Baptist Seminary, W. O. Carver and Harold Tribble, tried to moderate Bell's idealism. Warning him that precipitate action would brand him a radical and destroy his influence, they proposed a gradual campaign. Building on the surprising strength he mustered at New Orleans, Bell should first contact sympathetic members of the Social Service Commission in hopes of obtaining a favorable report from them. That failing, he should offer a comparatively mild resolution from the floor, holding in reserve an even stronger statement to advance if the messengers seemed favorable to his first proposal. They warned, however, that his confidence in the liberalism of the Richmond area was unfounded. The area was not progressive with respect to race, and the country's "big navy idea" dominated American public opinion.[35]

Bell followed their advice as best he could, pleading with Barton for a more advanced stand on issues. But Barton proved unyielding. Bell argued that the commission should be "out in front of our Southern conscience rather than bound by it." Barton reported that step-by-step the commission had expanded the Baptist conscience on social questions. He even asserted that "our Baptist people have not lagged behind but have really led the Christian bodies of America in taking sane, constructive positions on all social questions." Bell was amazed by what he read, although Barton's contradictory conclusion was nearer the truth: "You will recognize, of course, that no great serious minded body of Christians will go much if at all beyond their conscience in making united declarations on any question. . . . Those occupying positions of leadership have great responsibility . . . properly to understand and interpret, and to express the conscience and convictions of great constituency and not to violate this conscience and conviction so as to make their efforts futile."[36]

Tribble acknowledged that Bell had tried to follow proper procedures and despaired of more advanced leadership so long as Barton "does the thinking for the Commission." The only recourse was another challenge to the report at Richmond, with no better results than at New Orleans.[37]

Ever the persuader, Bell sought different avenues of influence. He submitted a lengthy rationale for Christian pacifism to his friend, L. L. Gwaltney, who edited *The Alabama Baptist*. In his own way Gwaltney was as much a mugwump as Bell, having taken numerous controversial stands on evolution, capitalism, and other issues. But he did not share Bell's pacifism and begged him to reconsider the essay. Gwaltney respected too much the right of freedom of speech and press to reject the article, but argued at length against his premises. He dismissed Bell's scriptural references contending that Jesus directed the Sermon on the Mount at his disciples, that pacifism could not be made an ethic for highly organized governments led by non-Christians. In an ideal world, such ethical notions might work, but not in the real world of Hitlerism and international lawlessness.

Bell would not relent and Gwaltney was as good as his word. Print it he did, and Bell must have been gratified by the response even if Gwaltney was not. Several influential Alabama pastors praised the essay as a "masterful presentation on the Christian attitude toward this entire situation." John Buchanan, influential pastor of Birmingham's Southside Baptist Church, which was one of the wealthiest and most influential congregations in the state, found himself "more in accord with the spirit and essence of this article than the resolution adopted by the Convention. I think it is unfortunate that the Southern Baptist Convention . . . declared war even before Mr. Roosevelt and the Congress had seen fit to do so." Montague Cook, pastor of Southside Baptist in Montgomery, agreed: "The position taken by the leaders of the Convention is an unfortunate one. They have left the Master. It is our duty to keep the teachings and method of Christ before the people. In such a way they will see that these who would lead them by the paths of rationalization into murder, are not worthy to be followed."[38]

Alabama friends such as Gwaltney were more willing to humor what they regarded as Bell's eccentricities than were denominational leaders who grew weary of his entreaties. To Bell's request for distribution of material on pacifism at the Southern Baptist Assembly grounds at Ridgecrest, North Carolina, J. E. Lambdin replied that the policy of the Sunday School Board was "to teach genuine Christian citizenship and to do nothing which would be interpreted as being disloyal. . . . With this in mind, it is not wise to have pacifist propaganda at Ridgecrest."

But Bell was indefatigable and repeatedly challenged Baptists to a different position. Even friends who shared some of his convictions warned that the SBC annual convention was controlled by emotion, not reason. When Bell sought to ask the Alabama state convention for funds to help conscientious objectors, Buchanan advised that such a request would be fruitless and would only provoke "unwise and unchristian" debate that would harm both the convention and conscientious objectors. Bell admitted that Buchanan was right. Baptist friends in other states concluded that no changes would be made until there were scores of funerals in the denomination.[39] And even that sentiment overestimated the liberalism of the rising generation of Southern Baptist pastors.

More painful perhaps than the rejection of his notion of social justice by right-wing elements within the denomination was the steady deterioration of religious affiliation by left-wing friends. Disillusioned by the church's halfhearted commitment to economic and racial justice, many of Bell's acquaintances drifted out of organized religion. One friend, who finally became a communist, best expressed the disillusion in a long and troubling letter:

> As far as ideals are concerned, Charlie, I have more than I ever had. As far as any mysticism is concerned—I have less than I ever had. I couldn't be completely honest any other way. You speak, too, of me being anti-capital. If there is that in my thinking—it's not on a personal basis. By that, I mean there is no ill-feeling in my heart for any individual, be he capitalist or what not. However, when I see the suffering and the growing decay caused by putting the control of everything into fewer and fewer hands—then my intense desire for the greatest good for the greatest number causes me to honestly and sincerely be opposed to that tendency in our economic sys-

tem. And I'm more and more convinced that the character of the men involved has very little to do with it. The march of mankind is straining at bonds to break into a more glorious day for everybody, and the favored position of a top few has the objective results of blocking this drive, and as a result thrusting mankind into starvation in the midst of plenty, war, and all the sufferings that follow.

. . . Division there is Charlie—deep basic division. A false sense of smoothing over this division under the guise of promoting unity just prolongs the honest facing of that division, and the clean-cut move to find an answer to it. America needs complete honesty desperately in this hour, but also fearless honesty that will delve right on down and face everything.

. . . I have an abiding faith in the great thousands of ordinary people. But it will take organization and rallying for their honesty and unselfishness to become the dominating thing in American life.[40]

More traumatic even than this was his brother's growing cynicism toward the church. Charles and Tartt had always been close, with the older brother an obvious source of intellectual and spiritual inspiration to the younger. While a student at Tulane, Tartt was still quite obviously under his brother's spell, idealistic and attracted to Kagawa, Gerald Nye, and the Fellowship of Reconciliation. But as the Depression deepened and war became a reality, Tartt drifted farther from his brother's world. During his work for a master's degree in economics at the University of Chicago, Tartt largely ignored his chosen field to probe new intellectual depths which he had missed at Tulane. Andre Malraux, Dostoyevsky, John Steinbeck, Thorstein Veblen, Frederick Engles, John Dos Passos, and Clifford Odets jarred him with new visions of the world. His previous reading had been "very puritanical," but his remedial education called old values into question. He was disappointed in Franklin Roosevelt for remaining in the reactionary Democratic Party. If only FDR would forge labor and the left into a new party it would be "a glorious start for a real progressive group." And he inquired politically of his brother: "Still content to call yourself a liberal and cooperate with anybody that comes along, or are you developing some more definite ideas about what you want and how to get it?"[41] Suspended between the values of his family and their religion and the new secular values emerging within the disillusioned intellectual community, Tartt challenged his older brother's conscience.

A Christmas reunion in the early war years provided the setting for a painful confrontation. Upon his return to Chicago, Tartt admitted how difficult it was to talk to his elder brother anymore. He felt intellectually out of place in Anniston, no longer sharing the same ideas, habits, and appetites that they once had in common. Recognizing his older brother's commitment to the Social Gospel, he could not comprehend Charlie's inaction in the face of so wicked a world. While sharing a meal with his brother's enlightened Anniston friends, Tartt could only think:

> Here sit a group of around 50 people, wonderfully well meaning in their desires to uplift themselves and others, individually well-adjusted to society, who have the dynamic for a revolution right here in the city. And further, they are all doing something about it. And yet they are losing a marvelous chance to make their efforts and hopes effective because they don't see beyond this concern with individual problems.
>
> . . . My goodness. Charlie, if people like yourself who certainly mean well aren't going to do anything about it, what is to be expected?
>
> . . . You have a leader and speaker, yourself. You have access to the press, Charles Dobbins. You have finances. You have freedom and courage. Why if a communist group had half what you have there they would be virtually running the town. I see no reason why, with a little political strategy, even if it means mass meetings, leaflets, anything at all, you couldn't put over some real reforms there in Anniston. And this very group—any church group for that matter—offers a great opportunity. Further it *should* be leading the revolution, both social and individual.[42]

What Tartt could not know in his youthful exuberance was how high the price of revolution in Anniston was and how painful were the wounds. Charlie knew only too well. The storms that he had loosed within the SBC had left him largely unscathed, but the controversies he stirred in Parker Memorial cost him dearly.

As early as 1937 Bell vowed to leave Anniston. Seminary friends found a more congenial church in Paducah, Kentucky, but members of that congregation found out about the controversial Oxford Group and sought Bell's pledge not to institute such activities in the Kentucky parish. This he would not give them and the negotiations ended. At this critical juncture his previous professor W. O. Carver warned him of the factionalism he was creating at Parker. Carver believed that Bell could become one of the most significant and prophetic leaders of the denomination, but he must exercise caution and restraint: "You can easily become a thwarted martyr to an ideal, instead of a compelling witness to and exponent of an idea—even of the Christ who incarnates the ideal."[43]

Caught between the extravagant expectations of his friends and brother and the pragmatic strategy of advisers such as Carver, Bell struggled to express his own convictions. In 1938 he resigned his pastorate at Parker Memorial. The occasion was an agonizing compromise he had made with the deacons regarding the Oxford Group. So divisive had the little fellowship become that he agreed to stop its meetings for two years in order to allow the church to put aside its internal strife. As logical as the agreement was for the sake of harmony, it so rankled his conscience and compromised him morally that he finally returned to the deacons to offer his resignation. But for the powerful position of his father and the active support of Harry M. Ayers, that would have ended his association with the church. However, a deacon employed at his father's bank caught the other deacons quite by surprise by proposing that if Bell felt compromised by his pledge regarding the Oxford Group, the church should relieve him of the obligation to honor the pledge. The resolution passed on a standing vote that some in the church interpreted as a strategy to keep Bell. Many members cared so much for Bell's parents that they could not bring themselves to publicly oppose their son.[44]

Local ministers and friends congratulated him on the support of his congregation, but one of his New York mentors in the Oxford Movement wrote more bluntly. Many of Bell's problems stemmed not from his adherence to the philosophy of the Oxford Movement but from his own impetuousness. Fundamentally Bell was an individualist and an isolationist who neither sought advice nor sustained a disciplined commitment to the Oxford ideas:

> I feel your tendency, Charlie, is to want to check something after it has reached a crisis instead of checking the policy which could have prevented the crisis. . . . It is not a question of courage or cowardice; it is a question of guided strategy thoroughly checked versus impulsive or routine or otherwise unguided courses of action. As things are, it seems to me you made people take up an attitude toward the Oxford Group which they do not understand and of which they have had no adequate demonstration. Of course, trouble results.
>
> . . . There is entirely too much laying down of conditions and entirely too little living of a life, if you ask my opinion, Charlie.[45]

Paradoxically Bell's younger brother advised a directly contradictory course. Disappointed that his elder brother had consented to the two-year moratorium in the first place, he advised "do absolutely what you feel that you should do with no compromises"; "to heck with what anybody else thinks; I hope you do what you will be absolutely satisfied with."[46]

In the end that is just what Charlie Bell did. The issue that ended his pastorate at Parker Memorial seems almost anticlimactic after the clashes on so many issues. Church members were determined to hang a plaque honoring Parker's members who served in the military and display a flag in honor of the righteousness of the nation's cause. Although Bell felt any national flag within the church identified Christ too much with an attitude of national exclusiveness, the flag itself was not the primary issue; the timing of the event primarily troubled him.

By displaying the flag after America declared war, it became a symbol of armed might. Despite Bell's objections, the deacons commissioned a US service flag with stars placed in the form of a cross. All other churches in the community had such flags, and they were determined that Parker would also.

Aware of their plans, Bell sought the advice of friends and family, who responded with ingenious if somewhat devious stratagems. One proposed to let soldiers in the congregation vote on whether they sought such symbolism in the church. With large numbers training for overseas duty at nearby Fort McClellan, he felt they had more important concerns on their minds. Others urged him to state frankly his own views but to abide by the majority decision of his congregation. By so doing he might educate them, if they did not dismiss him as pastor. Finally even Tartt understood the gravity of the situation and advised moderation. Bell should once again state his objections as fairly as possible, granting that some sincerely believed in a different course. He should not start with an ultimatum that if they displayed the flag, he would resign. His brother Alex offered similar advice, adding that Bell need not worry about the fate of wife Ann or son Charles III. He would provide financial support so long as they needed it.

Thus fortified, Bell faced his final battle at Parker. To identify the church with war simply because all the other congregations in Anniston were doing so was clearly unchristian. The crisis would come when they asked him to participate in the ceremony to hang the flag. And this he would not do.[47]

Bell was able to delay the final confrontation until D-Day in June 1944. But as news of the European invasion blared from radios throughout town, members trekked to the church determined to have their flag displayed regardless of their pastor's scruples. Nor could Bell back down on an issue, which for him was central to all religious values.

Some of his antagonists evidenced no spirit of Christian love, demonstrating perhaps how right Bell was, how much the war had dried up the wellsprings of love and goodwill. One anonymous parishioner wrote to his pastor, carefully noting that a carbon copy also had been sent to Bell's father:

> I want to congratulate you on your resignation. That is the best thing you have done for our church in ten or more years. Stick to your resignation. Don't let the two-faced ones in the congregation vote you back.
>
> . . . In your first resignation many voted to retain you because it was a standing vote and they did not wish to hurt your father and mother by voting against you. If it had been by secret ballot the only ones who would have voted to retain you would have been those crack-brained Oxford Movementites [*sic*].
>
> . . . The people are tired of a negro loving traitor to our flag. . . . The place for you is in a negro church in Harlem or Springfield, Missouri.

> ... The congregation is sorry for your mother and father, but they have no sympathy for you and your yellow to the core brothers. . . . A white person who believes in social equality is lower than the lowest negro alive. . . . A very potential danger to our South will be removed when you shake the dust of Alabama from your feet.[48]

Iva Cook, society editor of the *Anniston Star* and a longtime family friend, tried to be more reconciling. If ever he got "straightened out on your war attitude and the Negro question I am ready to throw my arms around you and fight for you."[49] From far and wide friends communicated their support. Fellow Baptists within the state and across the convention praised his courage. One of them expressed the prevailing opinion: "Thank God for you and men like you!" Word spread quickly and ministers of other denominations sent letters of support.

But perhaps the letters that meant most to Anniston's Pilgrim, sunk into his own "slough of despond," came from his parishioners. His efforts had not been entirely in vain, for laymen who could not leave Anniston risked much to defend him. In their letters they testified to his influence and their own spiritual maturity acquired through his guidance. One letter from an Annistonian put the entire matter in simple biblical perspective: "Jesus said, 'Darkness hateth the light because their deeds are evil.' In other words, when men's desires are to murder their fellow man contrary to God's law which reads 'Thou shalt not kill' naturally they want to find fault with those who teach the truth."[50]

Bell did not wait long to begin anew. The Fellowship of Reconciliation tendered him a position, but he declined, desiring to stay in the pulpit. On Bell's behalf, his old friend John Buchanan contacted Dr. Edwin McNeill Poteat, who then was teaching at Rochester Colgate Seminary. Buchanan believed Bell would be better accepted among Northern Baptists. Poteat bemoaned how churches "cut off their own noses to spite their faces," but could offer little encouragement: "Unfortunately the North is no more tolerant of men of his opinions than the South. . . . On the war issue, North and South are unanimous, and though the South may appear more volatile and ready to act more quickly, the North's moderation is nonetheless quite as resolute and decisive."[51]

On this score, Poteat was wrong. He wrote to the Rev. L. B. Moseley, a friend who was about to leave the pastorate of First Baptist Church, in Madison, Wisconsin, recommending the Alabama pastor. Moseley had followed Bell's career from his dramatic presentation at the SBC meeting in New Orleans through his prophetic essay on race in the *Christian Century* and assured him that the issues that had so divided Parker would not disturb the Madison congregation:

> In twelve years this church has supported me in preserving a free pulpit. I have never had any church that responded to the position of Jesus

> as I think this church has responded. Matters which trouble you in Alabama will be taken for granted here, unless you do too much about them. You understand that the Kingdom of God will not come without opposition. But this town listens and responds.
>
> . . . You can be a prophet and stay in Madison.

Moseley knew whereof he spoke, for his own spiritual pilgrimage had paralleled Bell's. A native of Selma, Alabama, he had attended Baptist Wake Forest University in North Carolina and Southern Baptist Theological Seminary before accepting a Northern Baptist pastorate. Numbered among his congregation were three black members, two Japanese Americans, many southerners, and scattered peoples from around the world.[52]

Bell enjoyed a successful and satisfying tenure in Madison before ending his career as pastor of First Baptist Church, in Pasadena, California, and retiring to Arizona. Although he mellowed a bit, especially on strategy and method, his basic convictions remained constant. Forged as they were in the cauldron of Anniston's religious fires, they were hard as steel.

Sitting on the front porch of Bell's family home in Anniston on a lazy summer day in 1972, two former parishioners of Parker Memorial Baptist Church reflected upon their separate spiritual pilgrimages. We had both changed, but my change had been the painless sort wrought by perceptive teachers at the Baptist college we shared in common and by the ethical liberalism of the 1960s. In many ways we sought the same kind of world and shared a common Christian ideology. But my commitment had cost little; in a perverse kind of way it was even fashionable. He had been mostly out of joint with his times and carried the scar tissue to prove it. Bell, eyes still afire with energy, recounted his dream of rural cooperatives. As he warmed to the subject, his voice became more animated. He leaned forward in his rocking chair, and his hands gestured vigorously as he said, "I feel that the American economy has simply got to come to some kind of principle where there is a fair division of our wealth. I mean I think all these social problems we are working on—it's foolish to continue hoping that we are going to resolve them until we resolve a more equitable distribution of our income. . . . You can't expect to have any kind of social justice with a man like Aristotle Onassis owning a thousand million dollars and some Negro boy here in Anniston not able to get an education. I mean revolution is going to come out of that. No way for any kind of social justice to be equated with that."[53]

—*Clearings in the Thicket: An Alabama Humanities Reader—Essays and Stories from the 1983 Alabama History and Heritage Festival*, 1985

My first published article about southern religion appeared at a time when historians were challenging nearly all inherited wisdom. And in at least some sense, so was I. It set the direction for my career.

First, I made clear my disagreement with many historians of religion as well as with C. Vann Woodward, the most influential historian of the South in my lifetime (and especially in my career). Woodward believed that the Social Gospel had no significant presence in the South. Convinced that the "burden of southern history" did not send the South spiraling quite that far out of the American religious orbit, I knew I would have to swim upstream a long way against the current. Second, I suggested that by linking three issues—liberal theology, ecumenism, and the Social Gospel—into one inextricable web, Woodward had made a strategic mistake. Many southern evangelicals, especially African Americans, decoupled this linkage. Social Gospel ideas could emerge from conservative theology as a literal interpretation of more than 2,100 passages of Scripture about Christian responsibility for the poor, the oppressed, widows, orphans, prisoners, the sick, and "strangers in the land." There were also the teachings of Jesus about the same subject. Biblical hermeneutic was open both to conservative ideas of individualistic private charity and liberal ideas of systemic social justice. Indeed, a recent biography of Baptist social gospel pioneer Walter Rauschenbusch emphasized his conversionist theology and attempts to establish balance between conversion/personal piety and activism/social justice.

Third, I began with the hypothesis that because urban problems were neither as extensive nor as long-festering in the newly industrializing South, Baptists outside the "Birmingham District" neither experienced the troubling consequences nor cared as much about them. But many of those who lived in affected areas sounded a great deal like Rauschenbusch or University of Chicago theology professor Shailer Mathews rather than some new species of evangelical merely interested in a bland regional variant of social Christianity. If they sounded like Social Gospel ministers, wrote articles like them, quoted them favorably, tried to implement their ideas, became involved in regional organizations such as the Southern Sociological Congress to accomplish their goals, brought them to Birmingham to speak, applauded their speeches, then waddling, quacking, wagging their tails, and acting very much like northern Social Gospel ducks on a pond down in Dixie probably made them so.

Finally, I emphasized the critical link between suppression of alcohol and Social Gospel reform. Just as the prohibition movement advanced the cause of woman suffrage, it also operated as a pivotal stimulant to the southern Social Gospel. In order to obtain their goal, ministers and lay people had to shed resistance to political involvement. Many rural Baptists had already done so in the 1890s when they played key roles as Populist agitators, orators, officials, and candidates. A decade later, ministers in fast-growing southern industrial cities made the same choices, a point I developed much more fully in my book Alabama Baptists.

Nor should we forget that despite historical depictions of prohibitionists as stuffy neo-Puritans trying to impose their religious opinions on everyone, alcohol abuse was a real problem, worse then than now, and usually most destructive to women and children. That is, it was a social problem for families both more extensive and destructive than child labor, industrial health and accidents, or the convict lease system. It is also worth remembering that Prohibition was a key weapon in the arsenal of many non-southern Social Gospel reformers even if the issue did achieve greater popularity in the South.

Rereading this essay in 2014, I realized that I could have qualified some statements and explained others better and more fully; I also noted that my conclusions mainly fit industrial southern cities such as Richmond, Louisville, Atlanta, Tampa, Jacksonville, Birmingham, Mobile, Nashville, Memphis, New Orleans, Dallas, and Houston. The industrial terrain where such ideas flourished was more circumscribed than in the urban North. But in relatively similar cities, remarkably similar religious debates, divisions, reforms, and activism occurred. That was my chief point in this essay, and one that I feel as strongly about nearly half a century later as I did then.

Chapter 2
Dissent in Zion
Alabama Baptists and Social Issues, 1900–1914

While much literature has been written concerning the Social Gospel in America from both historical and theological perspectives, very little of this literature has explored Southern Protestantism and social reform.[1] Charles Howard Hopkins dismisses the subject with one paragraph on the Southern Sociological Conference. Henry F. May completely ignores the progressive movement in the Southern churches. In a more contemporary analysis Samuel S. Hill Jr., contends that a major theme of Protestantism in the South has been its opposition to change and its advocacy of traditional ways.[2] Even Southern historians of eminent qualification have supported this conclusion. C. Vann Woodward observed three dominant religious movements in American Christianity in the early twentieth century: the trend toward church unity, liberalized theology, and increased emphasis on socialized Christianity. He concluded that the current of southern religious thought "ran counter to all three tendencies."[3]

Several recent studies of southern evangelical thought suggest a different conclusion. Kenneth K. Bailey notes the internal cleavage between social conservatives and progressives within Southern Protestantism and concludes that the region's social concern differed only in degree from Northern pronouncements on social problems.[4] Rufus B. Spain maintains that Southern Baptists in the late nineteenth century became increasingly involved in reform objectives for which they found biblical or moral precedent.[5]

These dissenting conclusions by Bailey and Spain offer the best setting for the study of Baptist thought in Alabama during the Progressive Era. Between 1900 and 1914 there was a substantial and vigorous intellectual assault on the social problems plaguing the nation, and the alternatives proposed by many Alabama Baptists were very similar to those popular in the activist Protestant churches of the Northeast. While this social concern was admittedly confined to urban areas and to Baptist leadership, it nonetheless won the most influential spokesmen for the denomination in Alabama: the editor of the denominational paper and the pastors of the largest and most powerful churches (powerful at least in terms of membership and financial contributions).

Perhaps the most significant revelation of the Baptist mind in Alabama was its changing attitude toward the role of church in society. In the last decades of the nineteenth century, Baptists as a denomination took little interest in social issues. This prevailing lethargy gave way to an expanding social awareness with the surge of reform sentiment in 1900. Underlying this new Baptist involvement was an altered view of the church and society. By no means did Baptists in Alabama believe that social service could replace individual regeneration; this is made abundantly clear in editorials maintaining that the traditional gospel could effectively improve society. Frank Willis Barnett, editor of the Birmingham *The Alabama Baptist*, warned against "institutional churches" which emphasized "filling a man's dinner-pail" rather than "filling his soul." This emphasis on individual renewal, however, is not unique to the South. Shailer Mathews, professor at the University of Chicago School of Theology and a prominent Northern advocate of the Social Gospel, preached that no social organization could ever replace the centrality of conversion.[6]

The significant fact is that Alabama Baptists traveled far beyond their traditionally exclusive interest in personal salvation. Barnett warned that Alabama Baptists must not reject the divine call to reform the social environment. The "Spirit of Jesus" motivated social change, and Baptists needed "to keep in touch with the great movements that today are moving like God's breath on the face of the earth, to feel those new yearnings that are swelling through the breast of humanity and slowly taking shape in brotherhood, social justice, unity of mankind."[7] In another searching editorial Barnett itemized the churches' opportunity for social service in solving the problems of worker exploitation, child and female labor, unsanitary and inadequate housing, and the failure to prevent industrial injuries and control diseases that led to poverty. "Here is the call which demands the best there is in our strong laymen and loving women."[8]

Other influential men concurred in this call for greater social concern. Washington B. Crumpton, secretary for Baptist Home Missions in Alabama and perhaps the most respected state leader, reflected the same attitude. There was a time, wrote Crumpton, when to say that a man was "conservative" was to imply that he was "safe," but "to be conservative now is to be hesitating, cautious, cowardly," for strenuous days demanded "progressives."[9] Alfred James Dickinson, influential pastor of the First Baptist Church of Birmingham, one of the largest congregations in the state, was both an advocate of the new "modernistic" theology challenging Fundamentalism and a proponent of the Social Gospel. After arguing that society was continually in flux, he concluded: "There are many of us who for a long time have doubted whether our programs for social improvement, and denominational betterment were best adapted to the changing conditions. . . . Are we doing, in view of the social situation in this state, what is most worth doing?"[10]

Another indication of the shifting intellectual milieu is found in the Baptist evaluation of the national Social Gospel movement and its various agencies. Editor Barnett surveyed the history of the "Men and Religion Forward Movement," the evangelistic cutting edge of the Social Gospel. This lay organization aimed at seventy principal cities. It was the largest and best organized of the social-reform groups and proposed a comprehensive system including a social-service organization for every church, church employment of social-service experts, passage of labor legislation, and similar measures.[11] Charles Stelzle, who headed its social-service program, in a multi-article series for *The Alabama Baptist* in 1912 and 1913 dealt with virtually every pressing social problem in America.[12] Barnett editorialized that the movement was simply a recognition that existing social conditions could not be tolerated. The genius of the organization was its realization that "no person can live unto himself and develop to full manhood. It is in his social relation that full individuality is realized." In a striking endorsement, Barnett contended that every act that helped another person nearer to God was sacred, "whether it is kneeling in prayer with face turned up to the Father, or whether it is compelling the owners of buildings to tear away walls that God's own daylight may penetrate the disease infected tenement, or loosen the bonds of child laborers, or banish saloons, or shut up houses of prostitution."[13]

His challenge to the status quo continued and intensified. The Men and Religion Forward Movement held its state convention in Birmingham in February 1912. Barnett praised the interdenominational group, whose speakers included Stelzle, a social worker, an expert in work with organized labor, and an authority on the YMCA. The next year he applauded the Presbyterian church for organizing a Bureau of Social Service and Northern Baptists for their Social Service Commission.[14] After paying tribute in 1912 to Jane Addams for a speech calling the church to involvement in social welfare, Barnett wrote that "in reality the true church of Jesus Christ and true social service are inseparably yoked together."[15]

Nor was Barnett alone in his concern for society. The new state Minister's Association, which A. J. Dickinson of Birmingham persuaded his fellow Baptist pastors to organize at the turn of the century, reflected Dickinson's social concern. The annual meetings included ministerial addresses on social issues. In 1912, for instance, Rev. Leslie L. Gwaltney spoke on "The Minister and the Labor Problem," Reverend Herman Ross Arnold on "The Minister in Politics," and Reverend J. D. Ray on "The Problem of the City."[16] Socially oriented sermons were even delivered infrequently at the annual state Baptist convention, as in 1909 when Reverend Joshua H. Foster of Anniston spoke on "Alabama Baptists and the Reforms of the Century."[17]

Some Baptists disapproved of their denomination's social concern, but the state organ of the Baptists left no doubt of its intention to continue espousing social awareness. The editor in 1907 considered "ultra conservatives" to be the chief threat to progress and warned that throughout history men who led "progressive movements of importance" had suffered attacks from reactionaries intent on preserving the status quo. When progressives departed "from the old and prevalent ideas, customs, and methods of procedure," conservatives impugned their motives and charged them with "disloyalty to the truth."[18]

A major consideration for the historian of thought is the motivation for this changing social ethic. The forces that apparently influenced Alabama Baptists differed at least in degree from the influences shaping the national advocates of the Social Gospel. With the exception of A. J. Dickinson, who was a devotee of the "Higher Criticism," which sought to demythologize the Bible, there were few theological "liberals" among advocates of reform. Editor Barnett and Secretary Crumpton, perhaps the most influential social critics in the state Baptist power structure, were both theological conservatives who bitterly contested Dickinson's advocacy of Higher Criticism.[19] They divided their writing between strictures against the inroads of theological heresy and stinging critiques of social conditions.

The Baptists of Alabama entered the economic and social arena more for practical reasons than from carefully reasoned theological principles. The two obvious factors motivating social awareness were economic uplift and prohibition. Poverty plagued Alabama, and adherents of the denomination favored reforms that often benefitted them. As will be noted later, this particularly influenced their view of labor problems. Perhaps even more important, the growing militancy over prohibition necessitated political action.

Frank W. Barnett, although hardly typical, illustrates the complex forces which shaped Baptist progressives. Born in 1865 into an affluent Black Belt family at Glenville, Barnett attended primary schools in St. Louis, Missouri, because of their high academic reputation and then studied at a private school in Paris, France. He returned to the United States and attended the University of Alabama and

Vanderbilt University. He subsequently traveled once again to Europe to continue his studies at the Sorbonne, the University of Vienna, and the University of Berlin. When he returned to the United States in 1888, he matriculated at the New York Law School and then the Southern Baptist Theological Seminary at Louisville, Kentucky. After practicing law in Barbour County, Birmingham, New York City, and Atlanta, he entered the ministry in 1895. He pastored churches in Tennessee and Georgia, resigning in 1901 to purchase *The Alabama Baptist*.[20]

Many Baptists became suspicious when he moved the paper from the sleepy capital city of Montgomery to the thriving coal and steel town of Birmingham, but they could not interfere since he owned the paper. A state Baptist historian concludes, however, that Barnett through his support of Prohibition overcame the initial reservations of many, to become quite popular and influential among Alabama Baptists.[21] Barnett, who needed ministerial support for Prohibition and his numerous other reform activities, denied that the pulpit should become a forum for partisan politics but affirmed the minister's active role in public affairs and even his holding public office: "If the preacher was heard oftener on political questions that effect [*sic*] the moral welfare of the community, it would be better for the State."[22] Barnett believed that politics in Alabama needed to be altered radically, holding in 1914 that the state's political life was "nothing but a perpetual sacrifice of temperance between the whiskey trust and big business," with public office being held by "the opportunists who publicly and brazenly wear the yoke of their masters."[23]

Other Baptist leaders adopted the same philosophy. State secretary Crumpton, a native of Wilcox County, Alabama, and a graduate of Georgetown College in Kentucky, served a term as president of the Alabama Anti-Saloon League. He warned that the "liquor power" had been in politics for a long time and suggested that preachers enter the political sphere to provide balance. As a young minister in Alabama, Crumpton first noticed the alleged power of the "liquor lobby" in the state legislature. Though he had previously been little involved in politics, he became a self-avowed lobbyist for prohibition at the state capital. He had no organizational backing and received no salary, but his opposition to the "liquor traffic" caused him to haunt the halls of the capitol at Montgomery and politicize before committees and individuals for prohibition. In 1881 he made the first temperance report to the Baptist State Convention and from that time on was the foremost champion of the cause among Alabama Baptists.[24] Prohibition catalyzed his active political life.

Rev. W. R. Whatley also concluded that the devil led the struggle to keep ministers out of politics; and a Baptist layman from South Alabama wrote that prohibitionists in his area were organizing political unions with officers in every beat of the county.[25] A. J. Dickinson favored statewide prohibition, admitted newspaper charges that he was a "political parson," and announced that since he belonged to the "church military and not the church millinery," he "wore no robes that may not be soiled in the service of humanity."[26]

Pastors oftentimes linked Prohibition to the solution of other social problems. They reasoned that political activity to prohibit liquor would also break the corrupt alliance between government and saloon, provide more money for the families of wage earners, and improve the "general social welfare of society." The best example of this juxtaposition of prohibitionist political activity and social concern came from the editorial pen of Barnett. He wrote in 1909 that any sincere minister must sometimes aggressively enter the struggle over grave social issues, particularly when they involved the "whiskey power." He attacked "ultra conservative and timid church members" who "elevate their eyebrows and rub their pious hands in deprecation" every time their pastor entered politics to improve the "moral welfare of mankind." Some laymen foolishly thought "that they can make men of God . . . talk and act as if Christianity had nothing to do with business, with pleasure, and with politics: as if it were simply a question of private life, with no social obligations." But he believed "in a Christianity that will make a man march up to the polls and vote for the right."[27]

The conclusion that politics was the legitimate vehicle for the expression of Christian ethics led some Alabama Baptists to radical positions on economic and social issues (at least "radical" when contrasted to previous Baptist thought in the state). The problem of poverty and the possible solutions reflect this advanced economic thought. Rev. Augustus Cleveland Davidson, native of Missouri and pastor of Birmingham's Southside Baptist Church, which was organized along the lines of a Northeastern "institutional church," wrote a series of articles in 1905 on social problems confronting the church. The first installment dealt with urban poverty. He suggested that poverty caused crime and disease and laid the blame for destitution at "the door of the present economic arrangements." In a subsequent article Davidson praised the ideas of urban critic Jacob Riis and proposed a program to eliminate poverty: short-term direct aid for the poor; agencies to train young people and heads of families in a useful occupation ("This is imperative. To fit one to be useful is second only to leading him to the Saviour."); and conversion.[28]

Davidson's third essay, strongly influenced by an environmental approach to poverty, concluded that tenements created juvenile crime. A church open day and night throughout the year afforded a partial solution to poverty. He proposed his program at Southside Baptist as a pattern for emulation: industrial schools for girls and women, night schools for boys and men where leisure time could be spent in reading and learning, and mission stations for workers. "Here then, is the need of strong churches in which the rich and poor unite. Churches able to provide means and appliances. Churches with many trained workers. Churches wisely located. . . . Churches that plant themselves in the midst of ruin.

. . . Around them all the social and industrial as well as the religious life of the people gather. Then only does the church fulfill it real mission."[29]

The social environment attracted much attention. Editor Barnett increasingly lamented the growth of urban poverty, slums, and subsequent social disintegration. He proposed in 1912 that Birmingham follow the example of New York by placing on each tenement, saloon, or house of prostitution a tin plate with the name and address of the owner so the public could trace the responsibility to its source—"the owner of the property."[30] Rev. L. L. Gwaltney, a prominent young pastor who gave an even more liberal direction to *The Alabama Baptist* as editor in the three decades after 1920, also took an environmental view of poverty and crime. He quoted sociologist Lester Frank Ward in 1908 to substantiate his premise that environment determined the difference between boys from the slums and from wealthier families: "one boy has the weeds taken away and the other is growing up in the midst of such social plants as are sucking and sapping his life."[31]

More radical alternatives than gradual economic reform infiltrated Baptist thought and stirred a lively dialogue. Barnett, though warning in an editorial in 1912 against turning the church into a "socialistic democracy of economic equality," reported in an earlier article that he had been interested in socialism since his student days in Paris, Berlin, and Vienna and advised all Americans to try to understand both Christian and agnostic socialism.[32]

When John Herbert Phillips, superintendent of Birmingham schools, delivered the 1909 commencement address at Howard College (a Baptist college in Birmingham, now Samford University), he contrasted the individualism and materialism of the nineteenth century with the socialism, which he predicted would characterize the twentieth century. Distribution of wealth would replace the production of wealth. While the individual would remain important, it would be the individual as a "social and institutional being, as a member of the state and of society. . . . Egotism must yield to altruism, and selfishness in individuals and in organizations must be sacrificed for the well-being of the race." The nineteenth century gave man a new material environment, the twentieth "must emphasize the ethical and moral aspects of life through social and economic organization."[33] Iconoclast A. J. Dickinson wrote for the state paper in 1904 a sermon which also suggested a "radical" economic course. Society created wealth, and the man of wealth owed rental to the society which provided it. He acknowledged that he was "socialistic enough to believe" that since wealth was a fortuitous gift of generations past, society had the right to demand "such portion thereof as she needs for her own adequate maintenance and growth."[34]

While few went so far as to question the capitalistic system, the excesses of monopoly capitalism aroused the ire of many Baptist leaders. Editor Barnett printed in 1901 a keen analysis of the financial empires of J. P. Morgan and John D. Rockefeller; since trusts had "no conscience or moral honesty," he feared the "monied aristocracy, into whose hands the government" was drifting. When a small group of men "by combination, can so control as to . . . supervene and inaugurate legislation to their wishes, and virtually rule the whole country, then it is time for good men and true to rise up."[35] Secretary W. B. Crumpton complained in 1902 that railroad trusts had eliminated competition in the South and concluded that "when the railroads all enter into one huge combine, we will all have reason to pray: 'Good Lord, deliver us.'" Barnett in 1903 praised St. Louis circuit attorney Joseph W. Folk (a Baptist layman) for exposing railroad bribery in Missouri and reprinted in 1906 a scathing attack on the beef trust by Ray Stannard Baker.[36]

"Trust busting" was also one of the most popular themes for commencement speakers at Howard College. In 1902 the alumni speaker, prominent Birmingham attorney Joseph T. Collins, devoted his speech to the subject. Editor Barnett applauded the discussion as a first step toward correcting a gigantic wrong.[37] Southern Baptist Theological Seminary professor John R. Sampey adopted the same theme for his 1906 commencement sermon. The country needed more men like Isaiah in public life, men of courage: "Experience and observation teach us that the corporations must be under the control of the government. It has been proven that these interests at times come in sharp conflict with . . . the people. . . . We need men at the head of our government and our states who will stand firm and say that you have invaded far enough on the people's rights."[38] Birmingham school superintendent John H. Phillips, the 1909 commencement speaker, argued that combinations of capital could "no longer go unchecked with their predatory processes of exploitation, but must be held accountable to a higher law than that of selfish greed and ambition."[39]

The plight of the laborer received more consideration between 1900 and 1914 than any other social issue except Prohibition. Attention focused on the unorganized worker and on child and convict labor. This interest is logical enough, since many urban Baptist churches at the beginning of the twentieth century contained a representative cross section of classes. For instance, the pastor of Ruhama, a prominent Birmingham church that served Howard College, reported that his congregation was divided into three parts: one led by a lawyer that represented the white-collar group, another composed of the families and faculty of the college, and a third led by a puddler who drew support from the workers in the factories and foundries.[40] Since many Baptists were industrial laborers, their problems were frequently matters of concern.

Numerous articles and reports surveyed the problem and advised change. A. C. Davidson of Southside Baptist devoted one of his series of thought-provoking articles in 1905 to the problems of capital and labor. Both had certain rights. The laborer possessed the "inalienable" right to sell his labor for any price he wanted and to organize into unions.[41] State missions secretary W. B. Crumpton devoted a portion of his mission reports to mill and factory workers, though his concern was more for their souls than for their economic plight. Mills that provided churches for their workers, Crumpton concluded in 1911, proved that corporations could be moral.[42]

Crumpton had bemoaned as early as 1902 the Baptist lack of interest in reaching the laborer: "When the Secretary stands before a country Association and pleads for sympathy and money to establish churches in the mill towns, he seldom gets either. . . . The average country Baptist cannot be made to see where there is any destitution in a city or town."[43] His analysis helps to explain the greater interest of urban pastors in the Social Gospel and social reform. Although Crumpton believed that the city churches bore primary responsibility for this labor ministry, he recommended employment of a full-time evangelist for the mill and mine workers, and the state convention endorsed this proposal in 1913.[44]

Baptists did some work to correct the prevailing apathy toward industrial labor. The State Board of Missions in 1903 listed a disbursement of $150 to construct a chapel in Anniston's factory district, and in 1913 the South Highlands Baptist Church was organized for miners in Bessemer.[45] Some pastors attempted to minister in various ways to laborers in their communities. Joshua Hill Foster, pastor of Birmingham's Ruhama Baptist Church, was deeply disturbed during a long industrial strike because some laborers were "starving to death." When his cow disappeared he searched for it until told that some miners had been seen killing the cow and dividing the meat. The pastor replied: "Well, they were starving. They're welcome to the cow."[46] Foster later moved to Parker Memorial Baptist Church in Anniston, where he organized missions at the net and twine mill, started a recreation program for young people, and originated the city's Chautauqua program to provide adult education.

William F. Yarborough, a native of Pickens County, Mississippi, and a graduate of Mississippi College, succeeded Foster as pastor of Anniston's Parker Memorial Church in 1909. Anniston was a northeast Alabama industrial town with a large foundry and mill population. Yarborough became distressed because his congregation, the sixth largest Baptist church in the state and one of the three leading churches in contributions, represented chiefly the privileged. He advocated the "abolition of class spirit in the church life, insisting that there was no distinction" between men in the sight of God. Motivated by this attitude, he persuaded the church to employ a social worker, whose ministry was directed to the mill families. Miss Linda Martin of Springfield, Missouri, a trained social worker, used a building donated by Parker Memorial to hold an afternoon school, and on Sunday the building was used as a Sunday school. Yarborough also emphasized evangelism and during the evolution of the mill ministry led the church in its most successful membership growth in years. While it cannot be proved that the mill ministry led to the rapid membership gain between 1910 and 1916, Yarborough's social interests were certainly accepted by the church and denominational leaders. He won the backing of his relatively elite congregation and left Parker years later to become executive secretary of the Alabama Baptist Executive Board, the highest office in the state Baptist structure.[47]

The Alabama Baptist editor Barnett also manifested sympathy for the plight of labor. In separate editorials from 1910 to 1912 he endorsed the decision of U.S. Steel to extend pensions to injured employees, praised the Federal Bureau of Mines for investigating mine explosions, and applauded the Bureau of Labor for condemning the seven-day work week in the steel industry.[48] Quickly rejecting a fatalistic acquiescence in industrial exploitation, Barnett argued that desire for profit by the corporations caused most labor problems. There would be no mine disasters, he wrote in 1913, "if coal mining were carried on for the benefit of the people instead of the making of profits." In an earlier article in 1912, he wrote that safety reforms were ignored by capitalists because it was more profitable to "work a man to get as much out of him as possible—'exploit him up to the last ounce of exploitability,' and when he drops out to fill his place with a new man—than it has been to restrict his work to his health limit."[49] Barnett proposed tighter state and federal control as a solution. Industry should be subject to inspection by state officials who would supervise all industrial establishments and have power to suggest and enforce changes; but he added that factory owners did not approve such an idea.[50] Barnett believed that the church must actively pursue such reforms, not just speak passively and abstractly of industrial justice. He wrote in a 1913 editorial entitled "Christ and Labor" that workers were disenchanted with the church for good reason: "Churches have frequently shut their eyes to the struggles of labor to get a minimum living wage; and have not heard the cry of the children who were being sacrificed in our mills; or cared when a fight was being made for shorter hours and better working conditions. It is of the utmost importance that the labor movement shall not be alienated from organized Christianity."[51]

Of all the social causes championed by the state periodical during the Progressive Era, none drew more enthusiasm from the editor than the cause of child labor. Articles and editorials condemning the use of children in mines, mills, and factories numbered in the dozens. Barnett praised the National Child Labor Committee, Sen. William E. Borah, Child Labor Day Sunday, Rev. Edgar Gardner Murphy, and almost anyone or anything attempting to abolish child labor. To purchase industrialization with the health of children constituted too great a price to pay for "progress." In 1907 the editor devoted the front page of his paper to pictures of children working in textile mills and coal mines and wrote emotional editorials describing their problems. Boys of nine and ten possessed lungs black from inhaling coal dust in the mines: "I have seen the 'merry' breaker-boys [boys who picked pieces of slate from streams of tumbling coal] with bleeding fingers. . . . Worse than all, I have heard the weeping of the mother who could not be comforted because her little boy had been engulfed in the great grinding stream of coal and smothered to death. I have seen little bodies torn by machinery in the textile industries, and the scarred hands and faces of the glass-house boys. A thousand times I have cried with the poet Hood: 'Oh God! that bread should be so dear, And flesh and blood so cheap.'"[52]

Barnett proposed positive denominational action to force legislative reform. After hearing the US commissioner of education speak on child labor in Birmingham in 1912, Barnett chided the pulpits for their silence: "It is time for us to learn here in Alabama that 'child labor means racial degeneracy, the perpetuation of poverty, the enlargement of illiteracy, the disintegration of the family, the increase of crime.'"[53] In many editorials he encouraged Baptists to join the National Child Labor Committee, write their congressmen and state representatives, and participate in Child Labor Day Sunday. He praised the 1910 Southern Baptist Convention, which passed a resolution opposing the abuse of children and censuring Congress for failure to pass laws prohibiting such labor. He did not excuse the system because of sectional pride: "the South is harboring a system of slavery more horrible than that which existed before the civil war, or which now exists in the Siberian mines—the slavery of child labor. Children from five to twelve years of age, working twelve and fourteen hours a day; babies . . . tramping wearily all day, before flying and buzzing machinery, pitiful little wrecks of humanity that wring the hearts of all who behold their thraldom, save their brutish masters the mill owners."[54]

To southerners who opposed federal regulation because it was aimed at the South he replied in 1910 that "so long as a child is thus employed anywhere on the face of the earth it happens to be some of our business, and we are in sympathy with those who want this evil brought out into the light."[55] The National Child Labor Law should be approved by all the public, he wrote in 1914; but he had warned as early as 1907 that human greed would oppose regulation, and this greed, represented by capital invested in factories, possessed great political power.[56] While his activity did not immediately end child labor in Alabama, it did contribute to an intellectual climate conducive to the political reforms during these decades.

Another major controversy raged in Alabama over the use of convict labor. The state leased convicts to private industrialists to provide cheap labor, break strikes, and create revenue for the state. Exploitation was common. Barnett in 1903 referred to charges of "peonage" in the use of convict labor and called for a complete investigation. Then in 1913 he praised a committee in Birmingham that went on record as opposing the system: " *The Alabama Baptist* is in hearty sympathy with the campaign to remove our convicts from the mines and lumber camps of the state, and to take steps . . . to abolish our system of hiring human beings to the highest bidder for cash, and throw off our cold-blooded commercialism, in which we have lost sight of the only true and proper purpose to be accomplished in dealing with this class, the prevention of crime, the reformation of the offender."[57] This was only part of his prison reform program, which also included separate reformatories for youthful Negro offenders and more humane treatment of prisoners in county jails.

It seems apparent that in economic matters influential Baptists showed a concern not unlike that of advanced devotees of the Social Gospel in other parts of the nation. The social attitudes of Alabama Baptist leadership in areas not directly involving economic reform reflect equally progressive ideas when considered in the context of the times. One of the most delicate problems which confronted the denomination, and one about which the Social Gospel nationally had little to say, was the "Negro Problem." Despite paternalistic notions to the contrary, Alabama Baptists before 1900 did almost nothing on a statewide basis either to help the Negro materially or to save his soul. But between 1900 and 1914 there was a growing conviction that white people carried some responsibility. Missions secretary W. B. Crumpton went up and down the state berating Baptists for their lack of material help to the Negro. In 1901 he reported to the state convention that Baptists should develop a plan of constructive aid. The next year the Mission Board recommended financial support for a chair of ministerial education at Negro Baptist Selma University, a program which was continued for years.[58]

Benjamin Franklin Riley, former president of Howard College, became so disturbed about worsening racial clashes that he gave up his Texas pastorate to work with Negroes. In 1909, with the encouragement of Crumpton, he organized the Southern Negro Anti-Saloon Federation with headquarters in Birmingham. Riley deplored the effort of prosaloon politicians to stir race prejudice by their attacks on the new group.[59] He wrote *The White Man's Burden* in 1910, a book on race relations that called for paternalistic help for the Negro.[60] Nor was he alone in asking for a new racial ethic. In a series of forceful editorials, editor Barnett opposed lynch law. The South, he said, could take no solace in the fact that lynching was a national problem. It was small comfort to a "right thinking man to know that pox afflicts a whole nation and not merely a single section."[61]

Some Baptists moved beyond a merely negative response to lynching and recommended new approaches to the "Negro Question." Barnett in 1904 praised a commission appointed by the Southern Baptist Convention to evaluate mission work among Negroes. He rejoiced that the commission included no racial "fire eaters," and he later chided some Alabama Baptists for discounting its work out of prejudice.[62] In 1904 Arthur James Barton, secretary for the newly expanded Southern Baptist work with Negroes, deplored the attitude that white people ought to "manage" Negroes: "We are dealing with the Negroes as fellow Christians, as fellow Baptists, as Christ's freemen. As such they are entitled to courteous and considerate treatment, and must have all of the individual . . . rights respected."[63] Pastor William Pugh Wilks, although a native of rural Pike County, Alabama, and not a college graduate, wrote an article in 1914 comparing the Negro to the New Testament Samaritans and calling attention to the responsibilities of the white people to help the black people.[64]

J. B. Albritton in September 1904 wrote the most iconoclastic article dealing with race relations, titled "The Spirit of Lawlessness." He inveighed against instilling racial prejudice in white youths over a cause that was lost forever. He noted that during election years there was suddenly much talk about the crimes of Negroes, as if they alone had done mischief; yet nothing was heard "about the crimes and punishment of white people though crime after crime is committed by them." He proposed a campaign against politicians who manipulated votes by appealing to race: "We object to give him [the Negro] an education. We object to his voting. We want him for our servant. We sell him all the liquor he can buy or drink, because we are in the liquor business for profit. We hate his color because the politicians tell us to. We are so perfect that we never see anything good in other people."[65] Certainly, few Alabama Baptists were egalitarian in this era. Yet any attempt to bridge the gap between races—even if only to evangelize or pass prohibition legislation or guarantee against lynching and the more overt forms of racism—moved Baptists beyond their nineteenth-century attitude of ignoring the Negro's very existence.

Another social issue to attract attention was public health. Barnett denounced food adulteration and satirized the opponents of federal legislation. He offered enthusiastic praise when Congress passed the Pure Food and Drug Act.[66] He was likewise concerned by tuberculosis. Citing national statistics concerning the indigent sufferers from this disease, he observed in 1910 that in Alabama no provision was made for such cases, and as a result patients had to be treated in jails or insane asylums. Barnett proposed that each town erect an institution to treat poor tuberculosis patients. Public schools should educate children about the disease, and open-air schools (recommended by the National Association for the Study and Prevention of Tuberculosis) should be provided in Birmingham.[67] Two such schools should be constructed for local Negro children: "The reactionary will protest against this act of wisdom, as usual; but if we are ever to get the best of tuberculosis in Birmingham and the south we must care for the negro also."[68]

Barnett believed that the best approach to national health problems could be found in closer affiliation between health departments of cities, counties, and states, all controlled by the national health service. He endorsed such federal legislation, noting that coordination of health activities by the national government was highly desirable in an age of concentration and unified control.[69] Federal action was necessary, he wrote in 1910, because conditions creating poor health were often controlled by financial interests more powerful than local civic authority.[70]

This same concern for the rights of society over the rights of individuals appeared in the struggle over conservation. Barnett saw the issue in 1909 in broader terms than the mere conservation of forest and mineral resources: lack of conservation caused poverty, and poverty meant the loss of educational and religious interest. The conservationist, he held, tried to instill a higher appreciation of things coming from the earth for the benefit of man and included irrigation, forestry, mining, good roads, and pure food in his area of concern.[71] Becoming specific, Barnett protested editorially in 1913 when a congressional bill threatened to turn Western national forests over to state governments. This would lead to private ownership by men who had grown rich by "looting the public domain."[72]

Like many national progressives, Alabama Baptist reformers viewed education as a key to economic and social progress. In 1902 *The Alabama Baptist* devoted an entire page to the work of the Southern Education Board. This progressive group (which included Booker T. Washington, George F. Peabody, Charles W. Dabney, Walter Hines Page, and Edgar Gardner Murphy) advocated free public schools for all Southern children. Subsequent articles in 1910 by Murphy and L. L. Gwaltney argued eloquently for universal education for all southerners of both races from the first grade through high school.[73] Barnett in 1909 endorsed a state law to allow each county to tax itself to provide better schools.[74]

This agitation led to specific progress when the state convention in 1910 appointed an education commission to survey needs and propose solutions. Since Alabama possessed no county high school system, the commission endorsed denominational academies to fill the gap between grammar school and employment or college. The state convention had first demonstrated interest in this philosophy in 1901 by purchasing the Scottsboro Academy for four thousand dollars. Before public high schools afforded serious competition in the next decade, local Baptist churches and the state convention created and operated nine secondary academies in the state.[75]

Barnett also commented on educational theory. In 1912 he praised "progressives" for taking control away from "conservatives" at the convention of the National Education Association (NEA). The convention declared itself in favor of uniform divorce laws, expanded industrial and agricultural education, instruction in sex hygiene, spreading the idea of international peace, increased teacher pay, woman suffrage, and credit for biblical literature courses. The editor praised the NEA for its vision, believing it would revolutionize American education.[76]

Immigration was another national issue to receive Baptist attention. *The Alabama Baptist* editor expressed some fear over the tide of immigration, but proved far more concerned for the welfare of the immigrants than most Americans in an age of growing exclusionism. Curiously, the Fundamentalist belief that God provided opportunity for evangelism through immigration moderated Baptist feeling toward immigrants. In 1907 Barnett called for modification of the Chinese Exclusion law because California Baptists felt it was "unchristian" to discriminate against the Chinese.[77] Birmingham Pastor O. W. Greer considered the flood of immigrants pouring into the steel city to be God's providential method of securing their salvation. He proposed that Baptists open schools to teach them English and provide a rudimentary education. Conversion would not come by evangelical confrontation but by involvement in their lives, by applying precepts of Christianity to their practical problems.[78]

This discussion by no means exhausts the areas of social concern of Alabama Baptists during the Progressive Era. Various leaders attacked prostitution in Birmingham, advocated national uniform marriage and divorce laws, circulated petitions opposing the Western opium trade in China, championed arbitration of international disputes, opposed American imperialism in the Philippines, attacked Belgian atrocities in the African Congo, questioned American armaments expenditures, and endorsed the worldwide peace crusade. In 1913 Walter Rauschenbusch, perhaps the most famous advocate of the Social Gospel, spoke on "The Social Program of the Church" at the Southern Sociological Congress in Atlanta. His speech summarized the credo of the national reform movement that had evolved within the American Protestant churches over three decades. He asked the churches to champion equal rights, uniform divorce laws, abolition of child labor, improved education, regulation of female labor, prevention of poverty, prohibition, conservation, health reform, protection of workers from industrial accidents, help for the aged, arbitration of labor disputes, a six-day work week, the gradual reduction in hours of labor, and a living wage.[79] Between 1900 and 1914 *The Alabama Baptist* and prominent clerics in the state endorsed with varying degrees of enthusiasm all of these reforms.

Although the denomination remained essentially Fundamentalist and devoted to a literal interpretation of Scripture, this by no means obviated a dynamic witness on the problems confronting society. While this witness was oftentimes confined to the Alabama Baptist administrative hierarchy and urban pastors and rarely penetrated the rural churches, it nevertheless reflected a growing intellectual climate of reform within denominational thought. Perhaps some reform advocates did more talking than acting, yet the presence of institutional church programs, church-employed social workers, and improved rural education suggests that many pastors were searching for ways to implement their theories. Most significantly, however, there was a change of attitude and philosophy that helped prepare the way for political and social change. One can conclude that many influential Baptist leaders and pastors in Alabama were forcefully committed to progressive social ideas and championed them with a courage and candor not subsequently excelled and perhaps not since equaled in the state.

—*The Journal of Southern History*, 1969

Appointment as Distinguished University Professor at Auburn University relieved me of one semester's teaching responsibilities each academic year. I filled the space with doctoral students writing mainly about religion and lots of off-campus lectures. I especially relished lay religious audiences such as the Southeastern Methodist Historical Society, which met in July 2003.

As often happened, issues of contemporary life and public policy seemed eerily reminiscent of patterns long established. Wherever possible, I tried to connect the historical dots. As one of my favorite novelists, Lee Smith of North Carolina, wrote in Oral History, *"nothing is ever over, nothing is ever ended, and worlds open up within the worlds we know."*

In this lecture, I constructed a narrative about Alabama Methodists paralleling my 1969 essay about the state's Baptists. The difference is application of the past to contemporary social ethics, which reflects my search for a "usable past." By reminding the audience how many of their spiritual forebears had worked to establish the Kingdom of God in Dixie, I hoped they would understand better their contemporary denominational debate about tax and constitutional reform, social justice, and poverty.

Chapter 3
Alabama Methodists and the Social Gospel, 1900–1930

During summer 2003 Alabama dipped into one of its periodic funding crises. The already inequitably funded state education system required more than a half billion dollars just to stay afloat. State prisoners had to be housed out of state because of inadequate funds for constitutionally mandated treatment. Many state agencies were being sued for unconstitutional provision of services (or lack thereof). The existing tax system, America's most regressive, taxed its poorest citizens at the highest national rate and its wealthiest at the lowest.

When reforms addressing many of these issues passed the state legislature, some political analysts claimed that the key to the outcome of a September public referendum would be what happened in the state's churches. Christian Coalition of Alabama proposed cutting government waste rather than raising taxes, arguing that the reform package was not family friendly.

On the other end of the evangelical spectrum, churches serving black and white parishioners roused from a long slumber and mobilized for an unlikely battle. Claiming the Bible as text and social justice as goal, lay leaders, clergy, and bishops staked out the moral terrain for a new social justice crusade. Susan Pace Hamill—a University of Alabama law professor, specialist in tax law, Methodist laywoman, and graduate of Samford University's theologically conservative Beeson Divinity School (where she wrote a thesis measuring Alabama's tax code against biblical standards of justice)—seemed an unlikely Joan of Arc carrying the flag of justice and leading her cohort into battle. Her crusade further emboldened Methodists who had already endorsed tax reform. Bishop Robert E. Fannin of the North Alabama Conference explained, "For the sake of children and the poor, we need both constitutional reform and tax reform." Republican Governor Bob Riley, a conservative Southern Baptist and champion of the tax reform package, appeared before the 2003 Alabama-West Florida Conference to argue that the Bible commanded Christians to love one another, especially the poor. Claiming that his reforms addressed moral issues by shifting the heaviest tax burden from the poor to the rich, he called for the church to mobilize its members for the September referendum. Bishop Larry Goodpaster interpreted the nearly unanimous delegate vote in favor of tax justice to be an indication of Methodist "understanding of the call to take care of God's people. The current tax plan is unjust."[1]

Reporters from the *Wall Street Journal* and other national news outlets were sufficiently amazed that evangelical southern Christians had suddenly discovered that the Gospel applied to issues of social justice and public policy that they called me for comment. I was not surprised at all. In fact, during the interviews my mind drifted back more than a hundred years to a theological gestation of immense importance.

In 1900 economic conditions were much more frightful. With the industrial New South in rapid construction and immigrants and rural people pouring into manufacturing cities such as Richmond, Tampa, New Orleans, and Birmingham, society became disrupted and chaotic. Slums could not house all the newcomers. The rate of child labor in textile mills, coal mines, and factories exploded. Women were drawn into the labor force by the so-called family wage that required all members work in order to obtain basic necessities. Trusts snuffed out competition and exploited workers. A system of racial apartheid engulfed black people. Women were denied fundamental rights available even to the mentally ill and to male children.

Where such conditions became most intense, in the Northeast and Midwest, churches adjusted the Gospel to new social realities. How could one save the souls of the poor or even attract a serious hearing amidst squalor, hopelessness, and degradation? As part of that adjustment, Christian leaders articulated the Social Gospel. The theology applied Christian ethics to the human situation in a collective way that went well beyond individual charity and personal conversion. Changing the social order became a priority equal to (and at least among a fringe, even greater than) individual conversion. Harry F. Ward, a Methodist professor at Union Theological Seminary in New York City, became one of the most liberal Social Gospel advocates.[2]

How one defines Social Gospel determines how widely it spread. In the classic work on the subject, Charles Howard Hopkins referred to it as "America's most unique contribution to the great ongoing stream of Christianity." He accepted the definition of University of Chicago professor and Baptist theologian Shailer Mathews as the "application of the teaching of Jesus and the total message of the Christian salvation to society, the economic life, and social institutions . . . as well as individuals."[3] Historian Robert Handy disagreed about the movement's uniqueness, tracing its origins to attempts to apply biblical impulses of justice and love to humanity. The Social Gospel seemed radical only because injustice within society was so extreme. Its leaders emphasized the power of the Gospel literally to reorder, reshape, and transform civilization. Beyond that common denominator, there is no single template to which all northern Social Gospel advocates conformed. Some promoted social justice as a higher Christian value than conversion. Others were more balanced.[4]

Historian George Marsden offered an alternative definition, arguing that the genuine test of the Social Gospel was "whether other aspects of Christianity are subordinated to, and in effect incidental to, its social aspects."[5] Advocates of this view insisted that the application of Christian ethics in the North took precedence over evangelism and should properly be called the Social Gospel. In the South, such hierarchy of values never took hold, and therefore whatever elements of social reform emerged should be referred to as "social Christianity," "social action," or "social concerns," but not full-fledged Social Gospel.[6] Actually, issues were hardly ever that simple in North or South. New research on Walter Rauschenbusch makes clear that his sermons in the German Baptist church in New York remained evangelical even after he became a crusading Social Gospel leader. He hardly ever referred to the Social Gospel while in his pulpit.

This semantic debate reminds me of a new scientific discovery. The person who makes the discovery often earns the right to name it. In this case, historians first discovered the application of Christianity to social ills in northern and midwestern industrial cities, so Protestant patterns of response there became normative. When historians finally realized that similar patterns existed in the South, they sought to distinguish regional from national patterns by using a different name for the Social Gospel.[7]

I will take a contrarian position that southern Protestantism developed its own full-blown Social Gospel tradition. It did not gain as strong traction as in the North for a variety of reasons: southern religion was more conservative and traditional; the region was more rural and had fewer large industrial cities; Social Gospel ministries paid stricter attention to whether they won professions of faith from recipients of social ministries; they went out of their way to skirt comparisons of their work to the northern Social Gospel for fear they would be condemned as theological liberals. They might establish a settlement house that functioned almost identically to one in Chicago or New York, but concern for how such ministries might be perceived in their denominations caused them to give these places names such as the House of Happiness or Goodwill Center. Their hope, it sometimes seems, was to sanitize social ministry by baptizing it with a generic name. Judged by historical inattention, this early attempt to camouflage their cause worked exceptionally well.[8]

John Patrick McDowell first offered a revisionist approach in a 1982 book about involvement of the Methodist Episcopal (ME) Church, South, and women in the Social Gospel. Samuel J. Shepherd Jr. followed in 2001 with an exhaustive study of the Social Gospel in Richmond, Virginia, between 1900 and 1930, including the significant role played by Methodists.[9]

As I have made clear elsewhere, criticism of such efforts came from conservative evangelicals who denounced its emphasis on the environmental sources of sin and claimed that a new coat of paint on the pen did not change the nature of the pig inside.[10] Furthermore, neo-orthodox theologians Reinhold Niebuhr and his brother, Richard, considered the Social Gospel naively optimistic because of its de-emphasis on original sin. Richard lumped it together with liberal theology in his famous dismissal: "A God without wrath brought men without sin into a kingdom without judgment through the ministrations of a Christ without a cross." Civil rights historian Ralph Luker added his criticism, arguing that the movement lacked focus, organization, "disciplined action and demonstrable achievements," although he does concede its seminal influence on Martin Luther King Jr. Historian Martin Marty joined the battle with his "two-party" thesis that American religion polarized between conservative/evangelical and liberal/Social Gospel factions, with little—if anything—gravitating from one camp to the other.[11]

If this is more than you ever wanted to know about both the definition of the Social Gospel and whether historians thought it actually existed in the South, I beg your indulgence. If you understand how thoroughly historians expected NOT to find it there, you can appreciate my surprise while working in the Birmingham-Southern College archives during the 1960s and 1970s and discovering a rich Social Gospel tradition in the ME Church.

The most important early interest came from women. Nationally, Methodist women created foreign and home mission societies in 1878 and 1880. In 1888 more than 200 home mission societies enrolled 3,500 members; by 1940 enrollment had grown to 300,000. These women constituted the strike force for the Social Gospel within the denomination. Institutionally, the intellectual incubator of such women was Scarritt College in Kansas City, Missouri, where Mabel

Howell, the school's first professor of sociology, proposed to create a new social order as well as a new individual. Scarritt opened in 1892 and became the training school for Methodist women entering home or foreign missions with many home missionaries essentially becoming urban social workers. The year Scarritt began, Methodist women also opened Wolff Mission School in Ybor City, Florida, for children of Cuban immigrants. They soon expanded their work to another school in West Tampa, and in 1904 established an Italian mission that enrolled 100 immigrant students. Within a decade, Methodists were running a night school with reading rooms and a gymnasium that supported six mission churches staffed by nine missionaries. What Tampa Methodists called "missions" were in the North called "settlement houses," and they functioned in the same way.[12]

Similar urban industrial ministries staffed by city missionaries became the vehicle for social ministries elsewhere. By 1899, seventeen special city missionaries worked in ten cities. After 1900 settlement houses became the common venue for such ministries, first in Nashville in 1901, followed by Atlanta, Dallas, and St Louis. Over the next four decades, forty-five Methodist settlement houses opened across the South. As a result, in 1902 the General Conference established the order of deaconesses despite opposition from many men. Over 300 "consecrated" deaconesses served as city missionaries as well as hundreds of others not officially so designated. Some, such as Lillie Meekin, who spent 20 years directing Mary Werlein Mission in New Orleans, and Minnie Boykin in Biloxi, Mississippi, became legendary for their work.[13]

Although some Methodists insisted these missions were not really settlement houses, that is certainly the way they functioned. A typical mission conducted a kindergarten for poor children, literacy classes, and boys and girls clubs; taught crafts and homemaking; provided hygiene programs; ran job placement bureaus; provided temporary lodging for homeless and transient men and women; and even offered medical treatment by volunteer physicians.

McDowell found that the southern home mission magazine *Our Homes* also recommended many books authored by northern Social Gospel ministers, especially Baptist pastor/theologian Walter Rauschenbusch. The magazine mentioned no conflict between social and personal ministries, emphasized the presence of the Kingdom of God in this world as the result of social reform and the influence of environment on human conduct. Methodist reformers endorsed better funding for public schools, fair treatment for labor, and restrictions on irresponsible corporations and trusts.

From modest beginnings in Ybor City, Methodists rapidly expanded social ministries. In Richmond, Virginia, the South's premier industrial city at the beginning of the twentieth century, Pastor Joseph T. Mastin of Trinity Methodist Church persuaded his congregation to provide temporary shelter for indigent men. City missionary George Wiley expanded this program into the Methodist

Institute, supported by local Methodist churches. Although a veteran evangelist himself, Wiley proclaimed that Richmond's mission field needed "baths more than . . . Bibles," children's clubs more than prayer meetings, nutrition more than tracts. The institute purchased the old United States Hotel and refurbished twenty-five rooms. In 1902 it cared for 700 transient men who worked at the facility to pay their board. The institute also provided a library, baths, playground, and boys club, with local physicians staffing its infirmary. Deaconesses soon added girls clubs. In time, Wiley added a night school, carpentry classes, and a job placement service that found work for several hundred men each year. A female board of visitors distributed food, clothing, and medicine to the neighborhood's poor. The institute, of course, also conducted regular worship and Sunday school classes.

In 1928 the Virginia Conference transformed Trinity Methodist into an institutional church, centering its urban missions there. Trinity functioned as a community center directed by a deaconess and assumed oversight of the Methodist Institute, Goodwill Industries (which accepted products for repair and resale), and the Wilson Inn, which had begun in 1912 to provide inexpensive board for young women moving to Richmond in order to find employment in the city's tobacco factories or as sales clerks, telephone operators, or stenographers.[14]

City churches proved extremely supportive of reform both in rural areas and urban.[15] Lucy Randolph Mason, the famous social reformer and CIO organizer, conducted a conference on the eight-hour work day at Broad Street Methodist Church in Richmond, urging churches to endorse the reform. John W. Shackford, her host pastor, observed that churches needed to "help men see the conflict of existing conditions with the standards of the Kingdom," and Trinity's pastor, J. T. Mastin, became first director of Virginia's State Board of Charities and Corrections and a preeminent prison reformer.[16]

Although Virginia's Methodist bishop, James Cannon Jr., played a prominent role in the Prohibition crusade and strongly opposed Catholic Al Smith's 1928 presidential candidacy, he was also an educational reformer, pushed for union with more liberal northern Methodism, and endorsed a host of domestic and international reforms.[17]

Similar ripples spread southward. James Myers, a New York Presbyterian and the industrial secretary of the Social Gospel–oriented Federal Council of Churches, visited North Carolina textile towns in 1929 to investigate growing labor unrest and violence. He scolded local clergy for their general indifference to the causes of labor and encountered few southern ministers sympathetic to his agency. But he also discovered that many textile strikers were deacons, Sunday school teachers, and other officers in Methodist, Baptist, Holiness, and Pentecostal churches.[18]

Georgia also produced a number of Methodist Social Gospel leaders. In fact, Atlanta rivaled Richmond for settlement work. Will Alexander, who had spent time as a Methodist pastor in Nashville, developed his interest in racial cooperation while organizing relief for unemployed workers in 1915. In 1920, he helped establish and then led the Commission on Interracial Cooperation (CIC), headquartered in Georgia's capital. Churchwomen, many of whom were Methodist, constituted core support for the Women's Department of the CIC. In 1911, Methodist women organized a settlement house for Negro children in Atlanta.[19]

Walter B. Hill, a prominent Methodist layman and leader of the Georgia temperance movement, became chancellor of the University of Georgia in 1898. He functioned in that strategic post as a progressive reformer who introduced a curriculum patterned after the University of Wisconsin and based on service to the state. He favored coeducation, was a racial moderate who served as a trustee of African American Paine College, worked to raise money for black education, and retained his populist views from the 1890s, endearing him to the state's small farmers.[20]

Conventional wisdom depicts the Upper South as more enlightened than the Deep South, the latter of which was unusually resistant to change and progressive ideas. But Alabama challenged this assumption. In 1900 Birmingham, located in Alabama's coal district, was poised to displace Richmond as the South's premier manufacturing city. Coal mines, iron and steel factories, coke ovens, railroad shops, and textile mills dotted the landscape for a sixty-mile radius around the city. Italian and eastern European immigrants, as well as poor white and black tenant farmers, poured into the region. Ten years later, Birmingham contained one of the highest proportions of immigrants of any southern city, with 6,000 first-generation immigrants and 10,000 more with at least one foreign-born parent. The city's percentage of black population led all American urban centers of at least 100,000 people.[21] Unions flourished, especially during the 1890s, 1910s, and 1930s. Although Mobile had entered a long decline after the Civil War when upland railroads stripped away the city's importance as one of America's busiest ports, large numbers of mills, factories, immigrants, and poor migrants created similar social problems there as well. Montgomery, Huntsville, and the rural Chattahoochee Valley—even small towns such as Anniston and Gadsden—added cotton mills and foundries. Methodists responded to these social problems in much the same way they had in Chicago, New York, Richmond, and Atlanta.

Birmingham became the primary setting for Methodist ministries for obvious reasons. They dominated Protestant white church membership within the city limits at the beginning of the twentieth century. In 1904 Methodists enrolled some 3,300 members in seven churches compared with only 1,575 Southern Baptists in three congregations. Methodists published the *Alabama Christian Advocate* in the city, a well-edited paper with a weekly circulation of 10,000. Rev. James H. McCoy, the editor, commented insightfully about a variety of social issues, including Prohibition, education, poverty, corporation abuses, and child labor, quite a change from 1900 when it took no stand on much of anything other than Prohibition. In 1901, 67,000 North Alabama and 51,000 Alabama-West Florida Methodists were organized in two conferences that nearly divided the state evenly with the state's 130,000 white Southern Baptists.

Powerful new forces beyond the influence of editor McCoy were also transforming religion in the Magic City. Shailer Mathews, Baptist Social Gospel exponent at the University of Chicago Divinity School, energized citizens with twelve lectures during spring 1906 on the life and teachings of Jesus to warm endorsement by the *Alabama Christian Advocate*.[22] The Missionary Training School in Nashville conducted short courses on urban and rural church renewal, designed to involve women in social ministries. One Methodist minister described Birmingham as a collective being, which loved, sinned, died, and passed into judgment. "It is one thing to live in a city," he wrote. "It is quite another thing to live for a city."[23]

Nashville's Methodist connection was important to unfolding events in Birmingham. The *Nashville Christian Advocate*, the denomination's leading newspaper, pursued the most liberal stance on labor issues of any southern church publication, questioning America's economic system and assailing the profit motive. Of all southern denominations during the 1930s, one historian argues that Methodists demonstrated the greatest concern for industrial workers, upholding their right to organize and adopting the expansive social creed of the Federal Council of Churches.[24]

The Woman's Board of Home Missions provided critical direction for Alabama Methodist women. It both organized and publicized social ministries. In Alabama, Nettie Erwin Webb, of Opelika, and Mrs. J. P. Jackson, of Birmingham, wrote insightful columns about social ministries for the *Alabama Christian Advocate*. Their columns described Methodist women who opened free kindergartens, worked among immigrants and the rural poor, established rescue homes for women, and sought to end child labor, as well as helped to achieve juvenile courts for youthful offenders, public health reforms, better housing and higher wages for industrial workers, the eight-hour work day, separate toilets for men and women in mills and factories, pensions for working women, female factory inspectors, and a minimum wage law.[25] In fact, the "Social Service" section of the *Advocate* endorsed almost all major national reforms advocated by the northern Social Gospel movement between 1900 and 1930. As social service editor, Mrs. J. B. Cummings wrote succinctly in 1913: "Many of the causes of this human wreckage lay in conditions in our social and industrial order which were, and are out of harmony with the teachings of Christ." She proposed changing the entire social fabric, not just individuals.[26]

Of course, Birmingham Methodists did not operate in a denominational vacuum. Many of the city's Baptists, Presbyterians, Episcopalians, Catholics, and Jews engaged in similar initiatives. Jewish charities, the WCTU Mercy Home, the Alabama Industrial School for Wayward Boys, the Birmingham Free Kindergarten Association, Salvation Army House, Rescue Home for "unfortunate women," Boys Club, Girls Home, Holy Innocents Hospital for Children, Hillman (Charity) Hospital, and Octavia White Home for Aged and Infirmed Old Ladies, all began between 1895 and 1915. Churchwomen organized the Birmingham Social Settlement Association specifically inspired by a 1911 lecture given by Jane Addams of Hull House to the National Child Labor Conference meeting in Birmingham. The County Board of Revenue, swept along by new social service currents, supported five new settlement houses for a total of seven in the city (one for black citizens, the other six for white citizens).[27]

None of these groups, however, matched the influence of Methodist women, who introduced both settlement house and free kindergarten movements to Birmingham. An article by deaconess Elizabeth Taylor in the *Alabama Christian Advocate* was the catalyst for the creation of the City Board of Missions in 1903. Women from home mission societies at St. John's and First Methodist established the board and opened the first settlement house in June of that year with a second soon to follow. Ten leading downtown churches ultimately supported the houses, managed by one minister and one woman from each congregation. Each was staffed by fully trained social workers. Six of the houses offered comprehensive social services that included free kindergarten, sewing and cooking classes, playgrounds, boys and girls clubs, adult recreation, daily child care for working mothers, night literacy classes, and free milk for babies.[28]

By 1908 the women had opened a Wesley House at Avondale Mills under the direction of a deaconess, enrolling forty children in its free kindergarten and fifty girls in sewing classes. At the end of the first year of operation, the ministry had outgrown its facility. By 1912 the initial session of the North Alabama Conference Woman's Missionary Society considered these facilities the heart of their urban ministries. They had also begun another Wesley House in Ensley that mainly served Italian immigrants working at the TCI mills. U.S. Steel was so impressed with the social improvements that it contributed financially to the settlement houses near its facilities.[29]

First Methodist, which had been a pioneer in settlement house work, steadily expanded social ministries. By 1931 its social service department furnished clothes as well as medical and hospital care to the poor; gave scholarships to needy boys and girls; paid tuition for teenagers to attend Berry School, Snead Seminary, and the state vocational school; established Goodwill Industries to provide jobs for the poor; funded the Eva Comer Cooperative Home for girls, in which board was based on salary; and funded Ensley's Wesley House and the Bethlehem House (a day nursery and kindergarten for African Americans).[30]

In the port city of Mobile, Methodist settlement work began in 1904 with acquisition of an old store with three attached rooms for social workers' quarters. Home mission societies established a City Mission Board and hired Mary Peery from Scarritt Training School and Estelle Haskins from a settlement home in Dallas to begin work similar to that in Birmingham. By 1905 the women had bought a new site on Canal Street closer to the heart of the city, employed a kindergarten teacher, and begun a day care nursery. In 1906 Miss E. M. Ganow, a seven-year veteran of New York City social work, assumed leadership of the Mobile house. Deaconess Almeda Hewitt added a free medical clinic with five physicians and employed five salaried workers and seventeen volunteers. Called the "best all around social agency in the city" by boastful Methodists, the settlement house by 1910 had added a detention home for juvenile offenders, a free public library, and a night school. By that year, the head resident was a nurse, and seven physicians staffed the dispensary and performed simple surgery.

In 1910 Leila Dumas, president of Mobile's Woman's home mission society, donated half the cost of a new institutional church to be constructed in the Mobile cotton mill district. The building's cost ($15,000) and $200 monthly expenses came largely from Dumas and other Methodist women. Dumas Institutional Church served a community of 400 poor white citizens, providing the area's only church or school. The impressive brick building had a chapel where Rev. J. D. Hartzog regularly preached; two large rooms on the lower floor for a medical clinic, library, and day nursery; and five living rooms for workers on the second floor.[31]

Settlement work quickly expanded to other locations across Alabama. By 1913 Methodists in Attala, a mill town adjacent to Gadsden, supported a deaconess working with textile mill people, and in Blockton, Methodists provided the same for immigrant coal miners. The following year Montgomery Methodists opened a Wesley House.[32]

Settlement houses mainly served urban workers, and the most progressive Social Gospel leaders sympathized with labor's attempt to unionize. Drawing from the consistent labor reform agenda of the ME Church, South's denominational paper in Nashville, editors of the *Alabama Christian Advocate* became reliable exponents of workingmen and women. The paper printed texts of speeches by southern bishops calling for a solution to labor problems. Speaking to the Alabama Conference Home Mission Boards, A. M. McMillan described problems of immigrants and slums, in addition to the conflict between labor and capital. McMillan believed the church must create a new economic environment centered in an "open church," utilizing its wealth and facilities to establish kindergartens, gymnasia, reading rooms, night schools, and other services.[33]

The paper's editor admitted that the church was losing the laboring masses but believed such defections were not inevitable. Unlike workers in the northern and western states, southern workers did not oppose the church "and are in the main very far from opposed to religion." He added that creating new churches alone would not solve the problem: "The poorer people will not be won by building chapels for them"; the "old order of things, simply preaching on Sundays," must give way to efforts to "better the conditions of living in the slums, in the tenements, in the factory settlements and wherever the blight of poverty and ignorance and vice rests upon men." One subscriber to the paper agreed, concluding that the most vital issue of the times was to demonstrate to workers that the church offered a way to ameliorate harmful social conditions. The church had to change, be true to its highest calling, or alienate workers. Industrial injustice and Christian apathy—"where we manifest no interest in his body, in the problems of his daily life that bear down on him and perplex him"—caused the laborer to doubt the church's concern for his soul.[34]

The Alabama Conference institutionalized its Social Gospel efforts in a Social Service Commission midway through the first decade of the new century. The agency's 1910 report argued that while "social salvation" could not replace personal conversion, it remained a critical element in the battle against "syndicated sin." Toward this end, the report endorsed a reduced work week, a maximum 10-hour day for women, and concluded that working conditions must not be determined by corporate greed but "upon the ground of health and public welfare." The 1911 report elaborated on the church's social task, maintaining that it must "work into the activities of society a constant force which will modify the whole social fabric and make a kingdom of God among men."[35]

Predictably, women's mission societies took the lead on justice for labor as on so many other issues. In fact, some elements of labor reform allowed Victorian women not inclined to support woman suffrage to advocate change. Like the temperance crusade, concerns for the health and welfare of mothers, the family wage that forced women out of the home and into the labor force or even into prostitution, and especially child labor, were considered issues entirely appropriate to woman's Victorian sphere of home and family.

Child labor particularly incensed them. During the decade between 1885 and 1895, the number of adult male textile workers in Alabama increased by 31 percent, adult women by 75 percent, girls under age 18 by 148 percent, boys under 18 by 81 percent. By 1900 a quarter of the state's textile workers were under 16, and by 1910, 1,000 children between ages 10 and 13 labored in cotton mills. The denomination's temperance committee entered the fray in 1901, calling on the next general assembly to endorse a law prohibiting the employment of children under age 12. A. H. Shannon, professor at Methodist-affiliated Millsaps College in Jackson, Mississippi, wrote an article on child labor for the *Alabama Christian Advocate*. Calling child labor morally wrong, he added that traditional solutions to the problem (moral suasion and individual philanthropy) had failed. Only agitation and legislation limiting the working age to 16 years would solve the problem. Editor McCoy added his opinion that child labor thrived because of industrialists' greed. "Industrial slavery" of children called for "swift and decisive reformatory measures."[36]

When industry lobbying killed a child labor reform measure in the 1902 legislature, McCoy unleashed his fury on arguments that regulatory legislation would scare off "foreign investment" in Alabama: "In other words, it appeared to be a good business proposition to barter away the poor white children of the state for a little more industrial development." Legislators, "drunk with sight of a new era of prosperity," sacrificed "Southern babes for Yankee dollars." Noting that 30 percent of Alabama's textile employees were under age 16, the largest percentage of any state, he implored the legislature to act.[37]

After the legislature enacted limited child labor reform the following year under intense lobbying from religious groups, Methodists demanded even more stringent laws in 1907. The *Alabama Christian Advocate* launched the campaign with a blistering attack on textile mills and coal mines for employing children. Arguing that legislative tax advantages extended to corporations were disproportionate to their worth to the state, McCoy wrote that if mills could not be run profitably without "levying tribute on children we had better let New England keep them." He also called for a limit on child labor under age 14, factory inspection to enforce existing laws, strict school attendance provisions, and liberal educational appropriations to improve schools. While he preferred state to federal regulation, he endorsed national restrictions if the state failed to act. After the legislature passed a compromise measure that limited work age to 12 years and work hours to 60 per week, the editor continued his agitation to establish true justice for children. At the 1913 second annual conference of the North Alabama Conference Woman's Missionary Society in Huntsville, Mrs. Arch Trawick spoke on the commandment "Thou shalt not kill," giving it a unique twist: "We allow laws which permit this to happen to women and children who toil." To fully appreciate the radicalism of such comments and actions requires one to remember that from the end of Reconstruction through the twentieth century Alabama's economic development strategy consisted of recruiting low-wage and low-skill industry, keeping taxes low, rejecting regulation of industries, and opposing labor unionism.[38]

As Alabama's workforce became increasingly manufacturing based, Methodists struggled hard to apply their ethical precepts to emerging industrial realities. All agreed that the denomination must redouble its efforts in mill towns and mining camps. At first, this emphasis consisted almost exclusively of personal evangelism. But as years passed, the social gospel impinged more and more on Methodist thinking. The *Alabama Christian Advocate* in 1902 summarized a speech given by the US Commissioner of Labor on how to obtain industrial peace after years of violent labor-management conflict. Socialism, factory inspection, and arbitration had all failed; religion alone held the answer. Man's treatment of his fellows depended on his own sense of justice, and social reform depended on religion. The same sentiment gained popularity at the 1903 General Board of Missions of the ME Church, South meeting in St. Louis. Officials called for organization of city mission boards to investigate labor problems and reattach laborers to the church. British and northern Methodists had done this with great success, speakers observed, and the South must follow their example. The editor of Alabama's denominational paper agreed. The growing complexity of industrial relations, McCoy wrote, exacerbated class differences. The old order of Sunday sermons no longer sufficed. Methodist efforts to eradicate slums and tenements and reduce poverty must follow the example of Christ who had ministered to physical as well as spiritual needs: "The average man will take our declaration of interest in his soul with a large grain of salt, where we manifest no interest in his body. . . . Doling out a few dollars" for home missions would not solve industrial problems.[39]

A 1905 missionary training school for Birmingham's Methodist preachers featured addresses by Methodist-related Vanderbilt professor Thomas Carter and Dr. E. O. Watson of Spartanburg, South Carolina. They discussed the need for vigorous action on child labor and other unjust industrial conditions and agreed that the South's dominant denomination would be the one most attentive to religious life in mill towns. Bishop Charles B. Galloway, addressing the ME Church, South general conference the following year added that brotherhood would prevail only when "the vast triumphs of commercial genius are converted into means for the betterment and not the oppression of the poor;" "The courageous application of the fundamental laws of righteousness and love to every great social and industrial problem is the chief duty of the church."[40]

Whereas Methodists had earlier touted mill village chapels and increased evangelism as the way to bring workers back into the church, by 1910 many favored application of the Social Gospel. That same year essays on cotton mill towns published in the *Alabama Christian Advocate* by Rev. Raleigh W. Greene of Montgomery advocated compulsory education, the end of child labor, and better housing as ways to reconnect workers to Methodism rather than preaching, because few mill people attended evangelistic services anyway. Greene argued, "The most religious thing may be to teach a boy the multiplication table, or give him a place to read or rest or bathe or play, and not a 'meeting.'" He admitted that he did not have all the answers, but "mere preaching is not doing the work"; and the new ministry must "touch . . . body and mind and heart, the home and social and business life."[41]

Despite increasing sentiment favoring individual workers and seeking ways to improve their welfare, few issues divided Methodists more sharply than unionism and strikes. Traditional and individualistic white southerners tended to oppose both as socialistic. Business opportunists proclaimed their own gospel that unionism constituted a barrier to southern industrial development. But even on this point, opinion began to change after 1900. Early century reports in the *Alabama Christian Advocate* recounted the organization of preaching services in mining camps and their salutary effect on the conduct of miners. The journal also noted that many mine owners and superintendents (presumably antiunion), as well as coal miners, were Methodists.[42]

Opinions began to change as the social gospel challenged the efficacy of traditional evangelism. The pastor of Birmingham's First Methodist Church sided with strikers demanding higher wages and better working conditions in 1900, and the *Alabama Christian Advocate*'s editorial page began a slow evolution. Workers had the right to organize unions to address their grievances just as capital organized into corporations and trusts. Both sides sought self-protection. But a strike used as a method of settling disputes pitted one powerful organization against another with little concern for what was morally "right" or for public welfare. Editors wrote that Christians should favor the weakest combatant because God did not always favor the strongest in such struggles. Binding arbitration offered a better way to resolve disputes because the entire social system suffered from disruptive strikes. During the 1902 national coal strike, the *Advocate's* editor criticized coal companies for initially rejecting arbitration, writing that their recalcitrance gave striking miners the moral high ground. He also endorsed the miners' chief objective: the right to organize. At the same time, he rejected labor demands for governmental ownership of mines as socialistic.[43] When a 1908 north Alabama coal strike turned violent, the editor rejected what he considered to be dangerous anarchism and endorsed the governor's use of state militia to restore order.

Out in the coal fields where Methodist ministers confronted such conflicts as close observers rather than theoretical abstractions, sympathy for miners was more pronounced. Rev. W. P. Blevins, who had preached to miners for six years, noted that Methodists were winning more converts on foreign mission fields than in Alabama mining camps. He complained that the membership of most coal town Methodist churches consisted of managers and supervisors rather than miners because they did not want to worship with company officials. If churches wanted to reach miners, they should provide reading material, social activities, a small gymnasium, baths, and a room devoted to literacy classes. Every large camp should establish a Methodist kindergarten and, if possible, employ a deaconess to begin social welfare programs. Laymen should regularly conduct services, "as often as possible by a miner in the interest of miners." Blevins's congregations enthusiastically endorsed his proposals.[44]

Rev. J. R. Nelson, secretary of the Mission Board, agreed with Blevins. He wrote that Methodist pastors seeking to convert coal miners must fully identify with them, which meant buying a miner's cap and carbide lamp, going down into the mine, watching what miners did, and sharing the danger. Presently, miners identified the preacher as a company man. Methodist pastors made a serious mistake when they opposed unions and instead should become at least advisory members of the United Mine Workers.[45]

This brief discussion of Alabama Methodists' encounter with urban and industrial problems between 1900 and 1930 does not begin to exhaust the denomination's involvement in Social Gospel causes. Reforms in education, public health, international peace, women's suffrage, even cautious calls for fairer treatment of African Americans, all gained currency within the denomination during these three decades.

Despite my attention to expanding Social Gospel influence, I caution that this stirring occurred within a theologically conservative denomination. Alabama Methodist advocacy of the Social Gospel drew its sources from simple biblical justice and pragmatic recognition that pietistic revivalism was no longer effective in converting the poor, immigrants, urban newcomers, and industrial workers.

Evidence of this continuing theological orthodoxy is nearly as compelling as evidence of growing interest in social justice. Not until 1918, half a decade after Alabama Baptists allowed women to vote at their state convention, did Alabama Methodists enact this reform. The 1914 conference acknowledged loss of the denomination's "most spiritual members to the Nazarenes and other churches," while expressing alarm at the silence of the Methodist press "in the face of . . . relentless propaganda of higher criticism in print and in school." The 1918 conference returned to that theme, condemning higher criticism of the Bible and suggesting that the denomination needed a good book burning. The 1923 North Alabama Conference argued fiercely about modernism, finally passing a resolution calling for the resignation of all Sunday school board officials in Nashville who were "not in accord with the teachings of the church." Delegates also denounced a speaker at a Lake Junaluska Sunday school conference who allegedly called the Bible a "cunningly devised fable." The 1929 conference adopted a resolution containing three of the five standards of the fundamentalist movement in order to "prevent any man or woman from preaching or teaching in our institutions of learning, churches, training schools, or Sunday Schools, or from editing any of our connectional literature, or from holding any other place or position in our Church, who does not believe in the inspiration of the Scriptures, the Virgin Birth, the death and resurrection of Jesus Christ, according to the Bible statements."[46]

This ambiguous legacy continued through following decades. Conflict over primary focus on evangelism or more balanced attention to both personal and social conversion, concern for laborers and the poor, and racial integration, divided Alabama Methodists for a century. Especially during the Civil Rights Movement, when most white Alabama evangelicals either sided with segregation or kept a discreet silence, a prophetic Methodist remnant risked denominational careers on behalf of their commitment to social justice. Methodism became too open to social justice to suit many of its members, who left for more racially accommodating and locally controlled Baptist churches, and too bound to conservative culture for others, who left for more politically, socially, and racially liberal denominations.[47]

After all these decades, Methodists still fight, duck, weave, compromise, accommodate, equivocate, and argue. It is precious little comfort to know that you are not alone in your conflicts. Baptists, Presbyterians, Episcopalians, and Lutherans, among others, were no closer to finding a consensus about commitment to personal evangelism and advocacy of social justice than when voters in the South's self-proclaimed buckle of the Bible Belt voted two to one against Riley and Hamill's tax reform proposals. But if we cannot always understand or accept the viewpoints of our spiritual ancestors, we can at least sympathize with them, for their dilemma remains our dilemma.

—Paper presented to the Southeastern Methodist Historical Society, Birmingham, Alabama, July 2003

Having begun writing a year earlier about religion in Alabama, I used this essay to position two elements of the state's religious energy—Prohibition and the Social Gospel—within the context of a specific political campaign. Whatever assumptions historians have about southern religious pietism, the "spirituality of the church," and its aversion to political activism, notable exceptions such as this suggest a more complex reality.

Oscar Underwood, Alabama's most powerful conservative Democrat and minority leader of the US Senate, ran for reelection confident of an easy victory. Instead, he encountered a meat grinder that came within a few thousand votes of ending his career. The unlikely coalition opposing him consisted of class-conscious union members, Social Gospel reformers, prohibitionists, the rapidly emerging Ku Klux Klan, the Alabama Farmers' Union, and newly enfranchised women.

At first glance these groups seem to be uneasy political bedfellows. But upon closer inspection, there was substantial overlap. A major theme of Social Gospel thought included better treatment of labor and recognition of their right to organize. It drew much of its political energy from the Prohibition and woman suffrage movements. Many ministers of working-class churches were bivocational coal miners, textile workers, or foundry laborers themselves. Others who earned their full-time living serving such people winced at the abuses they saw in the early stages of industrial capitalism: child labor, convict lease, health and safety hazards, and the autocracy of coal camps and mill towns.

More significant was conservative evangelical engagement by prohibitionists. Underwood was not only allied closely to planters, industrialists, and businessmen, he was also a leader of the statewide "wet" forces opposing Prohibition. Although many conservative religious leaders must have wondered about the company they were keeping with social gospelers, union members, and women suffragists, the temperance cause seemed worth the risk.

The result was a perfect storm of insurgency that nearly toppled Senator Underwood. Perhaps this 1919–1920 campaign foreshadows the 1960s and decades following, when evangelicals awakened from a long political slumber to form unlikely coalitions with Catholics, Mormons, Orthodox Jews, the Tea Party, and others on behalf of new pejorative moral crusades.

Chapter 4
Organized Labor, Reform, and Alabama Politics, 1920

Few areas of southern society have attracted so little attention as the region's economic history. This is especially true of the post–Civil War South.[1] Only in the last few decades have regional historians begun the tedious but vital work of analyzing the changes from rural-agrarian to urban-industrial society. Until this task is completed, it will be difficult to assess the importance of many trends taking place in the twentieth-century South.

One very important segment of economic history is the development of organized labor. While the South has never been a bastion of unionism, workers have infrequently exerted considerable influence on politics and economics. This has been particularly true when workingmen have sought a broader base of support among farmers or urban reformers. Organized labor in the state of Alabama has drawn some interest in recent years.[2] However, this research has been confined almost exclusively to the period before 1900. This article will attempt to demonstrate the way in which Alabama laborers joined a broader protest in 1920 to construct a powerful political coalition.

By the early years of the twentieth century, the Birmingham district was the focus of union activity in Alabama. The United Mine Workers (UMW) had tried unsuccessfully to organize the Birmingham region early in the century. During 1917 the UMW reentered the Alabama coal fields. The state's miners did not receive management recognition for their unions, but they did participate in the national coal strike that began in November 1919. Unionism also spread during these years to the state's iron and steel industry. The International Union of Mine, Mill, and Smelter Workers led the way, but companies rejected union demands and broke a general strike. As a result, Birmingham took little part in the great nationwide steel strike of 1919.[3]

Spurred by this organizing effort, the Alabama Federation of Labor had become increasingly active in state politics, dispatching lobbyists to the legislature and endorsing proposals favorable to workingmen. At its May 1919 state convention the federation voted resolutions to the legislature insuring mine safety, providing mine inspectors elected by miners, and endorsing enfranchisement for Negro men.[4] Nor were all Alabamians bitter opponents of organized labor in the early months of 1919. Even the business-oriented *Birmingham News* editorially praised the 1919 creation of a National Labor Party. The conservative editor of the *News* believed that the new party would bring workers' grievances into the open, turn workers' attention from the strike to the ballot, and absorb many workers who would otherwise drift into socialism.[5]

Events both within the state and across the nation rapidly broadened the chasm between labor and Alabama's business community. A miners' strike in the Birmingham district and attempts by the American Federation of Labor to organize schoolteachers in Jefferson County (Birmingham) created severe tension. On September 27, 1919, the Alabama legislature enacted an anti-strike law. On the national level a wave of walkouts and bitter disputes brought unprecedented labor disorder to the country and alienated much middle-class opinion.[6]

In the midst of such emotionalism the Esch-Cummins Bill was introduced in the United States Congress. This measure proposed to return America's railroads from government direction (where they had been during the First World War) back to private control. Organized labor waged acrid war against the bill and promised dire consequences to those congressmen who supported it. All ten of Alabama's congressmen, many of them elected with labor backing, voted against the Esch-Cummins Bill. But Senator Oscar Underwood, Alabama's presidential prospect who faced reelection in 1920, broke ranks and gave strong support to the legislation.[7] Underwood, constantly concerned about constituent opinion, instructed a political henchman to sample home state reaction to his call for law and order in labor-management disputes and his support of the Esch-Cummins Bill. The Alabama lieutenant detected no significant reaction even among labor groups (as it turned out, this was a sadly inaccurate reading of emotions within the state).[8] When Underwood announced for reelection in January 1920, the conservative press published a "ho-hum" announcement and evidenced no concern about his overwhelming reendorsement.

What Underwood and his supporters failed to grasp was a boiling tide of resentment afoot in Alabama, which nearly cost the powerful incumbent his seat and could have changed the political complexion of the state. Nationally, the AF of L announced in February 1920 that Underwood was one of six senators with the worst labor records in the nation and promised to help defeat him.[9] The Alabama Federation of Labor vowed that Underwood's championing of the Cummins bill would be his "valedictory, and swan song of the campaign, so far as the junior senator is concerned." The same sentiment was expressed among rank and file union members.[10]

Anti-Underwood feeling burst to the surface in a number of 1920 rallies. In the mining center of Walker County, the Committee of Allied Labor met at Jasper in February with more than one hundred delegates representing their unions. W. L. Harrison, president of the state Federation of Labor and a member of the Alabama legislature, addressed the group. He argued that the union men must vote as a bloc, and the delegates responded by nominating L. B. Musgrove, Walker County mine owner and a friend of organized labor, to run against Underwood. Not a single Underwood supporter could be found in the audience.[11]

Meeting after meeting reflected the same sentiment. The same day that the Jasper meeting occurred, February 15, a similar affair took place in Birmingham. Representatives of seventy-five Birmingham labor unions met to decide their political slate. After a five-hour conference, the unionists declined to make an endorsement in the US Senate race, but they did indicate that if no new candidate entered the contest, they would back Musgrove.[12] J. R. Rives, a union legislative lobbyist, bitterly opposed the incumbent Senator, saying that Underwood's attitude toward labor had changed radically.[13] Labor's state newspaper, the *La-*

bor Advocate, called Underwood a reactionary "related and associated" with a large coal and iron corporation which had "caused hardships and suffering among workmen," and endorsed Musgrove.[14] By late March, the state federation could report accurately to its members: "For this first time in Alabama, all branches of organized labor, including the Farmers Union, have recommended to their people, . . . one candidate for a high office [Musgrove] and have condemned the political course of his opponent [Underwood]."[15]

Organized labor also took steps to guarantee an effective statewide political campaign in behalf of Musgrove. A circular distributed by the state Federation of Labor to the Joint Labor Committee meeting in April 1920 urged all unions to publicize union endorsements. The circular was backed by the Alabama Farmers' Union, the Brotherhood of Railway Trainmen, the Brotherhood of Locomotive Firemen and Enginemen, the Order of Railway Conductors, and the Alabama Federation of Labor.[16] In Mobile, well-advertised labor rallies heard addresses by state union officials.[17]

Results of a labor campaign to register voters and pay poll taxes exceeded the wildest dreams of union leaders. In Mobile, P. G. DeWitt, secretary of the Central Trades Council, estimated that about 1,400 laboring people paid their poll taxes before the January 31 deadline. Political observers expected the largest labor vote in the history of Mobile.[18] In Jefferson County the Allied Committee had been established in 1919 to coordinate labor's political effort. The labor vote quadrupled in the county between 1919 and 1920, although total registration went up less than half, from approximately 18,000 in 1919 to 28,246 in 1920. The union claimed a county voting strength of 12,000 by 1920.[19] However, the organizing effort by labor sparked the Civitans to launch their own registration drive, which apparently offset some of the union gains in Birmingham. Miners in Walker County also conducted an effective registration-poll tax drive. Similar programs were followed around the state, and 1920 poll tax receipts doubled the 1919 figure.

Had organized labor been alone in its strenuous fight against Underwood, the result would not have been so significant. But labor leaders were able to fuse their campaign into a much broader framework, which sought economic and social reform on many levels. For years labor reform had been a major goal of the Social Gospel movement in the North. The left wing of Protestantism had often made league with Prohibition, social reform, and remedial labor legislation.[20] The late-blooming and loosely organized Social Gospel movement in the South also fostered this coalition, although the central issue seems to have been Prohibition rather than labor reform, reflecting the more agrarian base of southern society.[21]

Underwood had never championed Prohibition and was thought of in Alabama as a leading "wet."[22] As a result, a typical Musgrove assembly in 1920 was part union rally and part tent revival, with clerics assailing "demon rum" as fiercely as organizers damned Wall Street exploiters. At a Montgomery rally, Musgrove presented two speakers, Matt Bargainer of the Montgomery Central Labor Union, and Dr. W. B. Crumpton, president of the Alabama Anti-Saloon League and one of the most powerful and respected Baptist leaders in the state. In a Birmingham address, Musgrove joined his leadership in Prohibition to a statement that he would rather lose the election with labor endorsement than win without it.[23] Two weeks later in Anniston, Musgrove endorsed vocational education, welcomed labor support, and called Underwood "a representative of the Liquor Interests." Harry M. Ayers, progressive editor of the *Anniston Star* and leading Baptist layman, said that the Senator's reelection would be an endorsement of government by and for Wall Street trusts, calling Underwood the spokesman for "booze and business."[24]

The Prohibition crusade against Underwood was led by Rev. Brooks Lawrence, superintendent of the Alabama Anti-Saloon League. A Department of Justice official in Mobile wrote Underwood summarizing a conversation with the parson early in the campaign: "I saw Brooks Lawrence here yesterday and he was very talkative. He told me that they [Underwood's opponents] expected to make the *principal* issue against you 'Whiskey interests expect to make gigantic fight to capture Congress next election.' Also going to keep *labor agitators* in the field to keep labor vote poisoned against you."[25]

While prohibitionists were almost unanimous in their opposition to Underwood, not all of them rallied to Musgrove, who was an active Methodist with a consistent anti-liquor record.[26] A minor third candidate, Judge Samuel D. Weakley, had been a leader in the Prohibition and woman suffrage movements and had even more impeccable credentials than Musgrove. The *Birmingham News*, strongly behind Underwood, tried to split the powerful Prohibition bloc by praising Weakley as the logical prohibitionist candidate.[27] Lawrence, noting defections among his "dry" forces, tried unsuccessfully to persuade Weakley to withdraw and after some difficulty finally won Anti-Saloon League backing for Musgrove. An endorsement containing the signatures of 267 active and prominent prohibitionists representing forty-six counties publicly declared in favor of Musgrove.[28] In a master stroke, Lawrence persuaded William Jennings Bryan to stump Alabama in May, opposing Underwood as the greatest enemy of prohibition. The "Commoner" spoke at Albany, Huntsville, Anniston, Gadsden, Attala, and Montgomery, appealing for the election of Musgrove.

As one might expect in a time with strong nativist-Ku Klux Klan activity, Catholicism also entered the 1920 race. Apparently the Weakley camp initiated the "issue"; at any rate circulars accusing Underwood of pro-Catholic leanings appeared whenever Weakley spoke.[29] At a rally in Selma, "Parson" Gamble, the rector of the local Episcopal Church, flayed Underwood for making a speech honoring a Catholic friend. The audience of 150 mostly labor union men cheered loudly.[30] Musgrove picked up the argument and issued a statement denouncing the "Catholic political movement" in Alabama and saying that he would "rather wear the collar of Samuel Gompers, friend of President Woodrow Wilson and respected leader of the nation's organized toilers," than be supported by the Roman Catholic Church.[31] Apparently anti-Catholicism and Prohibition cut deeply into Underwood's support, for one friend wrote that ministers, especially Baptist and Methodist, were opposing the incumbent senator.[32]

One final group contributed to the curious potpourri challenging Oscar Underwood in 1920. Alabama farmers who were suffering from the general agricultural economic decline following the war blamed their US senator. Though Underwood still retained strong support in rural areas, he lost ground among some farm groups. C. M. Dinsmore, president of the Alabama Farmers' Union, was among the early Musgrove supporters. His organization politicked so successfully for the labor candidate that the Birmingham Chamber of Commerce, which owned the building where the Farmers' Union had its state headquarters, forced the Union to move its offices.[33] J. D. Wade, former Alabama commissioner of agriculture, also endorsed Musgrove, complaining that Underwood was trying to split organized agriculture and organized labor.[34]

Thus the disparate coalition of forces that challenged Underwood in 1920 included angry laborers, impoverished farmers, social reformers, religious idealists, and even anti-Catholic bigots. One frustrated Underwood friend complained that the opposition consisted of "the prohibitionists, the Unionists, the Suffragettes, the Bolshevists and where they could be prevailed upon, the Pulpit."[35] Though one can discount the political potency of the Communist vote in Alabama, this still must rank as one of the most interesting political movements in the state's history.

On the surface the Underwood camp seemed oblivious to the grassroot stirrings in Alabama. Optimistic reports continued to flow from campaign managers and filled pro-Underwood newspapers.[36] Privately, astute advisers warned of dire trouble. A confidential report by a Mobile newspaper correspondent noted strong anti-Underwood union strength in Selma and York, and prohibitionist opposition in south Alabama. Other friends wrote Underwood headquarters of active union campaigns for Musgrove in Leeds and Cullman, and all across Jefferson and Walker counties. John T. Cochrane—president of the Alabama, Tennessee, and Northern Railroad—reported that the situation was very close in Marengo, Wilcox, Washington, Choctaw, Sumter, and Pickens counties because of the railroad unions along his line. From Gadsden a leading lawyer wrote, "You are, of course, aware of the fact that there is no little stir and comotion [*sic*] among the labor class thruout Alabama."[37] J. A. Estes, an obviously shaken Bessemer lieutenant, wrote that a friend from Maplesville, a farming community in Chilton County, said that his area was strongly for Musgrove. Estes warned:

> We just can't keep from being a little worried about this situation: the union labor people will in a great majority be against you, and they have registered and paid poll tax more than ever before, many, many of them have paid up all their poll taxes which have accumulated since the Constitution of 1901 went into effect.
>
> ... Then we have been noticing for some twelve months or two years the union labor people have been working on the farmers, in an effort to get them to stand with union or organized labor in a political way.[38]

By March a consensus had developed in the Underwood camp that the campaign was lagging. His local organizations had entered the race overconfident and now were beginning to panic; his projected majority was too close. Underwood's manager sent an urgent appeal to Washington for the senator to return to the state and pump life into his campaign.[39]

When the senator returned in April for a whirlwind tour of the state, he adopted two strategies: publicly appeal to labor where possible and use opposition by the labor bloc to win conservative farmer and business support. Underwood had met the labor issue squarely at an earlier chamber of commerce dinner in Birmingham, saying that while he was not anti-union he did not think the unions should dictate policy. Dozens of copies of the Birmingham speech were sent throughout the state. In some speeches he blasted efforts to accentuate "class differences," a theme picked up by the Underwood press: "If our people are to be tagged and classified according to their various trades . . . , then legislated for or against in groups, have we not created a system which places new and artificial limits upon human achievement?"[40]

But Underwood also intensified his efforts to hold labor votes. He spent much of his speaking time disclaiming any anti-labor sentiment and became very defensive on the labor and liquor issues.[41] Polls were made among Birmingham laborers and W. A. Gunter, pro-Underwood mayor of Montgomery, was asked to speak to union rallies in his city. Gunter praised the history of unionism and urged the men to vote but also reminded the laborers that a public official had responsibilities to the entire community. It was as unfair, he said, to judge labor by a single incident in its history, as to judge a politician "by one or two incidents in that record and not by the whole." He praised compromise as the soul of government and warned against the "deception of demagoguery."[42]

If his vote on the Cummins bill destroyed Underwood's standing among laborers, it became the major rallying point for conservative supporters. The senator had always attracted conservative enthusiasm, but never more than in 1920 when he became a martyr to the alleged selfishness of the "labor conspiracy." R. I. Ingalls of Ingalls Steel Company in Birmingham blasted government meddling: "The Department of Labor seems determined to carry on its propaganda, which really means organized labor, at the expense of the tax payers."[43] Robert E. Spragins, a Huntsville attorney, advised the incumbent in a conference to run on a "straight fight against union labor"; Stanley C. Godbold of Camden said the prohibition lines were obliterated in Wilcox County and "the issue is the fight with organized labor"; Richard M. Hobbie, owner of a Montgomery wholesale grocery, wrote that "we all recognize the concerted opposition of Union Labor"; W. D. Null announced that he and his five sons "approve of your stand on class legislation, we do not think it for the good of our country [that] Union Labor should give orders to the balance of the people."[44] Even some friends of Musgrove were won by this appeal. A prominent Birmingham attorney wrote Underwood: "I have been closely identified with Mr. Musgrove on some matters, and our relations are of the friendliest sort, but I have come to the conclusion that you are right all the way around on the labor question which to my mind is the biggest thing the American people have to confront today."[45]

The senator and his friends certainly did all in their power to exploit this feeling in Alabama. Underwood sent a number of letters pointing to the labor blacklist of him and pleading for support against labor's attempt to "take control of the railroads of the United States." The *Sylacauga Advance* endorsed the incumbent, arguing that "organized labor is making an effort to gain legislative control of the American government. . . . The candidate who is seeking office through the vote of organized labor is dangerous."[46] The *Birmingham News* editorially blistered a March speech by Musgrove: "He boldly advocates that array of classes against classes. A very rich man himself, . . . he adds fuel to the radical flames of the day in advocacy of the union of the farmers and of the mine and factory workers for crushing capital and establishing a government of part of the people. . . . That is not only demogogy [*sic*], but is dangerous demogogy."[47] The *News* had certainly traveled a long way from its 1919 patronizing praise of a labor party as a desirable development for workers.

By the latter stages of the campaign, Underwood had become the champion of democracy against the sinister spectrum of the "labor bloc." A man from Georgia sent him a pamphlet denouncing labor and championing the "open shop"; an Athens attorney wrote that if the National Democratic Convention adopted "a plank that is satisfactory to Gompers [Samuel Gompers, president of the American Federation of Labor], in my judgment, we deserve defeat."[48] The senator observed the success of his campaign among conservative elements in Alabama and noted with pleasure his unanimous support among Birmingham businessmen.[49] Underwood's efforts also received a boost just before election day when the senator was elected Democratic leader of the US Senate.

Election results reflected the intensity of the senatorial race. Totaling first and second choice votes (to avoid a runoff in multi-candidate races, the voters cast first and second choice votes) Underwood won, with 69,130 to Musgrove's 61,360; tabulating only first-choice ballots, Underwood won a narrow race, 66,871 to 56,563. Musgrove carried the following counties: Jefferson, 9,934 to 9,833 (the only time in Underwood's long career that he lost his home county); Walker, 2,166 to 1,000; Tuscaloosa, 1,389 to 1,191; Etowah, 1,444 to 1,090; Calhoun, 1,749 to 1,439; and Shelby, Morgan, Marion, Lawrence, Houston, Geneva, Henry, Franklin, Fayette, DeKalb, Covington, Conecuh, Coffee, Clay, Clarke, Bibb, and Barbour. These returns clearly indicate the effectiveness of the coalition opposing Underwood, for Musgrove's strength was almost equally divided between labor influenced counties (Jefferson, Walker, Tuscaloosa, Morgan, Etowah, Covington, and Calhoun) and rural counties where Prohibition was the major issue (Shelby, Marion, Lawrence, Houston, Geneva, Henry, Franklin, Fayette, DeKalb, Conecuh, Coffee, Clay, Clarke, Bibb, and Barbour).

Labor solidarity emerges from a statistical analysis of this vote. The turnout in areas of labor strength was very heavy (as much as 50 percent over the previous high in Jefferson County).[50] In 1919, the state contained ten cities of 10,000 people or more: Anniston, Bessemer, Birmingham, Dothan, Florence, Gadsden, Mobile, Montgomery, Selma, and Tuscaloosa. These cities produced 47.8 percent of the state's manufactured products. Counties with the largest number of wage earners engaged in manufacturing (and hence with the largest potential labor vote) were, in order of size, Jefferson (Birmingham and Bessemer), Mobile, Etowah (Gadsden), Calhoun (Anniston), Montgomery, Madison, Chambers, Tuscaloosa, Talladega (with unorganized textile mills), Escambia, Morgan, and Covington.[51] Musgrove carried six of the twelve and missed winning the other six by narrow margins. Possibly even more significantly, he carried three of the four top manufacturing-urban centers in the state. Musgrove trailed badly in only the conservative Black Belt counties.

Numerous contemporary accounts support this statistical conclusion that labor voted as a cohesive bloc for Musgrove. Morgan County, which Musgrove carried by 584 votes, is a good case study. An Albany railroad worker and union member backed Underwood but noted that "the working men voted against you nearly solid"; another Albany citizen supported this contention by noting that of 1,291 voters in two labor precincts of the city, Underwood received only 314 votes. In Austinville and Hartselle, two additional centers of labor strength in the county, the vote also went for Musgrove.[52] Underwood carried the county by 150 votes outside of these union centers, but the labor "element became very active, and since the organization is new here, the members almost to a man followed the lead of the walking union delegate" and carried the Morgan County vote into the Musgrove column.[53]

Underwood and his lieutenants recognized the nature and strength of the opposition. The senator admitted that he had "never had a more strenuous fight, or opposition coming from so many different angles, but I am proud to say that I have not yielded to *class* demands."[54] Jelks H. Cabaniss, the senator's campaign manager in Jefferson County, offered a penetrating critique of what went wrong in the largest urban-labor county in the state:

> The result in this county is singular. There was a phenomenal cleavage between the working classes and the business interests. Instead of visualizing your main issue as a protest against aggression by organized labor leaders, they interpreted it as a contest of the well to do against the working man. In a county like Jefferson we could not satisfactorily overcome this point of view with the means at hand. The false impression was spread by Musgrove men in overalls to counteract it. The result was heavy majorities in centers where we were unable to obtain effectual workers. . . . In the eastern part of the city results were bad—centering around the railroad shops in Boyles and Avondale, and spreading into North Birmingham, Woodlawn and East Lake. The country vote was peculiarly unsatisfactory. It is really a labor vote, as every family in Jefferson County has members of his family in the mines and factories.
>
> . . . When the perfect organization is considered which was delivered to Musgrove by the Anti-Saloon League expanded by his complete control of organized labor and the farm union . . . , the [close election] result is a direct testimonial to yourself personally.[55]

The 1920 effort by organized labor marked a high tide of union influence in Alabama. The unionists elected many labor backed candidates, including two new members of the Birmingham Board of Education and US Congressman George Huddleston from Jefferson County.[56] Shortly after the election, national United Mine Workers (UMW) officers ordered a state-wide strike when Alabama mine operators refused to recognize the unions. About 12,000 of Alabama's 27,000 coal miners struck. Nearly three-fourths of the strikers were Negroes, which hindered the walkout. Violence erupted, the National Guard was mobilized, and after five months, the issue was submitted to arbitration. The governor, sole arbitrator, ruled in favor of the mine operators on every point and the operators' victory temporarily ended unionization of Alabama coal miners. After spending three million dollars in Alabama, the UMW had only a handful of members left.[57]

This election demonstrates that labor did indeed become a major force in southern politics by the 1920s. Unlike the Populist crusade of the 1890s when reform was concentrated in rural areas and on the farms, southern reformers three decades later looked to the cities for support. By widening their base to include social critics, religious reformers, and disgruntled farmers, Alabama laborers came within an eyelash of defeating a powerfully entrenched southern conservative. The 1920 Alabama campaign demonstrates that the North had no monopoly on labor activism and that the South's belching smokestacks and grimy mines could bring class warfare even to the land of sleepy magnolias and cool mint juleps.

—*The Alabama Review*, 1970

Tracing the origins and extent of Social Gospel thought in Birmingham through white Baptist and Methodist denominations left out nearly as much as it included. In some ways, individual Presbyterian and Episcopal leaders fit the national pattern that believed progressive religion was woven from a whole piece and not from individual scraps. Modernist theology, ecumenism, and Social Gospel activism particularly defined Dr. Henry Edmonds and Independent Presbyterian Church, arguably the most successful congregation in the city between 1915 and 1930. Arising from a split in South Highland Presbyterian, it was comparable to the divisions over modernist theology and the Social Gospel among churches in the North.

Paradoxically, another Presbyterian minister, "Brother" James Alexander Bryan, occupied the opposite end of the hermeneutic found in Matthew 25: 31–46, the most famous social justice passage in the New Testament. No single person in the city lived out more faithfully Christian pietism and charitable deeds, and no person in city history was more beloved by its teeming masses.

Although less numerous, Catholics and Jews competed with evangelicals both in building institutional identity and in proclaiming fidelity to social justice. Yet, their very presence also triggered the dark underside of politicized southern evangelicalism. No southern city experienced worse and more violent anti-Catholicism than Birmingham, and some leading bigots came from the ranks of the most theologically liberal and Social Gospel–oriented ministers. By the mid 1920s, Jefferson County had become the most Klan-infested area of the South, with its leaders estimating that more than half the county's Protestant ministers and at least that proportion of its laymen belonged to the hooded empire (including First Baptist Church Sunday school teacher, future Unitarian, and US Supreme Court Justice Hugo Black).

The connection between red-hot reform movements—such as Prohibition, moral purity, nativism, Social Gospel, and working-class political insurgency—and the Klan, reminds us that a religion of grace, generosity, and tolerance may also contain elements of judgmentalism, bigotry, and murderous violence.

Chapter 5
Religion in the Urban South
The Divided Religious Mind of Birmingham, 1900–1930

Recent years have seen increasing numbers of academicians struggling with religion as a critical instrument in the comprehension of American culture. Such historians as Kenneth K. Bailey, John Eighmy, and other interpreters of southern thought have demonstrated an increasing socialization of southern Protestantism during the twentieth century. Also, historians have treated their audiences to an increasingly refined insight into the urban South and the way in which Progressivism thrived in the metropolitan climate of the early years of this century. Industrialism in the South, as elsewhere, created complex problems that demanded substantial modification of nineteenth-century pietistic Christianity. Southern industrialism also produced a level of religious pluralism that resulted in at least a temporary increase in bigotry and intolerance. But there has been little effort to trace the interaction of church and urban South in order to determine how rural, agrarian religion adjusted to the complexities of industrial cities that sprang up among the wisteria, kudzu, and magnolia trees. Although Birmingham, Alabama, is atypical in both its late nineteenth-century origin and its unique heavy industrial economic base, it does serve as a fascinating case study in the socialization of southern religion.

It is ironic that two of the most notable symbols of twentieth-century Birmingham have been the giant statue of Vulcan perched atop the ore vein of Red Mountain and the Temple of Vesta dominating Shades Mountain. Leaders of the city in the heart of the Bible Belt have boasted that theirs was a "city of churches," while they also have identified it with the Roman god of metalworking and the Roman goddess of the hearth.[1] This curious mixture of paganism and evangelical Christianity is symbolic of the contradictory character of the city. Despite its many churches, it became nationally known as "Bad Birmingham," the city of minerals and murder. Although allegedly dominated by salvationists and otherworldly Baptists and Methodists, it also counted a large Catholic population, and for a time the Social Gospel flourished in the city. In theory affirming the brotherhood of man, the religious life of Birmingham was rigidly segregated by race. The Ku Klux Klan thrived on the city's racism and anti-Catholicism.

In religion Birmingham was a city of paradoxes. A number of factors shaped the city's religious attitudes. From Birmingham's earliest beginnings in the 1870s, local land companies provided free plots of land to encourage establishment of Christian congregations. Until the 1890s, most of the people pouring into the town were rural, evangelical southern Protestants, and despite the later arrival of immigrants who brought religious diversity, Protestants maintained their hegemony over community life. Leading businessmen were proud of their close association with one of the multiplicity of local sects, and the denominations pursued a sometimes unfriendly rivalry trying to enroll the community's "wealthiest and best."[2] Sermons traditionally emphasized individualism, salvation, and civic boosterism, while posing no challenge to the economic and social status quo. Yet the frontier mining nature of the city also gave it renown for moral looseness and for rip-roaring drunkenness and violence.

Birmingham, as a city of the "New South," could not escape the industrial and urban stresses that were transforming American life in the late nineteenth century, and her religious institutions strained under new pressures. Industrial urbanization brought social distress to the working classes and alienated them from the church, forcing pietistic Protestantism to begin dealing with the city's critical social problems. By 1900 the religious and ethnic homogeneity of Birmingham had relaxed as southern and eastern European immigrants poured into the region's factories and mines, giving it one of the highest proportions of immigrants of any Southern city. The religious census of 1906 revealed the pattern in unmistakable relief. The largest single denomination of the total church membership was Roman Catholic (7,965 members, 28.9 percent) followed by the National Baptist Convention (black, 4,029 members, 14.6 percent), and the Methodist Episcopal Church, South (3,919 members, 14.2 percent). Southern Baptists were a poor fifth (2,059 members, 7.5 percent). By 1916 the influx of immigrants had slowed, and the religious affiliation of the city's residents reflected a more typical Southern pattern: National Baptists were the most numerous (20,145 members, 26.1 percent of the total church membership), followed by the Methodist Episcopal Church, South (15,477, 20.1 percent); Roman Catholic (12,651, 16.4 percent); and Southern Baptist (8,420, 10.9 percent).[3]

In attempting to deal with the religious life of a community, one must come to terms with both the theological climate of ideas and the social expression of these ideas. Theology presents only minor problems, for evangelical Protestant Fundamentalism characterized the Bible Belt. Excluding Episcopal, Catholic, and Jewish minorities, black and white clergymen alike generally preached a Calvinistic doctrine of man's sinfulness, God's judgment, and the consequent imperative for man to repent and "be saved." The Bible was literally interpreted as the verbatim word of God. Such doctrines as the Virgin Birth, the Atonement, the physical resurrection of Christ, and immortality were equally sacrosanct. Sectarian independence was as fundamental as separation of church and state.

Although the foregoing description would summarize the religious convictions of the overwhelming majority of clergymen and laymen alike in the years from 1900 to 1930, a strain of religious liberalism provided variegation to the otherwise uniform theological landscape. A Unitarian congregation was established with its liberal influence, but more significant is the dissent within mainline Protestant churches. Within the Methodist Church there was liberal sentiment, particularly among the faculty of Methodist-related Birmingham-Southern College.[4]

Southern Baptists would appear an unlikely environment for religious iconoclasts, yet Dr. Alfred J. Dickinson, pastor of Birmingham's First Baptist Church, was the city's chief intellectual mugwump.[5] Upon becoming pastor of the Birmingham congregation in 1901, he accelerated his already active advocacy of the controversial "higher criticism" that sought to subject the Bible to all the canons of literary, historical, and archeological criticism used to examine any other piece of literature. He saw no conflict between evangelical concern and academic challenges to the literal interpretation of Scripture, and in a series of provocative essays in the state Baptist paper, he defended "higher criticism" against all comers.[6] Frank W. Barnett, a member of Dickinson's church and owner/editor of *The Alabama Baptist*, did not share his pastor's theological liberalism, but the same editorials that challenged liberalism defended the freedom of Baptists to take critical theological positions without fear of retaliation: "Let us shake off a false Baptist demagogy which, boasting of its own self-sufficing orthodoxy, becomes the worst of all tyrannies in striving to force its narrow tests upon all who are willing to receive with open minds truth from any source."[7] Barnett's successor as editor of *The Alabama Baptist* in 1919 was Rev. L. L. Gwaltney, whose defense of theistic evolution and science was in sharp contrast to the anti-evolution sentiment that thrived in the Bible Belt during the 1920s.[8] He spent his editorship arguing that science did not conflict with religion. In his declining years he wrote a manuscript pleading with Baptists to incorporate evolution and modern science in their religion so as not to alienate their young and informed people of all ages.[9]

Perhaps the most dramatic evidence of theological conflict in Birmingham came from the controversy that split South Highland Presbyterian Church and led to the creation of Independent Presbyterian Church. At the epicenter of the storm was Dr. Henry M. Edmonds. A native of Sumter County, Alabama, Edmonds became pastor of South Highland in 1913 but was barely settled when "a heresy-hunter was on my trail." The prominent layman, who had attended a "Fundamentalist Bible School," polarized the church against Edmonds, as he had against two previous pastors. Although cautious in his pronouncements, Edmonds's theological views on immortality, the divinity of Christ, the "second coming," human depravity, the Virgin Birth, and the Atonement were in no sense "orthodox."[10] Edmonds's antagonist also assaulted the pastor for his opposition to city blue laws that forbade movies and golf on Sundays, and for his social concerns. His antagonist chided, "You are trying to improve relations between husband and wife, between classes, nations, races. We ought to rejoice if those relations grow worse and worse, for when they become intolerable Christ will come again."[11] Finally, Edmonds was brought before the Birmingham Presbytery and censured for his views. He consequently withdrew from South Highland, together with a large segment of the congregation, and formed the unaffiliated Independent Presbyterian Church. Upon the invitation of Rabbi Morris Newfield, the church met at Temple Emanu-El for ten years, with night services emphasizing social action held at the downtown Lyric Theater.[12]

Ruhama Baptist Church experienced similar friction when Dr. Cecil V. Cook of Kentucky became pastor in 1910. A brilliant pastor and orator, he nonetheless suffered a brief and stormy tenure, charged by his congregation with tactlessness and liberal theological views.[13] Unlike South Highland, he had little support, and the church did not fragment when he resigned under pressure.

Sporadic evidence of liberal theology existed in Birmingham, and some clerics also sympathized with ecumenism. Throughout the first two decades of the new century, local congregations had cooperated on such issues as Prohibition and evangelization. While there was little demonstrable sentiment for church union among Birmingham clergy and laymen, there was sentiment for a more coordinated social and mission outreach. The focus of this interest was the Interchurch World Movement, an attempt to coordinate church energies in the service of evangelism and social ministries but not to compete with denominational agencies. On March 3, 1920, officials from New York held a conference in Birmingham to explain the movement. Churchwomen from throughout the state met at First Christian Church, while six hundred ministers discussed the same subject at the First Methodist Church. The ministers, representing every Protestant and evangelical faith in the state, endorsed the organization and returned to their congregations to explain its operations.[14]

The notable exception to this general enthusiasm came from the city's white Baptists. Ever fearful of ecumenism or even close cooperation, the Southern Baptist and Alabama Baptist conventions had rejected association with the movement. *The Alabama Baptist* conducted a forum on the subject based on correspondence from one hundred state pastors. The response was overwhelmingly negative, reflecting concern that it could lead to Catholic control, church union, or emphasis on social issues to the exclusion of individual salvation.[15] Despite his denomination's opposition, Birmingham Baptist iconoclast A. J. Dickinson enthusiastically endorsed the movement. It originated out of a basic human desire for progress, he argued, just as had missions, temperance, abolition of slavery, and women's rights. It was a movement for "effecting His Kingdom in the earth"; it was a community organization to serve the needs of the whole city, and this purpose could not be accomplished without cooperative church action.[16]

No matter how intently the climate of thought in Birmingham is studied, theology alone does not provide a complete picture of its religious life. The social manifestation of these ideas is equally significant. The demands of an industrial/urban community posed complex problems for the city's religious structure, and the response ranged across the theological spectrum.

Most representative of the older Fundamentalist attempt to wrestle with urban malaise was the remarkable ministry of Dr. James Alexander Bryan of Third Presbyterian Church. Fondly known to thousands as "Brother Bryan," he had come to Birmingham in 1888 and spent his entire life loving the city's volatile population. Although minister to a working-class church, friend of blue-collar workers and of black people, and an honorary member of most local labor unions, his sermons were evangelical with hardly a trace of Social Gospel influence.[17] A loner who believed in welfare organizations, he administered a personal program of vast relief supported by his own church, Jewish businessmen, saloonkeepers, and anyone else who offered help. He had no formal organization and kept no records. Yet, he organized a social ministry for Italian immigrants; brought the first district nurse to Birmingham to minister to the city's poor; literally lived at the city's mills, factories, and jails, helping laborers and criminals; and ended each midweek service at his church by inviting all who desired to have lunch with the pastor, so that the poor did not have to ask for food. He was so touched by the needs of others that he gave away his horse to a farmer whose beast had died and gave his food to those in greater need. Explaining his legendary ministry, which in time took on an aura of mystical unreality, Bryan wrote: "Ever since I have been a pastor my work has been partially among needy people. If there are no poor in your congregation, my humble advice is to get another charge or shut your doors. Social service alone will not solve the problem of the poor and hungry, nor can it alone fill the need of the breadless and bedless and jacketless . . . Christ taught us to pray, 'Give us this day our daily bread.' If He gives you your daily bread, you should divide with someone else. A woman came in the other day and said, 'Brother Bryan, one of your friends sent me a sack of flour, some meat and lard, and a half-ton of coal.' I saw Christ in that basket of food. People do not read their Bibles, they read you and me."[18]

Despite the individualistic nature of Bryan's ministry, his belief that all men—white and black, native-born and immigrant, poor and rich—were his brothers,[19] propelled him into an urban society festering with many kinds of hurt. His biographer maintains that Bryan had "by all odds relieved more suffering than any man who ever lived in Birmingham."[20] Apparently the people of Birmingham agreed; in 1920, when the *Birmingham News* announced a five-hundred-dollar award to the citizen who had rendered the greatest service to the city during the year, the selection committee was swamped with petitions from labor unions and private citizens nominating Brother Bryan. When he received the first annual award on January 9, 1921, a tremendous throng overflowed the largest theater in Birmingham and by the hundreds spilled over into the streets to honor the man who called them all his brothers.

The magnitude of social distress in the city caused most religious bodies to follow a more coordinated ministry than Brother Bryan's. The medium of expressing this concern was the Social Gospel, a movement pioneered in the North, but with substantial impact on the urban South as well. Two successive editors of *The Alabama Baptist*, writing from offices in Birmingham, championed social concern as fundamental to making the gospel relevant to modern city dwellers. Although both were theologically conservative, Frank W. Barnett and L. L.

Gwaltney turned the pages of their journal into a forum where they advocated control of trusts; political reform; better care for immigrants; and abolition of child labor, the convict lease system, and capital punishment.[21]

The issue that involved so many pastors in social activism was Prohibition. To achieve this moral objective the religious community had to forsake its passivism and enter politics. In 1907 the Woman's Christian Temperance Union and the interdenominational Pastors' Union made common cause against "demon rum," arguing that prohibition would not only reduce the city's legendary violence but also cure many of the community's social ills. Women and children wearing white ribbons surrounded polling places on October 28, 1907, and sang "When the Roll is Called Up Yonder," perhaps as a theological warning to male voters. Five thousand women and children paraded through city streets waving banners proclaiming "Save the Boys" and "Vote for Mothers." When Jefferson County went dry by 1,800 votes (although the city proper voted wet), crowds thronged the polling places singing—without regard to the irony involved—"Praise God From Whom All Blessings Flow."[22] Now fully aware of their combined political power, churchmen did not intend to relinquish it.

They turned their newfound muscle to Birmingham's unsavory moral climate. Saloons, dance halls, and brothels thrived along with the city's churches and emotional revivals. Murder, gambling, drunkenness, and prostitution characterized the city's national reputation more than did its fine steel.[23] The editor of *The Alabama Baptist* helped launch the cleanup in 1904 with a blistering editorial noting that Jefferson County had more murders annually than had occurred in all of Great Britain with a population of forty million people: "In Jefferson County when a man contemplated killing his fellow man he argues that with a little money and personal influence the probabilities are that he will be given a short prison sentence at most." The pulpits, he thought, should join the secular press to stop lawlessness in Birmingham.[24]

As part of this crusade, religious leaders sought the elimination of prostitution. The "oldest profession" was practiced openly and thrived on local customers as well as the weekend miners who flooded the city to gamble and to drink. City officials ignored the problem until 1905 when they sought to confine it to wards six and seven. Churchmen rejected this policy of segregating prostitution and continued a decadelong battle to rid the city of the practice altogether.[25]

Although partially defeated on the issue of prostitution, the city's religious forces won their struggle against Sunday amusements, to which Birmingham was not so deeply devoted. By 1908 they had pressured the city into passing ordinances forbidding such Sabbath pastimes as golf, baseball, tennis, football, hunting, shooting, gaming, card playing, and even dominoes.[26]

Reviewing church influence, one city historian concludes that Prohibition and moral reform in the first decade of the century resulted in clean amusements, increased church attendance on Sunday mornings, a firm insistence on law enforcement, and a moral climate unexcelled in the urban South.[27] Although this conclusion obviously is exaggerated, conditions had improved, and rigorous standards of morality had been enforced.

Concern for the social welfare of the community also helped politicize religion. The problems of labor in a blue-collar city not only were obvious by 1900 but also had alienated many workingmen from the church. Frank Barnett of *The Alabama Baptist* directed much of his attention toward remedying unjust labor conditions in his home city and chided the pulpits: "Churches have frequently shut their eyes to the struggles of labor to get a minimum wage; and have not heard the cry of the children who were being sacrificed in our mills; or cared when a fight was being made for shorter hours and better working conditions."[28] Infuriated by child labor, he exploded in dozens of editorials. After the state legislature postponed meaningful legislation in 1907, he stormed: "Let us call it [child labor] by its right name—murder. But if the death comes quickly enough, it is less cruel than the life to which such boys and girls are condemned."[29] He also propagandized for the end of the convict lease system, whereby many Birmingham area mine owners leased state convicts to work their mines.[30]

Editor L. L. Gwaltney, Barnett's successor, frankly advocated the Social Gospel, contending that he saw no conflict in it and the individualistic gospel of salvation. They were both elements of the complete gospel and neither could endure without the other; the minister who followed Christ "will also preach against the social vices and sins of the day. He will even tell armies what to do, and enter the realm of politics and insist that the levying of taxes must be just."[31]

Many local churches implemented the manifold social interests of Barnett, Gwaltney, and other clerics. Dr. Augustus C. Davidson, pastor of Southside Baptist Church, persuaded his congregation that it should pattern itself after Charles H. Spurgeon's famous "institutional church," to which were attached reading rooms, baths, a gymnasium, and other facilities. The church established a free kindergarten in the southwest part of town, an industrial school to teach workers' children to cook and sew, and a "Goodwill Center" among Birmingham's Italian community (with kindergarten, sewing classes, and Bible teaching).[32]

The Pastors' Union, aided by churchwomen, inaugurated various social ministries in the early years of the new century. The Free Kindergarten Association was formed in 1899 and provided three day nurseries or kindergartens for small children whose mothers worked. In summer 1908, women of the School Improvement Association opened kindergarten and settlement work in the basement of the Paul Hayne School.[33]

Methodists constituted one of the largest religious groups in the city and were active in social ministries. When the Pastors' Union proposed construction of a boarding house for working women, one Methodist layman pledged

$25,000. Women from St. John's and First Methodist churches created the City Board of Missions in 1903, and the board opened a settlement house in June of the same year. The home was situated in a working-class neighborhood and operated an "industrial school" for girls, a day school for children whose parents worked, a night literacy school for working boys, and a free kindergarten. The home ministered primarily to families working in the adjacent rolling mills and foundries. Between 1900 and 1905, some three thousand children attended church-sponsored kindergartens in Birmingham; most of the children came from blue-collar families, and the money for the schools was provided by the Methodist Christmas offering.[34]

The settlement house ministry operated so successfully that in September 1908 a "deaconess" (trained social worker) was employed by the Board of City Missions to open a Wesley House. By the end of the year the facility was in operation with a thirty-eight pupil kindergarten; the work grew so rapidly by 1909 that a larger house was purchased, an assistant was employed, and plans were begun for construction of an "institutional church." Another Wesley House was built directly behind Avondale Mills, one of the most prominent state textile mills. By 1912 it cared for eleven babies and forty preschoolers, enrolled thirty women in the "Mothers' Club," and conducted a night literacy program three evenings a week.[35]

The City Board of Missions expanded its social ministries in 1912 to five thousand Italian immigrants employed at the Ensley mills of Tennessee Coal and Iron Company (TCI). TCI donated a house, playgrounds, heat, light, and $2,000. The board, assisted by Ensley Methodist Church, employed Miss Dorothy Crim, a trained social worker, in October 1912. By 1913 two assistants had been employed, and the Ensley ministry included all the facilities of the Avondale house plus a boarding home for working girls.[36]

During these same years the Episcopal Church of the Advent became socially active. Its rectors focused their interests on the Boys' Industrial School, the Mercy Home for women, the Northside Community House, and social work among black people. When Rev. Middleton S. Barnwell became rector in 1913, a smaller rectory was purchased, and the older structure was devoted to social ministries, particularly a free neighborhood kindergarten. In a remarkable example of ecumenical social service, Barnwell joined Rabbi Morris Newfield of Temple Emanu-El and Dr. Henry M. Edmonds, pastor of Independent Presbyterian, to organize the Jefferson County Children's Aid Society, which subsequently spread statewide and became the Alabama Department of Child Welfare.[37]

Dr. Edmonds was perhaps the most independent minded of the city's clergymen. Infuriating many ministers by opposing church movements to ban Sunday movies and golf, he nonetheless retained their respect and was elected president of the Birmingham Pastors' Union. He also led his church in the most active social ministry of any area congregation. When Independent Presbyterian was established in 1915, the "Purpose of the Church" had listed service to humanity as second only to the individual search for God. In order to implement this purpose, Sunday evening services were held in the Lyric Theater, and a downtown office was maintained. A female member of the church staff was assigned the task of assisting the jobless, while a nurse was employed to serve the city's health needs (due to her excellent service to the church, she was subsequently employed by the city as the first public health nurse in Birmingham). The Northside Community House was established, although it was aided by several other congregations as well as Independent. In 1920 the church employed Miss Leila Winn as its city missionary to do case work that was brought to the attention of the church's Social Service Group.

The congregation also sponsored a Children's Fresh Air Farm, a project suggested by Edmonds and funded by the philanthropy of Robert R. Meyer. The thirty-acre farm on Shades Mountain provided summer nourishment and recreation for eight thousand poor children between 1920 and 1950, while doctors from the church performed over one hundred free operations needed by the children. The church also undertook "Winter Work," providing the poor with birthday parties for children, scholarships to school, weddings, baby showers, and other services of a continuing ministry. Independent Presbyterian, noting the disadvantage suffered by poor people of both races in the courts, also employed a lawyer who provided free legal aid.[38]

Much of Independent's social ministry grew from its services at the Lyric Theater. Held for ten years between 1915 and 1925, the services attracted every facet of urban Southern culture—black worshipers, who sat in a segregated upper balcony; gamblers; prostitutes; and the poor. One prominent "madam" of a "disorderly house" attended for many years, was subsequently converted, and became a regular member of Independent Presbyterian. Another convert from the services, formerly a prostitute, left a large bequest to the Atlanta YMCA when she died. Offerings from the services were used in local social work (for example, one offering purchased a new horse for a vegetable peddler whose animal had died).[39]

Since most of the city's charity and philanthropy was church motivated, virtually all denominations participated in social ministries. In 1895 the Ladies of Charity was organized, composed mainly from the membership of St. Paul's Catholic Church. This group appears to be the earliest Christian welfare agency in the city. Catholic St. Vincent's Hospital was opened in November 1900, and between its opening and 1904 it served over twenty-four hundred indigent patients. St. Vincent's nursing graduate Miss Marie Forsman became the city's first "district nurse" in 1907, with the responsibility of providing medical care to the city's poor white inhabitants. Catholics also established an orphanage at East Lake.[40]

Rabbis and Jewish businessmen not only contributed individually to city social agencies but also organized collectively. In 1890, the Daughters of Israel began Jewish social work in the city, followed by the Hebrew Relief Society (1897), and the Council of Jewish Charities, which coordinated activities.[41]

Most Birmingham pastors seem to have detected no conflict between social and spiritual ministries, viewing the Social Gospel as a practical necessity. Church membership during this epoch of "Social Gospelism" increased at a phenomenal rate indicating that the church was translating its spiritual interests in the poor and workingmen into social reality. The Methodist Wesley House ministry won the enthusiastic backing of denominational clergymen; the pastor of the nearest Methodist church to the Avondale Mills House praised the tremendous help it provided his parish in attracting mill workers.[42] Southside Baptist Church, founded in the mid-1880s, experienced the greatest spiritual prosperity in its history while operating as an institutional church.[43] For the city as a whole, church membership bounded from 27,578 in 1906 to 77,145 in 1916, nearly a 200 percent increase.[44]

In contrast with the social "liberalism" of Birmingham churches during the "Progressive" Era, the growing intolerance and bigotry that emerged full blown in the 1920s seem shocking. Rabid opposition to Catholics, Jews, immigrants, or any deviation from Protestant moral standards threw the churches into a frenzy. Whereas Protestants had organized politically to combat moral deviations earlier, many members added extralegal violence to political activism during the 1920s. Despite apparent contradictions, there are strong elements of continuity in the periods from 1900 to 1915 and 1915 to 1930. Both eras saw the churches deeply involved in social issues. During each period the church sought a restrictive, enforced community morality based on its own standards. In both, churchmen were activists, condemning forces that they felt encouraged religious and social diversity within the city.

Anti-Catholicism was a touchstone of the new period, although the theme had long been obvious in local Protestant circles. Baptist editor Frank Barnett, a leader in his denomination's socialization, believed that Catholics were a menace to American democracy and defended such organizations as the "Guardians of Liberty," a fanatical anti-Catholic cult organized in the second decade of the century.[45] As early as 1916 night riders burned a Catholic church and school near Pratt City. When two Birmingham public schools were destroyed weeks after the Pratt City incident, rumors spread that Catholics had burned them in retaliation. When federal agents warned of a plot to destroy other Catholic institutions, the local newspapers maintained a discreet silence. One newsman on the *Birmingham Age-Herald* staff was dismissed, allegedly for his negative expressions about the "True Americans," a local anti-Catholic group.[46] The same year Father James E. Coyle, pastor of St. Paul's Church, Alabama's largest Catholic congregation, wrote a rebuttal to the anti-Catholicism expressed by Baptist pastor R. L. Durant in the *Age-Herald*. The dispute broadened when the Birmingham Baptist Ministers' Conference passed a resolution supporting Rev. Durant's views.[47] Father Coyle's life was threatened in 1917, and federal authorities, learning of a plot to burn St. Paul's, persuaded the priest to place an armed guard on the church property at night.[48] By 1919 the editor of *The Alabama Baptist* not only believed that church union was a Catholic conspiracy, but also argued that there was only one struggle in the postwar religious world: Baptist democracy versus "Romanism's" monarchy.[49]

The 1920s deepened the chasm separating faiths. The city was characterized by religious zeal, the growth of civic and social clubs, population expansion, construction of the city's skyscrapers, financial problems, inadequacies in law enforcement and education, and the prevalence of social unrest.[50] Bigotry thrived in such an atmosphere. *The Menace*, a sometimes obscene anti-Catholic publication by Georgia's Tom Watson, was widely available at local newsstands.[51] The "True Americans" dominated city government with a motto of "No Catholics in Public Office." They defeated incumbent officials in the 1920 elections for refusing to fire a Catholic woman stenographer in the county treasurer's office, and they threatened to boycott businesses that employed Catholics.[52]

Even state politics became enmeshed in Birmingham's religious and ethnic strife. Incumbent US Senator Oscar W. Underwood, a resident of Jefferson County, simultaneously represented conservative political and economic philosophies and opposed the attempt of religious groups to prescribe individual choice through prohibition. Courageously opposing both Prohibition and the nativist sentiment of the "True Americans" and Ku Klux Klan, he became the natural target of an unlikely but comprehensible political coalition in Jefferson County. Methodists and Baptists, mobilized by the Alabama Anti-Saloon League, attacked Underwood for his "wet" record. They generally endorsed Jasper businessman L. B. Musgrove, who also had the backing of organized labor.[53] Religious leaders often joined labor spokesmen officiating at Musgrove rallies, and the editor of the state Methodist journal based his opposition to Underwood on the incumbent senator's "wetness," "anti-progressive" social philosophy and failure to support the more advanced "liberalism" of the Woodrow Wilson administration.[54] Pamphlets accusing Underwood of pro-Catholic leanings also circulated in the state.[55]

Although Underwood narrowly won the election (69,130 to 61,360), he lost Jefferson County (9,934 for Musgrove to 9,883), the only time in his long career that he lost his home district. Political lieutenants in Birmingham attributed his local defeat to the remarkable coalition forged by organized labor and the Anti-Saloon League.[56]

The Underwood election posed Birmingham's religious dilemma in sharp relief. The social concern of the churches had not changed suddenly to Klan-style bigotry. The nativist sentiment and battles against secularism of the 1920s were continuations of the earlier struggles to impose Prohibition and blue laws; all of these were attempts to dictate community morality by force. Many churchmen and laymen retained fairly "liberal" social attitudes, but felt that the Klan was working for a common objective: to preserve community moral standards.

There is certainly no question that Birmingham's white Protestant churches supported the Ku Klux Klan. The Klan's attempts to end bootlegging and its floggings of "moral undesirables" in the community usually elicited either praise or neutrality from the city's pulpits. The local head of the Klan estimated that 51 percent of the white Protestant ministers in the county were members of the Klan and that at least that proportion of the laity favored the organization.[57] Klansmen frequently interrupted church services in Birmingham during the 1920s to make a donation to the pastor for his support; such Klan processionals occurred at Inglenook Methodist, Pike Avenue Baptist, Virginia Mines Baptist, Avondale Baptist, Packer Memorial Baptist, Pentecostal Church of North Birmingham, Alton Methodist, Gate City Baptist, Irondale Baptist, and Antioch Baptist.[58]

Perhaps the most spectacular incident of religious intolerance during the 1920s occurred on the evening of August 11, 1921. Father Coyle a focus of Catholic-Protestant conflict, was shot to death by Rev. E. R. Stephenson, a Methodist minister and Klansman who specialized in performing marriages at the local courthouse. Stephenson's daughter had married a Catholic in a ceremony performed by Father Coyle. The enraged father of the bride admitted the shooting and was charged with second-degree murder, but the Birmingham community sympathized with Stephenson. His defense council, Hugo Black, a local attorney and active Sunday school teacher at First Baptist Church, won acquittal from a sympathetic jury. National opinion blamed the bigotry on the city's churches and the acquiescence of the press, while denouncing Birmingham as the "American hotbed of anti-Catholic fanaticism," where the "murder of a priest had been added to the achievements of bigotry."[59]

The religious mind of Birmingham was divided, however, even on Klan enforcement of morality. An increasingly vocal minority of ministers denounced the Klan and demanded that police curb its excesses. Although not all the denomination's ministers signed it, Methodist pastors passed a resolution condemning floggings in the city. Ministers such as Dr. Robert N. Simpson of First Christian, Rev. Jack Johnston of Eleventh Street Baptist, Dr. Henry Edmonds of Independent Presbyterian, Dr. J. E. Dillard of Southside Baptist, Rev. Theo Harris of Pike Avenue Baptist, Dr. W. R. Hendrix of Highlands Methodist, and Rev. Hans Reuter of Zion Lutheran all spoke out publicly against Klan violence.[60] When Father Coyle was murdered, Edmonds announced a sermon on the incident. Because Klan control of city government was almost complete, Edmonds's friends tried to dissuade him. Failing this, they attended his service at the Lyric Theater fully armed and scattered through the congregation determined to protect Edmonds should the Klan attempt any violence. Luckily, such an armed confrontation never materialized.[61]

Edmonds went beyond criticism of the Klan. He, Rabbi Newfield, and Father Eugene Sands, presiding priest at St. Paul's in Birmingham, also organized a Faith Panel, which toured Alabama and neighboring states speaking to civic clubs and colleges. He later aided local Jewish businessmen and Rabbi Newfield in reviving the National Conference of Christians and Jews to stem an ugly rise in anti-Semitism.[62]

Intolerance was not only personalized toward Catholics, Jews, and black people in Birmingham; it was also aimed at the entire climate of free thought. Anti-evolution sentiment was strong, and in 1928 a women's group sponsored a lecture by noted Fundamentalist Baptist minister Dr. John Roach Straton. Allegedly financed by the Klan, Straton's speech to a packed municipal auditorium verbally roasted Catholic Democratic Presidential nominee Alfred E. Smith.[63] On the opposite side of the issue was *The Alabama Baptist* editor L. L. Gwaltney, who quietly waged an energetic campaign for free religious thought. Appalled at the Fundamentalist attack on Baptist professors, he resisted their attempts to force teachers in Baptist institutions to sign statements of faith. The president of Birmingham's Howard College, which was Baptist affiliated, wanted to announce the willingness of his faculty to sign such a statement, but Gwaltney dissuaded him.[64] When a state Baptist pastor wrote an article attacking President William L. Poteat of Baptist Wake Forest University for his evolutionary ideas, Gwaltney refused to carry the article. The infuriated pastor told a prominent politico in his congregation about the incident, and the layman, who later ran for governor, demanded that Gwaltney carry the article as paid advertisement. Gwaltney again refused, and recalling the atmosphere years later, wrote that the same kind of "dogmatic faith" that had condemned Galileo's science "happened among Protestants of America, the Baptists included, during the second [third] decade of the twentieth century."[65]

Perhaps the energy diverted into Klan and Fundamentalist movements enervated the city's churches, for membership increased from 77,145 in 1916 to only 125,253 in 1926, a major decline from the nearly 200 percent growth of the 1906–1916 era. Between 1926 and 1936 church membership actually decreased from 125,253 to 109,945 in 1936, a 12.2 percent decline. Only eight of America's fifty largest cities experienced a decline during the same period, and Birmingham's was the fourth largest drop in the nation.[66] Although the cause of the decline is more complicated than any single issue, it seems clear that the atmosphere of constant controversy did not enhance the strength of the church in Birmingham.

Analysis of the city's church membership reveals that the largest single religious group in the city after 1910 was the National Baptist denomination representing Birmingham's black population. The African Methodist Episcopal church was close behind, and the preponderance of black churches necessitates further word about the religious expression of the 40 percent of Birmingham's population that was black.

The views of most white Protestants toward black individuals were paternalistic. They opposed lynching, favored education for black citizens, and even pleaded for better jobs, but beyond these attitudes few were willing to go.[67] Even a man so consistently liberal as Henry Edmonds viewed black people paternalistically and bemoaned the 1954 desegregation decision that he believed "ended the era of good feeling in the South between the races and halted the progress that was being made . . . under the earlier formula of equal but separate facilities."[68]

Despite such white attitudes, black people did make undeniable contributions to the religious life of Birmingham during the era. A Juvenile Court Association was organized early in the century comprised of one woman from each of thirty black churches. Its task was to take charge of black delinquents. In 1907 the women raised $2,000 and bought twenty-five acres of land near Montgomery. They built a six-room cottage and started an "industrial school" for black men, the beginning of Mt. Meigs Reformatory, which later became a state institution.[69]

The church was more central to the urban black subculture than to white society. Consequently, black people went to church more frequently and a larger proportion than white people were church members.[70] Preachers had high status, serving as political organizers and providing business leadership.[71] Two of Birmingham's leading black businesses were begun by clergymen: Rev. W. R. Pettiford founded the Alabama Penny Savings Bank, and Rev. T. W. Walker started the People's Home and Insurance Company. Black church societies also were more concerned with the social problems of the black community than were their white equivalents.

Other social interests of both black and white churches were similar. White Baptist pastor B. F. Riley assisted blacks in the organization of the Negro Anti-Saloon League in 1909 with national headquarters in Birmingham.[72] Black pastors also enthusiastically favored the Interchurch World Movement, demonstrating a more cooperative sentiment than their white brethren. One hundred seventy-three black delegates attended the Interchurch conference in Birmingham in 1920, and a special session was held on the last day of the conference at Sixteenth Street Baptist, the leading black church in the city. Black clergymen agreed that the movement would be helpful in promoting better race relations and in combating prejudice, injustice, and lynching.[73]

Whether black or white, the religious mind of Birmingham faced traumatic issues in the first decades of the new century. Responding to the evident challenges of the urban/industrial South, churches charted a new course that led them further and further from the otherworldly salvation gospel of the nineteenth century. Even the conservative individualists such as Brother Bryan demonstrated a social dimension not typical of rural Southern religion. At the opposite pole Henry Edmonds and A.J. Dickinson questioned traditional religious dogma, while black churches and Wesley Houses ministered to estranged laborers. Tragedy came when the attempts of the churches to remake society inadvertently lent support to "True Americans" and the Klan, whose tactics were inimical to Christianity. Reluctantly, chroniclers of southern thought must come to terms with the fact that the politicizing of southern religion was not always "good," that the same socialization that resulted in Social Gospel reform such as the abolition of child labor and injustice toward laborers also resulted in proscriptive morality and Klan-type intolerance. Perhaps Vulcan is an adequate symbol for the "city of churches," for sin and salvation as well as churches and violence existed in contradictory union during the first three decades of the twentieth century.

—*The Alabama Review*, 1977

On two occasions the University of Mississippi invited me to participate in the annual Chancellor Porter L. Fortune Jr. History Symposium. The first event focused on the newly developing field of southern labor history of which I considered myself one of the founders; the second, in October 1984, brought together scholars to discuss the burgeoning field of southern religion. By then, my initial enthusiasm for research about labor and poor white people had waned and my youthful fascination with religion had returned.

Having already plunged into the cornucopia of Baptist and Methodist archives available to me, I decided to broaden the scope of my research to the Presbyterian Church in the United States (PCUS), the southern manifestation of that venerable Calvinist tradition. Some theologians quibble with inclusion of the PCUS among southern evangelicals. Many patterns separated them from their Baptist and Methodist cohorts: The high position southern Presbyterians accorded Scottish Common Sense Realism; their convoluted Calvinist heritage; the strict educational requirements demanded of denominational ministers with resultant absence of bivocational, working-class pastors; the hierarchical doctrinal authority vested in presbyteries; and the revered doctrine of the "spirituality of the church" that restricted Presbyterian engagement with politics, even involving such seemingly obvious ethical issues as prohibition and child labor. Always suspicious of untamed emotions, most Presbyterians also became nervous at the spontaneous outburst of feeling often present in conversion experiences. For all these reasons, many historians of religion segregated Presbyterians from "evangelicals" (originally, Baptists and Methodists but later including restorationist Churches of Christ and by the late nineteenth century, Holiness and Pentecostal sects).

Although there is some logic to this argument, it ignores two salient points: during the great antebellum revivals, ministers of the three denominations were nearly interchangeable in the pulpits of August camp meetings, and in the early twentieth century, Presbyterian primary documents and biographies make the evangelical thrust of the church obvious and the highest priority. One may safely separate southern Episcopalians from evangelical narratives (although individual priests could preach "Jesus, and him crucified" with the best of evangelical preachers), but their Social Gospel antecedents were rooted deeper in ethical and cognitive concerns than as a new Gospel vehicle to save the souls of the poor and needy.

As in white Baptist and Methodist denominations, southern Presbyterians argued passionately and sometimes divisively about social justice. And with their better-educated clergy, high value of education, and ecclesiastical capacity to expel heretics and discipline dissenters (somewhat available to Methodist bishops but nearly entirely missing among congregationally governed Baptists), PCUS fissures have a much larger paper trail, a special advantage when I began my research.

Chapter 6

"Feeding the Hungry and Ministering to the Broken Hearted"

The Presbyterian Church in the United States and the Social Gospel, 1900–1920

As the Rev. Walter L. Lingle, pastor of Atlanta's First Presbyterian Church, browsed among magazines in that city's Carnegie Library in 1909, he happened upon an article by Ray Stannard Baker. The essay that attracted his attention dealt with Christianity and the nation's social problems. He read quickly through the article and noted Baker's enthusiastic reference to a new book by Baptist theologian Walter Rauschenbusch titled *Christianity and the Social Crisis*. Lingle moved through the stacks until he located the book and then read it with deepening interest. On the twentieth anniversary of that first discovery, Lingle delivered the James Sprunt Lectures at Union Theological Seminary in Richmond, Virginia. He chose for his subject the "Social Teachings of the Bible." Remembering his first reading of Rauschenbusch, he wrote: "It is a dynamic work. Since that time, I have read many volumes on the same general subject, but no other book has so stirred my soul as that first one."[1]

By the time the General Assembly of the Presbyterian Church in the United States (PCUS, the southern branch of Presbyterianism, as opposed to the Presbyterian Church in the United States of America, or PCUSA, which enrolled most non-southern Presbyterians) met in May 1911, Rauschenbusch's influence had spread. The Committee on Theological Seminaries, "in view of the growing importance of many social questions," recommended that all PCUS seminaries "adopt and teach a brief, practical course in Sociology." The recommendation was adopted, and within the month A. L. Phillips, the general superintendent of the Committee of Publication, wrote Lingle confidentially testing his reaction to becoming a professor at Union Seminary in Richmond. The most distinguished PCUS seminary wanted a professor to teach practical theology including subjects such as modern Sunday school, young people's societies, missions, church finance, and other issues involving a minister's adjustment to life in a modern society. Phillips had heard that Lingle advocated such changes "with great force and conviction" from the pulpit of Atlanta's First Presbyterian Church, which he pastored. His duties would also include teaching a new course on Christianity and the social order, a subject of growing interest to Lingle. So the times and the man met. Lingle resigned his pastorate and moved his family to Richmond where he began a new and influential ministry interpreting and advocating the Social Gospel.[2]

For many years historians simply ignored the Walter L. Lingles of the South. Treating the Mason-Dixon Line as an impenetrable barrier to reform, they discussed Populism, Progressivism, the labor movement and the Social Gospel as if such movements had never occurred in the South. With the discovery of a persistent reform tradition dating to the earliest years of the region, this notion has now been considerably modified. Recently intellectuals have even conceded that the South produced a highly developed culture, a notion that no doubt would have H. L. Mencken rejoicing in paradise, had he believed in paradise. Historians of southern religion have discovered numerous nineteenth-century urban pastors well educated in the theological ideas current in Europe, a rich and meaningful tradition of folk religion, and even a Social Gospel.

The Social Gospel is a concept generally applied to a specific period of American religious history, beginning in the late nineteenth century, flourishing between 1900 and 1920, and then slowly declining, although not without bursts of renewed vigor. Recent historians argue that the Social Gospel was not primarily a set of theological ideas, a new kind of Christianity, or a uniform movement. Experiences were more influential than ideas, especially those of urban pastors with the poor and with immigrants. Social Gospelers discussed theological ideas but filled their writings, lectures, and sermons with calls for action. Their primary concern was the city, which became a mission field for the conversion and Americanization of immigrants and the expression of Christian concern for the poor. The Social Gospel movement occurred in the context of change, excitement, and hope for a more just society. Although its critics viewed social Christianity as an aberrant, new form of Christianity, its advocates stressed their allegiance to traditional Christian concepts such as sin, conversion, salvation, regeneration, holiness, repentance, perfection, and the Kingdom of God. They merely attempted to apply such ideas to society rather than exclusively to individuals.[3]

Within the Social Gospel movement diverse elements competed for influence. The largest group was a conservative assortment of pastors, academics, and lay people who sought evolutionary change. They viewed the future with confidence in the emergence of a just social order. They were cautious and preferred the term "social service" to Social Gospel. They were suspicious of socialism, viewed the church as a mediating force between powerful special interests, and believed that efforts to remake society without converting individuals were doomed to failure. The reforms they advocated, such as settlement houses and institutional churches, were done *for* the working class, black people, and the poor. Shailer Mathews, professor of New Testament at the University of Chicago, was one of their leaders.[4]

A smaller, revolutionary Social Gospel faction was more pessimistic about the future of a country dominated by unregulated capitalism. But if Christianity could change the structure of society, social salvation might still be possible. The key, however, was to change structures, not individuals. These social activists worked for more drastic change, often endorsed socialism, and worked *with* the lower classes, believing that the church must take sides on social issues affecting the poor. Walter Rauschenbusch, professor of church history at Rochester Theological Seminary, was the primary spokesman for this viewpoint.[5]

The Social Gospel affected every mainline American religious group. Some it dominated, others it influenced but never controlled, while still others it touched only slightly. That it influenced the North more than the South is entirely understandable. There the problems of cities, immigrants, and urban class conflict, precisely the problems most frequently addressed by the Social Gospel, were pronounced. In the South, individualism, the predominance of a rural way of life, and the relatively modest size and complexity of cities presented fewer crises.

Nonetheless it is surprising that historians long ignored the primary sources of the Social Gospel in the South. Happily, the debate no longer revolves around whether the Social Gospel reached the South.[6] Rather the questions concern the extent of the Social Gospel's penetration, the relationship between ideas and action, the determination to redeem social structures rather than just to perform charitable good works, and the extent of its influence within southern denominations.[7]

To put the debate into context, several generalizations are important. First, the South's rural distinctiveness must be understood. Obviously a region with few cities would produce religious concerns somewhat different from a region with many cities. Second, the Social Gospel by no means swept the North and Midwest into a consensus on the role of religion and society. The resurgent Fundamentalism of the 1920s demonstrated the continuing diversity quite well. Third, even northern advocates of the Social Gospel acted from mixed motives, which often make it difficult to trace precisely the route from ideas to actions. A recent dissertation on the settlement house movement in Indiana notes that this quintessential Social Gospel reform was initiated not by radicals or socialists nor from a well-formed social philosophy. The ideas of settlement house social workers could best be called Christian humanitarianism, which defined sin as social maladjustment. They were not cultural pluralists, but "missionaries for the American way." They desired to convert Catholic immigrants not only to Protestantism but into proper Americans like themselves. Protestant settlement workers in Indiana generally attributed poverty to "a failure of will or character deficiency in the victim," not to structural problems within capitalism.[8] If in order to validate the Social Gospel the relationship of ideas to action must be precise, the concern for redeeming social structures paramount, and the extent of Social Gospel penetration pronounced, perhaps the Social Gospel did not exist in Indiana or the South.

The issue is too significant to hinge on a debate over semantics. Because so many of the South's liberals traced their roots to religious forms and ideas, it is tempting to treat this subject biographically. Candidates for such an approach are numerous: among them Edgar Gardner Murphy, Lucy Randolph Mason, Will Campbell, Aubrey Williams, Will Alexander, and Jimmy Carter. Virtually every recent historian who has tackled the South's twentieth-century liberal tradition has commented on the formative and unusually extensive role religion played.[9]

A more formidable and obscure challenge swirls around that solitary 1909 patron of the Carnegie Library in Atlanta. One is not so surprised to find numerous southern Methodist settlement houses for Methodists had prophesied a similar radical message in nineteenth-century England. And the anarchy of Southern Baptists always allows a heretic or two to slip under the ecclesiastical tent on the assumption that the only difference between orthodoxy and heterodoxy is my-doxy and your-doxy. But no more hostile environment could be found for the Social Gospel than the Presbyterian Church in the United States. The church, often viewed as the right wing of the Protestant Reformation, was theocratic, nationalistic, conservative, rationalistic, and sufficiently hierarchical and dogmatic to expel its worst malcontents.[10] If one can find in the PCUS a connection between theological ideas and social action, a fundamental critique of social structures, or influential linkage to mainstream Social Gospel organizations, leaders, and ideas, then such a discovery should lift the debate to another level.

Ernest Trice Thompson found no such phenomenon. In his splendid three-volume history of the denomination, he chronicled substantial social change between 1880 and 1920 but minimized the role of the Social Gospel. As did many others before him, he confined his research to denominational newspapers and official proceedings of presbyteries, synods, and the General Assembly. Although he mentions Walter Lingle and other Social Gospel leaders casually, he did not use their papers. Had he done so, what a treasure would have greeted him.[11]

The barriers to the Social Gospel that the PCUS erected were formidable. In addition to a religious hierarchy, which was, however, much more democratic and tolerant in practice than in theory, there were the individualistic, middle-class, and conservative economic and political values of most Presbyterians.

Like Southern Baptists and Methodists, Presbyterians rejected the new "higher criticism," which was long thought to be a concomitant of the Social Gospel. As best they could they sought to exorcise it from their body. After Lingle arrived in Richmond to teach at Union Seminary, he received letters leaving no doubt about the theological views of his friends. A student wrote for suggested theological reading: "I am a pretty strict Presbyterian of several generations back, but I have studied a good deal, and am not afraid of criticism, higher or lower; it can't hurt the Bible." A friend from Atlanta wrote Lingle about possible union of the northern and southern wings of Presbyterianism. He noted in his letter that a northern friend in the PCUSA desired unity also, "as soon as they could weed out about 20% of their cranks and heretics. This old brother knew what he was talking about, didn't he?"[12] Nor did Lingle stray far from biblical orthodoxy.

Some Presbyterians arduously desired to protect parishioners' minds from the poisonous wells of heresy. The secretary-treasurer of the Committee of Publication feared attempts to bring before the 1911 General Assembly a plan to require a censor. The committee had never practiced strict censorship because "Presbyterians have a way of doing their own thinking." But there was "a large element of conservative men scattered over the church who do not seem to understand the difficulties of our position." The issue arose again when the 1912 Assembly dispatched a pastoral letter condemning the International Graded Sunday School Lessons for disseminating "the theories of the school of radical criticism," deemphasizing redemption and the Holy Spirit, and including too much nonbiblical material. A resolution introduced at the 1920 General Assembly urged the Committee of Publication not to recommend or sell any publications that were "not in full accord with the fundamental belief of our Evangelistic Churches." A substitute softened the resolution only slightly by urging the committee to exercise "scrupulous care" concerning books recommended to Presbyterians.[13] Liberals occasionally rippled the theological waters but not enough to trouble Zion.

Although Presbyterians shared opposition to "higher criticism" with Baptists and Methodists, they were distinctive in their doctrine of the spirituality of the church. Dating back to the origins of the PCUS, the doctrine was partly rooted in New School–Old School theological debates and partly in the pre-Civil War struggle over slavery. A minority of northern Presbyterians condemned slavery and sought to use the church as a forum for abolitionist and pro-Union theory. As part of their rationalization of slavery, southern Presbyterians insisted that the church should not engage in secular politics. It had a legitimate prophetic role to stir the hearts of men who in turn should exercise their rights as citizens. But the institutional church was a spiritual not a social entity and must not soil itself with issues that would inevitably divide its fellowship and compromise its purity.[14]

Even conservative Presbyterians sometimes rankled under this doctrine, especially when the issue was demon rum. In 1907 a number of presbyteries from the Synod of Alabama petitioned the General Assembly to appoint a permanent committee on temperance. The assembly declined, replying that the position of the PCUS was well known already and such a measure "would involve the possibility of political entanglements." Not to be denied, the Presbytery of North Alabama in October 1909 endorsed statewide prohibition, which it called a nonpartisan and nonpolitical moral issue. Dissenters within the presbytery challenged the resolution as a violation of the Book of Church Order, paragraph 248, which established the principle of nonintrusion into civil affairs, but the prohibitionist faction won 14 to 7. By 1915 the issue had spread throughout the denomination. When the General Assembly congratulated the Woman's Christian Temperance Union and advised Presbyterians to support a constitutional amendment prohibiting the sale of alcoholic beverages, the Synod of Virginia vigorously opposed the action. Its delegates resolved that attempts to instruct citizens how to vote contravened the principles of the PCUS on the relationship of church to civil government.[15]

Within the denomination the desire to control alcohol abuse clashed with the doctrine of the spirituality of the church, but Walter Lingle decided his position early in the conflict. When a pastor in South Georgia near the turn of the century, his presbytery had turned out an elder who owned a distillery. Prohibiting liquor was the proper business of a Presbyterian as was the "need to carry Christianity into every department of life," Lingle assured a friend. He associated more active social Christianity not with radical departures from historic doctrine, but as a return to the teachings of Christ.[16]

Other moral questions called for the involvement of the church as well, none more so than child labor. D. P. McGeachy had been present when the Synod of Virginia debated the prohibition question in 1915 and had argued that in some cases the church should take a stand on questions involving politics. The debate became so heated that "for the sake of the peace of the house," discussion had been ended. The exchange had persuaded him to prepare a paper for the County Ministers Association on the subject "The Pastor and Social Service." He had read Rauschenbusch, Shailer Mathews, and Presbyterian James Howerton's book, *The Church and Social Reforms*, but remained confused. He asked Lingle to explain precisely what the Bible taught about social service. Although he wrote conservatives for their opinions also and planned to avoid either extreme position, he had already decided to plead for "preaching Christ" in "sermons on prohibition and child slavery [labor]." Was it not "pure cowardice" for Presbyterians to "never open our mouths over any question that might be in any degree political no matter how tremendous the moral issues are that are involved? I take the position that you have to answer questions like that with an 'It depends.'" Every situation had to be confronted as it appeared "keeping to the general principles of the spirituality of the church."[17]

Alexander McKelway experienced no such ambivalence. After completing his education at Hampden-Sydney College and Union Theological Seminary, he held pastorates in Virginia and North Carolina until 1898 when he became editor of the most influential PCUS state newspaper, the *Presbyterian Standard*, published in Charlotte, North Carolina. Although McKelway shared the racial ideology of his times, he differed markedly from conservative Presbyterians on the issue of social service. His special concern was the elimination of child labor, but he became involved in a multitude of social causes. As southern director of the National Child Labor Committee, McKelway urged Presbyterian ministers to use their influence for passage of federal legislation limiting child labor. To those who complained that this compromised the purity of Presbyterianism, he responded that "the church loses her hold on the conscience of men when she shrinks from uttering her voice for a righteous cause for fear of political entanglements."[18] A brilliant, acerbic propagandist and organizer, McKelway played a major role in the creation of the Southern Sociological Congress, was elected its first vice president, and used it effectively in his crusade against child labor. When President Woodrow Wilson hesitated to adopt the cause, McKelway bombarded him with propaganda until he finally capitulated in 1916. In that election year McKelway campaigned devotedly for Wilson and persuaded the Democratic Party to adopt twenty reform proposals for its platform, including the eight-hour day, a pension system, development of human welfare agencies, a national child labor law, and prison reform. After the Democrats accepted nearly all his proposals, he conducted a vigorous effort to win the vote of social workers and progressives from Theodore Roosevelt's 1912 Progressive Party.[19] Thanks to McKelway's spirited advocacy of child labor, the PCUS compromised its rigid adherence to the spirituality of the church. In 1908 the Rev. Dr. R. F. Campbell proposed a strong resolution to the General Assembly arguing that the legacy of child labor was "the disintegration of the family, the promotion of illiteracy, the destruction of church influences." The resolution urged employers and parents to obey laws already passed and to strive for more effective legislation. The resolution passed easily.[20] So effective was McKelway's lobbying and mobilization of southern churches that by 1910 all southern states had enacted minimum age laws. McKelway had found a way to translate Social Gospel ideas into legislative reality.

If McKelway's spirited campaign to save the children was the most serious early breach in the practice of the spirituality of the church, Dr. James R. Howerton's book was one of the earliest ideological challenges to that doctrine. Howerton was a professor of philosophy at Washington and Lee University and an influential Presbyterian minister. In 1909 he began delivering lectures on the church and social issues. In the mid teens he combined three lectures into a book entitled *The Church and Social Reforms*. Howerton unsuccessfully tried to harmonize the conflict between the Social Gospel and the spirituality of the church. In his third lecture/essay, titled "The Church and the Social Reforms of Today," he argued that both church and state sought the same end: the moral welfare of humanity. But the church must communicate a message of social salvation to its members, not act coercively or engage in secular reforms as an institution. The church must reform law by reforming lawyers, reform politics by reforming politicians, and reform society by reforming social leaders. But she could not improve society if such ethical reform was "merely incidental to the saving of the souls of lawyers, politicians, business men, and social leaders in another world." The Kingdom of God must be achieved in this world by reforming conditions, and the church must equip people to live ethically and deliver its message in such a way that all could understand it: "Let her preach the gospel as a rule of justification; but she must preach the law as a rule of life, and insist that obedience to it in all the relations of life is the only valid evidence of a saving faith. The epistle of James must be preached as well as those of Paul."[21] He described the church as a largely middle-class institution that ignored the poor. Capitalists and their allies paid their tithes in the belief that contributions absolved them from ethical responsibility for how they earned their money. He did not advocate socialism, arguing that this ideology was not germane. Christ was neither socialist nor anti-socialist, he taught neither politics nor economics. But he did teach ethics, which must underlie all political and economic theory. For all Howerton's prophetic prose, however, he was a transitional figure who could not bring himself to advocate a broader social role for the church beyond persuading its members, who in turn must courageously and individually change society.[22]

Although Howerton's book was widely read, its theological arguments made less impact than the practical experiences of Presbyterians. In denominations where the salvation of souls was paramount, structures quickly developed to promote evangelism. One such missionary enterprise slowly evolved in the remote vastness of the Appalachian Mountains. Presbyterians were no strangers to this land for among the early settlers were Scots-Irish Calvinists who scattered churches throughout the foothills. But further up the hollows and at the higher elevations institutions of all kinds were scarce. The Ladies Board of Missions, PCUSA, established the first denominational school for white students in 1879. Between 1885 and 1895 northern Presbyterians began thirty-one schools and sponsored thirty-four more during the following decade. The PCUS began its mountain work in 1881. The Synod of Kentucky authorized Dr. Edward O. Guerrant of Kentucky to devote his full time to mountain work. Guerrant founded the Society of Soul Winners, also called the American Inland Mission, in 1897 to raise money and to recruit home missionaries. Despite its conventional title and Guerrant's passion for saving souls, the society never disengaged from the social workings of mountain life. He had first traveled the mountains as a Confederate soldier and had been impressed with its beauty and the deprivation of its people. As a physician, Guerrant conducted clinics as well as revivals and believed no lasting change could occur in the mountains without education. Beginning with $360 and one mountain missionary in 1897, Guerrant organized the most extensive mission effort in the mountains. He raised in excess of $12,000 each year for more than a decade and supported as many as seventy workers. Although individual salvation never ceased to be his primary goal, he increasingly directed his efforts toward institutional work. In the process he won support of one PCUS agency after another. In 1898 the Asheville Presbytery offered its active support.

In 1911 the Executive Committee on Home Missions agreed to sponsor the work. Three years later the Synod of North Carolina proposed a new ecclesiastical jurisdiction for the mountains. Established in 1915, the Synod of Appalachia was created by combining parts of four existing synods (Virginia, Kentucky, North Carolina, and Tennessee).[23]

In time the Society of Soul Winners presided over a far-flung network of institutions, including Stuart Robinson School at Blackey, Kentucky (with eighteen teachers and 400 pupils); Highland Institute at Guerrant, Kentucky (fifteen teachers, 200 pupils); Madison Synodical School at Madison, West Virginia (eight teachers, 117 pupils); and Blue Ridge Academy, Hollow, Virginia (six teachers, 109 pupils). Some of the mountain schools were much more complex than their academic designation suggests. Highland Institute founded in Breathitt County, Kentucky, in 1908 included a church, farm, orphanage, and the only hospital in the county, with a resident physician and nurse. Guerrant regularly took medical personnel with him on trips into remote areas to provide medical care for the destitute people. He frequently conducted medical clinics next to his schools.[24]

Critics of mountain religion have generally dismissed it as traditional, otherworldly Christianity. Mountain preachers seldom preached on ethics, and when they did mountain people often resented such references. A visitor during the 1930s heard only one sermon on a social issue and that sermon condemned birth control.[25] But such critics were neither well informed nor even perceptive.

Presbyterians by 1910 had clearly opted for a mixture of spiritual and educational salvation. The PCUS operated mission schools for black students, immigrants, Indians, and mountain children, but by far the largest effort was in the mountains. Thanks to an individual who contributed $2,000 a year, the Home Mission Board and individual synods were able to expand Guerrant's work. They established schools such as Rabun Gap-Nacoochee in Georgia, Lees-McRae in North Carolina, Grundy in Virginia, Caddo Valley in Arkansas, and School of the Ozarks in Missouri. By 1910 the PCUS sponsored fifty-nine day schools with 1,343 pupils and 239 teachers. Each school combined Bible study and secular education, and most provided industrial/agricultural training for boys and domestic education for girls. The teachers served multiple roles: missionaries, educators, and church leaders, as well as social and community workers. The General Assembly considered mountain schools to be "the most important arm in the evangelization of the mountain people . . .," and the home missions committee employed a woman to represent mountain work before synodical Ladies' Societies. By 1914 the annual home mission budget for mountain schools had risen to $85,000, and by 1917 expenditures on the schools exceeded the entire PCUS home mission committee budget of 1907. Mountain work dominated the committee's proceedings; although it created a subcommittee on Mountain, Mill, City and Country Churches in 1910, its reports to the General Assembly for the next two years dealt exclusively with mountain work.[26]

As Guerrant's health declined, the home missions committee pondered the future of its Appalachian work. The legendary Dr. John C. Campbell, who headed the Southern Highlands Division of the Russell Sage Foundation, was deeply imbued with the Social Gospel and tried to influence the PCUS committee on mountain work to centralize the organization of schools under its jurisdiction. He also sought to minimize sectarianism and encourage interdenominational cooperation. He urged Presbyterians to honor President Wilson's first wife by creating the Ellen Axson Wilson Memorial Scholarship to support education in Appalachia.[27] His ideas heavily influenced PCUS policy between 1910 and 1920.

The Executive Committee on Home Missions agreed to assume responsibility for the Soul Winners society in February, 1911, although it employed Guerrant to oversee the ministry. Almost immediately the committee moved on Campbell's recommendations. It proposed a division of mountain work among Baptists, Methodists, and Presbyterians so as to eliminate duplication. The committee consolidated mountain activities under a superintendent who administered fifty missionaries and property valued at $49 million, containing forty-two mountain schools, 129 teachers, and 3,250 students.[28]

The transition from Guerrant's personal control to coordinated supervision by a committee in Atlanta created problems. William E. Hudson who was appointed superintendent of mountain work became involved in controversy with the Presbytery of West Lexington, Kentucky, when he tried to change the work. The superintendent of Riverside Institute wrote Guerrant resisting centralization: "None of the members of the Board have had experience enough to enable them to be familiar with the needs, yet they are the real determining factor in matters of government here."[29] Guerrant's death in 1916 at age 78 eased tensions somewhat.

Many of the schools became self-supporting and began to disappear in the 1920s and 1930s as public education spread through the mountains. But the Synod of Virginia still supported fifteen mountain schools in the mid-1920s, and the cumulative social impact of Guerrant's four decades of effort was enormous. Beyond the souls saved, thousands of mountain children who otherwise would have grown up illiterate received education. Hundreds of boys and girls unable to pay tuition received scholarships or worked their way through Presbyterian schools. Mollie Clark, a West Virginia coal miner's daughter, was one beneficiary. Her mother and father died when she was nine. She began attending a Presbyterian mission school at Shooting Creek, West Virginia, when she was age 12, was converted at 14, and remained at the school for seven years: "At first it was very hard for me to learn. I thought that no one loved me. I lived because I had to, and I wanted to die. When the teachers corrected me . . . I thought they were cruel to me. But with their patience I was convinced that they loved me, and that I was put into the world for a purpose." Later she entered Stonewall Jackson College, working her way through its high school program by serving in a dining room. The Woman's Auxiliary of the PCUS provided a scholarship to help with her expenses. Perhaps part of the money came from Mrs. Woodrow Wilson who took a keen interest in the schools and made a major donation to them. Such testimony emphasizes precisely what Guerrant had intended the schools to do: help Presbyterians convert Appalachian people. But inevitably the schools became more than agents of Presbyterian evangelism. They forced Presbyterians into ecumenical associations and led to conferences for mountain workers from various denominations. They led to the establishment of five PCUS orphanages and several hospitals.[30]

The mountain work also brought Presbyterians into an alien culture where either they had to adapt or force their charges to modify native Appalachian society. Culture shock worked both ways with many teachers disparaging mountain ways even as others followed the example of John and Olive Campbell. Many missionaries could not cope with the strange ways, isolation, and loneliness of the Appalachian frontier. One schoolteacher who left the Presbyterian school at Crossnore, North Carolina, recommended a classmate from the Presbyterian Training School she thought capable of standing the isolation there. Missionaries to the coal mining camps became agents of Americanization as fully as settlement house workers in Gary, Indiana. The Rev. E. E. Von Peachy, director of work among Hungarians near Holden, West Virginia, visualized his work in apocalyptic terms: "Failure to make Christian Americans out of these ignorant but willing and good Europeans may mean disaster; but success in our frontier work will mean peace, loyalty, faithful citizens of this great country." A pastor from eastern Kentucky desired a more hospitable and civilized environment than Grayson, Kentucky, which he described in the most unflattering terms: "The school is very poor, and I am sure I am not doing our children justice; every housekeeper here, practically, does her own work, it being impossible to employ servants. We have been doing our own work for more than a year, but my wife is not physically able to continue indefinitely."[31]

The same culture shock that drove many Presbyterians from the mountains opened opportunities for others that traditional southern society denied. Guerrant relied heavily upon women from the outset of his ministry. By 1910 the Society of Soul Winners supported twenty-five women working in the mountains of Kentucky and North Carolina and thirty-five teachers. They came from across America: two women on Turkey Creek in Breathitt County, Kentucky, came from Kansas and Iowa; two teachers at Canoe were North Carolina natives; at Athol the two mountain teachers were from New Jersey; Miss Ella Keigwin from Florida ran Ebenezer Mission in east Tennessee; Miss Alida Beyer, of Brooklyn, resigned her position as a city missionary in New York City to teach children in Kentucky and help carpenters build a church; Miss Mary Robertson, of Paris, Texas, directed a mission. Guerrant described the efforts of a female missionary in eastern Kentucky who went to an area without a church, Sabbath school, or preacher, twenty miles from the nearest town or physician to begin a Sunday school. She taught all who came that winter, spreading both the gospel and her short supply of medicines. She took in a woman whose drunken husband had tried to kill her. At the same historical moment that the PCUS east of the mountains adamantly resolved that women should not speak before mixed assemblies of men and other women, Guerrant quoted the apostle Paul: "I entreat thee, also, to help those women which labored with me in the Gospel."[32]

The women Guerrant described in his book were indomitable and apparently paid little attention to their previously limited spheres. The gospel had called them to a bold new ministry. Lizzette, whose last name Guerrant did not record, served as a missionary at Glencairn. A graduate of Converse College in South Carolina, she lived alone in a remote cabin, slept in a bed she built herself, taught a school with twenty-four children, and walked more than a hundred miles a month making her rounds. A Presbyterian minister was asked by his missionary daughter, Miss Clemmie Patton, of Decatur, Georgia, to preach at the mission she directed in Breathitt, Kentucky. After watching her direct the spiritual activities at the mission, he commented: "Some say that this is irregular; true, but if the work cannot be accomplished in a regular way, it must be done in an irregular way." What the people must have was Christ regardless of the methods. And the women proclaimed a gospel that was liberating in more ways than one. A female missionary described an arduous school regimen, which began at 8:00 A.M. with catechism and Bible verses, followed by religious instruction and lessons in reading, spelling, mathematics, and geography. After six days of this routine she conducted a Sunday school on the Sabbath. She expressed concern about girls marrying at age 14 or 16 and tried to broaden "their horizon" so they would not rush into marriage "so thoughtlessly."[33]

The desire to "save" Appalachian girls was a common theme of mountain missionaries. West Virginia missionary O. C. Huston sought a scholarship to the Presbyterian Training School in Richmond for a descendent of the Hatfields, a survivor of the famous feud: "I really do not know how she will make out, except this, she has the fighting blood of her forebears, and their stubbornness, which will be an asset, if she stands the strain of classroom work. I believe it is worth while to try her, if she will go, for if she comes out all right, she will be just what we need for some of these neighborhoods."[34]

The Training School for Lay Workers, founded in 1914, was the major source of female missionaries and teachers. Many of them took the two-year course of study in Bible, Religious Education, Missions, Personal Work, Christian Doctrine, Church History, Organized Woman's Work, and Social Welfare, and then worked in the mountains, mining camps, or urban settlement houses. Women teachers came from quite diverse backgrounds. In 1920 two Vassar College graduates wrote Lingle, who was then president of the Training School, that they wanted to teach in "a rural school in the southern mountains or do some kind of community service or health work." Helen Mathews who wrote Lingle was apparently a Protestant but her companion volunteer was Jewish. Lingle furnished a list of Presbyterian schools.[35]

Once they arrived in the mountains, the women quickly adjusted to unorthodox roles. Mary M. Sloop, principal of Crossnore School in North Carolina, declared war on the county's moonshiners, not that she disliked them personally: "I declare the smartest people on earth are the moonshiners. I just love 'em and they are the best friends I have in the county, even the ones I have arrested. And their children are numberless and as smart as their parents." County revenue agents shirked their duties causing Sloop to write: "if I didn't have a family, I'd surely take the job. Am sorter doing it any way, while my careful husband squirms at my audacity." She was determined to locate two Presbyterian missionaries for the moonshine centers of the county, although one suspects her enthusiasm for this ministry exceeded that of her male compatriots. Sloop also had an unorthodox notion of women's role in the church. In her attempt to recruit Miss Leyburn, a female missionary, she expressed hope that she could also attract a resident pastor. If so Leyburn's work would not be "so essential to the life of our church." But pastors were scarce and if none could be found, Leyburn's work would be "that of keeping alive and making to grow a very young and weak little church . . . and . . . if she did not call that a strictly church job, I'd like for her to find one that was."[36]

In the summers many pastors on vacation and theology students visited the mountains to preach, and the women welcomed and deferred to them. But during the hard winters the women led the struggling churches. When the Rev. R. P. Smith explained after one of his sermons that Presbyterians did not have enough ministers to assign them to the mountains on a regular basis, a mountain man responded: "We like to hear you fellows preach, and I am not saying anything against ye, but if we can't git both, send us the women teachers. These women teach our children books and good manners during the week and on Sunday they teach all of us a lot of what is in the Bible. Tell your folks to send us the teachers, we can git along mighty well for a good while yet just with them doing the work."[37]

Although Guerrant never intended his Society of Soul Winners to expand social opportunities for Presbyterian women or challenge the sexual assumptions of southern society, that was precisely its effect. Nor did he intend for education, orphanages, and health care to assume so large a role in its function, but he endorsed all these goals and without his blessing and assistance, the American

Inland Mission would have been nothing more than a series of remote preaching stations.

One reason the Social Gospel in the South has been so easily ignored is that it usually thrived in cities. When interjected into the world of rural America it assumed new directions. The Society of Soul Winners was one such form. The Country Life Movement was another. The progressive vision caught sight of declining rural America during the administration of President Theodore Roosevelt. Although the concern was not easily focused, it resulted in numerous conferences, books, and new initiatives to strengthen rural institutions. Virtually all the experts centered their attention on rural schools and churches as the critical institutions in stabilizing farming communities. They recommended that rural sociology be taught in colleges and seminaries, churches be consolidated, rural churches become social centers as well as houses of worship, and congregations build parsonages to attract full-time pastors and eliminate quarter-time and half-time churches.[38] Although the PCUS was not as strong in rural areas as Methodists and Baptists, it developed its own rural brand of the Social Gospel.

The crisis was obvious to all. A Presbyterian in Alabama remembered the decade of the 1890s as one in which PCUS ministers wanted "to leave a country field soon as a city pastorate beckoned." In 1913 the pastor of a small Presbyterian church in Paris, Tennessee, wrote that he could not live on his salary: "I want one single church in a town of good size or in a city." In 1918 the Presbytery of East Mississippi wrote Lingle that it needed pastors of several "group fields" (multiple churches) in rural areas.[39]

The PCUS began its formal effort to assist country churches almost simultaneous with the first national report on the subject in 1908. The Home Mission Board raised $1,500 to match private contributions of $1,000 to finance a conference for ministers in mountain and rural areas. The board paid expenses for a hundred rural ministers representing several denominations to attend the conference at the Presbyterian assembly grounds at Montreat, North Carolina. Many of the ministers were as poor as the people they served and also lacked education. So successful was the meeting that the board scheduled another in 1910.[40]

One intense but seemingly unlikely observer of this effort was Walter L. Lingle. As pastor of Atlanta's First Presbyterian Church and member of the Home Mission Board, he helped plan the 1910 conference. Unknown to most of his associates, Lingle's commitment to the country church dated back to seminary days when his request for such a parish as his first pastorate had been denied. Destiny had a different fate in store for him. At a strategic moment his visibility as a successful large church pastor and later as a seminary professor placed him as chairman of a committee on the problem of rural pastors for a conference in Chattanooga. Organized by the Southern Conference for Education and Industry, the Chattanooga meeting scheduled for April 1915, involved many progressive groups, including the Conference of Southern Women, the Southern Educational Council, and the Country Church Conference. The consortium chose the theme of "community," and designated the Rev. A. L. Phillips, general superintendent of the Presbyterian Executive Committee of Publication, to chair the Conference on the Country Church. Phillips asked his friend Lingle to research and recommend strategies for obtaining resident pastors for once-a-month country churches, factors to be considered in the location and construction of church buildings and parsonages, and the church's social and educational role in the community.[41] The Chattanooga meeting meshed nicely with a third PCUS Rural Church Conference planned for Montreat in 1916.

Lingle began preparation for the conferences in 1914. He invited a former student then pastoring a rural church to write an article for the seminary magazine he edited. The pastor, Willis Thompson, from a rural area near Springfield, Kentucky, actually first suggested the 1916 conference because of the serious conditions in rural areas. He had tried to reach the transient population of poor white tobacco farmers, but their tenancy made them so highly mobile that he had serious difficulties. His letter was a composite of condescension and concern:

> Without our numbers there is a welter of tenant tobacco-growers, roving yearly from locality to locality and made up of nominal "Baptists," nominal Campbellites, nominal Methodists, and nominal other things.... They are unmanageable and heartbreaking in their resistance ... to our work. I seem to have won their respect and attention ... but I shrink from thinking of their carelessness if one who woos them less fondly than I have should have charge of this field. I have learned how to preach to them also; for I won their respect through pastoral work solely. I have to preach so that the better class of people will find stimulus in the sermon and these poor Ishmaelites shall also have fire struck from them.... If they would but stay in one place, the task would be simple; I could rejoice in it, for they are sub-soil to my church work. But they rove perpetually.

Thompson attributed his enthusiasm for work among the rural poor to Lingle's guidance: "I had intended to write of what a real stimulus your influence at the Seminary afforded me.... It would not be heresy to say that I look eagerly for the modern viewpoint among the breathren in hope that it is with[in] them to back and invigorate the healthy conservatism of our church; but my watching is very discouraging at times."[42]

Thompson's faith in Lingle was not misplaced. Even as he composed his letter, Warren H. Wilson, superintendent of Country Church Work for the PCUSA Board of Home Missions, was advising Lingle about the proper elements to include in a rural church conference. Lingle had not stopped his reading of Walter

Rauschenbusch. Another favorite author was Wilson, whose research and writing had been inspired by Theodore Roosevelt's 1908 Country Life Commission report. Wilson's books, so eagerly devoured by Lingle, called the church to become a community center. Historically it had been too emotional and individualistic; now it must champion educational improvement and interdenominational cooperation. The major barrier to the spiritual mission of the rural church was not private sin and demonic powers; it was tenancy and rural poverty. In short, Wilson's ideas that so attracted Lingle expanded the Social Gospel into a rural setting.[43] When Lingle wrote Wilson for advice on the Chattanooga and Montreat conferences, the PCUSA minister responded enthusiastically and at length. He recommended that only pastors of small struggling rural churches be invited and suggested from his experience that the most popular courses would be in "Social Religion," the "Church and Community" or "Religious Sociology," and another in "Religious Pedagogy" or "The Teaching of Religion." He advised that the faculty be recruited from agricultural colleges and state universities: "I do not think that the school [conference] ought to become a place for missionary secretaries, or temperance advocates, or Sabbath observance exponents, or any other propagandists to tell their cause." Finally, the conference would have to pay the expenses of the rural ministers. Lingle was so impressed with Wilson's advice that he invited the northern Presbyterian to help him draft a "platform," which became the basis of Lingle's session at the Chattanooga conference.[44]

The July 1916 Montreat Conference on the Country Church allowed Lingle to develop his philosophy more fully. As the conference's organizer, he presented daily lectures on "The Social Teachings of the Bible," a topic that had come to dominate his teaching as well as his sermons. He also recruited the Rev. W. H. Mills, a professor of Rural Sociology at Columbia Theological Seminary and Clemson College and a specialist on the problems of country churches, to lecture each day. Lingle was so impressed by the applied Christianity of Mills that he also printed the professor's essays on the rural church in the *Union Seminary Review*.[45]

Lingle's advocacy of the Social Gospel in the country did not detract from his continuing interest in the urban South. From the vantage point of Atlanta, Lingle saw the problems created by a rapidly expanding city. He and a layman proposed in 1908 that the city's Sunday School Union purchase ten acres on the outskirts of Atlanta and construct a recreation center with tennis courts, a baseball diamond, croquet grounds, swimming pool, and picnic facilities. It should be located on a trolley line so Atlanta's children would have access to it. Such a development would indicate that the Sunday School Union cared for the "social and physical welfare of its members as well as for the spiritual." He also fought to prevent his congregation from selling their downtown site and moving the church to the suburbs. It was partly Lingle's involvement with urban problems that led to his appointment as a member of the PCUS Home Mission Board.[46]

The board was the PCUS agency most involved with the changing course of urban society. Its attempts to evangelize the city ran head on into new realities. The board's urban initiatives resulted partly from threats to traditional values. It defined its task as fitting the one million immigrants entering the United States each year "for intelligent citizenship." The "representatives of anarchy and atheism from the old world are organizing schools where their views are taught to their children. They combine together to root up every Christian and religious element from our educational system, and many of the Jewish population are joining them." As part of their strategy, the home mission committee proposed hiring Christian teachers and requiring prayer in public schools.[47]

Coercion alone could not solve the problem, however, so the Home Mission Board sought other strategies as well. Between 1908 and 1915 the board sponsored work among immigrants in a number of southern cities, including Tampa, Birmingham, New Orleans, and El Paso. It worked with other denominations to share responsibility. The board organized subcommittees to work with black, immigrant, Indian, and mountain people, along with mill workers, the country church, and city missions.[48]

As with most southerners, progressive Presbyterians did little to improve race relations. The home mission committee recommended the establishment of a segregated black synod in 1915. The Woman's Auxiliary supported the work of black Presbyterians at Stillman College in Tuscaloosa, Alabama, and raised substantial funds for the school. The director of the Woman's Auxiliary, Hallie Winsborough, took an active interest in the black population and supported the Commission on Interracial Cooperation, though she despaired at its excessive caution. Under her leadership, PCUS women sponsored conferences on race relations at the level of both presbytery and synod, capped by an annual summer conference at Stillman College.[49]

Lingle tried to improve race relations in Atlanta, a city infamous for anti-Negro violence and lynching during the first two decades of the century. Together with the pastor of the First Congregational Church, he proposed creation of a reformatory for black boys funded by public taxes as a way of separating them from prison and the convict lease system. Just as Warren Wilson was his inspiration on the country church and Walter Rauschenbusch on the Social Gospel, Marjorie Gray was a formative influence on his racial views. She was a northern woman who traveled south to teach at Atlanta University. She attended First Presbyterian Church where she listened intently to his sermons dealing with social issues. But she waited in vain to hear him address racial injustice. In a series of letters to him she communicated her disappointment and tried to educate him about conditions in the city. She described racial insults to black faculty and students at the university and told him that respectable black women feared for the morals of their daughters who worked as servants in the homes of white employers.

She also sent him essays by W. E. B. DuBois to read. Apparently her efforts succeeded.[50] In subsequent years Lingle became a leading advocate of desegregation in the Presbyterian church. But with progressive leaders such as Alexander McKelway so locked into a racist culture, these reforms were delayed for decades.

Other aspects of the urban Social Gospel became the subject of a major debate within the PCUS. Leading the forces of change was Walter Lingle. A native of Rowan County, North Carolina, and graduate of a denominational college and seminary, he was an ideal spokesman for social service. He read widely and kept his mind open to new theological concepts. He held a succession of important positions: pastor of Atlanta's First Presbyterian Church, professor of Christian sociology at Union Seminary, editor of the *Union Theological Review*, columnist for the *Presbyterian of the South* and the *Christian Observer*, president of the Layman's Training School in Richmond and later of Davidson College. These provided Lingle platforms from which he influenced the thinking and course of the denomination. Social activism was only one dimension of his ministry, a fact that aided him in battles with conservatives. Although he was devoted to social Christianity, conservatives respected him for his good judgment, opposition to alcohol and divorce, and hard work as a member of numerous agencies and boards. Northern churchmen found him a bit out of step before 1910. When he submitted an essay on Calvin to *The Interior* published in Chicago, the editor turned it down. His readers were "so heartily tired of Calvin that I really think a return to the subject some time later might be more efficient. Besides, a modern newspaper finds that it must indulge in history sparingly. The demand on it is for something up to date." The Atlanta pastor was not so out of touch with "up to date" matters as the editor might have thought. Rauschenbusch's ideas had already taken hold. Historian Ernest Thompson summarized Lingle best: he was "never so far in advance of the church that he could not gain a hearing but always far enough to broaden the church's viewpoint."[51]

When Lingle left Atlanta for Union Seminary in 1911, he entered the most influential phase of his ministry. His duties included teaching the new course in sociology authorized by the 1911 General Assembly. No such course had been taught previously, and he received numerous letters concerning its content. One Presbyterian minister wrote supportively that it was far better for a young theologian "to know something about the housing conditions of Richmondites than to be intimately acquainted with the family life of the Hittites; the Richmondites being still alive, and the Hittites having been a long time dead." Other ministers equated sociology and socialism and opposed both. Some were just confused. A prominent Presbyterian woman with six daughters thought the course was wonderful because her daughters could clarify their views on cards, theaters, and dancing.[52]

Lingle defined the course as an orientation to social service such as Christ had performed among the multitudes, an attempt to "translate into life the social and ethical teachings of our Lord." He rejected individualism, socialism, and communism as ways to solve social problems. The Christian ideal of social service worked best but was opposed both by conservatives who believed that Christianity contained no social message and by liberals who found nothing in the Bible except a social message. He proposed a middle position. He believed that the Kingdom of God was used in many ways in the Bible but one emphasized its earthly aspects. Although Rauschenbusch influenced him more than other theologians and ethicists, he frequently cited Shailer Mathews and Josiah Strong. His reading extended well beyond these three, however, and usually found its way into his courses, sermons, and correspondence. He read W. M. Clow's Social Gospel book *Christ in the Social Order*, as a possible text for his course, and borrowed a thesis entitled "Marxian Socialism and the Bible" written by a young Presbyterian student at the University of Chicago.[53]

Students felt his imprint. A young Presbyterian missionary in a remote area of Alaska clearly bore Lingle's ideological stamp. He criticized a Congregational missionary for his "soothing syrup, socialism and social service that makes me tired. If a man is drowning he does not want a bottle of milk, he wants a life preserver." But the former student championed "the value of social service for it has its place, one which the Church in the past has failed to give it. . . . Have enjoyed reading Rauschenbusch's 'Social Principles of Jesus X'." To his request for further reading about socialism, Lingle recommended a balanced list including H. C. Vedder's *Socialism and the Ethics of Jesus*, John Spargo's *Socialism*, Arthur J. Balfour's *The Case Against Socialism*, and Father Barnard Vaughan's *Socialism From the Christian's Standpoint*.[54]

Almost as important as his classroom was Lingle's editorship of the *Union Theological Review*. He turned that journal into a forum on the Social Gospel. He reviewed current and controversial books by all major Social Gospel figures as well as Warren Wilson's works on the country church. He organized series dealing with social issues, including one on the proper role of the church in society. Because of the intense debate within the PCUS on the social message of the church, he asked moderators of the northern and southern churches to respond to his question "What is the business of the Church?"[55]

As a lecturer, preacher, and essayist, Lingle gained even more attention within the church. His sermon manuscripts are preoccupied with social problems, especially unjust economic conditions, and his favorite source was Walter Rauschenbusch. In a sermon titled "The Bible and Money," he traced America's social problems to the accumulation of vast wealth in the hands of a few individuals. The accumulation produced two problems: an idle class of rich and social unrest among the poor. Money was not inherently bad, but abuses of money such as paying unfair wages were evil. Lingle also rejected the notion of a market economy:

"We are too apt to let the wage scale be determined by the laws of political economy, and not by the teachings of Christ." His sermon on "Wealth and Social Problems" was more specific. He cited 1916 income tax data showing the incomes of the nine richest men and a wide disparity in wealth between them and the rest of society. The problem was the concentration of power to control money markets, prices, and wages, a condition that created social unrest. He summarized Christ's teachings about wealth and treatment of the poor using Rauschenbusch's book *Christianity and the Social Crisis* as a source. As an example of proper Christian stewardship, he cited his Atlanta friend John J. Eagan, a Presbyterian layman who had shocked the business world by allowing his workers to elect the Board of Operators and share company profits. Lingle attributed poverty to a multiplicity of sources: war, drunkenness, sloth, improvidence, ignorance, physical or mental defectiveness, crime, and dishonesty; but he also traced it to environment, industrial oppression, changing technology, and inadequate wages. The Bible denounced those who oppressed or neglected the poor and who taught that the Church as a corporate body should provide for them. But he proposed no specific strategies to correct economic abuses except the application of private ethics and the collective involvement of the church in caring for the poor.[56]

Although he devoted less attention to other subjects, he did not ignore them altogether. In his sermon on "The Family and Social Problems," he attributed blame for faltering marriages and disintegrating families not only to drunkenness and immorality, but to child labor, tenement houses, and slums. His discussion on "Christianity and the Race Problem" raised a series of extremely troubling questions for southerners: "Is our treatment of the Negro Christian? Do we know the Negro, especially the educated Negro? Should Negroes receive equal treatment with the Whites in respect to schools, courts, housing, streets, sanitation, travel, etc.? Would Jesus draw the color line in His church? How shall we treat Negro delegates and commissioners who attend Church meeting and General Assemblies? Should Negroes be entertained in hotels with the Whites at meetings of the Pan-Presbyterian Council and other similar religious gatherings?"[57]

Such sermons and lectures increased his popularity. Invitations to preach poured into his Richmond office, often with requests for specific sermons on Christianity and social problems. One Presbyterian minister engaged in the ultimate form of flattery after reading Lingle's sermon on "The Teachings of Jesus and Modern Social Problems." He decided to preach it himself.[58] The president of the North Carolina Conference for Social Service invited Lingle to address the organization's fourth annual state conference in 1916. The Charlotte, North Carolina, Ministerial Association recommended that the city's pastors preach the Sunday morning of the conference on Christian Social Service. That evening they planned a combined service to hear Lingle preach. Conference officials asked the seminary professor to refute the "current opinion that there is a sort of conflict or incompatibility between individual Christianity and social Christianity." Lingle gladly accepted, offering a choice of three sermons that would fit the themes. From the National Board of the YMCA came a request to lecture at the Southern Student's Conference on Christianity about the world crisis of 1918. The National Chautauqua invited him to lecture nationwide on the social teachings of Jesus and contemporary problems.[59]

Editors also sought his essays. He popularized most of his writings for Presbyterian newspapers and Sunday school literature. In 1916 the editor of *The Westminster Teacher* asked Lingle to prepare a series of lessons for the quarterly on "The Social Teachings of the Bible." He wanted the lessons to provide discussion, not lead to yes or no answers.[60]

But Lingle's best-known publication was a collection of papers delivered as the James Sprunt Lectures at Union Theological Seminary in 1929. Published under the title *The Bible and Social Problems*, they contained basically the same material he disseminated so widely in sermons between 1915 and 1920, though presented in a more systematic way. Chapters on "The Bible and Poverty" came directly from his sermon. But his essay on "The Church and Social Reform" was more pointed and direct. Ministers must study the social problems of their communities and then preach about those problems from the pulpit, not to engage in partisan politics but in order to apply the social and ethical teachings of Christ. Church courts should deal with conflicts between labor and capital as well as with private ethical matters. They must define clearly which of Christ's teachings governed labor and which management, because "Jesus' ideal for the world is that the Kingdom of God should come on earth as it has already come in heaven."[61]

Although Lingle was the most influential Social Gospel spokesman within the PCUS, he was by no means a voice crying in the wilderness. A. W. McAllister, a prominent businessman and moderator of Orange Presbytery, opened the 1914 meeting with an address urging churches to pay more attention to social problems. As a result of too much emphasis on individual aspects of religion, workingmen were ignored and were leaving the church. That same year, the Rev. Stonewall J. McMurry, speaking at Austin Seminary in Texas, warned that the church could not ignore the injustice of wages and the maldistribution of wealth. A. M. Scales, ruling elder in Greensboro, North Carolina, and a former governor of the state, argued that Presbyterians would attract unchurched people if they were more committed to social service.[62]

So long as such advice was directed at individual members, even conservatives within the PCUS could agree. The General Assembly in 1914 adopted a report drafted by a joint committee of the PCUS, PCUSA, and the Associated Reformed Presbyterian Church on the relationship of the church to social reform. The report urged members to practice Christian principles in all social relations, encouraged the creation of voluntary organizations devoted to social reform, and recommended the Federal Council of Churches of Christ in America as a cooperative vehicle for Christian social service. Conservative Presbyterians did not object to that portion of the report urging individual members to action, but they did oppose the Federal Council.[63]

The debate was soon joined by Presbyterians who believed that individual action, efficacious though it might be, could not dramatically change complex social institutions. They proposed to organize Presbyterian institutions in such a way as to alter urban life. Their campaigns against child labor and alcohol had already won them allies among moderates, but now the boldest pastors and laymen proposed more sweeping changes.

The development of institutional churches among Presbyterians began as part of the Home Mission Board effort to reach immigrants. Plagued by illiteracy, poor housing, inadequate medical services, and a lack of child care and recreational facilities, immigrants had more immediate concerns than the welfare of their souls. Often Catholic in background and preoccupied by "this worldly" problems, they did not frequent Presbyterian churches. The Home Mission Board sought to reach them by a ministry more balanced between spiritual and physical needs. In 1910 it planned an institutional church that would offer a variety of social services for immigrants in El Paso and for black people in Louisville. With the cooperation of Central Presbyterian Church in Kansas City, the board began an institutional church for the city's 6,000 Italians. Begun in 1908, it had a kindergarten, sewing school, boys and girls clubs, and cooking and English classes, as well as preaching services. Institutional work among Italians in Birmingham was even more developed. Presbyterians organized a settlement house at Ensley, Alabama, under the direction of an Italian pastor and American social workers. The pastor conducted a night school, preached, and conducted Bible study. The women taught a kindergarten with seventy students from five nationalities. The Woman's Missionary Union in the city paid part of their salaries. Miss Agnes Avery taught a night school at the settlement house and directed domestic science classes and boys and mothers clubs. Presbyterians also rented a house in the industrial suburb of Pratt City where Miss Ramelle Anderson opened a day school and conducted other social ministries. Similar work was begun among Cubans in Tampa and among Hungarians in St. Petersburg. Sometimes the work prospered as in Pratt City, and at other times vigorous Catholic opposition stopped it as in Ensley.[64]

Although the PCUS did not become as deeply committed to settlement houses and institutional churches as Methodists, enthusiasm for such ministries did spread. In 1910 a church leader proposed to Lingle that First Presbyterian Church in Atlanta become the foundation for a "great Institutional Church" like Wesley Memorial Church in the city. He proposed attaching a Presbyterian hospital and various social service agencies to the church.[65] Lingle left Atlanta months later, so nothing came of the proposal, but he did take the idea with him to Union Seminary, which was a fertile climate for such notions.

Presbyterian seminaries were not unaware of the new theological currents surging through America. The PCUS Committee on Theological Seminaries urged curriculum innovations to accommodate the new ideas. Not only did Union employ Lingle to teach Christian sociology, but other seminaries quickly followed suit. The Presbyterian Theological Seminary of Kentucky added four new courses in 1915: Christian Sociology, Christian Ethics, Religious Education, and Christian Missions. Columbia Theological Seminary employed an expert in rural sociology and established a chair of Christian Ethics and Apologetics.[66]

Because the primary emphasis of the seminaries was theological, applied ethics and practical training for social service did not attract great interest. Consequently in 1911 the General Assembly created a special committee to investigate the possibility of a school for lay people. The committee, headed by the Rev. H. H. Sweets of Louisville who was deeply involved in the mountain work, reported that the denomination badly needed assistant pastors, Sunday school superintendents, teachers, nurses, and social workers, but had no institution to train them. In 1914 the General Assembly created the Training School at Richmond and established a curriculum consisting both of traditional courses (English Bible, Church History, Presbyterian Standards, Home and Foreign Missions) and innovative ones (City Missions, Day Nursery, Country Church).[67] Under Lingle's presidency the Training School staffed most of the Social Gospel agencies of the denomination, including its settlement houses, institutional churches, and mountain schools.

Church conferences at Montreat also popularized the Social Gospel. In addition to summer conferences devoted to the country church, the annual home missions conference typically dealt with social ministries. The 1917 session featured programs on Stillman College, West Virginia coal miners, and mountain schools. Lingle frequently led Bible study on some aspect of Christianity and social problems.[68]

Concrete results of such courses and conferences can only be inferred. But individual churches, presbyteries, and synods did organize interesting new ministries. The First Presbyterian Church of Roanoke, Virginia, established a mission in the cotton mill village with a church building and "annex for social work." In 1914 the pastor asked Lingle for the name of a student who could direct the ministry. A pastor in Concord, North Carolina, addressed a similar inquiry to Lingle a year later. The First Presbyterian Church had sponsored a mission church in the mill village that was nearly self-supporting. He believed that the new pastor "must be one of or with" the textile people to be successful. In 1917 First Presbyterian of Gastonia, North Carolina, sought an assistant pastor to take charge of work in the mill village. The Gastonia congregation, however, was not so anxious that the new pastor identify with the workers. The president of the mill was an officer in First Presbyterian and would provide his support, which lent special meaning to the pastor's request that the student have "practical judgment and horse sense." These inquiries especially interested Lingle. He had once pastored in Rock Hill, South Carolina, which contained a number of mills. At a ministers' meeting he had suggested that the Baptists, Methodists, and Presbyterians divide the villages, with each assuming responsibility for specific areas. Ministers endorsed the proposal enthusiastically, except one Baptist preacher who blocked the joint venture. When Lingle returned many years later, all three denominations had rival churches in each mill village, all of them weak and inefficient. That experience left Lingle committed to ecumenical cooperation in church ministries.[69]

Such local concerns seemed minor as international tensions increased. Although antiwar sentiment is often associated with liberalism, conservatives within the PCUS were strangely ambivalent and divided on the issues of war and peace. In 1912 the editor of the *Presbyterian Standard*, one of the most influential and conservative journals, condemned war: "It is a hopeful sign of the times that Christians are lifting a more united voice against war.... the Christian is pledged to keep out of it, and, so far as in him lies, to keep everybody else out of it. No Christian parent should send a son to West Point or Annapolis. Why should boys of Christian households be taught the art of making hell."[70]

One explanation for such advice from a conservative Presbyterian weekly was the doctrine of the spirituality of the church. As the United States drifted into the First World War, federal officials sought to mobilize churches on behalf of the war effort. It was not a difficult task because Christians were caught up in the chauvinism of the times. But Presbyterians absolutely committed to denying the church a formal voice in issues of public policy extended their doctrine to the war. As with social questions in general, Presbyterians disagreed on this crisis. When a Wilmington, North Carolina, pastor proposed to display the American flag in his church, the *Presbyterian Standard* rejected the practice as inappropriate. The editor reminded his readers that during the Civil War northern Presbyterians had displayed the American flag whereas southern churches had refused to unfurl the Confederate ensign. Southern Presbyterians believed that separation of church and state should be absolute. When the church covered the pulpit with the nation's flag it proclaimed itself an ally of the state, an alliance both unholy and unscriptural. But many Presbyterians wrote the paper objecting to this position. International affairs caused the editor no small amount of doctrinal trouble. When some Presbyterians chided the Federal Council of Churches for sending a delegation to Paris in 1919 on behalf of the League of Nations, the editors of the *Standard* defended the council by arguing that some political questions contained "a legitimate moral side" that allowed the church to speak.[71]

Perhaps the confusion of the *Presbyterian Standard* reflected the divisions among Presbyterians concerning the justice and morality of war. The Lingle family was deeply divided on this issue. Walter Lingle reluctantly supported the war. His brother Thomas, a professor at Davidson College, was so enthusiastic a supporter of the allies that he volunteered to serve as a YMCA representative with the American Expeditionary Force in France. But a third brother, W. H. Lingle, who was serving as a missionary in China, thought the war iniquitous. He and Thomas conducted such an acrimonious debate that it destroyed their relationship. He had read many books sent by his brothers in an effort to justify the war: "but they have not convinced me, and there is no book that can convince me. I do not believe Christianity and war are reconcilable, and I hold to Christianity. I do not believe that Jesus Christ would approve war under any circumstances." Americans must put Christ above Theodore Roosevelt and Woodrow Wilson, he wrote, and he doubted Wilson could have been elected had the people known he would lead them into war. His daughters, both students in America, violently disagreed with him. Margaret wrote to her uncle that she did not understand how her father could be so "absolutely pro-German after all they have done." But her father held his ground, relieved that though his daughters were caught up in America's "war madness," at least he had no sons to become "cannon fodder."[72]

The war and his family's division about its morality made a profound impression on W. L. Lingle. In his 1929 Sprunt Lectures he devoted an entire essay to "The Bible and War." He traced its causes to class, racial, and national hatred, greed, selfishness, yellow journalism, national chauvinism, and the glorification of war. Because God's ideal was peace, the church should preach against such forces. It must actively seek righteousness and justice between nations.[73]

War and its aftermath also partly explain the increasing conservatism within the PCUS. In 1919 immigration threatened to overwhelm the country. Strikes, social conflict, and disorder spread fear and nativism among the middle class. The 1919 General Assembly, discussing the implications of the postwar world, warned that the church must convert and Americanize the new wave of immigrants. The alternative was ominous: "If Bolshevism, the labor question and the race problem should form a coalition, Christian civilization itself will tremble in the balance."[74]

The real challenge to the fundamental structure of American society did not emanate from radical conspiracies of workers, political radicals, and black people, as Presbyterians believed. It was more subtle and close to home, and its source was American women.

The saga of Presbyterian women between 1900 and 1920 reveals the complex interaction of Christianity and culture. Denominational women could not escape involvement with the secular issues of their times: feminism, divorce, birth control, middle-class rebellion, women's suffrage, and working women.

No denomination more adamantly resisted expanding the role of women. James Woodrow, a professor at Columbia Theological Seminary, decried the "perversion of women's influence" evidenced by "male women, female lecturers, public speakers and preachers, and all 'woman's rights' advocates." The same year, Robert L. Dabney, professor at Union Theological Seminary in Richmond, opposed women as preachers or teachers and castigated southern ministers for allowing women a larger sphere in church life. The year of this "abomination" was 1879. In 1897 the West Lexington Presbytery inquired of the General Assembly whether women should be allowed to speak before a mixed audience containing men. The assembly cited the Old School Assembly of 1832 and the General Assembly of 1872, both of which approved meetings of pious women to talk and pray but cited both I Corinthians and I Timothy as prohibiting women from teaching, exhorting, or leading prayer in "public and promiscuous assemblies."[75]

Even attempts by southern Presbyterian women to organize missionary societies met stiff resistance. Denominational leaders attacked the societies as efforts to displace the organized church without scriptural authority, to provide undue prominence to one phase of church work to the injury of others, and to obscure the unity of the church. The Synod of Virginia offered more clearly anti-feminist reasons. In 1899 it issued a report misnamed the rights and duties of women, misnamed because it dwelt on duties and listed few rights:

> the woman was created out and for the man. . . . The first law of government is, 'thy desire shall be unto thy husband, and he shall rule over thee'. . . .
>
> The family, the home, is by the Scriptures made the special sphere of woman . . . 'wandering from house to house' characterizes those on whom the censure of the Holy Spirit falls heavily. . . . The home and the family, the last and strongest bulwark of society, of the state and of the church, the 'Woman's Movement' tends to undermine and destroy.[76]

When the General Assembly finally allowed the creation of separate female organizations, the Standing Committee on Women's Societies, consisting of twelve men, recommended that the Woman's Missionary Union (WMU) be placed under the control of the presbytery. In that way the Presbyterian WMU, unlike the Southern Baptist equivalent, was not autonomous and did not control its own finances.[77]

Contact with more enlightened regions did little to alter the minds of male southern Presbyterians. A former member of W. L. Lingle's church staff in Atlanta moved to Central Presbyterian Church in Denver, Colorado. The church had a sharp-tongued Scottish pastor and a woman secretary-treasurer. During one of the Rev. McNeill's Wednesday evening sermons in 1915 a woman interrupted him and spoke to the congregation at length, after which McNeill raged at that "fool American woman" who "didn't hesitate to drag her confounded impertinence right into the holy of holies." That incident was sufficient to convince the transplanted southerner: "These western women are so ugly and as they vote here in Colorado there is no abiding with them. They take such a hand in church affairs. Every church business affair I preside over there are the women to deal with. If I ever have a church no woman shall even lift a voice in affairs. . . . by all means oppose voting for women."[78]

Presbyterian women listened to such diatribes but paid them little heed. By 1900 they had organized 1,000 missionary societies and thirty presbyterial unions. In 1904 the Synod of Texas allowed the first synodical union for women. But they still were embarrassed at how poorly developed their work was compared with other denominations. Hallie Winsborough, a Kansas City housewife with six children, decided to change that situation. In her quiet but determined way she won support in the Missouri Synod for a woman secretary for Home and Foreign Missions. Opposition to the proposal came mainly from east of the Mississippi. The Rev. M. L. Lambdin of Montgomery, West Virginia, wrote an article for the *Presbyterian Standard* arguing that the proposal undermined the conservative and scriptural position of the PCUS. He denounced it because women already had enough influence and because it was part of the "rapidly growing evils and ominous signs of the times . . . the widespread feminine sex unrest." This was a "neurotic species of disease, that renders the unhappy victim . . . discontented with her divinely ordained sex limitations" and led to a rationalistic denial of Bible teachings on "the priority of man and subordination of woman in the home, the church, and the state." Other Presbyterian men were less restrained. They referred to the proposed secretary as "unwomanly," "a limited pope," "a woman bishop," and "an ecclesiastical suffragette."[79]

Surprisingly, most church leaders supported the appointment, demonstrating the change in attitudes that was occurring. The *Presbyterian Standard* printed articles on both sides of the issue, one of which took a more liberal view of Timothy and Corinthians and reminded church members that Phoebe had served the New Testament church and surely must have spoken in the presence of men. The author opposed ordaining women as ministers or elders but conceded their right to teach a mixed class, pray, prophesy, serve as a deacon, or even "preach the Gospel." He urged men to "help women of our church who labor in the Gospel" and give them a general secretary for woman's work if they wanted one. His view prevailed. The Executive Committee approved the request from Winsborough at its January 9, 1912, meeting, and the General Assembly concurred at its annual gathering.[80]

The choice as first Superintendent of the Woman's Auxiliary was both obvious and fortuitous. Winsborough presided from headquarters in Kansas City. She organized a Woman's Council composed of women presidents of synodical groups and proved amazingly effective as a fund raiser for Presbyterian causes. In 1913, the first full year of operation, the Woman's Auxiliary raised $74,000 for missions. So successful were the efforts of women that the 1914 General Assembly urged pastors and sessions to encourage women's societies and each presbytery and synod to appoint a permanent committee on women's work. Unfortunately the assembly did not change its practice of taking all the money women raised and then parceling a portion back to support their work. Like W. L. Lingle, Winsborough was conservative enough to make her social views palatable to a traditional denomination. When Lingle asked her to recommend a female principal for one of the training schools, Winsborough carefully qualified her recommendation of Miss Barbara Lambdin of Berry School in north Georgia. Although Lambdin had proper qualifications, Winsborough added, "Of course, I believe very strongly that no woman reaches the full development of her powers who has not been wife and mother. These experiences give her understanding and sympathy, a comprehension of problems and ability to handle them which comes to women in no other way. However, the wives and mothers who are in position to take such work, during their middle years are few and I feel sure you do not want an old lady as they reckon old ladies now days. Miss Lambdin is a woman of rare spirituality. Is older than she appears and has been a teacher."[81]

Such traditional views allowed her to effectively expand the influence of women within the PCUS without causing a backlash among men. By 1919 there were 2,347 women's societies with 65,405 members. Together, they contributed $565,000 to missions. Women studied for mission work in PCUS seminaries and constituted a substantial proportion of students at the training school in Richmond. In 1913 Austin Seminary in Texas enrolled twenty-seven men studying for the ministry and three women preparing for foreign missions. More significantly PCUS schools, churches, settlement houses, and agencies actively recruited women for jobs. In 1918 the home mission committee asked Lingle to recommend a female graduate of the training school to work in the settlement house at Ensley, Alabama, for a salary of $50 per month plus a room. The pastor of Independent Presbyterian Church in Savannah, Georgia, planned new work and needed a senior seminary student *or* a woman from the Training School with missionary spirit and the capacity to hold prayer meetings and direct Sunday school. But his liberation was only partial. If he employed a woman, he added, she should be capable of doing stenographic work and looking after the office in the mornings. Despite such limitations, women were charting a new course within the denomination. In 1917 two women were elected trustees of the Training School, the first women ever selected for such a position. Three years later women were added to all executive committees. Also in 1920. Winsborough was invited to address the General Assembly on behalf of the Women's Auxiliary, with only one dissenting vote. Although it may seem a small victory in retrospect, the invitation thrilled Winsborough, who must have remembered twenty years earlier when PCUS policy prohibited women from addressing "a mixed assemblage."[82]

Such victories did not come easily. After 1912 reluctant male Presbyterians contested every forward step taken by women, making female progress all the sweeter.

In some churches women sought to organize societies and men tried to prevent them. A church that met at Union Theological Seminary in Richmond and contained many faculty families instructed its women's society to withdraw from the Presbyterial Union. Leaders of the session contended that the General Assembly's plan for women's societies encouraged women to speak before mixed assemblages. They cited three women who advocated the plan publicly as the logical consequence of such initiatives. The congregation was badly split, with some seminary faculty fearing the session's action would make the seminary appear reactionary. At each annual General Assembly resolutions were proposed condemning the more liberal position taken on "woman's position in the Church," almost always citing I Corinthians 14 and I Timothy 2 as authority for silencing women in the church. In each case the General Assembly's action reaffirmed the position of the 1880 Assembly, which had rejected ordination for women but left other issues to "the discretion of the Sessions and the enlightened consciences of our Christian women themselves." Although women were excluded from the presbytery, they were allowed to hold the office of deacon.[83]

The *Presbyterian Standard* maintained a neutral stance concerning the decision to recommend a woman superintendent, but it soon returned to a more conservative stance. In 1918 the journal attacked the Methodists and Baptists for extending representation to women, arguing that the logical result of such action would be ordaining women to preach. Presbyterian women had not yet disparaged the Apostle Paul "but they show symptoms. They will be heard from by and by. Paul was an Old School Presbyterian and that kind is getting scarce." The editor had to wait less than four months for the assault. He had an explanation for why aggressive women disliked Paul: "Simply because he tried to get self-assertive and obstreperous women to behave themselves in church and married women to recognize the husband as head of the house. For these well-meant efforts of his, some women can never forgive him." The editor also opposed woman suffrage. In a particularly ugly editorial, he discussed Frederick Douglass and Elizabeth Cady Stanton. He described Douglass as "a negro with a white wife" who favored woman suffrage and social equality. He hinted darkly that when woman suffrage leaders visited Douglass they went for long private walks with him in the garden. Stanton wrote a "Woman's Bible" and denied the divinity of Christ. Current leaders of the suffrage movement meddled with social questions and dabbled in politics. They sneered at religion, belittled the home, encouraged marriage outside the sanction of the church, and supported divorce. And even "good and pure" women were joining their cause.[84]

One such woman was Clara Lingle, wife of Thomas W. and sister-in-law of W. L. Lingle. A gifted speaker, she became deeply involved in all phases of the woman's movement. She participated in the North Carolina Federation of Women's Clubs and the North Carolina Conference for Social Service. In 1915 she traveled to Raleigh where she and Dr. Anna Howard Shaw addressed the legislature on behalf of woman suffrage. Her husband supported her completely, often accompanied her on speaking trips, and even tallied audience size and reaction. When her husband volunteered for YMCA service with the AEF in France, she moved the children to Chapel Hill where she became advisor to the Division for Women, Bureau of Extension, at the University of North Carolina. Her assignments included lecturing to women's groups, correspondence, and preparation of study outlines on female welfare and education. In many ways the job was a continuation of the volunteer work she had performed for six years. She remained active in Presbyterian affairs, participating in the Chapel Hill church and teaching a course in parliamentary law for the 1918 Woman's Summer School of Missions.[85]

Although the two Lingle brothers applauded her work, her liberation complicated her husband's life. In 1916 students at Davidson College denounced T. W. Lingle as a teacher. They accused him of sarcasm, unfairness, and pedantry, among other failings. Davidson's president confronted Lingle about his alleged inadequacies and warned him that he must improve or face dismissal. But Lingle claimed his real problem was two or three people "who cannot tolerate in this town a woman who has attained to the prominence, popularity and service all over North Carolina that Clara has." The simplest way to rid themselves of his wife was to "magnify my faults and weaknesses and get rid of me." Whether a rationalization of his own inadequacies or a genuine example of Presbyterian sexism, the incident did demonstrate the marital tensions that accompanied the attempt of Presbyterian women to establish separate identities.[86]

Walter Lingle demonstrated the same commitment to women's rights as on all social questions. In his sermons on the family written during this era, he emphasized the revolt of women. Perhaps thinking of his sister-in-law Clara, he discussed their role in business, the professions, society, and politics. He called for a calm and careful rethinking of women's roles, discussed both the Bible's teachings on women and the feminist movement, and then told his congregation that "Jesus evidently placed women on an equality with man." But he could not bring himself to endorse the ordination of women. A young North Carolina pastor wrote that his session had appointed two deaconesses and inquired about the proper procedure for installing them. The session desired to ordain them. Lingle was "pleased to see how progressive and up-to-date your Church Session is" and endorsed the selection of deaconesses. But to ordain them would be contrary to the Book of Church Order and the provisions of the General Assembly. He proposed instead a public installation of the deaconesses without ordination. In a sermon on "Poverty and Social Problems," Lingle proposed that churches appoint a committee of deacons to assist the poor and then added almost as an afterthought in his sermon notes "might add deaconesses." But as late as 1925 he believed the PCUS would "unite unanimously on the idea that we will have no women preachers or elders." Beyond that one restriction, however, the PCUS had reached no consensus. Indeed, the issue was so heated in 1915 that when Lingle sought articles for the *Union Seminary Review* on "The Place and Work of Women in the New Testament Church," one minister he asked to write an essay replied: "Did I not know that you were a very amiable man and a lover of your brethren, I might suspect you of trying to get some of us into trouble. This is certainly a thorny subject. I . . . am not at all sure of being able to prepare the article you request."[87]

As Presbyterian women gradually developed their own internal network of contacts and supporters, a comparable network evolved among social activists. Although such networking is well known within the business world, it has not been studied carefully in the church. Because Social Gospel advocates within the PCUS were a deeply committed minority, they sought each other's company and advice. The Atlanta circle related to Walter Lingle provides an excellent example. The Rev. Dunbar H. Ogden pastored Central Presbyterian Church across the street from Georgia's capitol. He was not only a personal friend of Lingle's, but the two were equally committed to the social ministry of the Presbyterian church. In 1913 he shared with Lingle his opinion of a new book entitled *Christ in the Social Order*. The book was orthodox from the standpoint of the PCUS, challenging individual members to involvement but not the church. Ogden was disappointed in the author who "lacked the fire that I wish linked with conservatism." The book was "too largely a defense of the present order." When a staff member left his church a few years later, Ogden wrote Lingle asking for a young seminarian who could reach the boarding houses and apartments near his church: "In working out this down town problem there will be a large amount of ministry to the poor, and the man who takes the work must have sympathy toward this class and wisdom in helping them practically. This feature of the work will also mean close co-operation with other Christian forces in the working out of our city wide problems." The person would also be responsible for a new ministry to inner-city blacks. Lingle often used Ogden at Montreat conferences to help liberate the PCUS "from the death grip of reactionaries." In 1915 Ogden wrote to his friend that he had been invited to deliver two series of addresses in Birmingham and planned one topic on "The Social Message of the Bible": "You see how you have been leading me out. I trust that your platform has not been tainted past fumigation." Lingle recommended Ogden as Professor of Church History at Union Seminary; however, the idea did not appeal to his Atlanta friend: "I would enjoy the life, but I feel a desire to be in the very thick of the fight while the strength of young manhood is mine." But later, in his senior years, he might enjoy the challenge of delivering lectures "on the Social message of the Bible."[88]

Ogden's most famous parishioner at Central Presbyterian was another friend of Lingle's, John J. Eagan. Born in Griffin, Georgia, Eagan inherited money and began a distinguished business career in Atlanta. A devoted churchman, he served as superintendent of the Sabbath School at Central Presbyterian for twenty years, as an elder, and a member of the Home Mission Board. He contributed generously to mountain schools, served as chairman of the subcommittee on mountain work, chairman of the board of Berry Schools, and began Rabun Gap-Nacoochee School in north Georgia. He provided books, especially on social ministries, for Union Seminary, and engaged in the private charities expected of such philanthropists. In his application of the Gospel to society, he was as cautious as Ogden and Lingle. Although he read widely in the new sociological literature, he was unsatisfied by its exclusive emphasis upon changing society. Nor did socialism appeal to him: "The tendency of modern socialism is to exalt 'Thou shalt love thy neighbor as thyself' above the first and great commandment," causing many people to serve humanity as their only effort to love God.[89]

But during the second decade of the century he also became deeply committed to social justice. He read widely on "the Negro problem" and sought racial cooperation. The works of Social Gospel advocate Josiah Strong particularly influenced him. Although he wished the term "sociology" could be replaced by "Christianity," that would be possible only when the church assumed its social obligations. "I am convinced that a careful study of the life of Christ will convince one that He was tremendously concerned about the bodies as well as the souls of men," he wrote Lingle. "You know better than I the proportion of His ministry that was devoted to healing the sick, feeding the hungry and ministering to the broken hearted." He rejoiced when Lingle left Atlanta for the seminary because he believed seminaries devoted too little attention to practical work. Applied Christianity should rank equal in the curriculum to systematic theology, and he believed that Union Seminary students should spend more time among the needy people of Richmond.[90]

Eagan certainly practiced in Atlanta what he preached to Richmond. He became an active member of an interdenominational Social Gospel group the Men and Religion Forward Movement. Atlanta was one of ninety cities where the group organized a chapter, and Eagan was elected president at its first meeting. The first task of the organization was a successful campaign against prostitution. Next came the purchase of a home for unwed mothers, prison reform, Prohibition, support of child labor legislation, and economic justice for workers. The organization became involved with organized labor in 1913 when it supported a strike by the Typographical Union against a Baptist publishing house. Months later laborers at the Fulton Bag and Cotton Mills in Cabbagetown, a poor white community in southeast Atlanta, organized a union. The company promptly fired seventy-eight union members, and the Men and Religion Forward Movement again supported the workers. The group's executive committee published a weekly bulletin in the *Atlanta Constitution* to state their view of social issues and injustice. The movement also helped organize public meetings to publicize the wretched mill conditions that led to unionization. *The Journal of Labor* expressed gratitude to John Eagan and ministers who spoke at labor rallies and so loyally supported workers. Eagan as president of the group addressed one of the mass meetings where he talked of the necessity of applying Christian principles to the solution of labor problems. The Men and Religion Forward Movement also endorsed labor legislation pending in the state legislature. A historian has called the Atlanta group's involvement with labor justice one of the major deviations from individualistic southern religion and Eagan the primary architect of that policy. Perhaps it was not coincidental that during the labor disputes Eagan was reading Walter Rauschenbusch's book *Thrice Born Men*.[91]

Eagan continued both his active public involvement in the Social Gospel and his private commitment to social justice. In 1919 he was elected first president of the Council on Interracial Cooperation, which he helped found. Two years later in 1921 he turned over his enormously profitable American Cast Iron Pipe Company to its employees. His outline for the corporation's management was simple but radical: a reasonable living wage must be paid to the lowest paid workman; constant employment must be provided every employee; and the Golden Rule must govern all relations between employer and employee. Management-labor relations were coordinated by a Board of Operatives elected annually from among workers by their peers.[92] In a sense the reorganization of the company into a venture of cooperative capitalism was the culmination of his long Social Gospel pilgrimage.

Lingle's network of allies stretched beyond Atlanta and involved many of his former students. Of the hundreds who owed him gratitude for their theology and social consciousness, none was more intriguing than Witherspoon Dodge. Just out of seminary in 1913 Dodge became pastor of Central Presbyterian Church in Anderson, South Carolina. He considered Lingle the formative influence in his seminary career and maintained contact through the years. Unlike Eagan, Ogden, and Lingle, Dodge fits the model of a revolutionary advocate of the Social Gospel. He frequently clashed with church elders because of his unorthodox theology and reform minded sermons. He considered even Lingle to be too cautious and conservative. After volunteering to write articles for the *Union Seminary Review* to balance the journal's "reactionary views," he declined to do so because he was too busy fighting for "civic and social righteousness" and because his article would be "so full of Christianity and so lacking in traditional theology" that it would never be allowed into print anyway.[93]

Perhaps he was correct. The activities of Lingle, Ogden, Eagan, Dodge, Winsborough, and others were not warmly received in many church quarters. The major Presbyterian forum for those who opposed the Social Gospel was the *Presbyterian Standard*. It seldom deviated from Old School Presbyterianism and the doctrine of the spirituality of the church. The editors attacked "social service," the term used by Social Gospel advocates within the PCUS, because it ignored saving souls in order to minister to slums, factory districts, and "submerged classes." The editors did not object to better wages or shorter hours, old-age pensions, or other reforms. But social service had a vision limited to the present and trusted too much in civil legislation. Their advice was to transform society by saving souls: "Make the tree good, and the fruit cannot be evil. Convert Zaccheus, and he will restore fourfold for all that he has gained by extortion. Is not this the one all-inclusive mission of the Church?"[94] The paper was loyal to that creed throughout the decade. It denounced aggressive women and opposed woman suffrage. When Walter Rauschenbusch died Lingle wept; but the *Standard*'s editor thought the theologian's conception of Christianity shallow, his influence and teachings "far from wholesome." In 1913 coeditor R. C. Reed condemned sociology and socialism, prompting Lingle to respond that Reed did not understand the difference between the two. Reed conceded his ignorance but did not change his mind. That began a long and testy correspondence. When Lingle demanded that the PCUS denounce lynching, Reed responded that the church "should not go into politics in order to secure social and political reforms." Lingle wrote Reed denouncing the tendency within the PCUS to ignore "current evils" and praised the tendency of "the Church at large" "to seek *social, industrial*, and *political* reforms through means of civil legislation." Reed responded that Jesus had not agitated for social or political reforms, to which Lingle replied that Jesus certainly did teach ethical principles "which cut right at the heart of the social evils of the day," and James "spoke out against those who did not pay a sufficient wage."[95]

Reed was not convinced. In 1918 he praised a pamphlet titled "The Social Ministry of the Church to Those Outside of Its Membership" for its sound theology. Containing essays written primarily by members of the PCUS, the pamphlet affirmed the exclusively spiritual character of the church. One of the essayists, Dr. W. Irving Carroll, had "hit the nail most squarely on the head" when he wrote: "As to the social mission of the Church to those outside of its membership, may I simply say that it has none! None, absolutely none. Its one work is the . . . salvation, not the education, nor the civilization, nor the social uplift, of lost sinners." Reed agreed: "This is the doctrine that needs to be proclaimed upon the housetop, and written in golden letters over the doors of all our church buildings." What was needed, he added later, was "Old Time Religion," not the "uplift of humanity." Although the paper did not advise neglecting the poor, it did deplore the church's neglect of the rich: "The influence of the rich for good or evil is so much greater than that of the poor that the church should feel deeply concerned to enlist them for Christ."[96]

Conservative editors were by no means the only critics of the Social Gospel. When a prominent Presbyterian in Alabama wrote the history of the PCUS in his state, he devoted special attention to the failure of settlement house ministries among Italian steel workers, which he blamed on too much Social Gospel influence and too little Bible study and evangelism.[97]

Virtually all of the animosities, disagreements, and ideological divisions within the PCUS focused finally on one issue: ecumenism. Conservatives blamed interdenominational groups for diluting Calvinist doctrine and fostering heresy. The first round in the decadelong debate began in 1908 with the organization of the Federal Council of Churches of Christ in America. The council became involved in all aspects of social ministries including child labor, labor-management conflict, trusts, Prohibition, divorce, and international arbitration. Such involvements ran counter to the doctrine of the spirituality of the church. The PCUS joined the Federal Council, provoking furious criticism and causing the General Assembly to vote to withdraw in 1911. But the Assembly reversed its actions and reaffiliated in 1912. Despite annual debates and bitter conservative opposition to the affiliation, moderate leaders managed to defeat their attempts to withdraw from the Federal Council until 1931.[98]

The council's critics directed their fire at its Social Gospel proclivities. They attacked its leaders, such as University of Chicago professor Shailer Mathews, and its programs. During the 1912 General Assembly debate on reentering the council, the Rev. R. C. Reed, coeditor of the *Presbyterian Standard*, opposed reaffiliation because the council "meddled with political matters, which we opposed as a Church." In 1914 a number of presbyteries urged the PCUS to withdraw. Their petition was defeated but not before the newly created Committee on the Relation of Christian Faith and Social Service was instructed to inform the council that the General Assembly did not approve of its social service programs. The mood in 1915 was better. The General Assembly congratulated the council on its efforts to help country churches, improve rural life, and strengthen the family. But the Assembly again denounced its involvement with secular matters extraneous to the mission of the church.[99]

The Federal Council had its defenders within the PCUS, especially W. L.

Lingle. In 1913 he served on one of the council's commissions, and through him council defenders tried to counter opposition within the church. A Greensboro attorney urged Lingle to use his considerable influence to educate Presbyterians by writing articles explaining the council's work. Lingle moved quickly to do so using literature furnished by the council. The secretary of the Federal Council denied that it deemphasized "the spiritual background of social reconstruction," and urged Lingle to emphasize that point in his articles. Dr. J. R. Howerton, whose book on the Social Gospel influenced so many Presbyterians, also used his influence to quiet critics and served a term as the council's president.[100]

As fiercely as the two sides contested this issue, the Interchurch World Movement created even greater furor. Lingle once again stood at center stage in the controversy. In 1920 he addressed a conference of the Interchurch World Movement in Richmond. His topic, "Christianizing The Industrial Order," reflected the Social Gospel direction of the organization and so impressed some Methodist and Episcopalian delegates that they invited him to give the same address in their community. Conservatives opposed the new organization, conceding its noble objectives but fearing that it would seek uniformity, "minimize creed," and "shock our ideas of the sphere of the Church."[101] Concern about the General Assembly's position caused both advocates and opponents to bombard Presbyterian papers with articles.

But before the 1920 General Assembly met, another issue loomed even larger. For those supporting ecumenism, the logical first step was to heal the historic breach between the two wings of America's Presbyterian Church,: the PCUS and PCUSA. W. L. Lingle vacillated on the question, favoring unification early in the century, opposing it in 1911, and equivocating in 1918. He devoted the January, 1918, issue of the *Union Seminary Review* to a series of position papers on the subject. The General Assembly in 1917 had appointed a committee to study the possibility of federation, but the PCUS was deeply divided. Some authors favored organic union of all Presbyterian churches, others wanted a federation that left each intact, and some opposed all forms of merger. Those who favored organic union also tended to be the ones most sympathetic to social service.[102]

Debate on the issue swirled across the pages of Presbyterian papers for two years. Although Lingle did not favor merger until a clear consensus supported it within the PCUS, he did defend organic union in theory. He wrote that he had "never been able to see any great principle of the Gospel or Presbyterianism separating the Presbyterian Churches of America." When a minister disagreed with this advice because the PCUSA made pronouncements on political and social issues, Lingle retorted that even southern Presbyterians spoke on such issues, especially on temperance. His antagonist admitted that the PCUS did occasionally violate its own principles by passing resolutions on social questions, but insisted that the PCUSA did so much more frequently. Thornton Whaling, professor at Columbia Seminary in South Carolina, led the campaign against Lingle. Although Whaling accepted cooperation between the two bodies, he vigorously opposed organic union. The debate intensified in 1919 when the First Presbyterian Church of Louisville, Kentucky, voted to join the PCUSA. At the 1919 General Assembly, many synods and presbyteries denounced the union movement. But advocates, including Lingle's longtime friend Dunbar Ogden of Atlanta, urged union talks between the two churches.[103] The debate became increasingly nasty in 1919 with acrimonious personal correspondence and an allegation by Ogden that Whaling "was after" him at the meeting of his presbytery. The newspaper debate became so intense that editors suggested it cease.[104]

As the decade closed the issues unleashed by twenty years of conflict came together at the 1920 General Assembly. Opponents of Presbyterian union and the Interchurch World Movement mobilized all their resources against Social Gospel ecumenism. The first decision faced by the Assembly provided delegates a clear choice. Five men were nominated as presiding officer, among them seminary professors Lingle and Whaling. Four roll calls and three hours later, delegates elected Lingle moderator. Later a majority report favoring participation in the Interchurch World Movement won 136 to 103 over a minority report proposing that the PCUS withdraw. Lingle as moderator then refused to vote on a tie when conservatives requested that a questionnaire on membership in the group be sent to all PCUS congregations. By not voting, Lingle defeated the proposal. His friend John Eagan congratulated him on keeping the PCUS in the Interchurch World Movement. He believed that the united movement of the church even with its imperfections was better than sectarian competition. Lingle savored his victory, aware that the real issue had been his theology and the issues he had championed for a decade:

> When I was nominated as Moderator, I felt that the Assembly was face to face with the question as to whether the general position that I took in my articles was correct, or whether the position of my leading critic, who was also nominated, was also correct; in fact, when I was nominated without any seeking on my part, and without my knowledge, I just asked the Lord to show me in that election whether I had been right or wrong. Somehow I feel that the election was His answer to that question. . . . Perhaps I put the wrong interpretation on all of this, but somehow I feel that it is the Lord's answer to my challenge to the Church to cultivate the spirit of love and unity and fellowship with the other great Presbyterian bodies of this country.[105]

Thus vindicated in his own mind, Lingle expanded his vision within an increasingly conservative church. He followed the Sprunt Lectures in 1929 with a series of hard-hitting Social Gospel sermons in the 1930s and advocacy of desegregation in the 1940s and 1950s. John Eagan continued with his interracial work and his collectivization of American Cast Iron Pipe until his death in 1924. Witherspoon Dodge despaired of ever reforming Presbyterians, became a Congregational minister in Atlanta during the 1920s and a CIO organizer in the 1930s when he was nearly stoned to death by an antiunion mob at Gaffney, South Carolina.[106] The PCUS withdrew from the Federal Council of Churches in 1931, resisted desegregation, and was able to reunite with its northern wing only in 1983, when many conservative congregations withdrew to join the Presbyterian Church in America. Many Social Gospel dreams from those early years died in subsequent decades. But it was a goodly fight they made and a bright fire they kindled.

—*Religion in the South*, 1985

On two occasions, colleagues at Carson-Newman College, a Baptist liberal arts college in Jefferson City, Tennessee, invited me to present the Carlyle Marney Lectures. Honoring the most influential Southern Baptist pastoral theologian of his generation, who relished his nickname of "renegade Baptist," Marney was one of the few Southern Baptist ministers to make a theological impact beyond his denomination and region during the decades between the Great Depression and the 1960s. While pastor of First Baptist Church, Austin, Texas, and Meyers Park Baptist, Charlotte, North Carolina, his published sermons reached a sufficiently wide audience for Time *magazine to name him one of the nation's five most influential Baptist preachers. Princeton, Harvard, Yale, the University of Chicago, Union Theological Seminary in New York City, Duke, and Vanderbilt all invited him to lecture to their students and faculties.*

To many fellow Southern Baptists, however, Marney was contemptuously more heretic than hero. He referred to them as evangelical holy rollers while expressing opinions generally sympathetic to modernist theology and Social Gospel causes. I was aware of this when I sat down to write this lecture in his honor.

I decided to describe two people as intriguing as Marney although also equally obstreperous. George Lawrence Ridenour shared Marney's Appalachian Tennessee roots as well as his Carson-Newman and Southern Baptist Theological Seminary pedigrees. There the similarities end. I discovered little about Ridenour's remarkable and strong-minded wife, Agnes Whipple, but there was plenty of evidence that she worked as hard in their Appalachian ministries as he did.

Together, they make a wonderful cautionary tale about reading too much into sources. On one hand, they were traditional, conservative, Southern Baptists who opposed modernism, ecumenical religious endeavors, labor unionism, pentecostalism, dancing, and even birth control. On the other hand, they relished the sociological application of religion to the problems of Appalachia, launched innovative community health centers, libraries, and youth programs, and advocated expanded rights for tenant farmers. They also warned denominational leaders not to disrespect Appalachian people by depicting them as quaint or degenerate "yesterday people" in order to solicit home mission contributions. For historians seeking evidence for a southern variant of social Christianity quite different from the Social Gospel but nonetheless devoted to changing social structures, the Ridenours strengthen their case.

Chapter 7
Southern Baptists and Appalachia
A Case Study of Modernization and Community

America's long fascination with Appalachia has been dominated by two conflicting images. The first is of Appalachia as quintessential America. Its people are original stock. Its folk traditions are the oldest, richest, and best preserved. Its population consists of the purest Anglo-Saxon stock. Its cultural values of individualism, familism, elemental Christianity, and pride are the values that made this nation great.

The other view depicts Appalachia as the prototype of American primitivism. At the core of American culture is embedded esteem for modernity, tolerance, education, industrialization, urbanization, sophistication, and refinement. Appalachia exists at the periphery of these values, a fringe that tolerated and preserved such bizarre and disagreeable practices as moonshining, violence, incest, family feuds, herb medicine, and midwifery.[1] Working from these two dominant ways of understanding Appalachia I will try to insert Southern Baptists into the story.

The religious equivalent of the notion that Appalachia is essential America can be found in the religious generalizations that seem so compatible to Baptists. The essential religious values of Appalachian Christians were those of historic American evangelicalism: individualism, emotionalism, conservative moral values, democracy, and a strong sense of community. These, by the standards of many American evangelicals at least, constitute "good religion." Unfortunately, bizarre religious practices swirl around the periphery of this core: fatalism, otherworldliness, intolerant fundamentalism, pentecostalism, and snake handling.

For instance, one important center for pentecostalism was an area of Appalachia clustered around Cleveland, Tennessee. And certainly the most bizarre expression of pentecostalism——snake handling——originated in the mountains.[2] As a consequence of such "aberrant practices," many Southern Baptists saw Appalachia by 1900, as a quasi-savage land, a region of worthy traditions gone astray, of deprived and deluded people who needed religious attention and missionaries nearly as badly as darkest Africa.

Appalachian Religious Values and Essential Evangelicalism

At the core of all Protestant Christian theology is a belief that harmonized with Appalachian values. Each individual is terrifyingly responsible for her own fate. The point is so obvious that I will not belabor it. Although in his 1990 Carlyle Marney Lectures Michael Carter properly balanced individualism with the stress that rural congregations place on community and teamwork, I would still place individualism near the core of both Appalachian and Baptist practice.

Presumably both Southern Baptists and Appalachians were otherworldly, not so much in the formal theological meaning of that term as in the generic sense. At the center of the cosmos is an entire range of events over which humans have no control. As an agrarian people who depended on nature for their livelihood, Appalachian people and Baptists looked to primary not secondary causes. Like the ancient Hebrews, they implored God to restrain the storms or bring the rains that watered thirsty fields. An impetuous Alabama Methodist layman, Billy Grizzard, prayed for rains at a special community meeting during a serious drought in the 1830s. Wasting no time, Grizzard got right to the point: "Good Lord, send us a root-soaker and a gulley-washer."[3]

In North Alabama I discovered a wonderful piece of piety in the face of Appalachian reality. A mountain family, who believed they could control their stubborn team of oxen only by hollering profanity, began attending a revival meeting being held in a nearby settlement. One by one each member of the family was saved, leaving only one teenage boy outside the sacred circle. Neighbors anxious for the boy's salvation pressed him for an explanation of his apparent indifference to the moving of the Spirit of God. The boy offered a practical explanation: "Dad went down there and got religion. Mom she went down there and got religion. John went down there and got religion. If I went, who'd drive the oxen?"

Fatalism also commands our attention. Often misjudged to be a passive acceptance of events that might be altered but for the resignation of Appalachians, I prefer to think of this characteristic as an entirely logical reaction of a largely powerless people to events beyond their control. How was one to prevent tornadoes such as the one that blew away the schoolhouse and killed the children at Rye Cove? The family cemetery of my wife's people adjoining Hatchett Creek Presbyterian Church in Clay County, Alabama, raises a question as old as Job: M.Y. and J. P. Swindall buried two infant sons. John Manly was born on September 1, 1884, and died on October 21, 1886. An unnamed son was born and died on April 9, 1887. G. J. and E. L. Berry lost two daughters, both age 2. I. W. and M. E. Jones buried four children there, three daughters ages 17 to 20 and a son age 22. Many of my wife's Appalachian ancestors must have wondered with Job: "Why let men go on living in misery? Why give light to men in grief?"

Where Appalachian folk had some real options they were often not so fatalistic as historians have imagined. Ask the owners of coal mines how resigned United Mine Workers (UMW) members were to conditions during the 1930s. Or read the letters from uneducated bivocational Baptist preachers sent from Appalachia to President Franklin Roosevelt during the New Deal. In such sources one finds as much righteous indignation in the presence of human injustice as resignation.

Anecdotal evidence abounds on this point as does the rich vein of Appalachian folklore. There is the story of the frontier Presbyterian preacher who always carried his rifle to preachings in order to protect himself from Indian attack. When a Calvinistic parishioner questioned his faith, admonishing "When your time is up, your time is up," the preacher responded, "I carry my rifle because the Lord may mean it's the Indian's time that is up."

Democracy is not only one of the abiding legacies of Appalachia, it is (or at least historically it was) also one of the hallmarks of Baptists. Jacksonian notions of the universal worth of white men found a hospitable reception in the mountains. So did resistance to authority, whether the authority of federal revenue agents or centralized religious bureaucracies. Baptist pastors were usually bivocational men drawn from the common people. When they received pay at all it was seldom more than a pittance. The democratic assumptions governing Baptist congregations and the egalitarian assumptions of parishioners sparked rapid growth in the years after the Revolutionary War and the Second Great Awakening.[4] I could go on but, hopefully, my first premise is clear: Appalachia and Baptists share many assumptions and values.

The anti-missionary and Landmark movements of the early and late nineteenth century began to change the mountain region. At least in the opinion of Southern Baptists, Appalachia became a region less hospitable to them. By the late nineteenth century, when Southern Baptist consciousness neared full development under the influence of New South urban and industrial values of progress and modernity, the mountain region seemed alien to them.

This sense of religious alienation corresponded to a new American characterization of Appalachia. Although not appearing until 1981, Anne Rivers Siddons's novel *Fox's Earth* is set in Athens, Georgia, beginning about 1900. The story describes four generations of manipulative, determined, strong willed, and (at least to this male) terrifying Yancey women, struggling out of poverty into affluence. The progenitor of the family, Cater Yancey, was a fundamentalist preacher–textile worker from the Georgia highlands who moved south to the edge of the mountains in order to put his wife and children to work in a cotton mill. I will let Siddons take the story from there: "Like many of the people of the Southern Appalachians, the family of Cater Yancey were a strange, insular lot, half pagan-wild, half sternly Presbyterian, both traits legacied from the Scots who had first found refuge in those hills after the defeat of Bonnie Prince Charles at Culloden."

Any stereotype omitted from that paragraph appears in the next, which deals with the inclination of the family toward incest. No wonder Cater was "illiterate, ill-clad and eerily aberrant by the time he reached puberty." His uncle had killed his father with an axe and carried off his mother "to earth in his hidden cabin across the mountain." Cater's madness was largely a heritage of the grandmother who had raised him with a "ringing gift of tongue and a worshipful terror of a strange and privately perceived God of the Old Testament. When the old woman died and left him alone in the bare cabin, he had already preached for three or four years, sporadically, to congregations of perhaps a dozen people in tiny churches huddled meanly in the mountains, and he went down out of the mountains with the thought of working in the mills only until he could establish himself as a preacher and choose a regular church." Unfortunately, fondness for moonshine, sexual relations with his daughter, and religion too emotional even for other poor white textile workers made it hard for him to find a pastorate.

Admittedly Siddons's stereotypes of Appalachian religion seldom transcend the cognitive level of trashy modern novels and such Hollywood pablum as the *The Dukes of Hazzard* and *The Beverly Hillbillies*. But in 1900 a fair number of Americans, including most Southern Baptists, viewed the mountain region much as Siddons did: a vast, dark, foreboding land of benighted, quaint people, quasi-if not wholly primitive, who desperately needed rescuing.

Meanwhile, in the mountains lived a vigorous, religious folk who did not realize they needed saving. A Baptist former college president, Joseph C. Smiddy, of Wise, Virginia, told me a story during the 1970s that perfectly symbolized the differing assumptions about Appalachia. A prolonged blizzard had dumped six feet of snow on the mountains and hollows around Wise. After snow remained on the ground for nearly six weeks, the local rescue squad became concerned about the fate of Granny Jane Collins, who lived alone in a log cabin on High Knob. Snow plows and bulldozers feverishly labored to clear a path to Granny Collins's door. Rescue workers anxiously knocked, only to be greeted by a sprightly, perturbed women who announced, "I contributed to you-uns last summer." Like most Appalachian Christians at the turn of the century, Granny Collins did not realize she needed saving. But be saved they must, and Southern Baptists mobilized for the rescue effort.

In a 1991 doctoral dissertation for the University of Kentucky, Keith Harper contends that efforts by the Home Mission Board (HMB) to aid Appalachian and Ozark mountain schools between 1890 and 1920 may provide the best example of how Southern Baptists combined their social and missionary concerns. He notes that several streams of ideology drove their efforts. Baptists argued that mountain people descended from the purest ethnic stock but needed help to develop their churches and schools. Social and economic change threatened mountain people and their traditions unless they changed drastically. Yet they seemed incapable of coping with the forces of modernity.

As Baptist ethicist Victor Masters put it, "Their number is millions. Their blood is the most pure Anglo-Saxon blood in America. Their habits and manners are simple: they are like children." Or as Albert E. Brown, who headed the Southern Baptist Convention (SBC) mountain ministry, wrote in 1911 after nearly a decade of educational reform: "The moral tone has greatly improved, crime has lessened, feuds have disappeared, respect for law [has been] inculcated," local churches and prohibition sentiment strengthened, and mountain people had added to their houses guest chambers with bureaus, wash bowls, and other "conveniences." Such improvements, he believed, represented the "response of mountain people to advanced ideas of home life."[5]

Such comments from Baptist reformers exactly fit the dominant historical interpretation of southern Progressivism. Most historians now argue that the reform movement that flourished in the South between 1900 and 1920 contained strong elements of social control. Well-educated, urban middle-class reformers, operating usually from evangelical Christian assumptions of social justice, tried to impose their own mores and notions of modernity on simple, poor, uneducated folk, whether these unfortunates were black, immigrant, mountain people or textile workers.[6]

Although Harper recognizes elements of such paternalism in Baptist thought he pushes beyond this simplistic analysis to suggest a more complex range of issues: incipient social gospel concerns, a desire for some degree of empowerment, a strong commitment to community.

Unlike northern denominations that sent missionaries directly to the mountains, the HMB worked in cooperation with state Baptist mission agencies in Appalachian states. The HMB chose Albert E. Brown of Asheville, North Carolina, to head the ministry. Brown's father had been the first president of Mars Hill College (an Appalachian Baptist school located near Asheville), and he was assistant corresponding secretary of the North Carolina Baptist State Convention when selected for the new job.

Whereas Presbyterians funded their mountain schools much better than Baptists, they raised most of the money outside the mountains. Baptists argued that such a practice encouraged dependency. They boasted that they raised most of their money within the mountain communities themselves. Local communities not only bore primary responsibility for fund-raising to build the schools, they also assumed the burden of operating them. The close ties between school and community resulted in many graduates of the institutions remaining in the mountains to work following their graduation.[7]

By May 1922, the HMB operated thirty-seven schools employing 229 teachers and enrolling more than 6,000 students (175 of them studying for the ministry). The distribution of schools was not surprising. Although nine states contained SBC-sponsored mountain schools, North Carolina led with eight, followed by Tennessee (seven), Arkansas (six), and Kentucky and Virginia (five each).[8]

Typical of the schools was Stockton Valley Academy near Helena, Tennessee. Begun in 1909, it was located "off the beaten track" among the rural mountain people it was designed to reach. By 1922-1923 enrollment at Stockton Valley had reached 148, of whom twenty-eight boarded at the school at a cost of

$9 a month. Like the local students, boarders could pay part of their tuition and board through a work program if they needed to do so.[9]

The Baptist program of mountain education contained both expansive endorsements of native ability and demeaning paternalism. One commentator noted in 1923 that mountain children, "unspoiled by the deterioration of customs and manners in the last few years," had both the brain and brawn necessary "to revitalize the world." But another endorsement for a Virginia mountain academy concluded: "The average mountaineer is absolutely without emotion, cool and reluctant to accept new ideas, and if you appeal to him it must be to what he calls his 'horse sense.' He is naturally a religious creature, very often, it is true, sadly misguided; but this only proves that they should have larger opportunities for Christian education."[10]

By the 1930s mountain Baptist schools began to disappear as states constructed local public schools throughout the region. Although academies remained in Tennessee in 1932 (Cosby Academy, Harrison-Chilhowee Institute, Smoky Mountain Academy, and Watauga Academy), the HMB turned its attention to other ministries. This new effort was led by the remarkable Una Roberts Lawrence, whose oversight of a number of HMB social ministries deserves more attention than it has received. As a way of examining Southern Baptists and the sense of community in Appalachia, I will focus on one case study from the 1930s in Tennessee.

Few states felt the blow of the Depression or the change of the New Deal more than Tennessee. The extent of deprivation probably explains the ambivalence of Baptist response. Early in the New Deal the state Baptist newspaper editorialized about the Tennessee Valley Authority (TVA) efforts to transform mountainous East Tennessee. Calling the experiment "State Socialism," the editor of the *Baptist and Reflector* described TVA's efforts to clear forests, build resettlement communities, and establish community churches.

Although the editor boasted that Baptist democratic polity made it possible for the denomination to work "under any form of government," he warned that socialism could easily become communism, a philosophy rooted in infidelity. Furthermore, Baptists would not tolerate TVA's campaign to establish "Unionism" (interdenominational churches) within the new model communities being built. He called for a massive Southern Baptist counterattack in East Tennessee, involving doctrinal emphasis, increased field workers, and better funding.[11]

As part of this initiative the HMB conducted an extensive religious survey of each Appalachian mountain county in five Southern states. The survey dismissed urban populations within the counties so as to focus exclusively on rural life. It sought to identify the proportion of population claiming church membership, location of mountain missions and schools, and possible links to local boards of education, Cooperative Extension services, health departments, and other helping agencies. Lawrence even added a category for surveying industrial development because, she contended, reaching miners required some sort of goodwill center delivering social ministries, whereas working with farmers necessitated strengthened rural churches.[12]

As the data accumulated, the strength of Southern Baptists in Appalachia became apparent. For instance, in Tennessee forty-eight of Anderson County's seventy-two churches were SBC congregations. In Claiborne County the figure was sixty of eighty-three; in Hawkins forty-four of 120; Meigs thirteen of thirty-eight; Monroe forty-one of eighty-five; Roane thirty-five of ninety-eight; and Sevier fifty-one of ninety-one. Other counties were outside the SBC empire: Bledsoe had only two SBC congregations among its thirty-one churches; Clay had two of twenty-seven; Fentress three of twenty-four; Grundy two of thirty-two; Marion eight of sixty-four; Pickett one of sixteen. For reasons that will become clear momentarily the ratio in Campbell County is particularly important. Of the county's eighty-eight churches, forty-seven were Southern Baptist.[13]

Lawrence and the HMB dispatched a special emissary to supervise work in Campbell County and vicinity. George Lawrence Ridenour was typical of Southern Baptists who had directed the denomination's Appalachian ministries since 1900. He was a local man, well educated and deeply committed to uplifting his people.

Ridenour was born in a log cabin located in the center of the area occupied by the new Norris Dam reservoir. When residents had to be removed—their churches closed and their cemeteries relocated—Ridenour felt the pain as much as they did. Both his paternal and maternal ancestors were pioneers whose earthly remains rested in this sod. He attended a log school in Sugar Hollow and was converted at age 15 during a revival at Old Sugar Hollow Church. Although his father earned a living as a schoolteacher, the short terms common to area schools limited Ridenour's formal education. He had to intersperse a job logging around school terms to help provide a living for his family. He estimated that he spent only seven months in actual high school classes. After graduation he entered Carson-Newman College, paying his way by teaching short-term courses in mountain schools from July through September and then heading for Jefferson City.

After graduating from Carson-Newman, he taught briefly before entering graduate school at Vanderbilt and later the University of Tennessee. During the First World War he spent a year in the Army and then returned to teaching. He served as school principal in a large mining camp and preached at the local Baptist church. This experience led him into the ministry, and he left Tennessee for Southern Baptist Theological Seminary, where he completed the BD and PhD programs, specializing in the sociology of religion.

Service in a Campbell County mining town had wetted his appetite for sociology. Years of observing labor conditions and industrial relations shaped his formal education. One of his favorite pastoral illustrations compared spiritual blindness to an occasion when he had been lost in the underground blackness of a coal mine. Unfortunately, I know little about Ridenour's remarkable wife and helpmate, Agnes Whipple Ridenour.

The needs of their Campbell County neighbors brought the Ridenours back to East Tennessee to spend their lives in service to the people of the Cumberland Mountains. Unlike many ministers who insist that nothing they learn in an academic environment helps them in the real world, Ridenour vowed that all the sociological and theological theory he learned in school helped him directly in the actual work of Campbell County. Back home under sponsorship of the HMB, Ridenour led the church and cemetery relocation efforts when TVA began construction of Norris Dam. More importantly he used his intimate knowledge of the county and its people to demand that the government agency alter policies that threatened to disrupt and destroy their lives.[14]

In G. L. Ridenour a blend of Appalachian culture, Baptist theology, and sociological theory created a strange mixture. On an entire range of issues, he was predictably and conventionally Southern Baptist. One of his driving goals was to save his people from the three sins of ecumenism, modernism, and socialism.

TVA brought to the mountains many social planners who proposed to redesign Appalachian culture to their more enlightened standards. Theirs was a secular version of the Appalachian missionaries who had come to save mountain people from their benighted ways a generation earlier. An Interdenominational Regional Committee of the Council for the Southern Mountains and the Tennessee Valley coordinated religious activities, establishing interdenominational ("Union") Sunday schools and preaching points in the Norris Dam resettlement areas. The agency consisted of twenty-six constituent denominations, such as Disciples of Christ, Presbyterians (US and USA), Methodists, Congregationalists, and Episcopalians. Notably missing were Southern Baptists, Primitive Baptists, the Church of God, and other Appalachian groups. On Thursday evenings neighboring pastors spoke. On Tuesday evenings TVA social workers conducted recreation programs that included dancing. The key component of the committee's work was the notion "that the situation at Norris Dam calls for [a] united religious program."[15]

Ridenour spent a good portion of the next few years trying to defeat this effort. In an article published in the *Baptist and Reflector* in March 1935, he attacked activities of the Save the Children Fund in Campbell County. The program's leader, Ruth Parker, had served as a YWCA missionary in China and as a Presbyterian missionary to American Indians, as well as doing a stint with the Friends Service Committee in Appalachian relief work. Her pedigree did not impress Ridenour. He read printed materials published by the Save the Children Fund and warned Tennessee Baptists that the nondenominational organization proposed birth control and other "modernistic tendencies." Ridenour warned, "We do not need birth control taught. We need Christ preached."[16]

Ridenour used all his efforts over the next few years to block such heretical teachings. Appealing for more help from the HMB in 1935, he warned that otherwise he would have to turn his work over to the Federal Council of Churches. The following year he chided an American Sunday School Union missionary who opposed his efforts to open a medical clinic and attacked a TVA official at Cumberland Homesteads for demeaning Appalachian religion. In 1938 he claimed that Congress of Industrial Organizations (CIO) leaders also sought to replace Baptist Sunday schools with union Bible study. As an antidote to such mischief, Ridenour proudly recounted his success at recruiting a young Baptist preacher from "the heart of the mountains" to attend a preachers' school at Jefferson City, presumably thereby assuring his denominational orthodoxy.[17]

Nor were Ridenour's social and political attitudes unpredictable. Many of the sites where he ministered were mining camps such as Bear Wallow, Turley, and Rich Mountain, where the UMW were organizing. In his 1933 article for the *Baptist and Reflector* he left no doubt as to his view of the UMW, which he labeled a vanguard for "the agitator and the Red." In 1938 he reported to Lawrence on his work among miners at Rich Mountain. During the summer some preachers working with the CIO "who were boldly advocating Communism" tried to gain a foothold in the community and launched a strike. At Turley two preachers accompanied Marshall Musick of Harlan County, Kentucky, on a UMW organizing drive. Musick's son Bennett had been killed by company thugs three years earlier in Kentucky. Despite this tragedy Ridenour had no sympathy for the delegation, reporting that one of their aims was to destroy the Baptist Sunday school and replace it with an interdenominational meeting. The CIO wanted to destroy all religious work, which was bad enough. But even worse, ordained Baptist preachers, paid by the CIO, had led this effort. Ridenour denounced them as "without exception" men who had never pastored churches. Conversely he endorsed the young Baptist pastor of a congregation at Clinchmore because he related well to coal companies.[18]

Mining company officials usually received Ridenour's applause. At Westbourne the local coal company helped him establish a library "in order to keep the Federal Council of Churches worker out of the camp."[19]

Nor was Ridenour friendly toward Pentecostal sects that were multiplying throughout the mountains. In his 1933 *Baptist and Reflector* article he warned that holy rollers threatened to overrun Campbell County. In 1936, he reported to Lawrence that the long narrow hollows echoed "with all the wild orgies that Holy Rollers can put on in a meeting." Indeed he and his wife came to believe that one of their primary ministries was to bring enlightenment to "the great holiness population that has been untouched." Unfortunately the class consciousness and emotionalism of pentecostalism was infecting Southern Baptist preachers, whose revival services resembled holy-roller services.[20]

All this is pretty predictable stuff. But Ridenour's Appalachian consciousness, strong sense of community, and formal training in sociology created another dimension to his ministry. In correspondence with Lawrence, he warned against using a description of Appalachia proposed for a HMB journal. Citing a publication of the Save the Children Fund (*Schoolplace in the Foothills*), he attacked religious groups that tried to raise money and volunteers by depicting Appalachian culture in demeaning ways. "As a native," he wrote, "I know how most of the natives feel about the publicity in regards to [mountain superstitions]." In fact one reason for his opposition to well-meaning ecumenical efforts by TVA officials was the condescension they manifested toward Appalachian religion. In one of his letters to Lawrence he quoted a speech by the assistant manager of the Cumberland Homesteads resettlement community to the 1936 Tennessee Social Workers Conference:

> The religion of many of our homesteaders is primarily emotional, narrow, and primitive, not involving any intelligence. We saw from the beginning that if they had half a chance they would split and fight over religion, and our whole program would be wrecked, leaving just another stranded community. So we build them a community church, where they can all worship and work, and believe as they please.
>
> . . . Some of the old fashioned ones have reared up and said that the young folks are going to Hell, because they dance. They declare they don't want anyone teaching in Sunday School, or clerking in the store, who dances. These objectors are a minority, but they are a vociferous minority. We don't want to dictate to them of course, we simply ask them for tolerance. It is a matter of re-educating them—it is a lot harder to re-educate the emotions than to teach them new business methods, or methods of farming.

Such New Deal meddling with community religious mores infuriated Ridenour. He organized a committee of Baptists to meet with TVA officials and won support from a majority of the local committee to eliminate dancing from the recreation program. The success of any mountain missions effort, he wrote, depended on the leadership of native preachers who possessed "a true biblical knowledge and evangelistic zeal."[21]

Ridenour's sensitivity to local mountain ways governed his attitude toward governmental attempts to impose ballroom dancing and nondenominational religious institutions. But his background in sociology drove his program of social ministries. Although Ridenour carefully specified that reform efforts were always designed to convert the soul, he nonetheless built his evangelical efforts around social ministries to unemployed coal miners and displaced tenant farmers.

In the same 1933 *Baptist and Reflector* article that revealed Ridenour's scorn for ecumenical social and religious ministries, opposition to birth control, and concern about Communist influence, the Baptist minister outlined a program of social ministries. Two photographs with their captions illustrated conditions. One depicted decaying houses in a coal mining community and appealed for clothes and shoes. The other captured more than a score of children in the village, fourteen of them suffering from pellagra, all more than 15 percent underweight, three with goiter, and others who were tubercular. For them Ridenour had begun a relief program designed to treat malnutrition and illness.[22]

As poverty conditions worsened after 1932, evidence of economic and social disintegration became more obvious. In one mining camp Ridenour found many cases of colitis (an inflammation of the membrane of the large intestine). The displacement of mountain people in the Norris Lake region, together with the location of a Civil Conservation Corps (CCC) camp in the vicinity, led to an outbreak of syphilis among young people. Ridenour and his wife began a treatment program, assisted by a physician who was Baptist as well as a native of the region, and who directed the TVA's health program. Together they planned a program of social activities through Baptist churches (no dancing, of course!) that would provide "a wholesome social environment" for youth. The missionary blamed the outbreak of venereal disease on CCC boys from New York City, but acknowledged that the scourge was not confined to the local "down and out"; it had spread to the "up and out" as well.[23]

Unfortunately many area religious leaders opposed the clinic and medical work. Some objected because the Ridenours directed part of their efforts to curing syphilis patients. Other preachers and denominational workers were steeped in religious and medical superstition. While examining a 17-month-old toddler for colitis at their Caryville clinic, the Ridenours discovered a filthy cord holding three pieces of rattlesnake spine. The child's mother explained that a preacher had killed the snake, blessed the bones in the name of the Father, Son, and Holy Ghost, and attached them in order to frighten away the witches and demons responsible for the infant's sickness. The modern medicine applied by the Ridenours cured the infant and converted the mother from her faith in the "adulterous holy roller" preacher.[24]

Ridenour described other forms of superstition as well. Parents brought a tubercular child to him whom they had treated by placing a pan of cold water under her bed. A "charm doctor" treated a 13-year-old girl with a nearly severed toe by wadding up a pack of cigarette papers, inserting them in the wound, binding the foot in a dirty rag, and reciting a verse of Scripture from Ezekiel. The result was an infection that nearly cost the teenager her foot.[25]

Ridenour related such stories to Lawrence so she could publicize the needs of Appalachia's poor in *Home and Foreign Fields*, the HMB journal. Such stories generated the contributions necessary to purchase the medicine and supplies used at the six centers the Ridenours established. But Ridenour recognized that such appeals were a double-edged sword. Even as they cut away parsimonious Baptists from their money, they also severed non-Appalachian people from respect for Appalachian culture. Indeed, after itemizing the horrific medical superstitions of his mountain neighbors, he thought better of this strategy. Lawrence wrote to him, proposing to use his appalling examples in an article for *Home and Foreign Field* that would horrify Southern Baptists and generate generous offerings. Ridenour thought poorly of such a tactic. He warned that mountain people resented outsiders who depicted the bizarre and unusual as typical of Appalachian culture.[26]

To address the social, nutritional, medical, and educational problems that Ridenour identified in his articles and letters, he established multi-purpose community centers. Housed in abandoned churches and buildings from the Norris Lake reservoir basin or in coal camp structures, the centers provided a variety of services: mission Sunday school and worship services; free medical and dental care; community library; craft shops for boys and sewing rooms for girls; and Vacation Bible Schools.[27]

As Ridenour conceived his new work, distinctions between social ministry and evangelism were blurred. His proposed twenty daily Vacation Bible Schools, designed to reach 1,700 children ages 5 to 17, contained as "one of the most important features" a clinic that provided medical and dental examinations. The VBS/Clinic at Caryville treated a total of 222 school and preschool children during a two-week encampment in July 1936.[28] Although much of this activity consisted of routine Southern Baptist organizational work, Ridenour argued that traditional Baptist missionary and enlistment programs did not work in communities undergoing TVA displacement, coal mine layoffs, disruptive strikes, and resettlement of tenant farmers.[29]

At the same time, Ridenour acknowledged that medical work was not his chief concern. In the best evangelical tradition he insisted that there was "no point to giving health talks and medical examinations apart from the reality of training . . . people in a vital religion. Unless the people find Christ we have failed." Medical ministry merely gained entrance to a community so as to facilitate the more important work of evangelism.[30]

During the mid-1930s, George and Agnes Ridenour opened centers in Westbourne, Pioneer, Caryville, Red Oak, Hutsons, Turley, and Rich Mountain. As this work developed, they moved to more remote locations at Sand Gap, on Stinking Creek, Laurel Branch, No Business Creek, and Tackett Creek.

Staffing the centers presented a problem. The Ridenours worked at all of them.

But as the number of centers expanded, additional staff became essential. This the missionaries supplied through determined recruiting. Ridenour persuaded Eva Brewer, resident nurse at Louisville's WMU Training School for women, to help them during summer 1935. He also obtained the services of a new graduate of that institution, Edna Earl Hutcherson. From his alma mater, Carson-Newman College, he recruited two coeds to conduct Vacation Bible Schools. Both were foreign mission volunteers, and one had also worked in a Good Will (social) Center in Nashville.

Ridenour used older graduates of his Vacation Bible School to conduct programs in the most destitute communities. County health officers and local physicians volunteered to staff the clinics. In remote areas Ridenour used his title, Doctorate of Theology, as "sufficient authority for examinations and the dispensing of simple medicines." He also conducted baby clinics to educate new mothers about rudimentary nutritional, hygienic, and medical practices. During one Appalachian spring, Ridenour boasted that he made as many sick calls as any area physician. "And the pity of it was," he wrote Lawrence, "my services were the only ones that these poor families have."[31]

Ridenour's ministries varied from center to center, but medical services seemed to attract the greatest response from mountain residents. At the Caryville Clinic in June 1935, the staff immunized seventy-two preschool children against diphtheria and inoculated older youngsters. Twenty-four of these children also accepted Christ and were baptized, reinforcing the link between social ministry and conversion. At the mining village of Rich Mountain, where coal miners were stranded after the mine went into receivership, Ridenour's wife conducted a hot lunch program each school day and examined children for infected sinuses, ears, feet, tonsillitis, and malnutrition. Less than a quarter of the children received milk, and three had developed rickets. Nearly a fifth were underweight. Among her favorite patients were two bright children of a crippled Italian coal miner. Because the Italian family were strangers, Appalachian natives felt no compulsion to help, leaving them stranded, hungry, and sick. By contrast, most of the Sunday school children attending services at Laurel Branch and No Business Creek were descended from families involved in the Hatfield-Turner feud, and were "not . . . typical backward type of children but fine looking, healthy mountaineers."[32]

Some centers included libraries. In Westbourne, Ridenour raised $300 to furnish a room as a library to serve a relocation community of 2,000 people. He also helped TVA officials organize a regional library in Campbell, Union, Anderson, and Claiborne counties, although he protested that most of the religious books were "modernistic."[33]

Raising money to fund such varied ministries consumed much of Ridenour's time and energy. As with Southern Baptist mountain schools during the previous generation, he relied heavily on local donations. But he also used his friendship with Una Lawrence and the HMB to obtain money from nonmountain SBC sources. In one letter he appealed for 1,000 books for a library to serve a community where few people had gone beyond elementary school. In other letters he begged for medicine and milk for children and promised that for only $100 a month he could fund all his ministries in the Campbell County area. Encampments designed for children languished because most came from families too poor to furnish food for them.

Although he always tried to have campers perform work in order to preserve their pride and make them feel that they had paid their own way, the truth was that he relied on contributions from WMU societies, Sunday school classes, and individual Baptists to furnish food and medicine for most of them. A camp designed for twenty young mountain preachers ran into the same problem. They had no money for food. The costs of the retreat amounted to only $3 per person, but that sum amounted to more than most of them earned as salary from their congregations in an entire year.[34]

These ministries targeted primarily an industrial subculture within East Tennessee. But Agnes Whipple Ridenour expressed similar concern for tenant farmers. Many widows and orphans relocated by the Norris Dam project were entirely destitute. As a consequence she decided to organize Baptists in defense of tenant rights. First, she met with the Baptist Association to discuss what could be done to help. She invited forty tenants who had been displaced and had no jobs to meet with the association's executive committee. They asked the Campbell County Baptist association to send resolutions to the Tennessee State Executive Board and the SBC pleading for help.

Their presentation moved Agnes deeply: "I'm telling you it was a pitiful crowd. They are all Baptists and they do not know whom to look to for help except their brethren. It seems to me that as a denomination we ought to take an official interest in it." Fearing that TVA did not intend to address their problems, Agnes met with the heads of the agency's legal and public relations departments. Failing in this initiative, she urged Lawrence to persuade "some of our higher up organizations" to exert pressure on TVA. The government agency should be forced to provide relief for tenant farmers displaced by construction of its dams. She located a plot of 32,000 acres above Lafollette which the owner was willing to sell to TVA. Then displaced tenants could resettle on land in their home county among their own people, churches, and cemeteries.

As superintendent of the Campbell County Associational WMU, she also wrote TVA director Arthur Morgan, who was president of the University of Tennessee. The local WMU proclaimed that when TVA displaced tenant families "Christian women must do something" because of the "suffering among sick people, women and children" caused by such policies. After recounting several particularly pathetic cases, the WMU demanded a prompt response from Morgan and vowed to take up the issue at the 1935 SBC scheduled in Memphis.[35]

The Ridenours' combination of parochial evangelicalism and social ministries can be interpreted in many ways. Their exposure to advanced theological and sociological education at Carson-Newman and Southern Seminary may have influenced them favorably toward Social Gospel ideas. But their attacks on ecumenism, modernism, unionism, and Communism, in addition to their support of mining companies and local elites, suggest an alternative explanation. Their Appalachian roots, respect for traditional mountain values, and firm connection to local churches and institutions provided them a strong sense of community.

The Ridenours' reading of the Gospel suggested two preeminent callings. First and foremost, their task was to win their mountain neighbors to a transforming personal Christian faith. Second, the compassion emanating from that faith compelled them to address the social and economic distress of their neighbors. If Baptist pietist traditions and otherworldliness proved incapable of successfully addressing these problems, they would use sociology and good sense to find new ways. This divergence culminated in the creation of community centers where they dispensed health services, food, clothes, and library books. They pioneered community organizations, which were designed to pressure TVA officials to change offensive policies. And if TVA refused, they threatened to take their case to the SBC in order to rally it to the defense of the weakest and least powerful of its East Tennessee parishioners. Thus did a sense of the social and religious responsibility for their community deflect Southern Baptist faith in strange new directions for Agnes and George Ridenour.

—*Carson-Newman Studies*, 1994

My first two books were biographies of Florida politicians, the second being Rev. Sidney J. Catts. A Baptist preacher from Alabama, Catts set small town and rural Florida aflame in 1916 with his anti-Catholic bigotry. His gubernatorial victory that year despite having virtually no money and the universal opposition of the Democratic Party apparatus (although not necessarily its rank-and-file voters) stunned the nation. Running as a Prohibitionist after the state supreme court robbed him of his rightful nomination, Catts became the only independent in history to win the state's highest office. As I researched his story, I was amazed at how infrequently biographers of southern political figures located their narratives in religious context.

Despite a campaign of demagoguery worthy of Louisiana's Huey Long or Georgia's Tom Watson, once in office Catts (like them) championed the humblest white citizens, fostering prison, education, and infrastructure reforms while largely ignoring the alleged "Catholic menace" that had propelled him to power. Borrowing from the Bible and Christian teachings both for his campaigns and his reforms, Catts also mobilized the well-honed rhetorical skills and knowledge of plain folks' beliefs, foibles, and phobias characteristic of evangelical preachers.

At the heart of this case study is a larger truth about evangelicals. Mythologically other-worldly (the assumption that they worried exclusively about reaching heaven rather than righting wrongs) does not reflect the reality of either southern religion or politics. Catts was not dubbed the "stormy petrel of Florida politics" because he obsessed about the pearly gates. He earned that title by raising hell from Pensacola to Key West about what he thought was wrong in America, especially about Catholicism in Florida.

One further truth emerged from his career. Evangelicals could engage in self-delusion. However much they might rationalize their politics as a calling from God, divine summons seemed to parallel personal ambition. In the case of Catts, he convinced himself that his sacred causes justified appalling ethical lapses culminating in scandalous reports of ties to professional gambling and counterfeiting. Whether contrived by his political enemies or symptomatic of his increasing cynicism, Catts's career made it more difficult for self-proclaimed moral reformers after him. Nevertheless, governors such as Robert Martinez, George Wallace, and a hundred others were more likely to water their arid campaigns from the same wells of Scripture and popular religion than politicians elsewhere. Whether their opportunism better served Christian ethics, personal ambition, or public cynicism is another matter.

Chapter 8
Religion at the Polls
A Case Study of Twentieth-Century Politics and Religion in Florida

Florida politicians show up in strange places. While working as pop music writer for the *Birmingham News*, Shawn Ryan authored a column on March 2, 1990, about Governor Robert Martinez's attempt to purge Florida record stores of obscene material. A special session of the Florida legislature had just pulverized the governor's anti-abortion legislative package. Martinez sought to recover by ordering an album by 2 Live Crew, *As Nasty as They Wanna Be*, removed from record store shelves in Dade County. The fact that the governor of a state with more than its share of adult bookstores and pornography palaces should have targeted records as an issue on which to take his stand probably tells more about political strategy than religion. He explained to a *Newsweek* reporter, "If you answer the phone one night and the voice on the other end begins to read the lyrics of one of these songs, you'd say you received an obscene phone call."[1]

The fact that Governor Martinez, no bluenose Puritan, took this position emphasizes how enduring religio-moral values are to American political discourse and how, generally, Florida historians have overlooked the subject. Martinez's responses speak to important historical traditions in the state long ignored by historians, who by and large do not take evangelical religion as seriously as do ordinary citizens. This article will explore these trends, using Governor Sidney J. Catts's career as an example of the historic practices at work. Although the times and issues changed from nativist xenophobia in 1916 to moral majoritarianism in 1990, the importance of religion in defining the contours of political debate in Florida remain constant.

The political activity of religiously affiliated people demonstrates some very important patterns that have shifted dramatically over the past century. When the century began, Protestants and Catholics operated at predictably opposite ends of the political spectrum. Nativist and anti-Catholic feeling ran so high that organizations such as the American Protective Association, the True Americans, The Guardians of Liberty, and the Ku Klux Klan could often count on a solid Protestant vote merely by identifying the religious affiliation of a candidate or the local extent of the "Catholic conspiracy."

By the 1980s Catholics and Baptists were politically if not ecumenically unified on a wide range of issues: opposition to abortion, support for prayer in public schools, and federal aid to church schools, just to name three examples. Fundamentalists have largely controlled the Florida Baptist Convention, severed relations with Stetson University, and generally have more in common with conservative Roman Catholics than with moderate Baptists. In fact, the growing contemporary preoccupation with moral and family issues threatened to redefine the contours of American politics during the 1980s. If historians could ignore the religious context of Florida politics for nine-tenths of the century, they have a lot of catching up to do during this decade.

The claim of historical oversight needs some qualification. Historians David R. Colburn and Richard K. Scher pay brief attention to the formal religious affiliation of Florida governors. They correctly note that nine of fifteen governors between 1900 and 1955 were Baptists (make that ten of fifteen if one includes Albert W. Gilchrist, who although christened an Episcopalian spent his adulthood active in a Baptist church).

Of course such statistics must be weighed against the political opportunism of several generations of southern politicians who knew well that church membership was good politics. Hence David Sholtz converted from Judaism to Congregationalism. Even Congregationalism might seem a little strange to the state's Baptists, but during the Great Depression there were more important problems to consider. And at least Sholtz would not perplex voters with talk of bar mitzvahs and Hanukkah celebrations. Duncan Fletcher, who faced the constant threat of embarrassment from his wife's Unitarian-Universalism and Spiritualism, kept careful ties to Jacksonville's First Baptist Church. Senator Park Trammell was a more consistent Baptist, but his biographer suggests this may well have been due more to his wife's devotion than to his own.

The last Baptist to serve as Florida's chief executive was Acting Governor Charley E. Johns, a Baptist businessman and legislative power broker who served most of Daniel McCarty's term from 1953 until 1955 after the governor died of a heart attack. It may be instructive that of the four governors to whom Colburn and Scher attribute the lowest public ethics, two (Catts and Johns) were Baptists, and the other two (Haydon Burns and Claude Kirk) were Methodist and Episcopalian.[2] Whether Johns's practice of voiding state contracts in order to award new ones to political allies dealt a death blow to Baptist governors is unknown. Likely the changing religious and political demography of the state had more to do with the eclipse of Baptist influence. Florida's increasingly heterogeneous political landscape dominates the post-Johns religious affiliation of the state's governors: two Episcopalians, two Methodists, a Presbyterian, a member of the United Church of Christ, and a Roman Catholic.

Religion often became an issue of controversy in twentieth-century Florida's public life. Scholars have shown that in 1928 and again in 1960 evangelical Protestants bolted the Democratic Party in large numbers rather than vote for a Catholic presidential nominee. In 1978 Robert L. Shevin lost a runoff for the Democratic gubernatorial nomination to Robert Graham partly because he was Jewish and from Miami.[3] Which of these facts hurt him more is a matter of speculation.

Despite such passing recognition, no systematic treatment of the religious context of Florida politics exists. In their biographies of Napoleon Bonaparte Broward and LeRoy Collins, Samuel Proctor and Tom Wagy do not analyze religion extensively. The book on Florida governors by Colburn and Scher devotes half a page to religion and only lists denominational affiliations. Although Wagy ignored religion as a topic, like several other essayists, he correctly emphasized religio-moral values as the source of Collins's courageous stand for racial justice. Speaking to Presbyterian churchmen, Wagy notes that Collins challenged them to go "All the Way for Christ" when racist mobs howled at their doors or when innocent people were fired for their kindness to black people. The governor warned that no legal resolution could end racial injustice because the issue involved "moral rights" and "principles of brotherhood." To demand that African Americans "stay in their place," forgoing their legitimate rights, was "not a Christian point of view." Although Wagy makes it absolutely clear that Collins's religious and moral presumptions underlay his racial assumptions and provided his most effective arsenal against Florida's racists, religion does not play a role in the story. A passing reference to "Presbyterian" is all that appears.[4] Contemporary commentators on Rueben Askew's courageous advocacy of school busing frequently mentioned his religious values, but whether historians seeking other motives do any better explaining his actions remains to be seen.

A number of studies have recognized the significant correlation between religion and political action nationally. They have shown that 57 percent of Catholics who voted for president in 1960 identified themselves as Democrats. Among Jews the figure was 66 percent. Among Baptists it was only 47.6 percent. In fact, Baptists have been moving toward the Republican Party since Harry Truman, one of their own, carried Baptist counties on his way to the 1948 Democratic upset victory. In 1956 Adlai Stevenson received 50 percent of the Baptist vote, Lyndon Johnson carried 49 percent in 1964, Hubert Humphrey got only 24 percent (George Wallace and Richard Nixon split the other 66 percent) in 1968, and George McGovern received 25.5 percent in 1972. Jimmy Carter, of course, dramatically reversed this downward cycle in 1976, winning 57 percent. But 1976 was the "year of the Evangelical," when news magazines ran features on born-again Christians, and Jerry Falwell launched the Moral Majority. Although Carter did better among self-styled evangelical voters than Democrats normally, he still failed to woo most of them from the Grand Old Party (GOP).[5]

By 1980 many evangelicals who had voted for Carter four years earlier repented and returned to the house of their fathers, now made more hospitable by the presence of Jerry Falwell and assorted Southern Baptist luminaries. In fact, in 1976 many new right evangelicals rejected Carter as a religious imposter. Third Century Publishers rushed out a "Christian's guide" in 1976 to help evangelicals elect "God-directed candidates." The guide denounced Carter while rejoicing in the election of Mickey Edwards in Oklahoma, Bob Durnam and Bob Badham in California, and John Myers and Dan Quayle in Indiana.[6] Specific Florida data tying Carter's declining popular vote from 1976 to 1980 to religion are impossible to produce. But if evangelicals nationwide were disappointed in Carter's performance, it seems logical that some of his eroding support in the sunshine state stemmed from disillusion among his born-again 1976 supporters.

The Christian right thrived during the 1980s when presidents Ronald Reagan and George Bush granted its leaders unparalleled access to the White House. Bush and Vice President Quayle spoke to the SBC, although neither was Baptist, an honor that, incidentally, was not bestowed upon Jimmy Carter, who was a born-again believer and one of their own.

Nor did religious rightists return to the traditions of their fathers in 1992. Despite an unprecedented Democratic ticket composed of two Southern Baptists and one spouse whose opposition to nasty record lyrics sound like Governor Martinez's, white southern evangelical and fundamentalist Protestants opted for a politically correct Episcopalian. Admittedly Clinton's reputation as a womanizer made this defection easier to understand than the 1980 desertion of Carter, but by and large the religious right seemed capable of forgiving sins of the flesh more easily than sins of ideology.

Clinton-Gore in fact won a majority of Catholics, Jews, black Protestants, and religious liberals and narrowly lost mainline Protestants—usually a GOP bastion. But Bush won decisively among the 17 percent of the electorate that identified itself as "white born-again Christians." He took 61 percent of that vote compared with 23 percent for Clinton and 15 percent for Perot. In ninety-six heavily Southern Baptist counties in eleven southern states, including Florida, Bush won 46 percent to Clinton's 40 percent. Bush's three strongest states were Mississippi, Alabama, and South Carolina. Among the 40 percent of Alabama voters who listed themselves as "white born-again Christians," Bush beat Clinton 67 to 23 percent.[7]

Victories by religious right candidates in Oklahoma, California, Indiana, and Michigan make clear that Florida has no monopoly on voters whose ballot choices are swayed by religious issues. But the denominational mix is significantly different according to region. For instance, 58 percent of Baptists in the mid-1970s resided in the South, while only 16 percent of Roman Catholics and 19 percent of Jews lived in Dixie (64 percent of Jews live in the East, 10 percent in the Midwest, and 7 percent in the West; for Roman Catholics 41 percent live in the East, 28 percent in the Midwest, and 15 percent in the West). Even within the South the pattern varied. The traditional Bible belt South is a Baptist camp.

In Alabama, Baptists represent 31 percent of the population, in Arkansas 26 percent, in Georgia 28, Kentucky 26, Mississippi 32, North Carolina 25, Oklahoma 26, South Carolina 28, Tennessee 28, and Texas 22.[8] Florida is notably absent from states of the Baptist dispensation, although that would not be the case if the discussion pertained only to north Florida. The Bible Belt meanders across state boundaries well into central Florida before it encounters a solid barrier of religious heterogeneity constructed from immigrants drawn from every state and a multitude of foreign countries.

Florida politics in the twentieth century can be analyzed in numerous ways. The most famous description is "every man [and woman] for himself [herself]," reflecting the politics of factionalism. The rise of a strong Republican Party is changing that characteristic by forcing Democrats to impose some unity and order onto its natural and preferred state of anarchy. Supreme Court cases mandating one person/one vote, with the resulting transfer of power to southern Florida, took a long time to bring results, but now a south Floridian can become governor. The rapidity of population growth in Florida creates the greatest political flux of any southern state, making reelection an unusually risky venture.

Today's conventional political wisdom is tomorrow's ancient history. Courthouse gangs and party elites have come and gone with such regularity since the 1960s that one needs a scorecard to keep up with the players. In many ways Florida is the most nonsouthern of southern states. In politics, as in religion, it drifts ever closer to national patterns. Other than Sidney J. Catts, Florida cannot even claim a respectable demagogue. Kirk tried but fell far short of Catts's high standard.

Two givens characterize the state: religion is an increasingly important barometer of political behavior, and Florida is a different sort of southern state. From these two facts one may draw an obvious conclusion. Scholarly discussion of twentieth-century Florida politics must focus less on politicians and political processes and more on religious context.

Precisely how would attention to religious context enrich our understanding of Florida's political processes? The administration of Sidney J. Catts offers a concrete historical example. He was admittedly the only preacher-governor in the state's history, but, as references to Robert Martinez, Robert Shevin, LeRoy Collins, and others illustrate, he was by no means the only governor to address issues directly within the context of religious and moral assumptions. Catts was elected governor as an Independent Prohibitionist in 1916, was defeated handily by Duncan Fletcher for a Senate seat in 1920, and then lost close gubernatorial contests in 1924 and 1928. How did religion affect Catts's career and produce these outcomes?

In 1916 Florida's Negro Baptists led all denominations with 70,000 members, and Southern Baptists accounted for the largest number of white Protestants in the state with 57,732 members organized in 686 churches. The Methodist Episcopal Church, South trailed just behind with 51,505 communicants. Roman Catholics lagged in fifth place with only 24,650 members, or 7.5 percent of the total church population. The Catholic Church ranked sixth in terms of the value of its property.[9]

These rankings remained fairly constant for a decade. In 1926 Florida's 528,000 church members (a 57 percent increase from 1916) were divided among the same three leaders: Southern Baptists (white) 103,000; Negro Baptists 98,000; and Methodist Episcopal Church, South (white) 74,000. The number of Roman Catholics had increased to only 39,000.[10]

Catts understood the world of white southern evangelicals as well as any man in Florida. Indeed, he had served a long apprenticeship as a Baptist pastor in Alabama prior to living in Florida. Here, he honed many of his basic approaches to life and religion.

One skill nourished by the southern evangelical church, but little understood by historians, was the power to persuade an audience. At the heart of any evangelical religious process is the ability to move people to action: to accept Christ as personal savior, to change conduct, to tithe, to assume a position of service or ministry. Clergymen assumed roles of leadership in southern politics, and many Florida Populist leaders were evangelical preachers. In the next generation many preachers carried the banner of progressivism, as did Sidney J. Catts.

Offspring of a black belt Alabama planter family, Catts attended several schools before deciding on a career in law. Following a short stint at Cumberland University Law School in Tennessee, Catts practiced law briefly before feeling "called" to the Baptist ministry. As with every other decision in his life, he defined this one in religious metaphors. He described his decision to enter Florida's 1916 governor's race in similar terms: "For weeks before I announced, I could not sleep at night. I felt a call that I was trying to resist. I firmly believe, and was finally convinced that I was called of God to make that race. And after I got into the fight I was more and more convinced of the truth of my vision."[11] Catts needed a near-messianic confidence in his own vision and mission. He had resided in Florida only five years; had no money, contacts, or name recognition; and was ignored by both the press and his own party.

A second skill Catts learned in Alabama churches also served him well at Florida political rallies. Churches that place the pulpit in the middle of the church send a powerful symbolic message: the sermon and not the liturgy is central. The ability to move a congregation of people to voluntary action to change conduct or society is no small accomplishment. One person who heard Catts preach called him "a power in the pulpit." Another termed him "one of the best impromptu speakers I ever listened to." In his 1904 race in Alabama's Fifth Congressional District against Thomas Heflin, one correspondent described his campaign through the hill country: "The people here have not heard anything to equal this address since the days of the campaigning of the lamented William I. Samford [former governor]."[12] When Governor-Elect Catts visited Birmingham in December 1916, curious citizens asked him to speak about his recently ended campaign, which had created such a national sensation. He obliged with an hour-and-a-half address. The newspaper reporter described a speech "of gripping intensity with a narrative filled with dramatic incidents, interspersed with humorous happenings." The "more impassioned parts of the speaker's address were cheered to the echo," and when Catts finished the audience cheered for more.[13]

Unfortunately, the two parts of Catts that were so interchangeable to him—religion and politics—confounded historians who insist that the expression of Christian faith in Dixie was essentially otherworldly and escapist. The actions of Pat Robertson, Jerry Falwell, Jesse Jackson, the Moral Majority, and Operation Rescue in the last decade of the twentieth century place this assertion on weak ground. Sidney Catts's career casts doubt upon the premise as applied to the first decades of the century.

In its mildest form, southern religion called for moral rearmament. A revivalist sermon at Catts's Fort Deposit church in July 1894, for example, attacked "ballot box stuffing as a common practice that Democrats used to count out Populists in that election year, Blind Tigerism, Waltzing, vulgar anecdotes and such things."[14] This curious philippic, blending public and private and political and personal morality, points to themes that extend throughout Catts's Florida career. He frequently engaged in political campaigns on behalf of prohibition. As pastor of Tuskegee Baptist Church, he also kept careful watch for heretical racial views at Tuskegee Institute. As a speaker at the 1904 Alabama Baptist Convention, he spoke on "The Preacher and Politics." He had precise notions on the subject. As pastor of Mt. Willing Baptist Church, he had just completed an unsuccessful campaign for Congress against a demagogue who taught him well how to appeal to the masses.[15]

The religious world of Sidney Catts was also obsessed with the menace of immigrants, particularly those who were Roman Catholic. In 1894 the nativist American Protective Association came to Mobile, Alabama, where it waged war against a Catholic candidate for mayor. During these decades all three of Alabama's major cities—Mobile, Montgomery, and Birmingham—elected Catholic mayors. Evangelicals grew increasingly uneasy about the link between the Vatican and American politics. *The Alabama Baptist* editorialized in 1894: "There is one peculiar fact about Catholicism. Wherever it prevails you observe a low state of morals. Marital ties set lightly. Fornication and adultery are common. The Sabbath has been changed from a holy day to a holiday. Gambling is fashionable. Saloons are numerous and prosperous. . . . There is no question that rum and Romanism go together. Indeed, the very stronghold of rum in this country is Romanism."[16]

How deeply such attitudes penetrated Catts's consciousness soon became apparent. Speaking at Tuskegee Institute on the "Persecutions and Martyrdoms of the Church," Catts described ecclesiastic and secular history as a battle between papist and democratic forces. He reasoned that "every movement of Jehovah seems to be directed against the temporal power of the Pope, and for enlightenment and good government." Historical evidence appeared on every hand: Italian unification was a blow to the power of the church, as were Andrew Jackson's incursions into Florida.[17] Catts was discovering what many Florida politicians would learn: bad history can make good politics.

But the most complete revelation of Catts's remarkable blend of religious context and political opportunism came in his December 1916 speech in Birmingham. So many critical elements of Florida's political tangle were unraveled there. He was introduced that evening by Dr. A. J. Dickinson—pastor of First Baptist Church, graduate of the University of Chicago, theological liberal, pastor to Hugo Black (who may well have been in the audience), advocate of social Christianity, and himself a future candidate for public office. The man who presided at the meeting, a man with the last name Dozier, was one of the leading anti-Catholic luminaries in the city. Dickinson opened the meeting with a simple premise: no one should be allowed to vote who held obligation to any agency or institution higher than America. Dozier also announced a meeting of the Ku Klux Klan to be held in the same hall immediately after Governor-Elect Catts finished his speech.

Catts no doubt swelled attendance at the Klan meeting by his remarks. He stated that his decision to run for governor resulted from "the pernicious influence" and "domination of the Jesuits." He entered the campaign to force the other candidates to explain where they stood "on the principles of our organization" (The True Americans?). But they clearly "knew nothing about our American platform and they cared less." "I had been lecturing in every little church and schoolhouse scattered over the state every night after I finished my work. . . . I had informed the people in the country on the menace which threatened our state."

What was the menace? Less than one-fifth of Florida's population was Catholic, he warned (the real figure was nearer one-fifteenth, but that was too low to frighten the common folk), yet they held two-thirds of all offices in Florida (a bit of ministerial hyperbole, like estimating the size of a revival congregation). Catholics, through "unseen and invisible methods," controlled government and the press: "The Catholics were about to take Florida and I told the people about it wherever I went. I was trampling on their toes and raising the devil to such an extent that many of the Catholics wanted to kill 'Old Catts.'" Weary of harassment from police and threatened with assassination, he spoke "with both hands on big pistols which were loaded in every chamber." Eschewing towns, he campaigned in the country, taking a collection at each stop to get him to the next.

His campaign to take "our public schools out of the hands of those holding allegiance to a foreign potentate" triumphed despite attempts to steal the election from him. Lest Catts appear exclusively as the hero of this crusade, he acknowledged that he did have friends in high places: there was God, of course, but also Tom Watson, Catts told his hushed audience, "the greatest leader of our cause, Americanism." At this point the crowd broke into thunderous applause.[18]

Thomas E. Watson, former leader of Georgia Populism and still a spokesman for rural, southern plain folk, began publishing a series of articles in 1909 on "the Roman Catholic Hierarchy" in his *Jeffersonian* magazine. The paper had many subscribers in Florida between 1910 and 1916, and secret anti-Catholic societies spread like wildfire under the stimulus of Watson's acid-tipped pen. The paper's emotional excesses help explain how sane, kindly people became so mesmerized by Catts's crackpot mixture of religious bigotry and pseudo history. Italics and bold-faced type, all-capitalized letters, and red-inked headlines added a sense of urgency to the torrid prose. The series on "The Roman Catholic Hierarchy: The Deadliest Menace to Our Liberties and Our Civilization" began in August 1910 and ran for twenty-seven months. It was so successful that the series spawned an even more lurid sequel titled "The History of the Papacy and the Popes." Published in book form, the exposes enjoyed wide circulation until banned from the mail for their salacious content during the First World War.

A sample of what rural Floridians were reading just prior to and during Catts's gubernatorial campaign helps explain his phenomenal rise to power. Article titles do justice to the finest grocery story tabloid: "The Murder of Babes," "The Sinister Portent of Negro Priests," "How the Confessional is Used by Priests to Ruin Women," "One of the Priests Who Raped a Catholic Woman in a Catholic Church,"; and "What Happens in Convents." Watson probably provided the most prurient reading available to an entire generation of Florida evangelicals.[19]

Such activity slowly changed the state. In 1910 the nativist Patriotic Sons of America helped defeat St. Augustine Catholic congressional candidate Lewis W. Zim. Four years later US Senator Nathan P. Bryan, a Methodist layman, appointed Peter Dignan postmaster of Jacksonville. Dignan was a respected member of the city council and was also a Catholic. Billy Parker, a newly arrived immigrant from Pennsylvania, used the appointment as the catalyst for a series of bitter speeches on Jacksonville street corners vilifying Catholics in general and Dignan in particular. It was Parker who apparently organized Jacksonville's chapter of The Guardians of Liberty and circulated its paper, *The Menace*, across the state. Soon Protestant backlash to the Dignan appointment reached such proportions that anti-Catholic groups persuaded Baptist governor Park Trammell to abandon his already announced candidacy for the First Congressional District and to enter the Senate campaign against Bryan.[20]

The best expression of the cumulative effect of all this propaganda on Florida residents is contained in a brief, bigoted, but eloquent correspondence to Park Trammell in May 1916. One writer was M. F. Green of Perry, Florida, located squarely within north Florida's Bible Belt: "I think most of us of Florida [in Taylor County at least] has enough of Bryanism, Negroism, and Catholicism, they can all go to H— for my part."[21] Trammell had tuned his ear to Florida's religious discord as finely as had Catts. Senator Trammell had stopped white teachers from instructing black pupils in a Catholic school and arrested three sisters who persisted in their educational tasks. William Collins, chief of police in Okeechobee, wrote Trammell congratulating him for removing white teachers from Catholic schools enrolling black students. He also deplored a Catholic paper circulating in Florida that criticized the way Trammell had handled the matter. S. G. Bartow, exchange editor of *The Menace*, wrote Trammell from the Aurora, Missouri, headquarters of The Guardians of Liberty. He requested information regarding Florida's new law restricting white teachers from instructing black students for use in a forthcoming issue of *The Menace*. The masthead of Bartow's stationary carried a logo that was playing well in the sunshine state: "The Roman Catholic Political Machine: The Deadliest Menace to Free Institutions and Liberty." R. C. Boulvare wrote Trammell eight days later from Kendrick, Florida, boasting of his membership in an anti-Catholic organization claiming 15,000 members in Florida: "We are . . . instructed to vote for Catts and Trammell!"[22]

It was true, as Fuller Warren wrote in 1949, that Sidney Catts "hanged the Pope to every oak tree in West Florida during the years between 1910 and 1925."[23] But Catts did not purchase the rope. He arrived in a state already seething with religious animosity and xenophobia. To understand Catts's remarkable 1916 Florida race without understanding his evangelical roots or the religious context of his political campaign is like *Newsweek* trying to comprehend Robert Martinez's assault on 2 Live Crew without reference to a Florida religious mindset fed up with cultural sewage. Historians who ignore religious context are constantly surprised when they encounter men like Sidney Catts and Robert Martinez in American politics. More careful attention to religious popular culture would reduce the surprise.

—*The Florida Historical Quarterly*, 1994

In a perfect world, this chapter would have been written a decade earlier as my first venture into southern evangelicalism rather than the one that launched my second decade of discovery. For my imperfection, I will blame both the infancy of the field of inquiry and my deeply flawed education. As the product of Alabama's horribly underfunded public schools and a parochial state Baptist college, I had lots more to learn than I realized (although I concede to no southern religious historian of my generation greater fidelity to primary sources). But I lagged badly in placing this research into a broader theological and philosophical perspective. Put another way, I did not begin my exploration of southern religion by asking big questions. I started by revealing startling vignettes I was discovering in labor archives, denominational newspapers, church records, and oral histories.

My primary tutors in a long career of in-service learning were Sam Hill and Donald Mathews. Hill, my beloved friend and longtime sparing mate, far exceeded me both in education and erudition. His study at Southern Baptist Theological Seminary, Vanderbilt, Cambridge, and Harvard, conditioned him to begin all scholarly inquiry with the topology, existential meaning, and sociological implications of religious experience.

Mathews, who grew up in a holiness Methodist tradition in Idaho but honed his conversion experience in the rarified atmosphere of Yale University Divinity School and a Duke doctoral program, brought both family biography and a sharp theological mind to subjects such as the centrality of the Christian Crucifixion narrative, God's righteousness and humanity's faith, divine wrath and human waywardness, and punishment and its psychological damage.

As I corresponded and conversed with, listened to, and read books by Hill and Mathews, I experienced what some pentecostals might call a second baptism of the Spirit. Unable to unwind my life in order to access what they knew from challenging graduate seminars and internationally famous professors, I did what generations of Americans had done before me: I plunged as deeply as teaching a 13-course-per-year class load at Samford University permitted into reading (sociology of religion, psychology, psychiatry, anthropology, folk culture) in a process of self-education.

This essay, written to present in 1979 at the University of Alabama in Birmingham, is the result of that 10 years of learning to think bigger, of asking anthropological questions inherent in the study of all religions—not the specific question, is this "good" or "bad" religion, but the more general and nonjudgmental question, what role does this religion play in the lives of those who believe it to be true. From 1979 forward, I employed raw materials obtained in archives to construct a larger and more convincing theological and philosophical edifice.

Recovering American religious history is imperative if we are to understand the way in which Americans thought about human nature and destiny. Church historian Sam Hill, focusing specifically on the South, has maintained that the solidarity of religion is as important as politics and race to southern distinctiveness. No other region has been so uniformly evangelical Protestant. In the 1960s membership in Baptist and Methodist churches constituted nearly 80 percent of the total church affiliation in six southern states. Adding Presbyterians and Disciples of Christ, the total in Alabama for the four evangelical churches was 90.9 percent of the total, 88.3 in Arkansas, 93 in Georgia, 93.9 in Mississippi, 87.5 in Tennessee.

Obviously, any serious attempt to understand the southern mind must begin by grappling with the region's evangelicals, and this task is not easy. One observer of the southern church in the 1920s wrote with more perplexity than insight: "Religion in the South is infinitely puzzling. It is a paradox, dead and yet alive, unprogressive and narrow but a powerful force."

This chapter asks four questions: (1) Who are southern Evangelicals? (2) What do they believe? (3) What function did religion serve for them? (4) What was their approach to culture? Like most academicians, I have more answers than questions, so I limit this discussion to white evangelicals who have organizational roots in the Protestant Reformation—namely Baptist, Methodists, and Presbyterians.

Chapter 9
One in the Spirit, Many in the Flesh
Southern Evangelicals

Who Are Southern Evangelicals?

Defining mainstream southern evangelicals is not as easy as it may first appear. In the late eighteenth century they were mainly economically insecure frontier folk with a strong bias against the aristocracy. The Anglican Church with its commitment to the upper class sought to perpetuate a hierarchical social system. Powerless common people came to despise the established church and condemned the sins they associated with the social class it represented: horse racing, gambling, and slavery. Southern folk religion became a volatile, defiant movement of alienated lower-middle-class and lower-class white people. Nor was the animosity one-sided. Upper-class communicants in the Episcopal Church had no use for the theology or character of evangelicals. One aristocratic Virginian described Baptists in unflattering terms: "Some of them were hair-lipped, others were blear eyed, or humpbacked, or bow-legged, or club-footed; hardly any of them looked like other people."[1]

Of course, not every frontiersman was religious. In 1800 only one in fifteen Americans was a church member, and religious literacy, especially on the southern frontier, was astonishingly low. A piece of religious folklore described a preacher's witness to a woman in a remote backwoods cabin. Asked if she had any religious convictions, she replied: "Naw, not my ole man, neither. He was tried for hog stealing once, but he warn't convicted."

No wonder evangelicals attacked the frontier with such fierce determination. Circuit riders and missionaries led revivals that saved the souls and changed the lives of tens of thousands. By 1850 an estimated one in seven Americans belonged to a church, twice the percentage of fifty years earlier.

But the intervening years had also changed southern evangelicals. No longer were they primarily powerless, defiant, lower-class folk. Many of them had become small planters or prosperous yeoman farmers. Although a disproportionate share of wealth and political power still resided in the hands of Episcopalians, evangelicals shared enough to become conservative defenders of much that they had criticized earlier, including slavery. By the 1830s, few southern evangelicals raised their voice in protest against the "peculiar institution," and by 1844–45 they had repudiated the increasingly anti-slavery stance of their northern brethren and established their own ecclesiastical organizations.

More subtle changes occurred during the same years. Bonds of professionalism grew among ministers. More of them attended college and afterwards established academies to train their children and those of their parishioners. Denominational colleges mushroomed and ecclesiastical bureaucracies developed to manage tract societies, home and foreign mission agencies, denominational newspapers, and the other trappings of organized religious life.

Not all evangelicals made the transition into affluence. The result was internal class divisions that matched the earlier cleavage between Episcopalians and Evangelicals. These differences resulted in the birth of the Disciples of Christ and the Cumberland Presbyterian Church, and animosity between missionary, anti-missionary, and Landmark Baptists. Although these controversies had theological dimensions, class elements were more significant. In most cases the dissenters were poor and mountain white people, those closer to the frontier experience who resented the increasing religious sophistication of their wealthier and more politically powerful lowland brothers. The Calvinistic antimission Baptists objected to all human means of conversion, believing that the sinner's fate was in the hands of God alone. They rejected revivals, missionary and tract societies, and church discipline in matters of drinking and personal vices. They especially resented educated missionaries who came to the mountains and moralized about how quaint and backward the Primitive Baptists were. By 1844 there were some 900 antimission preachers; 1,622 churches; and 68,000 members. For the next fifteen years a battle raged within southern folk religion, especially in the Piedmont and Mountain counties, which left permanent marks on the folk religion of the South.[2]

The years from the Civil War to the Second World War were difficult ones for most evangelicals in the South. Many rural churches combined middle class and poor in a fellowship of mutual acceptance. Congressman Brooks Hays, a former president of the SBC who lost his seat in the House of Representatives because of his courageous stand for racial moderation during the Little Rock desegregation crisis, described the democratic congregation of his boyhood in Russellville, Arkansas: "In Western Arkansas at the turn of the century, the typical congregation covered the whole spectrum of community life. There was an admirable reflection of it in the emphasis upon equality. My first Sunday School teacher was a blacksmith. Later I was instructed by a coal miner, whose gnarled hands symbolized for me the hardships of the period's life. There sat on the same pew with my parents the woman who did my mother's washing. 'Miss Helen,' mother called her. Her vote in church conference had the same weight as my mother's and father's, and her presence on that third pew with them remains for me an authentic symbol of Baptist democracy."[3]

In larger towns, however, internal class divisions became pronounced. "Uptown" churches catered to middle-class merchants and professionals and maintained little contact with their co-religionists in the mill town. Most industrial workers—such as miners or textile mill workers—if religious at all, were Methodists or Baptists. But then, so were their bosses. After 1900 urban churches developed greater interest in labor problems but neglected the plight of churches in the rural areas.

Since World War II, southern Evangelicals generally have enjoyed unprecedented prosperity, and most have moved into the middle class. Their support of the economic and social status quo is well known. Brooks Hays noted that his childhood Baptist church in Russellville, Arkansas, had moved to a more prominent corner and served a more prosperous constituency. A newer Baptist church, following less formal ways, now serves the town's poorer folk. Yet, the diversity that developed in the nineteenth century remains, primarily in the rural-urban dichotomy that is so basic to understanding modern American culture.

More than any denominations, southern Methodists and Baptists remained powerful among the poor white population in the rural South. Of the 35,000 Southern Baptist churches in 1977, 14,000 were rural and 4,000 more were in villages of less than 500 people. Many of the churches were small; 69.4 percent of all Southern Baptist churches enrolled less than 300 members in 1977.[4]

Obviously, southern evangelicals changed and diversified between 1800 and 1977. The perceptions of reality, class interests, and the proper function of religion differed greatly between evangelicals who were scratching out a subsistence life in the remote mountains of Appalachia and their brothers in Christ who taught at the University of North Carolina or owned banks in Birmingham. The differences still exist, even after the homogenizing effect of post-1945 affluence.

What Do Evangelicals Believe?

What do southern evangelicals believe? They constitute a "southern church" with a common ideology forged in the early years of the nineteenth century. Until 1800 theology in the South was as varied as in other American regions; but in the next three decades southern evangelicals developed remarkably similar patterns of thought, different in some ways from their European theological roots.

The initial element in this process was the second Great Awakening, which gained fame on the Kentucky frontier at Cane Ridge and spread rapidly. Sectarian differences were temporarily put aside for oneness of the spirit.

Despite the emotional extremes and social eccentricities of the revivals, (more souls were made than saved was the common charge), they produced a remarkably enduring set of characteristics. Rather than viewing the camp meetings as essentially a social event with a thin religious veneer, one should view them as the anvil upon which plain folk religion was forged. The common people who preached and exhorted without benefit of much education made folk religion democratic. The camp meeting songs, which were both rousing and easily sung, contained a coherent system of religious symbols important to frontier people. Appeal was to the heart more than to the head, and conversion was the dominant religious experience. The quest for personal holiness which followed conversion took an individualistic course; reform was inward and aimed at the individual, not outward and aimed at society. Theology was heavily laced with Calvinistic notions of the sinfulness of man and the need for repentance. Services were less liturgical, reliance on biblical authority more complete, the importance of good, popular preaching greater than was true among other American Protestants.[5] These elements became the essence of southern folk religion.

Some of these elements are so important as to demand elaboration. Democracy was both the chief strength and weakness of southern evangelicals. It kept them responsive to the common people, but it also enslaved their churches and institutions to the prejudices of the people. One conservative president of the Southern Baptist Convention (SBC) phrased it well: "Democracy, such as Southern Baptists have, is like a log raft. You cannot guide the thing very well; you wallow all over the place; and your feet are always wet—but you can never sink a log raft. If you keep trying, you eventually get to a destination."[6]

Equally important was individualism. The notion that each person was responsible for his spiritual welfare fitted perfectly into a society renowned for its independence. One southern woman caught the spirit of southern folk religion perfectly in a legendary dictum: "What I am, I am, and nobody can't make me no other."

The centrality of conversion is apparent in the hymnology, organizational structure, and priorities of southern evangelicals. Seldom in the history of Christianity have so few people produced so many home and foreign missionaries or devoted so much of their material wealth to convert others. Although southern evangelicals would cringe at the comparison, perhaps only the Jesuits brought such zeal to their tasks. This unity on the central religious issue is the force which held urban and rural, conservative, moderate, and liberal evangelicals together. They could slay each other with biblical quotations on race, evolution, the millennium, and women deacons, and then reunite on behalf of world evangelical outreach. This denominational loyalty, grounded in the imperative of evangelism, also made them cautious about the Fundamentalist Movement which historically insisted that loyalty to creed was more important than loyalty to denomination.[7] Although southern evangelicals generally adopted fundamentalist theological positions, they were not prominent in the Fundamentalist Movement until the 1920s. Even then the most caustic Fundamentalists spent more time attacking other southern evangelicals than anyone else and quickly lost influence in their own denominations. J. Frank Norris, the most famous Southern Baptist example, lost his influence in Texas and led his church out of the convention.

Although I would concede that emotion played a major role in southern folk religion, historians and sociologists have made too much of this. Not all practitioners of the religion of the head lived north of the Chesapeake, nor were all southern evangelicals empty-headed pew jumpers. Emotional religion earlier had found brilliant intellectual support in Jonathan Edwards and New England's New Light theologians. Conversely, Barton W. Stone, the father of the Cane Ridge revival of 1801 and himself a founder of the Disciples of Christ, regretted the emotional excesses of the great revivals. He argued his case in theology complicated and obtuse enough for even the most dogged systematizer.[8] In later years southern clergymen revised rational orthodox theology to serve the needs both of religious liberalism and conservatism.[9]

If emotion played a larger role for a longer time in southern folk religion than it did elsewhere, that is partly because the South remained a frontier longer than most sections, and as Richard Hofstadter brilliantly revealed some years ago, the frontier mind, whether religious or secular, tends to be anti-intellectual.

The South's preoccupation with original sin and guilt, in fact its altogether melancholy and pessimistic outlook on man, must be understood within the broader context of western man's post-Renaissance humanism. The rather grim medieval estimate of man gave way to an almost naive optimism about his potential by the time of the eighteenth-century Enlightenment. Within this cycle of views, the religious pessimism that dominated southern folk religion seemed strangely out of step with American theology before 1939. But it does not seem so quaint since the advent of Neo-Orthodox theology. With Reinhold Niebuhr's post-1940 writings, especially *The Nature and Destiny of Man* (1941), *The Children of Light and the Children of Darkness* (1944), and *The Irony of American History* (1952), sin ceased to be a dirty three-letter word. Even psychology and psychiatry are not of one mind anymore (witness Karl Menninger's *Whatever Became of Sin?*). What appeared as strangely regional theology before the 1940s has become at least acceptable, if not fashionable, perhaps yet another example of the southernization of America. Coupled with the rapid growth of fundamentalist religion in other regions since World War II, this exportation of southern evangelical thought demands far more attention than it has received.

What Functions Did Southern Evangelicalism Serve?

Focusing on the interaction of religious values and secular culture is only one way to examine the third question, the functions served by evangelical religion. Examining how evangelicals sought to reform social and political injustices usually ends in a serious indictment of southern religion. Coming at religion from a more internal perspective—how it contributed to the southerner's sense of self-worth, how it helped him make sense out of social reality, how it contributed to and helped maintain a sense of community—raises different questions and allows a more positive assessment.

The South's lack of originality in the classical art forms was balanced in part by its contributions to folk music, folk architecture, and folk art. I would add that the deficiencies of rational and systematic theology just catalogued should be weighed against the positive functions served by folk religion. Historian David Potter emphasized the fact that folk culture, with all its faults, provided a relatedness and meaning that urban industrial society was rapidly losing in the nineteenth century.[10] To be sure, ties of kinship and family are important in folk culture; as the saying goes, given time any two southerners can establish kinship. But evangelical religion was the cement that held southerners together despite the vagaries of time and history. Modern Americans are still wrestling with the question of how best to achieve a sense of belonging; but no one living in the age of the Peoples Temple, Moonies, Jesus Freaks, and a thousand communes and cults can seriously challenge the importance of a sense of community.

The conventional view of the southern church is that its overriding concern for personal conversion made evangelicalism so individualistic that it had neither time nor interest for the community. True, up to a point. But equally important was its insistence on bringing the individual into intimate relationship with other people. A central function of the Great Revival between 1800 and 1815 was to substitute the order and discipline of Christian society for the disordered frontier world of violence and irresponsibility. Evangelicals rejected the emotional sterility and intellectual coldness of rational religion for a folk religion that emphasized social intimacy and mutual respect (offering the right hand of fellowship, love feasts, dinners on the ground, identifying terms such as "brother" and "sister," praying with arms around each other, greeting other Christians with a kiss, foot washing). Even church discipline had at its core the desire to help restore the chastised to a harmonious relationship with the Christian community.[11]

The organization into very small religious groups provided a tremendous source of strength in the face of trouble, and of troubles there seemed no end. An unhurried stroll through any nineteenth century graveyard impresses one with the mortality of man. A thousand inscriptions proclaim that "as for man, his life is like grass; he grows and flourishes like a wild flower. Then the wind blows on it, and it is gone, and no one sees it again":

> Theresa Scott
> Darling Daughter of Theodore and Effie Scott
> Born August 10, 1845–Died January 15, 1847
>
> David Jessup
> Born July 12, 1872–Died March 10, 1877

Add to the ephemerality of life, its drudgery, monotony, exhaustion, and for many its poverty, and one has described the life experience of most nineteenth-century southern evangelicals. Their goals and hopes were seldom realized. They had less than their fair share of money and power. So, conventional wisdom informs us, they retreated into an otherworldly, escapist religion. W. J. Cash, describing the "Years the Cuckoo Claimed," 1914 to 1930, chronicled the rise of emotional religion, of traveling evangelists and faith healers. He wrote, "Beset with difficulties beyond his control and comprehension, increasingly taken in his vanity, puzzled, angered, frightened, the common white tended, like his fathers before him in the early days of the nineteenth century and in the Reconstruction time, to retreat into otherworldliness and, in the solace and the hope he found there, to resign himself to his lot in this world as of no more moment than a passing shadow cast in the sun by a cloud."[12]

In recent years both Jewish and Christian scholars have attempted to make biblical sense out of "the reality we live in." Historically, a major function of both religions has been to help people understand social reality. In Europe the sense of being a people depended heavily on religious identification. When the immigrants came to America, their religion was the cement that bound ethnic communities together.[13]

In much the same way, their brand of evangelicalism provided the ethnic southerner a coherent view of his place in the world. A major theme of camp meeting hymns was the assurance of salvation, in contrast to preaching and exhorting that emphasized man's lostness. Conversion, the central theme of evangelicals, brought a new world view. Anticipation of the glories of heaven replaced the hopelessness of the present world. This "canaan language" provided a bond of fellowship between black and white evangelicals. Many common people of both races, for quite different reasons, viewed existing conditions as intolerable and hoped for a different world to be created by divine intervention.[14] Such religion can be called otherworldly and escapist; indeed, that is the way in which most scholars view it.

I prefer psychiatrist Robert Coles's view that religion, at least for the rural poor, is an inescapable part of human meaning; in that sense, it is never wholly escapist.[15] A sociological survey of white Tennessee tenant farmers during the late 1930s documented Coles's point. In times of trouble, tenants found a resource: "If He had not stood by me, I would not have lived through the trouble I have had." Asked what difference it would make in their lives if they became convinced that no loving God cared for them, one tenant replied: "I'd feel like I was lost." Another responded: "Wouldn't have any encouragement then sure enough. Would just end it up sometime."[16]

That southern evangelicals left many tasks undone, I would not debate. But in the rush to discover what was wanting, one must not ignore the functions evangelicalism served: the affirmation of personal worth, the ordering of a chaotic world, providing an explanation of social reality, and creation of a sense of community.

What Was the Relationship of Southern Evangelicalism to Southern Culture?

No subject demonstrates better the problems of understanding southern evangelicals than their relationship to culture. It is axiomatic among intellectuals that religion is the servant of culture. One study of Southern Baptist social thought (incidentally, a study considered to be revisionist by church historians because the author actually discovered some Baptist social thought) was entitled *Churches in Cultural Captivity*.

The inability of southern religion to escape the confining pressures of culture is, of course, not unique to Southern Baptists or even southern evangelicals. Witness, for instance, the bitter divisions among Northern Baptists during the 1920s over evolution or more recently between liberal and conservative wings of the Missouri Synod Lutheran Church. Advocates of change always accuse their brothers of being culture bound. Yet, one has to admit the basic thesis of W. J.

Cash, Sam Hill, Martin Marty, H. Shelton Smith, and many others, that southern evangelicals have been more faithful to southern culture than they have been to the radical ethics of Christ.

This thesis becomes increasingly difficult to understand when one examines it within the context of cultural pluralism. Assuming that white Baptists in Jefferson County, Alabama, are the servants of culture, which subcultures are served by Church of the Covenant, Berney Points, Vestavia Hills, Mountain Brook, Beverly, and Powderly Baptist Churches? These churches obviously appeal to quite different classes, espouse different theologies, and serve different social needs. Some of them serve aspiring lower-middle-class families who resent any threat to their mobility. Others represent upper-middle-class people who "have arrived," who oppose social change, belong to the chamber of commerce and voted for Republican James Martin for the US Senate. Still others serve blue-collar people who hold tenaciously to fundamental theology while belonging to labor unions and voting for Democrat Donald Stewart for the Senate. One of these churches caters to well-educated, politically liberal people who prefer a religious climate of openness and questioning. All these are legitimate human needs that religion helps meet. Jimmy Carter's election demonstrated to many Americans the diversity and sophistication of evangelicals. Church historian Martin Marty has said that Carter's election did as much to bring Southern Baptists into the mainstream of American Protestantism as John Kennedy's election in 1960 did for Catholics.

Southern evangelicalism always has served several subcultures. Perhaps it has not served as many as religion in other regions, hence its appearance of homogeneity; but its social thought has always been more diverse than most church historians have realized.

The long-recognized barriers to political action—excessive individualism, otherworldliness, fear of secular corruption, the view that politics and the exercise of political power is inherently evil—did not keep southern evangelicals from active involvement in politics. They never adopted the repudiationist stance that called for the Christian to reject the secular world. The royal governor of North Carolina in the 1770s blamed rebellious Separate Baptists for the Regulator Movement. To the north, in Culpepper County, Virginia, Anglican officials arrested Baptist preacher James Ireland for preaching his "vile, pernicious, abhorrent, detestable, abominable, diabolical doctrines." It is no surprise, then, to discover that southern evangelicals constituted the core of support for the American Revolution in the otherwise Tory South. As a consequence of their political involvements, they emerged from the war with enhanced respect and considerable support among the South's common folk.[17] In the years that followed the Revolution, evangelicals played a major role in the establishment of religious freedom in state constitutions, the growth of education and temperance reforms, and the defense of slavery, perhaps the preeminent political issue of the times.[18]

Such involvements have been acknowledged, but they constitute only a small portion of the story. I want to emphasize two more crucial areas of interaction between southern white evangelicals and their culture, both having to do with the quality of rural and urban life.

One key to understanding the evangelical's reaction to his culture is bivocationalism. Many ordained evangelical ministers did not earn their livelihood preaching. They worked full- or part-time secular jobs and preached in addition to that. In 1976, for instance, 27 percent of all Southern Baptist churches were pastored by men employed in secular jobs. In churches of less than 300 members, 51 percent of the pastors were bivocational. Among music ministers serving the 35,000 Southern Baptist churches in 1978, 24,000 were part-time or voluntary workers, earning their livelihood elsewhere.[19] Bivocational ministers quite literally lived in two worlds, including a secular one that subjected them to the same frustrations, exploitations, and insecurity as their parishioners.

Perhaps the most obvious example of bivocationalism occurred in the rural South where it greatly influenced the way in which rural ministers viewed society. Presumably no more conservative American ever lived than the individualistic, rural, southern evangelical. What always puzzled me about that assumption was that counties that were made up of precisely this kind of person staged the Populist revolt of the nineteenth century. Most of those who have tried to explain this contradiction have examined the wrong evidence. If he surveys the state denominational newspapers, for instance, he does not learn what all evangelicals thought about Populists. Instead, he learns what Baptist or Methodist entrepreneurs who usually ran privately owned, run-for-profit newspapers thought. If he examines state or conference religious minutes and annual reports, he learns what the best educated pastors of the most prominent and wealthy churches thought.[20] Based on such evidence, he might think that only rural atheists voted the Populist ticket.

Let me balance this elitist approach to evangelicals by suggesting what was happening among Alabama's common folk at the fork of the creek in the 1890s. Many evangelical farmer-pastors concluded that the only economic salvation for themselves and their parishioners was some form of government help. Since ministers possessed both community respect and oratorical skills, they became the natural leaders of the Populist cause. In Alabama, Baptist pastor Samuel M. Adams served as president of the state Farmers' Alliance, as head of the Populist Party, and was elected to a term in the state legislature. A conservative newspaper reporter heard the Baptist preacher address a farmer's institute in 1891 and commented, "Mr. Adams is an easy and fluent speaker, but if he had stuck to his text we think it would have been more in accord of our idea of a Farmer's Institute. He is so full of politics that it was a hard matter for him to keep in the road."[21]

When chastised by fellow ministers for his political forays, Adams replied that "many of our brethren do not understand the true condition of the country" or they would be more concerned with the economic injustice in America.[22] Adams was closer to the feelings of the evangelical small farmer in the state than the editor of the state's Baptist paper. The editor of *The Alabama Baptist* had little sympathy for Populists and worried constantly about reports of unrest in the churches. Many Baptist pastors had "gone wild over politics." Laymen were so engrossed over secular issues that "they talked politics during Sunday School and outside the church, not coming into worship until after the prayer and Scripture reading." So bitter had the 1892 elections been that the editor of *The Alabama Baptist* warned that churches had been disturbed and "Christ's work neglected at many points." A country preacher wrote that his members became absorbed in politics, bad feelings were engendered, and a general coldness prevailed. The pastor of a church in rural eastern Alabama complained that his parishioners had more politics than religion. The pastor of Shiloh Church in Pike County wrote in 1893 that the political strife of the previous year had been a greater curse to the churches than even "the whiskey traffic."[23] Baptist leaders, trying to explain why an unprecedented number of their pastors were running for public office, noted that many of them were impoverished farmers.[24] Obviously something was amiss in the rural Zion.

The quality of rural life improved only marginally after the turn of the century. By 1916 half the rural churches in America were in the South and within those churches bivocational ministers labored. Many of them pastored more than one church; some of them pastored as many as four or five. Many of these marginal churches had no educational program and no organizations for women or children. Of the total 44,300 white Baptist and Methodist churches in the South in 1916, 82 percent were rural; and of those, 90 percent had preaching only once a month. Some 80 percent of these rural churches were served by absentee pastors. Of 3,430 Presbyterian churches in the South in 1913, 271 had no pastors.[25] Nor did conditions improve markedly until after World War II. As late as 1947 there were still 1,946 Baptist churches in Alabama that met irregularly and 1,600 Baptist churches that relied on bivocational preachers.

Statistics do not capture the depth of deprivation of many southern evangelicals. In the mountains of southwestern Virginia in 1915 one untrained Baptist minister pastored two churches for a year. He spent three weeks in revivals and earned a total salary of $13.20. With his family, he lived in a two-room cabin on thirty acres of rented land. He worked for a neighbor part-time in exchange for a horse to plow his corn field. On alternate Sundays he walked to his churches, one of which was six miles away, the other was five miles. In the same region another pastor worked at a grist mill all week and earned an annual salary from his churches of less than $30.[26] Dr. J. W. Lester, Alabama's rural minister of the year in 1949, began preaching full-time in 1932 in four rural churches near

Alexander City. Eagle Creek Baptist Church paid him $36.47 for the year; the salary at Rockie Creek was $33.00; New Salem paid him nothing; and Elam paid $215.66; a total of $285.23 for the year.[27]

Such conditions spawned two reactions. First, some denominational leaders developed greater interest in the quality of rural life.[28] Denominational colleges began to offer courses in rural sociology. The 1913 meeting of the Southern Baptist Home Mission Board created a special rural ministry called the Department of Enlistment (the title is important; when Evangelicals tried to reform society it was imperative that it be done in the name of evangelical outreach). This agency employed fifteen ministers to work with rural Baptist associations to try to reduce farm tenancy, improve the quality of home and farm life for rural southern women, reform farming practices, encourage the formation of rural organizations that would reduce the isolation, soften the individualism, and stimulate the social lives of rural people. Dr. Lester, one of the missionaries appointed under the new program, not only preached on original sin; other sermon titles included "The Relationship of Wise Land Use to the Churches, the Schools, the Homes, and Other Social Agencies," "And He Will Heal Their Land" (the damaging consequences of soil erosion), and "The Rural Church Faces the Future." He studied rural sociology, ultimately becoming so expert that he was asked to lecture at Baptist seminaries and at Auburn University. He showed films in his churches on sanitary methods of milking cows. After he retired from his rural pastorate in Alabama, he became head of the Rural Church Department at Clear Creek Baptist School in the mountains of eastern Kentucky where the average preacher-student was age 30 and had a ninth-grade education. He assigned them books on rural sociology including Arthur Raper's 1936 indictment of farm tenancy *Preface to Peasantry*. While he taught the men, his wife traveled the remote hollows of Appalachia teaching six hundred mountain women the Laubach literacy program so that they could spread education among isolated and poverty-stricken mountain people.

The Methodist Bureau of Christian Social Relations began studying problems of the rural South as early as 1912. In 1930 the Woman's Missionary Council created the Committee on Rural Development, which proposed an extensive program of community reforms to improve rural life in general and especially the plight of rural women.

A second reaction to rural blight was more in the Populist tradition. Particularly among angry evangelicals in the Southwest, socialism thrived between 1910 and 1924. Socialist-minded evangelical ministers used camp meeting strategies and the religious idiom to transform secular socialism into a transcendent faith in universal brotherhood and economic justice. Clinging all the while to their individualistic culture traditions, they fought tenaciously against the domination of capitalistic large scale agriculture, urban values, and wealthy town churches.[29]

To say that southern evangelicals ignored the problems of rural America is not accurate, although they awakened to those problems more slowly than evangelicals in other regions.

Interest in urban problems increased slowly among a people so overwhelmingly rural. Most Methodists and Baptists at the turn of the century feared the city and believed it corrupted morals and loosened family ties. One Baptist leader captured the spirit of most evangelicals when he wrote, "Men, like hogs, are bred in the country to be consumed in the towns."[30]

Among people directly affected by urbanization, attitudes began to change rapidly after 1900. Two dissimilar groups of evangelicals contributed to urban reform. On one hand, there were denominational leaders well educated in national currents of thought. Many of them were influenced by the social Christianity becoming fashionable in the urban North and Midwest. The other group consisted of working-class preachers, themselves coal miners or textile mill workers, who carried their class interests into the pulpit.

For decades historians denied the existence of the Social Gospel in the South, but recent research has demonstrated that scholars, like evangelicals, do make mistakes.[31] As workers deserted the church because they believed it cared nothing for their problems, sensitive clerics in increasing numbers advocated change. Temperance was the preeminent reform of the era, and it was usually viewed as a matter of social and not private morality. Because Prohibition demanded that evangelicals enter politics, it produced a generation of shrewd, effective church lobbyists. Once involved in the political process, many evangelicals enlarged their reform agenda.

The changes they proposed addressed almost all the major urban-industrial problems of the day. In Birmingham, for example, Dr. Henry M. Edmonds led the congregation of Independent Presbyterian Church into a broad Social Gospel program. His church, the result of a split within more fundamentalist South Highland Presbyterian Church, helped organize the Jefferson County Children's Aid Society, hired a female member of the church staff to assist the jobless, a nurse to aid the poor, and a social worker for the Northside Community House; the church also constructed the Children's Fresh Air Farm, which provided summertime nourishment and recreation for 8,000 poor white children between 1920 and 1950.

Women in the Methodist Episcopal Church, South, began a settlement house ministry in 1893. Situated in working-class neighborhoods, the Wesley and Bethlehem Houses provided day schools where working women could leave children, night literacy programs for working boys, and free kindergartens. Such a house was opened in Birmingham in June 1903. So successful was the initial effort that additional houses were built behind Avondale mills and for Italian steelworkers at Ensley.

Methodists in Mobile began an even more ambitious program in 1904. By 1910 Mobile's Wesley House was called "the best all around social agency in the city." In addition to the services provided by the Birmingham settlement houses, the Mobile facility operated a free medical dispensary that took care of sick indigents without charge. In 1910 a staff of five doctors performed surgery at the house with scaled charges based on income.[32] By 1920 there were at least forty-four such Methodist settlement houses serving both races in the urban South.[33]

Baptists had more difficulty institutionalizing their social concerns. The editor of Alabama's denominational newspaper from 1901 until 1919 was Frank W. Barnett. Although a theological conservative, he edited a reform newspaper that treated nearly every social question of the time. On labor conditions in Birmingham, he wrote: "Churches have frequently shut their eyes to the struggles of labor to get a minimum wage; and have not heard the cry of the children who were being sacrificed in our mills; or cared when a fight was being made for shorter hours and better working conditions." Next to temperance, the issue that he addressed most frequently during these years was child labor. He urged Baptists to write their legislative representatives and to join the Alabama Child Labor Committee; by such policies, he organized a powerful lobby. When the legislature postponed reform in 1907, he thundered, "Who keeps a lobby, day in and day out, watching these bills? Who appears at hearings, trying to have them defeated or amended in such a way that they fail? . . . The attorney of cotton manufacturers, of glass manufacturers, the paid representatives of the oppressors are there, but who represents you and me in our earnest desire to see justice done to the children?" When his plea fell on deaf ears, he wrote: "Let us call [child labor] by its right name—murder. But if the death comes quickly enough, it is less cruel than the life to which such boys and girls are condemned." Largely due to his efforts, the second session of the 1907 Alabama legislature passed a child labor bill that was called the "most effective child labor law that has thus far been enacted in the South."[34]

Middle-class reformers risked very little with such proposals because they were also endorsed by progressive businessmen, teachers, lawyers, and even some southern politicians. On more "radical" questions such as collective bargaining, strikes, and socialism, Evangelicals were generally cautious. Many mill and mine owners were influential laymen who used religion as a method of social control. Liston Pope, in his classic study *Millhands and Preachers*, quoted an obituary from the *Gastonia Gazette* (North Carolina) describing a deceased mill worker: "He served his church and pastor well, and was a bulwark of safe conservatism and orthodox religion in all the church courts."[35] Such wealthy parishioners donated land for churches, paid for buildings, and subsidized ministers' salaries. Denominational leaders, in turn, were properly deferential, praised the civic mindedness of pious laymen, and opposed strikes.[36]

As in the Populist movement, however, the bivocational minister who labored in mine or mill often approached these problems quite differently. During a particularly violent 1914 strike in the West Virginia coal fields, miners held a meeting in Wellsburg. The mixture of native-born white people and immigrant miners from Italy and eastern Europe applauded incendiary speeches denouncing capitalism. *The Wheeling Majority* (West Virginia) ended its account of the rally with a matter-of-fact sentence: "After Mr. Levinski [a national organizer for the U.M.W.] had spoken in their own language to the Slavish and Polish, the audience was requested to turn out in a body that night and attend the revival service at the Tabernacle now being conducted in Wellsburg."

Six years later, in 1920, miners struck the Red Jacket Coal Company in Mingo County, West Virginia. In May of that year 500 miners held a rally in Matewan, West Virginia. A preacher named Combs "made a radical talk" denouncing the company. Urging miners to refuse to sign contracts with the company, Combs said that any miner who signed it was "not as good as a yellow dog." Any superintendent who would ask a fellow human to sign such an agreement "carried a gizzard around in a heart's place."

When West Virginia's labor dispute degenerated into a bloody war in 1922, the man who led the miners was Rev. John Wilburn, who had pastored the Baptist Church in Blair, West Virginia, since 1915. To supplement his preacher's salary he mined coal side by side with his parishioners. An organizational genius who did not confine his talent to the Sunday school, Wilburn established armed patrols that gained control of Blair Mountain and the passes leading to it. At one briefing he harangued his troops, suggesting that they lay siege to the town of Logan and that they take no prisoners. Intercepted on the march to Logan by sheriff's deputies, the miners fought a pitched battle that resulted in deaths on both sides. Before the affair ended, the US Army was sent to the area and the air force conducted a bombing raid on Blair Mountain to dislodge the parson and his troops. John Wilburn was tried for treason and other charges and convicted of murder but later pardoned.[37]

Such events were not as rare as the scarcity of written records indicate. Oral histories are only now giving such poorly educated evangelicals a voice, and what we are hearing does not coincide with long-accepted stereotypes. One Baptist minister in Greensboro, North Carolina, left a powerful narrative of the 1930s. He had entered the textile mill to work at age 15 and had progressed well before "surrendering" to the call to preach. He praised the company for its support of churches and preachers' salaries (his church paid a generous salary of $2,060 a year). When the workers organized in the 1920s and went on strike, he tried not to take sides ("our work not bein' mill work but the salvation of souls"). But as parishioners came to him to express their grievances, he began to change his mind, finally concluding that southern textile workers ought to organize. He looked to

Washington for help, and his congregation sent him to Franklin D. Roosevelt's 1933 inauguration. He reported his impressions to the church when he returned: "But as I stood there in that vast throng watchin' Hoover go out and Mr. and Mrs. Roosevelt come in, I felt like weepin'. I thought, one man of big promise goes out and another comes in, and like always the people go on in need. When the people is helped, it'll be when they've waked up to their rights."[38] Even if such memories are flawed by time and are sometimes self-serving, they do suggest another dimension of the southern evangelical mind.

Who were the mainstream southern evangelicals? A mixture of rural farmers and urban workers and businessmen, rich and poor. What did they believe? Essentially they were individualistic and felt more comfortable with a religion that consoled the heart than with one that troubled the mind. The function of their religion? To help them understand the world they lived in, to comfort them in times of trouble, to provide a sense of personal worth. Southern evangelicalism's relation to culture? Diverse, depending on class and time and needs. Whatever the southern mind was, we will never comprehend it until we understand southern religion.

—*Varieties of Southern Evangelicalism*, 1981

In 1986, nearly a decade after I began to subject my research to larger questions, the Alabama Humanities Foundation sponsored a conference on Religion in the South where I shared the podium with Donald Mathews and Sam Hill. By then I had made another friend who substantially expanded my education.

Anne Firor Scott, of Duke University, was one of the feistiest, toughest, and brightest historians I ever met. We became fast friends in 1979 when I invited her to deliver the Ralph Draughon Lecture at Auburn University. She had already written the first in a trilogy of illuminating books, The Southern Lady: From Pedestal to Politics *(1970).* Making the Invisible Woman Visible *(1984), and* Unheard Voices: The First Historians of Southern Women *(1993) followed thereafter. She was to southern women's history what Sam Hill was to southern religious history, one of its original pioneers and most perceptive interpreters. To complete the comparison, the two burgeoning fields exploded simultaneously in the 1960s and 1970s.*

Scott taught me to ask a new set of questions. How do women both privatize and socialize religion? How does private spirituality liberate women at the same time that cultural religion often shackles them? How do women utilize stealth strategies of compromise and even submission to infiltrate and overcome male hegemony over religious institutions? Are these really stealth strategies, or is the "Sambo thesis" of submission applicable to women as well: following thousands of years of biblically based submission, did many Christian women become like the stereotypes that many male ministers proclaimed? Did Christian women's work so widely applauded by male evangelicals ultimately undermine their traditional authority? How did such efforts interface with the woman suffrage movement? Was it easier for the "new woman" to break through boundaries of gender in spheres such as religion, which men generally conceded as appropriate for Victorian women, rather than areas such as business, commerce, or politics, which men believed inappropriate? Because earlier essays in this anthology have dealt extensively with Methodist and Presbyterian women, I edited this published essay to focus on Baptist women.

This was my initial foray into women's history. As with my initial exploration of evangelical history, it was incomplete and flawed. It also expressed my own profound disillusion with the fundamentalist (or, as they prefer to call it, "conservative") takeover (or, as they prefer to call it, "correction") of the Southern Baptist Convention (SBC) beginning in 1979. As much because of the SBC's demeaning theology of women as because of my opposition to fundamentalist SBC theology, I agreed to election by my church as "messenger" to numerous SBC national conventions during the 1980s. I voted each year against resolutions to end all abortions whatever a woman's circumstances and against resolutions denying women ministerial ordination (because, according to the majority of the brothers and sisters, they were first in the Edenic fall). For decades after that 1984 SBC meeting, I kept on my office wall the cleverest cartoon I ever read. A Greenville, South Carolina, newspaper depicted an Appalachian woman busy at her quilting frame, cat perched on a chair while listening to an old-fashioned radio quoting the resolution. The caption contained her commentary delivered to the cat: "Now that's what I call holding a grudge."

After a decade of such silliness, I conceded defeat and agreed that my friends John Boles and Sam Hill had been partly correct. The dominant direction of white southern evangelicalism had been opposed both to social justice and modernity. And I had personally been on the losing side of twentieth-century religious wars. Yet, embedded in that demeaning 1984 SBC resolution about women was one fact supporting my arguments: 42 percent of the white evangelical messengers like me had voted against it.

Chapter 10
Women, Society, and the Southern Church, 1900–1920

The month of June 1984 was a busy one for the Kansas City convention center. Early in the month the Women's World Exposition focused on the expanded role of women in American society. In late June the American Society of Medical Technology discussed the dizzying pace at which new techniques and machinery were transforming health care and creating problems in medical ethics. Sandwiched between these two meetings was the 127th SBC. Among other actions, Baptist messengers to the convention formally resolved their opposition to abortion for any reason other than to save the life of the mother and received resolutions opposing Planned Parenthood, in vitro fertilization and artificial insemination, genetic engineering, and endorsing scientific creationism. But the messengers reserved their sharpest words for women. Resolution Three precipitated one of the sharpest reactions in the history of the convention:

> Whereas, The Scriptures attest to God's delegated order of authority (God the head of Christ, Christ the head of man, man the head of woman, man and woman dependent one upon the other to the glory of God) distinguishing the roles of men and women in public prayer and prophesy (I Cor. 11:2–5); and
>
> Whereas, The Scriptures teach that women are not in public worship to assume a role of authority over men lest confusion reign in the local church (I Cor. 14:33–36); and
>
> Whereas, while Paul commends women and men alike in other roles of ministry and service (Titus 2:1–10), he excludes women from pastoral leader-

> ship (I Tim. 2:12) to preserve a submission, God requires because the man was first in creation and the woman was first in the Edenic fall (I Tim. 2:13 ff); . . . .
> Therefore, be it Resolved, That we do not decide concerns of Christian doctrine and practice by modern, cultural, sociological, and ecclesiastical trends or by emotional factors; . . . and that we encourage the service of women in all aspects of church life and work other than pastoral functions and leadership roles entailing ordination.[1]

Of course the Scriptures were not so exclusive a source, nor were "modern cultural, sociological, and ecclesiastical trends" so entirely absent from the proceedings as Baptist conservatives implied by their resolution. The Bible did not mandate that the Resolutions Committee would contain eight men plus a male chairman. And the convention immediately preceding the SBC in Kansas City was the National Right to Life Committee whose 1,000 delegates heard a videotaped address by President Ronald Reagan and the Rev. Jerry Falwell of Moral Majority. To many Americans in 1984 preserving the stability of the American family required the inequality of the sexes. That was the sociological climate in which the SBC met in Kansas City.

Public reaction to the 1984 SBC demonstrates more than just misunderstanding of contemporary Southern Baptist life. It reflects a misreading of mainstream southern Protestantism as well.

The virulence and stridency of Fundamentalist Southern Baptists reflect their anger at what they believe to have been moderate and liberal control of the denomination and its institutions. They believe that most "grassroots Baptists" share their contempt for faculties of the six denominational seminaries and personnel of most SBC agencies. From their vantage point, the 1984 convention was historic because it was "a turning point in the SBC's return to its Biblical roots and heritage."[2]

The convention certainly demonstrated how deep is the fissure within America's largest Protestant denomination. On the question of adopting Resolution Three, which opposed the ordination of women, 4,793 messengers (58.03 percent) voted yes and 3,466 (41.97 percent) voted no.

Had there been no overt social challenge to the Baptist messengers, perhaps the women's issue would have passed without notice at all or as no more than a codicil to Resolution 10 that denounced godless Secular Humanism. But the denomination contained an increasing number of female seminarians and Baptist churches that ordained women as ministers and deacons, and such insidious liberalism demanded action. As if to confirm the crisis, another meeting occurred at Kansas City two days before the SBC began. Women in Ministry, SBC held its second annual meeting at the Radisson-Muehlback Hotel. Membership had doubled since its first meeting at Pittsburgh in 1983. It produced a newsletter and received substantial support from the Woman's Missionary Union, which allowed the group use of its reserved space in the headquarters' hotel. In their small group meetings the women shared experiences of rejection. One doctoral student at Southern Baptist Theological Seminary, the daughter of a Baptist pastor, recounted preaching in churches where the pulpit had been removed to keep a woman preacher from desecrating it. Another remembered her "call" to the ministry while hanging out wash thirty-six years earlier, but thought the message must be meant for her husband. She gradually changed her mind, and after years of perseverance, became pastor of a small rural Alabama Baptist church. Addresses by Lynda Weaver-Williams, co-pastor of Goshen Baptist Church in Goshen, Kentucky; Debra Graffis-Woodberry, associate pastor of Ridge Road Baptist Church, Raleigh, North Carolina; and Elizabeth Barnes, a PhD candidate in Theology at Duke University, described a "new womanhood" humbled by suffering, a "gentler more tolerant people" more likely to reduce the war, violence, and poverty so widespread in modern societies. The Baptist women denied that they were radicals, but admitted they were firmly resolved. As Weaver-Williams observed, "There are many out there who oppose us. Some are men who think we want too much and some are women who think we don't want enough"; "part of our faith is to wait and not to be negligent"; "God doesn't ask us to be successful but he does ask us to be faithful." It was to counter such pressure from within the denomination that 58 percent of SBC messengers in 1984 sought to restrict the rights of Baptist women.

Such conflict has been a constant element of the southern church, usually ignored by popular journalists and as frequently underestimated by historians. The attitude of southern Protestants has been stereotyped as otherworldly; if they did not reject secular society altogether, they certainly lived in constant tension with it. As early as 1805 the minutes of the Elkhorn Baptist Association in Kentucky recorded a query from Glens Creek asking "Is it right for Baptists to join in and assemble at barbeques on the 4th of July? Answered No."[3]

Historians have recently discovered a much more complex southern religion, one divided along class, social, racial, and sexual lines. Because the complexity is far too great for a discussion of all the social issues encountered by even one denomination in the first years of this century, I will focus on only one. Southern churches obviously did not first encounter the shifting role of women in 1984. Nor did they confront the issue alone. Women's pressure for change, the scriptural proof texts used by both sides, and conservative reaction characterized the battle that raged between 1900 and 1920. It left indelible marks on all southern evangelicals.

Southern churches historically had not sought to expand the horizons of women. Conversion provided them some measure of psychological and social freedom both from the constraints of culture and from their often more worldly husbands. In the nineteenth century, when American society generally recognized the authority of the husband over his spouse, southern women used their Christian discipleship to set certain limits on a man's authority. He must not restrict her worship or Christian conscience. Women were allowed to testify freely against men in ecclesiastical trials and the church brought women together in a public body. Within congregations women organized their own prayer groups and missionary societies. Within these they not only established warm social relationships with other women but also refined leadership skills as officers, parliamentarians, and lobbyists for their special causes. They developed skills that were later employed on behalf of woman suffrage and other social reforms.[4] Long before women were allowed in most professions, southern denominations allowed single women to follow their calling as missionaries. Some southern women even became role models because of their faithfulness in pioneering new mission work. The most obvious was the legendary Charlotte Diggers "Lottie" Moon. A native Virginian and graduate of Virginia Female Seminary (Hollins College), she taught school briefly before volunteering as a missionary. The Southern Baptist Foreign Mission Board appointed her as a missionary to China in 1873, where she ministered for nearly 40 years. Within the denomination, Moon became the quintessential missionary whose life often slipped across the boundary of biography into mythology.

Because of the less centralized ecclesiastical organization of Southern Baptists, the role of women in the denomination was more complicated than for the Methodist and Presbyterian women. Separate Baptist congregations in the Colonial South ordained deaconesses and at least some women preached, though probably without formal ordination. Baptist women formed mission societies in South Carolina as early as 1811. But Separate Baptist union with the more traditional Regular Baptists and a change in the philosophy of the deaconate from an office primarily devoted to ministry to one more concerned with budget and business management limited female opportunities. Beginning in 1872 the SBC included a report on "Woman's Work" at the annual convention, although a man always presented the report. In 1876 Baptist women in South Carolina formed the first Central Committee of Baptist Women, primarily as a way of raising money for missions. In 1882 the SBC authorized appointment of a woman as Superintendent of the State Central Committees. The woman would be salaried and would coordinate women's efforts within the denomination. But the Foreign Mission Board was too timid to appoint women to such positions, so delegates from several state Central Committees met in 1888 in Richmond and formed the Woman's Missionary Union (WMU) as an auxiliary of the SBC. Although not officially a part of the convention nor subject to its supervision, the WMU has cooperated with the SBC and has been its primary support agency for foreign missions. In fact the Home Mission Board, jealous of the affection women heaped upon the Foreign Board, often pled for equal treatment. In 1891 the Ladies Society of First Baptist Church of Dallas listened politely to the director of home mission work in Texas.[5] Immediately after his plea for home missions, the women voted to send every penny in their treasury to foreign missions. Independent control of their treasury, a freedom not enjoyed by Presbyterian women, gave them power that male SBC officials could not ignore. Women's Missionary societies, organized under the direction of all female WMU leadership, spread quickly. By 1911 SBC churches contained more than 10,000 societies and contributed annually nearly 240,000 dollars for missions.[6] More daring women even challenged Pauline doctrine restricting the pulpit to men. In a celebrated 1891 incident, Atlanta's First Baptist Church (pastored in the 1980s by SBC President Charles Stanley who allied with the Fundamentalist, anti-feminist wing of the denomination) split over an invitation to evangelist Mattie Gordon to preach there. The church's young people urged that she be invited but their elders rejected the woman preacher.[7]

Like their Presbyterian and Methodist counterparts, most Southern Baptist men viewed such tendencies with alarm. In official resolutions, editorials in denominational papers, and books and pamphlets, they made clear their opposition to more public roles for women. Among their targets were coeducation, ordination of women, women speaking to mixed assemblies, and woman suffrage. Changes in Baptist attitudes toward women between 1900 and 1920 appear modest compared with current attitudes. But these changes occurred within the context of late nineteenth-century Victorian social values. To understand the iconoclasm of the changes, one must comprehend the conservative nature of the society in which they took place. In 1868 one Southern Baptist editor rejected female education because he believed that woman's minds, like their bodies, had less strength than men's; by way of compensation, he emphasized that their minds, like their bodies, had more beauty and symmetry. Six years later, in 1874, a writer for the *Religious Herald* denied both the intellectual and spiritual equality of women because Eve, not Adam, was deceived by the serpent. Referring to woman as "man's chief ornament," he believed she was incapable of producing any great literature, inventions, or legislation. J. R. Graves, conservative Tennessee Baptist editor and a founder of the Fundamentalist Landmark Movement, was ambivalent. As a strict Biblical constructionist, he accepted women deacons on the authority both of Scripture and Baptist history. But he also cited Paul's prohibition against women as public speakers or preachers both of which were "contrary to her womanly nature and at variance with the law of God."[8]

Nor were such attitudes confined to a populistic, poorly educated fringe of the denomination. Most well-educated denominational leaders held views only slightly more moderate. Dr. Lansing Burrows, a graduate of Wake Forest and Princeton universities, occupied some of the most prestigious pulpits in the denomination, including the First Baptist Churches of Lexington, Kentucky; Augusta, Georgia; and Nashville, Tennessee. From 1881 until 1913 he was the Recording Secretary for the SBC and later served three terms between 1914 and 1916 as president of the SBC. Among his sermons is a series preached in 1872 on "Woman's Position in the Church." In ten consecutive Sunday night sermons, he reviewed the Biblical history of women concluding that in spiritual matters she stood on an equal basis with men; but in temporal matters such as ordination or public speaking and teaching, women should not "usurp" man's role. Public life would strip away her modesty through which she exercised her greatest influence: "Let her lose her modesty lo! she has lost her power; her pressing forward into the mad throng, her mingling with the boisterous, struggling creation of busy men, her grasping the guiding reins of a fickle and passionate public, makes her the crushed toy of the cruel world. The ship dashing wildly without compass has more hope of the unseen harbor than the woman casting herself upon the turbulent water of public opinion. But let her wield her powers in that sphere in which God's Scripture places her, and lo! she becomes that mysterious magnetic power which draws the needle of the compass to the unerring poles of duty, right, and honor." Her proper sphere was the home and the education of youth: "Disdain not this humble ministry, my sisters; it is God's plan; it answers your own cravings; it is endorsed by your own tender intuitions."[9] The series of sermons explained the function of biblical women in such a way as to limit the spheres of contemporary women.

Baptist seminary professors were little more supportive. Dr. John A. Broadus, one of the denomination's luminaries, authored a pamphlet in 1890 titled "Should Women Speak in Mixed Public Assemblies." Denouncing the practice that Broadus attributed to northern Methodists and midwestern female temperance advocates and the influence of the woman suffrage movement, he cited I Corinthians and I Timothy as restricting women from speaking to groups that contained men.[10] Broadus's colleague at Southern Baptist Theological Seminary, Professor H. H. Harris agreed in an essay he wrote for the *Religious Herald*. He took his counsel both from Paul's instruction to the church at Corinth and from history. When women demanded a public role, what resulted historically was the substitution for marriage of copartnership dissoluble at will, the withdrawal of men from churches to lodges, men's clubs, and saloons, and the loss of "woman's queenly power." Harris presumably clinched his case by warning that if women insisted on standing in the pulpit while men sat and listened, they should also stand on the streetcar while men occupied the comfortable seats.[11]

Concluding that even more needed to be said on the subject, T. T. Eaton, Fundamentalist and influential editor of the *Western Recorder*, wrote a pamphlet in 1895 titled "The Bible on Women's Public Speaking." Relying on the familiar proof texts in I Corinthians and I Timothy, he denied that Paul's advice pertained to a specific church or unique conditions found in Corinth. Women must not speak in public nor even teach Sunday school where men were present. Biblical women might have prophesied but there was no record that they did so before men. He posed the issue in simple terms: women could obey Scripture or they could follow the disruptive spirit of their times where heresies such as Spiritualism, Theosophy, and Christian Science allowed women to speak in public.[12] Some Baptist men even opposed the new Baptist Young People's Union because it allowed young girls to speak in assemblies attended by teenage boys.

Although such views represented an overwhelming consensus in the late nineteenth century, the mood was changing. Some Baptists began to experience misgivings about the subordination of women. Professor H. H. Harris wrote his denigrating 1896 essay in the *Religious Herald* in response to an article by Dr. T. C. Johnson, of Charleston, West Virginia, in which he favored allowing women to both speak and pray in public. Fred D. Hale, of Owensboro, Kentucky, wrote the same paper in 1895 denouncing the idea that women were intellectually inferior to men as "a heathen notion": "She can think as profoundly, reason as logically, and put her thoughts into clear, vigorous, and beautiful language as her supposed to be intellectual superior. Women can write as good books, articles or editorials, frame as good laws, render as just decisions, construct as good arguments, reach as wise conclusions . . . and do everything else that required a well-balanced and highly-cultured intellect as well as men in like circumstances can do." But even Hale thought women's place was in the home. Dr. William H. Whitsitt, president of Southern Seminary and theologically more liberal than Professors Broadus and Harris, quipped that when Catholic women wanted to preach, the church sent them to convents; when Baptist women wanted to preach, "we don't know what to do with them."[13]

Although many Baptist women accepted and even endorsed the theology of female subordination, others began to challenge it. In 1891 Mary T. Gambrell of Meridian, Mississippi, used *The Baptist Basket*, a Baptist woman's magazine, to deny that women's mission activities required men to guard "the pulpit against the sacrilegious tread of feminine feet." Another woman in the same journal approved the practice of some women in Indian Territory who kept their maiden names after marriage, chose their own husbands, divorced them if they were lazy or tyrannical, and demanded to be consulted on family business matters. As early as 1885 some Baptist women's societies restricted meetings to women only. When denominational leaders requested the WMU to allow a man to write its reports, women leaders of the organization replied that theirs was a "Woman's Missionary Union, and there is no need for gentlemen to frame our resolutions." When Dr. John A. Broadus published his pamphlet denying the right of women to teach men, a Baptist woman in Kansas who was church clerk and also a trustee of her congregation protested that her public speaking had resulted in much activity favorable to the Kingdom of God.[14]

The rapid change in attitudes between 1900 and 1920 resulted from many intersecting forces. Try as they might, Southern Baptists could not escape the bounds of secular culture, and momentous forces were loosening Victorian ties. Youthful rebellion against middle-class values, the destabilizing influences of the First World War, rapid increases in the number of middle-class women attending college, wartime necessity for women to work both as volunteers and for salaries, the liberalizing tendencies of the Social Gospel, the new "Higher Criticism" infiltrating northern churches, and the woman suffrage movement all accelerated the pace of change.

The spearhead for this change within the Southern Baptist Convention was the Woman's Missionary Union, led by the remarkable Annie Walker Armstrong. A native of Baltimore on the northern fringe of SBC territory, Armstrong led in framing the 1888 WMU constitution. As Corresponding Secretary of the WMU from its inception until her stormy resignation in 1906, she was a brutally frank, shrewd infighter who could charm or shame men, outmaneuver or verbally castigate them, or threaten to sue them if the occasion demanded. A single woman who spent much time in her Baltimore jail ministry, she was an indefatigable worker and a tough, inflexible protagonist. She not only refused to accept a salary for her work but even financed much of her travel from her own funds. So arduous was her work of managing sickly parents and the WMU that in 1898 she wrote Dr. J. M. Frost, head of the Sunday School Board, to propose (one suspects not very seriously) that the WMU be consolidated with the Sunday School Board, with Frost serving as head of the combined agency. Characteristic of the strong minded Armstrong, she demanded that the new headquarters be located in Baltimore.[15]

Determined to dominate the Baptist Woman's organization, she clashed frequently with WMU president Fannie E. S. Heck, a well-educated single woman from North Carolina who had led the organization in her native state from its beginnings in 1886. Heck believed the national president of the WMU should be its chief spokesman and clashed repeatedly with Armstrong. Both of them shrewdly cultivated the support of men who headed SBC agencies, although Armstrong possessed the best survival instincts.[16]

After orchestrating a compromise by which Heck agreed to refuse a new term as president, Armstrong turned her attention to other matters. In many ways she spanned the chasm between two epochs, although in independence, temperament, and political sagacity she belonged entirely to the age of the "new woman." She worked closely with black women to help organize WMU's in their churches. Despite her short-lived suggestion to combine the WMU and Sunday School Board, she fiercely defended the autonomy of her organization. When Frost tried to force her to accept a salary by arguing that the Sunday School, Home, and Foreign Missions boards should determine her salary, Armstrong responded that as an auxiliary of the SBC the officers of the WMU were appointed by neither the convention nor by its boards. Her organization had made the three boards the custodian of its funds but the Women's Missionary Societies through their representatives could withdraw such funds at any time. Frost clearly understood her warning.[17]

Despite her frank and sometimes menacing demeanor, Armstrong was theologically conservative. Like most Baptist men, she believed that women should not be ordained or speak to mixed audiences. While on a WMU tour of Oklahoma in 1902, she was "horrified" when two pastors in Oklahoma City asked her to speak at their Sunday evening services. Both pastors were from Kentucky and imbued, she feared, with unorthodox views. She rejected both invitations as inappropriate and wrote a Baptist leader proudly: "Please note that although in the West, I did not adopt Western ideas."[18]

Another example of the transition from one generation of female leadership to another came over the decision of Southern Baptists to create a Training School for Women Missionaries in Louisville. The primary impetus for this move came from Southern Seminary faculty, their wives, and Baptist leaders concerned about the lack of formal preparation available to women missionaries. Unwilling to accept women into seminary classes, they proposed an extension of the seminary taught mostly by seminary faculty and their wives. Kentucky WMU leaders enthusiastically endorsed the project and provided most of its support. Armstrong, however, was not enthusiastic. When the idea was first proposed, she urged that Southern Baptist women who desired to attend such an institution attend the Northern Baptist Training School, a strange proposal indeed since the northern institution had no prohibitions against women speaking before mixed audiences, which Armstrong opposed. It seems likely that her primary concern was that the new school would function under seminary direction rather than WMU control. At any rate, she reluctantly endorsed creation of a separate school under WMU control and blocked attempts to provide WMU funding for the institution in Louisville which opened in 1902. Her opposition contained a strange mixture of feminist and traditional ideas. Officially she said that her only concern about the Louisville Training School was her opposition to training women as preachers. But in letters she emphasized the opinion of some Northern Baptist leaders that young men studying for the ministry should avoid marriage. Some Baptist friends greeted her concerns with amusement, others with ridicule. A rumor began to circulate that her opposition to the Training School derived from fear that it would become a matchmaking institution. It is uncertain whether she was motivated by concern that single women studying at the school might be pressured to marry male seminarians. But that is certainly a possibility. And those who favored the Louisville School used the issue to ridicule her. T. P. Bell wrote in Georgia's *Christian Index* in 1906 that fear of the Training School becoming a matchmaking agency "might well have arisen in the fertile imagination of some maiden lady of uncertain age, who has come to look upon marriage as a dreadful thing, and especially a marriage between two Christians whose hearts are one in the service of the master."[19] He also called absurd the allegation that the school would train women to become preachers. The Georgia paper published additional attacks, some even more directly aimed at Armstrong. Nor did Armstrong shrink from the combat. She wrote one Baptist leader: "We are told in God's Word 'Vengeance is mine; I will repay saith the Lord.' If not in this world, in eternity. Dr. Bell and some others will, I have not the slightest doubt, be made to realize that God is not only a God of love but also of justice. If I did not recognize this and was not trying to shape my actions according to what I believe God requires, I should have long before this placed in the hands of some eminent lawyers proofs which I hold that the editors of the INDEX, some of the Professors of the Seminary, the wife of the Financial Agent of the Seminary, . . . and others had been guilty of libel and had suits instituted accordingly."[20]

In her noncooperative, belligerent, and independent style, Annie Armstrong was probably the best representative of the "new woman." She treated men who headed SBC Boards as equals and demanded that they treat her the same. She chided them frankly and even condescendingly on occasion, as if her vision of Christianity was clearly superior to theirs. She was uncompromising, a shrewd strategist, and a relentless protagonist who never forgot a grievance. But in her theology she was a literalist. Despite her ability to work with men when necessary, she seemed almost to champion a separatist mentality, with women controlling their own spheres. Perhaps underlying her rejection of women speaking before audiences that contained men was a more basic rejection of men and a fear for WMU autonomy in any close association with male dominated SBC agencies.

But the tide of change was running against her. By shrewd lobbying and by threatening to resign, she narrowly defeated a resolution at the 1905 WMU convention endorsing establishment of the Louisville Training School. A year later she was forced to make good on her promise to resign as Corresponding Secretary when the WMU both endorsed and agreed to help fund the institution. Subsequently, the Training School became a major factor in preparing women to follow their own careers and in turning Baptist life in a more liberal direction.

Perhaps the person most responsible for the success of the Training School was Annie E. Eager. Her husband George B. Eager taught Bible and pastoral theology at Southern Baptist Theological Seminary from 1900 until 1920. Before his teaching career, he had served in the 1890s as pastor of Montgomery, Alabama's historic First Baptist Church where he had taken a keen interest in political reform and civic morality. He believed the church should become involved in political reforms, and he urged that barriers restricting women be removed. Annie Eager was a perfect match to her husband. While they lived in Montgomery she had led the Boys' Reform School and Montgomery Infirmary associations and served as president of the Alabama State Federation of Women's Clubs which was to play a key role in Alabama's progressive reform movement. She led the 1905 attempt to persuade the WMU to bolt Annie Armstrong's leadership and endorse the new Training School, which was successful two years later at Richmond when the WMU voted overwhelmingly to adopt the institution in Louisville. Annie became chairman of the Board of Managers, a member of the faculty, and a counselor to the young women.[21]

Along with Annie Eager, the most formative influence came from Maude R. McLure who became principal of the school when it came under WMU control in 1907. A native Alabamian, McLure, like so many other women leaders of the times, was born into an affluent home where she had all the advantages of education, travel, and refinement. She married and bore a son before the deaths of her husband and mother, and the loss of the family fortune forced her to earn a living. "Suddenly thrust forth into the world," she began to teach, first at Cor College and then as principal of the Training School. A sensitive person who constantly sought "God's will," she also charted a course for her institution which greatly broadened the vision of young women.[22]

Although Eager and McLure played leading roles in the development of the Training School, many seminary women lent support. Among the faculty were at least three seminary wives: Mrs. Eager, Mrs. B. H. DeMent (whose husband became president of New Orleans Baptist Theological Seminary in 1917), and Mrs. William J. McGlothlin (whose husband earned a PhD in history at the University of Berlin in 1901, taught at the Seminary until 1919, then became president of Furman University and president of the SBC from 1930 until 1933). Miss E. S. Broadus, daughter of a former seminary president, also played a key role in creating the school.

Women students took some regular seminary courses with male students, where they often led their classes academically. In March 1916, for example, fourteen women took exams in Old Testament; eleven made between 90 and 98, and three made a perfect score of 100. Of the 108 men taking the same course, only one made 100. The WMU proudly reported these results as positive proof of the intellectual ability of women to compete with men. In addition to Bible study, women took courses in city missions, church music, sewing, and cooking. These domestic skills were applied to ministries other than caring for husbands. The seminary women taught cooking and sewing to women in settlement houses. By 1917 enrollment reached sixty-two women; fifty of the school's graduates served as missionaries in that year, while others taught in mountain schools, served as city workers among immigrants, as social workers in urban settlement houses, or as missionaries to women and children in the South's cotton mill villages. In 1912 the WMU purchased a Good Will Center that was used as a settlement house in a working-class Louisville neighborhood. Students from the Training School assisted Miss Emma Leachman, Baptist city missionary and also a member of the Training School faculty, in operating the house. The settlement contained a branch of the Free Public Library, a free clinic complete with a physician and nurse, girls and boys clubs for child laborers, a music club which furnished lessons, handicraft classes, Sunday school and Vacation Bible Schools. The WMU provided the funds to rent, renovate, furnish, and operate the house. The rationale for this funding was that the Settlement House was a teaching extension of the Training School. Women from the school also worked at Louisville's other seven settlement houses, including one which served black people. In addition they received training at City Hospital, the alms house, and the Home for Incurables. Such activity required extensive fund-raising, a task which the WMU had skillfully performed for some time. In a winter 1917 drive, Louisville WMU leaders raised $30,000 in the city toward a total goal of $150,000. Much of it came from non-Baptists, a testimony to the impact of the school's social ministries.[23]

Although the Training School did not go out of its way to challenge Baptist views on gender, its very existence and widespread ministries redefined women's roles. Specific lesson plans are unavailable but visiting speakers often provided women a new understanding of their worth. At the 1917 commencement, Dr. H. C. Wayman preached on "Woman's Place in the Work of the Master." Paradoxically, his text came from Paul: "I commend unto you, Phoebe, our sister, which is a servant of the church which is at Cenchrea: that ye receive her in the Lord as becometh saints . . . for she hath been a succorer of many." A number of Jesus's disciples were devoted women, he added, "a future prophecy of the place of women in the church."[24]

Twenty years earlier Wayman's sermon would have been heretical, but it seemed conventional enough in 1917. Baptist life had undergone a remarkable transformation in the first decade-and-a-half of the new century.

As with many Progressive-Era reforms, the change in attitudes toward women began on local and state levels, and then gradually percolated to the national scene. Alabama provides a useful example. In 1892 the editors of *The Alabama Baptist* noted with scorn the creation of political clubs for women. They congratulated southern women for avoiding "the craze of woman suffrage and 'woman's sphere in politics." Three years later the editor softened his view of the "coming woman" when the Detroit Methodist Episcopal Conference voted to admit women delegates: "What is the need of it all, and the good of it all, we have thus far been unable to see. But if there is necessity for it let her come."[25]

Few Alabama Baptists saw any point to such changes either. When Professor H. H. Harris wrote his essay instructing women to be subordinate to men, *The Alabama Baptist* praised the article and reprinted it. A woman identified only as Mrs. O. J. B., of Buena Vista, read the learned professor's advice and wrote the paper a letter of approval. The Reverend H. C. Hurley, pastor of the Baptist church in Jasper, joined the pamphleteers in 1896 with a 25-page effort titled "The New Woman and the Church." For seventy-five cents one could read that the "New Woman" was incompatible with traditional Christianity, that women should neither speak in public nor hold a position of authority within the church.[26]

But women found ways to evade such restrictions. One response was the creation of separate women's groups. Increasingly women attended Baptist associational meetings, which generally coincided with a county's boundaries, held separate sessions, and elected their own officers. In 1896 Baptist women formed such organizations at Scottsboro in the Tennessee Valley and in the industrial cities of Birmingham and Anniston. Through these WMU sessions, women began raising money for missions and pressing for a larger role in official state convention life.[27] At the 1909 Alabama Baptist State Convention, the all-male messengers unanimously invited Grace H. Wilkerson, of Birmingham, to address the convention on her work with aged ministers. Although the invitation seems routine by later standards, the Baptists to whom she spoke were mostly men who only recently had rejected the right of women to speak to mixed assemblies. She disarmed any lingering chauvinists in her audience by a touching and shrewd introduction: "I am a daughter of a minister; you are my brothers; and so I come without fear and with much assurance that you will aid women in this worthy and beautiful service." State leaders called her skillfully presented speech a highlight of the convention.[28]

By 1912 women routinely addressed the Alabama Baptist Convention. At its annual meeting in Jasper that year a female teacher at the Baptist Orphans Home, "poised and thoughtful," discussed the ministry to orphans. At that same meeting, Dr. Charles A. Stakely, who pastored Montgomery's First Baptist Church (and whose wife later became president of the national WMU and an articulate advocate of the Training School), joined H. S. D. Mallory, Dr. A. J. Dickinson (who pastored First Baptist in Birmingham), and other theological and social liberals to propose changing the convention constitution to allow women messengers from the WMU, associations, and churches. After a lively discussion, the convention unanimously instructed a committee to bring a report authorizing the admittance of women messengers.[29]

Parallel developments occurred throughout SBC territory. Baptist historian and seminary professor W. J. McGlothlin, whose wife taught at the Training School, served as chairman of enrollment for the 1909 Kentucky Baptist General Assembly. In his official role he raised the question of whether women sent by churches and associations should not be enrolled as messengers. His proposal launched a spirited debate. J. W. Porter, conservative editor of the *Western Recorder*, registered his solemn protest against admitting women messengers. But M. P. Hunt responded that many southern and all northern state Baptist conventions accepted women messengers. Nor did any Scripture prohibit their acceptance. L. W. Doolan also relied on Scripture: "Christ said there is no male or female in the kingdom. There is at least one woman here sent by a church. Shall we refuse her and others like her?" Judge Blakey, of Frankfort, appealed to the Baptist tradition of church autonomy. Since churches and associations decided their own messengers, the state convention should accept any person they selected. The vote overwhelmingly admitted women as full-fledged messengers to the assembly. The Tennessee Baptist Convention joined Kentucky in accepting women messengers in 1911.[30]

The first challenge to the national Southern Baptist Convention occurred in 1885 when two women were among the seven messengers from Arkansas. One of them was Mrs. J. P. Eagle, wife of the speaker of the Arkansas House of Representatives; the other, Mrs. M. D. Early, was the wife of a prominent pastor. Both were unprepared for the furor their presence caused. M. D. Early admitted that he at first objected to his wife's selection as a messenger but argued that the SBC constitution contained no restriction prohibiting women. He concluded by saying, "The question before this Convention is, Shall the Baptist ladies of this country, who have sent more money into the vaults of this Convention than the men, be excluded from a part of its deliberation?" The convention appointed a five-man committee to consider the issue. Although all probably opposed admitting women messengers in principle, three were strict constructionists who reported that in the absence of any specific prohibition, women must be admitted. But the Convention substituted the minority report that excluded women by a vote of 202 to 112. The Convention also inserted the word *brethren* in place of messenger to constitutionally prohibit women messengers in the future. For the next twenty years women who attended the SBC were seated in the balconies, a place they probably remembered had been reserved for slaves before the Civil War.[31]

Opinion changed rapidly after 1900 as state conventions began to accept women messengers. When T. B. Bell finished reading the report on Woman's Work to the 1910 SBC, J. B. Gambrell of Texas responded with a warning to his brethren: "Paul said help those women who labor with me in the Gospel. He did not say manage them. That is their strong point, and when the young pastor tries to manage these women he will have all sorts of trouble on his hands. Go slow in trying to manage our Baptist women."[32] In 1914 R. H. Coleman of Dallas tried to change the constitution to its pre-1885 wording, but the reaction was so volatile that the convention refused to act. In 1917 more than a thousand women registered for the WMU meeting that preceded the convention and many of them were seated in the balconies when Coleman reintroduced his proposal. The female gallery greeted his proposal with applause, but it sparked "one of the most acrimonious debates and difficult parliamentary tangles of the Convention." Coleman's resolution passed, but convention president J. B. Gambrell ruled erroneously that a constitutional change required a two-thirds vote of messengers enrolled, not those in attendance, and the issue was lost again. During the next year many Baptist leaders endorsed Coleman's change. The editor of the Texas *Baptist Standard* wrote: "The woman question is not settled; and we confidently expect after a few years, when certain brethren will have learned the way of the Lord more perfectly, to see the elect sisters admitted to the Convention on the same basis as the men, just as we do in Texas." The wait was short. Coleman reintroduced his resolution in 1918 at the convention in Hot Springs, Arkansas, which immediately passed it by an overwhelming vote. When the tally was announced, the male messengers and female observers arose and spontaneously joined in singing "Blest be the tie that binds." The editor of the *Religious Herald*, a paper once filled with articles admonishing women to stay in their place, noted that the Convention had given "tardy recognition" to Baptist women and urged that they be appointed to every convention board.[33]

Accompanying Baptist enfranchisement of women was a more profound change in attitude. Support for woman suffrage became a standard against which to measure male support of women's rights, and many Baptists failed the test. J. W. Porter, who led the resistance to allowing Kentucky women as messengers to the Baptist General Assembly, accused the suffrage movement of being antisouthern with an ultimate goal of establishing the Negro as the dominant force in southern politics. Militant suffragists, he cautioned, were "getting mighty common, just about as common as pig tracks, and just about as valuable." He also accused them of rejecting motherhood, favoring lower birth rates, and even repudiating marriage. In a grand summation he wrote: "The feminine demons, knowingly or otherwise, are pointing womankind to the path that leads to harlotry and to hell." Porter was not alone in his apocalyptic prophecy. The editor of the *Christian Index* considered politics too vulgar for refined ladies. The Rev. J. P. Greene added that men were not fitted by God to run the home, nor women to run the government. He called woman suffrage an "evil enchantment."[34]

Such opinions are neither exceptional nor surprising; they characterized Victorian thought. What *is* surprising is the extent of dissent and the prestige of the dissenters. Editor James B. Gambrell of the *Baptist Standard*, of Texas, considered opposition to woman suffrage futile and reminded Texas Baptists that they had long allowed women to vote in church meetings. In 1917 the Texas state convention endorsed equal suffrage. Both *The Alabama Baptist* and Georgia's *Christian Index* endorsed the Nineteenth Amendment. The editor of *The Baptist World*, published in Louisville but circulated throughout the SBC, endorsed woman suffrage and in 1912 urged that women pay no heed to the "crystalized delaying precedents established by the men." They should press directly for what they wanted despite the resistance of "men from the dark ages." The editor quoted favorably Dr. E. L. Powell, of Louisville, who noted that men had controlled education in Kentucky for a hundred years, and it was a scandal with the second highest rate of illiteracy in America. Nor did he have any sympathy for the notion that keeping women disfranchised protected them from "the rough usages of the world": "such reasons of opposition are not well founded either in reason or common sense, because the ideal which the woman must realize concerning herself must be realized and created by the woman herself, and not by man. Man's attempt to fashion an ideal woman fail for the reason that it is impossible for him to understand what her conception of the truly ideal is."[35]

But the toughest woman's issue for the church was ordination. Biblical literalists fixed on this as the central test of scriptural integrity. Dr. Charles A. Stakely, who earlier helped Alabama women obtain admission to the state convention, spoke to the 1912 Missionary Society at Southern Baptist Seminary. His sermon on women took the theological position that the experience of grace was a call to preach, and women were not exempt. Jesus had received and blessed ministries of women. Pheobe had served the church as a deaconess, an official church position. "In most lines of service" women could work as successfully as men; in some lines they could excel men; in a few they were almost exclusively qualified. As a rule women were also better equipped for an intelligent grasp of Christianity and "these women are not going to sit under an ignoramus for a preacher."[36]

Dr. J. B. Moody is a rare example of a preacher willing to admit a complete shift of opinion during the era. Early in his career he denied scriptural authority for women preachers. But in a book titled *Women in the Churches*, he renounced that view as based on tradition. He claimed that several New Testament words were translated "preach" and in some sense women were called to preach: "To deny this is madness." Perhaps they should not stand behind the pulpit on Sunday but they could certainly preach "in a private and unofficial way." He rejected the notion that women should be silent in church, urging them to relate their Christian experiences in any appropriate way except as a fully ordained minister. The editor of *The Baptist World* also stopped just short of ministerial ordination, supporting the offices of female deacons and prophetesses. He considered the prohibition against women's service in Scripture a local problem limited to Corinth and not generally applicable. He also reminded recalcitrant men that when the WMU started "many of the wise brethren solemnly shook their heads in disapproval of the innovation." Baptist churches responded by ordaining a number of deaconesses but apparently no ministers.[37]

Southern Baptist women wasted no time availing themselves of the new opportunities. At the 1919 Convention 475 messengers registered. Of these, ninety-nine were women just from the state of Alabama. From Arkansas thirty of 127 messengers were women. When Southwestern Seminary opened in Fort Worth, Texas, in 1908, women were admitted on the basis of complete equality with men.

Other changes came more slowly. Not until 1964 is there concrete evidence of a woman ordained to the ministry by a Southern Baptist Church. A few women served on Southern Baptist Convention boards in the 1920s, but only five served on the powerful SBC Executive Committee between 1927 and 1958. As late as 1971 only 4.53 percent of the members of all convention agencies and boards were women. Although one-fifth of all graduates from Southwestern Seminary are women, in 1970 only 10.5 percent of the faculty were female. Not until 1963 did the SBC elect a female second vice president and never have the messengers elected a woman president.[38] On the other hand, Baptist reaction to the 1984 resolution on women was tremendous. Protest meetings in Baptist churches in Virginia, Kentucky, North Carolina, and Georgia drew thousands. And the General Association (Convention) of Virginia in 1984 became the first state convention to approve the ordination of women.[39] Southern Baptist women and their allies also began *Folio*, a newsletter circulated throughout the denomination.

Change swept the South in almost every sphere of society between 1900 and 1920, and it did not escape that most central southern institution: the church. One reason that resistance to woman suffrage and a redefined role for women met no greater hostility than it did was because the major three Protestant denominations developed more open and accepting attitudes. Just as a conservative culture had imprisoned the church throughout the nineteenth century, a more progressive society haltingly liberated it in the twentieth. Most men and some women resisted the changes, but as the 1920s began church women had made major improvements in their status. They had put to rest a central theological argument of the nineteenth century that had denied them the right to speak before audiences containing men. They had organized powerful women's missionary societies under their own direction, which increased their influence in the church and provided them money-raising and leadership skills. Gradually they turned these skills to secular pursuits. They won the right to serve as voting delegates to denominational meetings and receive professional training at denomination seminaries and training schools. They used this training in more socially engaged ministries. They recognized that God had not ordained them for a separate and subordinate sphere within the church. And they first visualized a world in which they might respond to God's call to preach and minister without first asking a man if he had heard the same message.

—*Religion in the South Conference Papers*,
Alabama Humanities Foundation, 1986

Of my some thirty published articles, book chapters, and books dealing with southern religion, this essay is my favorite for these reasons: It reflects the maturation of my self-education; it teases larger meaning out of the most arcane local history; I began a love affair with rural, poorly educated, fundamentalist Christians entirely different from me, folks (to use a wonderful biblical allusion) called "salt-of-the-earth people."

Martin Marty, a historian of religion at the University of Chicago Divinity School and winner of the Pulitzer Prize in History, may have suggested my name to James P. Wind (Lilly Endowment program director in religion) and James W. Lewis (executive director of the Louisville Institute for the Study of Protestantism and American Culture). At any rate, they asked me to join a new multi-year project. Their hypothesis was simple and self-evident: denominationalism, the primary American contribution to Christian religion, was being displaced by congregationalism. Annual surveys revealed that fewer and fewer believers remained in the denominations of their birth. The nation was moving toward boutique religion where people satisfied spiritual yearnings through a congregation (or, increasingly, a series of congregations corresponding to passages in their lives). The Eli Lilly Endowment funded their study of congregationalism and the two volumes entitled American Congregations *that the project produced.*

My assignment was a rural congregation in the South. In order to utilize my strengths, I made two decisions: It would be a church in Alabama, and it would be Southern Baptist. Given Alabama's ruralism and the kudzu-like SBC canopy overspreading the "Heart of Dixie," those decisions did not much narrow my choices. So I added two other criteria: The church should span the state's entire history, and it should have complete records. Although ambivalent myself about how divine providence works, I could not escape the implications of ensuing events. The archivist of Samford University's phenomenal Baptist history collection informed me that Mt. Hebron Baptist Church, a still rural congregation south of Leeds, had been formed in 1819, the year Alabama obtained statehood, and had maintained a perfect run of church records. When I told my wife this good news, she commented offhandedly that her father had pastored Mt. Hebron while a poor ministerial student at Howard College in the early 1930s. Indeed, when I began reading records and oral histories conducted with members by my graduate research assistant, I learned that W. Albert Smith, who served the church from 1929 until he graduated college in 1932, was one of the congregation's most beloved pastors, as was his successor, Rev. Fred E. Maxey.

Whereas my father-in-law's diaries left no doubt that he was an orthodox lifelong Southern Baptist minister—fundamentalist in theology but winsome, tolerant, and non-judgmental in temperament—Fred Maxey was anything but *orthodox. Called as Mt. Hebron's pastor after preaching a successful revival in Leeds's out-of-business movie theater in 1932, he had earlier in life been a religious skeptic while working as a labor negotiator in the southwestern Virginia coal fields. Converted in 1924 at the Walnut Grove Church of the Brethren, he survived during the initial years of the Great Depression as an itinerant evangelist advertising on his newsletter's masthead that his "Christo-centric" ministry was "Fundamental," "undenominational," and "Pre-Millennial," all buzzwords for independent fundamentalist. Once called as pastor of Mt. Hebron, he became beloved by poor tenant farmers and unemployed coal miners, both white members of his own church and a larger biracial cadre in the vicinity. He became their compassionate advocate to local New Deal social agencies. More intriguing, he became a keynote speaker at rallies sponsored by the Communist Party, which had established a southern beachhead in nearby Birmingham. According to the historian of Alabama Communism, Maxey had become a member of the party (although I doubt that). With the words of anthropologist Clifford Geertz (*The Interpretation of Cultures*) ringing in my ears (at the core of religion was the "drive to make sense out of experience, to give it form and order," a drive every bit as compelling as any biological urge), I plunged into those priceless records.*

CHAPTER 11
"A Special Feeling of Closeness"
Mt. Hebron Baptist Church, Leeds, Alabama

My initial visits to Mt. Hebron Baptist Church demonstrated many of the persistent themes of evangelical rural religion in America: crises within rural society reflected in the church, extreme individualism and traditionalism, fundamentalist theology, lack of class barriers, democratic polity, ambivalence about the believer's relationship to the world, and a strong sense of community. My first visit came on a cold winter's morning in February 1989. A young layman filled the pulpit in place of the pastor, who was ill. The young man had recently responded to God's call to preach and was taking Bible courses to prepare for his new career. He made the day's announcements and then stepped back into the choir where he added his voice to a choir of six. When the anthem ended, he moved into the pulpit, opened his Bible, and instructed his congregation to turn in the New Scofield reference Bible to the page from which he read (a passage from Revelation 3).

His exegesis concerned the hypocrisy of the ancient church at Sardis. His application focused on religion in America. He denounced large churches which, like Sardis, had neglected their true mission to win souls for the lesser task of meeting the needs of the community. Selecting an agricultural analogy, he compared the modern church to a hull which when opened contained no bean. But his jeremiad was not confined to the empty churches of urban America. Even Mt. Hebron showed signs of spiritual decay. Like all the other powerless churches, it was shackled to tradition and had forsaken the ministry of soul-winning. The enfeeblement of the church reflected the moral collapse of the nation. Americans had forsaken Christian values. The old verities and benchmarks no longer anchored American society.

His homily completed, he began the invitation, issuing a general call for professions of faith and transfers of membership. No one came. More earnestly now, he admonished the deacons to come forward as a pledge of their prayers for the renewal of Mt. Hebron. Then he asked all members who would join in this commitment to come and stand with him. Gradually the congregation of sixty or so thinned to three adolescents sitting to my left, each apparently determined to resist the invitation, but each also wavering. Finally one of them, a girl, rose slowly and headed for the side aisle, followed in a moment by her two male companions. Now the entire congregation made a semicircle at the front of the church, all of them facing my wife and me who were now the only persons still seated. Noting our obvious discomfort, the young minister quickly dismissed the service with prayer and hurried to speak to us. He greeted us warmly, apologized for any embarrassment he might have caused, adding that the spiritual fires of Mt. Hebron had burned low and only the infusion of new fuel could set the spirit aflame again.

Easter night my wife and I returned to hear Pastor James Blair preach. Obviously more comfortable in the pulpit than the young layman had been, he proclaimed a gospel of renewal and hope. Repeatedly citing the absolute authority of the Bible and using no notes, he paced from one side of the pulpit to the other. He delivered his extemporaneous message in conversational style, not in the random shouts that might have punctuated pulpit oratory in an earlier age. An occasional dramatic gesture was his only concession to bygone days.

Such descriptions have long been the stuff of humorous undergraduate lectures and disdainful academic scholarship. Yet the nexus between those services and Mt. Hebron's historical experience contains far more profound meaning.

Believers at Mt. Hebron expressed their faith through a set of sacred symbols shared by all: the Cross, believer's baptism, the Lord's Supper, extending the right hand of fellowship, laying-on-of-hands for those set apart for special ministry, and the use of special designations such as "brother" and "sister." The sacred symbols and rituals of the church produced consecrated behavior—worship, discipline, revivals, singings, homecomings—which shaped the life of generations of believers. They wrestled with questions of suffering and community disaster, not considering how to avoid suffering but how to make physical pain, personal loss, or worldly defeat meaningful and how to comfort those who experienced it. The motivations and expectations growing from powerful religious symbols gave meaning to life and helped determine right conduct in one's relations to neighbors. Encounter and commitment mattered more than detachment and analysis in the religious cosmos of Mt. Hebron. At the core of religion was the "drive to make sense out of experience, to give it form and order," a drive which was as real and pressing as biological needs.[1]

Religion operated in two ways. On one level it provided meaning that allowed a person to make sense out of the realities of existence. But it served a social function as well by relating persons to a sacred community made up of people who perceived reality in similar ways and shared common symbols and aspirations. After all, there were many "realities" within Alabama's rural society: moonshining, violence, indigence, alienation, incest, wife and child abuse, and financial corruption, to name only a few. So the distinctive evangelical Christianity practiced at Mt. Hebron integrated people into a very specific "reality" within many competing realities, a concrete and sacred "world" within many larger worlds. The shared symbols touched people at different points with varying strength. Sometimes a person sought to pull away, but the web exerted even greater effort to keep the wayward pilgrim within the sacred community.

Evangelical Protestantism enabled a rising lower and middle class on the southern frontier to achieve identity and solidarity. The new birth on which this new community rested resulted from a conscious act of choice. The order and discipline which this community required replaced the former disorder and social anarchy of a chaotic frontier. Special symbols of social intimacy such as laying-on-of-hands, greetings with a kiss, and extending the right hand of fellowship became powerful bonds for this spiritual community. And the community was expansive enough to offer a place for the poor, for women, and for African Americans living within a secular society that offered no such opportunities.

Bivocationalism bound the religious community into an especially democratic arrangement. All that was needed for a Baptist minister to preach was a sense of divine calling; education, even literacy, was not a prerequisite. Because churches often consisted of poor folks and because members often believed a minister should work at secular tasks to earn a living, salaries, when paid at all, remained low. This assured that no professional class of ministers remote from a people would arise.[2] Such a religion might seem excessively individualistic; indeed, its primary thrust was toward the individual, a thrust which suited it nicely to southern culture. But southern evangelical religion often transcended this personal ethos for a more collective approach to the world, as in Bible, tract, and education efforts, home and foreign mission societies, and programs for the poor, blind, and Indians.[3]

Mt. Hebron Baptist Church was a product of the first phase of settlement of the Alabama frontier. Located in the Upper Cahaba River Valley in the southern foothills of the Appalachian Mountains, the region was settled at the end of the First Creek War (1812–1814). Tennessee soldiers who had fought across eastern Alabama in Andrew Jackson's army received land through lease-sale agreements. Many of the pioneer families came from Tennessee, obtained their lands in this way, and began farms and Mt. Hebron Church at almost the same time. Many families that were to play a major role in the life of the church settled in the decade after 1815.

Hezekiah Balch Moor and his wife, Virginia ("Gincy"), left Tennessee with their two children in late 1816 or early 1817. They came by ox cart and settled near the St. Clair-Jefferson county line in the northern part of the valley. Moor had served as a physician under the command of General Andrew Jackson and claimed a grant of land. The third of his fifteen children, Joseph, born in 1817, was ordained to preach at Mt. Hebron and became moderator of the Canaan Baptist Association. The church also ordained Hezekiah Moor Jr., who pastored Bethel Baptist, a mission of Hebron located in St. Clair County.[4]

John McLaughlin and his wife, Margaret, claimed bounty land in 1821. He had soldiered through the valley under the command of General John Coffee, one of Jackson's lieutenants. He fought again in the Second Creek War (1834–1836) as a member of McAdory's 4th Mounted Alabama Infantry. McLaughlin led a family resettlement from Tennessee that resulted in his brother purchasing land in the northern end of the valley adjacent to his. Like the Moors, the McLaughlins produced large families. William C. McLaughlin, the second son, who was born in 1821, bought land next to his father and served as the eighth pastor of Mt. Hebron, affectionately known to inhabitants of the valley as "Pastor Billy."[5]

The Mitchell Pool family came to the region from South Carolina in 1819 with six daughters and three sons. The Pools settled in the southern end of the valley near where Mt. Hebron was organized. Among the twelve charter members of the church were three Pools: John, Huldah, and William.[6]

An Indian trail split the Cahaba Valley, running southwest from the future village of Ashville in St. Clair County to Montevallo in Shelby County. In the 1820s the trail became a stagecoach route, called the Ashville-Montevallo Road, with inns and post offices at frequent intervals. Flanked by the Cahaba River on the north and mountain ridges to the south, it was not ideal farming country. Unlike the rich bottomland of the Tennessee Valley in northern Alabama or the magnificent ebony soil of the central Alabama Black Belt, this earth yielded a good living only to the hardiest and most determined. Early settlers staked out claims to an entire section of 640 acres or more, and some acquired the slaves necessary to farm such extensive domains; but more typical were small yeoman farmers who scratched out a living on twenty to forty acres worked by hordes of their "younguns." Rural traditions and values took firm root. Seventh-generation descendants of these early settlers still live in the valley, some on the same land originally cleared by their ancestors.[7] Descendants of some founders of Mt. Hebron still claim a place in the pews each Sunday.

Mt. Hebron Church owed its existence to the Rev. Hosea Holcombe, a legendary figure who in 1818 pastored the first Baptist congregations in the region. A Virginian of limited formal education, Holcombe had entered the ministry in 1805 and moved to South Carolina where he preached for thirteen years before joining the westward movement into Alabama. While in South Carolina he came under the influence of Luther Rice and Richard Fuller, Baptist leaders who pioneered foreign missions and led in the establishment of the State Convention of South Carolina. Holcombe retained their evangelical fervor, founding five churches in the region that would one day become Birmingham.[8]

When Holcombe arrived in the state in 1818, Alabama was part of the "Old Southwest," still a raw frontier quite unlike the more sophisticated and stable Atlantic seaboard from which he had come. He later estimated that in 1820 the new state contained no more than fifty Baptist churches, all small and struggling.[9] Problems abounded. Creek Indians still posed a psychological threat if not a physical one. The Creek War of 1812–1814 had opened eastern Alabama to settlement, but Creeks remained on some of their lands until their removal in the late 1830s. The Upper Cahaba Valley was just to the north of the Creek Nation in a no-man's-land between Creeks, Cherokees, and Chickasaws, hunted by each but occupied by none. The first settlers moved into the valley only months after the decisive Battle of Horseshoe Bend in 1814, and Mt. Hebron began services only five years after that bloody engagement. Violence, drunkenness, and disorder accompanied the general anxiety about safety from Indian attack. Internal migration, the severing of family and community ties occasioned by moving, the arduous labor entailed in clearing new land and building houses and farm buildings, all added to the perils of marginal land and difficult transportation. The Cahaba River was not navigable, and transportation for five-hundred-pound cotton bales was difficult if not impossible. The valley produced corn, wheat, potatoes, and many other food crops but relatively little cotton. The marginality of the economy compounded problems inherent in pioneer life: extreme individualism, competitiveness, and a spirit of noncooperation. Added to all these problems, illness, disease, and frightfully high rates of infant mortality created a theological climate of fear and impending doom. Many early settlers had families by multiple wives because of the high female mortality rates in childbirth. Gincy Moor—wife of Hezekiah, mother of fifteen children, two of them sons ordained at Mt. Hebron—died in 1862; Hezekiah later married a widow and began a second family. John C. Pool, descendant of one of Mt. Hebron's charter members, died along with four of his children in a February 1884 tornado.

Inscriptions on tombstones in the cemetery behind Mt. Hebron Church speak eloquently of the impermanence of life on the Alabama frontier.

Evangelical religion offered a coherent view of every person's place within this capricious world. To women facing the perils of childbirth, to men confronting drought or flood, the simple message of good news dispensed by rural congregations was welcome. Religion contained obvious social benefits for such congregations. It brought isolated people together, provided young people opportunities for courtship, and offered a community center for activities. But first and foremost the gospel of the fall, redemption, and ultimate vindication and glory of humanity provided balm for the soul. Tiny quarter-time churches allowed an opportunity for socializing only once a month or at infrequent camp meetings or protracted revivals. But comfort for the soul and the certainty that God was in charge and would work His will from among all the discordant and evil events of life provided constant solace.

Nor was such religion escapist. Despite much Zion talk about ultimate causes and destinations—Canaan land, the New Jerusalem, Heaven—the Baptists of the Upper Cahaba Valley lived very much in the real world amidst real problems. But most of these problems were beyond their control: natural disasters such as droughts, floods, tornadoes, deaths in childbirth, and diseases; and man-made disasters such as wars, depressions, and political oppression. They exerted all the efforts of hard work and citizenship that were within their power, voting for those who favored their causes and influencing policy. Alabama was as close to a pure white democracy as America knew at the time, providing universal manhood suffrage, a legislature controlled by poor and yeoman farmers, and a tax system that taxed according to one's wealth. For problems that resisted such efforts, they had to trust in the providence of God. There is no evidence that evangelical religion kept the people of Mt. Hebron in a syrupy world of religious platitudes. Quite to the contrary, some members owned slaves, fashioned a defense of their peculiar institution from Scripture, and condemned many of the sins believed to be rife among their social betters, the large planters and aristocracy. Antebellum tirades against gambling, drinking, the theater, and dancing were as much rooted in class grievances as in theology.

The symbols and rituals of evangelical religion, its rousing hymns and thunderous sermons, provided a providential message for a frontier folk. Sin and depravity threatened on every hand. One needed only to look about to observe the consequences of such wickedness. The wage of sin was death. But praise be to God who from his abundant grace offered a gospel of redemption and renewal, of entry into a holy community of restoration and ultimate glory! The much-maligned camp meeting revivals offered hope not only to individual souls but to the community of the saved. Salvation created not only a new person but a new community, a people of God. It was this need—for self-discipline and restraint, for order and meaning, to control violence within families and among neighbors, this necessity for one to live responsibly in relations with friends and community—that nourished the crop that Hosea Holcombe harvested. The Great Revival that began at Cane Ridge, Kentucky, in 1800 had set the forces in motion. And as that revival swept across the South, conditions in the Cahaba Valley were ideally suited for religious awakening.[10]

Hosea Holcombe brought his message to a responsive community. During the last week of August 1819, some seventy-five days before Alabama became a state, seven men and five women established Mt. Hebron Baptist Church. Holcombe preached one service a month, and William White donated land in what was then Shelby County but would ultimately be included in Jefferson County. As early as 1827 the congregation had a building. In 1836 the expanding congregation relocated and rebuilt. A tornado destroyed this building in 1884. The new building was much like the former one, a white frame structure with tower to the left of the front entrance, and two doors, one opening into the women's side of the church, the other into the men's domain. This building could no longer contain the crowds by 1922, and the congregation constructed a larger edifice, which burned after being struck by lightning in 1954. The present building—a low, simple brick structure—lacks the simple elegance of the earlier frame buildings or the ecclesiastical grandeur of the typical Greek revival church. The location of all the buildings since 1838 is a too-small plot beside the strategic Montevallo-Ashville Road. It nestles in a valley five miles south of Leeds, a New South industrial town that began about 1881 in the shadow of Birmingham, which is located in Jones Valley across several mountain ridges to the west. There in the southern part of the Upper Cahaba Valley the little church beamed forth its light.

The founders provided an "Abstract of Principles," which provides ample insight into their mission. They formed Mt. Hebron Church because all who were "favored with the dispensation of God" should "embrace his covenant, acknowledge his government, profess his name and unite in the faith and fellowship of the gospel." A strong sense of religious community prevailed among them as they covenanted "to endeavor to keep the unity of the spirit in bonds of peace," to meet together at "all convenient seasons," "to sympathize with each other and to pray with and for each other," and to contribute part of their substance to conduct worship and help needy members. Because of the "diversity of sentiment among professing Christians," they believed it necessary to adopt a set of principles, namely belief in one true God which was three persons in the Godhead; faith in the Old and New Testaments as the "word of God" and the only rule of faith and precept; God's "free electing love" expressed through Jesus Christ that beckoned "God's chosen" to be "called, regenerated, and sanctified"; man's original sin and incompetence to save himself; justification by the righteousness of

Christ through faith; the certainty of a final judgment; the practice of baptism and the Lord's Supper, ordinances for all "regularly Baptized" true believers; the ministration of a "regularly Baptized," "called," and ordained minister; resurrection of the dead; eternal punishment for the wicked and joy for the righteous; the sanctity of the Lord's day; the obligation to support the gospel; and the duty "to pay . . . conscientious regard to civil government and to give our support as an ordinance of God."[11]

"Rules of Decorum" reflected the democracy of the southern frontier. At church conferences held monthly, motions made and seconded would be put to a vote. A simple majority would prevail but must act with "due respect to the minority, and if possible convince them, but if they cannot, the minority shall submit to the majority." To assure order, the rules provided that a member who chose to speak should rise to his feet and address the moderator. Upon being recognized, the member could speak on the subject under debate "without casting reflections" on any member who had spoken previously. No member could speak more than three times on a single subject without permission of the church, nor miss more than one conference without sending an excuse. If a member missed twice without excuse, the congregation appointed a delegate to cite the miscreant to attend the next meeting. No member could bring charges against another without first "taking gospel steps" to resolve the conflict, and any member accusing another without sufficient evidence had to satisfy the accused.[12]

Taken together, the "Abstract of Principles" and "Rules of Decorum" provided a doctrinal basis for Baptist polity. The modest Calvinism of the abstract still allowed for aggressive proselytizing. The formation of the church created a special religious community, set apart from the world, which covenanted to associate together, help one another in physical need, live in peace, and accept a common body of doctrine rooted in Scripture and in historic Reformation Christian practice. Aside from the distinctive Baptist requirement to be "regularly Baptized" (i.e., immersed), the abstract was neither narrow nor sectarian. The decorum assured that democracy and order would prevail in their proceedings just as they hoped it would permeate secular society. If the sacred community prevailed, it would require Herculean efforts by God's chosen community, efforts of attendance, involvement, and commitment not required or even possible elsewhere in their lives.

Discipline

Historian Donald Mathews contends that the terms "order" and "discipline" were central to the southern evangelical's conception of the Christian life. After carefully studying antebellum evangelicals in Mississippi, historian Randy J. Sparks agreed that "the disciplinary process was at the very heart of the evangelical experience."[13] Evangelical churches made heavy demands on their members as part of a separate and holy fellowship. The purpose of such discipline was not to punish the wanderer but to recall the person to faith and to full fellowship within the community. Since Baptists believed that once a sinner was saved the person could not "fall from grace," the purpose of church discipline had more to do with the boundaries of a sacred community than with assurance of salvation. Bound together in the wonder of Christ's redeeming love, Baptists believed that the sins of a brother or sister inflicted pain on the entire family. In the life of Mt. Hebron, congregational disciplining of a member compared closely to parental restraint of a child. The intent was not to exclude the child from the family but to clarify the boundaries of accepted conduct, to forewarn that, if an offspring valued participation in the family, then that child must observe certain standards of conduct. Such restrictions were not designed to hinder the rebellious so much as to keep the family coherent, stable, and mutually committed. The scriptural basis of such discipline was Matthew 18: 15–17.

Words became important symbols in Mt. Hebron's disciplining. The congregation began the process by "citing" a brother or sister, a process that involved appointing a committee of two or three men to investigate and bring the wayward one before the next church conference. Usually the accused appeared promptly and either "acknowledged" the sin and asked forgiveness or "gave satisfaction" to the congregation. Only when the accused refused to appear, would not deny the charge, or, if acknowledging it, would not repent, did the congregation act. In fact the conference seemed anxious not to take action, repeatedly delaying decisions and appointing new committees to reason with the accused. Only when all efforts at reconciliation failed did the congregation "exclude" or "excommunicate" the brother or sister from "fellowship." Clearly, this threatened loss of place in a valued community was a powerful stimulus to reform. Most accused either energetically and promptly denied the charge or repentantly confessed their sins and asked forgiveness. No sin seemed too grievous to forgive; confessions of immorality, alcoholism, gambling, dancing, slander, swearing, fighting, or swindling—all received immediate forgiveness and restoration.

Mt. Hebron's members realized the poor clay from which humanity was crafted and offered the most generous conditions of restoration. They cited their brothers for "drinking too much" or "drinking to excess," not for drinking. They encouraged inquiries about ethical conduct that might be unclear. And periodically the church simply wiped the ethical slate clean in what might be called a "Baptist dispensation": past sins forgiven but from this day on members must abide by strict ethical standards!

Sins against family weighed more heavily than personal impiety such as drinking, dancing, or swearing. The wording of one 1830 disciplinary action was particularly harsh: Brother Lungley was "excommunicated for inconstance in marrying another man's wife." But the congregation anxiously awaited repentance. In September 1857 the church cited Brother Marion McDanal for "immoral conduct." When he acknowledged that he had "done wrong and gave satisfaction" of his repentance, "he was acquitted."[14]

During the first decades, the church primarily disciplined personal habits on a disordered frontier. But as the frontier receded, the congregation cited members more frequently for sins against the collective community. The first such reference appeared in March 1841, when the congregation excluded Brother John Kelly "for violating the law of our state." Ten years later, in October 1851, amid the prosperity of the cotton boom in the Gulf South, the church brought charges against Brother D. A. Ellington for taking illegal tolls at his mill. In January 1853 the congregation excluded Brother John Watson for passing worthless paper banknotes for genuine money. In March 1866, the church cited Brother Isaac Looney for signing over his property to his wife in order to avoid paying his debts. Although personal ethical grievances still predominated, the church increasingly sought to stabilize the life of a society beyond the sacred community. Paradoxically, after the defeat of the Confederacy in 1865, the church seemed to renew its devotion to controlling the private lives of its members and chastening society. During the 1870s and 1880s the church handled an unprecedented number of cases as if to make up for the sins that must have caused the awful judgment of God between 1861 and 1865.[15]

By the last three decades of the nineteenth century the church faced an unprecedented crisis, which it also sought to contain with church discipline. Until these decades Mt. Hebron had absorbed Methodists and Presbyterians into its fellowship but seldom lost its own. When such an event had occurred, the culprit was usually a woman who left for another denomination either because of marriage or discontent with Mt. Hebron. In either circumstance the church had acted firmly and harshly, excluding them from membership. But these isolated instances paled in comparison to the "comeoutism" of the 1870s.

What triggered the crisis is hard to tell, but it clearly involved a deep sense of dissatisfaction with mainstream evangelical southern churches. The exodus of members from Baptist and Methodist congregations swelled the Church of God, the Holiness Church, and other Pentecostal and Holiness sects. Departing members resented the church's growing assimilation of secular culture, yearning for a purer ecclesiastical order. Spreading poverty and rising rates of tenancy increased class divisions within churches. Political divisions between conservative Bourbon (Redeemer) Democrats and independent-minded and more radical Greenbackers, Grangers, Alliancemen, and Populists split congregations. Fueled by a multitude of causes, tension mounted in this rural Zion.[16] As with all other matters of discord and disharmony, members relied on church discipline to contain the damage to their sacred community, which they increasingly perceived in sectarian form.

Periodically Mt. Hebron had expelled members for heresy, but the church's rigid adherence to its original statement of principles and the denominational loyalty of its pastors minimized the influence of schism. Mt. Hebron's one concession to Baptist heterodoxy came in 1868 during a period when it had trouble retaining a regular pastor. The church voted to adopt foot-washing as an ordinance.

More serious trouble arose in September 1871, when the congregation excluded seven people for joining another church. Mt. Hebron expelled others in October, and in November church minutes mentioned the new congregation by name, Sherman's Church, so named for a man who lived in the vicinity of Mt. Hebron. Three more members left Mt. Hebron for Sherman's Church in January (all were excluded) and others apparently followed (approximately thirteen in all), contributing no doubt to the congregation's steady decline in membership from 109 in 1861 to 35 in 1902 (though the largest percentage of this loss resulted from the withdrawal of black members). Luckily Sherman's Church was short lived and only a momentary threat. In addition to excluding heretical members, the congregation took steps to shore up denominational loyalty. In October 1877 members voted to add "Baptist" to the official title of the church, and in July 1878 the congregation elected delegates to the Baptist State Convention. Although the church had been active in regional associations—the Cahaba Association in 1819, the Mt. Zion Association in 1823, the Canaan Association in 1833, and the Cahaba Valley Association in 1867—this is the first reference to participation in the state convention.[17]

The ecclesiastical rigor of church discipline appeared more severe than it really was. Not only did members immediately forgive a penitent sinner, they also softened the language of discipline. Even when a committee cited a member, it did so in ways that symbolized the unity of the sacred community. Minutes referred to miscreants as "brother" and "sister" even when they had committed sins of adultery and heresy. If the sinner proved recalcitrant, the congregation excluded the slacker; but the break in fellowship was often temporary. One principal function of the annual summer revival was to call the excluded to repentance and renewal. Seldom did a revival season pass without joyous reunions as sinners reentered the sacred circle. Church clerks filled the minutes with symbolically significant words. Those guilty of acts of "nonfellowship" were "excluded from fellowship" and then later "made a statement to the community" and were "restored to fellowship." Of 376 members who belonged to the church between 1819 and 1865, the church excluded fifty-five. Of these fifty-five, the church restored at least ten to fellowship. No doubt the extreme pride and individualism so renowned among southerners caused many disciplined members to join other denominations or leave the church entirely. But this cultural pattern only accentuates the significance of those who repented of their sins with contrite and humble hearts.

One function of discipline was to define the boundaries of sacred community. This function encouraged members to challenge vague or ambivalent teachings by asking for clarification. Better to avoid a breach in fellowship by asking interpretations of doctrine than to risk exclusion.

During the frontier stage of Mt. Hebron's existence, when community mattered most and individualism posed a threat to church order, the minutes contain many inquiries resolved in conference. In January 1837 a church conference resolved that none of its members should make or sell "ardent spirits unless for medical purposes." Any member who became drunk more than twice would be excluded. In May 1839 Brother Hezekiah Moor Jr., inquired as to whether it was wrong for a member of Mt. Hebron to take his or her seat "among the world, and not among the members of the Church" during communion. The answer helped strengthen the sacred community; the congregation voted that such practice was wrong. During communion members should sit among their own. More mundane inquiries poured in: Was it wrong to "pitch dollars on the Sabbath day in sport"? Yes! Was it "consistent with Christianity for a man to marry his wife's niece"? The congregation believed such practice "to be consistent." In December 1852 members resolved against "dancing, playing cards for sport or otherwise, nor engage in vain plays nor allow the same in his or her house."[18]

The "Hebronites," as they were called within the community, also tempered church discipline with periodic wholesale revisions, reversals, and suspensions. These occurred mainly when social, economic, and political unrest threatened to engulf the church.

The first such crisis began in 1861. Although hostile armies did not traverse the Cahaba Valley, Mt. Hebron did not escape unscathed. A partial list of church members who served in Confederate armies contains seven names among the congregation of 104. Lists of church members in 1865 indicate that one-third of the members were slaves, so nearly 10 percent of the total white membership (and 27 percent of the estimated white men) fought in the conflict. This put an extraordinary strain on the church. In October 1861 Bradley White wrote from his bivouac in Auburn, acknowledging his sins and asking restoration. The church not only restored him, it also appointed White and three of his comrades-in-arms from Mt. Hebron to "watch over each other" and inform the church of any "misdemeanor" committed while in service. Letters of acknowledgment soon arrived from two other soldiers seeking absolution at long range. It was granted, though not without some resistance in one case. Thus did the sacred community extend itself even to distant battlefields, to men in danger of their lives. But it is unlikely that the soldiers or members back home paid much attention to misdemeanors during the next half-decade. In the preoccupation with surviving, discipline declined.

With war ended and the disaster of Reconstruction descending, Mt. Hebron had to rethink its theology. Convinced that a just God must have acted according to His will, how could a southerner make sense out of historical tragedy? Had a decline in Christian conduct precipitated the ruinous outcome of the war? In February 1866 the church resolved to "strike out all complaints against those that have taken any act in plays and dancing, drinking, and so on and commence with our resolution and inforce them strictly." What followed was the most rigorous application of church discipline in Mt. Hebron's history. Members scrambled to qualify previous sins under terms of the "wipe out law," and the congregation granted generous terms. A rash of exclusions followed, the severity of which threatened the fragile stability of the church. Realism once more outweighed moral judgment. In February 1867 the church agreed "to suspend rules against parties and drinking for the present and inforce them strictly hereafter." For a while the church relied on arbitration of disputes rather than on punitive discipline.

When this crisis passed, cases of discipline mounted rapidly during the remainder of the century. Exclusions, the withdrawal of black members, and the heresy of Sherman's Church reduced the congregation to only thirty-five members in 1902, the smallest figure since the early days of the church. Mt. Hebron abandoned church discipline altogether in 1904. The only recorded cases of exclusion between the Populist revolt which divided the church in 1892–1893 and the end of church discipline in 1904 were cases involving members who joined another denomination. The steady membership decline ended what the Populist revolt had begun: the luxury of exclusion in a church barely able to attract enough members to survive.

Although the church took no formal action to suspend discipline in 1904, no further cases appeared in the minutes until the congregation adopted a new order of decorum amid another historic crisis in December 1934. In that month the congregation issued a blanket dispensation similar to the ones it had granted in 1866 and 1867. Members voted "to let the past conduct be the past and forget and never allow it to come up in the church"; but "from this date on we do agree to comply with all the church rules and decorum of this Hebron Baptist Church." This discipline primarily affected polity and procedures, not personal conduct. Deacons had to attend church conferences. If the church appointed a committee to hear grievances between members, the decision reached by the committee would be final. If the committee could not agree, it would turn the matter over to the entire church for action. Active members must attend church at least once a month unless providentially hindered. All grievances or charges of misconduct would be referred to a church committee created for that purpose.

The renewal of church discipline was short lived. At church conferences the moderator would ask for "acknowledgments," and occasionally a member would confess a sin and ask prayers and forgiveness. The last such recorded confession occurred in September 1945. Discipline had become a matter of individual conscience, and confession a method of maintaining harmony within the church family, not a way by which the sacred community imposed its standards through collective action.

The decline of discipline after 1900 demands an explanation. At its most basic level, discipline functioned as a method of establishing and preserving values and defining the boundaries of acceptable conduct within the religious community. But the twentieth century brought a more complex definition of values. Matters such as dancing were no longer moral issues that were as central or as compelling as they had once been. The congregation had more difficulty imposing its values upon an increasingly pluralistic and tolerant society. At the same time, the religious community successfully imposed many of its notions upon the secular society. Progressive reforms such as Prohibition made the state a partial arbiter of private conduct and lessened the need for church discipline. If discipline was designed to keep the world out of the church, it was less necessary in a time when world and church seemed to be converging. Right conduct was subsumed under broader notions of good citizenship and community conformity. Protestant standards of personal conduct permeated society, and true Americanism became synonymous for a while with what had once been the ethos of Mt. Hebron.

African Americans

The relationship of church discipline to religious community is nowhere more apparent than in the way it affected African American slaves and women. It was in the historic tangent where southern evangelical Christianity touched race and gender that Mt. Heron left its most lasting impact upon secular society.

Baptist attitudes toward slavery underwent a slow metamorphosis between the Revolutionary War and the Civil War. The zeal for freedom following 1776 confirmed the abolitionist sentiments of many Baptists. But the expansion of cotton cultivation and slavery muted such sentiment and gradually turned southern evangelicals into ardent defenders of slavery. They rationalized that a literal reading of Scripture supported slavery and that the presence of so many slaves constituted an unparalleled opportunity for evangelism. Actually they made only halfhearted efforts at evangelizing slaves until the creation of the Southern Baptist Convention (SBC) in 1845. After that date they frequently favored teaching black people to read the Bible, among other reforms. Following the creation of a regional church, secular southerners could no longer oppose reforms by arguing that they stemmed entirely from meddling Yankee abolitionists-evangelicals.

Several keys unlock the complex relationship between black and white Baptists. Although African Americans did not experience religious equality, they did obtain rights not granted by secular governments. Under Alabama law after 1832, slaves could not be taught to read and write, could not testify in court, and could not meet separately in groups. Informal social contacts between the races were governed by a complex hierarchical caste system that denied all forms of social equality. Yet within evangelical churches slaves entered a religious community by an act of free will (commitment to Christ or transferal of membership). They were baptized in the same creeks with white congregants; offered the same "right hand of Christian fellowship;" were brought before the church for discipline in the same way; were exonerated, forgiven, excluded, and restored in the same process; allowed to give testimony,; sometimes preached to both black and white congregations; and worshiped in the same services with white members (although often in a separate area of the building).[19] White evangelicals often taught them to read Scripture (a violation of the law) and recognized the sanctity of their marriages and the inviolability of their families.

The extent of shared rituals varied from congregation to congregation. Black churches existed in cities, but rural congregations usually combined races both for purposes of economy of effort and ease of social control. That way white churchgoers could monitor how ministers interpreted Christianity to black members of the flock. Some rural churches used the terms "brother" and "sister" uniformly without regard to race; others used such familiar terms only for white members. Some minutes recorded only the first names of slaves but the full names of white parishioners. Membership lists sometimes separated the names of white worshipers and slaves; others mixed them; some omitted the names of slaves altogether. In matters of discipline slaves sometimes testified against slaves, sometimes acknowledged their own sins, sometimes were the objects of charges by white members, and infrequently watched passively as whites cited other whites for mistreatment of slaves. In extremely rare cases slaves testified against white members.[20]

Even if white people intended the Gospel as a form of social control, slaves often appropriated the symbols and rituals in different ways. Masters expected obedience as the result of the Christian message; but slaves obtained a sense of joy, meaning, and spiritual liberation. Different perceptions of spiritual symbols and white notions of black inferiority assured that the sense of religious community experienced by black and white church members would be different.[21] Within each racially mixed church, three sacred communities existed: whites with whites, blacks with blacks, and whites with blacks.

Mt. Hebron tended toward the liberal end of this continuum of Christian relationships. Of 376 names recorded in church minutes between 1819 and 1865, fifty-one were names of slaves and two those of free black people. The church book recorded only the first names of slaves and always listed them as "a servant of " (eg, "Pattey, a servant of R. S. Shepherd"). Their names are listed chronologically among white church members in the order in which they joined Mt. Hebron, not separately by race. In many cases slaves joined the church although their masters did not belong. That seems to be the case with planter R. S. Shepherd, who was not listed among church members although eleven of his slaves were. Other slaves joined at the same time as their masters. Peter and Mark, servants of John McDanal, were listed as numbers 134 and 135, and McDanal as member number 136. Mary and Pattey, servants of B. White, came as members 193 and 194; Nancy E. White, presumably B. White's wife, came as member 192. Many slaves joined long before their masters and may even have influenced the white families to join. John, a servant of Isaac Cameron, entered Mt. Hebron as member number 72; his mistress, Sara Cameron, became member 100. Rose, servant of William Watson, joined the church (number 78) long before her master (number 266).

The church did not remain all white for long after its founding. In October 1825 Peter, "a colored person, servant of John McDanal," joined. Most slaves came by profession of faith, though some came by letter of transfer. Usually the congregation routinely dismissed slaves when they desired to transfer elsewhere (perhaps because they were sold to another plantation). A curious exception to that pattern occurred in March 1829, when the church granted letters of dismissal to "black brethren" belonging to a Dr. Shackleford. But at a June meeting white member Jesse Sparks reported that three of the "black brethren belonging to Dr. Shackleford, wish their letters to remain in this church." This intriguing conflict between Shackleford, his slaves, and the church is not further explained, although in December the black brethren did request their letters that the church had first granted and then retained. Whatever the complex factors operating in this case, obviously the congregation respected the right of the three slaves to determine for themselves whether or not to request their letters. However Shackleford obtained their transfer, whether through persuasion or coercion, the church would not grant the letters so long as the three slaves resisted. Only when they themselves sought their letters did the church honor the requests.

When a slave is mentioned in church proceedings, the prefix "black brother" or "black sister" is usually appended, although no slave was accorded a last name. That was not the case with free men of color. Ned Potter joined Mt. Hebron on June 14, 1832, and is always called by his full name when mentioned in the minutes. Like many of his white brethren, he fell victim to church discipline. In July 1833 two white men cited Porter. In August the congregation excluded him from fellowship for drunkenness and swearing. In February 1855 the church received by letter Isaac Johnson, "a colored man." Although the minutes do not specify whether he was slave or free man, the use of his full name suggests that he was a free man of color.

Slaves also answered frequently to charges. Church minutes record the names of seven male slaves subjected to discipline and two female slaves. In January 1836 members excluded Bob and Abram for quarreling on the Sabbath. In August 1852 the church excluded Elijah for lying. Allegations of unruly and disorderly conduct typified charges against black men: the church cited two for quarreling, two for fighting, one for lying, one for nonattendance, and one for Sabbath violation.

The two women cited seemed to have committed offenses that struck more fundamentally at the racial order. In March 1846 a two-man committee cited "Sister Julia," a slave of C. Thompson. They charged that she disobeyed her master and ran away. For this offense the church excluded her. In September 1858 the church cited Mary, a slave belonging to a man named Herring, for "unchristian conduct." The church appointed her master, apparently a church member, "to inform her of the charge and report to next conference her reply." This practice differed from the normal practice of allowing members personally to answer charges made against them. Because her master investigated the charge and presented her reply, it is no surprise that the membership excluded her.

Having a white reply on behalf of a slave was uncharacteristic of earlier discipline cases. In February 1848 two men appeared before the church to acknowledge that they had engaged in fighting in self-defense. Brother Lowery was white, Brother George was a slave. Both spoke in their own defense, and each asked to be retained. The church forgave them and retained fellowship with both men. George was not so lucky the second time around. When he acknowledged the same sin seventeen months later, the church excluded him from fellowship.[22]

The strangest episode in the interracial history of Mt. Hebron occurred in 1854 and demonstrates the way in which close religious fellowship blurred the secular boundaries of race. In January 1855 the congregation considered a report that "some brethren" had attended "a Negro ball, and engaged with the blacks in dancing." The church appointed an unusually large committee of five white men to investigate. The committee reported in January 1855 that several church members had attended a gathering on the Shepherd plantation during the Christmas holidays. At least eleven of Shepherd's slaves belonged to the church, so such an assembly might not seem strange except for the circumstances. White people other than masters seldom visited slaves in their own cabins. Furthermore, the committee reported that "one or two [white] members engaged with them in [fiddling and dancing] . . . (to wit) Samuel P. Dyers, Leonard B. McDonald, Manson Glass, Bradley White, Smith White, and Samuel W. White."

The entire congregation took up the charges in February. Three of the accused gave "satisfaction" and were retained. But the other three failed to exonerate themselves and were excluded from fellowship.

Barely four months after the resolution of the interracial Christmas dance, the church cited Sister Audea Harris. The sensational report alleged that Harris had been seen visiting the Negro quarters on the Shepherd plantation. Harris explained through the committee to the July church conference that she had been processing Mrs. Shepherd's will. As part of those duties she had "called at a negro cabin but says she has not made a habit of visiting" Negro houses and "disapproves such conduct." The church accepted her explanation and took no action.[23]

The two episodes reveal much about race relations. The unusual length and detail of the account in church minutes and the unprecedented size of the investigating committee indicates the extent of concern. Having brought the two races together in sacred community, white members now scrambled to define the limits of their fellowship. White and black worshipers could share hymns, communion, baptism, the right hand of fellowship, discipline, and sermons; but they could not share the slave quarters or fiddle and dance together. The specter of six white men dancing with black women at a Christmas party was bad enough. But a female church member frequenting a slave cabin alone raised sexual questions of even greater magnitude. Mt. Hebron Church, having first blurred racial distinctions in the process of defining religious community, now tried desperately to reorder and redefine those distinctions within a larger secular society that absolutely would not tolerate acts of racial iconoclasm.

This close attention to church discipline reflects Mt. Hebron's concern for the spiritual welfare of its slave members. But the interest appears in other aspects of church life as well. In January 1828 members agreed to build an addition to the meeting house for "the accommodation of Black persons." Apparently between 1825 when the first slave had joined and this addition some three years later, slaves had worshiped with white churchgoers. The new addition allowed the spatial separation within the building that white members deemed necessary. This symbol of hierarchy and separation indicates both the limits of community and the determination of white members to minister to the spiritual needs of slaves even at considerable inconvenience and the allocation of precious financial resources.

Four years later, in March 1832, "Brother Anthony," slave of Willis H. Jones, was "liberated by the church to preach the Gospel so long as he keeps in good order." "Liberate" did not mean to free physically, which was beyond the power of the church in any case. But use of the term, which the church minutes do not employ when describing ordination of white worshipers, is significant, as is the unusual qualification (so long as he "keeps in good order"). One may assume Anthony kept in "good order" and continued his ministry of preaching to his flock in Mt. Hebron and environs because the minutes make no further mention of him.

Of course the Civil War and emancipation altered all of these arrangements, but not so suddenly as one might expect. Denominational leaders in Alabama differed sharply over the future course of black-white relations when the war ended. The Rev. I. T. Tichenor, a distinguished minister, businessman, and college administrator, chided Alabama Baptists in 1865 for having tolerated antebellum laws that denied black people the ability to learn to read Scripture. White Baptists should welcome freedmen into church fellowship, teach them to read the Bible, and share communion with them.

Not all Alabama Baptists agreed with this proposal. Some churches established committees to speed the withdrawal of black members, and one association in the Tennessee Valley refused to accept a black church into its fellowship, urging black Baptists to create an association of their own. Many white Baptists expressed triple concerns: fear that black churchgoers would want to remain with them; fear lest meddling northern Baptists try to proselytize among them, thereby working both religious and political mischief; and fear lest black brethren create churches under the leadership of ignorant and overtly political black pastors. In a variety of ways white church members made it clear that any continued relationship would be on their terms, not on terms of religious or social equality. Interracial churches would not select black pastors, deacons, Sunday school teachers or other officers. Nor did most white churches make much effort to dissuade black members when they began to leave.[24] Black Baptists chose to create churches that they controlled, met their religious needs, and allowed them to realize the full possibilities of religious community. But the fact that the patterns of their churches so closely matched the ones from which they came confirms the strong element of biracial community even in the churches that slavery wrought. Given the paternalism or outright hostility of many white Baptists, it is no surprise that virtually all black believers withdrew from interracial Baptist churches during Reconstruction, and most did so within months of emancipation.

Once again Mt. Hebron proved an exception to the rule. Perhaps the relatively small number of black people living in the Upper Cahaba Valley and the stable and long-term religious association inhibited quick resolution of the issue. Whatever the cause, separation occurred slowly. In October 1865, six months after the Civil War ended, the church received "black sister Emley by letter." The familiar designation of "sister" remained, but so did the condescendingly familiar given name without surname. The church continued to exercise discipline over both races. In March 1866 the congregation considered charges of immoral conduct against Salley, a "black sister," and excluded her. In January 1872 the church excluded a black member, now listed by full name as Alse McDanal, because he had joined the exodus to the heretical Sherman's Church, which apparently was interracial. The final reference to black members in church records occurred in November 1873 when sisters Mary and Matilda Looney transferred their letters. After that date the church consisted of white members only, reflecting the broader patterns of segregation spreading rapidly across southern society.

Ironically, however, the Looney sisters were not the last black persons to attend Mt. Hebron. Despite hardening racial lines and the steady progress of Jim Crow laws, local tradition and Christian goodwill once again defied stereotypes in the twentieth century. Present member Margie Poole Martin remembers a black woman who attended the church. An elderly couple, the Jim Doroughs, hired the black woman to live with them and help them with chores. She accompanied them to church "just as regular as can be." The church building contained a large potbellied stove, and a bench nearby belonged to her.[25] So in the twentieth century as in the nineteenth, community existed within community. The congregation exempted a single black woman from racial exclusion but made sure she had her own bench, to emphasize that racial boundaries still mattered in congregational life.

Women

Evangelical churches divided by race also designated roles according to gender. Baptists in early Virginia and South Carolina represented a back country frontier people opposed to a Tidewater gentry dominated by men. The history of discipline within these early churches reveals how forcefully evangelicals attacked so-called masculine virtues—competitiveness, violence, gambling, drinking, swearing, horse racing, and Sabbath desecration (especially hunting on the Sabbath). Added to this inferential evidence is the fact that most congregations were disproportionately female (one estimate claims a ratio in all southern churches of 65 percent female to 35 percent male). Although male evangelicals were as "manly" as their secular counterparts, they belonged to churches that glorified "feminine" virtues such as nonviolence, emotional expressiveness, kindness to neighbor and stranger, humility, and pursuit of collective rather than individual goals.[26] One of the strengths of religious community was its capacity to encourage and nourish human growth and potential, "motherly" characteristics within the complex division of roles according to gender.

"Family religion" became common in the South. Society at first expected the male head of family to establish religious standards for his family. But when men shirked this responsibility, pressure shifted toward women as pivotal in the public and private life of evangelicalism. In the process of directing and arbitrating the family's religious life, many women consciously or unconsciously experienced a fascinating metamorphosis paralleling the religious experience of slaves. Evangelical religion became a force for restraining abusive husbands and rowdy sons, a method of establishing "psychological distance" between themselves and worldly husbands, which allowed them, for the best of theological reasons, to place loyalty to God above obedience to husband in at least the most sacred spheres of life. Christianity allowed women to secure both a separate sexual identity and a group gender identity. In time they could speak and vote their minds in church conferences.

The church also provided antebellum women their chief means of public identity. The great awakening that swept the South after the Cane Ridge revival of 1800 even allowed women to become "exhorters." Such women appeared in a formal role to urge sinners to respond to the tugging of the Holy Spirit.[27] And the separate doors and seating within frontier churches must not be considered exclusively a matter of sexual separation. Segregating women and girls from men encouraged emotional bonding with other women. Mt. Hebron experienced many of these patterns. Although men slightly outnumbered women in the first few months of the church's existence—seventeen men and eleven women among the first twenty-eight members—the pattern quickly became more typical. New members added during 1828 included eleven white and three black women, six white and two black men, or a total of fourteen women to only eight men. A ten-day camp meeting in October 1848 brought in twenty-eight white and three black women, nineteen white and two black men, for a total of thirty-one women to only twenty-one men. By December 1865, Mt. Hebron contained twenty-six male members and forty-seven female members, a ratio of 65 percent female to 35 percent male, virtually identical to one historian's estimate for the southern church.[28] Interestingly, the church in 1865 divided the membership list by gender, whereas previously it had listed names in the order in which persons had joined the church.

Religious symbols confused gender identification. As with black slaves, women shared freely and equally in most of the common rituals. Like black churchgoers, they initiated a relationship to Christ and his church by an act of free will. The congregation extended baptism, the right hand of fellowship, communion, and discipline without regard to gender. But other practices stemmed from women's separation into a sphere reserved for them. Like black congregants, they sat in a separate section of the church, and this segregation lasted at least until the 1920s, within the memory of women who still belong to Mt. Hebron.[29] Like black members, women were excluded from leadership roles within the church. No woman's name appears as an officer or as a member of any committee until February 1830, when a Sister Nance served on a committee to cite another woman for a discipline violation. But appointing a woman to a discipline committee was not common practice. In infrequent cases where the church appointed women to such committees, the accused was also a woman. Women never investigated charges against men, but men frequently conducted investigations involving women. Although the evidence is not conclusive, it appears that women did attend church conferences from the early years of the church, but it is not clear when they began to vote on ecclesiastical matters. Certainly they were considered full members of the church from the moment of their profession of faith and baptism.

Throughout the history of Mt. Hebron, disciplinary matters most clearly revealed the complex gender relations within the sacred community. From the first recorded case of discipline in 1826 until the last in 1904, church minutes describe at least 242 cases brought before the church. Of these complaints 181 accused men (172 citations of white men, 7 of slaves, and 2 of free black men) and 61 charged women (58 white women, 2 slaves, 1 free black woman). So in a church that was 65 percent female, women stood accused of only 25 percent of the ethical and religious violations. The 35 percent minority of men committed 75 percent of the breaches of acceptable conduct.[30]

Analysis of the types of offenses committed reveals gender differences even more sharply. Although women held no offices, they strongly influenced the ethical standards of the church. The "sin" most frequently cited in discipline cases was alcohol abuse. It is now clear that excessive consumption of alcohol often accompanies other activities destructive to family and community values: fighting, gambling, wife and child abuse, adultery, and other "disorderly" conduct. Of the fifty-four cases of "excessive drinking," "too much drinking," "intoxication," "whiskey-making," and so on, all involved men and all but one a white man. So far as the formal discipline of Mt. Hebron was concerned, drunkenness was an exclusively male sin and the one most frequently cited. Of the eighteen cases of swearing cited in church minutes, every one involved white men. Gambling, card playing, disorderly conduct, and Sabbath violation appear as exclusively male sins, as do a series of unethical business practices (unlawful use of public funds, swindling, and overcharging). Charges of quarreling, fighting, and anger affected twenty-three men but only one woman. The church also excluded one man for wife abuse. Conversely, some categories of "sin" belonged to women. Charges of heresy resulted in the exclusion of three women but were never brought against a man.

A few moral breaches seemed to affect both sexes. The church cited thirty-two men and twenty women for dancing, six women and five men for falsehood/slander, eight men and four women for nonattendance, fifteen men and thirteen women for joining another denomination, and four men and two women (one of them a free black woman) for immorality/adultery.

Quite clearly discipline meted out by Mt. Hebron served to protect women and families from the worst aspects of frontier life and to socialize and "civilize" men in a way defined by women. This fact tends to mitigate the absence of women on committees appointed to cite wayward members. They might not often serve on such committees, but they heard the charges and they either cast votes or influenced decisions on whether to exclude miscreants.

Another curiosity of disciplinary proceedings was the frequency with which women rejected the jurisdiction of the church over their private conduct. Such cases usually involved dancing, as did an instance in 1857. After being cited for this violation in February, Sister Martha Jane Byram acknowledged the conduct in a March conference but refused to "make satisfaction"; the church excluded her from fellowship. In April 1869 Sister Jiney McDanal also refused to give satisfaction on dancing charges and met the same fate. Many other members charged with dancing asked forgiveness at that same conference, and the church retained them in fellowship. In 1852 Elizabeth Hall obtained a letter dismissing her from Mt. Hebron. But in May of that year the conference excluded her and asked that she return the letter. Sister Hall refused a man's request for her letter and the church voted to report her to the association. She finally capitulated to this threat in July.

Women frequently left Mt. Hebron for other denominations, but often this decision involved marriage or the dictates of husbands or families. Some incidents of exclusion of women for joining Presbyterian or Methodist churches carry the mitigating reference in church minutes that the sister *had married* and joined another denomination. Church minutes for September 1832 refer to "Sister Annie" who "to satisfy her family, joined the C. Presbyterians." No such clarifying reference ever appears in regard to a man.

Another crisis of conscience and family loyalty could occur when the congregation cited a spouse or family member. On numerous occasions independent-minded members of Mt. Hebron refused to recant and were excluded. Often family members remained loyal to them and requested a "letter of dismission" as protest against church action. Unless a member remained in good standing, that person could not transfer membership to another Baptist church. So an excluded person would often "give satisfaction" in order to return to good standing and then immediately request a church letter of dismissal allowing transfer to another Baptist church. Frequently the unoffending spouse would also request a letter. Many such cases appear in church minutes, and in all but two cases they involved a wife loyally supporting her aggrieved husband.[31] Twice the church charged women with offenses, and their husbands loyally stood by them. In August 1839 the church found Sister Mary Whitfield guilty of slandering Elizabeth Kelley and excluded her. At the same meeting, her husband, George Washington Whitfield, requested that his name be withdrawn from church rolls. In March 1851 Sisters Harris and McDanal and Brother McDonald investigated an "evil report" circulating about Sister Elizabeth McDanal. Two of the members accepted the report as true (it seems likely that the Sister McDanal on the inquiring committee was a relative and perhaps dissented), and the church excluded

Elizabeth McDanal. In May a relative, John McDanal, requested his letter, and in January 1852 Elizabeth's husband William requested dismissal. In May 1853 William, Elizabeth, and Francis McDanal, another relative of the prominent family, moved their letters back to Mt. Hebron. In April 1880 the church cited Mollie Courson for dancing, and she immediately acknowledged her sin. But in August Ann Courson, probably Mollie's mother, requested a letter of dismissal. Clearly family ties often meant more to spouses and family members than good relations with a sacred community.

What is equally fascinating is the infrequency with which a wife left the church when the church cited her husband. In fact the recorded cases of family solidarity in such crises makes even more significant the numerous exceptions to this pattern. Usually after the church cited a man the minutes contain no reference to a wife seeking a letter of dismissal. Although the case is not altogether certain, it appears that most women chose loyalty to Christ and his church over loyalty to spouse, perhaps because many devout women believed the discipline meted out to their husbands was entirely appropriate. Such a case occurred in July 1848, when Mt. Hebron members excluded William Watson for hunting on the Sabbath. Sister Watson remained an active member of the church, and in November 1848 served on a committee to cite a sister who had joined the Presbyterian Church.

Because the central function of the church was preaching and the primary task of deacons and trustees was fund-raising and administration of church business, women obviously did not fit into the hierarchical structure of Mt. Hebron. During much of the nineteenth-century services consisted of nothing more than preaching once a month on Saturday followed by a church conference. Annual camp meetings and protracted revivals afforded women few roles other than preparing meals or boarding a visiting preacher.

Development of a more complex educational structure after 1900 extended greater opportunities to women. The Woman's Missionary Union (WMU) provided a place for women to develop leadership and parliamentary skills and socialize with other women. It also became Mt. Hebron's primary advocate of missions, especially of community ministry to the poor and sick.

Mt. Hebron's most important denominational affiliation was the annual associational meeting. The early records of the church mention no delegates elected to the Alabama Baptist or Southern Baptist conventions, but the church seldom failed to send a delegation to the nearby associational meetings. The church always elected male messengers until 1919. During the years between 1900 and 1917 Alabama and Southern Baptists furiously debated the propriety of allowing women to serve as messengers (delegates) to the statewide denominational meeting. Many biblical literalists insisted that this reform contradicted Scripture. Mt. Hebron's minutes contain no reference to the issue. But seven years after the state convention allowed women to serve as messengers (1912) the church apparently elected its first female delegate to the association when it selected Mr. And Mrs. G. C. Chaney.[32] It may not be altogether coincidental that this rural Baptist congregation elected its first woman messenger in 1919, the same year Congress approved the nineteenth amendment extending to women the right to vote. In 1921 the church again selected the Chaneys as well as Mr. And Mrs. A. L. Dorough and Mrs. Ellen Moore, giving women a three-to-two majority. Since many of the male members had begun working in coal mines and steel mills by the 1920s, they could not attend the daylong associational meetings. Although male messengers often attended in the evening, women regularly outnumbered men during the daytime sessions that made policy and transacted business, none of which of course was binding on the fiercely independent local Baptist congregations.

Hard times during the 1930s further eroded male dominance. With men desperately seeking employment or demoralized by the Great Depression, women assumed a larger role in church life. They had long furnished all Sunday school teachers except for the two men's classes. A historic event occurred on February 23, 1930, when the pastor, a Howard College student, asked a prominent WMU leader, Mrs. McDanal, to conduct a prayer meeting. The Rev. W. Albert Smith was no liberal or theological iconoclast, but the church was experiencing difficulty finding a man willing to serve as deacon or in other leadership roles, so Mrs. McDanal's service seems to have been more an act of ministry in time of need than an example of theological liberalism.

Other breakthroughs occurred four years later. Previously, business matters had been largely beyond the influence of female members, although they had proven quite adept at raising money for missions through the WMU. But on December 16, 1934, the church appointed Mrs. Joe Dorough as secretary of donations. That same month the church revised its decorum to reestablish a committee to hear grievances or complaints of misconduct toward members. It appointed Mrs. Annabel Moore as one of three committee members.

Post–World War II social upheaval accelerated the pace of change within the church. Mt. Hebron's Sunday school organization in May 1946 listed female teachers for twelve of fourteen Bible classes. When the church selected messengers to the associational meeting in September 1947, it elected four women, and it again elected an all-female contingent a year later. Women regularly led in prayer at church meetings, and in February 1958 a female missionary to migrant workers spoke from the pulpit at a regular Sunday morning worship service. During Youth Sunday in March 1957, a boy "brought the morning message and Earline McLaughlin spoke on missionaries at the evening service." Although the minutes do not clarify the difference between a boy/man "bringing a message" and a girl/woman "speaking" at a service, apparently the church regarded both as regular services. At the end of Miss McLaughlin's "speech," she gave an invitation, and Margaret Ann Skelton accepted Christ as her savior, undoubtedly the supreme test of a "sermon" from a Southern Baptist pulpit.

Numerous subtle tensions over gender surfaced in the 1960s. Women began to resist the traditional annual all-day singing because they had to cook to feed the singers, most of whom were not members of the church. When the church left the matter of refreshments for the annual revival to the discretion of the WMU, the ladies decided that everyone should bring a supper on the Saturday evening of the revival, in place of a few women preparing refreshments for each night of the services. Their work retiling the nursery floor, making curtains, and raising money for new choir robes and church kitchen equipment left little time for preparing refreshments. Obviously Mt. Hebron's women had decided their Christian ministry did not consist mainly of preparing meals for men.

In summer 1964 the church employed a female choir director to replace a man who had resigned. Her modest pay of $20 a week barely covered her travel expense, but Mrs. Davis served faithfully and well. She tried to resign in 1969, but the entire church gave a banquet in her honor and persuaded her to stay on until 1974. In September 1975 the deacons proposed to raise money to build an educational building and entrusted the task of being the fund-raising chairman to Mrs. Ester Oglesby, who was nursery director and teacher of the woman's Sunday school. The deacons instructed her to select her own committee members. When Mt. Hebron's pastor resigned in 1981, the church elected a pulpit committee consisting of three deacons and their wives, who would elect their own chairman.

The good folk of Mt. Hebron through the generations insisted on rigid adherence to biblical admonitions regarding the subordination of women and the hierarchical nature of the family. Yet the church did respond in numerous ways to societal shifts in the understanding of the appropriate role of women in society. Women established their own networks whereby they raised money for missions and held offices from president down within the WMU. Many established the priority of Christ in their lives even when husbands did not share the same vision. They influenced the church's concept of proper ethical conduct and molded Mt. Hebron's use of discipline toward social objectives that helped protect them from violence, drunkenness, and discord. They might not hold the offices of pastor or deacon, but they made their voices heard nonetheless.

Pastors

The men who provided leadership to Mt. Hebron were as unpredictable a group as the women who filled the pews. Few generalizations fit all of them, although some do provide helpful categories. Between 1819 and 1980 the church employed thirty-six pastors. "Employed" is almost too strong a word to describe their relationship to the congregation. Most were bivocational men who earned a primary salary in a secular vocation. Others studied at nearby Howard College, the leading Baptist institution in the state. The fortuitous proximity of the college allowed the church to use faculty and ministerial students as revival speakers, interim pastors or guest preachers when pastors were ill or out of town, and regular pastors. In fact Mt. Hebron had a long association with the eastern end of Jones Valley, later the East Lake suburb of Birmingham. Hosea Holcombe, pastor of Ruhama Baptist in East Lake, founded Mt. Hebron. In 1887 Howard College moved from Marion to East Lake, across the street from Ruhama Church, continuing the close relationship.

During most of its history Mt. Hebron, like most rural churches in the South, was quarter-time. Throughout the nineteenth century members met once a month, usually on Saturday. During the 1920s the church experimented with services twice a month, but reverted to older traditions by the early years of the Depression. Not until the late 1930s did the church begin weekly services on a regular basis.

Because the membership consisted mainly of farmers and working-class people, the church struggled financially. This fact limited what it could pay pastors and embroiled it in financial crises. Low pay kept its pastors poor, as both church records and oral history attest.

Not until the 1960s did the church select a pastor for an indefinite period of time. Before that, members elected their pastor annually. The process followed the most elemental democratic practice, with members lining up behind their favorites. Many times the church conducted a kind of preach-off, bringing in several visiting preachers for trial sermons and then voting to elect the one which the congregation liked best. Such elections were often temporarily divisive. In September 1945 members nominated three candidates for pastor. Then they voted on whether to conduct a secret ballot or a public, standing vote, and decided on the latter. The beloved former pastor (1935–1944), Fred E. Maxey, received twenty-three votes, a preacher named Fullmer got twelve, and the Rev. Earnest Faulkner was elected with twenty-nine. At the same conference, members elected Mrs. Fred Maxey Jr. to the post of church clerk; she was daughter-in-law of the former pastor. Whether because of the rejection of his father or for some other reason, Fred Maxey Jr., and his family left the church and affiliated with Bold Springs Presbyterian Church, although they rejoined Mt. Hebron in 1953. In 1948 the church unanimously decided to delay calling a preacher for three months in order to hear a variety of them, but split sixteen-to-eleven over whether to pay visiting preachers. After one of the deepest splits in Mt. Hebron's history in 1954, members voted on two nominees by having all who favored the Rev. Jim Brunner move to one side of the auditorium (thirty-two moved to his side) and those preferring the Rev. Gene Crocker (a former pastor) to stand on the other side (thirty-four moved to his side, giving him the pastorate). In September 1947 a member proposed calling a pastor for an indefinite period of time in conformity with general Baptist practice, but members tabled the motion by a three-to-one vote. In 1959 the church voted on whether to keep the present pastor, the Rev. Albert I. Bowman, or to elect a new one. The vote of thirty-five-to-thirteen favored a change.

Low pay contributed to the general instability. In the nineteenth century many rural Baptists believed the church should not pay the pastor a regular salary. He was one of the people, though divinely called, and should earn his living by the sweat of his brow like his parishioners. What was good for Paul and Silas was good enough for Mt. Hebron.

The long tradition of bivocationalism had some salutary effects. It guaranteed a pastor close to the people, one who spoke their language, shared their beliefs, and knew their problems. No gulf of formal education or theological learning stood between pastor and people. Although many church historians have depicted this practice as a liability to spiritual maturity, it was most certainly a stimulus to growth. Rural Baptist churches became the churches of the common people. Affluent planters and businessmen, the well educated and the culturally refined, might find a more hospitable worship environment, but the plain people flocked to Baptist churches.

From their meager earnings the plain folk gave what they could, which was never very much. During the early years members subscribed money in various special solicitations for the pastor's salary, associational offerings, mission gifts, building funds, and other causes. By the 1930s the church followed the Southern Baptist pattern of adopting a single, unified budget which included all items. The church also urged members to adopt the biblical principle of the tithe. This change over time in church finances is clearly reflected in historic patterns. In August 1837 Mt. Hebron's members decided it was "not expedient to employ a minister to ride and preach for us next year." For the remainder of the year the church did without a regular parson while soliciting funds for a salary in the future. In October 1906, with membership near a historic low, members raised $18 for a pastor. In November 1921 the church anguished over how much to pay the preacher. Not until 1935 did the church begin to consider a parsonage. During the middle 1930s the church paid the pastor only $20 a month, when it could raise that much. But some members still walked to church themselves, and many others still traveled by wagon. By 1948 postwar prosperity and the emphasis on tithing and a unified budget allowed the church to raise the salary to $25 a week, though the Rev. Eugene Crocker recommended cutting his salary in 1950 because low contributions made it impossible to fully pay him anyway. In a move which reflected the church's precarious finances, members voted in 1951 to raise Crocker's salary to $50 a week if the church could pay that much, or to $45 if it could not. The church raised the salary to $55 a week in 1954, to $300 a month in 1960, $400 in 1966, $500 in 1974, and $160 a week in 1980. The beloved Rev. Willie B. Harris, who served a record seventeen years as pastor between 1962 and 1978, earned his primary living at a local company and had to terminate his pastorate when the company moved to Atlanta in 1978.

Irregularity of pastoral leadership may explain Mt. Hebron's occasional flirtation with heterodoxy. During the years when the church adopted foot-washing (1868) and lost many of its members to the heretical Sherman's Church (1871), the congregation apparently had no regular pastor. Although minutes from the Reconstruction period are fragmentary, they list no names of pastors from 1855 until 1874, and contain another gap from 1874 until 1878. Nor is a pastor listed for the critical years from 1897 until 1902, years of economic decline and political turmoil when church membership dropped. Conversely, when the church began to rely heavily on the state denominational college for its pastors, it became much more orthodox, adopting Southern Baptist literature and organizational structure.

Despite its problems, lack of pay did not keep Mt. Hebron from attracting a steady supply of able pastors. The first, Hosea Holcombe, was the premier denominational leader of his time in Alabama. During his years as pastor of Ruhama, Mt. Hebron, and numerous missions, he helped establish the Alabama Baptist Convention in 1823, became its first domestic missionary, served for six years as its president (1833–1838), helped establish a manual labor institute, wrote the first history of Alabama Baptists (1840), and fiercely resisted the antimissionary Primitive Baptists, who took over many congregations and led them out of the missionary fold.[33] Although Mt. Hebron apparently lost members to the antimissionary movement, it remained loyal to Holcombe's vision through good times and bad.

Subsequent pastors were like Holcombe in that their evangelical zeal outweighed their theological education. They came mostly from the area. The eighth pastor (1874, 1892–1894), the Rev. C. McLaughlin, grew up in the church, son of one of the valley's earliest settlers. The Rev. Joseph Moor and his brother Hezekiah Jr., also descended from early families and grew up in the church. Mt. Hebron ordained Joseph in May 1847 and Hezekiah in November 1856. Hezekiah became pastor of Mt. Hebron's mission church, Bethel Baptist.

The Moor brothers were only two of nine men ordained by Mt. Hebron, which also licensed (indicating permission to preach) eight of its sons to the ministry. Although the congregation respected the right of any man, however simple, to hear and respond to God's call to preach, it did exercise careful scrutiny. The name of Anthony, the slave "liberated by the church to preach the Gospel," does not appear in the church history. Nor do the names of two white members licensed to preach.[34] The church licensed John Lowery in 1854 but later asked him to surrender his license because he had not used it. In August 1874 the church licensed

J. W. Owens to preach, but in September reconsidered its action and recalled his license, though it did grant him the "liberty to exercise in public at home."

Jacob Lawler served Mt. Hebron as its third pastor in 1829–1830. Lawler moved from his native North Carolina to Tennessee and from there to Alabama in 1814. Elected a Shelby County judge in 1825, he soon began preaching also. Although he continued to pastor churches until his death in 1838, he did not seek to escape the temporal into some ethereal world. He served as a state legislator, receiver of public monies, US congressman, and trustee of the University of Alabama.[35]

Infrequent services and limited pastoral duties made such dual careers possible. The Rev. Henry Cox, who pastored Mt. Hebron in 1833 and again from 1838 until 1844, agreed to preach "as often as convenient." When reelected pastor in 1843 by the apparently satisfied congregation, Cox consented "to attend occasionally."[36] His duties consisted of one preaching service and one church conference per month plus occasional funerals and marriages, all performed for a congregation of only fifty or so members.

Between 1829 and 1981 minutes contain the names of thirty-four pastors together with their terms of office. Their tenures averaged only 3 to 4 years, and even that figure is distorted by two long terms of ten and seventeen years. Deleting those two periods of service, the remaining thirty-two pastors averaged only 2.7 years. So continuity of leadership was not characteristic of the church.

The Rev. W. Albert Smith (1929–1932) was born in 1905 in Clay County, Alabama, one of the state's poorest white counties. His father—a ne'er-do-well who farmed, traded horses, and cut meat—did not set a good example for the boy. Jealous and occasionally violent, he abused his wife and ultimately caused her to leave him, although they never formally divorced. The gentle Albert survived both the poverty and the domestic violence of his childhood. He worked in a textile mill to help buy necessities, although such efforts delayed his high school graduation until he was twenty-one. A mill church afforded the peace and serenity lacking in his family. His decision to enter the ministry led him to the Baptist college in Birmingham in 1929. Despite help from the mill's owner, a job became imperative. Mt. Hebron called him as pastor in 1929, and he continued to lead the church until he graduated in 1932 and headed for Southwestern Baptist Theological Seminary in Fort Worth, Texas. The pay of $20 per month at Mt. Hebron did not include eggs and vegetables, which members lavished on their pastor, nor gargantuan country meals eaten in their homes. Smith was remembered as a good pastor and a kind person; his age, particularly, appealed to the youth. He enjoyed being with them and shared their fishing trips and baseball games.[37] After struggling through seminary during the depths of the Depression, he and his wife returned to Alabama where he became pastor of a series of small-town churches and a respected denominational leader.

Although vigorously Bible-oriented and unquestioning of biblical authority,

Smith seldom if ever mentioned "literalism" or "inerrancy." The necessity to minister to vast human needs left him no time for biblical polemic. Perhaps he was fundamentalist in the elemental sense of that term. But at Southwestern he came into contact with critical approaches to biblical scholarship and seemed to have no trouble reconciling science, history, and biblical authority. He took for granted biblical miracles, the Virgin Birth of Christ, the authority of the Bible, the Atonement, and the bodily resurrection, and assumed other Baptists did also. But he lacked a fundamentalist temper. He was tolerant and open-minded, and avoided controversies both at Mt. Hebron and at his later charges. He was far ahead of his times on racial issues. While pastoring in the Tennessee Valley, he drove to Courtland once a week to teach theology to black Baptist preachers, often accompanied by his two youngest children, one of whom vowed to grow up to become "a black Baptist preacher." He kept his openness and tolerance on racial issues pretty much to himself during the tumultuous years of the 1950s and early 1960s, but like Mt. Hebron he represented a Christian ethic that personalized race relations in such a way as to remove some hard edges from racism.

The Rev. Fred E. Maxey represents a different tradition in the pastoral history of the church. Maxey became pastor following a good deal of conflict over a new order of decorum in December 1934. He conducted a three-week revival in the church during March 1935, with five professions of faith to show for his efforts. Apparently church members were impressed because, when their current pastor resigned in April 1935, they immediately employed Maxey to take his place. Thus began a ten-year tenure that became one of the best loved in the church's history.

Unlike Albert Smith, Maxey came from another state and religious tradition. A native of Virginia, he practiced law and became a labor negotiator before moving to Taylor's Valley in southwestern Virginia in 1922. A religious skeptic when he arrived, he was converted in 1924 at the Walnut Grove Church of the Brethren. That church licensed him to preach, and Maxey became an evangelist, preaching in tabernacles, brush arbors, tents, store buildings, and barns in twenty-six states. He also held pastorates in Texas and Indiana before coming to Alabama. His skills as a speaker and his aggressive evangelistic style served him well. Maxey arrived in Leeds in January 1935, to preach a citywide revival. He rented an old theater building and preached the first night to an audience of forty, who apparently came thinking they would see a movie. Maxey had neither fuel for a fire nor money to buy any, so a Baptist preacher-miner provided some coal for the theater's stove. The revival continued into February and attracted the attention of some Mt. Hebron members, who invited Maxey to preach a revival at Mt. Hebron, perhaps unaware that he belonged to a different denomination.

At the time, in February 1935, Maxey published a newsletter for supporters titled "Christo-Centric." He headed his publication with the theological descriptions: "Fundamental," "Undenominational," and "Pre-Millennial." His February letter described the eight "Dispensations." His dispensational Pre-Millennialism identified him firmly with the fundamentalist tradition of the nineteenth century. However, the prospect of a new base of operations in Alabama—and perhaps some changes in his own doctrinal beliefs—led him to become a Baptist and the new pastor of Mt. Hebron in April 1935. The next newsletter listed Leeds, Alabama, as its home and omitted from its masthead the three words "Fundamental," "Undenominational," and "Pre-Millennial."[38] Whether this change reflected the economic desperation of the Depression, an opportunistic change of course, or the culmination of a long theological odyssey is uncertain.[39] Although Mt. Hebron would not have disputed fundamental theology, it was not a fundamentalist church in the sense of strident, intolerant dogma or interdenominational commitment to restrictive theology or to a political program. Had members thought much about theological questions, they would have affirmed the fundamentals propounded by Maxey's publication. But they were too busy surviving to waste time on such idle speculation.

The Maxeys had five children, too many to feed on a salary of $20 a month, so members gave them food. They were so poor that when Maxey departed for one revival he left his wife and children only large bags of red beans and rice, which became their diet three meals a day until he returned.

Though he lacked formal theological training, Maxey possessed a keen legal mind and considerable skills as a communicator. His background as a labor negotiator in the Appalachian coal fields served him well at Mt. Hebron, where a number of his members were miners.

The church proved amazingly tolerant of his constant absences as he preached at revivals, perhaps because when he preached at Mt. Hebron he did so with such good effect. A three-week revival he preached in September 1935 brought eight additions. So popular was he that church minutes during his decadelong tenure ceased mentioning an annual call, and in December the church committed itself to building his family a parsonage, the church's first.

Although a traditional evangelist in theology, Maxey was innovative in the structure of his meetings. He held preaching services at night and Bible studies in the morning. After his revivals ended, he conducted sessions to train new converts and involve them in church life. He also divided men and women into separate groups and talked to them about marriage, relationships, and sex. Although he always had his wife attend the sessions with women, some men objected to the meetings and would not allow their wives to attend. Those who came heard Maxey's frank advice that sex was an important aspect of marriage and should not be considered dirty or a chore. God intended sex to be a joyous and wonderful part of life.

Maxey also proved unorthodox in his political and racial ideologies. His skills in labor arbitration brought a tempting offer. During the Franklin D. Roosevelt administration a Department of Labor official visited Maxey in Leeds and offered him the princely sum of $15,000 a year to work for the Labor Department as a negotiator. His inability to provide for his family tempted him to take the post, but in the end he remained at Mt. Hebron. He did use his ties to the Democratic administration, however. People on welfare or without food contacted him frequently, and he intervened with the state welfare bureaucracy to obtain work for them. His assistance even extended to black people who visited the parsonage seeking help. Maxey tried to aid them with relief administrators, an activity that apparently did not sit well with some local folk. On one occasion Maxey received a telephone threat from the Ku Klux Klan warning him to stop interceding for Negroes. In East Tennessee he preached a sermon titled "The Cross of Christ or the Cross of the Klan," and the hooded order sent a delegation to visit his service and warn him to stop meddling in race relations. But Maxey's best-kept secret was his flirtation with the Communist Party. The party had established its southern base of operations in Birmingham, and Maxey began to write for one of its newspapers, the *Southern News Almanac*. His "Pulpit in Print" column charged the church with failing to live up to its biblical mandate to care for the poor and proclaimed Jesus to be a radical. He tried to fuse Christianity and Marxism, and spoke at rallies opposing the poll tax and advocating the right of black citizens to vote. Although it is unlikely that his congregation knew the extent of his radicalism, it is worth remembering that many of them were tenant farmers and coal miners who had much to gain from a more just economic order. Certainly his radical egalitarian racial ethic was wildly at variance with the world of his parishioners, which makes his continued popularity with older members of the congregation even more remarkable.[40]

Apparently his skills as evangelist and negotiator mitigated any opposition within Mt. Hebron about his frankness over issues of sexuality, personal contacts with black residents, or frequent absences. His close ties with Democratic officials, assistance in getting poor members relief jobs, evangelistic preaching, and thorough Bible studies endeared him to members. Annabel Moore reminisced about her favorite minister: "He taught me so much about the Bible and how to live close to God and meant very much to me." The entire community respected the Maxey family, and Leeds residents later elected his grandson mayor.

Connections

Mt. Hebron's warm relationship with Maxey reflects its long tradition of connectedness to churches of other denominations. Nor was this unusual for rural congregations, which often behaved quite differently from denominations that sought to draw distinctions between their doctrines and practices and those of sister groups. Mt. Hebron's members did not confine community to a narrow sphere. The congregation evidenced a keen interest in the religious life of the valley and the church universal of which it recognized itself to be only a small part.

Members of Mt. Hebron assumed a role of leadership in the various Baptist associations to which the church belonged. The church first elected delegates to the Cahawba Association in August 1825. Pastors and members served terms as moderator (chief officer) and on many of its committees.

During special occasions at nearby Methodist and Presbyterian churches, Mt. Hebron often suspended its own services so members could attend the others. Because all the churches in the valley conducted services only once a month, devout Christians often attended a different church each week, developing Christian friendships across denominational lines. The Great Revival of 1800–1820 had created a southern evangelical church remarkably similar in its basic conception of the acts of God, the nature and destiny of humanity, the reality of sin, and the imperative of repentance and salvation.[41] Children who grew up in one church moved easily to another, depending on friendships, marriage, and personal preferences. Concepts such as Fundamentalism and neo-Orthodox theology, ecumenism or parochial denominationalism played little role in the religious life of the valley. Methodists and Presbyterians, who were kin and neighbors of Mt. Hebron members, might dispute small matters of polity and practice but united on larger issues of meaning and purpose. Of eight members interviewed in 1989, everyone mentioned family connections to nearby Methodist and Presbyterian churches. Annabel Moore grew up in a Methodist family before joining Mt. Hebron. Maggie Dee Wilkinson's family belonged to Bold Springs Presbyterian Church before joining Mt. Hebron in 1952, but had often attended the Baptist church for singings, homecomings, decoration days at the cemetery and for revivals. J. T. Poole's father was also Presbyterian, though the family attended Mt. Hebron so regularly that many members assumed he was Baptist.[42]

As late as 1946 members of other denominations held offices in the Sunday school. Although all church officers belonged to Mt. Hebron, newly joined members often held these posts. The church elected Fred Maxey Jr. to the post of Sunday school superintendent in July 1953 after his family returned from Bold Springs Presbyterian Church in January. Members elected a man baptized in March 1953 as Baptist Training Union director in July.

The ease with which members moved back and forth across denominational lines reflected the simplicity of joining Mt. Hebron. All one had to do was profess faith in Christ or express desire to become a member. If the person had been previously baptized by immersion, even within a non-Baptist church, the congregation admitted the brother or sister without further action. For instance, on September 13, 1964, members accepted a new member by statement of previous baptism from Chelsea Church of God. But when Fred Maxey Jr. joined from a Church of the Brethren background, the congregation decided they had better baptize him again to make sure it was done properly. That night they took him down to the creek on Edwards's farm, turned their car lights on, and immersed him in the waters. Members thereafter called him a "moonlight Baptist."

Lack of emphasis on doctrine explains this ease of movement as well as the periodic heterodoxy of Mt. Hebron. People unaccustomed to Southern Baptist literature, organization, and procedures adopted whatever material and mode of operation made sense to them. In 1945 each Sunday school class voted on its literature. Some used Southern Baptist material; others used the independent fundamentalist Scofield Bible literature. In May 1946 the congregation voted to use only Southern Baptist Sunday school literature; but in September 1948 the church decided to try International Sunday school materials for two months. During the 1930s and 1940s the church adopted the standard Baptist church organizations: Training Union, Woman's Missionary Union (WMU), and brotherhood and youth programs. In 1956 members adopted a "standard" Sunday school graded according to age. By this period earlier flirtations with foot-washing were an aberration of the past. In fact when a member requested use of the church building in order to christen her baby, the church clerk wrote that "this is against the rules of a Baptist church," and members unanimously denied the request.

Although the church developed close ties to the local association and to a lesser extent with the state convention, its connection to the Southern Baptist Convention (SBC) was remote. The Woman's Missionary Union followed the lead of the national women's groups more closely than it followed any other segment of the church. But the national WMU had no formal ties to the SBC and was a fully independent auxiliary. Not until 1979, the first year of fundamentalist victory within the denomination, did Mt. Hebron's minutes record a messenger to the SBC's annual meeting. Although the pastor and his wife often traveled to the convention after 1979, few lay people could afford such a trip. Hence the battle for control of the denomination remained remote to Mt. Hebron. When asked how church members viewed the convention-wide controversy over the inspiration, authority, and inerrancy of Scripture, Annabel Moore responded: "We discussed that some, but when they have conventions they almost get in a fight. It has been in the news and we're so sorry about that, but in Hebron Church, it's just lovely now and we'd never think about having any trouble or anything. Everybody loves each other and why we just enjoy our life as we meet there on Sundays and prayer meetings."[43]

Mt. Hebron's connection to its community confounds the traditional notion that fundamentalist churches ignore secular social institutions. Just as Fred Maxey reached out to unemployed members and the community's black citizens during the 1930s, the church had existed within both sacred and secular communities. Distinctions between the two became blurred. Because the farming area south of Leeds had no school, Mt. Hebron established one before the Civil War.

Classes met in the church until the community joined together about 1915 to build a schoolhouse adjacent to the church. In 1859 John G. Moor, descendant of a prominent pioneer family that also furnished many members to Mt. Hebron, taught the school. Prominent families—among them the McDaniels, Baileys, DeShazos, Moors, Doroughs, and Fosters—sent their children to the school. It continued to prosper after the turn of the century until the rural consolidation and school bus programs finally caused its discontinuance in 1942.[44] During the Depression, Auburn University home-demonstration agents used the school building as a community center to teach poor families how to make mattresses and learn crafts to supplement incomes. After the school closed in 1942, the Mt. Hebron Extension Homemaker's Club turned the building into a clubhouse and community center for educational and social programs—canning, sewing, cooking, and hygiene. Many female church members joined large crowds of women attending the monthly meetings.[45] In 1951 the church voted to cooperate with the Home Demonstration Club and Mt. Hebron Cemetery Association in repairing the well at the clubhouse, which all three would then use.

Recalling club meetings, Annabel Moore spoke of "wonderful memories" of a time before women worked for salaries, when they had time on their hands and enjoyed spending it together.[46] So the ties of community that developed within Mt. Hebron expanded outward to a larger secular community.

Mission

If asked to name the central function of Mt. Hebron, most members will not answer to discipline members, to forge community, or to build schools. Members defined the primary function of their congregation as winning people to faith in Christ and enrolling them in his church. But people won to faith in Christ are not simply related in a new way to their creator. They are related in a new way to other believers.

The church directed much of its energy and resources toward conversion. In the early years, revivals, camp meetings, or protracted meetings formed the central agenda of the church. One such protracted meeting in July 1838, conducted with four other churches, added sixty-one members. As early as October 1827, members decided to "hold meeting" in the neighborhood of a Captain Nance. This revival at Hopewell Meeting House attracted enough new members to justify services there every third Saturday. In December members voted to name this new "arm of the church" Bethel. But disagreements soon troubled the fellowship. Members stopped attending Bethel, the mission declined, and the mother church chided its offspring for accepting a member who came from a Separate Baptist Church without requiring re-baptism. Finally in December 1832 Mt. Hebron dismissed sixteen of its members to reconstitute Bethel. In 1845 Mt. Hebron appointed six brethren to meet on fourth Sundays at a cabin on Bear Creek for services. Four years later the church established a campground for meetings and also began services in a settlement where many members had joined Mt. Hebron during an October revival. A protracted meeting of ten days in September 1858 added fifteen new members by profession of faith, six by letter, and seven by restoration to fellowship. By 1858 the church had established a mission on "Shole" (Shoal) Creek, which flourished during the next few years. As a result of such evangelistic outreach, Mt. Hebron's membership grew from 107 in 1856 to 133 in 1858. The loss of black members and the Sherman Church schism reduced membership from 100 members in 1869 to 72 in 1871. Although Mt. Hebron experimented with different meeting times and weekends for services, membership declined throughout most of the remainder of the century. The church could not obtain pastors, drifted away from Baptist doctrine, and seemed to lose its evangelistic zeal. Perhaps Reconstruction, rural poverty, the spread of sharecropping, and political dissension simply left its members too little money and energy.

Whatever the reason for decline, conditions improved after 1902. Revivals became more frequent and successful. The community seemed to stabilize. A 1910 revival added eight members by profession of faith; seven more came in August 1913, and twelve more joined in a September 1921 meeting. The 1920s brought such prosperity that the church temporarily began services twice a month. Fred Maxey strengthened this resurgence during his pastorate in the 1930s. A revival he preached in July 1938 added thirteen members by profession of faith, and his September 1939 meeting brought in eighteen more. He began morning and evening services weekly.

Another expression of the church's missionary interest came in the form of contributions. From its earliest association with the Cahawba Association, Mt. Hebron donated money to what Baptists then called "domestic missions." In 1830 the church could contribute only $3, but it faithfully gave what it could. By 1832 Mt. Hebron had doubled its original gift. In 1846 several members pledged $1 each to the cause of domestic missions. By 1950 the church determined to send the entire evening offering for statewide missions, and the following year the church added a $20 donation toward purchase of a mission bus for Howard College. Mt. Hebron also tithed its income (10 percent) to the Cooperative Program of the Southern Baptist Convention, which in 1925 replaced individual fund drives with a single unified budget. As the church became increasingly aware of local needs, it shifted emphasis in 1956, allocating 1 percent of its funds for associational missions, 2 percent for state missions, and 7 percent for the Cooperative Program, a formula it modified again in 1963 and 1964. Increasing financial needs among local people required an allocation of 2 percent each for local and associational missions and 6 percent for the Cooperative Program. For a church that perpetually experienced financial woes, such an allocation of funds demonstrated its historic commitment to missions. And figures did not include special WMU offerings for foreign and home missions at Christmas and Easter.

The Persistence of Community

The geographical area in which Mt. Hebron Church functioned changed dramatically between 1819 and the 1980s. The valley had begun as a rural frontier; by the 1870s, Leeds had become an industrial suburb of Birmingham. Whereas Mt. Hebron's members had originally been farmers, more of its male members began to mine coal or work in iron and steel mills. By the 1970s the community experienced additional dislocation resulting from the steady decline of smokestack industry and the growth of economic sectors of the economy that did not well suit the folk south of Leeds. Urban sprawl south of Birmingham moved slowly up the Cahaba Valley toward the church, threatening to overwhelm it with apartments, condominiums, and fashionable housing projects. With Leeds moving south and Birmingham moving north, the rural-minded Mt. Hebron community seemed an anachronism. Their narrow strip of rural Alabama had contracted to less than ten miles by 1990. Sunday school enrollment steadily declined from more than a hundred in 1967 to barely fifty in the early 1980s. Perhaps the sense of community was more important when life was risky and people were powerless. As life stabilized and conditions improved, the sense of community was not restricted to the religious life of Mt. Hebron.

Each change within the larger community left its impact on Mt. Hebron. Each infusion of new members created tensions between old-timers basically satisfied with the church and its work and younger, more aggressive newcomers bent on change.

Almost all of the current members who are in their seventies and eighties grew up in farm families. Of seven current members interviewed, each one grew up on a farm. The father of one was a farmer-miller, another a farmer-carpenter, a third a farmer–coal miner, but all seven traced their values and origins to rural life. None had very much education. Only one continued beyond high school, obtaining secretarial training at a business college. Most of them did not finish high school. Of five interviewees who listed occupations, one became a farmer, one mined coal and worked for a steel manufacturing company, and three women married men who became coal miners, industrial workers, or farmers. The economic fluctuations of the Birmingham coal and steel district affected them dramatically. Tied to a farm economy in the nineteenth century, Mt. Hebron was suspended between agricultural and industrial worlds in the twentieth century.

Because so many of the members of Mt. Hebron represented families with deep ties to the valley, membership represented more than a joyous occasion of conversion. Joining Mt. Hebron became a way of identifying with one's roots, of continuing tradition, and affirming family. Although most accepted Christ during revivals, a gradual process usually led to conversion, not a dramatic emotional experience.[47]

Once bound together in sacred fellowship, members, who were neighbors and often also relatives, helped with each other's needs. In the early days such concern did not find its way into church minutes. But by the 1930s the decline of farming and the perilous cycles of industry had created new problems. An economy built around subsistence farming had given way to an industrial wage system. Layoffs, depressions, recessions, plant closings, catastrophic diseases, high medical bills—all these and more brought new problems to the valley. A membership so small and close that the church cut its own Christmas tree and drew names for presents could not ignore human misery.

Historically the church had expressed part of its concern through local missions. This heritage had provided the church a vision larger than itself. The women of the WMU best exemplified this tradition. Although small, the congregation regularly adopted an orphan from the Baptist Children's Home to support, gave clothes to needy families and Birmingham's Jimmy Hale Mission, prepared meals for widowed black women at holiday seasons, visited and cared for elderly members, contributed to the sick who could not afford medical care, and performed a multitude of other charitable services. After World War II this impulse toward sharing became global. In June 1946 the church voted $25 for world relief and rehabilitation.

In 1952 young pastor Gordon T. Walker expanded this world vision. Deeply concerned about the spiritual welfare of postwar Europe, Walker joined a Youth for Christ team bound for France and Germany. The church granted him a three months' leave of absence. In long, detailed letters from Berlin, Walker described the wretched conditions in refugee camps. He told of helping a displaced couple in their twenties who had no coats and only the clothes they wore. When he returned, he preached about the poverty, the emptiness of state-supported churches, and the judgment of God on humanity. These sermons obviously touched an emotional current within the congregation. Layman Fred Maxey Jr. proposed that all contributions over $100 collected the first Sunday of each month be given to a clothing station sponsored by evangelicals in France. The church also gathered 161 boxes of clothes for refugees.

Despite these global efforts, members reserved their greatest concern for friends and neighbors. In January 1947 the church appointed a committee for the needy. In November 1948 members voted to buy radio batteries for a poor family. In 1954 members gave $80 to buy a wheelchair for a member.

By the 1960s the growing number of community financial problems convinced members of Mt. Hebron that individual acts of charity must give way to a more systematic policy. So the church voted to redistribute missions spending and created a local missions budget of 2 percent of all contributions available for those in need. During the next three decades, Mt. Hebron appropriated thousands of dollars to help its own members and people who lived in the community: in 1965, $15 to the Hyde family; in 1966, $50 to the Albert Chambers family; 1967, $35 to Mrs. Flora Yarbrough; 1970, $50 to a local family whose house burned and $55 to the Phillips children; 1971, $75 to Jerry Thompson, whose house had burned, and $50 to church member Archie Dison, who had been sick and unable to work. In 1972 the church gave Dison additional money and in 1973 provided funds to a seriously ill member. In 1974, Mt. Hebron loaned money to Eddie Gosnell, a church member, to pay his tuition at Howard College, allowing him to repay the loan by mowing the church lawn and from earnings on a summer job. By fall 1977 the church provided Bertha Mae Chambers between $30 and $40 per month and assisted the Larry Standifer family as well. In 1979 members helped the Steve Atkinson family, who had lost a son. Because demands on the local missions funds had been so great, the church had to limit appropriations to $50 a month, less than the Atkinsons needed. A member solved this dilemma by contributing $215, to be added to the $50 from local mission funds. By fall 1979 at least one person received the maximum $50 from the local funds every month, and many months the church helped several families.

Mt. Hebron demonstrated its concern for the community in other ways as well. In 1967 the church began a community youth program open to all white families. Available to any "young people of the community" over age eight, the program used the old schoolhouse as a recreation building. The church appropriated $75 for film rental, and a local man coordinated the program. Every other week the church showed films and sponsored recreation.

Although members responded to a changing society as best they could, tensions between old ways and new were inevitable. Members with roots that sometimes extended back seven generations valued the plot of land on which four successive church buildings had stood. Debates over the shape and location of church buildings seem trivial to casual observers. But to Mt. Hebron's people and to many other Christians such matters were of great consequence. Two entrance doors and separate seating for men, women, and children, and slaves had reflected a profound white male notion about the hierarchical arrangements of Christianity. A plain, unadorned church building with a pulpit in the front center emphasized the role of preacher, proclamation, and conversion. And location tied people to their roots, to ancestors now departed. On this ground members had attended their first Christian services and their first school. Here their ancestors lay beneath the sod of a cemetery gently sloping up the hill behind the church. Nearby they had disappeared beneath the baptismal waters of the Little Cahaba River and risen to new life in Christ. But members who joined during the 1930s, 1940s, and 1950s had fewer ties to the community and more concern with parking places and youth programs, sufficient building space for a spacious sanctuary, and an education building for an expanding Sunday school. The differences finally came to a head in 1954.

The crisis was precipitated by a fire that destroyed Mt. Hebron Church. Until then all had seemed well within the congregation. The missionary journey of the Rev. Gordon Walker had energized the church and added to its membership. Rising income during these prosperous years allowed the church to increase the pastor's salary. Energetic new members held most church offices and brought a level of enthusiasm to Mt. Hebron unseen in years. In fact members had begun to remodel the church when lightning struck the building on August 9, 1954. Within forty-five minutes the building, which had been constructed of heart pine in 1922, had burned to the ground.

In a spirit of unity and dedication the congregation vowed to rebuild and set about the task of raising money. All went well until the planning committee recommended that the church authorize it to negotiate the purchase of six acres a short distance away. The new site would provide room for a larger building and adequate parking. The church would sit back farther off the road, allow the parsonage to be located elsewhere, and permit expansion of the cemetery. Opponents of this move cited added expense and sentimental attachment to the place of their ancestors.

At a business meeting on August 29, 1954, Fred Maxey Jr. proposed to buy the new site, and the Rev. Walker seconded his motion; fifty-four members supported the motion and only six opposed it. But when the church voted whether to build on the old site or the new, forty-five voted for the old site and only thirty-six for the new. On October 17 Walker announced at a Sunday morning service that he believed God wanted the church to re-vote on the site of the new church. He believed God desired the congregation to move. Walker asked those who favored the new site, or at least were willing to support it, to move to the left side of the church. Those who believed God meant the rebuilding to occur on the current site should stand to the right. Those who were neutral or unsure of God's will should abstain from voting. The vote went overwhelmingly for the new site, forty-four to eighteen. But that night the deacons called another church conference. They announced that they had conferred with another pastor, who had advised them that in a case where two votes occurred with varying results, a third vote should be held. Furthermore, only baptized members of Mt. Hebron or those who had come by letter could vote. The minutes record no additional ballot, but Walker resigned in December, announcing his plan to enter seminary. The vote to name his replacement, a thirty-four/thirty-two split, confirmed the deep division within the church. On December 12, forty-eight members, including Fred Maxey Jr., the Rev. Walker, and most key Sunday school officials and church officers transferred to Leeds First Baptist Church; four additional members left the following Sunday.[48] The fifty-two members who departed shortly afterwards formed a new congregation: Valley View Baptist Church. The thirty members who remained at Mt. Hebron began to plan how to rebuild on the location so dear to them. Thanks to the sacrifices of those who remained and the generosity of one of their more affluent members, Mt. Hebron moved into its new building in 1955.

Those who remained behind perceived the issue as a dispute over the location of the church. The leader of those who left understood the controversy in more complex terms. Maxey believed that the Rev. Gordon Walker, young and brimming with evangelical zeal, had led the church toward strong commitment to evangelism and church growth; but Walker "was young, was inexperienced, and I think said things instead of approaching people where they were." Maxey also explained the crisis as more fundamental than merely a dispute over location of the church. Members disagreed over growth. The Maxey-Walker faction wanted the church to move in a different direction, to reach new people, and to build educational space; older members remained satisfied with the church as it was, more committed to its traditional course.[49]

Although some members exchanged harsh words and many left, this split was only the worst of many in the life of Mt. Hebron. Anti-mission Baptists had left for the Primitive Baptists early in the nineteenth century. During subsequent decades, members left because church discipline offended them. In 1871 a substantial number had left for Sherman's Church. And without exception those on both sides of the 1954 controversy who were interviewed in 1989 maintained that individual relationships with the community remained good. Fred Maxey Jr. believed that the split had left no lasting effect; he loved his neighbors, and they loved him. Annabel Moore was one of only four members who withdrew and then later returned to Mt. Hebron. She remembered the strong feelings on both sides, but also believed time had healed the wounds. Now the members of Valley View "love us and we love them." The chairman of Mt. Hebron's deacons at the time of the dispute, who remained at the old site, visited older members seeking advice during the controversy and then talked with those who threatened to leave. But he could not reconcile the two groups. Margie Poole Martin believed that those who left did not depart as enemies of the ones who stayed. As years passed, they returned to visit Mt. Hebron on Memorial Day and other occasions.[50]

The Calvinist cosmology that had allowed their forefathers to make religious sense out of flood and drought, war and pestilence, served them as well. Margie Poole Martin described the split as a way of forming a new and prosperous church. T. C. West explained that every event, even the lightning that destroyed the church building and the split, "works for the best for them who love God (Romans 8:28)." Annabel Moore recalls that when the split occurred and those who left formed

Valley View Baptist Church nearer Leeds, "there wasn't a building anywhere around Valley View, so it must have been God's leading because all of a sudden houses sprang up all around it." Fred Maxey Jr. expressed a similar theology: "I don't think the Lord is the author of confusion, but I think he allows [it] to happen and now we are reaching people that Mt. Hebron would have never reached and no one else in Leeds has reached."

Although Mt. Hebron slowly recovered and even grew momentarily (Sunday school attendance returned to above a hundred in the 1960s), the space limitations and traditionalism of its members continued to hinder the church. By the 1980s Valley View flourished and Mt. Hebron languished, its Sunday school attendance reduced to fifty or so faithful souls. In 1982 the Rev. James Blair became pastor and injected new energy into the congregation. Like so many of his predecessors, Blair is a bivocational minister and sells building materials as well as preaching. Under his ministry the church has grown slowly to a Sunday school attendance of 60, with 90 in worship services and a resident membership of 188 (1989).

But not all churches are expected to grow, expand, and begin new programs. In some locales caught between old ways and new, between farms and cities, between tradition and modernity, between the elderly and the young, perhaps it is enough just to survive and to provide a place of meaning and caring. In 1989 Mt. Hebron's sense of sacred community seemed as strong for those who remained as ever before.

In some ways the members have changed. None we interviewed favored reinstituting church discipline. Margie and J. T. Poole could not remember Mt. Hebron excluding a member and did not think it a good idea. T. C. West remembered an uncle who lived up a hollow from the valley who once gave a dance and was turned out of the church. West's father played the banjo and one of the deacons played the fiddle for the dance. The church cited all three, but his father and the deacon asked forgiveness for a deed neither believed to be wrong: "It hurt the church. Some of them never did come back. My uncle who had the dance, he moved his membership down to the Presbyterian Church." Although a fine Bible scholar and deacon, West saw no good purpose to such a practice. Annabel Moore also remembered exclusions. The church turned out two members during her lifetime: "I never had such feeling in my life. It was like God had shut the door on them. I don't believe in it. I would not vote for it and I didn't. . . . It was the coldest feeling I ever had. It broke my heart because one of them was my friend, a lady, and the other was making whiskey and selling it." Maggie Wilkinson agreed, opposing exclusion on biblical grounds, believing as Baptists do that "once saved always saved; you might stray, but you'll come back. When you stray, people need to pray for you, not push you out."[51]

Tastes in theology also changed with the passing years. T. C. West contrasted preaching "intended to frighten you—that you were going to hell for what you did and what you didn't do"—to modern sermons that emphasize love. He remembered such shouting in Mt. Hebron that boys who could not stand the pressure would jump out of the windows during services. Explaining his own theology he reasoned: "Fear is misleading to people who don't understand. With the fear of God, it's not that you're scared of him, that's not it. You love him enough to want to do what he says, that's the fear of God."[52]

In other ways members have changed little. For them Mt. Hebron still represents an anchor of stability in a turbulent world. They rely on its fellowship for their social activities, treasure its sense of community, and draw strength from it during times of personal trouble. Although elderly members are concerned that conditions have changed, that they see less of each other than they once did, and that they have less time to help one another, they still believe Mt. Hebron contains a special closeness and fellowship.

Conversion remains at the core of religious experience at Mt. Hebron. Annabel Moore grew up the youngest child in a family that did not attend church. Her mother died when she was a small girl, and her father, left with eight children to rear, did the best he could. She eloped at age 16 and became a Christian after the birth of her first child. Maggie Wilkinson accepted Christ at age 12 or 13 during a 1934 revival. T. C. West responded to a series of tragedies which subjected him to emotional stress.[53]

But conversion has never been an end in itself. Extending the right hand of fellowship follows conversion and baptism. This historic and symbolically important gesture involves more than a physical ritual. It opens a sacred inner community to a child, stranger, or newcomer. Of course the new convert now determines the boundaries of sacred community rather than the church doing so with discipline as in the old days. But if one seeks it, this inner community works as well as it ever did. The testimony of four members makes this clear.

Remembering the Great Depression of the 1930s, Annabel Moore recalls typical Sunday mornings: she would draw water from her well, gather vegetables from her garden, cook lunch over a wood stove, and then gather her children for their walk down the road to church (the Moores had no car). She described her life during those years not in the bleak hues of depression but in the warm tones of community: "Wonderful life! We'd come back home and . . . a lot of times the preacher would eat with us." Asked if she still spent more time in church activities than in other social involvements, she responded that the church "*is* our social life." Maggie Wilkinson agreed that she and her husband had few social outlets beyond the church. T. C. West also agreed, saying he attended church functions four or five times a week, "every time the door is open."[54]

Every person interviewed talked about "a special feeling of closeness" at Mt. Hebron. One member claimed that because members grew up together, "I don't think it's [closeness] nowhere else but here." Margie Poole Martin added: "We're more like brothers and sisters than we are neighbors." J. T. Poole, asked to name the best attribute of Mt. Hebron, did not hesitate: "Make a stranger feel at home."[55]

Once again recalling the 1930s, Annabel Moore explained, "Times were very difficult but I tell you we visited each other, we quilted for the church, and we had the best time . . .; we were close to each other and saw each other all the time." Both Annabel Moore and Maggie Wilkinson experienced tragedy—the loss of their spouses and illness. And each time they suffered, the church responded. This love moved them deeply. Moore explained: "I just have the deepest feeling. I'm the happiest, I feel it's heaven when I get down there and sing and worship with the others. It's just part of my life and I don't reckon the door ever opened that I wasn't there." Maggie Wilkinson added, "Everyone loves one another. Most people who live there have lived there all their lives. . . . Everyone knows what you need, you don't have to call them, they'll come to help you." T. C. West reminisced about church neighbors who had helped build his house and later surrounded him with love when his wife died: "It has been a wonderful place to live, this valley. I tell you right now there's plenty of love over here."[56]

Young women work now, and their social lives no longer revolve exclusively around the church. The pluralism of a hectic secular world has eroded exclusive loyalties to Mt. Hebron. But enough of the old ways survive that a young bivocational lay preacher could still base his sermon, the first I ever heard there, on a sacred community set apart from the world. Conversion was central to his vision. Ancient traditions both bound members of Mt. Hebron together as family and hindered their divine mission. So urgent was the task that all members must choose sides, come forward, and stand beside their preacher in a symbolic gesture of separation from the world and commitment to each other. That February 1989 Sunday morning their faith drew more heavily from their past than any of them realized.

—*American Congregations, Volume I: Portraits of Twelve Religious Communities*, 1994

As I entered the final year of my four-decade teaching career, I completed the final revisions for my presidential address to the Southern Historical Association (SHA). I chose a broad topic that combined my nearly half century interests in politics, labor, poor whites, religion, and the 1930s. During two earlier research trips to the Franklin Roosevelt Library and Archives at Hyde Park, New York, I had become familiar with the Clergy Papers. Some 8,000 letters from southern ministers written to the president in 1935 not only described conditions in their communities but also provided insights into their racial and class backgrounds, conceptions of God, and understanding of a just and Christian nation. My wife, Dorothy, and I methodically ploughed through the letters as primary source for my address.

Once again employing collateral insights from psychology, sociology, anthropology, and folklore, together with my earlier research in labor and political history, I made a wide sweep across the South's religious terrain. SHA members gathered that November weekend in Memphis to celebrate the association's 70th birthday mostly without knowledge that seven decades earlier few of their predecessors taught, researched, or wrote about religion. That is unfortunate because religion provided the poor as it had for millennia the biblical and ethical arguments for a full scale assault on injustice. More importantly, it allowed them to maintain dignity and a sense of self worth, even when they could not overcome intractable injustice.

As SHA president, I also raised money to attract more African American historians than typically attended the SHA. Nearly half a century earlier the SHA had met in Memphis following the Brown v. Board *decision. The 1955 program focused on the implications of the ruling and included Nobel Prize winner William Faulkner and educator/civil rights leader Benjamin May. I spotlighted the career of a non-attendee, John Hope Franklin, preeminent historian of black America, who had refused to speak when the Peabody Hotel, the convention headquarters, refused him a room. In 2004 SHA's secretary explained this earlier snub to the hotel's convention manager and mentioned my name as incoming president. The person remembered hearing about the incident in his southern history class at Auburn University. Needless to say, the Peabody Hotel (as well as city officials) expunged past sins with generosity and attention beyond my wildest expectations.*

Despite his impending 90th birthday, Professor Franklin spoke to a special gathering of Memphis power brokers, to the opening session of the convention, and to a luncheon I hosted for all professors at historically black colleges and universities. After an exhausting four days of honors, dinners, speeches, and a pre-90th birthday party (plus the luxury of the Peabody's presidential suite that, he joked, was larger than his house), he told me that the convention had been a highlight of his career. Of equal importance to me, the biracialism of that week symbolized one of the threads binding black and white southerners together: "Rich and poor have this in common: The Lord is the Maker of them all" (Proverbs 22:2).

CHAPTER 12
Religion for the Blues
Evangelicalism, Poor Whites, and the Great Depression

May Jordan lived a hard life. Before her death in October 1914 at age 25, she spent most of her time helping her father and family survive on a small farm in remote Washington County, Alabama. The sandy soil made agriculture difficult and forced many of the county's residents, black and white alike, to trap animals in the swamps along the Tombigbee River and sell their furs.

But anyone who reads the diary she kept between December 1912 and March 1914 recognizes that her poverty did not diminish her sense of self-worth, family solidarity, community identity, or religious faith.[1] Indeed her family's poverty enhanced her delight in simple pleasures,in her storytelling and singing and especially in her theology. Yes theology, for that is what it was: a distinctive way of understanding God, of explaining the meaning of life, of making sense of her own social reality, and of relating her powerless self to an omnipotent God, to ultimate vindication and justice.

Religion was the topic May most frequently mentioned in her diary as a subject of conversation with other women. Although a proud and independent woman—who often spent nights alone in the wilderness while her father tramped down some dirt path impassable to wheeled vehicles, bound for a remote trapper's cabin—May centered her diary entries on God, community, and her family instead of gender.[2]

Community for her revolved around Buck Hill Baptist Church, a rural congregation made up of people like herself. The church building also served as her school, which was no inconvenience to worship services since they were held only once a month anyway. Each August the church conducted a singing school to educate members in shape-note singing, and in September the entire community assembled for a protracted revival. Born-again believers were baptized in nearby Pine Barren Creek.[3]

Her father Eugene was a "faith doctor" without a formal ministerial portfolio who, according to family legend, had cured his daughter from a high fever triggered by meningitis and had "raised" a dead woman at a church service. He also supplemented his meager income from the family's 160-acre federal homestead and his fur trade by selling patent medicines. May contributed income as "an agent for an herb company."[4]

On the first page of her diary, May explained the source of her relentlessly upbeat outlook on life: "There is church every 3rd Sunday. . . . And I sure enjoy going To preaching. We never can learn to much about our Saviour Who suffered so upon the cross And humbled hisself when he could but lift his hands and strike [his enemies] down."[5]

Running throughout the diary is a Calvinistic sense of God's providence. During the final spring fur-buying trip in 1913, May wrote that "if it is the Saviours will," she and her father would venture out again the following winter. Noting the beauty of Washington County's wildflowers, forests, and sunsets, she contemplated "how good our Saviour is to us all." On a cold December night, she rejoiced that the "Blessed Saviour has given us plenty of fine lighter to burn." Unable to reach home one freezing winter evening, she concluded that "our Blessed Saviour seen fit to make the night so dark until we could not see to drive."[6]

In a theological refrain common to most Christians, May appropriated religion to explain suffering. To those who complained "of so much sorrow," she advised, "But if they will only love and trust the Blessed Saviour . . . they will find more happiness and not so much sorrow."[7]

Not that May Jordan was Pollyannaish about life. Living with eight siblings on a poor farm afforded no opportunity for false piety or religious pretension. She filled her diary with lighthearted jokes and folklore at the expense of hypocritical preachers and ignorant believers. She acknowledged that she often had "the blues," and she and her father compromised their high regard for Sunday as a day of rest when they were forced by economic necessity to dress furs. But on those Sundays when church met, worship restored her soul: "The Sabbath has closed with every one as happy as A Lark."[8]

In his book *The Irony of Southern Religion*, John B. Boles traces the origins of May Jordan's sort of evangelicalism back into southern religious history. Focusing on the ironic correlation between the intent and outcome of southern religion, he emphasizes how antebellum evangelical folkways, over time, came to shape the faith of the leadership classes. In turn, many in the lower classes rejected the emerging religious consensus to embrace new holiness and Pentecostal expressions of faith.[9]

Boles's work flows into a rich stream of recent research and writing. Randy J. Sparks and Paul Harvey wrote recently that few areas of southern history during the past four decades have produced more solid scholarship than religion. The historiography of antebellum evangelicalism has attained maturity, though the study of the past century and a half lags behind.[10] Yet even the more recent past now proves alluring to an impressively gifted generation of historians.

Actually, scholarly inattention to recent decades may not be all bad because too much attention to the post-Second World War era can distort the historical meaning of evangelicalism. In our own neo-fundamentalist age, when mega-churches often become in effect precinct headquarters for local Republican Party candidates with Christian Coalition endorsements, one can easily be misled about the historical complexity of southern evangelicalism. Intellectuals find much to dislike in the politicized emotionalism, supernaturalism, anti-intellectualism, exclusivity, and intolerance of the new political religious right.

Scholars have less trouble identifying with African American Christianity, even though that form of southern religion is no less emotional, supernatural, provincial, politicized, or otherworldly than poor-white religion, and black Christianity often manifests the same kind of intolerance toward women, homosexuals, and other religions. Yet for half a century historians and sociologists of the African American religious experience have crafted sensitive, nuanced, balanced scholarship on the black church and its role in creating and sustaining black communities.

Indeed, the past three decades have produced such a cornucopia of scholarship about black Christianity that the outpouring represents nothing short of a watershed in our understanding of American religion. The scholars' names alone read like a historian's who's who: John B. Boles, Eugene D. Genovese, Lawrence W. Levine, John W. Blassingame, Charles Joyner, C. Eric Lincoln, Albert J. Raboteau, Sylvia R. Frey, and Leon F. Litwack, to name a few.[11]

The fact that balanced studies of poor-white evangelicals of more recent decades seem less common can probably be attributed to a multitude of reasons. The poor-black church represented a minority race that was perceived by many Americans as being oppressed. The poor-white church represented a submerged fraction of a dominant race, most members of whom, in the South at least, were perceived as doing the oppressing. In addition, middle-class people lumped the religious practices of poor white people into the same category of emotional excess that they believed characterized poor-black religious ritual and practice. Such practices did not particularly appeal to intellectuals either.

Given such assumptions, those who seek to find value within poor-white religion must turn to the interior world of social coherence and cosmic purpose, intellectual terrain usually occupied by anthropologists, sociologists, and psychologists. Within this interior world, issues such as self-worth, equality, interpersonal acts of kindness and charity, a sense of community, hope in a world of adversity, ultimate vindication in a world of powerlessness, emotional release in a world of drab routine, and social stability in a world of violence and familial dysfunction rise to central importance. Rather than escapist, such functions appear to many social scientists to be essential to personal hope, wholeness, and well-being.

The historiographical trajectory of studies about poor-white religion has followed a pattern similar to that of poor-black religion, with the earliest writing most strongly negative. In his 1942 study of Gastonia, North Carolina, Liston Pope describes how mill-village pastors and churches, many of them subsidized by mill owners, betrayed the class interests of their parishioners. Although Pope notes the emergence of class-based white sects, some of which did support workers, he depicts the sects as essentially renouncing the prevailing culture and social structure, expressing feelings of persecution and abuse, and adopting a theology of strict Biblicism, sectarian non-cooperation, and otherworldliness.[12] Other sociologists of the era agreed with Pope about the essentially reactionary nature of southern poor-white religion. In a 1966 article George L. Maddox and Joseph H. Fichter argue that traditional religion often impeded social change and slowed reform.[13]

Novelists have made similar claims. Writer Erskine Caldwell created a tobacco-road theology to match the characters in his novels. The son of an open-minded, ministerial father who belonged to a generally fundamentalist southern denomination (the Associated Reformed Presbyterian Church), Caldwell was exposed to Calvinistic, fundamentalist, and pentecostal religion as a young man. In a memoir entitled *Deep South*, he traces religious ecstasy and preoccupation with heaven to Appalachian hunger, poverty, and despair. Poor-white religion was "the only available narcotic to dull the pain of living." "Evangelism," he continues, "has always promised more for the future than any government can provide for the present." Poverty and isolation spawned "hell-fire-and-brimstone," a "pearly-gates-of-heaven" religion that appealed to "impoverished and unenlightened Southerners of Anglo-Saxon descent." Fundamentalist dominance of mountain sects, he adds, has led "inevitably to reactionary and ultra-conservative principles and conduct in secular life" as well as to racism and extremism, all of which explained Appalachian backwardness. Caldwell describes one demeaning example after another of rural, mill-village, and mine-village preachers. Sects such as the Assembly of God, the Church of God, the Church of the Nazarene, and the Church of God in Christ rejected contemporary political, economic, and social concerns in favor of "religious exhibitionism" usually associated with "night clubs and other places of theatrical entertainment."[14]

Similar comments about pentecostals, although less satirical, became a staple of social-science research following the Second World War. Experts concluded that pentecostalism resulted from a crisis in social identity. Or it emanated from the sociopsychological distinctions between conservative and liberal people, with conservatives clinging desperately to religion in search of a steady anchor in a chaotic world. Or pentecostalism derived from the social disorganization occasioned by rural-to-urban transitions. Or pentecostalism owed its growth to cultural protest against declining morality, ecumenism, higher criticism of the Bible, Darwinism, the Social Gospel, and secularism. Or pentecostals were ignorant people who lacked the power of oral expression; hence they spoke in tongues. Or they were psychologically troubled and filled with anxiety; were psychotic or neurotic; and could not establish satisfying interpersonal relationships (psychologists applied social-psychosis theory particularly to Appalachian snake handlers). One mainstream Southern Baptist professor of psychology describes tongue-speakers as possessing "weak egos, confused identities, high levels of anxiety, and unstable personalit[ies]."[15]

As with interpretations of black Christianity, the past four decades have markedly improved both factual knowledge and analytical sophistication about poor-white religion. Cultural anthropologist Clifford Geertz provides a useful starting place for rethinking such religion in his 1973 book *The Interpretation of Cultures*. "For an anthropologist," Geertz writes, "the importance of religion lies in its capacity to serve . . . as a source of general, yet distinctive, conceptions of the world, the self, and the relations between them." He continues, "The drive to make sense out of experience, to give it form and order, is evidently as real and as pressing as the more familiar biological needs." Rather than being rooted in inductive experiences from daily life, religious belief stems from the acceptance of authority, which transforms those experiences. The issue is not how to avoid suffering or to gain power, status, and wealth, but how to make pain bearable and bestow meaning on personal loss, worldly defeat, and poverty. In such a process, faith, commitment, encounter, and relationships are more important than skepticism, detachment, contemplation, and analysis. Humans need to have "a meaningful framework for orienting themselves to one another, to the world around them, and to themselves." This framework creates "webs of significance" by which they relate themselves to reality. Religious rituals (such as glossolalia, divine healing, and other so-called miracles) fuse the world as lived with the world as magic.[16]

I first realized the full implications of Geertz's hypothesis in conjunction with a project at the University of Chicago on congregationalism in American life. Asked to write about a single fundamentalist congregation in the rural South, I selected a mainly poor-white country church east of Birmingham. Historically the congregation of Mt. Hebron Baptist Church consisted of small farmers, tenants, mill workers, and coal miners. So wretched were their circumstances and marginal their social status during the 1930s that these Baptists employed Fred E. Maxey, a fundamentalist Nazarene evangelist, as their pastor—a man who spoke at communist rallies, wrote for the local communist paper, and may have been a party member himself. Older members of the congregation remember Maxey not as a dangerous radical but as a beloved pastor who helped them obtain jobs and ministered to them in their suffering. His efforts for them (and on behalf of unemployed black members of the community) earned him a Ku Klux Klan cross-burning but also rallied his members to a sense of sacred meaning and community. Or to use Geertz's phrase, Mt. Hebron provided a meaningful framework for orienting members to one another and to the world around them.[17]

The evidence for this conclusion came from a series of oral histories with members. Because the Mt. Hebron community had no school or community center, classes met in the church early in the twentieth century. During the 1930s, home demonstration agents used the building as a place to teach poor families crafts and how to make mattresses. Distinctions between sacred and secular roles blurred as the church became the community's primary social institution, especially for women. Reminiscing in the late 1980s, members praised pastoral theology that morphed from terrifying hell-fire-and-damnation to a gentler emphasis upon free grace. Rituals such as baptism, extending the right hand of fellowship, homecomings, all-day singings, and dinners on the ground forged powerful ties between members. In the 1930s, female members recalled that the church constituted their entire social life beyond their own families. One member remembered being present "every time the door is open." Another remarked about "a special feeling of closeness" at Mt. Hebron: "I don't think it's [closeness] nowhere else but here."

Annabel Moore remarked about the Great Depression: "Times were very difficult but I tell you we visited each other and saw each other all the time." During her illness and the death of her husband, the church responded with assistance and love, and she reciprocated: "I just have the deepest feeling. I'm the happiest, I feel it's heaven when I get down there and sing and worship with the others. It's just part of my life and I don't reckon the door is ever opened that I wasn't there." Maggie Wilkerson added, "Everyone loves one another. Most people who live there have lived there all their lives. . . . Everyone knows what you need, you don't have to call them, they'll come to help you." J. T. Poole, when asked to name the best attribute of Mt. Hebron, did not hesitate: "Make a stranger feel at home." Margie Poole Martin declared: "We're more like brothers and sisters than we are neighbors." T. C. West concluded, "It has been a wonderful place to live, this valley. I tell you right now there's plenty of love over here."[18]

The insights I derived from oral histories at Mt. Hebron were similar to those that Harvard child psychiatrist Robert Coles absorbed from his interviews with poor black and white southerners. Rejecting the traditional view of southern folk religion as escapist, otherworldly, and discouraging the poor from confronting economic and political realities, Coles focuses on the way such religion afforded the rural poor a sense of dignity, self-worth, and promise of future vindication. Such recognition allowed them to endure poverty while maintaining social cohesion despite repeated economic and political failures.[19]

Whereas some intellectuals adopted "caricatures" that transformed sincere and passionate believers "into opiated and deluded victims, or into philosophically duped and neurotically afflicted patients," writes Coles, he found rational behavior based on the need of poor people to link their experiences to social reality. In poor people's prayers, supplications, acknowledgments of faith, protestations, and affirmations of belief, Cole finds their need for coherence and "reassurance that somewhere one is being noticed and somehow [one] does matter, after all."[20]

"'Grace' and 'charity' and the 'forgiveness of sins'... and 'redemption through faith,'" all had real and precise psychological and social functions. Expressive worship "foster[ed] joyfulness"; released pent-up emotions, "resentments and fears and qualms"; and brought relief, "peace[,] and calm as well as excitement." Their faith did not make the poor simpleminded. They still had theological doubts, problems, and questions. They understood "existential despair," even if they lacked the words to express it.[21]

There was also a distinct social dimension to such religion. Historians over the past generation have noted that poor-white beliefs in equality and justice contributed to the rhetoric, rituals, and success of the Farmers' Alliance, Populist Party, socialism, and other forms of political radicalism. Drawing upon the idiom of rural evangelicalism, organizers from such groups as the Farmers' Alliance, the Southern Tenant Farmers Union, and the Communist Party tried to transform personal faith into political action.[22] Other historians have explained how such religion assisted the poor to cope with modernization.[23]

As mainstream Baptists and Methodists were absorbed into the middle-class poor white people in the same denominations became increasingly sectarian. Among Baptists, the Primitives or Old Regulars remained largely lower class. Mainly rural as well, Primitives lived up to their name—imposing strict standards of personal conduct, rejecting denominational bureaucracies and institutions, and insisting on the absolute autonomy of their congregations and the egalitarian values of their ancestors. Such rituals as foot-washing and the simple designation of members as "brother" and "sister" emphasized the democratic origins of Primitive Baptists and their emphasis upon humility. With strength in the most remote parts of the South (Appalachia and Wiregrass-Piney Woods regions), their economic and political marginalization matched their religious isolation.[24]

In Appalachia sectarians even defined gender relationships. Historian Robert S. Weise emphasizes the "household localism" that located familial authority in the male head of the family. He argues that such authority was reinforced by Old Regular churches, which limited leadership and preaching to men.[25] But Deborah Vansau McCauley's study of traditional Appalachian churches (Old Regular, Separate, and Missionary Baptist congregations and Pentecostal and holiness sects) highlights a different aspect of their practice, the widespread selection of "eldresses" and "deaconesses" representing women leaders who achieved "relative equality" and sometimes considerable respect and distinction.[26]

Other aspects of traditional Appalachian churches include the value they placed on ordinary believers as opposed to hierarchical elites; the egalitarian conversion experience (being "born again") as the entry point for membership into a sacred community; the emergence of revival preachers as persons of significant social status; "the chanted, spontaneously composed sermon[s]"; the emotional and/or ecstatic services; the oral transmission of culture; the church as a gathering of equals; and the prevalence of democratic rituals, such as baptism, footwashing, the Lord's Supper, laying-on-of-hands, the kiss of charity (the so-called holy kiss), and extending the right hand of fellowship. Although McCauley rejects Erskine Caldwell's assumption that these churches were part of "a subculture of poverty and the product of powerlessness and alienation," her individual portraits of leaders and sects offer much support for that conclusion. So anxious is she to emphasize the agency and respectability of the people she describes that she does not follow the logic of her narrative. These churches were a mixture of the very poor and people moving into the lower middle class. But their theological emphasis upon equality, ultimate vindication, and the value of ordinary people as opposed to wealthy, educated elites represent classic poor-white religious themes that go all the way back to colonial times.[27]

Although pentecostalism moved beyond Appalachia, the region was a fertile "seedbed" for it. Characterized by "otherworldly hope," "antagonistic" relationships to the secular world, occasional "aberrant social behavior," and emotional zeal, sects formed as the result of a vast religious "comeoutism" in the decades straddling the end of the nineteenth century. Incorporating elements of religious populism (though with far more variety to it than its political cousin), the sects bore a multitude of names: Churches of Christ, Church of God, Assemblies of God, Pentecostal Holiness Church, the Pillar of Fire Church, United Holy Church of North Carolina and Virginia, and Triumph the Church and Kingdom of God in Christ, as well as numerous independent Baptist congregations.[28]

David Edwin Harrell Jr., senior scholar of the movement, describes this phenomenon in class terms: "The most tangible single explanation for the southern sectarian revival . . . was poverty—the grinding, pervasive, unrelenting poverty of millions of white Southerners between the Civil War and World War II. Deprivation has always been the breeding ground for religious zealots."[29] Like black churches, southern poor-white sects thrived by providing voice to marginalized people. Characteristic of such churches, Harrell notes, was the affirmation of poor people in the Kingdom of God (Jesus favored outcasts, and in His kingdom the first would be last, the last first). Otherworldly hope was less about escapism than it was about ultimate vindication and hope for a miracle that would "bypass the repressive machinery of society."[30]

Harrell's location of the sources of southern pentecostalism in poverty is confirmed by some scholars and disputed by others. Robert Mapes Anderson, John B. Holt, David L. Kimbrough, Charles Y. Glock, Mickey Crews, and Paul K. Conkin support Harrell's argument about the lower-class origins of pentecostalism.[31] Deborah V. McCauley, Grant Wacker, and J. Lawrence Brasher take the opposite point of view, arguing that pentecostals came mainly from the middle class.[32]

Similar arguments swirl around the racial and gender ideologies and practices of Pentecostal/holiness sects. Scholars contend that sects on the margins of American life, with no social status to lose by unconventional attitudes about race and gender, were often more open to black people and women than mainstream denominations. Many sects were racially integrated. They also allowed women leadership positions as preachers, evangelists, and missionaries, especially in the chaotic early decades of the twentieth century. But as sects moved "from back alley to uptown" after the Second World War, their prejudices and restrictions more nearly mirrored those within mainstream southern culture.[33]

Trying to absorb such a huge body of data, theory, and analysis across so broad a chronological span leaves the mind whirling. But plugging these generalizations into a specific historical context such as the Great Depression makes analysis manageable. The years from the late 1920s to the beginning of the Second World War constituted a historic transition for poor white people. On one side of the depression were increasing rates of farm tenancy, rural desperation, fierce industrial conflicts between labor and management, and sharp class divisions within churches. On the other side of the war were economic mobility, rapid technological change, the collapse of farm tenancy, the decline of the coal-mining workforce, migration, and the movement of "third force" religious sects into mainstream respectability. If historians are to understand the ways poor-white churches reflected specific class values, there is no better place to look than during these transitional years.

The South's religious landscape during the 1920s and 1930s reflected both the depths of the region's economic problems and the strength of its religious convictions. According to the 1926 *Census of Religious Bodies*, 54 percent of US adults belonged to churches; the Southeast led all regions with a membership rate of 61 percent. But the region's large membership was scattered as a result of the rural distribution of its population. The average church in the Southeast claimed only 137 members.[34] In New England in 1936 the property of a rural church had an average value of more than $17,000, whereas rural churches in the South averaged slightly more than $3,000. Property of churches of the Southern Baptist Convention (SBC) had an average value of $9,500; Assemblies of God, $3,300; and the Church of God only $1,500.[35]

A 1922 SBC survey of the denomination's rural churches revealed troubling patterns. More than a third of farmer members of SBC congregations were landless tenants. One-quarter of SBC churches contained fewer than fifty members. More than a third of country churches reported no baptisms for the year. Nearly one in five had no pastor. Less than one in three had a pastor who lived in the church community. Only about one in five pastors had college and seminary training; almost half had neither. The average quarter-time pastor earned $145 a year and was not provided a parsonage. This data persuaded the denomination's preeminent sociologist to declare that something was "*radically wrong* with the present day country church." He traced the problems in part to absentee landownership and farm tenancy.[36] Similar statistics portrayed Pentecostal churches as being even more impoverished.

Another southern rural church specialist expressed concern that rural churches were dying in areas of heavy white tenancy. In twenty-one North Carolina cotton and tobacco counties with high rates of white tenancy and illiteracy, the percentage of adults who did not belong to churches in the early 1920s ranged from 27 to 77 percent. In Edgecombe County three-fifths of the population were tenants, and four-fifths were not church members. Tenants who moved to town for industrial jobs were also less likely to join a church. By the mid-1930s, 60 percent of farm owners in the South belonged to churches, compared with only 34 percent of tenants.[37]

White tenants dropped out of church for a variety of reasons. They most often cited lack of appropriate clothes, which seems to have been a particular concern for women who were members of churches that enrolled a variety of socioeconomic groups in a single congregation. Clothes were less of a problem in uniformly poor Pentecostal and holiness churches.[38] There was only one church (a Baptist congregation) in Cleveland, Mississippi, where Kathleen Knight, daughter of a white Delta sharecropper family, lived. She remembered that her parents made sure she and her siblings had appropriate clothes and went to church. But her parents had no such clothes and stayed home. Lillie Mae Flynt Beason related a similar memory of parents who made sure their children had churchgoing clothing even when they did not.[39]

Demeaning attitudes toward poor white citizens, whether intended or not, deepened class divisions. In many mill villages and mining camps, churches represented distinct classes, with Methodists and Presbyterians most frequently enrolling middle and upper classes, Baptists split, and Pentecostal and holiness congregations tending toward lower class. Mrs. L. A. House grew up Methodist in a farming community and visited a church of that denomination when she moved into a Sylacauga, Alabama, mill village. She soon left for Mignon Baptist Church, she explained, because most management people and the mill owners were Methodists while she felt more comfortable among ordinary Baptist laborers like herself.[40] Elsewhere in Alabama, a Baptist women's missionary report deplored the class divisions in a south Alabama community where five churches and one mission enrolled mutually hostile socioeconomic classes. Another study found similar conditions in other parts of the state. In the town of Brundidge, a new Baptist pastor invited a tenant farmer family to attend services, only to discover that some of the "hoity-toity type people didn't want them in the church."

The pastor's wife invited a poor white woman to a Woman's Missionary Union meeting with the same result: members "let us know they didn't care to have her in the church."[41]

Another barrier to poor-white church attendance was company subsidies for working-class churches or preachers. Historians have long believed that textile and coal company officials encouraged Baptist and Methodist churches in mill towns because those denominations preached a gospel of work, along with an otherworldly obsession with being born again and obtaining heavenly rewards instead of social justice in this world. Companies often contributed both to church maintenance and preachers' salaries.[42] The companies even used a check-off system, withdrawing from salaries whatever contributions workers wanted to make to the churches.

Although some workers praised such philanthropy, others considered it manipulative and self-serving, offering it as a reason for their lack of church participation. Although active in Sylacauga's mill village Baptist church, Mrs. L. A. House remembered clashes between her pastor, who opposed dancing, and the company's recreation director, who encouraged it in the mill's community center. Mill officials visited services themselves to determine whether or not the pastor of a company-subsidized church was challenging company policies. Coal miner Luther Smith believed that Pratt Consolidated Coal Company in Walker County, Alabama, hired preachers for the community's Baptist, Methodist, and holiness churches who could "get along with the company officials." Timber worker Cecil Spencer explained that his lumber town in West Florida built and furnished a church and paid half the pastor's salary. Three southwestern Virginia coal miners offered conflicting versions of the company church. Lloyd Vick Minor remembered that the Stonega Coal and Coke Company in Imboden provided the church building, but he believed the company did not interfere with his Methodist pastor. Minor's foreman father recalled the company's voluntary salary deductions for the church and the large attendance by both supervisors and miners, and he also denied any company pressure on pastors to conform with company policy. But miner Glen Carter believed that the Blue Diamond and Benedict coal companies for which he worked controlled the churches and that preachers did what the company "wanted 'em to do. And most of 'em, when they come in there . . . if they didn't do as they [the company] wanted to and preach as they wanted 'em to, they didn't stay long." Yet he added that most miners respected their ministers.[43]

This mixed testimony does provide some external evidence for evangelical religion as a capitalist device to manipulate poor white people. But much evidence also suggests countervailing effects. A team of researchers from the University of North Carolina at Chapel Hill, led by Jacquelyn Dowd Hall, conducted extensive interviews with North Carolina textile workers and accentuated the role evangelicalism played in forging a sense of community among them. Joining sects such as the Church of God, Pentecostal Holiness, or Wesleyan Methodist emphasized workers' independence from the mainstream religion of owners and uptown folks who lived outside the mill village and often considered themselves socially and morally superior to mill workers. Contributing to the sense of empowerment that sectarianism afforded them was the fact that some mill owners tried to keep sects out of their villages. One owner complained that so-called holy rollers (a derogatory term applied indiscriminately to both pentecostals and holiness sects) "just tear up a village and a community, keep folks at the meeting till all hours of the night so that they are not fit to work the next day, and they keep such meetings going for two months with shouting and carrying on. Here they are the sorriest sort of folks and not desirable in the community on general principles."[44] Belonging to a sect, then, became one way in which cotton mill people forged an autonomous culture.

Sectarian churches also ministered to the spiritual and physical needs of members. The churches dispensed charity during strikes and depressions. They especially inspired women to demand their rights. They provided prophetic Biblical language to mobilize against the oppression of the poor by the rich. A Mrs. Ellington angrily wrote David Clark, editor of the *Southern Textile Bulletin*, during the 1930s textile strike in Charlotte: "You and I know that the truth will stand when this world is being destroyed by fire, and the Clarks and mill owners will have passed beyond to face the Divine Creator of us all." And the churches crafted a theology of patient confidence in God's provision. A Bynum, North Carolina, textile worker explained, "If I hadn't had the faith in God, I'd never have got by. I feel like if I hadn't, I wouldn't be here today. 'Cause He's really stood by me in hard times and rough times. I've been really down and out. But with God, somehow, someway, something come along. Made a way."[45]

Sometimes sectarian churches also challenged prevailing class arrangements. One bivocational preacher in a Greensboro, North Carolina, mill village, who began textile work at age fifteen, finally became a full-time preacher of a company-subsidized congregation of more than five hundred members. Although he tried to avoid taking sides in strikes, by 1938 he had seen enough. A fierce, partisan Democrat and admirer of Franklin Roosevelt, he preached a sermon during that year's textile strike, taking his text from James, a New Testament book admonishing the application of religious faith toward the goal of social justice: "Go now, ye rich man, weep and howl for your miseries that shall come upon you. Your riches are corrupted, and your garments are moth-eaten." His exegesis comforted his own poor flock at the expense of mill owner Herman Cone.[46]

To be sure, many accounts by poor white people do reflect a resignation to injustice. Bill Holmes, a Primitive Baptist preacher in western Tennessee, explained: "My heart ain't set on the comforts of this earth. Heaven, sweet heaven, is my home and—oh—I'm beginning to git homesick."[47] But by no means did such a theology preclude more subtle and subversive sentiments.

Margaret Jarman Hagood conducted interviews in the 1930s with white North Carolina tenant farm women for her dissertation at Chapel Hill. She recorded a woman who consoled herself amid a life of backbreaking exertion with a Bible verse that admonished her to "Be content with your lot" in life. But the woman quickly added, "Tenants ain't got no chance. I don't know who gets the money, but it ain't the poor. It gets worse every year—the land gets more wore out, the prices for tobacco gets lower, and everything you got to buy gets higher. Like I told you, I'm trying to 'be content' like the Bible says and not to worry, but I don't see no hope."[48]

Hagood also discovered a "strange contradiction to the ordinary limiting of women's vocations," contained in three accounts of women preachers who had conducted revivals during the previous year: "They were given unqualified praise by husbands, wives, and children. In one case they declared that the woman was the best preacher they had ever heard and repeated bits of her life and her sermons." Apparently, Hagood concludes, the usual poor-white restrictions on women's roles did not apply to "the Lord's work." Hagood also found that the most loyal church attendees were all holiness women.[49]

A recent dissertation by James D. Ross Jr. finds similar multiple levels of religious meaning in the failure of the Southern Tenant Farmers Union (STFU) in Arkansas. He traces the collapse of the union to the disconnection between, on the one hand, the rank-and-file commitment to fundamentalist religion and individual landownership and, on the other hand, the allegiance of union leaders to atheism, secularism, collectivism, and the Social Gospel.[50]

Historian Elizabeth Anne Payne applies such generalizations to a specific person, Myrtle Lawrence, considered by STFU leaders to be their finest white female organizer. Born in the clay hills of Lamar County, Alabama, Lawrence dropped out of school after only two weeks in first grade to chop cotton. By 1937 she and her husband had sharecropped twenty-eight cotton seasons in three states. Illiterate and mother to a large family (she named two daughters, born in wintertime, Icy Jewel and Snowbank), she was "devoted to" Taylor Springs Baptist Church. Indeed she joined the STFU after apparently thinking it was a church organization to help sharecroppers. She took her union pledge from a Baptist minister, not unusual in a union where an estimated 60 percent of organizers were black and white ministers, who sometimes enrolled entire congregations. STFU meetings followed the pattern of poor folks' worship services, with prayers and hymns, vivid testimonials, and moving sermons and exhortations, followed by brief union business sessions and much socializing. Women breast-fed their babies, and worshipers spat in tin cans, while dogs and children wandered in and out of the building. There was no certain time to begin or to end. Black and white people often met together, typical of life on the margins of southern society.[51]

These primitivist religious folkways, of course, did not constitute the image that union founders H. L. Mitchell and Clay East wished to cultivate. Socialist leader Norman Thomas shared their views. By the 1930s American intellectuals had laid aside the angst and estrangement of Paris's left-bank bohemians for the causes of social change and revolution. Now the "masses" embodied not so much philistinism and bigotry as nobility and innocence. Erskine Caldwell had crafted new literary heroes whose degeneracy was rooted less in personal choices than in economic and political exploitation.

Mitchell understood this metamorphosis, and this son of a Baptist preacher-turned atheist feared that women such as Myrtle Lawrence would tarnish the union's image. For all Mitchell's economic radicalism, he wanted noble southern ladies, not fundamentalist women, to represent the union. Lawrence was not only a Baptist believer and a charismatic speaker; she also water-witched and had ecstatic visions. Except for the embarrassment of illiteracy and disfigured teeth (a byproduct of pellagra), Lawrence never doubted her ability or tried to mask her poor-white culture.[52]

In 1937, during National Sharecroppers Week, "thousands of New Yorkers attended a meeting" that featured three Arkansas sharecroppers, including Lawrence. Senators Robert LaFollette and Robert Wagner attended, as did presidential candidate Norman Thomas. But Myrtle Lawrence stole the show with her "spit can" wrapped in "bright pink paper." While the political notables orated, the front rows riveted their attention on Lawrence. Henrietta McGhee, an African American organizer, told Mitchell after the meeting that she had never been "so embarrassed in her life as by that old white woman making everyone think the union folks were all just like those Tobacco Road people they had heard about."[53]

Historian Payne unwraps this scene, revealing a long-hidden tangle of issues involving race, class, gender, power, and religion. Leftist New York intellectuals viewed Lawrence as an exotic primitive, as compelling as Ralph Ellison's invisible man was to the city's Communist Party sophisticates. H. L. Mitchell was also appalled by such a "tobacco roader" despite her unrivaled organizing and speaking skills. He refused to allow her to volunteer for work in the union's Memphis headquarters, where office manager Evelyn Smith Munro (who was both a socialist and a feminist) recalled Lawrence as "not the kind of woman who interested me at the time. Of course, now I would be completely fascinated by her, but then I was put off by her appearance and mannerisms." Mitchell and Munro sought nobility, someone worthy of a Dorothea Lange portrait of exhausted grandeur, a Mona Lisa for the crackers.[54] Instead of nobility, they got authenticity—a snuff-dipping Southern Baptist who located social justice and democratic values in primitive Biblicism and the equality of all before God. Her support system came not from comrades in the union but from her brothers and sisters in the Baptist church.

But evangelical culture made her no less a radical. Growing up poor and illiterate among the cotton fields of North Alabama, she understood both economic exploitation and the shared interests of poor white and black people. Her parents taught her to respect African Americans, an attitude she carried with her to the YWCA Summer School for Women Workers in Industry at Black Mountain, North Carolina. Her history professor there, visiting from Vassar College, was especially impressed with Lawrence's commitment to racial equality. Of black people, Lawrence told one English class, "They eat the same kind of food that we eat; they live in the same kind of shacks that we live in; they work for the same boss men that we work for; they hoe beside us in the fields; they drink out of the same bucket that we drink out of; ignurance is a kill'n' them just . . . the same as it's a kill'n' us. Why shouldn't they belong to the same union that we belong to?"[55]

The point of Payne's biography is much larger than the story of one white female sharecropper and union organizer. The broader message concerns the way in which American social activists and liberal intellectuals marginalized poor white people whose fundamentalist culture so often obscured the deeper meaning of their lives.

That generalization would have been doubly true had Lawrence followed a growing trend and been pentecostal or holiness instead of Baptist. As early as 1914 Methodist officials in Alabama regretted the departure of "many of our most spiritual members to the Nazarene and other churches."[56] Historian Herman Clarence Nixon, native of an Appalachian hill county in the same state, wrote in the early 1940s about a holy-roller congregation that had been built near the site of a defunct, burned Methodist church. He concluded that Baptists and Methodists had lost the old-time revival fervor to holiness and Church of God congregations, which were thriving in rural regions and mill villages.[57] Ila Hendrix, a coal miner's wife in Alabama, explained that she, her husband Benny, and their children attended a Nazarene church rather than one of the more numerous Baptist and Methodist churches because the Nazarene congregation better suited their needs.[58]

Across the state border in Perry County, Mississippi, a brush arbor went up in the fall of 1931, and a holiness revival began. At first, neighbors came to gawk and ridicule, but slowly they began to observe respectfully and attentively and then participate. The better-to-do in the community became alarmed and criticized the excessive emphasis upon "holiness or hell, the baptism of the Holy Ghost, which was revealed in unknown tongues, and any pleasure or diversion [which] was held up as a besetting sign." But one by one residents joined the new fellowship, and a majority of county residents soon expressed sympathy for the miraculous events unfolding. One teenager testified that after intensive prayer to receive the Holy Ghost, he walked out "under the stars one night when suddenly everything seemed lighter. He look up and saw that the stars were falling and one fell in his mouth and the power of the Holy Ghost came upon him and he was able to speak in other languages."[59] The revival birthed a Church of God that drew its members mainly from other congregations.

Conversions, of course, involved social consequences. A white Alabama coal miner and bootlegger served prison time because of his wife's "crazy religion." She became a "holy roller kind" and turned him in to the Talladega County sheriff; then she left to build a new life for herself and their children working in a cotton mill. In the northern part of the state on Lookout Mountain, a coal miner who had lost his home, job, a son, and a son-in-law to violence told a different story. He lived by the Ten Commandments and a simple code of right and wrong. Although he had joined a Church of God and had repented his bootlegging, he still believed federal laws against making whiskey infringed upon his personal liberty. Nevertheless, he proclaimed to an interviewer that "the church has done for him through love and sympathy what the state could not do through force and fear of prison."[60]

Whatever the attraction, sects multiplied like the South's legendary kudzu. In Coffee County, Alabama, according to one account, holiness and Pentecostal congregations were growing fastest. In the Cumberland County, Tennessee, community of Browntown, where most white dwellers were illiterate and half were on relief, mainline religion was declining in the 1930s, while the Holiness Church had surpassed the Baptist in significance. Examination of a Mississippi Delta community revealed only one church, a holy-roller assembly meeting on one of the farms. In Tarboro, North Carolina, another survey reported that emotional sects were gaining such a foothold that children came to school exhausted because "they were kept up late the night before to attend a church meeting."[61]

One of the finest 1930s community studies began in Tuscaloosa County, Alabama, in 1934. Two University of Alabama professors, Paul Terry and Verner Sims, hired O. N. Andrews, a newly married Auburn graduate from rural Chambers County, to conduct field research for them. Andrews's father had struggled throughout the early 1930s to hold on to his two-hundred-acre farm, finally using his mules as collateral for a seed loan. He even sold the trophy his son had won in a livestock contest to pay for the boy's tuition at Auburn University. Reared as a member of the mainline Christian Church and married to a Baptist woman, young Andrews was shocked as he surveyed the religious life of the Gorgas community (called "Upland Bend" in the ensuing book).[62] The community contained seven churches, the oldest Baptist and Methodist, the newest Nazarene and Church of God's Children. The oldest five churches shared many characteristics, although the major Baptist church contained mostly landowners while a smaller Baptist congregation enrolled nearly equal numbers of owners, tenants related to them, and unrelated tenants. Four of the ministers were bivocational, and none of the churches conducted services every Sunday.[63]

The most fascinating phenomenon that Andrews encountered involved the newly formed Church of God's Children. Begun in 1933, its services were substantially different from the others. Even the Nazarenes had won grudging community acceptance, but not the Church of God's Children. Members of the new church lived in an isolated, "half-mile square . . . surrounded by woods." Only two or three church families owned their houses, and they were "small," "crowded," and "untidy." Members were indifferent to education because "Jesus didn't have to go to school to have some sense." One of nineteen congregations of that denomination in Alabama, all very small, the church had only thirty-seven members. But those thirty-seven made up in commitment what they lacked in numbers, meeting every Wednesday and Saturday nights in addition to nearly all day on Sunday. They held two revivals in the summer. Despite their ardor, free-will offerings to pay their pastor averaged only about 85 cents a week. They claimed regular divine healings, spoke in tongues, and were Biblical literalists. Lengthy descriptions of their spontaneous and emotional services explained why community leaders were so hostile to the new congregation. One man dismissed them completely: "All of them are a bunch of damn fools." Another added: "Something should be done to scatter these people, because they are raising too many children who are mimicking them like a bunch of apes." A third man "puzzled" over the meaning of the new church: "I have thought about these people quite a bit. Frankly I don't know how they can be helped, for they refuse to associate with better people or to listen to outsiders. They are steeped in ignorance and poverty and being in that condition, they have become insane in their religion."[64]

Such a demeaning characterization would hardly have fit historian Bill C. Malone, who grew up in the small community of Galena, Texas, eighty miles east of Dallas. Son of an East Texas tenant farmer, Malone noted in a recent autobiographical essay his mother's conversion to pentecostalism from Methodism. Both volunteers from the area and occasional itinerant revivalists conducted services in the Tin To Pentecostal Church, which she attended with her children. Shouting, testifying, speaking in tongues, spirited music with guitar accompaniment, and other manifestations of the spirit brought consolation and joy. "Music, then, was . . . her salvation, as it was for me," Malone writes. "She sang to dispel her loneliness, to voice her frustrations, and to praise her God." The pentecostal culture that was the solace of his mother's salvation was the beginning of his distinguished career.[65]

Americans in general might have had even more difficulty understanding such religion than the residents of Gorgas, Alabama, or Galena, Texas, because people in other areas only rarely encountered it. But that isolation would not last long.

The massive dispersal of poor whites between 1930 and 1960 would drive millions of them to California and the midwestern industrial states. This migration did not introduce Southern Baptists and pentecostals to the Pacific coast or the Midwest, but it certainly accelerated the growth of their numbers there. Although many migrants initially visited local churches in their new homes, the newcomers often felt unwelcomed and disagreed with the liberal theology they encountered. Gravitating toward conservative Landmark Baptist churches or Pentecostal and holiness sects—which already existed in both the Midwest and California—they sought to preserve their ethnic identity in much the same way all immigrants do. C. R. Collier, a Southern Baptist migrant from Arkansas in the 1930s, visited a Northern Baptist congregation but did not like it much. Their theology was too liberal, and they "didn't appreciate us fellas coming out here anyway."[66]

Jim Hammitte left his coal-mining job in southeastern Kentucky in 1942, bound for the war plants in Detroit. Most of his fellow migrants, he recalled, were Baptist, Methodist, Church of God, or Church of Christ. They contrasted with the northern working-class people with whom they mingled, a population that was overwhelmingly Catholic. That made for an uneasy workplace environment: "Far as talking religion and politics, that was two subjects I stayed away from in Detroit. I didn't choose to talk that or express my feeling on it . . . and [you] didn't get that close to know them, exactly what their ideas [were]." In Kentucky he had attended church two or three times a week. In wartime Detroit, long work shifts and the inconvenient location across town of churches like "we grew up in" caused him to find excuses not to attend. He began to send his children with more devout neighbors to these churches.[67]

Rich as community studies and oral histories are for revealing poor-white religious experiences during the 1930s, there is an even better source. In September 1935 Franklin Roosevelt launched a new era of politicized religion. A letter was mailed over the president's signature to nearly 122,000 of the nation's 200,000 clergy; 100,000 letters reached their intended destinations, triggering 30,000 responses. Ostensibly soliciting "counsel and advice" in his clergy letter, the president was more interested in winning support for his 1936 reelection effort. Roosevelt received more than he bargained for. In the letter, he inquired about conditions in ministers' communities and their opinions about various public works programs and the new Social Security Act. Fairly typical of the responses were those from Alabama, where 327 ministers responded, 79 percent of them favorably and 5 percent critically (many of the negative letters criticized the New Deal from the left for doing too little).[68] Some writers can be identified as poor white citizens because of their denomination or geographical location. Others poured out their life stories, identifying themselves as poor.

Southern states produced slightly more negative responses than other regions.

One reason was the recent repeal of Prohibition. Ministers of all economic backgrounds chided the president for allowing a return of the roadhouse and honky-tonk. Others denounced Roosevelt for playing golf on Sunday, coddling the poor, plowing under cotton and slaughtering livestock, destroying the Protestant work ethic, and promoting the Social Gospel.[69] One critic believed that only "an Old time Pentecostal Revival of Holy Ghost power," war, or Christ's return to earth could prevent national disaster. The country had turned from "priceables of Righteousness to Modernism and Communism."[70] Rev. George F. Wolf of North Carolina warned that "people are like a pen of hogs as long as you poor slop into the trought they will drink and some try to stand in the trought to keep the rest out and when the slop give out they will throw of there heads and try to nock the bucket out of your hands so look out president when you have to stop putting out."[71]

Many letters critical of the New Deal came from pastors of textile churches. The pastor of two Methodist mill churches in South Carolina complained about labor agitators who inspired rioting, vandalism, strikes, and violence. Another Methodist pastor in a Spartanburg mill village deplored discord and strife, condemning labor for fomenting bitterness. The pastor of a North Carolina mill church was convinced that anyone who wanted a job could find one.[72]

Occasionally Roosevelt's letter was intercepted by unintended recipients. That happened in Gastonia, North Carolina, where church members authorized a poorly educated seventy-two-year-old woman (the only one among them who could write) to respond to the letter their pastor had set aside without consulting them. "As for our preacher he are a big tond preacher," she wrote: "He don't go among the mill peopel. [H]e are afraid he will get a gurm from them or see some of ther poverte. So my naber wanted me to rit you and tell you if wer gaine to help the old peopel to get a pednthen to do so for the old one wer nead it bad so thay cold get a Dr. To come to them."[73]

Other poor-white evangelicals had better luck. Their pastors were proud to represent them. Many interpreted the president's instruction as literally as they did the Bibles they read, sending Roosevelt lengthy lists of indigent members. In careful, handwritten letters reflecting their limited educations, clergymen implored Roosevelt to assist specific widows, orphans, elderly, and all indigents. They listed ages and addresses, as well as detailed physical conditions. From eastern Tennessee, Rev. W. M. Worley explained: "this people that I am menthon hant got no way in the world to make a living they are to old to get a job in eny factory are public work." They were "bound to starve are freze one because they have no way of getting eny wood are eny thing."[74]

Because rural ministers often served churches consisting largely of tenants and sharecroppers, many of the letters focused on tenancy. A series of letters from different sections of Georgia described the problems. From Appalachian Georgia a Methodist pastor with a circuit of "pure blood Anglo-Saxon" residents chided Georgia Power Company for ignoring their pleas for electricity. Roads were only fair, no one had electrical power, and three hundred people had no pure drinking water. Another minister wrote of proud people who wanted work, not a dole. Many others were too elderly or sick to continue arduous physical labor, but they had no choice because the New Deal's cotton allotments were too small to provide tenants and small farmers sufficient income to survive. A minister from the other end of the state wrote that tenant shacks "were rotting down. South Georgia is rotting down." A Methodist who pastored near Augusta estimated the annual incomes of sharecroppers close to his church at only $40 to $50, with which they were obliged to buy clothes, pay physicians, and send their children to school: "The real condition is really appalling: Luxuries are unknown, necessities are positively lacking." Pastors could not survive because tenants had no money to pay their salaries. He would get by some way, "God being my helper but it is stated out of a heart that aches for the want and actual suffering of our country people."[75]

Elsewhere the news was no better. A bivocational minister/schoolteacher from Bell County, Kentucky, wrote of coal mines closed because of labor conflict, tenant farmers with no resources, and 60 percent of the children in his one-room school of fifty without shoes or decent clothing. The pastor of a Methodist church in a fishing village on the North Carolina coast reported prices of fish that would not sustain the families of fishermen, who were deserting the Democratic Party for socialism.[76]

Two Church of God pastors sent similar reports. The bishop of the denomination in Alabama complained that New Deal programs in the Tennessee Valley had countervailing impacts. Tennessee Valley Authority jobs paid good money for those fortunate enough to obtain them. But they also raised the cost of living to unaffordable heights for those without jobs and even for those on relief work. The result was much suffering as winter approached. From Fannin County, Texas, a minister of the same denomination reported that his members worked from "daylight till dark" for 75 cents a day. The county needed salvation, and he believed the depression to be punishment for the nation deserting God. But while he waited for his fellow citizens to repent, the Texas pastor believed that someone needed to do something about the two men who ruled the county and controlled all relief jobs.[77]

Hundreds of letters included a dual message. Along with reports about conditions in their communities, ministers sent descriptions of themselves. Usually they made the obvious connection between their poverty and the indigence of their congregations. Most poor-white churches (Methodists being an exception) could not expect help from denominational agencies. What they raised from their own members would have to suffice. They were one with their flocks not only in spirit and doctrine but also in suffering.

Many of the letters came from ministers who also worked as small farmers and tenants. Small landowners complained that their cotton allotments were too small, their mortgages were being foreclosed, and they would soon become tenants. A farmer/preacher/turpentiner from Florida estimated his combined income at $40 a month. To many of the letter writers, that would have been a princely sum. W. J. Crowder of Tellico Plains, Tennessee, described himself as "one among the porest class of people I guess you do not . . . know the kneeds. Christ said you have the pore with you all ways you may do them good when you will. [G]od love the charful giver." Although the nation must repent or perish, Crowder believed, "thare may be a man in the whale belly that will bring the message that will bring us repenteus."[78]

At the bottom of the ministerial ladder were preachers who had become farm laborers. F. D. Coppin of Paxton, Texas, had preached the gospel wearing a donated, patched suit since the early 1920s. He received a salary of thirty dollars a month from his church of two hundred members and earned a dollar a day working the cotton fields. Alton Pury of Dresden, Tennessee, had pastored poor country churches, though none could afford him presently. He had one cow and a battered car and fed his wife and two children by doing farm labor, when he could get it, for 75 cents a day. A preacher from Texarkana, Texas, gave the parable of the prodigal son a sardonic twist: preachers were "living on the husks which the swine did eat."[79]

Roosevelt Elliott, a sharecropper/preacher in Knox County, Kentucky, lacked sufficient clothing and bedding to stay warm, and he could not get on relief rolls. He both appealed for help and provided the president a fundamentalist version of gender relations. President Roosevelt should fire female relief workers and hire only needy men: "Women having controle of the office force . . . in other words being head boss [was wrong] . . . Let men have authority over women and not the women over the men," which would be "more pleasing to the sight of God. . . . I do not believe our nation or any nation" can prosper "so long as women have authority over the men because it is against God's Holy and Divine Word and His will."[80]

Three poor-white women preachers saw the issue differently. Maggie L. Cheek preached in a sawmill camp in Whaleyville, Virginia. Since the sawmill had closed in 1920, the only employment available to residents was picking cotton. Poor widows such as herself had suffered terribly and welcomed any help the New Deal offered. Ida S. Lynch (known as "Sister Ida") identified herself as an ordained minister in the Bible Church of God. She had preached in North Carolina and Virginia for thirty-six years. When she answered Roosevelt's letter, she was working among the poor in Richmond's slums, prisons, and hospitals. God had called her to do "mercy work" as a child, but her labor as a city missionary produced no salary. When she begged wages for her work, people "scoffed openly." She offered to visit the White House to help the president craft a plan to give a tithe of federal revenues to the "Lords missionaries" working with the "poor and needy." Roosevelt did not respond to her offer. Anne M. Hunter did not pastor a church, but she was "an evangelist and a woman in the bargain. I'm not one of the salaried preachers, but live and carry on my work by free will offerings." The widowed mother had been left stranded in Florida when her car broke down and strong winds shredded her gospel tent. She had never accepted relief despite the fact that she preached to people too poor to pay her expenses. Her sermons sought for her hearers both their "social betterment as well as their spiritual upbuilding," and she vowed that she knew their problems better than the "big preachers." Many on relief did not deserve it, she wrote, while poor children went hungry. If the government could waste so much money on the undeserving, she knew no reason why the New Deal could not buy her a new tent and a car.[81]

Similar testimonies came from mining camps and textile villages. The wife of a textile-mill pastor in Florence, Alabama, made the family's clothes and served as a source of income by working at a knitting mill. Their church, like most in the village, was in debt, received few contributions from poor members, and needed repairs. A Kentucky preacher/coal miner told a similar story of men out of work (himself included). A Tennessee coal miner/preacher was also out of work, leaving him, as well as his church members, without food, clothes, or schoolbooks for their children.[82]

Other letters were less specific but just as desperate. Three farmer/pastors of the Missionary Baptist denomination from South Carolina, Georgia, and Tennessee lived in the "back woods" among poor farmers. Preachers in their communities barely had enough education to read the Bible. One eighty-year-old preacher was nearly blind and suffered from pellagra. His only income came from the poor churches he still served as pastor despite his age and infirmity. He was too proud to beg and too feeble to labor. "Who will care for us?" he wondered when he was forced to retire. Another pastor with little education, age 77, praised old-age pensions. Although he believed "the Lord would provide for him," he was "in hard luck now."[83]

The most pathetic letters came from such elderly ministers who had preached all their lives to poor congregations for virtually nothing. Many were in poor health. Denied access to Social Security payments because they were considered self-employed, they envisioned no solution to their indigence short of the poorhouse. P. R. Warren, of Jonesboro, Arkansas, complained that he could obtain no pastorate because churches preferred younger men. Deeply in debt, he grieved for the "untold misory from the lack of food and clothing" as elderly people "sit in their little old huts that is not fit . . . to house cattle and no food no clothes no fual—and it looks to me that if it were not for government and the hopes that they would soon receive some relief that they might pray god to die before winter comes on." R. E. Houston, of Baskin, Louisiana, a First World War veteran with eight children, agreed. Living in a community where "ninety-five percent have nothing witch to survive the winter on," he knew "people need Christ most of all, but they must have metureal help" as well. J. H. Hooker, of Bibb County, Georgia, was a retired 86-year-old Free Will Baptist preacher living in the county poorhouse. Forced to write with a pencil because he had no ink, he begged for help "for we are crazy to get out of this place and get to where we can spend what days there is left for us in peace an quietness."[84]

Dozens of ministers swallowed their pride and sought jobs on public relief, only to discover that as pastors they were considered by relief officials to be employed, even if they earned nothing from their preaching. Some of them worked as day laborers for less than a dollar a day, or they preached full-time for less than $200 a year. Some had been turned out by congregations that could no longer pay them anything, and they had to live on charity from hard-pressed relatives. Rev. K. V. Judd, of Greenburg, Kentucky, had a more sinister explanation. As a lifelong Republican (even though he had voted for FDR), he believed that local Democratic relief officials had denied him work because of his political affiliation. He tried to "lead our people to obey our rulers and leaders" whatever their party, "so I think you should see that us poor ministers that is down and out should get some of the money that is being wasted for every thing but the right thing."[85]

Other preachers used their good standing or influence to obtain relief jobs. Like many secular relief recipients, ministers complained about too few hours of work and too little pay, of favoritism and shabby treatment. But most praised Roosevelt for what little they received. Rev. N. J. Joyner, of Camden, Tennessee, had "spent the best years of my life preaching to the poor." Now he was one with his people, depending upon his Works Progress Administration job to support his wife and son. Although M. C. White, of Pelham, Georgia, an 86-year-old minister who was crippled and partially blind, worked digging ditches for so little money he could barely afford to buy bread, he praised Roosevelt, remembering that "Old Hoover made a corn bread cutter out of me." And anti-New Deal Georgia governor Eugene Talmadge was no better than Hoover. He made White "think of a switch engen—he goes first one way and then another. I am afraid if Talmadge is the [only] chance to help me I will get might hungry."[86]

M. C. White was not the only minister to express political preferences in his letter. Long before the Moral Majority or Christian Coalition, many white ministers used their pulpits for overtly partisan purposes. Class grievances boiled to the surface of many of their letters. Some ministers wrote to Roosevelt that they preferred the quasi-religious Townsend plan (a $150 pension for every American past age 60) to the Social Security Act. But most praised Roosevelt for his unprecedented concern for the poor, vowed their support for him, and pledged to do all they could to reelect him in 1936.

Harris Gilliam, a Nazarene Sunday school superintendent in Monteagle, Tennessee, who had no previous interest in politics, was committed to the "welfare of our people" and promised his support. J. W. B. Pannell, pastor of a blue-collar church in Tarrant, Alabama, who was about to lose his house to foreclosure, called FDR "the victim of more traitors than any man since the days of Jesus." Another letter writer, a lifelong Republican from the GOP bastion of Winston County, Alabama, had cast his first Democratic vote for FDR. A. C. Stevenson, a pastor from Hollytree, Alabama, also proclaimed himself and his congregation "for the 'New Deal' one hundred per cent." S. L. Loudermilk from Florida praised Roosevelt and advocated government ownership of public utilities as well as provision of a house and land to every family. W. P. Powell, a Church of Christ minister from North Carolina, believed that God had planted ideas such as old-age pensions and relief work in Roosevelt's heart "because the Bible do say 'the strong must bare the infirmity of the weak.'" Thomas A. Little, of Marshville, North Carolina, who identified himself as an "old cuntry pasor," supplemented his praise with Scripture, and he urged Roosevelt to declare a Jubilee year to forgive all debts: "The banks unload on the farmer. Why not unload this once on the capitalist and give us a Juber Lee." A Kentucky pastor declared Roosevelt to be the greatest American president. W. V. Brown, pastor in Cycle, North Carolina, believed no company should be allowed profits of more than two or three million dollars in one year. Businesses should be compelled to divide any additional revenue with their employees. D. P. Baker, a 77-year-old pastor in Lancaster, South Carolina, hoped FDR would win in 1936 and then be "elected dictator of the U.S.A." A pastor from the same state believed Roosevelt had saved America from violent revolution.[87]

Letters from five ministers of textile-mill churches scattered across the South challenged generalizations about mill-village pastors made by Liston Pope based on his experiences in Gastonia, North Carolina. The letter writers strongly favored labor, FDR, and the New Deal. A pastor from Porterdale, Georgia, believed workers had a right to join a union and congratulated FDR for extending such rights. Two ministers from the textile city of Columbus, Georgia, agreed. J. W. Miller, a textile worker and preacher, had lost his mill job to the stretch-out system and believed that "the money kings are trying to force the country back to the DARK AGES. When we see these little ones in our midst suffering from malnutrition or slow starvation, it is enough to embitter all our hearts and mind toward the rich, for they seem to sneer at us in our cry for help." Andrew L. Stewart wrote that Columbus textile officials treated workers "like slaves. . . .

They exploit[ed] the peoples and the wages of those that are working," refused to meet with workers, and had reinstated sweatshop conditions. Pastors from North and South Carolina expressed similar views.[88]

Coal-camp pastors were equally laudatory of FDR for gaining their church members the right to join unions. Companies had controlled houses, churches, schools, courts, and politics and had compelled families to shop in company commissaries, where prices were a third higher, and to join company unions. L. D. Spears, a miner/preacher from Central City, Kentucky, protested that officials robbed miners with pencils in the company store as certainly as thieves robbed them with guns.[89]

Literal reading of the Bible did not always furnish a conservative critique of America either. Orion S. Rowlett, of Webster, Florida, praised the New Deal and condemned the rich: "These great men are litterly building scaffolds as Haman of old to hang their own necks on! They cannot hide their sins. The working people all know this and they hate them for it, and this hatred is acumilating as steam in a boiler." A lifelong minister in Bell County, Kentucky, "pointed out that the principles of the New Deal are the word of God" and that the "monied interests . . . had coulralled the money in America. . . . Your fight for the public ownership of private utilities and all natural recorces is something I am sure God is going to use to cary on a successful culmination despite senators congressmen editors and preachers that oppose." A pastor from a working-class church in Charlotte, North Carolina, heard one man refer to FDR as "Jesus" when Congress enacted the National Recovery Act (NRA). And a pastor from Mt. Airy in the same state considered that piece of federal legislation the finest ever passed to help poor people: "And may God bless thoas good men who said good buy NRA. You know that the Good Book said pray for thine who despitefully use you, and we surly feel like praying from those 9 men [on the Supreme Court who struck down the NRA]."[90]

Carrying such sentiments one step further, a pastor from Boonesville, North Carolina, was using his lifelong commitment as a "starnch Dimocrat" and his ministerial role as a "public man" to speak on behalf of FDR. Rev. J. N. Parker from North Georgia had won election to the state legislature, where he had supported the New Deal and opposed Governor Eugene Talmadge. A pastor from Cedartown, Georgia, boasted that he had helped elect FDR in 1932, with Roosevelt carrying forty of the forty-two votes in the man's rural precinct. A pastor near Monticello, Georgia, held a meeting, attended by both white and black farmers, at Reids Chapel Baptist Church. After a brief debate, the assembly had declared FDR to be the greatest world leader since Moses and Aaron had led the Hebrew people out of bondage. On a series of Sunday mornings, Grant T. Mills, of Apex, North Carolina, told his rural churches "that Pres. Roosevelt was following more nearly the program of Jesus than any president we have ever had."

He illustrated each of his points (the declaration of a year of Jubilee for debt forgiveness, God's concern for the poor, help for the blind, setting the wounded free) with Scripture. E. K. Ison, pastor in Robinson Creek, Kentucky, spoke at a Democratic mass meeting to elect delegates who would support FDR at the state party convention. G. K. Fortinberry, of Amite, Louisiana—a veteran of the First World War and a country pastor earning less than $25 a month—pledged to speak a good word on behalf of FDR in all his churches.[91]

True enough, in 1935 many fundamentalist preachers still inhabited a world that shunned politics, rejected the secular world, and awaited transportation to a heavenly kingdom beyond the troubles of the world. But as Clifford Geertz and Robert Coles explain, even that religion is comprehensible as a way of making bearable the abuse, defeat, and powerlessness of a life full of pain. As the poor-white members of Mt. Hebron Baptist Church in Alabama testified, such religion could provide "a special feeling of closeness" that contrasted with the conflict and anonymity of the world around them. They created, to use Geertz's term, "webs of significance" to explain the social reality of their times. But many of them no longer dwelt in such a disorderly world, having found in politics and unionism a realization of their Biblical vision of justice. If, as Geertz argued, the importance of religion is to be found in its capacity to serve as a source of general conceptions of the world, self, and the relations between them, then evangelicalism served a powerful function for disconsolate, desperate, angry poor white people who flooded the White House with their Jobian tales of woe between September 25 and December 31, 1935. And seen from that perspective, the bittersweet religion of May Jordan does not seem strange, escapist, or inconsistent at all.

—*Journal of Southern History*, 2005

Although I had long since severed my Southern Baptist (SBC) connections in favor of the more moderate Cooperative Baptist Fellowship (CBF), I remained active in the Baptist History and Heritage Society (formerly the Southern Baptist Historical Commission, which I had chaired before its secession from the SBC). Now inclusive of other Baptist traditions (including northern and African American groups), the organization sponsored a national gathering to celebrate the 400th anniversary of Baptists (1608–2008).

I was invited to speak and decided to merge historical Baptist demands for church-state separation, forged by the denomination's experience of persecution, with its more recent heritage as the South's unofficial state church. As long as Baptists (and other Christians who thought like them, including lots of Catholics they had long reviled) controlled the state, they were content for it to prescribe school prayers, install replicas of the Ten Commandments in public places, divert state taxes to private Christian schools, ban abortions, embed Biblical views of marriage in state constitutions, deny religious freedom to Muslims, and in other ways establish a quasi-Christian state religion.

I decided to use my lecture to explain this historic reversal through sharply diverging judicial philosophies of two Alabama Baptist judges from two different generations, US Supreme Court Justice Hugo Black and State Supreme Court chief justice Roy Moore. Perhaps no biographical comparison reveals more clearly the changes in southern white religion.

The South's judicial battle over God has been shoved to the fringe of southern religion by its fierce culture war brawl on center stage. Of course, they are related. When a denomination jettisons one of its founding principles, historians should pay attention.

Chapter 13
Conflicted Interpretations of Christ, the Church, and the American Constitution

Not long after I arrived at Auburn University in 1977, the president of the institution (who held a PhD in philosophy from Yale University and was an ordained Baptist minister and military chaplain) claimed that the school was the largest Baptist university in the world. No matter that Auburn was in fact a state-funded land-grant university. Of the 20,000 students enrolled, nearly half identified as Baptists.

Such homogeneity in religion is hardly surprising in a state where more than

90 percent of the population affirms belief in God, where three in four adults consider themselves to be born again (compared with only one in three nationally), where nearly two million of Alabama's 4.5 million people belong to Baptist churches, either black or white, and where two of every three church members are Baptists.

Traditional Baptist enthusiasm for the doctrine of separation of church and state seemed like a reasonable assumption given such religious homogeneity. So when a columnist for the university newspaper, *The Plainsman*, editorialized that the idea of separation of church and state was neither a Baptist idea nor indigenous to American democracy, but a communist concept borrowed directly from the first Soviet constitution, I assumed the student not only had gotten his chronology wrong but also his history.

Having attended an Alabama Baptist university myself, I knew better. Dismissing the incident as an aberration resulting from poor education and America's culture wars—and believing no idea so constitutionally sacrosanct and so deeply ingrained in Baptist history as separation of church and state could be endangered—I shrugged off the article and its ominous implications. This assumption was not my last mistake, but it was one of my biggest.

My mistaken confidence was rooted in the denominational history that was part of my generation's lifeblood. What follows is a brief summary of this inherited wisdom.

John Smith and Thomas Helwys led a group of General (Armenian) Baptists (1608–1609) who were part of the separatist communities that thrived in seventeenth century England and which briefly resettled in the Netherlands (Amsterdam). Another segment of the separatist community settled in Leyden, also in the Netherlands, and shortly thereafter embarked for the New World on the *Mayflower*. As if to confirm their decision to flee England, Thomas Helwys was confined to Newgate prison when he returned home. Before his death in confinement, he wrote in the flyleaf of a book: "The king is a mortall man and not God. Therefore hath no power over immortall soules of his subjects, to make lawes and ordinances for them, and to set spirituall lords over them."[1]

Considered by Baptist historians to be "the first statement of absolute religious liberty to be written in English,"[2] Helwys's contention that religious liberty was an absolute right for both Christian dissenters and nonconformists turned out to be no more popular in Puritan New England than in Anglican Old England. By the middle of the eighteenth century, Roger Williams (who briefly called himself a Baptist) had entered the wilderness of Rhode Island to escape the Puritan theocracy. Baptist pastors John Leland and Issac Backus had gone to jail for opposing the use of public funds for private churches.[3]

Meanwhile in Virginia, Thomas Jefferson and James Madison had won popular support from Baptists for a bill establishing religious freedom. Madison's famous *Memorial and Remonstrance*, presented to the House of Burgesses in 1785, helped win acceptance of Jefferson's crusade for religious liberty. Like Roger Williams, Madison argued that in matters of religion, citizens were accountable to God alone. No civil magistrate was competent to "employ religion as an engine of civil policy." Legal establishment of religion harmed both it and the civil state, and "in no instances have they been seen the guardians of the liberties of the people."[4] While Virginia's Tidewater Anglican aristocracy—including Patrick Henry, John Marshall, and Richard Henry Lee—favored an established church supported by public funds, Jefferson pressed for his "Statute for Establishing Religious Freedom," which passed the legislature in 1786. It proclaimed "that no man shall be compelled to frequent or support any religious worship, place, or ministry whatsoever, nor shall be enforced, restrained, molested, or burthened in his body or goods, nor shall otherwise suffer on account of his religious opinions or belief; but that all men shall be free to profess, and by argument to maintain, their opinion in matters of religion, and that the same shall in no wise diminish, enlarge, or affect their civil capacities."[5]

Although the authorship of the First Amendment to the US Constitution is uncertain, Madison no doubt influenced the theory if not the exact wording. After many alterations, Madison's conference committee opted for brevity and simplicity of language: "Congress shall make no law respecting an establishment of religion, or prohibiting the free exercise thereof."[6] Those sixteen words proved to be among the most contentious in American history, and generations have argued about their meaning. Were they designed to keep Congress, but not the states, from establishing a single church or religion? Were they intended to prevent government meddling, but not public observance?

Following the closely contested and highly divisive 1800 presidential election, in which Federalists accused Thomas Jefferson of being an atheist among other things, the new president took opportunity to argue his own understanding of the First Amendment. When Baptist supporters in Danbury, Connecticut, sent their congratulations on his victory and urged him to set aside a day of fasting for national reconciliation, Jefferson responded by explaining his interpretation of the First Amendment: "Believing with you that religion is a matter which lies solely between man and his God, that he owes account to none other for his faith or his worship, that the legislative powers of government reach actions only, and not opinions, I contemplate with sovereign reverence that act of the whole American people which declared that their legislature should 'make no law respecting an establishment of religion, or prohibiting the free exercise thereof,' thus building a wall of separation between Church and State."[7]

Lest someone misunderstand his meaning, Jefferson elaborated four years later in his Second Inaugural Address: "In matters of religion, I have considered that its free exercise is placed by the Constitution independent of the powers of the general government."[8] Though religious himself and sympathetic to the Christian impulse, Jefferson spent his life reinforcing the "wall of separation" about which he wrote Danbury Baptists.[9]

Nineteenth-century Baptists found little to disagree with in Jefferson's interpretation. Francis Wayland, president of Baptist-affiliated Brown University in Rhode Island and arguably the finest Baptist theologian of his time, noted that Baptists had often been the object of state-directed persecution and favorably quoted Roger Williams as saying, "I desire not that liberty to myself which I would not freely and impartially weigh out to all the consciences of the world beside. . . . All these consciences, yea, the very consciences of the Papists, Jews, etc., ought freely and impartially to be permitted their several worship, their ministers of worship, and what way of maintaining them they freely choose."[10] Though nineteenth century Baptists often endorsed the practice of a generic form of Protestant piety in public education, they strongly denounced Catholic efforts to obtain government funding for parochial schools. Beyond that issue, the intersection of government and generic civil religion (inclusion of the words "In God we trust" on national currency, for instance) caused Baptists little concern.

The American Revolution, of course, destroyed the "confessional state" and ushered in a free market of religious ideas that spawned literally hundreds of religious groups and a religious eclecticism unparalleled elsewhere in the world.[11] This religious pluralism resulted in 130 religious lobbies that presently maintain offices in Washington, DC, all trying to shift public policy in the direction of their beliefs. Thankfully, no single group ever approached a religious majority in America (Catholics with some 65 million adherents and Southern Baptists with 16 million come closest), thus making some level of tolerance a necessity for all.

Not only did Baptist historians throughout the nineteenth and twentieth centuries endorse separation of church and state, they proudly claimed that their denomination played a significant (some denominational "triumphalists" even claimed a predominant) role in establishing this unique American ideology.[12]

Nor was the state of Alabama with its overwhelming Baptist population reluctant to affirm the doctrine. The state's 1901 constitution acknowledged "the favor and guidance of Almighty God" in its preamble and then in section three of its "Declaration of Rights" enunciated the classic Baptist conception of religious freedom much more elaborately than even the US Constitution: "That no religion shall be established by law; that no preference shall be given by law to any religious sect, society, denomination, or mode of worship; that no one shall be compelled by law to attend any place of worship; nor to pay any tithes, taxes, or other rate for building or repairing any place of worship, or for maintaining any minister or ministry; that no religious test shall be required as a qualification to any office or public trust under this state; and that the civil rights, privileges, and capacities of any citizen shall not be in any manner affected by his religious principles."[13]

This pronouncement was not just idle theory. Indeed, a Supreme Court justice from within Alabama Baptist ranks probably did more to solidify and expand the wall of separation than any other single person in the twentieth century.

A native of Clay County (a predominantly white hill county in east-central Alabama that had been a populist political stronghold during the 1890s), Hugo Black came from a Jeffersonian heritage reinforced by Baptist individualism. After moving to Birmingham to practice law, he joined First Baptist Church in 1907 and taught the Baraca adult Sunday school class for more than two decades. For Black, the ethics of Jesus—treating all people fairly, promoting social justice, defending the vulnerable and the powerless—were more important than personal spirituality, which he left to his wife, Josephine, herself the daughter of a Presbyterian minister. His Sunday school class attracted an array of working people and professional men who heard much more about unjust conditions in Birmingham than about some futuristic spiritual millennium.

Despite the political opportunism that led to his membership in the Ku Klux Klan that dominated Birmingham politics during the 1920s, Black possessed a strong moral compass that drove his politics to the left. As US Senator during the 1930s, Black provided the New Deal one of its most reliable southern advocates.

Black's pastor at First Baptist, Alfred J. Dickinson, represented the most liberal theological wing of the denomination, having been imprinted with modernist theology during his studies at Harvard University and the University of Chicago. Like his famous parishioner, Dickinson cared less about evangelism than about social justice, and in 1918 resigned as pastor in order to run for Congress as a labor reform candidate. More social worker than evangelist, Dickinson endorsed evolutionary biology, higher criticism of the Bible, separation of church and state, and expressed impatience with "noisy conversions and ecclesiastical whoopee."[14] His successor as pastor, James R. Hobbs, had less influence on Black but had himself contemplated a career in law and politics before opting for the ministry.[15] Black, who cared little about what he considered to be esoteric theological questions such as the divinity of Christ or heaven and hell, once told his son, "Understand I cannot believe. But I can't not believe either."[16]

His son inquired how Black could reconcile such agnosticism with teaching Sunday school and serving as deacon at First Baptist. The senator responded that he taught only those parts of the Bible that he selected, and he didn't have to listen to the preacher. The Bible contained more positive advice for living a constructive life than any other book, and he considered the Golden Rule to encompass the essence of all religion. During his Washington residence, Black seldom attended religious services, and when he did, he went to a Unitarian church.[17]

No doubt Black drew much of his unorthodox theology from Dickinson's modernism. In an interview late in his life, Black described Dickinson's sermons as "prose poetry" that soared over the heads of his congregation. And he remembered vividly his pastor's 1918 race for Congress on a platform that was anti-Catholic and which strongly favored separation of church and state.[18]

Black's initial opportunity to add judicial planks to Jefferson's "wall of separation" came in the high court's 1947 case *Everson vs. Board of Education.* The case involved a New Jersey statute that authorized local school boards to reimburse parents for the cost of transporting students to both public and private schools. The plaintiff challenged state repayment for travel to parochial schools. Although Justice Black did not believe New Jersey had breached the Constitution in this case, he argued passionately that "neither a state nor the Federal Government" could "enact laws aiding one religion over another, force or influence a person toward or away from a church, belief, or disbelief, punish a person for profession or nonprofession, levy a tax to support religious activities or institutions, or participate in the affairs of any religious organization." "In the words of Jefferson," Black concluded, "the clause against establishment of religion by laws was intended to erect 'a wall of separation between church and state.'"[19]

Black's introduction into a Supreme Court decision of Jefferson's language to Danbury Baptists reflected the jurist's deepest convictions about the First Amendment's role in American life: "It is my belief that the part of the Bill of Rights which protects free speech, free religion, and a free press constitutes the real bulwark of liberty and that a suppression of these rights would destroy our nation as democracy."[20]

Black was not the first justice to enunciate the principle, even if he did insert Jefferson's memorable metaphor. Four years earlier, Justice Robert Jackson had put the matter succinctly (*West Virginia Board of Education v. Barnette*) in a case involving Jehovah's Witnesses' children who were being required to salute the American flag in violation of their religion: "If there is any fixed star in our constitutional constellation, it is that no official, high or petty, can prescribe what shall be orthodox in politics, nationalism, religion, or other matters of opinion or force citizens to confess by word or act their faith therein."[21] The Supreme Court subsequently quoted this language in five 1980s decisions, one of which, *Wallace v. Jaffree*, originated in Alabama.

Following the Everson decision, Black had a more important rendezvous with destiny. The New York State Regents composed and recommended, although they did not require, that public schools begin each day with a twenty-two word prayer: "Almighty God, we acknowledge our dependence upon Thee, and we beg Thy blessings upon us, our parents, our teachers and our country." Five parents protested that the prayer violated separation of church and state. Black desperately wanted to write the majority opinion in this case, and Chief Justice Earl Warren acceded to his request.

As he labored over his manuscript, Black told his wife that people had been tortured in Europe, their tongues cut off or their eyes gouged out, all in the name of religion. Indeed, his lifelong grievance against Roman Catholicism (like that of his Birmingham pastor, A. J. Dickinson) had been rooted in its long history of religious persecution. Imbued as he was with the moderate Christian realism that constituted the primary force in American Protestantism at the time, and fashioned by his intense Baptist individualism, Black sought to protect American democracy (which, as he understood democracy, was the secular expression of Protestantism).

As Black prepared to write the 1962 *Engel v. Vitale* decision, he became more historian than lawyer. He began his research with the Anglican *Book of Common Prayer* and then moved to John Bunyan's *Pilgrim's Progress*, which he kept on his desk throughout his revisions. The selection of Bunyan's work was a strong clue to his decision. Bunyan, a Baptist pastor in Bedford, England, had been imprisoned for twelve years (1660–1672) for violating the Clarendon Code which had sought to regulate nonconformist activities. For instance, the 1662 Act of Uniformity exacted compliance with the revised *Book of Common Prayer* and its liturgical practices. This, Bunyan refused to do.[22]

Black's clerk at the time remembered that the judge had the appropriate "religious references on his fingertips," and sent him back and forth to the library to retrieve them. By the fourth draft of the decision, it contained more history than law. The fifth and sixth drafts added even more history. Except for the opening statement of facts in the case, *Engel v. Vitale* is almost entirely a narrative of church-state relations in England and America between the sixteenth and eighteenth centuries. Thinking perhaps of Thomas Helwys and John Bunyan, Black wrote: "It is a matter of history that this very practice of establishing governmentally composed prayers for religious services was one of the reasons which caused many of our early colonists to leave England and seek religious freedom in America." Colonists knew "from bitter personal experience" the dangers of government extending official approval for one form of religious expression over another. The fact that the prayer observance of students in New York schools was voluntary did not exempt it from First Amendment restrictions because when government bestowed its power and prestige on a particular religious belief, the indirect result was to pressure religious minorities to conform. Each state government as well as the federal government "should stay out of the business of writing or sanctioning official prayers and leave that purely religious function to the people themselves."[23]

While rendering the majority opinion, Black's body language reflected the passion of his argument. According to one reporter's account, he leaned forward and his voice trembled with emotion when he cited the Founding Fathers' belief that religion was "too personal, too sacred, too holy to permit its 'unhallowed perversion' by a civil magistrate."[24] His wife, Elizabeth, described his delivery as "almost like a sermon because he had drawn on his long period of teaching Sunday school class in Birmingham."[25]

In light of later events, the furious reaction to the Engel decision is worth noting. Of the thousand letters he received concerning the ruling, the most approving came from Baptists, Jews, and Quakers. Having just completed twenty-five years on the bench (he was one of only sixteen previous justices who had served as long), Black was convinced that the positive Protestant response to the court's decision insulated the nation from demands by some outraged Congressmen to amend the Constitution in order to permit prayer in schools.[26] Not all Protestants were so supportive. Seventy Baptist ministers met with Black in May 1964, representing congregations upset by his ruling. He urged the pastors to educate their people about the history of religious persecution.[27] One irate woman consigned him to hell in a condemnatory letter. In a rare response to a critic, he suggested where she might go as well: to a library (because he was certain she did not possess the book in her own home) and ask for a book called the Bible. She could open it and read the chapter where it said "pray in your own closet."[28]

In his home state, leading Baptists rallied to Black's cause. Although many lay people, a few influential pastors, and Methodist Governor George C. Wallace denounced the ruling, Leon Macon, a religious conservative and editor of the *Alabama Baptist*, praised the Engel ruling. When one of Alabama's Baptist congressmen, Albert Rains, warned state Baptist executive secretary George Bagley of negative reaction to the ruling stirred up by Wallace, Bagley wrote all white Baptist ministers in the state. He explained the threats to church-state separation, denied that the Engel decision prevented prayer in schools, and urged pastors to educate their congregations and contact their congressmen in support of Engel and against a pending constitutional amendment to override the decision. Congressmen reported that Bagley's letter accomplished its mission. Their offices were inundated with resolutions from churches opposing any tampering with the First Amendment.[29] Black's old political friend and former Alabama attorney general Harwell G. Davis, who had recently retired as president of Samford University, the state's largest Baptist college, defended Black's decision vigorously, writing his niece three days after the Engel decision: "The basic premise of the First Amendment is that people must be left to say their prayers in their own way, and to their own God, without express or explicit coercion from any political office holder. There are not many people with religion and intelligence who will think this constitutional principle wrong on mature second thought. To those who think prayer must be recited parrot-like in public places in order to be effective, the sixth chapter of Matthew, 1 to 19, might be reflected upon."[30]

Such letters not only revealed the deepest convictions of many Southern Baptists, they also reflected the collective experience of many non-Baptist citizens who had reservations about their Baptist neighbors and lawmakers. As Black clearly perceived, Catholics, Anglicans, and Puritans were not the only ones who threatened religious minorities. In a state where two-thirds of all church members were Baptists, they could be the agents of religious oppression.

As in most American states where one religion or denomination predominated, Baptists could and did make life difficult for religious minorities. In 1939 and again in 1946 members of the Jehovah's Witnesses offended local custom and broke nuisance laws with their door-to-door solicitations and contrarian beliefs. Rosco Jones and his wife, Thelma, preached and witnessed so fervently in Opelika and Auburn neighborhoods that ministers and lay people of other denominations had them arrested. Grace Marsh plied her evangelical calling among shipyard workers in the Gulf coast port of Chickasaw near Mobile. Her child refused to salute the American flag and family members were pacifists in accordance with Witness teachings. Like Rosco Jones, she was arrested. Jones and Marsh appealed their convictions (*Jones v. Opelika, Marsh v. Alabama*) through the federal appellate system to the US Supreme Court. In both instances, the high court expanded First Amendment protection of free exercise of religion to include the actions of these two obscure Jehovah's Witnesses.[31]

A generation later, the children of an agnostic African American attorney, Ishmael Jaffree, and his Bahai-believing wife, told their parents that teachers were conducting prayers in their Mobile public school classrooms. The city was a fundamentalist stronghold whose political strength radiated through the community from its center in two Southern Baptist mega-churches, Cottage Hill and Dauphin Way. The Jaffrees protested what they viewed as unconstitutional religious compulsion, and the city's conservative religious community rallied at the state capitol in Montgomery. A sympathetic Christian right governor, Fob James, and an equally agreeable legislature, rushed through a "moment of silence" law, allowing teachers to lead students in meditation or voluntary prayer. In US District Court, Chief Judge W. Brevard Hand, of Mobile, issued a bizarre decision that upheld the state law, ruling (*Wallace v. Jaffree*, 1982) that previous Supreme Court application of the First Amendment to all fifty states had been a mistake. He believed that the First Amendment prevented Congress from establishing a national religion, but did not prevent individual states from doing so. If Alabama chose, it could authorize more than a state prayer; it could establish Christianity as the state religion. Preventing Christian expression actually favored a different religion, "secular humanism." The Constitution, he wrote, "does not protect people from feeling uncomfortable. A member of a religious minority [including school children] will have to develop a thicker skin if a state establishment offends him." Chiding the US Supreme Court for misreading history and informally changing the Constitution, he flung down the gauntlet against federal judicial tyranny as blatantly as George Wallace had challenged federal political tyranny.[32]

When the Jaffree case reached the US Supreme Court, Justice Stevens in his opinion for the five-justice majority struck down the Alabama law whose clear intent was to promote prayer. Citing Justice Robert Jackson's 1943 admonition (*West Virginia Board of Education v. Barnett*) that no official could prescribe orthodoxy in religion or force citizens to confess their faith by word or act, he also sharply rebuked Judge Hand for overstepping his judicial authority.[33]

Justice William Rehnquist vigorously dissented, rejecting the nearly forty-year tendency (since the 1947 Everson case) to read the Bill of Rights as though Roger Williams, Thomas Jefferson, and James Madison had written it. The "wall of separation," Rehnquist argued, was a misleading metaphor that appeared only in Jefferson's private letter and which had no constitutional force. The First Amendment did not require governmental neutrality so far as religion was concerned, but only prohibited establishment of a national church. Since George Washington himself had proclaimed national days of prayer, perhaps the Supreme Court had strayed from the original meaning of the Establishment Clause.[34]

Rehnquist was an associate justice and a judicial dissenter in the 1985 Jaffree case. By the 1990s, he was chief justice and primary architect of a correction after decades of judicial activism. His colleagues now included Justice Clarence Thomas, an African American, Republican conservative who agreed with Rehnquist that fifty states could establish fifty theocracies so long as the establishment was nonpreferential.

This new mood on the high court paralleled deep cultural divisions within the nation that gave rise to politicized white religion in the form of two Virginians, Jerry Falwell who founded Moral Majority and Pat Robertson who formed the Christian Coalition. And even some religious moderates believed that Hugo Black's rendering in the Engel case had gone too far. Opponents argued that Black's argument rested on sparse historical evidence concerning the intentions of the framers of the Constitution and accused him of judicial activism. Neo-orthodox theologian Reinhold Niebuhr disagreed with Black's reasoning. Catholics, Black's old nemesis from his Klan days in Birmingham, denounced the Engel decision even as they strenuously opposed reading the Protestant King James version of the Bible in public schools.[35]

A decade and a half later, Pat Robertson, founder and president of Christian Broadcasting Network and of Christian Coalition, opened a new graduate-level institution named Regent University to educate a cadre of committed Christian intellectuals in how to wage war against Satan and his minions. Schools of law, divinity, business, education, counseling, government, and communication recruited faculties with degrees from Yale, Emory, Oxford, and Cornell, among other notable institutions. Diverse in their theological conservatism (they included evangelicals, fundamentalists, charismatics, and pentecostals), both faculty and students impressed modernist visitors who (unlike fundamentalist Bob Jones University in South Carolina) were invited to the Virginia Beach, Virginia campus to lecture. No less a liberal luminary than Harvey Cox of Harvard University had some kind things to say about Regent faculty following a lecture there.[36]

Not that Regent is without controversy. Law school faculty prepare legislative drafts and constitutional amendments that religious right congressmen introduce. It also helps staff the American Center for Law and Justice, a sort of religiously conservative shadow of the liberal American Civil Liberties Union. In July 1994 the law school suffered a major embarrassment when the university's law review suddenly withdrew an article asserting that Christian theology justified killing doctors who performed abortions. Publication seemed to be a case of bad timing. Abortion physician John B. Britton and his security escort, a retired Air Force colonel, had just been murdered at a Pensacola, Florida, abortion clinic by a Christian anti-abortion activist.[37]

Creation of Regent University coincided with a major Christian right effort to rewrite American history. The life and teachings of Jesus Christ, their leaders insist, inspired the settlement of America. And the triumphalist unfolding of American history represents God's favor bestowed upon the new Jerusalem as certainly as the glory of David's capital city represented the covenant theology that gave rise to the first Jerusalem. In home schools and private religious academies, the new Christian right teaches an alternative theocentric version of American history, or "heritage studies," from texts written for that purpose. Their leaders conduct tours of the site of the Danbury, Connecticut Baptist church which was the recipient of Jefferson's famous letter. At that very place, they preach that Jefferson only intended the "wall of separation" to prevent government from meddling with religion, not to restrict religion from shaping government. In this version of history, Hugo Black, a Ku Klux Klansman overcome by Satan, had led the stampede toward secularism, abortion, and homosexuality, breaking the sacred covenant that had resulted in American prosperity and power. What followed was the Great Depression (never mind the chronological problem here), the Kennedy assassination, Vietnam, drug addiction, AIDS, global warming, 9/11, and the Iraq war. Their purpose is to reclaim America's godly heritage, defeat activist judges, and restore the Constitution to its original purpose.[38]

The chief guru of this revisionist Christian history is David Barton, a self-taught historian and Christian conservative activist who lives near Fort Worth, Texas. Delivering some 250 speeches and sermons a year from a selection of memorized scripts, Barton uses his WallBuilders ministry like an Old Testament prophet used the Torah. His books, tapes, and videos have sold more than a million copies. He served as vice chair of the Texas Republican party, campaigned for the GOP in 2004 in the pivotal state of Ohio, and has access to the highest national echelons of the party. *Time* magazine in 2005 named Barton one of the 25 most influential American evangelicals.

Barton was raised in a sleepy ranching town of 400 citizens and attended Oral Roberts University on a math and science scholarship in preparation for a high school teaching career before changing his major to religious education.

He attended his parents' fundamentalist church, where Barton later taught math and science in the church's school, coached basketball, and served as principal.

Intrigued with early American history in general and the Founding Fathers in particular, Barton began to read and collect original documents about the Constitution and early Republic. Convinced that almost all of the nation's founders were deeply Christian, he developed an encyclopedic knowledge of their lives and committed long passages of their speeches and writings to memory. Focusing especially on Jefferson's memorable phrase "wall of separation" as applied in the Everson and Engel cases, Barton insists that this single misinterpretation has plagued America for half a century. In fact, Jefferson meant only to protect religion from government intrusion, and the Bible was the early American source book for every facet of society, government, law, business, and family.

From his collection of 70,000 original documents written before 1812 and stored in a concrete vault on his ranch, Barton has constructed a revisionist Christian history of America. In Barton's speeches, the Constitution intended the judiciary to be the weakest branch of government and never envisioned the doctrine of judicial review of congressional legislation. In his book *Restraining Judicial Activism*, he lists such judicial overreaches as *Roe v. Wade*, *Lawrence v. Texas* (which struck down Texas's anti-sodomy laws), and *Wallace v. Jaffree* as examples of judicial tyranny. His book *The Myth of Separation* repudiates the entire Jeffersonian–Hugo Black legacy in American judicial history. In his spare time, Barton teaches an annual clinic for like-minded law students. American historians who have carefully studied Barton's writings have found a multitude of mistakes and distortions and have even called his work anti-historical. The *Myth of Separation* contained so many misquotes and inaccuracies that Barton had to publish a retraction (retitling the book *Original Intent*). Barton's historiography is in the tradition of Parson Weems, whose biography of George Washington sought to reclaim the first president for Christianity despite the president's beliefs.[39]

If David Barton was the behind-the-scenes research engine for the Christian right version of American history, Judge Roy Moore was the movement's confrontational public presence. If Hugo Black was the Rousseau of Alabama Baptists, Roy Moore was their Savanarola.

Moore grew up in a poor, working-class Baptist family on Sand Mountain, an almost all-white Appalachian foothills region of small farms stretching across northeastern Alabama. After graduating from the US Military Academy in 1969, he served a tour of duty in Vietnam before earning a law degree at the University of Alabama in 1977. Voters in the small industrial town of Gadsden at the foot of Sand Mountain elected Moore circuit judge of the 16th Judicial District in Etowah County where he might well have labored in obscurity but for his flamboyant display of religious icons. In addition to opening sessions of the court with prayers by local ministers (he did not invite rabbis or Catholic priests), he installed a replica of the Ten Commandments in his courtroom. The American Civil Liberties Union (ACLU) sued to have the plaque removed, and Montgomery County Judge Charles Price ordered Moore to cease prayers in his courtroom and either to remove the commandments or add other historic documents to the display.

Price's spring 1997 ruling, which Moore quickly appealed, launched a new phase in America's culture wars. On April 12, 1997, a pro-Moore rally in the state capital attracted a crowd from across America estimated at between 20,000 and 25,000 people. Speakers at the event read like a who's who of America's religious right. Ralph Reed, executive director of Christian Coalition of America, vowed that as long as there was breath in his body, the commandments would remain on Moore's courtroom wall. He also compared the audience that day to the one Martin Luther King Jr., had addressed in Montgomery thirty-two years earlier at the end of the Selma-to-Montgomery march. Donald Wildmon, president of the American Family Association, argued that the real issue was not prayer or the Ten Commandments, but judicial decrees that threatened religious freedom. Alan Keyes, a black conservative author and two-time Republican presidential contender, called judicial decisions such as Price's the greatest danger to American freedom. Alabama attorney general Bill Pryor, later appointed by President George W. Bush to a federal judgeship, vowed to prevent the ACLU and federal courts from destroying constitutional democracy. Governor Fob James compared the "wall of separation" to the Berlin Wall erected by East German Communists and vowed to call out the Alabama National Guard if necessary to keep the Ten Commandments on Judge Moore's wall. Moore won the loudest applause of all when he vowed not to seek higher office: "I'm not running for anything, but I'm not running away either." Ironically, the *Birmingham News* devoted one half page of its April 13, 1997, edition to the rally and the other half page to Hugo Black and the Engel decision that the rally sought to overturn.[40]

Moore suffered the first in a long series of judicial reversals in federal court and at the same time launched a national crusade to establish the right to public expression of religion. In a 1998–1999 law review article, he insisted that federal courts had incorrectly interpreted the First Amendment to deny the sovereignty of God in American life. Furthermore, the sovereign God was not a Jewish or Muslim God, but a distinctly Christian God. Borrowing freely from Judge Hand's Jaffree ruling, Moore agreed that individual states could establish specific religions even if Congress could not. By leaving religion undefined, Moore wrote, the court "has opened the door to the erroneous assumption that, under the Establishment Clause, religion could include Buddhism, Hinduism, Taoism, and whatever might occupy in man's life a place parallel to that filled by God, or even Secular Humanism, which might be defined as man's belief in his own supremacy and sufficiency." Supreme Court rulings essentially provided federal protection for these apostate religions.[41]

With such grave matters at issue, Moore reneged on his intention not to run for public office. After his election as chief justice of the Alabama Supreme Court, he dispensed with simple plaques containing the Ten Commandments in favor of a five-thousand-pound slab of granite engraved with the Mosaic laws that he had placed in the state Supreme Court foyer in the dead of night without notifying other justices. The ensuing storm of controversy, Moore's defiance of a US Supreme Court order to remove the offending material, his removal from office after a showcase hearing by a panel of Alabama lawyers, and daily mass rallies outside the state Supreme Court building (complete with pilgrims who bowed down before the piece of granite, or ran their hands over its surface in the manner of medieval petitioners rubbing sacred relics) turned the affair into high religious drama and fodder for late night television comedians. It also earned Moore the same kind of fanatical national following that had galvanized around Governor George C. Wallace following his dramatic "stand in the schoolhouse door" at the University of Alabama in 1963.

The 11th Circuit Court of Appeals made short work of Moore's state's rights claim that as the highest officer of the Alabama court system, he had "discretionary power" to decide which federal court orders the state would obey. In unusually blunt language, the judges vowed that their order in this case "will be enforced" and "the rule of law will prevail." Commenting on the ruling, the *New York Times* reminded its readers: "Alabamians, who have given the nation great jurists like Justice Hugo Black and Judge Frank Johnson, Jr., deserve far better—and if Justice Moore decides to run for re-election, they should insist on it."[42]

While waiting for the next gubernatorial election to test his popularity with Alabama voters, Moore placed his "holy rock" (as detractors called it) on a truck, and began a national speaking tour where he espoused his judicial philosophy in churches and meeting halls, raised money for a new foundation devoted to his cause, and built a national following among conservative Christian activists. Once again borrowing a page from George Wallace's play book, Moore assumed that by demonstrating how popular Alabama views were across the nation, he could transfer national support into state political preference. Moore, like Wallace before him, was "standing up for Alabama."

Unfortunately for Moore and his cause, he badly misjudged home state opinion. An October 2003 poll by Capital Survey Research Center indicated that the state that had produced both Hugo Black and Roy Moore appreciated the ambiguities of church-state issues. While 76 percent of voters supported the display of the Ten Commandments in public places and 88 percent endorsed school prayer, only 35 percent believed that exclusive Judeo-Christian religious symbols should be displayed in public places, and only 13 percent were willing to restrict school prayers to Christians and Jews. Alabamians by 56 percent believed religion and government should be kept separate, and 83 percent agreed that the state should recognize all religions and favor none; 59 percent believed that Moore should have obeyed federal court orders; 53 percent supported associate justices who had the monument removed; and only 33 percent said they would vote for Moore if he ran for governor.[43] Closer to the 2006 state elections, a poll in the Mobile *Register* found little change in these numbers, with incumbent Republican Governor Bob Riley defeating Moore in a hypothetical Republican primary, 43 percent to 35 percent.[44]

Moore's race for governor in 2006, inspired an entire slate of like-minded candidates for the Alabama Supreme Court. His ally on the court, Associate Justice Tom Parker, ran for chief justice. Parker launched his campaign with a January 1, 2006, op-ed column in the *Birmingham News* attacking his eight fellow Republican justices for commuting the death sentence of a convicted murderer who was only age 17 when he committed the crime. Parker's colleagues were merely applying the US Supreme Court precedent from the March 2005 *Roper v. Simmons* decision in which the high court ruled five to four that it was unconstitutional to execute someone for a crime committed when the person was younger than age 18. But this mattered not at all to Parker. His colleagues "chose to passively accommodate—rather than actively resist" an incorrect US Supreme Court ruling, Parker wrote, adding that the role of a state Supreme Court was not to be subservient "to whatever liberal majority of the US Supreme Court says." He might even urge the state court to ignore a US Supreme Court ruling on the death penalty, religious freedom, or some other compelling issue.[45]

Parker recruited three conservative lawyers to run against incumbent Republican justices in the June party primary as part of a larger strategy to expand Moore's base of operations. Christian conservatives entered candidates in Republican primaries in Georgia, Iowa, and California as well, making Moore's strategy part of a nationwide effort. Campaigning in churches and mobilizing an army of zealous foot soldiers, the crusade won support from a number of fringe groups: Republicans for Conservative Judges; Vision Forum (a home school Christian group located in Texas); Vision America (another Texas-based, religious right organization which had helped organize the 2003 Montgomery protests); and Conservative Christians of Alabama.[46]

The season of summer primaries wilted conservative hopes that had blossomed so profusely in springtime. Ralph Reed, caught up in the Jack Abramoff scandals and accused of funneling Indian casino gambling money into Alabama in order to defeat a state lottery, lost his GOP primary race to become Georgia's lieutenant governor. Moore received only 33 percent of the Alabama GOP primary vote against incumbent governor Bob Riley. Tom Parker lost his race for the GOP chief justice nomination by nearly the same margin, as did all three of his allies in the associate justice races.[47]

This battle was nothing less than a contest for the soul of the Republican Party in the South, a match between well-educated business people and fiscal conservatives on one side and grassroots Christian conservatives on the other. And even in the most institutionally religious region of America, Christian conservatives lost badly. Outspent by huge margins, marginalized by allegations that they were radicals whose judicial philosophy would reverse the 1803 *Marbury v. Madison* case (which had established the principle of judicial review of congressional enactments), condemned for an ideology that would allow any state court to ignore a federal court order and thus create chaos in America's judicial system, even Americans who had misgivings about high court rulings regarding separation of church and state deserted them.[48]

Meanwhile, America, Alabama, and the rest of the South grow more religiously diverse by the day. In 1955, sociologist Will Herberg described mid-twentieth century religious diversity in the title of his book *Protestant, Catholic, Jew*. But Professor Charles H. Lippy has noted recently that a work exploring the same subject half a century later would require a title nearly as long as the book: Protestant, Catholic, Jew, Muslim, Hindu, Buddhist, Sikh, Bahai, etc. By 2000, America was home to more Muslims than Presbyterians or Episcopalians and nearly as many as Jews. The US also contained more than a million Hindus and 900,000 Buddhists. By 2050, demographers estimate there will probably be as many Muslims in the United States as Southern Baptists.

Sun Belt prosperity, low taxes, and warm winters brought new religious groups pouring into the South.[49] By 2000, the Jewish population in southeast Florida was larger than Boston, San Francisco, Philadelphia, or Washington, DC. Georgia and Virginia each contained nearly 70,000 Jewish residents.[50] And a meeting of the Birmingham Islamic Society in January 2000 drew between 1,500 and 2,000 Muslims.[51]

Such diversity strengthens the work of Baptists and other evangelicals who adhere to older traditions of church-state separation. The Baptist Joint Committee for Religious Liberty, a lobby in Washington, DC, which represents a coalition of fourteen Baptist groups, more than half of them southern-based, continues to advocate the historic denominational position on separation of church and state. So does a south wide coalition called "Mainstream Baptists." In January 2008, former Southern Baptist presidents Jimmy Carter and Bill Clinton, together with eighty leaders of forty Baptist organizations, will host a meeting in Atlanta that is expected to draw 20,000 people to a "Celebration of a New Baptist Covenant" (including church-state separation). As if to certify the deep divisions within the American Baptist family, Southern Baptist officials rejected an invitation to participate, calling the conference "voodoo ecumenism."[52] The Baptist Center for Ethics and the Baptist History and Heritage Society, both headquartered in Nashville, continue to publish books to educate Baptists about their historic adherence to church-state separation. So does the national journal *Baptists Today*.[53]

Unfortunately, this reclaiming of traditional dissenter principles and the implosion of the Christian right in the 2006 election cycle can mislead observers. In Alabama, for instance, the unincorporated town of Brooksville decided to govern itself according to the Ten Commandments, King James Version, to vote in churches, and to unite church and state. In Pike County, Alabama, the only Jewish students in public schools were teased, mocked, and proselytized by Christian students until they finally sued.[54] Though they won in court, the Jewish families decided to move north to find a more tolerant environment.

When the executive director of the Washington, DC-based Americans United for Separation of Church and State was asked in 1997 where he would rank Alabama among states at risk for blurring the line between church and state, he replied that it, along with South Carolina, headed the list of endangered states. In May of that year, a member of the South Carolina State Board of Education concluded a discussion about whether placing the Ten Commandments in public schools would offend other religions such as Muslims or Buddhists by saying "Screw the Buddhists and kill the Muslims . . . this nation was found to worship, honor, and glorify Jesus Christ."[55] He later apologized for his offensive language though not for his preference for an all-Christian America.

Nationwide, a 2004 Opinion Research Corporation poll found Americans deeply divided on this historic American principle. Slightly less than half of those surveyed, 49 percent, believed that keeping religion and government separated was important to American democracy. But 29 percent believed the separation had become irksome and should be less strictly interpreted by the courts. Another 20 percent saw no reason to separate church and state at all, causing the executive director of the Council for America's First Freedom to call the results "disquietening."[56]

Whether two new Supreme Court justices, John Roberts and Samuel Alito, appointed by President George W. Bush, will tip the scale toward so-called "originalists" who emphasize the "original intentions" of the Founding Fathers, remains undetermined. Liberal Justice Stephen Breyer argued in a case on December 5, 2005, that if the originalists were correct, then America might as well have "nine historians on the court." Conservative justice Antonin Scalia fired back that he had rather have nine historians than nine ethicists.[57]

A court that Baptist Hugo Black once led on issues of religious liberty and which had few Catholic justices by the early twenty-first century contained no Protestants at all. And the historical perspective of those justices and that branch of Christianity about separation of church and state is quite different from that of Protestant dissenters whose memory of European oppression by state churches grows dimmer with each passing year.

Perhaps George Orwell was correct when he wrote that the one who controls the past also controls the future. As Orwell understood, this reality meant that the battle for control of the historical narrative would always be fierce. And the current battle among evangelicals over judicial activism, the Supreme Court, and separation of church and state, makes him seem like a prophet.

—Lecture to Baptist History and Heritage Society

After my retirement in 2005, I stopped writing for professional journals and spent more time writing books and op-ed pieces about public policy. But I still relished speaking on university campuses and lectured on average fifty times a year for the next decade. I did not submit those lectures for publication, but two of them reflect my postretirement interest in religion. Both continued the essential theme of the previous forty years: southern religion is complex and becomes more diverse with each passing year. And white Christians have become as politically partisan as their black brothers and sisters.

Chapter 14
The South's Battle over God

Christianity can be compared to a homemade stool with four legs, each one symbolizing a dimension of religion: belief; ritual; personal ethics; social ethics. Unfortunately for the inept craftsman, the legs vary in height and in that way are like southern religion. It strongly emphasizes belief and personal ethics while mostly ignoring ritual (except for Catholics, Orthodox, and high church Episcopalians). Social ethics ebb and flow with the times, tend to thrive in and even define black churches, but are nearly absent in many white evangelical congregations. Mainline churches tend to be a bit more balanced, though usually tilted toward one leg or the other. As for belief, the range of evangelical Biblical opinion is fairly narrow and literalistic, but the scope of doctrinal interpretation even within the same denomination can be broad, divisive, and lethal. Although evangelicals seldom officially rank the importance of the legs, they clearly value belief above all else.

Personal ethics tends to be important but malleable. Evangelicals once took a hard line (as reflected in harsh church discipline cases) on most moral deviation from biblical absolutes: adultery, fornication, divorce, swearing, unethical business dealings, and Sunday recreational activities. They even added a few sins not in the Bible: bans on alcohol, dancing, attending movies, "mixed" swimming, and gambling. As American cultural and social norms changed, so did they. Unlike my childhood, few sermons now reign down damnation on parishioners for divorce or moderate use of alcohol. Those who dance, swim together, attend movies, or engage in Sunday recreation, no longer need divine absolution, and some of these activities even occur on large church "campuses."

Other than homosexuality and abortion, which have risen to the status of penultimate sins, sermonic admonitions about personal frailty have declined dramatically. Conversely, except for a few outliers in all denominations, the personal sins of greed, materialism, and neglect of the poor (which are central to Scripture) have mostly disappeared into a theological black hole.

Whether the South remains (or ever was) America's most religious and pious region depends entirely on which of the four legs one considers most important to the stability of the stool. By the standard of belief, polling data reinforces the South's claim to Christian predominance. Judged by the importance of the other three, the South's self-proclamation of Biblical fidelity and Christian exceptionalism rings hollow.

Southern novelists have actually done a better job than some historians of depicting the grotesque tilt of the stool. Here is how Catholic novelist Walker Percy described the flawed angles of traditional Protestantism and Catholicism:

"There are only three ways to go. One is their way out there, the great whorehouse and fagdom of America [the North's secularism, hedonism, and materialism]. I won't have it. The second way is sweet Baptist Jesus and I won't have that. Christ, if heaven is full of Southern Baptists, I'd rather be in hell with Saladin and Achilles. There is only one way and we could have had it if you Catholics hadn't blown it: the old Catholic way."[1]

"The Southerner started out a skeptical Jeffersonian and became a crooked Christian. That is to say, he is approaching and has almost reached his essence, which is to be more crooked and Christian than ever before. Do you want a portrait of the New Southerner? He is Billy Graham on Sunday and Richard Nixon the rest of the week. He calls on Jesus and steals, he's in business, he's in politics."[2]

You might want to make a mental note of how Percy separates pretentious piety and corrupt ethics. We will revisit this insight later.

While Percy is hard on southern religion, he is no fan of northern secularism either: "The Northerner is at heart a pornographer. He is an abstract mind with a genital attached. His soul is at Harvard, a large abstract locked-in sterile university whose motto is truth but which has not discovered an important truth in a hundred years."[3]

Not entirely fair to Harvard, or to southern evangelical Protestants, but he does perceptively call attention to regional religious differences. The North prefers its religion vague, abstract, tolerant, and generic. The South prefers its religion specific, concrete, exclusive, and sectarian. To southern evangelicals, heaven is so identifiable it can be located on a map, perhaps because their physical world was so often inhospitable. The North, wallowing in its innocence, prosperity, and success, was more at home in this world and less anxious to depart for the next.

Not to pick on Baptists unduly, but then again the largest southern evangelical empire has not fared well in regional literature. Harper Lee isolated Primitive Baptists for this exchange between Miss Maudie and Scout about women, intolerance, and exclusion:

> "foot washers believe anything that's pleasure is a sin. Did you know some of 'em came out of the woods one Saturday and passed by this place and told me me and my flowers were going to hell?"
>
> "Your flowers, too?"
>
> "Yes ma'am. They'd burn right with me. They thought I spent too much time in God's outdoors and not enough time inside the house reading my Bible."
>
> . . .
>
> "That ain't right, Miss Maudie. You're the best lady I know.
>
> "Miss Maudie grinned. Thank you ma'am. Thing is, foot-washers think women are a sin by definition. They take the Bible literally, you know.
>
> . . .
>
> "Miss Maudie stopped rocking, and her voice hardened. 'You are too young to understand it,' she said, 'but sometimes the Bible in the hand of one man is worse than a whiskey bottle in the hand of [another]."[4]

What southern evangelicals consider pious righteousness, Lee depicts as either self-righteousness or hypocrisy.

Eudora Welty shared Lee's resentment at triumphalist Southern Baptists. In *The Optimist's Daughter* she describes the religious exuberance of the poor white, unsophisticated, ne-er-do-well Chisom family: "you can't curb a Baptist. Let them in and you can't keep 'em down. . . . When the whole bunch of Chisom's got to going in concert, I thought the only safe way to get through the business alive was not say a word, just sit still as a mouse."[5] What they believed to be a helpful dose of religious community, the Optimist's Daughter interpreted as superficial and intrusive interruption.

Welty's fellow Mississippian, William Faulkner, affirmed the Christian faith of black southerners while ridiculing the hypocrisy of white people. Being a Southern Baptist, he told students at the University of Virginia in 1957, was "an emotional condition that has nothing to do with God or politics or anything else. . . . It came from times of hardship in the South where there was little or no food for the human spirit—where there were no books, no theater, no music, and life was pretty hard and a lot of it happened out in the sun, for very little reward and that was the only escape they had. I think that is the human spirit aspiring toward something. Of course, it got warped and twisted in the process."[6]

Despite my respect for Faulkner's perceptive insight about the sociological roots of religion in the poverty of the southern masses, his argument that Southern Baptist religion has nothing to do with God or politics reflects more his bad experiences with evangelicals than contemporary religious or political reality.

But then Southern Baptists would expect nothing more from the South's greatest modernist writer and exponent of ethical relativism. Faulkner does offer a wiser explanation of Isaac McCaslin's view of God and religion in *Go Down Moses*: "There are some things He said in the Book, and some things reported of Him that He did not say. And I know what you will say now: That if truth is one thing to me and another thing to you, how will we choose which is truth? You don't need to choose. The heart already knows. He didn't have His Book written to be read by what must elect and choose, but by the heart, not by the wise of the earth because they don't need it or maybe the wise no longer have any heart, but by the doomed and lowly of the earth who have nothing else to read with but the heart."[7]

Southern evangelicalism, as Faulkner notes, has often been a religion for hard times, not educated minds.

Faulkner, Lee, Percy, and Welty wrote at a time when Southern Baptists completely dominated the South's religious landscape. And truth is that Baptists sometimes do engage in megalomania. Witness Fundamentalist Memphis pastor and former Southern Baptist Convention (SBC) president Adrian Rogers who told the *Indiana Baptist* newspaper "this is going to sound like megalomania but I believe that the hope of the world lies in the West. I believe the hope of the West lies in America. I believe the hope of America is in Judeo-Christian ethics. I believe that the backbone of that Judeo-Christian ethic is evangelical Christianity. I believe that the bellwether of evangelical Christianity is the Southern Baptist Convention. So I believe in a sense, that as the Southern Baptist Convention goes, so goes the world."[8]

Sometimes people sound like megalomaniacs because they talk like megalomaniacs—which may mean they are megalomaniacs.

Religious Diversity and Pluralism

The religious environment that shaped the prose of the Southern literary renaissance is changing fast. But even in earlier times, the South's regional Christianity was more complex than it seemed. There were black and white Baptists, male and female Baptists, rich and poor Baptists, urban and rural Baptists, Free Will Baptists, Landmark Baptists, Missionary Baptists, Seventh Day Baptists, Primitive Baptists, Progressive Baptists, and National Baptists as well as Southern Baptists. Now there are also Cooperative Baptists and the Alliance of Baptists, and all these just in the South. Restorationists formed the Churches of Christ, Christians and Disciples of Christ. Then, of course, there were Presbyterians, Methodists, Lutherans, and Episcopalians of various persuasions and theologies. And the fastest growing southern sects are black and white pentecostals such as the Church of God, Assemblies of God, and Church of God in Christ, along with independent megachurches.

Nor does this traditional description of southern sectarianism take into account the region's burgeoning religious pluralism. Immigration patterns reshape religion every year as more Hindus and Muslims, Catholics, and Jews pour into the Sun Belt. Some 9 percent of American Catholics lived in the South in 1945, a percentage that doubled by end of century. By 2000 more than 10 percent of all American Jews (644,000) resided in Palm Beach, Broward, and Dade counties Florida, an increase of 30 percent between 1980 and 2000. This was the highest concentration of Jews in the US outside of New York City.[9]

Needless to say, when evangelicals feel compelled to witness about Jesus Christ in order to convert Jews, the religious debate is no longer evangelical versus secularist, as numerous angry articles in the southern Jewish press made clear. By the turn of the century, Southern Baptists and Jews took the field against each other, disputing aggressive evangelism initiated by the International Mission Board of the SBC. One deeply offended reader of the *Deep South Jewish Voice* reacted angrily,

> The Southern Baptist press release states, on Rosh Hashana . . . Southern Baptists will be praying they find [God's] Son.
> I didn't know He was missing. Have they tried putting Him on milk cartons? . . .
> Shouldn't they be looking for Him? There's a lot of them. Do they really need our help? It seems like they have more searching to do themselves before they worry us. . . .
> Leave us alone. (Yiddish for 'leave us the $A#! Alone, < insert "South Park" insult>.)[10]

Religious pluralism not only separates religions, denominations, and sects into warring factions, it also divides them internally. Many Orthodox Jews agreed with certain Southern Baptist political and social objectives, especially about God's special concern for the state of Israel. Many theologically conservative black Baptist congregations, attracted to the efficiency and employee pension plans of the SBC, have become dually aligned with that mainly white juggernaut as well as with their own black national conventions. In the unlikely setting of Birmingham, Alabama, twelve predominantly black Baptist churches belong to the mostly white Birmingham Baptist Association which consists of 139 congregations. They include the 5,000 member Sixth Avenue Baptist Church, the city's largest and most prestigious black Baptist congregation. By 1992 the SBC had become the most ethnically diverse denomination in America excepting only the Catholic Church, with 6,000 ethnic churches worshiping in 100 languages and serving 102 ethnic groups. By 2000, the SBC claimed to be the largest Spanish-speaking evangelical religious body in the world and had 1,400 predominantly black churches with 400,000 members. Eighty predominantly black Southern Baptist churches were being organized every year.[11]

It was a good thing, too, because otherwise the SBC would have experienced steady membership decline. After years of internal bickering and theological turmoil, the nation's largest Protestant denomination declined by 162,000 members during 1998, its first membership drop since 1926. Annual baptisms, which had exceeded 400,000 during some years of the 1970s, topped that number only twice in the fifteen years before 1999 despite a fundamentalist takeover of the convention.[12]

How Religious Is the South?

So extensive had the Deep South's religious turmoil and pluralism become by the 1990s that even scholars began to question the region's claim to be the nation's "Bible Belt." In order to evaluate this controversial data, we need to define the issues that make a society religious. Does religiosity consist of belief, spirituality, or ethics? And if ethics, what kind of ethics, personal or social? Do we measure religious commitment by church attendance? Reading the Bible? Anti-abortion policies and opposition to homosexual marriage? Practicing Biblical patterns of sexual morality? Divorce rates? Ethical treatment of women and African Americans? Commitment to social justice as expressed in concern for the poor, fair tax policies, and care for children? Walker Percy was on to something when he separated orthodox purity of religious belief from ethical conduct.

The context for any debate about regional Christianity begins with the fact that America is the most religious industrialized nation. A 2002 poll by the Pew Research Center reported that 59 percent of American respondents said that religion was "very important" in their lives compared with 33 percent in Britain, 30 percent in Canada, 27 percent in Italy, 25 percent in South Korea, 21 percent in Germany, 12 percent in Japan, and 11 percent in France.[13] Furthermore, a study by Baylor University sociologists in September 2006 found that previous polls had actually overestimated the number of Americans who said they had no religious affiliation; their data listed the figure at only 11 percent.[14] Another report, analyzing data generationally, found that Generation Xers were considerably more religious than the generation of Baby Boomers who abandoned organized religion in substantial numbers during the 1960s and 1970s.[15] But overall, Gallup polling data revealed little change in religious indicators during the half century between 1947 and 1997. In 1947, 95 percent of Americans said they believed in God compared with 96 percent half a century later; earlier, 73 percent believed in an afterlife, in 1997, 71 percent. In both years, 41 percent said they attended church at least once a week and 90 percent said they prayed.[16] After substantial membership losses by many mainline American denominations during the 1960s, 1970s, and 1980s, most stabilized and some even grew slightly during the 1990s.[17]

Unfortunately, polling data seems contradictory. A recent study indicated that actual church attendance does not correspond with Gallup polling claims. To state the matter another way, lots of American Christians lie to pollsters about how often they attend church.[18]

Within mostly Christian America, some polling data also suggested less regional differentiation than stereotypes claimed. A 1990 Glenmary Research Center survey opened the debate about whether the Deep South could legitimately claim to be the nation's Bible Belt. Although religious sociologists agreed that the Pacific Coast was the least religious region of America, the South Central (Alabama, Mississippi, Tennessee, and Kentucky), Southwest (Texas, Oklahoma, Arkansas, and Louisiana), and South Atlantic (Florida, Georgia, North and South Carolina, West Virginia, Virginia, Maryland, and Delaware) regions showed little variation in either religious beliefs or church attendance. Utah actually had the highest rate of church membership in 1990, with North and South Dakota, Minnesota, Wisconsin, and Massachusetts also listed in the top 10. Conversely, Kentucky and Tennessee ranked 23rd and 24th, Virginia 31st, Arkansas 34th, Florida 36th, and West Virginia 44th. Birmingham enrolled 61 percent of its population in churches compared with Provo, Utah, with 97 percent; La Crosse, Wisconsin, 90 percent; Dubuque, Iowa, 83 percent; Chicago 68 percent; Philadelphia 62 percent; and even New York City (which to the southern mind was the capital of the Empire of Evil, where *Sex and the City* characterized daily life more than church attendance), enrolled 61 percent, the same as in Birmingham.[19]

Religious demography can also be misleading unless seen in broader sociological context. For instance, it may be true that Generation Xers during the 1980s and 1990s were more institutionally religious than Baby Boomers, but the millennial generation that followed is the least religious of any in the history of polling. And even Generation Xers viewed religion as a vast religious smorgasbord. In 1958 just four of every hundred Americans had left the denomination in which they were raised. By the late 1980s, more than a third had done so. At least 60 percent of Americans had spouses who belonged to another denomination[20] (in my youth during the 1950s, an interfaith marriage included a Baptist who married a Methodist, which has now become a source of amusement). Within life cycles, the Barna Research Group released a poll in 2006 indicating that 6 in 10 teenagers involved in a church will probably not continue their spiritual commitment into early adulthood. Perhaps that explains the apparent contradiction of high church membership in New York City, where youthful and elderly religious affiliation are merely the generational bookends to *Sex and the City* in between.[21]

THE ENDURING BIBLE BELT

Having used all this data to qualify southern evangelical triumphalism, I can make the opposite case by focusing on different data. Virtually every poll of religious belief during the 1990s located the Bible Belt between the Potomac River and the Rio Grande, running straight through Appalachia and the Ozarks, including the slopes on both sides. A 1992 Gallup Poll found that 40 percent of Americans read their Bible at least weekly; in the South 55 percent did so. A 1989 poll of Birmingham residents found that Bible devotional reading was their number one lifestyle, ahead even of fishing, hunting, and watching sports on TV (surely not including Auburn and Alabama football games!). As one might have predicted in a region characterized for more than a century by conservative Protestantism, 30 percent of southerners engaged in systematic Bible study (black respondents more than their white counterparts) compared with only 22 percent in the Midwest, 15 percent in the West, and 13 percent in the East. A 1994 Gallup survey concluded that southerners were also far more likely (by roughly 20 percent) than people in other regions to consider religion "very important."[22]

An Alabama survey found that 99 percent of those polled believed in some sort of heaven, 95 percent believed in hell, and 86 percent believed in Satan or an evil spirit (compared with national polls that revealed 80 percent of Americans believed in heaven and only 60 percent in hell). More than half (53 percent) the Alabama respondents agreed that "every word of the Bible comes straight from God and is completely free of error" (a surprising 38 percent believed the Bible, although inspired by God, contained historical and scientific errors).[23]

The 1994 annual *Atlanta Journal-Constitution* Southern Life Poll devoted its survey to religion and noted similar regional distinctions. Whereas only 52 percent of Americans living outside the South believed the Bible was literally true historically and scientifically, two out of three southerners believed that it was as reliable concerning history and science as on theology. Eight in ten southerners believed that angels and the Devil exist. More than nine in ten southerners believed adultery to be wrong even if it seemed to be as popular there as elsewhere. And African Americans tended to be more biblically literal and conservative than white believers (perhaps reflecting more about education than race; black people were the poorest educated southerners, and increases in educational attainment corresponded to steep declines of belief in biblical literalism). Although southerners were also more likely to believe they had a responsibility to witness to their faith and support missionaries, only 52 percent of them considered converting people to their faith to be "very important" (this regional decline in evangelical fervor must be balanced by the corresponding decline in similar attitudes outside the South, where only 32 percent felt that personal witnessing was "very important").[24]

What are we to conclude from all this data about belief and personal spirituality? Southern popular religion is conservative. It is emotional, revivalistic, evangelical, pietistic, and experiential. It is isolated and insular. It is biracial. It appeals especially to poor and powerless people. None of this should surprise us, for this summary not only characterizes southern religion, it is also a good, general description of southern culture. And that is both good and bad.

Religion rooted in culture tracks many of the best patterns in the culture. It also tracks some of the worst. Imprinting southern religion with southern culture results in parochialism and fatalism but also increases the importance of place, community, kinship; rootedness; piety; and the centrality of honor, charity, and attention to primary rather than secondary causes (God as the source of life without assistance from creatures crawling out of the primal ooze).

One of the first books that I read about southern religion back in the early 1960s was James Sellers's *The South and Christian Ethics*. Although his thesis was the necessity for more evangelical engagement with social justice and especially racial integration, Sellers appropriated all the wisdom of the southern literary renaissance on behalf of the importance of rootedness, personalism, and concreteness as opposed to philosophical abstraction; a longing for stability over a preference for progress and modernity at the expense of tradition.[25]

Despite their high regard for tradition, southern evangelicals are not stupid. They know the world is changing and that they have to adjust to it. Bill J. Leonard, a Texas Baptist and dean of the Divinity School at Wake Forest University, specializes in evangelical religion within the Appalachian subregion. After speaking to a group of Appalachian ministers about mountain religion, an older minister asked him: "Tell me something, son. Do you think we'll ever go back to havin' two week revivals again?" Leonard responded: "I doubt it. The times have changed. For example, traveling to this meeting [at Ginny Wiley State Park in Kentucky] I could not help noticing all the satellite dishes sitting outside rural mountain houses. Now instead of a two week revival, folks get 185 channels." Distractions were not new, Leonard continued, recalling the story of a mountain boy who returned home from town one day and said excitedly, "Grandma, if you ever go to just one circus, you'll never go to prayer meeting again."[26] Add Walmart, Arkansas football, Little Rock, MTV, HBO, and a hundred other diversions to the circus and it is safe to say that the old time religion at the little church in the wildwood will never hold the same unitary place of affection in southern culture that it once did.

But before we brood too much about lost innocence, let us not forget all those modern megachurches at the intersections of southern life. Nor should we forget how robust modern evangelicalism is. In 1776, 6 percent of the US population belonged to a church. In 1800 the figure had risen to only 8 percent, by 1850 to 15.5 percent, and by 1900 to 37.7 percent. By 2000, 86.2 percent of adults belonged to "Christian Faith Groups." Indeed, 33 percent of Americans currently worship at congregations that are evangelical, espouse an inerrant Bible, affirm the centrality of a personal relationship with Jesus, and promote personal evangelism. And that 33 percent does not include authentic evangelicals worshiping in mainline Protestant and Catholic churches.

Personal spirituality is thriving in the South as well. A 2006 poll of senior adults found that nationally 69 percent listed health care as their chief concern. In Birmingham 72 percent of seniors ranked spirituality first.[27] And southerners continue to spread the word of salvation by word of mouth, on the back of currency, on the covering of cotton bales, in restaurants and on office signs, even in public bathrooms and on bumper stickers (my favorite is "Christians' Retirement Benefits Are Out of This World").[28] Evangelicals oppose gay marriage and abortion, attend church regularly, believe the Bible is the literal word of God, believe it is important to spread their faith, believe the only hope for salvation is through personal faith in Jesus Christ, believe they are part of the American mainstream, but also believe they have to fight hard just to make their voices heard within the political dialogue of their times.[29] They represent, many religious historians contend, the fourth Great Awakening in the religious history of America.[30]

Although southern evangelicals may not be first in line to advocate systemic tax reform and equitable funding of public schools, they are year after year the most charitable Americans in terms of the percent of their income given to the less fortunate.

They are also among the most biblically literate Americans. I realize that southern evangelicalism can be and often is anti-intellectual. Almost always there is some level of tension between the religion of the heart and the religion of the mind. But when weighing the truth of religious faith against the truth of modern science, for instance, southern evangelicals are not much different from other Americans. In a 2003 poll Americans were three times as likely to believe in the Virgin Birth of Jesus (83 percent) as in evolution (28 percent).[31] Perhaps this is further evidence of the southernization of American religion.

Of course, there are plenty of stories such as that of Alabama native E. O. Wilson, of Harvard University—a two-time Pulitzer Prize–winner, arguably the most influential evolutionary biologist in the world and creator of sociobiology—who was baptized in the First Baptist Church of Pensacola, Florida, but who is no longer a believer. Southern Baptists can make it hard for an evolutionary biologist to retain both faith and profession. Woodrow Wilson also briefly departed the faith. The future president had an intense religious conversion at age 17 and then a crisis of faith at Davidson College. Later, he placed a sign on his door during a protracted revival at Princeton where he was in graduate school: "I am a Christian, but studying for exams."[32] Woodrow Wilson eventually returned to his faith; E. O. Wilson did not. Nevertheless, the Harvard biologist remains a civil scholar who displays tenacious courage in defending his views. He has strong affection for the South and refrains from criticizing its religion. Were the two Wilsons permanently imprinted by southern evangelicalism? Is the southern attachment to kin, community, and place, its sense of moral absolutes, its tenacious defense of truth as it understands truth, a product of southern evangelicalism, or does it merely coexist within a broader cultural cohabitation? Let me illustrate the problem for you: the University of Chicago was founded as a Baptist university. Currently the number of Nobel Prize winners on its faculty ranks second in the world only to Cambridge University.[33] Is that because the university was once Baptist and espoused soul liberty, the priesthood of the believer, and commitment to truth without fear of consequences? Or is that because the university long ago detached itself from Baptists?

Recently the journal *Religion & Public Education* published an article about religious literacy. The article was based on a study at the University of North Carolina at Chapel Hill, one of the region's finest state universities. What struck me about the study was how much more my father, who never graduated high school much less college, knew about Christianity and the Bible than did students at UNC. While 81 percent of them knew that Genesis is the first book of the Bible, only 54 percent could name the first two books. Only 30 percent could provide anything at all approximating the first of the Ten Commandments. Although 82 percent could name the four gospels, only 22 percent knew that the New Testament was originally written in Greek. Only 18 percent could place the Reformation in the correct century, and only 14 percent could give even the vaguest definition of Zionism. Not a single one correctly identified the Social Gospel.[34]

That poll reminded me of an episode in January 1984 when Auburn University played Michigan in the Sugar Bowl with an outside chance of winning a national championship. Auburn won a boringly tight defensive battle, and the following week I picked up a copy of *The New York Times* to read the paper's take on the game. Ira Berkow, an essayist for the *Times*, noted for placing sport in a broader social context, penned a column entitled, "At Wit's End with 'We're No. 1.'" Following only cursory comment about which university had the best claim to the mythical national football crown, he descried a new (to him) phenomenon of football: fans displaying signs, banners, and even bed sheets with biblical passages written on them. The one he cited—Job 3:16—seemed intended "to give the stamp of celestial approval to football."[35] Of course, that had nothing whatever to do with the passage's intent. As I perused Job 3:16 ("Or why was I not hidden in the ground like a stillborn child, like an infant who never saw the light of day?"), I was not surprised that the otherwise erudite Mr. Berkow could find no football application of the Scripture (although the passage might deeply trouble evangelicals with its hint of infanticide or abortion). My main point is not to poke fun at Berkow, but to emphasize how obvious his error would have been to an uneducated waitress in Batesville, Arkansas, to a mill worker in Little Rock, or to a long-distance truck driver in Dallas. They would have known immediately that the passage scribbled on the bed sheet was John 3:16, and that the intent was conversion, not the celestial affirmation of football.

Knowledge as well as religion can be regionalized. What people in the South consider essential knowledge—biblical literacy—may be less important than encyclopedic knowledge of wines on the Pacific Coast or of the stock market in the Northeast. Knowledge may also be nationalized rather than regionalized according to class, age, race, income, and education. But I have a hunch that wherever in America you find churches with names like the "Outreach Endtime Deliverance Church" or the "First Independent All Nation's Holy Church of God," you are likely to discover people who journey with a religious vision different from other Americans (those two churches can be found along Highway 231 between Montgomery and Dothan, Alabama).

Such churches are the sacred preserve of down-and-out Americans, black and white. In our centuries-long national conversation about poverty, we often forget that differences among white ethnic groups in America are enormous. In one landmark 1974 study by the University of Chicago's National Opinion Research Center, researchers divided white Americans into seventeen ethnic and religious backgrounds and then scored them by educational attainment and family income. Contrary to prevailing wisdom, White Anglo-Saxon Protestants (WASPs) were nowhere near the top. In fact, there was greater variation between groups of white Americans than between white and black Americans. WASPs living in the Midwest and South constituted the bottom eight educational and income categories and ten of the bottom twelve. White Baptists were in 17th (bottom) place overall, and it made no difference in their ranking whether the white Baptists lived in California or Arkansas (where many poorly educated present-day Californians originated before their 1930s migration westward). This is pretty solid evidence that their low ranking is more culturally derived than geographically determined. Many of the nation's elites tend to dismiss such people and their religious proclivities by stereotyping them as fans of NASCAR and professional wrestling, mocking their manufactured homes, and ridiculing their Fundamentalist and Pentecostal religion. Thus the source of exterior images of the Ozark and Appalachian hick/ridge runner, "Joe Six Pack," "good old boys and good old girls," "trailer trash," "snake handlers," and all the rest.[36]

The result of this disconcerting and altogether unnecessary distortion of religion and culture as understood by outside secular elites and inside religious folk represents a sad chapter in American history. One subculture seems oblivious of the other, or if aware, wholly ignorant of the other.

The pivotal issue in understanding a religion different from our own is merely becoming acquainted with it. For instance, in the 1976 presidential contest Jimmy Carter introduced Southern Baptists to America's media and democratic power brokers, earning a cover story in *Newsweek* magazine entitled "Born Again! The Evangelicals." Southern evangelicals were amazed to learn that what they understood from Vacation Bible School on seemed to be a startling revelation to most nonsouthern adult Americans. Historians argue that Carter did for Southern Baptists in 1976 what John Kennedy had done for Catholics in 1960: legitimize them and integrate them into the American political mainstream.[37]

Ethics: Personal and Social

Opposition to drinking alcohol, attending movies, dancing, listening to blues and rock-and-roll music, "mixed bathing," and other sins of the flesh, set southern evangelicals apart even from their own larger culture. Imagine the reaction of northern draftees (and even many secular southern soldiers) sent to Camp Blanding, Florida, on the shores of Lake Kingsley during World War II when they read a billboard proclaiming: "Bathing Beach for Christians. No Drinking or Belly-Rub Dancing Allowed."[38]

As the sign at Lake Kingsley indicated, southern evangelicals advocated strong ethical principles but applied the principles mostly to personal moral conduct such as "belly-rub dancing." Establishing social justice and eradicating systemic inequality received scant attention. Contradictions within both the personal and social ethics of evangelicals became grist for the fiction of Percy, Lee, Welty, Faulkner, and others. One example of the contradictions is the post-1960s evangelical enthusiasm for the anti-abortion movement. Yet, one study found a disturbing pattern: states that imposed the most restrictive access to abortion also spent the least money on health, day care, and housing for poor families.[39] Conversely, countries such as Belgium and the Netherlands, where abortion was legal and covered by national health insurance, reported an abortion rate of 7 per 1,000 women compared with the US rate of 22 per 1,000. Could Belgian and Dutch national health care systems that provided lifelong support from fetus through old age be a better remedy for abortion than anti-abortion laws?

And since abortion begins with an act of sexual intercourse, what are we to make of the 2003 Youth Risk Survey that reported the percentage of high school students who said they were sexually active? Mississippi led all states with 61 percent of its high school students admitting they were sexually active, followed by Alabama at 57 percent. The top states were all southern and border states.[40]

In Alabama, citizens also had the nation's highest divorce rate as the twentieth century came to an end. More than one in three births were to unmarried women. Alabama ranked 12th in one-parent families, 7th in child hunger, 5th in life-threatening low birth weights of babies, 3rd in births to teens, 6th in infant mortality, and had one of the nation's highest poverty rates at 18 percent.[41] Mississippi, Louisiana, and Arkansas were close behind Alabama. Failure in so many quality of life issues is no endorsement of evangelical values.

Even isolating personal ethics to traditional sexual teachings, the South does not excel. Nationally, Baptists are more likely to divorce than any religious group other than non-denominational Protestants and are more likely to do so than either atheists or agnostics.[42] Southern teenagers are more likely than their peers in other regions to sign a pledge promising sexual abstinence until marriage. But a Northern Kentucky University survey of 600 teens who signed the pledge reported that 61 percent broke it within a year. Of the 30 percent who said they had kept the pledge, more than half had engaged in oral sex.[43] I suppose they have adopted Southern Baptist Bill Clinton's definition of what it means to "have sex," but this is still an unconvincing witness to the private, ethical, sexual restraint and fidelity conservative Christians expect of believers.

Of course, the most shocking inconsistency between southern evangelical pretensions and actual ethical conduct involves poverty, racism, and sexism. The most evangelical states generally have high poverty rates, the lowest number of women holding public office and better paying jobs, and the worst historical record on racial justice. Sam Hill's book *Southern Churches in Crisis* documented the incredible gap between evangelical white claims about God's universal love and the political reality in the states they dominated. Alabama—home to the 1963 children's marches in Birmingham, the terror bombing of 16th Street Baptist Church, and the state trooper attack on Civil Rights marchers on Selma's Edmund Pettus Bridge—became the poster child for racial injustice and violence, and the world cannot fail to notice that at the time all this was happening nearly one in four of its citizens belonged to white Southern Baptist churches. James Sellers (*The South and Christian Ethics*) quoted a letter in 1962 to the editor of the *Nashville Banner* from a man in Columbia, Tennessee, who claimed that the only southern support for integration came from "the muckheads, bubbleheads, block-heads, wart-heads, sob sisters, starry-eyed do-gooders, pink-punks, pin-head punks, egg-heads, bleeding hearts and de-segregation buzzards." Another letter writer insisted that segregation was not a religious issue: "God is the author of segregation. He is a God of segregation."[44] Among congregationally governed churches, Christians mobilized politically only when members reached a consensus that made some topic a moral issue (abortion or homosexual marriage, for instance). When the congregation could not reach consensus, it declared the issue to be political and thus beyond the scope of the church (poverty, sexism, and racism).

Black people commented on this phenomenon. "So far as the Anglo-Saxon civilization is concerned," black Baptist pastor W. B. Johnson wrote in 1899, "it may be compared to the religion of Buddha, Brahmin, Confucius, or Mahomet, for there is less Christianity in the Anglo-Saxon civilization as PRACTICED than in those religions which are called heathen. Then brethren, let us preach Christianity and not Anglo-Saxon civilization."[45]

Novelists also pointed to the contradiction. Shirley Ann Grau in her 1965 Pulitzer Prize winning novel *The Keepers of the House* puts these words into the mind of Abigail when describing her half-black, half-white cousin and teacher: "They taught me my Bible lessons the exact same way. And to this day I am very good at spotting signs of Negro blood and at reciting the endless lists of genealogies in the Bible. It's a southern talent, you might say."[46]

In fairness to southern evangelicals, by the 1960s when Grau wrote that novel many no longer believed that God was a segregationist or that the Bible was a text for maintaining separate schools. As British historian Mark Neuman has demonstrated, even white Southern Baptists were deeply divided over segregation. Most missionaries, denominational leaders, college and seminary faculties and students, Woman Mission Union officers, and others slowly but surely undermined support for segregation and even maneuvered a resolution through the SBC supporting the Civil Rights Act of 1964.[47] But this very breach between an enlightened (opponents called it "liberal") leadership and a reactionary rank-and-file also hastened fundamentalist control of the SBC a decade later. Similar splits occurred among southern Methodists and Presbyterians.[48]

Southern evangelicals are not only more divided than ever, they no longer dominate the South's religious landscape as they once did. Pockets of religious diversity are becoming contiguous majority zones of Jews, Catholics, and pentecostals, with scattered pockets emerging of Muslims, Hindus, New Age spiritualists, agnostics, and even atheists. Battles over God have changed direction but certainly have not diminished. And I am increasingly confused about what it now means to be a southern Christian.

—Lecture at Lyon College, Batesville, Arkansas, 2006

To argue about God's politics is as silly and excessively anthropological as a debate about God's color or sex. Southern religion once reverberated with arguments (mainly within different racial communities) over whether God was black, white, red, yellow, or brown. Now the rhetorical terrain has shifted to whether God is blue, red, or purple. Unfortunately, Christians seem unable to help themselves: they must determine whether God is a Democrat, a Republican, or undecided.

Southern African American evangelicals fully embraced politics as early as Reconstruction. Southern white evangelicals generally avoided partisan politics (although Populism and the New Deal tested their restraint) until the 1960s. By the twenty-first century, black and white southern churches functioned organizationally as surrogate Democratic and Republican campaign headquarters, with steeples and crosses lending their sides symbolic heavenly endorsement. This lecture evolving as it did over three presidential election cycles tracked the political polarization of southern religion.

Chapter 15
God's Politics
Is Southern Religion Blue, Red, or Purple?

In 2008, Uwe Romeike, his wife, and their seven children, fled what they considered to be religious oppression in Baden-Wurttemberg, Germany, and relocated in Morristown, Tennessee. Romeike, who taught music, also worked as pianist at the local First Baptist Church.

Both push and pull factors inspired the family uprooting. They chafed at German laws forbidding parents from homeschooling their children because the nation's high court had ruled that placing all children together regardless of religion, race, language, values, or belief taught them tolerance and prevented the development of "parallel societies." As a result of the family's old-fashioned views and religion, the two oldest children experienced ridicule and bullying in school. From the official German point of view, the issue was not the Romeike's religious freedom but the government's determination not to permit fringe groups with fanatical ideologies (such as Nazis in the 1920s) to operate outside the post war liberal consensus.

Honoring German law, the US State Department sought to deport the Romeikes because of consular agreements with our European ally, a decision that the conservative majority on the US Supreme Court upheld. US officials, however, understood the potential political firestorm if legal immigrants claiming refugee status because of religious and social persecution were forced to return to their country of origin. So, a day after the Supreme Court ruling, federal officials indefinitely delayed the Romeikes' deportation, which established no legal precedent for other cases but also avoided insulting an important US ally.

In my youth during the 1940s and 1950s, this would have been viewed as a shrewd federal resolution of a potentially divisive international legal tangle. Not so in the modern religious South where white evangelicals had a larger point to make.

The Virginia-based Home School Legal Defense Association had urged the family to apply for asylum in order to publicize the issue of home schooling in America and inflame the issue in Germany. Tilman Goins, Republican representative of the mountainous eastern Tennessee Morristown district in the state legislature, incorrectly condemned Germany's homeschooling restrictions as a 1938 Hitlerian promulgation. Dean Haum, the Romeikes' pastor at First Baptist Church, denied that the family fit the rubric of "illegal" immigrants because they "are not on welfare, they're not asking for handouts. They're hard-working" (all of which would have applied to lots of illegal Hispanic immigrants who were devout Catholics but found neither sanctuary nor support at First Baptist Church).

A spokesman for the Southern Baptist Convention injected political commentary into the incident: families who believed like the Romeikes were no longer welcome in Barack Obama's America because heterosexual married couples with stable, disciplined children represented "the antithesis of this administration's political agenda." The town's mayor, a retired businessman, announced that town residents were prepared to hide the Romeikes if the federal government did not relent. Even native born American Christians feel persecuted, he added, because "God is being pushed out"" of the public square.[1]

The Romeike saga represented a rupture in white southern evangelical opinion about appropriate ministerial comment about politics. Southern Baptist pastors and denominational officials publicly criticizing President Harry Truman (who fervently advocated a universal single payer federal health care system) or President Dwight Eisenhower (who sent the 101st Airborne Division into Little Rock, Arkansas, to enforce federal court rulings to integrate schools) would have been confined to a fringe of hot heads occupying the last redoubts of total resistance churches.

Most white pastors in the South avoided public politics altogether before 1954. If they voted at all, they kept their preferences to themselves lest it trouble ecclesiastical waters and make upward ministerial mobility even harder than it already was. Powerful southern congressional delegations contained less than their representative share of Southern Baptist men (there were no Southern Baptist female congressmen except for a rare special appointment after a congressional spouse died). One's religious affiliation mattered so little that many candidates omitted reference to it entirely, and well-heeled Episcopalians, Jews, Catholics, and Presbyterians were proportionately more likely to be elected than Southern Baptists or pentecostals.

Many white evangelicals in those days really did believe this world was not their home, they were just passing through. When Southern Baptists did enter the huskings, they were as likely to be racial and economic moderates such as Brooks Hays of Arkansas as reactionaries such as South Carolina's Strom Thurmond.[2]

News that southerners argue about God is not news at all. Their denominational and doctrinal battles are legendary. But my contention that southern religion can be defined politically either as "red," "blue," or "purple" appears to some as startling news indeed.

Let me begin with the national religious context from which the South is either diverging or toward which it is converging (depending on your viewpoint). Although many of the primary spokesmen of the Religious Right—Jerry Falwell, Paige Patterson, Paul Pressler, Albert "Al" Mohler, Richard Land, Pat Robertson—were Southern Baptists, the influence of Moral Majority and Christian Coalition extended well beyond one region or denomination.

In 2008, journalist Christine Wicker, herself a fallen-from-grace Southern Baptist (I know Southern Baptists believe that to be impossible, but they will make an exception for Wicker), wrote a book provocatively titled *The Fall of the Evangelical Nation*. It discusses both strengths and weaknesses of the Religious Right in American politics.

Wicker begins her book with this comment: "Evangelical Christianity in America is dying. The great evangelical movements of today are not a vanguard. They are a remnant, unraveling at every edge. Look at it any way you like: Conversions. Baptisms. Membership. Retention. Participation. Giving. Attendance. Religious literacy. Effect on the culture. All are down and dropping. The idea that evangelicals are taking over America is one of the greatest publicity scams in history, a perfect coup accomplished by savvy politicos and religious leaders, who understand media weaknesses and exploit them brilliantly."[3] Updating her analysis, a March 2014 poll of "millennials" (ages 18–35) found them to be the most politically liberal and least religiously connected of any generation polled in US history. And the Southern Baptist Convention lost 800,000 members in ten years to 2015.

Using extensive data collected during the past quarter century, Wicker challenges the predominant assumption that theological fundamentalism and its political shadow, the Religious Right, is a juggernaut plowing under anything standing in the path of creating an American theocracy. Let me summarize her main points.

The generally accepted idea that 25 percent of American adults are evangelicals who twice elected George W. Bush president; oppose abortion and gay rights; supported the Iraq War; justify the torture of captured combatants; demand lower taxes; favor corporate America; question the separation of church and state; and promote prayer, posting the Ten Commandments, and teaching Creationism in public schools, is at best an exaggeration. According to Wicker, this estimate of evangelical strength derives largely from replies to pollsters' questions about religious affiliation, how many members these denominations claim, and denominational positions on political and social issues. Problem is, careful scrutiny of denominational claims and actual membership statistics don't jive. People remain on church rolls long after they move, drop out, or change denominations. For instance, the Southern Baptist Convention claims 16 million members but can locate only half that many. The other half is AWOL. Sunday school attendance, which measures the level of concentrated Bible study as a percentage of worshipers, declined sharply from 85 percent to 69 percent between 1991 and 2005. Utilizing multiple categories to indicate levels of enthusiasm (such as financial contributions, participation in mission groups, and worship attendance), Wicker estimates the true number of devoted, deeply loyal Southern Baptists at around four million. Nationwide, the National Association of Evangelicals (NAE) claims to represent 61 denominations (not including the SBC), containing 30 million members. But by counting the actual members claimed by each of the sixty-one groups, Wicker arrived at a figure of only 7.6 million. When she asked NAE officials how they arrived at their numbers, no one knew or even bothered to defend the estimate. Of these nearly 8 million, Wicker estimates between two and four million are deeply committed believers.[4]

Complicating this over-reporting of evangelical success is the under reporting of its decline. Currently the percentage of nonbelievers (which doubled between 1990 and 2001 from 8 percent to 14 percent, from 14 million to 29 million adults) is increasing faster than the number of evangelicals. Furthermore, a 2004 Pew Forum on Religion and Public Life identified 67 percent of the US population as Christian but not self-described as evangelical or pentecostal. The total membership of mainline Protestant denominations (Methodists, Congregationalists, Episcopalians, Lutherans, Disciples of Christ, etc.) that lean moderate to progressive slightly outnumbers evangelicals and pentecostals trending conservative.[5]

Southern Baptists, often viewed by secularists as the biggest and baddest hombres patrolling the evangelical frontier, actually are experiencing a gut-wrenching identity crisis. Having won control of the largest American Protestant denomination by accusing moderate Southern Baptist leaders of being closet liberals who had departed from their evangelical roots, fundamentalist leaders of that denomination now try to explain why the number of both baptisms and members are declining under their watch. In 2007 they pledged to baptize one million people. But the total harvest of their well-organized and passionately conducted crusade was only 372,000, which represented a 4.15 percent decline from the previous year and fewer people than the SBC had baptized in 1950 when alleged moderates and liberals controlled the denomination. And even many of those 372,000 new members were Baptists being dunked for a second or third time or converts from other denominations. When SBC researchers that year tried to locate denominational churches performing as well as the average SBC church had fifty years earlier, they could find only twenty-two churches out of 4,300 that met their criteria. Even more critical for the future, within the millennial 18–34 age group SBC baptisms fell by 40% between 1980 and 2005. Nationwide, evangelicals are growing slower than the US population.[6]

Probing yet one layer deeper in sociological data, Wicker discovered that grouping all evangelicals/pentecostals into a single political category is a mistake. As I have argued in books, articles, and lectures for decades, Baptists do not all think alike. To believe that democratically organized churches whose members stretch across gender, ethnic, racial, and class lines, produce homogeneity of anything—worship style, theology, political ideology, or social attitudes—is naive, uninformed, and far-fetched. Using supposed definitions of core evangelical beliefs, respected evangelical pollster George Barna documented my premise: he found that 25 percent of self-described evangelicals do not believe homosexuality is morally wrong; 27 percent do not believe abortion is a sin; 32 percent don't think smoking marijuana is evil; and 40 percent do not believe that sex between unmarried people is forbidden.[7]

Wicker cites other factors eroding evangelicalism as well. Contrary to conventional beliefs, megachurches (defined as the 1,200 congregations enrolling between 2,000 and 36,000) boast members who tend to be better educated and wealthier than smaller churches (leading some critics to refer to them as "country clubs for the sanctified" or "Wal-Marts for selling Jesus lite"). They are also loaded with debt and often have a difficult time transitioning to new leadership upon the death, retirement, or resignation of the founding charismatic pastor.

There are other threats to evangelicalism as well. Many evangelical churches have an increasing retention problem among 18–35 year olds, who tend to be more socially tolerant and concerned with issues such as poverty and the environment and who are less obsessed with homosexuality and abortion. The SBC, for instance, now estimates that 88 percent of SBC teenagers leave their churches after high school graduation. Presently in America, 21 percent of 21–45 year olds never attend religious services compared with 14 percent in 1972–1976. Rebellion against what many consider narrow-minded, mean-spirited evangelicals has also spread to the general population. Asked to evaluate eleven groups in terms of respect, non-Christians in one poll rated evangelicals 10th, ahead only of prostitutes. Even more worrisome to evangelical leaders, few Christians of any theological persuasion actively witness to their faith. The SBC estimates that only 16 percent of members regularly witness to others. Secular university culture also erodes evangelicalism, challenging its strong resistance to rationalism, evolutionary biology, environmental determinism, and much of modern psychology. As we shall see, immigration; religious diversity; demographic changes in courtship, marriage, and family patterns; and shifts in attitudes about women's role in society pose additional challenges.[8]

Having expelled moderates from the SBC, fundamentalists fell on fellow believers. This should have been no surprise. Once your own religious belief and practice become normative for judging other believers, all denominational and political alliances become transitory: work with those who loosely agree with some of your objectives; then when your coalition routs the enemy, turn on insufficiently orthodox fellow believers. In its October 9, 2010, issue, *The Economist* described the multiple tensions rumbling through the SBC: Calvinists from the Reformed tradition versus evangelical fundamentalists; charismatic-pentecostal elements versus fundamentalists who reject their emphasis on the role of the spirit.[9]

The same year that Wicker's book made the best seller lists (2008), historian Allan J. Lichtman wrote *White Protestant Nation: The Rise of the American Conservative Movement*. Tracing modern conservatism back to the 1920s and post World War I fears that secular, pluralistic, and cosmopolitan forces threatened America's national identity, Lichtman concludes that modern conservative ideology is grounded less in specific issues such as fear of centralized government, higher taxes, or more government regulation, than in dual visions of America as a White Protestant nation and a country whose national greatness is determined by private enterprise. Like Wicker, Lichtman forecast a Religious Right implosion rooted in political disillusion.[10]

If we broaden the evangelical family to include its disparate ethnic, racial, and economic components, the idea of a single religio-political faction becomes unsustainable. Applying this complex description of evangelical Christian subculture to specific American political campaigns complicates many of our assumptions about the Religious Right.

Religion and Politics in Recent America

There have been three pivotal presidential elections in my lifetime so far as American religion is concerned. The first occurred a half century ago in 1960 with the election of John Kennedy, a Catholic, to the presidency. The second, in 1976, installed Jimmy Carter, a born-again Southern Baptist, in the White House. The third in 1980 established the potential power of America's Religious Right. In all of American history from 1792 to 1976, Americans had elected only two Baptist presidents, Warren G. Harding and Harry S. Truman. During the following sixteen years, they elected two more, Jimmy Carter and Bill Clinton. Curiously, the last three Baptist presidents came from the center of the Democratic Party. Mike Huckabee, the Republican runner-up for the party's nomination in 2008, represented the social and religious right wing of his party.

Ironically, both support for and opposition to segregation launched southern evangelicals, black and white, onto a sea of political conflict not entirely unfamiliar to them. In the middle of the nineteenth century, for instance, white evangelicals had mobilized the Bible and their faith on behalf of slavery, Pauline admonitions of subservience to the established political and social order, and southern nationalism. Black slaves, meanwhile, preferred the Exodus narrative and harnessed the cause of freedom to their understanding of God's providential deliverance. After the Civil War, white evangelicals entered politics with a vengeance on behalf of regional civil religion rooted in personal ethics (prohibition, sexual purity, Sabbath observance). Despite a passing nod to the doctrine of separation of church and state, that doctrine was more a theological convenience useful in their battles against Catholics lobbying for state funding of parochial schools than a deeply felt or even thoroughly understood conviction. Black evangelicals during those same years were preaching a different civil religion of liberation theology and radical change in order to achieve a more just world.

Those who seek the origins of the deep polarization that has created red and blue America—where we live in neighborhoods of like-minded people, sip latte or wine in like-minded ideological coffee shops or bistros, and attend churches surrounded by Democrats or Republicans who hire similarly inclined pastors—might begin looking in the 1960s. Before that time most white southern evangelical pastors either did not vote at all or voted for Democrats. Then came the culture wars of the 1960s. David Edwin Harrell, the preeminent historian of American pentecostalism, explains that it was as if a thoughtless man had walked up to a pit bulldog sleeping in front of a warm fire and kicked it hard. If you do that, don't be surprised when the dog bites you. Secularizing American culture gave evangelicals a series of vigorous kicks to the solar plexus. Predictably, evangelicals mobilized and fought back. By 1979, Jerry Falwell had organized Moral Majority. In 1986 Baptist pentecostal evangelist Pat Robertson used the vast audience tuned to his technologically sophisticated Christian Broadcasting Network and its *700 Club* to launch his presidential campaign. In 1990 he organized Christian Coalition of America. Pentecostal superstar Jimmy Swaggart of Louisiana, evangelist Jim Bakker of North Carolina, Oral Roberts of Oklahoma, and Falwell all weighed offers to endorse George Bush or Robertson in

1988, and most backed Robertson. Probably no quartet of southern evangelicals ever spread more terror among secular Americans without actually taking life than Swaggart, Roberts, Falwell, and Robertson.[11]

It is also worth remembering that in 1988 not one but two Baptist preachers entered the presidential primaries, Robertson for the Republicans and North Carolina native and Baptist minister Jesse Jackson for the Democrats. Jackson's Rainbow Coalition also inspired fear, but mainly among southern white evangelicals.

With issues such as feminism, abortion, pornography, promiscuity, school prayer, and posting the Ten Commandments in public buildings capturing hearts and headlines, the newly mobilized Religious Right began to influence or even determine elections across the country. Working- and middle-class white religious people of all denominations, especially in the South but by no means limited to that region, began to vote more heavily Republican. Secular, suburban, well-educated and higher income Americans began to leave the Republican party headed in the opposite direction.[12] When Democrats such as Jackson courted southern voters, they did so in the familiar Sunday morning surroundings of African American churches. But the familiar black church endorsements suddenly had a white competitor, the Christian Coalition "surveys," which made it clear how Democrats and Republicans stood on those issues near to Jesus's heart, such as the legal right to own assault weapons and the necessity to keep property taxes low as well as to restrict abortion and homosexuality. So politicized had evangelicalism become that during the early 1990s, six of seven politicians in the succession order to the presidency belonged to SBC churches (President Clinton, Al Gore, Richard Gephardt, Trent Lott, Newt Gingrich, and Jesse Helms). Ponder these names and ideologies and you have additional evidence for the diversity of evangelical thought.

By 1997, polling data found deep political divisions within American religion. Although Christians supported both the political left and right, 54 percent of Christians who supported the right believed the Bible was literally true compared to only 4 percent of Christians on the left. On the right, 98 percent believed salvation was found only in Jesus, compared to 64 percent who believed that on the left. The Christian right drew 81 percent of its strength from self-described evangelicals, and the left only 27 percent (and most of those were black evangelicals).[13] By the 1990s, in an historic reversal unparalleled in US religious history, Catholic conservatives and Southern Baptist officials were holding regular meetings in Nashville to forge a common Religious Right political agenda.[14]

Bush presidential advisor Karl Rove understood these developments better than other political strategists and perfected a GOP strategy in response to them. He created a religious core to the party of Lincoln by generating ballot referenda guaranteed to bring out Religious Right masses: ballots to ban abortion and same-sex marriage, stem cell research, cloning, and assisted suicide. *The New York Times* reported during the 2004 election cycle that Republicans sent mass mailings to voters in Arkansas and West Virginia showing a Bible with the word *banned* across it, together with a photo of a man on his knees placing a ring on the hand of another man with the word *allowed*. The "liberal agenda," the mailout continued, sought to remove "under God" from the Pledge of Allegiance.[15]

The political militancy of the Religious Right alienated many well-educated, fiscally conservative Republicans. Indeed, the most extreme evangelical militants sounded pretty much like the radical Muslim Imams whom they despised and who had established theocracies across the Middle East.[16]

Damaging the Christian Right even more than internal divisions and wildly inaccurate claims was a series of scandals in the spring of 2005. Revelations that Republican lobbyists had laundered Mississippi Choctaw Indian gambling money to Ralph Reed (former head of Christian Coalition of America) in order to defeat a lottery referendum in Alabama confirmed what Democrats in the state had claimed. In fact, documents subsequently revealed that of the one million dollars spent by Alabama Christian Coalition to defeat the lottery, $850,000 of it had come from a Choctaw casino foundation.[17] The revelations probably cost Ralph Reed his GOP candidacy for lieutenant governor of Georgia and badly damaged the credibility of Alabama Christian Coalition. The Alabama and Georgia chapters subsequently withdrew from the national organization, claiming that Christian Coalition of America had turned liberal by supporting an increase in the minimum wage and environmental reforms.

By the 2006 midterm elections, the Religious Right had learned the meaning of a piece of ancient wisdom: "Whom the gods would destroy they first made mad with power." So-called values voters complained that the GOP courted them at election time and forgot them afterwards. A former deputy director of the White House office of Faith-Based and Community Initiatives wrote a book (*Tempting Faith: An Inside Story of Political Seduction*) claiming that members of the Bush administration privately ridiculed conservative Christian allies as "boorish," "nuts," "goofy," "out of control," and "ridiculous."[18] A vice president of the Southern Baptist Convention concluded that "conservative Christians are somewhat disenchanted with Republicans." An Associated Press-Ipsos poll conducted in September 2006 found a surprisingly high 42 percent of white evangelicals disapproved of President Bush's performance as president.[19] And this disillusion preceded Republican Congressman Mark Foley's sex scandal, which unraveled in October 2006. Two leading figures in Falwell's 1979 Moral Majority movement explained in their 1999 book *Blinded by Might* that "religious conservatives, no matter how well organized, can't save America. Only God can." National Religious Right columnist Cal Thomas became ever more critical of the Bush administration, and he was soon joined by Paul Weyrich of the Free Congress Foundation, one of the founders of the Religious Right.[20]

Of course, most thunder from the right originated in white churches. Although African American evangelicals in the South generally espoused similarly conservative attitudes toward homosexuality, prayer in schools, and posting the Ten Commandments, they also distrusted the Republican party, were economically liberal, and voted overwhelmingly Democratic.

The 2008 election cycle demonstrated how deep the fissures went. MSNBC's Chris Matthews, commenting on Mike Huckabee's primary victories in the Bible Belt South, gushed that the Southern Baptist minister from Arkansas "practically owns the place." Not quite. As Millsaps College historian Robert S. McElvaine pointed out in a late October blog, Obama out-polled Huckabee by nearly two to one in Bible Belt presidential primaries. And November presidential exit polls indicated that the evangelical vote nationally split 55 percent for John McCain (who claimed to be Southern Baptist though he had not been baptized in a SBC church) to 43 percent for Obama. George W. Bush, by contrast, had won 78 percent of the evangelical vote four years earlier.

On election day in 2008, black evangelicals overwhelmingly voted for Obama. White evangelicals, especially in the South, voted for McCain/Palin by similar huge majorities. According to historian McElvaine, of the 225 counties where McCain scored at least 10 percent higher than George W. Bush had in 2004, all but one (in Alaska) were in the South, and most were in the Ozarks and Appalachia. Those counties were overwhelmingly white, lower income, less educated, more rural, less diverse, and 32 percent Southern Baptist.

The more biblically conservative white evangelicals were, the more likely they were to vote for McCain. Only 17 percent of evangelicals who voted for Obama believed the Bible to be the literal word of God. Of those who attended church weekly and voted for McCain, 58 percent believed the Bible was literally true.

A brief disillusion with Bush and revelations about Republican political and sexual scandals damaged the GOP and drove some white evangelicals back toward personal pietism. Although Ed Hindson, contributing editor of Jerry Falwell's *National Liberty Journal*, continued to promote conservative Christian political activism, other leaders urged evangelicals not to become "useful idiots" of a political party. National observers began to describe a "new evangelicalism," which kept its distance from partisan politics. They argued that neither political party was the "Party of God."[21]

The 111th Congress that met in January 2009 epitomized evangelical diversity. A total of sixty-six self-identified Baptists served in the Senate and House, the second largest religious delegation behind Catholics. They belonged to the SBC, three major African American denominational groups, the moderate American

Baptist Churches USA, the General Baptist Conference, the Cooperative Baptist Fellowship, the liberal and gay-friendly Alliance of Baptists, and the Association of Welcoming and Affirming Baptists. In the House, Baptists split evenly between Democrats and Republicans. African Americans constituted 33 percent of House Baptists. In the Senate, Baptists Robert Byrd (D-West Virginia), John McCain (R-Arizona), and Mitch McConnell (R-Kentucky) held key leadership roles but shared no common ideology.[22]

As disillusion with the GOP and disagreement about how closely evangelicals should identify with the new Tea Party wing of the party spread, it appeared briefly that conservative southern white Christians might retreat once again into less politicized religion. But the 2012 election cycle ended that illusion. At first, southern GOP primaries demonstrated that white evangelicals had little enthusiasm for Mormon candidate Mitt Romney, partly because Southern Baptist evangelist Billy Graham (now in his 90s) had pronounced Mormonism to be a non-Christian religious cult. But after Romney won the party's nomination, Graham's son and successor, Franklin, removed the controversial statement from the Billy Graham Evangelical Association website and made it clear that authentic Christians should vote for the Mormon.

By November 2012, white evangelicals had made their peace with Romney. Never in the history of southern religion, not even when white Protestants stormed the electoral barricades trying to defeat Catholic John Kennedy in 1960, had white evangelicals so completely abandoned God's spiritual provision for them in favor of human political mobilization. Declaring Sunday, October 7, 2012 (a month before political armageddon), to be "Pulpit Freedom Sunday" (and ironically citing as precedent the long black church tradition of public endorsement of political candidates), some Southern Baptist and Pentecostal pastors engaged in acts of civil disobedience. From their pulpits, they publicly denounced President Obama and endorsed his opponent in violation of the 1954 Johnson Amendment that prohibited churches and other tax-exempt organizations from making political statements. Like the short-lived government deportation order of the Romeike family, federal officials had never rigorously enforced the Johnson Act anyway, particularly not on black churches where pulpit endorsements had been common practice for 150 years. Nationwide, 1,500 white pastors engaged in civil disobedience that Sunday morning. Alabama stood near the top with twenty-one self-identified pastors denouncing Obama or his policies. Dr. Jimmy Jackson—former president of the Alabama State Baptist Convention and pastor of Huntsville's Whitesburg Baptist Church—led the dissenters. In a stem-winding 45-minute sermon entitled "The Great Divide," Jackson proclaimed his defiance of the 58-year-old federal restriction: "God disagrees with Obama," who had violated biblical injunctions on issues ranging from same-sex marriage to abortion.

Jackson received support from Baptist layman and Gadsden megachurch member, Roy Moore, the "Ten Commandments" former chief justice of the Alabama Supreme Court. Moore insisted that though the US Constitution prohibited establishment of a state religion, the 10th Amendment permitted a state to do so. Running successfully on the Republican ticket to regain his seat atop the state's highest court, Moore described the Johnson Amendment as "an egregious violation of church and state." As for pastors who endorsed candidates, "Those pastors are simply testing that proposition, and I think they will be proved right." Although some readers of the article on AL.com disagreed with religious endorsements, others insisted that such disobedience of federal law was a valid exercise affirming "a Christian's duty to choose God, not man, no matter what government office they hold."[23]

Ironically, Moore, Jackson, Morris, and others, sounded not only like black pastors who endorsed Obamacare and the president's reelection a few Sundays later but also like Muslim clerics in the Middle East who demanded imposition of Sharia (Muslim religious) law over secular government enactments.

In November 2012, the unprecedented mobilization of a declining evangelical base fell far short of victory. National exit polls revealed that regular church attendees split 59 percent for Romney to 39 percent for Obama, while occasional church attendees reversed that pattern by a 55 percent to 44 percent margin. Those who never attended church preferred Obama by 62 percent to 34 percent. Self-described born again Christians proved Romney's strongest base, voting for him 79 percent to 20 percent for Obama, slightly higher than even Romney's fellow Mormons. Protestants broke 57 percent to 42 percent for Romney, but Jews (by a 69 percent to 30 percent spread) backed Obama. Catholics narrowly favored Obama (50 percent to 48 percent), although those who regularly attended mass strongly favored Romney. Conversely, Hispanic Catholics voted for Obama by a 75 percent to 21 percent margin. Black Christians constituted Obama's strongest base by 94 percent to 5 percent nationally.

Among the ten most religious states as defined by rates of church membership in 2011, nine were in the South, led by Mississippi and Alabama (the other was Utah). None of the ten voted for Obama in 2012. Among the bottom ten religious states (led by Vermont, New Hampshire, and Maine), only Alaska voted for Romney. Evangelicals voted for Romney, a Mormon, by an even higher percentage than they had voted for self-proclaimed Baptist John McCain four years earlier, and by the exact same margin they had provided George W. Bush over John Kerry in 2004 (78 percent to 21 percent). Comparisons of white evangelical margins in "purple" swing states reflect the same pattern. In Florida, which narrowly voted for Obama, white evangelicals cast 24 percent of the total vote and favored Romney by a 79 percent to 21 percent margin (compared to McCain, 77 percent to 21 percent in 2008).

Predictions that many white evangelicals would simply refuse to vote in an election between Obama and a Mormon after opposing Romney in GOP primaries proved incorrect. In four of five southern states, white evangelical turnout as a percentage of total vote actually increased, and in another state it remained the same as in 2008:

Percentage of white voters by state who identified themselves as "evangelical Christians" in the 2012 presidential election (with % who voted for Mitt Romney)

Mississippi	50%	Romney won 95%–5%
Alabama	47%	Romney won 90%–10%
North Carolina	35%	Romney won 79%–20%
Virginia	23%	Romney won 87%–17%

In two of these four states, Romney's margin over McCain among white evangelicals actually increased.

The only two southern states where the percentage of white evangelical voters significantly declined between 2008 and 2012 were Virginia (from 28 percent of the total vote to 23 percent) and North Carolina (from 44 percent to 35 percent, a decline that nearly cost Romney the state).[24]

Perhaps a 2004 Zogby International Poll of US voters helps make sense out of such confusing data. Analysis of self-proclaimed "moral values voters" in the November election between George W. Bush and John Kerry that year had concluded that voters meant quite different things when they voted their "morals": 33 percent cited greed and materialism as society's most urgent moral concern; 31 percent named poverty and economic justice as highest priorities; 42 percent chose the war in Iraq as the issue most influencing their vote. In the "One Campaign Poll," 90 percent of evangelicals agreed that the new administration whoever might be president should fight to reduce AIDS and poverty. Painting the political ideology of American or southern evangelicals with either too bland or too contrasting colors is a risky venture.

When the new 113th Congress convened in January 2013, two Muslims, three Buddhists, a Hindu, and one congressman who answered "none" when asked for his religion reflected the nation's trend toward religious pluralism and secularism. Twelve other congressmen did not specify a religious affiliation. One of the three Buddhists, Hank Johnson, of Georgia, was an incumbent southerner who won reelection in 2012. Protestants continued to dominate (56 percent of all congressmen), but their numbers continued to decline from 75 percent in 1961. Though Catholics were the big religious victors in 2012 (winning 163 seats compared with 156 in the 112th Congress and constituting 29 percent of Congress but only 22 percent of US population), Baptists (split nearly evenly between Democrats and Republicans, and black and white members) also increased their numbers by five to seventy-three members (13.7 percent of all congressmen, a bit lower percentage than their 17 percent of Americans who identified themselves as Baptists). The comparative number of Baptist congressmen in 1969 was only fifty-three.[25]

My point in all this data is that politicized religion is complex. Before generalizing about southern evangelical political preferences, one must determine whether the evangelicals are black, white, or Hispanic; poor or rich; urban or rural; men or women; high school dropouts or PhDs. At present, most historians, sociologists, political scientists, and even journalists understand that southern evangelicals are not marginal, displaced persons wandering aimlessly in the desert of American politics. They are not politically dumb or unsophisticated. Nor do they all agree with each other or vote the same way. That may not be everything evangelicals wish for, but it is much more than they have received in the past. At least they are no longer politically ignored.

—Lecture first presented at Lyon College in Batesville, Arkansas

Notes

Foreword

1. John B. Boles, "The Discovery of Southern Religious History," in Boles and Evelyn Thomas Nolen, eds., *Interpreting Southern History: Historiographical Essays in Honor of Sanford W. Higginbotham* (Baton Rouge: Louisiana State University Press, 1987), 541.

Introduction

1. *Birmingham News*, July 3, 2005.
2. *Birmingham News*, February 29, 2008.
3. US Bureau of the Census, *Religious Bodies, 1916, Part I* (Washington, 1919), p. 123.
4. Lisa Miller, "Harvard's Crisis of Faith: Can a Secular University Embrace Religion Without Sacrificing Its Soul?" *Newsweek*, February 22, 2010, p. 43. For a contradictory view, see "Matters of faith find new prominence at universities," *Birmingham News*, May 4, 2007. Although denominational schools featured "religion," "Bible," or similarly named departments primarily to educate ministers for their congregations, wider and broader studies of comparative religions developed late and at first mainly among learned ministers outside the academy (unlike in European universities, where such interest originated in philological scholarship); see James Turner, *Religion Enters the Academy: The Origins of the Scholarly Study of Religion in America*. (Athens: University of Georgia Press, 2011).
5. Walter B. Posey, "The Protestant Episcopal Church: An American Adaptation," *Journal of Southern History*, XXV (February 1959), 3–30.
6. Wayne Flynt, "Religion for the Blues: Evangelicalism, Poor Whites, and the Great Depression," *Journal of Southern History*, LXXI (February 2005), 3–28.
7. Wayne Flynt to Mavis Bryant, December 18, 1981; Flynt Papers, Samford University Archives, Birmingham, Alabama.
8. Wayne Flynt to David R. Goldfield and Paul Escott, June 11, 1987; Flynt Papers.
9. Wayne Flynt to NEH, November 27, 1979; Flynt Papers.
10. Wayne Flynt to Donald G. Mathews, Nov. 1972; Mathews to Flynt, Nov. 27, 1972; in Flynt Papers.
11. Martin Marty to Flynt, Apr. 20, 1978; Flynt Papers.
12. Samuel S. Hill to Flynt, May 2, 1977; Flynt Papers.

Chapter 1

The text of this chapter originally appeared in a slightly different form as "Growing Up Baptist in Anniston, Alabama: The Legacy of the Reverend Charles R. Bell, Jr." in *Clearings in the Thicket: An Alabama Humanities Reader—Essays and Stories from the 1983 Alabama History and Heritage Festival,* edited by Jerry Elijah Brown (Macon, GA: Mercer University Press, 1985), 147–82.

1. *Editorial, The Anniston Star* (January 5, 1954).

2. Joshua Hill Foster, *Sixty-Four Years a Minister* (Wilmington, North Carolina First Baptist Church, 1948) 54.

3. "Parker Memorial Baptist Church, Anniston, Alabama, 1887–1937," anonymous manuscript, Church Records Division, ABHS, Samford University Library, Birmingham, AL. Hereafter Bell Papers.

4. Harry M. Ayers, *Parker Memorial Baptist Church, Anniston, Alabama, 1887–1937* (n.p., n.p.) 31.

5. Oral history with Charles R. Bell Jr., January 28, 1972.

6. W. O. Carver to Charles R. Bell Jr., January 18, 1941; Sam Hobbs to Bell Jr., May 14, 1942; John H. Bankhead to Bell Jr., April 27, 1942, Bell Papers.

7. Erman L. Crew, *History of the Baraca Class, Parker Memorial Baptist Church, Anniston, Alabama, 1904–1976* (n.p., n.p.). Copy in ABHS.

8. H. M. Cox to Bell Jr., July 20, 1937; Khalil Watim to Bell Jr., April 23, 1938; Henry R. Luce to Bell Jr., November 28, 1941, Bell papers.

9. Oscar Causey to Bell Jr., May 15, 1936; D. M. Key to Bell Jr., May 14, 1936; R. B. Shipley, Chief, Passport Division, to Bell Jr., April 17, 1936, Bell Papers.

10. Oral history with Charles R. Bell Jr.

11. Tartt Bell to Bell Jr., undated, but sometime in March 1936; F. M. McConnell to Rev. Herman S. Ray, February 19, 1936, Bell Papers.

12. K. Brooke Anderson to Bell Jr., May 5, 1937, Bell Papers.

13. Bell Jr., to Franklin D. Roosevelt, October 3, 1935, PPF 21-A, Clergy Letters, Alabama, Box 4, FDR Library, Hyde Park, New York.

14. Anderson to Bell Jr., May 5, 1937; E. R. Brown to Bell Jr., May 13, 1937; Gemiann Patton to Ann and Charlie Bell Jr., September 1943; Arle Brooks to Bell Jr., July 27, 1943; Clarence Jordan to Bell Jr., July 13, 1944, Bell Papers.

15. Oral history with Charles R. Bell Jr.; Annie G. Perry, et al. to Bell Jr., September 19, 1943, Bell Papers.

16. Lucy R. Mason to Bell Jr., July 25, August 25, and October 25, 1937; oral history with Charles R. Bell Jr.

17. Willard Uphaus to Bell Jr., February 14, 1939; Yelverton Cowherd to Bell Jr., December 6, 1941; Walter P. Reuther to Bell Jr., July 8, 1944, Bell Papers.

18. George W. Carver to Bell Jr., October 26, 1932; Robert Lee Moffett to Bell Jr., June 4, 1944, Bell Papers.

19. Hugo L. Black to Bell Jr., May 10, 1937, Bell Papers.

20. Lister Hill to Bell Jr., November 2, 1942; J. H. Bankhead to Bell Jr., October 28, 1942, Bell Papers.

21. Virginius Dabney to Bell Jr., March 22, 1944, Bell Papers.

22. "A Member" to Bell Jr., January 31, 1944, Bell Papers.

23. Anonymous to Bell Jr. undated but January 1944, Bell Papers.

24. Oral history with Charles R. Bell Jr.

25. Louise J. Moses to Bell Jr., October 13, 1939, Bell Papers.

26. Louise O. Charlton to Bell Jr., August 29, 1938, Bell Papers; oral history with Charles R. Bell Jr.

27. Harry F. Ward to Bell Jr., November 15, 1938; W. B. Bankhead to Bell Jr., December 15, 1938; Sam Hobbs to Bell Jr., December 12, 1938, Charles Bell Papers, Samford University Archives.

28. Tartt Bell to Bell Jr., undated; John H. Bankhead to Bell Jr., September 27, October 28, 1942; Harry M. Ayers to Bell Jr., August 18, December 3, 1942; Lister Hill to Bell Jr., October 19, 1942, Bell Papers.

29. Tartt Bell to Bell Jr., undated; Lister Hill to Bell Jr., May 22, 1944, Bell Papers.

30. Tartt Bell to Bell Jr., undated; A. J. Muste to Bell Jr., April 30, 1943; W. M. Hammond Jr., to Bell Jr., December 15, 1942; Dan Whitsett to Bell Jr., May 26, 1943; Lewis F. Kosch to Bell Jr., June 9, 1943, Bell Papers.

31. *Time* (May 31, 1937): 57–58; unidentified clipping, Bell Papers.

32. Charles Dobbins to Bell Jr., May 17, 1937; Hugh Peterson to Bell Jr., January 5, 1938, Bell Papers.

33. Edward A. McDowell Jr., to Bell Jr., October 4, 1937, Bell Papers.

34. Lonnie W. Meachum to Bell Jr., July 29, 1935, April 7, 1937, January 21, 1941; Maxie C. Collins to Bell Jr., August 1, 1939, Bell Papers.

35. Arthur J. Barton to Bell Jr., August 2, 1937; Harold W. Tribble to Bell Jr., February 16, 1938, Bell Papers.

36. Barton to Bell Jr., April 19, 1938, Bell Papers.

37. Harold W. Tribble to Bell Jr., April 25, 1938, Bell Papers.

38. L. L. Gwaltney to Bell Jr., June 3, 1941; John H. Buchanan to Bell Jr., June 13, 1941; Montague Cook to Bell Jr., June 16, 1941, Bell Papers.

39. J. E. Lambdin to Bell Jr., June 10, 1934; John H. Buchanan to Bell Jr., February 4, 1942; John W. Inzer to Bell Jr., April 28, 1942; James H. Ivey to Bell Jr., undated, Bell Papers.

40. S. J. to Bell Jr., August 5, 1940, Bell Papers.

41. Three letters from Tartt Bell to Bell Jr., all undated but between 1936–1942, Bell Papers.

42. *Ibid.*, sometime in the early 1940s.

43. Edward A. McDowell Jr., to Bell Jr., September 27, 1937; George D. Heaton to Bell Jr., November 17, 1937; W. O. Carver to Bell Jr., September 9, 1937, Bell Papers.

44. Oral history with Charles R. Bell Jr.

45. "Sam" to Bell Jr., October 10, 1939, Bell Papers.

46. Tartt Bell to Bell Jr., undated, Bell Papers.

47. "Jim" to Bell Jr., February 1, 1944; Ralph T. Templin to Bell Jr., October 12, 1942; Tartt Bell to Bell Jr., November 8, 1942; Alex Bell to Bell Jr., undated; Bell Jr., to "Jim," undated, Bell Papers.

48. "A Member" to Bell Jr., June 13, 1944, Bell Papers.

49. Iva Cook to Bell Jr., undated, Bell Papers.

50. For samples of reactions, see S. J. Ezell to Bell Jr., June 30 1944; "Jim" to Bell Jr., July 10, 1944; H. Ross Arnold to Bell Jr., June 30, 1944; Dr. T. W. Ayers to Bell Jr., October 4, 1944; Sam Eby to Bell Jr., August 2, 1944. For reactions from within Parker, see especially John L. Cottrell to Bell Jr., June 19, 1944; Alex and Nan Hall to Bell Jr., June 21, 1944; W. B. Crabb to Bell Jr., June 15, 1944, Bell Papers.

51. John H. Buchanan to Edwin McNeill Poteat, July 3, 1944; Poteat to Buchanan, July 12, 1944, Bell Papers.

52. L. B. Moseley to Bell Jr., August 6, 1944, Bell Papers.

53. Oral history with Charles R. Bell Jr.

Chapter 2

The text of this chapter originally appeared in a slightly different form as "Dissent in Zion: Alabama Baptists and Social Issues, 1900–1914," *The Journal of Southern History*, Vol. XXXV, No. 4, Nov. 1969, 523–42.

1. For a brief but helpful survey of recent historiography of American Protestantism, see Paul A. Carter, "Recent Historiography of the Protestant Churches in America," *Church History*, XXXVII (American Society of Church History: March 1968), 95–107.

2. Charles H. Hopkins, *The Rise of the Social Gospel in American Protestantism, 1865–1915* (New Haven, CT: Yale University Press, 1940); Henry F. May, *Protestant Churches and Industrial America* (New York: Harper and Row, 1949); Samuel S. Hill Jr., *Southern Churches in Crisis* (New York, Chicago, and San Francisco: Peter Smith Publisher, Incorporated, 1966), 29.

3. C. Vann Woodward, *Origins of the New South, 1877–1913* (Baton Rouge: Louisiana State University Press, 1951), 450.

4. Kenneth K. Bailey, *Southern White Protestantism in the Twentieth Century* (New York, Evanston, and London: Peter Smith Publisher, Incorporated, 1964), 164.

5. Rufus B. Spain, *At Ease in Zion: Social History of the Southern Baptists, 1865–1900* (Nashville: Vanderbilt University Press, 1967), 149.

6. Frank Willis Barnett, "Editorial," *The Alabama Baptist* (Birmingham), October 5, March 26, February 5, October 1, 1913.

7. *Ibid.*, June 19, 1912.

8. *Ibid.*, November 13, 1913.

9. Washington B. Crumpton, *The Alabama Baptist* (Birmingham), July 3, 1913.

10. Alfred James Dickinson, *The Alabama Baptist* (Birmingham), April 4, 1906.

11. Hopkins, *Rise of the Social Gospel*, 296–97.

12. Charles Stelzle, "Series of Articles," *The Alabama Baptist* (Birmingham), October 9, 16, 23, November 6, 20, 1912; March 19, 1913.

13. Frank Willis Barnett, "Editorial," *The Alabama Baptist* (Birmingham), November 22, 1911.

14. *Ibid.*, February 7, 1912; April 2, 1913.

15. *Ibid.*, February 14, 1912.

16. *Annual of the Alabama Baptist State Convention, 1912* (Birmingham 1912), 75. On microfilm in ABHS.

17. Manuscript copy in ABHS.

18. Frank Willis Barnett, "Editorial," *The Alabama Baptist* (Birmingham), August 14, 1907.

19. For a brilliant and vigorous debate between Modernist and Fundamentalist spokesmen among Alabama Baptists, see Birmingham's *The Alabama Baptist,* June and July 1906 and January 12, February 9, June 1, 1910. The battle was renewed in February and March 1913.

20. Clipping in Baptist Biographical File, ABHS.

21. A. Hamilton Reid, *Baptists in Alabama: Their Organization and Witness* (Montgomery: Alabama Baptist State Convention, 1967), 184.

22. Frank Willis Barnett, "Editorial," *The Alabama Baptist* (Birmingham), November 8, 1905.

23. *Ibid.*, April 1, 1914.

24. Washington B. Crumpton, *A Book of Memories, 1842–1920* (Montgomery: Baptist Mission Board, 1921), 193.

25. Reverend W. R. Whatley, *The Alabama Baptist* (Birmingham), September 1, 8, 1909.

26. A. J. Dickinson, *The Alabama Baptist* (Birmingham), October 13, 1909.

27. Frank Willis Barnett, "Editorial," *The Alabama Baptist* (Birmingham), October 6, 1909.

28. Reverend Augustus Cleveland Davidson, *The Alabama Baptist* (Birmingham), March 1, 15, 1905.

29. *Ibid.*, March 29, 1905.

30. Frank Willis Barnett, "Editorial," *The Alabama Baptist* (Birmingham), July 10, 1912.

31. Reverend L. L. Gwaltney, *The Alabama Baptist* (Birmingham), October 28, 1908.

32. Frank Willis Barnett, "Editorial," *The Alabama Baptist* (Birmingham), December 4, July 24, 1912.

33. John Herbert Philips, *The Alabama Baptist,* (Birmingham), June 2, 1909.

34. A. J. Dickinson, *The Alabama Baptist* (Birmingham), July 20, 1904.

35. Frank Willis Barnett, "Editorial," *The Alabama Baptist* (Birmingham), February 21, 1901.

36. *Ibid.*, June 18, 1902; April 22, 1903; July 25, 1906.

37. *Ibid.*, June 4, 1902.

38. *Ibid.*, June 6, 1906.

39. John Herbert Philips, *The Alabama Baptist,* (Birmingham), June 2, 1909.

40. Joshua Hill Foster, *Sixty-four Years a Minister* (Wilmington, NC: First Baptist Church, 1948), 52.

41. A. C. Davidson, *The Alabama Baptist* (Birmingham), April 19, 1905.

42. W. B. Crumpton, *The Alabama Baptist* (Birmingham), April 12, 1911.

43. *Annual of the Alabama Baptist State Convention, 1902* (n.p., n.d.), 5, ABHS.

44. *Ibid.*, 1913 (Birmingham, 1914), 15.

45. *Ibid.*, 1903 (n.p., n.d.), 13; and "History of Sunday School of the South Highlands Baptist Church, Bessemer, from 1913 to 1936," anonymous MS, Church Records Division, ABHS.

46. Foster, *Sixty-four Years a Minister*, 54.

47. "Parker Memorial Baptist Church, Anniston, Alabama, 1887–1937," anonymous MS, Church Records Division, ABHS.

48. Frank Willis Barnett, "Editorial," *The Alabama Baptist* (Birmingham), May 11, 1910; October 2, 1912; August 30, 1911.

49. *Ibid.*, May 7, 1913, October 30, 1912.

50. *Ibid.*, October 30, 1912.

51. *Ibid.*, June 18, 1913.

52. *Ibid.*, February 13, 1907.

53. *Ibid.*, October 9, 1912.

54. *Ibid.*, July 24, 1907.

55. *Ibid.*, May 25, 1910.

56. *Ibid.*, February 4, 1914; February 6, 1907.

57. *Ibid.*, June 17, 1903; June 25, 1913.

58. *Annual of the Alabama Baptist State Convention, 1902*, 5.

59. Benjamin Franklin Riley, *The Alabama Baptist* (Birmingham), June 30, 1909.

60. Benjamin Franklin. Riley, *The White Man's Burden* (Birmingham: B. F. Riley, 1910).

61. Frank Willis Barnett, "Editorial," *The Alabama Baptist* (Birmingham), September 21, 1904. For other strong editorials opposing lynching, see *ibid.*, May 18, 1904; April 10, 1907.

62. *Ibid.*, August 31, September 14, 1904.

63. Arthur James Barton, *The Alabama Baptist* (Birmingham), September 21, 1904.

64. Pastor William Pugh Wilks, *The Alabama Baptist* (Birmingham), April 8, 1914.

65. J. B. Albritton, *The Alabama Baptist* (Birmingham), April 8, 1914.

66. Frank Willis Barnett, "Editorial," *The Alabama Baptist* (Birmingham), January 30, 1907.

67. For Barnett's series on the tuberculosis problem and his recommendations for change, see *ibid.*, June 1, February 16, 1910; September 18, 1912.

68. *Ibid.*, September 18, 1912.

69. *Ibid.*, November 6, 1912.

70. *Ibid.*, September 21, 1910.

71. *Ibid.*, July 28, 1909.

72. *Ibid.*, March 5, 1913.

73. Edgar Gardner Murphy and L. L. Gwaltney, *The Alabama Baptist* (Birmingham), July 16, 1902; September 21, 1910.

74. Frank Willis Barnett, "Editorial," *The Alabama Baptist* (Birmingham), August 25, 1909.

75. Reid, *Baptists in Alabama*, 187–88.

76. Frank Willis Barnett, "Editorial," *The Alabama Baptist* (Birmingham), August 14, 1912.

77. *Ibid.*, May 22, 1907.

78. Pastor O. W. Greer, *The Alabama Baptist* (Birmingham), January 22, 1913.

79. For the text of this address, see *ibid.*, November 19, 1913.

Chapter 3

The text of this chapter originally appeared in a slightly different form as "Alabama Methodists and the Social Gospel, 1900–1930." Paper presented to the Southeastern Methodist Historical Society, Birmingham, Alabama, July 2003.

1. *Birmingham News*, June 4, 5, 2003. Susan Pace Hamill's research was published and became a central argument in the debate about Alabama tax policy and social justice: *The Least of These: Fair Taxes and the Moral Duty of Christians* (Birmingham, AL: Sweetwater Press, 2003).

2. David Nelson Duke, *In the Trenches with Jesus and Marx: Harry F. Ward and the Struggle for Social Justice* (Tuscaloosa: University of Alabama Press, 2003).

3. Quoted in Christopher H. Evans, *Perspectives on the Social Gospel: Papers from the Inaugural Social Gospel Conference at Colgate Rochester Divinity School* (Lewiston, New York: Edwin Mellen Press, 1999), xv; see also, Hopkins, *The Rise of the Social Gospel in American Protestantism, 1865–1915*.

4. Robert T. Handy, "The Social Gospel in Historical Perspective," *Andover Newton Quarterly* 9 (January 1969): 175–77; for a broader discussion of different approaches among non-southern social gospel advocates, see Evans, *Perspectives on the Social Gospel.*

5. George Marsden, *Fundamentalism and American Culture: The Shaping of Twentieth Century Evangelicalism, 1870–1925* (New York: Oxford University Press, 1980), 254–55.

6. Robert D. Linder, "The Resurgence of Evangelical and Social Concern, 1925–75," in *The Evangelicals: What They Believe, Who They Are, Where They Are Changing*, ed. David F. Wells and John D. Woodbridge (Nashville: Abingdon, 1975), 206–7; see also Betty Brandon, "A Wilsonian Progressive—Alexander Jeffrey McKelway," *Journal of Presbyterian History* (Spring 1970).

7. C. Vann Woodward, *Origins of the New South, 1877–1913* (Baton Rouge: Louisiana State University Press, 1951), 450, 452; also Carl N. Degler, *Place Over Time: The Continuity of Southern Distinctiveness* (Baton Rouge: Louisiana State University Press, 1977), 23.

8. These historians emphasize Southern hostility to the Social Gospel: Samuel S. Hill Jr., *Southern Churches in Crisis* (Boston: Beacon Press, 1966) and *Southern Churches in Crisis Revisited* (Tuscaloosa: University of Alabama Press, 1999) new introduction; John B. Boles, "The Discovery of Southern Religious History," in *Interpreting Southern History: Historiographical Essays in Honor of Sanford W. Higginbotham*, ed. John B. Boles and Evelyn Thomas Nolen, (Baton Rouge: Louisiana State University Press, 1987).

9. John Patrick McDowell, *The Social Gospel in the South: The Woman's Home Mission Movement in the Methodist Episcopal Church, South, 1886–1939* (Baton Rouge: Louisiana State University Press, 1982); Samuel J. Shepherd Jr., *Avenues of Faith: Shaping the Urban Religious Culture of Richmond, Virginia, 1900–1929* (Tuscaloosa: University of Ala-

bama Press, 2001); see also Stephen R. Prescott, "The Social Gospel and The American South: An Historiographical Appraisal," in *Perspectives on the Social Gospel: Papers from the Inaugural Social Gospel Conference at Colgate Rochester Divinity School*, and Carolyn DeSwarte Gilkes, "Sisterhoods of Service and Reform: Organized Methodist Women in the Late Nineteenth Century, an Essay on the State of Research," *Methodist History* 24 (October 1985): 15–30.

10. Wayne Flynt, "Dissent in Zion: Alabama Baptists and Social Issues, 1900–1914," *Journal of Southern History* 35 (November 1969): 523–42; Wayne Flynt, "Religion in the Urban South: The Divided Religious Mind of Birmingham, 1900–1930," *Alabama Review* 30 (April 1977): 108–34; Wayne Flynt, "Alabama White Protestantism and Labor, 1900–1914," *Alabama Review* 25 (July 1972): 192–217; Wayne Flynt, "Organized Labor, Reform, and Alabama Politics, 1920," *Alabama Review* 23 (July 1970); Wayne Flynt, "One in the Spirit, Many in the Flesh: Southern Evangelicals," in *Varieties of Southern Evangelicalism*, ed. David Edwin Harrell Jr. (Macon, Georgia: Mercer University Press, 1981), 23–44.

11. Evans, *Perspectives on the Social Gospel*, xvi, xvii; Ralph Luker, "Interpreting the Social Gospel: Reflections on Two Generations of Scholarship," in *ibid.*, 6–7.

12. McDowell, *The Social Gospel in the South*, 3–4, 12, 23, 26; Nancy A. Hewitt, *Southern Discomfort: Women's Activism in Tampa, Florida, 1880's-1920's* (Urbana: University of Illinois Press, 2001), 183–84.

13. McDowell, *The Social Gospel in the South*, 13, 61–64.

14. *Ibid.*, 15, 20–25, 32, 34–35, 39, 41, 43–45.

15. For examples of rural reform efforts, see McDowell, *The Social Gospel in the South*, 12.

16. Shepherd, *Avenues of Faith*, 22, 143–44, 169, 199, 286.

17. For Cannon's little-known activities on behalf of social justice, see Robert H. Hohner, *Prohibition and Politics: The Life of Bishop James Cannon, Jr.* (Columbia: University of South Carolina Press, 1999).

18. Elizabeth Fones-Wolf and Ken Fones-Wolf, "Lending a Hand to Labor: James Myers and the Federal Council of Churches, 1926–1947," *Church History* 68 (March 1999): 62, 64, 67, 72–73, 80.

19. J. William Harris, *Deep Souths: Delta, Piedmont, and Sea Island Society in the Age of Segregation* (Baltimore: Johns Hopkins University Press, 2001), 286; David M. Reimers, *White Protestantism and the Negro* (New York: Oxford University Press, 1965), 89, 148; see also Martha Tovell Nesbitt, "The Social Gospel in Atlanta: 1900–1920" (PhD diss., Georgia State University, 1975).

20. Thomas G. Dyer, *The University of Georgia: A Bicentennial History, 1785–1985* (Athens: University of Georgia Press, 1985), 153–73.

21. Blaine Allison Brownell, "The Urban Mind in the South: The Growth of Urban Consciousness in Southern Cities, 1920–1927" (PhD diss., University of North Carolina, 1969), 19–20.

22. *Alabama Christian Advocate* (Birmingham), July 21, 1906.

23. *Ibid.*, January 11, April 5, 1906; quoted in Arthur J. Moore, "A Christian Obligation to His City," *Circuit Rider* III (December 11, 1927): 1.

24. Billy H. Wyche, "Southern Attitudes Toward Industrial Unions, 1933–1941" (PhD diss., University of Georgia, 1970), 99–100; see also Arthur E. Shelton, "The Methodist Church and Industrial Workers in the Southern Soft Coal Fields," (DD diss., Boston University School of Theology, 1950).

25. Nettie Erwin Webb and Mrs. J. P. Jackson, *Alabama Christian Advocate* (Birmingham), August 3, 1911, May 22, 1913, April 9, May 7, 1914.

26. J. B. Cummings, *Alabama Christian Advocate* (Birmingham), April 24, 1913.

27. Edward S. LaMonte, "Politics and Welfare in Birmingham, 1900–1974," (PhD diss., University of Chicago, 1976), 96–112.

28. Elizabeth Taylor, *Alabama Christian Advocate* (Birmingham), November 26, 1903.

29. *Alabama Christian Advocate*, January 21, July 22, 1909; June 9, 1910; February 8, April 25, December 12, 1912; March 6, September 25, 1913; *Minutes of Women's Missionary Society, North Alabama Conference, 1912* (Birmingham: American Printing Co.), 41–42. The local TCI steel company became an industry leader in what business historians describe as "social welfare capitalism."

30. Estelle Whorton, "The History of the First Methodist Church of Birmingham," (BS thesis, Howard College, 1931); 12–15.

31. *Alabama Christian Advocate*, July 6, 1905, July 19, 1906, August 1, 1907, October 15, 1908, April 1, May 27, 1909, March 17, April 28, December 8, 1910, May 25, November 9, 1911, December 19, 1912, February 27, 1913; *Minutes of the Alabama Conference, 1908*, 43.

32. *Minutes of Women's Missionary Society, North Alabama Conference, 1913*, 35–36, 56–57; *Alabama Christian Advocate*, September 3, 1914.

33. A. M. McMillan, *Alabama Christian Advocate* (Birmingham), April 13, 1905.

34. Editorial, *Alabama Christian Advocate* (Birmingham), May 14, 21, 1903, April 12, 1906.

35. *Minutes of the Alabama Conference, 1910* (Nashville: Publishing House of the Methodist Episcopal Church, South, 1910), 42–43; *ibid.*, 1911; 43, both at Birmingham-Southern Library; see also Wayne Flynt, "Alabama White Protestantism and Labor, 1900–1904," *Alabama Review* XXV (July 1972); 192–217.

36. *Journal of the North Alabama Conference, 1902* (Birmingham: Leslie Printing Co., 1902); 42; *Alabama Christian Advocate*, September 11, 1902.

37. Editorial, *Alabama Christian Advocate*, September 18, 1902; for further angry denunciations of industrial exploitation of children, see *ibid.*, August 28, September 25, November 6, 1902, January 22, February 5, 1903, September 6, December 20, 1906.

38. *Ibid.*, January 17, 24, August 1, 1907, June 26, 1913; *Minutes of Woman's Missionary Society, North Alabama Conference, 1914* (Decatur: Decatur Weekly News, 1914), 53; for similar attacks on child labor, see *Alabama Christian Advocate*, February 14, May 9, August 15, November 21, 1907, December 1, 1910, March 16, 1911, January 4, April 25, July 4, October 17, 1912, June 26, 1913. For contrasts between the social gospel proposals advocated by many Alabama evangelicals between 1900–1920 and the state's (South's) conservative political and business leaders, see James C. Cobb, *The Selling of the South: The Southern Crusade for Industrial Development, 1936–1980* (Baton Rouge: Louisiana State University Press, 1982); and Cobb, *Industrialization of Southern Society, 1877–1984* (Lexington: University of Kentucky Press, 1984).

39. Editorial, *Alabama Christian Advocate* (Birmingham), April 3, 1902, May 14, 21, 1903.

40. *Ibid.*, January 26, March 9, 1905, May 10, 1906.

41. Rev. Raleigh W. Greene, *Alabama Christian Advocate (*Birmingham), April 28, 1910.

42. *Alabama Christian Advocate*, January 17, August 22, 1901, March 27, 1902, June 11, October 22, 29, 1903, May 12, 1904, October 5, 1905, November 12, 1908, March 11, 1909, March 9, April 6, 1911.

43. *Ibid.*, July 3, 10, 17, August 21, 28, September 11, October 9, 16, 23, 1902, March 28, 1912; *Birmingham Age-Herald*, April 13, April 16, 1900.

44. Reverend W. P. Blevens, *Alabama Christian Advocate* (Birmingham), June 6, 1907, July 30, August 6, 13, 27, 1908.

45. Reverend J. R. Nelson, *Alabama Christian Advocate* (Birmingham), April 28, 1910.

46. Marion E. Lazenby, *History of Methodism in Alabama and West Florida* (North Alabama and Alabama-West Florida Conference of the Methodist Church, 1960), 599, 613, 650, 659, 669, 685.

47. Theological liberalism did attract a following among some ministers and church women and especially at Birmingham-Southern College. For racial divisions within the church after 1930, see Charles Marion Prestwood Jr., "Social Ideas of Methodist Ministers in Alabama Since Unification," (PhD diss., Boston University, 1960); Peter C. Murray, "Christ and Caste in Conflict: Creating a Racially Inclusive Methodist Church," (PhD diss., Indiana University, 1985); Thomas L. Parker, "In Search of Identity: The Methodist Church in Alabama and West Florida, 1950–1980," (MA thesis, Auburn University, 1996); Donald E. Collins, *When the Church Bells Rang Racist: The Methodist Church and the Civil Rights Movement in Alabama* (Macon, GA: Mercer University Press, 1998). The Methodist social gospel tradition survived even if it never again thrived as between 1900 and 1930. The Upper Sand Mountain Parish, a cooperative social ministry of 11 small rural Methodist churches on a farming plateau in northeast Alabama, represented that tradition in the 1980s and 1990s. The United Methodist Church also began Greater Birmingham Ministries, one of the state's premier biracial social ministries, which took a leading role in tax and constitutional reform.

Chapter 4

The text of this chapter originally appeared in a slightly different form as "Organized Labor, Reform, and Alabama Politics, 1920," *The Alabama Review*, July 1970, 163–80.

1. Gerald D. Nash, "Research Opportunities in the Economic History of the South After 1880," *The Journal of Southern History*, XXXII (August 1966), 308–24. Prof. Nash calls for additional study of organized labor (319). C. Vann Woodward also has pointed to the serious omission of research in the area of southern organized labor; see *Origins of the New South* (Baton Rouge: Louisiana State University Press, 1951), 228–31.

2. Besides periodical literature, two significant works have examined organized labor in Alabama: Holmn Head, "The Development of the Labor Movement in Alabama Prior to 1900" (Master's thesis, University of Alabama, 1955); and Robert D. Ward and

William W. Rogers, *Labor Revolt in Alabama: The Great Strike of 1894* (Tuscaloosa: University of Alabama Press, 1965).

3. For a very brief summary of Alabama union activity, see US Department of Labor, *Labor in the South*. Bulletin No. 898 (Washington: Government Printing Office, 1947). Hereinafter cited as *Labor in the South*.

4. See Alabama Federation of Labor Resolutions, in Oscar W. Underwood Papers, Department of Archives and History, Montgomery, Alabama. Hereinafter cited as Underwood Papers.

5. Editorial, *The Birmingham News*, November 26, 1919.

6. For an example of conservative Alabama reaction to this national upheaval, see Leander Poole to Oscar W. Underwood, Sept. 29, 1919, Underwood Papers.

7. For a thorough treatment of Underwood's career, see Evans C. Johnson, "Oscar W. Underwood: The Development of a National Statesman" (PhD dissertation, University of North Carolina, 1953).

8. Oscar W. Underwood to Leander Poole, Oct. 1, 1919 and Poole to Underwood, Sept. 29, 1919, Underwood Papers.

9. *The Birmingham News*, Feb. 21, 1920.

10. *Labor Advocate*, Feb. 7, 1920; for a sampling of rank and file sentiment, see Letters to the Editor from R. A. Statham and J. L. Busby in Jan. 10, 1920, issue of *Labor Advocate*.

11. Walker County *Mountain Eagle*, Feb. 18, 1920.

12. *The Birmingham News*, Feb. 16, 1920.

13. R. S. Wetmore to Oscar W. Underwood, July 21, 1919, Underwood Papers.

14. *Labor Advocate*, March 20, 1920.

15. *Ibid.*

16. A copy of the circular is in the Underwood Papers.

17. One advertisement for an anti-Underwood speech at the Mobile Labor Temple asked, "Are Our Alabama Working Men 'Damned Slackers and Traitors' as Mr. Underwood said?" See flier in Underwood Papers.

18. P. G. DeWitt, *The Birmingham News*, Feb. 13, 1920.

19. *Ibid.*, Feb. 16 and Apr. 22, 1920.

20. For an excellent summary of the connection between the social gospel and labor in the North, see Charles Howard Hopkins, *The Rise of the Social Gospel in American Protestantism, 1865–1915* (New Haven, CT: Yale University Press, 1940).

21. To place this campaign in the broader context of Alabama progressivism and religion, see Allen W. Jones, "Political Reforms of the Progressive Era," *The Alabama Review*, XXI (July 1968), 173–94; and Sheldon Hackney, *Populism to Progressivism in Alabama* (Princeton, NJ: Princeton University Press, 1969), especially chapters 11–14.

22. For an excellent study of the 1920 campaign, see Evans C. Johnson, "Oscar W. Underwood and the Senatorial Campaign of 1920," *The Alabama Review*, XXI (January 1968), 3–20. Johnson focuses on prohibition as the central issue (14) along with the farm vote; he pays little interest to labor, however.

23. Text of Musgrove's Birmingham Speech of Mar. 25, 1920, in Underwood Papers.

24. *Birmingham News*, Feb. 18 and May 4, 1920.

25. Walter (last name missing) to Oscar W. Underwood, Feb. 7, 1920, in Underwood Papers. Emphasis by the author.

26. For a brief study of Musgrove which sheds light on the blending of labor and religious forces see Winfred G. Sandin, "Lycurgus Breckenridge Musgrove," *The Alabama Review*, XX (July 1967), 205–15.

27. To see this strategy emerge, note *The Birmingham News* editorials, March 26 and 30, 1920.

28. *The Birmingham News*, March 19 and 25, 1920.

29. J. B. Long to Oscar W. Underwood, Apr. 20, 1920, Underwood Papers. One of the circulars can be seen in the Underwood Papers, Apr. 22, 1920.

30. Lloyd M. Hooper to Oscar W. Underwood, Apr. 25, 1920, Underwood Papers.

31. L. B. Musgrove, *The Birmingham News*, Apr. 24, 1920.

32. James B. Ellis to Oscar W. Underwood, May 15, 1920, Underwood Papers.

33. C. M. Dinsmore, *The Birmingham News*, April 1, 1920.

34. J. D. Wade, *Labor Advocate* (Birmingham, AL), Mar. 6, 1920.

35. J. W. Knight to Oscar W. Underwood, May 15, 1920, Underwood Papers.

36. For instance, see *The Birmingham News*, March 14, 1920.

37. For these confidential reports see: Rice Gaither to Frederick L. Thompson, April 17, 1920; H. T. Caffey to Oscar W. Underwood, March 16, 1920; George A. Blinn Jr. to Oscar W. Underwood, Mar. 23, 1920; J. B. Leeth to Oscar W. Underwood, April 10, 1920; John T. Cochrane to Floyd M. Hooper, May 6, 1920; J.B. Locke to Oscar W. Underwood, February 16, 1920; all in Underwood Papers.

38. J. A. Estes to Oscar W. Underwood, Apr. 26, 1920, Underwood Papers.

39. Lloyd M. Hooper to Oscar W. Underwood, Mar. 25, 1920, Underwood Papers.

40. *The Birmingham News*, Feb. 13, 1920.

41. For instance, see reports of his speeches at Huntsville and Gadsden, *The Birmingham News*, Apr. 6 and 8, 1920.

42. Manuscript of a Speech of W. A. Gunter, February 1920, Underwood Papers.

43. R. I. Ingalls to Oscar W. Underwood, May 24, 1919, Underwood Papers.

44. For these sentiments in more detail, see: Robert E. Spragins to Oscar W. Underwood, May 20, 1920; N. D. Godbold to Oscar W. Underwood, Feb. 27, 1920; Richard M. Hobbie to Oscar W. Underwood, Feb. 5, 1920; W.D. Null to Oscar W. Underwood, May 5, 1920; all in Underwood Papers.

45. Fred Fite to Oscar W. Underwood, Feb. 27, 1920, Underwood Papers.

46. *Sylacauga Advance*, quoted in *The Birmingham News*, May 2, 1920.

47. *The Birmingham News*, Mar. 28, 1920.

48. W. T. Sanders to Oscar W. Underwood, June 14, 1920, Underwood Papers.

49. Oscar W. Underwood to G. A. Ward, Mar. 11, 1920, Underwood Papers.

50. One Birmingham paper reported unparalleled interest, registration and turnout in Jefferson. See the *Birmingham Age-Herald*, May 12, 1920.

51. US Bureau of the Census, *Fourteenth Census of the United States: 1920. Manufactures* (Washington: Government Printing Office, 1923), 21–25.

52. W. A. Vantreese to Oscar W. Underwood, May 16, 1920: J. K. Knight to Oscar W. Underwood, May 15, 1920; Elizabeth Simpson to Oscar W. Underwood, May 17, 1920; all in Underwood Papers.

53. Tennis Tidwell to Oscar W. Underwood, May 15, 1920, Underwood Papers.

54. Oscar W. Underwood to Thomas F. Ryan, May 14, 1920, Underwood Papers. Emphasis by the author.

55. Forney Johnston to Oscar W. Underwood, May 13, 1920, Underwood Papers.

56. For labor endorsed candidates, see *Labor Advocate*, April 10, 1920.

57. *Labor in the South*, 159.

Chapter 5

The text of this chapter originally appeared in a slightly different form as "Religion in the Urban South: The Divided Religious Mind of Birmingham, 1900–1930," *The Alabama Review*, April 1977, 108–34.

1. To complete the irony, the Temple to Vesta built by Birmingham Mayor George Ward later was converted into a Baptist church.

2. See John R. Hornady, *The Book of Birmingham* (New York: Dodd, Mead, and Co., 1921), 4–7; George M. Cruikshank, *A History of Birmingham and its Environs* (2 vols., New York: Lewis Publishing Co., 1920), I, 270–86. A fascinating perspective is offered by Blaine Brownell, who suggests not only that pastors were important in instilling a sense of civic responsibility and unity of purpose in their congregations, but also that "success" in the ministry meant promotion from a rural church to an urban one; thus, coming to terms with urban problems as well as not alienating one's own congregation were both measures of a pastor's "success" and hence contributed to his status. See Blaine A. Brownell, "The Urban Mind in the South: The Growth of Urban Consciousness in Southern Cities, 1920–1927" (PhD dissertation, University of North Carolina, 1969), 181, 202–16.

3. US Bureau of the Census, *Religious Bodies*, 1916, Part I (Washington, 1919), 123. In 1920 the city population counted over six thousand immigrants and more than ten thousand citizens with at least one foreign-born parent. Most of these came from Italy or Russia. The city was 40 percent black, and the religious diversity intensified. In that same year the following churches were represented: White: Adventist (1), Southern Baptist (33), Christian (5), Christian Science (1), Church of God (1), Congregational (1) Evangelical (1), Greek Orthodox (1), Lutheran (2), Methodist Episcopal Church, South (37), Methodist Protestant (1) Presbyterian (25), Protestant Episcopal (6), Roman Catholic (13), Unitarian (1). Black: Adventist (1) National Baptist (64), Church of God (4), Congregational (1), Episcopal (1), Methodist (37), Presbyterian (Black) (2), Sanctified (2); as well as 3 Jewish temples; *Birmingham City Directory*, 1919–1920, XXXIV (Birmingham, 1920), 59–62.

4. See Charles Marion Prestwood Jr., "Social Ideas of Methodist Ministers in Alabama Since Unification" (PhD dissertation, Boston University, 1960).

5. For an excellent thesis exploring Dickinson's theology, see John H. Burrows, "The Great Disturber: The Social Philosophy and Theology of Alfred James Dickinson" (MA thesis, Samford University, 1970).

6. For examples of the liberal/fundamentalist exchange, see *The Alabama Baptist*, August 15, November 21, 1906, February 5, 19, 26, April 2, 23, 1913, September 22, 1915.

7. Frank Willis Barnett, "Editorial," *The Alabama Baptist* (Birmingham), August 16, 1916.

8. Rev. L. L. Gwaltney, *The Alabama Baptist* (Birmingham), January 3, 1917, November 6, 27, December 11, 1918.

9. L. L. Gwaltney, "This I Leave With You," unpublished manuscript in ABHS.

10. Henry M. Edmonds, *A Parson's Notebook* (Birmingham: Elizabeth Agee's Bookshelf, 1961), 72–86.

11. *Ibid.*, 73.

12. For extensive discussion of the theological clash that split South Highland, see *ibid.*, 72–96; and *The Independent Presbyterian Church of Birmingham, Alabama* (Birmingham: Independent Presbyterian Church, 1950), 8–10.

13. Fanna K. Bee and Lee N. Allen, *Sesquicentennial History: Ruhama Baptist Church, 1819–1969* (Birmingham: Ruhama Baptist Church, 1969), 139.

14. *The Birmingham News*, March 4–7, 1920.

15. *The Alabama Baptist*, February 5, 12, 1920.

16. A. J. Dickinson, *The Alabama Baptist* (Birmingham), December 11, 1919, January 1, 1920.

17. See J. A. Bryan, *A Collection of My Sermons* (Birmingham, n.d.).

18. Quoted in Hunter B. Blakely, *Religion in Shoes* (Birmingham: Birmingham Publishing Company, 1967), 43.

19. For a summary see Dewey Robinson, "The Life of Dr. J. A. Bryan," unpublished manuscript, 1934, in ABHS.

20. Blakely, *Religion in Shoes*, 43.

21. For general surveys see Wayne Flynt, "Dissent in Zion: Alabama Baptists and Social Issues, 1900–1914," *Journal of Southern History*, XXXV (November 1969), 523–42, and Robert F. Crider, "The Social Philosophy of L. L. Gwaltney, 1919–1950" (MA thesis, Samford University, 1969).

22. Martha C. Mitchell Bigelow, "Birmingham: Biography of a City of the New South" (PhD dissertation, University of Chicago, 1946), 109–11; *The Alabama Baptist*, November 6, 1907.

23. Nationally famous evangelist Sam Jones, who held a great revival meeting in the city in the 1890s, called Birmingham a "hell-hole."

24. Editorial, *The Alabama Baptist*, October 12, 1904.

25. *Ibid.*, February 27, 1907, June 19, 1912, June 18, 1913.

26. Bigelow, "Birmingham," 212–13.

27. Hornady, *Book of Birmingham*, 6–7.

28. Frank Willis Barnett, "Editorial," *The Alabama Baptist* (Birmingham), June 18, 1913. For a general survey of Birmingham Baptist attitudes toward social issues, see Flynt, "Dissent in Zion," 523–42.

29. *Ibid*, February 13, 1907.

30. *Ibid*, June 25, 1913.

31. L. L. Gwaltney, *Forty of the Twentieth or the First Forty Years of the Twentieth Century* (Birmingham: Birmingham Printing Company, 1940), 126–27.

32. James F. Sulzby Jr., *Annals of the Southside Baptist Church, Birmingham, Alabama* (Birmingham: Birmingham Printing Company, 1947), 88.

33. Bigelow, "Birmingham," 153.

34. *The Alabama Christian Advocate*, March 6, 1901, November 26, 1903.

35. *Ibid.*, January 21, July 22, 1909, June 9, 1910, February 8, 1912.

36. *Ibid.*, November 7, December 12, 1912, March 6, September 25, 1913.

37. Mittie Owen McDavid, *Church of the Advent: Its History and Traditions* (Birmingham: Press of Birmingham Publishing Company, 1943), 44–65.

38. For excellent discussions of Independent Presbyterian's far-flung social ministries see *The Independent Presbyterian Church of Birmingham, Alabama*, 14–40, and Edmonds, *A Parson's Notebook*, 96–99.

39. Edmonds, *A Parson's Notebook*, 96–97.

40. Bigelow, "Birmingham," 149.

41. *Ibid.*

42. *The Alabama Christian Advocate*, April 25, 1912.

43. Sulzby, *Annals of the Southside Baptist Church*, 89.

44. US Bureau of the Census, *Religious Bodies*, 1916, Part I, 123.

45. Frank Willis Barnett, "Editorial," *The Alabama Baptist* (Birmingham), November 6, 1912.

46. Charles P. Sweeney, "Bigotry in the South," *The Nation*, CXI (November 24, 1920), 586.

47. For the resolution, see *The Alabama Baptist*, March 29, 1916.

48. Charles P. Sweeney, "Bigotry Turns to Murder," *The Nation*, CXIII (August 31, 1921), 232.

49. Frank Willis Barnett, "Editorial," *The Alabama Baptist* (Birmingham), April 24, 1919.

50. These characteristics are noted as formative patterns in the Ku Klux Klan dominance of Birmingham. For an excellent study see William Robert Snell, "The Ku Klux Klan in Jefferson County, Alabama, 1916–1930" (MA thesis, Samford University, 1967).

51. Sweeney, "Bigotry in the South," 586.

52. Sweeney, "Bigotry Turns to Murder," 232; also see Snell, "Ku Klux Klan in Jefferson County," 25.

53. *The Alabama Baptist*, December 11, 1919, January 1, 1920; *The Alabama Christian Advocate*, April 22, 29, May 6, 1920. For a fuller discussion of this race see Wayne Flynt, "Organized Labor, Reform, and Alabama Politics, 1920," *Alabama Review*, XXIII (July 1970), 163–80.

54. Editorial, *The Alabama Christian Advocate* (Birmingham), January-April 1914.

55. J. B. Long to Oscar W. Underwood, April 20, 1920, Underwood Papers.

56. Forney Johnston to Oscar W. Underwood, May 13, 1920, Underwood Papers.

57. Snell, "Ku Klux Klan in Jefferson County," 161.

58. *Ibid.*

59. Sweeney, "Bigotry Turns to Murder," 232. *The New York World* blamed the religious press for its failure to take a stand against the Klan; quoted in Snell, "Ku Klux Klan in Jefferson County," 161.

60. Snell, "Ku Klux Klan in Jefferson County," 92 ff; also see *Birmingham Age-Herald*, July 11, 18, 19, 24, 1927.

61. Edmonds, *A Parson's Notebook*, 98.

62. *Ibid.*, 197, 215.

63. Snell, "Ku Klux Klan in Jefferson County," 200.

64. Gwaltney, *Forty of the Twentieth*, 140.

65. Gwaltney, "This I Leave With You," 40, 65.

66. US Bureau of the Census, *Religious Bodies*, 1936, Part I (Washington, 1941), 71–72.

67. For fuller treatment of this subject see Wayne Flynt, "The Negro and Alabama Baptists During the Progressive Era," *Journal of the Alabama Academy of Science*, XXXIX (April 1968), 163–67.

68. Edmonds, *A Parson's Notebook*, 283.

69. Bigelow, "Birmingham," 155.

70. *Ibid.*, 218.

71. The political function of the black pastor was frequently criticized by white ministers; for example, see *ibid.*, 215–16, and *The Alabama Baptist*, October 22, 1902.

72. *The Alabama Baptist* (Birmingham), April 21, 1909.

73. *The Birmingham News*, March 7, 1920.

Chapter 6

The text of this chapter originally appeared in a slightly different form as "Feeding the Hungry and Ministering to the Broken Hearted: The Presbyterian Church in the United States and the Social Gospel, 1900–1920," *Religion in the South* (Jackson: University Press of Mississippi, 1985), 83–137.

1. Walter L. Lingle, *The Bible and Social Problems* (New York: Fleming H. Revell Co., 1929), 7.

2. *Minutes of the General Assembly of the Presbyterian Church in the United States, 1911* (Richmond, Virginia: Presbyterian Committee of Publication, 1911), 27. Hereafter cited as *Minutes, PCUS. Ibid., 1910*, 60: A. L. Phillips to W. L. Lingle, May 24, 1911, Walter L. Lingle Papers, Historical Foundation of the Presbyterian and Reformed Churches, Montreat, North Carolina. Hereafter cited as Lingle Papers.

3. For a splendid article on the nuances of the Social Gospel, see Winthrop S. Hudson, "Walter Rauschenbusch and the New Evangelism," *Religion in Life*, 30 (Summer 1961), 412–430.

4. *Ibid.*; for example, see Shailer Mathews, *The Social Teaching of Jesus: An Essay in Christian Sociology* (New York: Hodder and Stoughton, 1897).

5. See Walter Rauschenbusch, *Christianity and The Social Crisis* (New York: The Macmillan Company, 1907).

6. In an excellent book titled *The Social Gospel in the South: The Woman's Home Mission Movement in the Methodist Episcopal Church South, 1886–1939* (Baton Rouge: Louisiana State University Press, 1982), John P. McDowell briefly surveys the literature. Ronald C. White Jr., and C. Howard Hopkins recognize the presence of such a southern dimension in their book, *The Social Gospel: Religion and Reform in Changing America* (Philadelphia: Temple University Press, 1976), which contains a useful chapter, "Voices from the New South." Dewey W. Grantham's excellent study, *Southern Progressivism: The Reconciliation of Progress and Tradition* (Knoxville: University of Tennessee Press,

1983), discusses the Social Gospel in a chapter entitled "Social Justice." There and in his final chapter, "The Reconciliation of Progress and Tradition," he properly limits the extent of commitment to change while arguing that progressives were reformers seeking social justice. Southern churchmen played a major role in his chronicle of reform.

7. John B. Boles and Samuel S. Hill presently argue that though the Social Gospel existed in the South it was of little consequence and existed largely "on the very fringes of southern Protestantism" (to use Boles's term), or that the Social Gospel "has been present in only minor and occasional forms, and never dominant" (to use Hill's term). Ronald C. White Jr., although willing to concede the existence of the Social Gospel in the South in his 1976 work, was not so sure in 1984. Reviewing McDowell's book, he suggests that McDowell perhaps confused social concern with the Social Gospel and that no linkage is made between ideas and actions. See John B. Boles, "Religion in the South: Recent Historiography," paper presented at the Southern Historical Association, November 6, 1982; Samuel S. Hill's review of McDowell's book, *The Journal of Southern History*, 50 (February 1984), 139–40; and Ronald C. White's review of McDowell's book in *Church History*, 53 (June 1984), 268.

8. Ruth Hutchinson Crocker, "Sympathy and Science: The Settlement Movement in Gary and Indianapolis to 1930" (PhD dissertation, Purdue University, 1982), especially 482–483. The extent of religious settlement house work in Gary and Indianapolis appears to be roughly comparable to that in Birmingham and Atlanta, although in 1911 only 45 of the nation's 413 settlement houses were in the South. But this percentage does not deviate substantially from the South's proportion of major cities.

9. See Hugh C. Bailey, *Liberalism in the New South: Southern Social Reformers and the Progressive Movement* (Coral Gables: University of Miami Press, 1969); Morton Sosna, *In Search of the Silent South: Southern Liberals and the Race Issue* (New York: Columbia University Press, 1977); Anthony P. Dunbar, *Against The Grain: Southern Radicals and Prophets, 1929–1959* (Charlottesville: University of Virginia Press, 1981).

10. See T. Scott Miyakawa, *Protestants and Pioneers: Individualism and Conformity on the American Frontier* (Chicago: University of Chicago Press, 1964), 4.

11. See Ernest T. Thompson, *Presbyterians in the South, Vol. II, 1861–1890* (Richmond: John Knox Press, 1965), 413; *ibid., Vol. III 1890–1972* (Richmond: John Knox Press, 1973), especially 265–69.

12. S. R. Church to W. L. Lingle, March 13, 1914; S. W. Carson to W. L. Lingle, June 5, 1913; Lingle Papers.

13. R. E. Magill to W. L. Lingle, April 14, 1911, Lingle Papers; *Minutes of the PCUS, 1912*, 42; *ibid., 1920*, 63–64.

14. E. T. Thompson discusses the doctrine of the Spirituality of the Church thoroughly in his three volumes on the PCUS.

15. *Minutes of the PCUS, 1907*, 57; *ibid., 1910*, 44–45; *ibid., 1915*, 29.

16. W. L. Lingle to Dr. John T. Thomas, December 30, 1916, Lingle Papers.

17. D. P. McGeachy to W. L. Lingle, undated but probably in 1915 or 1916, Lingle Papers.

18. Quoted in Bailey, *Liberalism in the New South*, 179–80.

19. *Ibid.*, scattered throughout, and Grantham, *Southern Progressivism*, 191–99.

20. *Minutes of the PCUS, 1908*, 19.

21. James R. Howerton, *The Church and Social Reforms* (New York: Fleming H. Revell, 1913), quotation on 83.

22. *Ibid.*, see especially his final chapter.

23. Thompson, *Presbyterians in the South, Vol. III*, 101–5; David E. Whisnant, *All That Is Native and Fine* (Chapel Hill: University of North Carolina Press, 1983), 37–39; *Minutes of the PCUS, 1914*, 43; *ibid., 1916*, 12.

24. Thompson, *Presbyterians in the South, Vol. III*, 105; *Minutes of the PCUS, 1914*, 104.

25. For such views, see Elizabeth R. Hooker, *Religion in the Highlands: Native Churches and Missionary Enterprises in the Southern Appalachian Area* (New York: The Home Missions Council, 1933).

26. *Minutes of the PCUS, 1916*, 31; *ibid., 1914*, 43; *ibid., 1917*, 105–6; "Minutes of the Home Mission Board," Research Center of the Historical Foundation, PCUS, Montreat, North Carolina, February 15, 1910; *ibid.*, 1910–1913. Hereafter cited as "Minutes of the Home Mission Board."

27. See John C. Campbell, *The Future of the Churches and Independent Schools in our Southern Highlands* (New York: Russell Sage Foundation, 1917); Mrs. Olive D. Campbell, *Southern Highland Schools Maintained by Denominational and Independent Agencies* (New York: Russell Sage Foundation, 1921); O. D. Campbell, *The Life and Work of John Charles Campbell* (Madison: University of Wisconsin Press, 1968).

28. "Minutes of the Home Mission Board, 1911," 60–61, 76–77, 106, 127, 153, 180, 185; *Minutes of the PCUS, 1912*, 44; *ibid., 1913*, 58.

29. W. E. Hudson to W. L. Lingle, January 14, 1915, Lingle Papers; G. E. Drushal to Edward O. Guerrant, August 17, 1915, Edward O. Guerrant Papers, Research Center of the Historical Foundation, PCUS, Montreat, North Carolina.

30. "Appalachia" file, Henry H. Sweets Papers, Historical Foundation of the Presbyterian and Reformed Churches, Montreat, North Carolina; William E. Hudson, '*The Least of These': The Beneficenses of the Synod of Virginia* (Richmond: Presbyterian Committee of Publications, 1926), 113–14; William E. Hudson to W. L. Lingle, February 28, 1914; E. E. Lane to W. L. Lingle, January 30, 1913; R. E. Magill to W. L. Lingle, January 12, 1909; all in Lingle Papers; Rev. Edward Marshall Craig, *Highways and Byways of Appalachia: A Study of the Work of the Synod of Appalachia of the Presbyterian Church in the United States* (Kingsport, Tennessee: n.p., 1927), 67.

31. Mary N. Sloop to W. L. Lingle, ? 23, 1918, Lingle Papers; *Minutes of the PCUS 1917*, 107; Ora C. Huston to W. L. Lingle, July 21, 1919, and H. A. Love to W. L. Lingle, February 11, 1918; Lingle Papers.

32. Edward O. Guerrant, *The Galax Gatherers: The Gospel Among the Highlanders* (Richmond: Onward Press, 1910), especially 59.

33. *Ibid.*, 73–76, 182–83.

34. Ora C. Huston to W. L. Lingle, September 10, 1919, Lingle Papers.

35. William E. Hudson, '*The Least of These*,' 60–65; "Students Who have Attended the Assembly's Training School," 1916–17, ms. in Lingle Papers; Helen Mathews to W. L. Lingle, May 11 and 14, 1920, Lingle Papers.

36. Mary M. Sloop to W. L. Lingle, ? 23, 1918, and February 12, 1918; Lingle Papers.

37. Rev. R. P. Smith, *Experiences in Mountain Mission Work* (Richmond: Presbyterian Committee on Publications, 1931), 46, 61.

38. For examples of the rural expression of Progressivism and the Social Gospel, see William L. Bowers, *The Country Life Movement in America, 1900–1920* (Port Washington, NY: Kennikat Press, 1974).

39. James Williams Marshall, *The Presbyterian Church in Alabama*, edited by Robert Strong (Montgomery: The Presbyterian Historical Society of Alabama, 1977), 288; Stanford Binkley to W. L. Lingle, November 28, 1913; W. L. Downing to W. L. Lingle, February 18, 1918; Lingle Papers.

40. R. E. Magill to W. L. Lingle, January 6, 1908, Lingle Papers; "Minutes of Home Mission Board," November 1910, 41.

41. Willis Thompson to W. L. Lingle, October 13, 1914; A. L. Phillips to W. L. Lingle, February 20, 1915; Lingle Papers.

42. Willis Thompson to W. L. Lingle, October 13, 1914, Lingle Papers.

43. For Lingle's reading of Wilson, see W. L. Lingle to Dr. A. P. Bourland, March 20, 1915, Lingle Papers. For a sample of Wilson's ideas on the rural church, see Warren H. Wilson, *The Church of the Open Country* (New York: Missionary Education Movement of the United States and Canada, 1911), and Wilson, *The Church at the Center* (New York: Missionary Education Movement of the United States and Canada, 1914).

44. Warren H. Wilson to Walter L. Lingle, October 20, 1914; A. P. Bourland to W. L. Lingle, April 2, 1915; copy of "The Southern Conference for Education and Industry, Chattanooga, April 27th-30th, 1915"; all in Lingle Papers.

45. Copy of brochure, "Montreat N.C. Program, 1916," in Lingle Papers; Rev. W. H. Mills, "The Church's Duty to the Country Church," *Union Seminary Review* (W. L. Lingle, editor), 31 (October 1919–July 1920), 39–45.

46. F. Wade Vaughan to W. L. Lingle, March 31, 1908; Gracy H. Hampton to W. L. Lingle, October 29, 1911; Lingle Papers.

47. *Minutes of the PCUS, 1911*, 33–34.

48. "Minutes of the Home Mission Board," May 12, 1908, 122; *ibid.*, December 15, 1908, 136–37; *ibid.*, March 9, 1909, 143; *ibid.*, May 11, 1909, 149; *ibid.*, October 12, 1909, 160–61; *ibid.*, October 11, 1910, 38.

49. For a thorough discussion of racial views within the PCUS, see Joel Alvis, "The Bounds of Their Habitations: The Southern Presbyterian Church, Racial Ideology and Civil Rights, 1945–1972" (Ph.D. dissertation, Auburn University, forthcoming).

50. Rev. H. H. Proctor to Walter Lingle, October 4, 1910; Marjorie Gray to Walter Lingle, undated but probably 1910; Lingle Papers; and Alvis, "The Bounds of Their Habitations."

51. Nolan R. Best to W. L. Lingle, July 14, 1909, Lingle Papers; Thompson, *Presbyterians in the South, Vol. III: 1890–1972*, 265.

52. Quoted in Lingle, *The Bible and Social Problems*, 12–13.

53. *Ibid.*, 29–32; W. L. Lingle to George H. Doran Co., November 28, 1913; William T. Hanzsche to W. L. Lingle, February 27, 1918, and Lingle to Hanzsche, March 2, 1918; Lingle Papers.

54. J. L. Hughes to W. L. Lingle, March 20, 1917; Lingle to Hughes, April 25, 1917; for

a similar letter referring a reader to Social Gospel materials, see Lingle to Stanley White, April 20, 1918; Lingle Papers.

55. List of "Books on Home Missions," in Lingle Papers; W. L. Lingle to J. S. Lyons, June 23, 1913; W. L. Lingle to R. M. Russell, June 25, 1913; Lingle Papers.

56. "The Bible and Money," "Wealth and Social Problems," "Poverty and Social Problems," sermon manuscripts in Lingle Papers.

57. "The Family and Social Problems," "Christianity and the Race Problem," sermon and discussion outline in Lingle Papers.

58. J. J. Hill to W. L. Lingle, September 15, 1916; E. D. Brown to W. L. Lingle, April 20, 1916; Lingle Papers.

59. A. W. McAlister to W. L. Lingle, December 14 and 20, 1915; Margaret E. Burton to W. L. Lingle, March 11 and May 21, 1918, Lingle to Burton, March 19, 1918; W. L. Lingle to R. A. Swink, May 17, 1920; Lingle Papers.

60. John T. Farris to W. L. Lingle, June 29, 1916, Lingle Papers.

61. Lingle, *The Bible and Social Problems*, 176–77, 191.

62. Thompson, *Presbyterians in the South, Vol. III: 1890–1972*, 265–66.

63. *Ibid.*, 268–69.

64. "Minutes of the Home Mission Board," April 5, 1910, April 4, 1911; *Minutes of the PCUS, 1911*, 84–85; *ibid., 1914*, 107–8; *Presbyterian Standard*, February 13, 1918.

65. D. W. Brannen to W. L. Lingle, January 3, 1910, Lingle Papers.

66. *Minutes of the PCUS, 1912*, 62–63; *ibid.*, 1915, 80d.

67. *Ibid., 1911*, 30; *ibid*, 1912, 64; *ibid., 1913*, 70n-70p; *ibid., 1914*, 26–28.

68. Programs for Montreat Conferences for 1916 and 1917, copies in Lingle Papers.

69. Head to Lingle, January 16, 1913; W. Bruce Buford to W. L. Lingle, April 28, 1914; A. D. Wauchope to W. L. Lingle, March 4, 1915; James H. Henderlite to W. L. Lingle, February 23, 1915 and January 29, 1917; W. L. Lingle to Rev. A. B. Bass, January 29, 1918; Lingle Papers.

70. *Presbyterian Standard*, August 14, 1912.

71. *Ibid.*, August 14, 1912, January 30, February 27, April 17, October 9, 1918, March 19, 1919.

72. W. H. Lingle to W. L. Lingle, September 8 and June 13, 1917; Margaret Lingle to W. L. Lingle, April 29, 1917; Lingle Papers.

73. Lingle, *The Bible and Social Problems*, 162.

74. *Minutes of the PCUS, 1919*, 87–88.

75. See Lois A. Boyd and R. Douglas Brackenridge, "The Evolving Role of the Southern Presbyterian Woman: Blessed Inconsistencies," *Presbyterian Women in America: Two Centuries of a Quest for Status* (Westport, CT: Greenwood Press, 1983), 207–8; *Minutes of the PCUS, 1897*, 16.

76. Quoted in Thompson, *Presbyterians in the South, Vol. III: 1890–1972*, 387–388.

77. *Minutes of the PCUS, 1911*, 67.

78. L. Sorrows to W. L. Lingle, undated but in 1915, Lingle Papers.

79. Thompson, *Presbyterians in the South, Vol. III: 1890–1972*, 388–89; *Presbyterian Standard*, May 15, 1912.

80. *Presbyterian Standard*, May 8 and May 15, 1912; "Minutes of Home Mission Board," December 12, 1911, 115, and January 9, 1912, 119; *Minutes of the PCUS, 1912*, 60.

81. See Hallie Paxson Winsborough, *The Woman's Auxiliary Presbyterian Church U.S.* (Richmond: Presbyterian Committee on Publication, 1927); *Minutges of the PCUS, 1914*, 38, 62; *ibid., 1913*, 58, 70d; (Mrs.) W. C. Winsborough to W. L. Lingle, March 23, 1918, Lingle Papers.

82. *Minutes of the PCUS, 1913*, 33; *Ibid., 1919*, 31–32; *ibid., 1920*, 20; S. L. Morris to W. L. Lingle, April 30, 1918; Neal L. Anderson to W. L. Lingle, November 19, 1919; Lingle Papers.

83. W. C. S. to Rev. T. C. Johnson, May 5, 1914, Lingle Papers; *Minutes of the PCUS, 1916*, 48–49, 76–77, 80a-80b; *ibid, 1917*, 68–69.

84. *Presbyterian Standard*, May 29, September 18, and October 16, 1918, February 4 and March 3, 1920.

85. Thomas W. Lingle to W. L. Lingle, February 19, 1915; Clara L. Lingle to W. L. Lingle, October 3, 1917; Montreat Program Schedule, 1918; all in Lingle Papers.

86. W. L. Lingle to T. W. Lingle, March 11, 1916; T. W. Lingle to W. L. Lingle, March 14, 1916; Lingle Papers.

87. Eugene Alexander to W. L. Lingle, May 2, 1918; W. L. Lingle to Charles R. Hemphill, November 24, 1915; Hemphill to Lingle, December 6, 1915; Boyd and Brackenridge, "The Evolving Role of the Southern Presbyterian Woman," 212; and undated sermons in Lingle Papers, "The Family and Social Problems" and "Poverty and Social Problems."

88. Dunbar H. Ogden to W. L. Lingle, January 2, 1913, January 15, 1914, March 30, 1915, October 14, 1915, October 30, 1913; all in Lingle Papers.

89. Theron H. Rice to W. L. Lingle, April 15, 1902; Rev. C. I. Stacy to W. L. Lingle, November 16, 1908; Stacy to Lingle, November 10, 1908; R. P. Smith to W. L. Lingle, April 22, 1909; John Eagen to W. L. Lingle, April 26, 1909; Eagan to Lingle, September 23, 1911; Lingle to Eagan, January 31, 1912; Eagan to Lingle, April 10, 1913; Eagan to Lingle, December 17, 1910; all in Lingle Papers.

90. John J. Eagan to W. L. Lingle, August 10, 1912, Lingle Papers.

91. Harry G. Lefever, "The Involvement of the Men and Religion Forward Movement in the Cause of Labor Justice, Atlanta, Georgia, 1912–1916," *Labor History*, (Fall 1973), 521–35; John J. Eagan to W. L. Lingle, April 4, 1916, Lingle Papers.

92. For an excellent though obviously subjective summary of Eagan's career, see Robert E. Speer, *John J. Eagan: A Memoir of an Adventurer For the Kingdom of God on Earth* (Birmingham: American Cast Iron Pipe Company, 1939).

93. Witherspoon Dodge to W. L. Lingle, December 15, 1913, October 27, 1916, February 28, 1917; Lingle Papers.

94. *Presbyterian Standard*, September 18, 1912.

95. *Ibid.*, September 4, 1918; R. C. Reed to W. L. Lingle, March 21, 1913, September 15, 1916; Lingle to Reed, September 12, 1916; Lingle Papers.

96. *Presbyterian Standard*, August 28, December 4, 1918, June 11, August 20 and 27, November 12, 1919.

97. Marshall, *The Presbyterian Church in Alabama*, 340.

98. For an excellent discussion of the PCUS and the Federal Council of Churches, see Thompson, *Presbyterians in the South, Vol. III: 1890–1972*, 248–301.

99. *Presbyterian Standard*, May 29, 1912; *Minutes of the PCUS, 1913*, 67; *ibid., 1914*, 48; *ibid., 1915*, 39–40; *ibid., 1919*, 55.

100. Charles S. MacFarland to W. L. Lingle, March 26 and September 15, 1913; A. M. Scales to W. L. Lingle, March 20, 1913; Lingle Papers; *Presbyterian Standard*, April 3, 1912.

101. T. A. Painter to W. L. Lingle, March 29, 1920, Lingle Papers; *Presbyterian Standard*, March 17 and May 19, 1920.

102. W. L. Lingle to Rev. Jere A. Moore, April 4, 1911, Lingle Papers; *Presbyterian Standard*, February 6 and April 24, 1918.

103. For progress of the debate, see the *Presbyterian Standard*, February 26, March 12 and 26, August 13 and 20, September 24, October 15 and 29, November 12, December 3, 17, 19, 1919; W. L. Lingle to Rev. A. M. Fraser, September 8, 1919, Lingle Papers; *Minutes of the PCUS, 1919*, 47–48.

104. W. M. McPheeters to W. L. Lingle, May 19, 1920, Lingle Papers; *Presbyterian Standard*, November 12, 1919.

105. *Presbyterian Standard*, May 26, 1920; *Minutes of the PCUS, 1920*, 11; W. L. Lingle to Miss Mamie Bays, June 1, 1920; John Eagan to W. L. Lingle, June 4, 1920; W. L. Lingle to J. S. Lyons, June 1, 1920; Lingle Papers.

106. See Lingle's sermon, "The Bible and Poverty," and his discussion topics, "Christianity and the Depression," "Christianity and War," "The Church and Social Security"; Witherspoon Dodge, "Free Enterprise," unpublished manuscript in Stetson Kennedy Papers, Southern Labor Archives, Georgia State University, Atlanta, Georgia.

Chapter 7

The text of this chapter originally appeared in a slightly different form as "Southern Baptists and Appalachia: A Case Study of Modernization and Community," Carlyle Marney Lecture, Carson-Newman College, *Carson-Newman Studies*, Vol. VIII (Fall, 1994): 79–99.

1. For these ambivalent images of Appalachia, see especially: Rodger Cunningham, *Apples on the Flood: The Southern Mountain Experience* (Knoxville: University of Tennessee Press, 1987); Henry D. Shapiro, *Appalachia On Our Mind: The Southern Mountaineers in the American Consciousness, 1870–1920* (Chapel Hill: University of North Carolina Press, 1978); David Whisnant, *All That Is Native and Fine: The Politics of Culture in an American Region* (Chapel Hill: University of North Carolina Press, 1983); and J. W. Williamson, *An Appalachian Symposium* (Boone, NC: Appalachian State University Press, 1977).

2. See David Edwin Harrell Jr., *All Things Are Possible: The Healing and Charismatic Revivals in Modern America* (Bloomington: Indiana University Press, 1975); Mickey Crews, *The Church of God: A Social History* (Knoxville: University of Tennessee Press, 1990).

3. Samuel S. Hill, editor, *Religion in the Southern States* (Macon, GA: Mercer University Press, 1983), 8.

4. *Ibid.* See especially chapters on Tennessee, Kentucky, and North Carolina.

5. Quoted in Louis Keith Harper, "Southern Baptists and Social Christianity, 1890–1920," PhD diss. University of Kentucky, 1991, 136–37, 161–62, 164.

6. For examples of such historiography, see especially: Walter I. Trattner, *Social Welfare or Social Control: Some Historical Reflections on Regulating the Poor* (Knoxville: University of Tennessee Press, 1983); Dewey W. Grantham, *Southern Progressivism: The Reconciliation of Progress and Tradition* (Knoxville: University of Tennessee Press, 1983); and William A. Link, *The Paradox of Southern Progressivism, 1880–1930* (Chapel Hill: University of North Carolina Press, 1992).

7. Harper, "Southern Baptists and Social Christianity," 145, 153–54, 163–64.

8. Mabel Swartz Withoft, *Oak and Laurel: A Study of the Mountain Mission Schools of Southern Baptists* (Nashville: Sunday School Board of the Southern Baptist Convention, 1923), 16, 139.

9. *Ibid.*, 119.

10. *Ibid*, 134, 138.

11. *Baptist and Reflector*, April 19 (1934 or 1935?), copy in TVA file, Mountain Missions Box, Home Mission Board Papers, Southern Baptist Archives and Historical Commission, Nashville, Tennessee. Hereafter cited as TVA file.

12. "Approaches to Survey of Appalachian Mountain Region," undated but during the 1930s, in TVA file.

13. Tabulation of churches, Mountain Survey File, Mountain Missions Box, HMB Papers.

14. "George Lawrence Ridenour," TVA file.

15. Press release entitled, "Church Also at Work in Tennessee Valley Development," undated but probably 1933 or 1934, in Mountain Survey file.

16. *Baptist and Reflector*, March 23, 1933, copy in TVA file.

17. G. L. Ridenour to Una Roberts Lawrence, July 22, 1935; Ridenour to Lawrence, June 25, 1936; Ridenour to Lawrence, March 26, 1936; Ridenour to Lawrence, October 19, 1938; Ridenour to Lawrence, July 11, 1936; TVA file.

18. *Baptist and Reflector*, March 23, 1933; G. L. Ridenour to Una Roberts Lawrence, June 25, 1936, and October 19, 1938; Ridenour to Lawrence, July 22, 1935; TVA file.

19. G. L. Ridenour to Una Roberts Lawrence, August 26, 1935; TVA file.

20. *Baptist and Reflector*, March 23, 1933; G. L. Ridenour to Una Roberts Lawrence, July 22, 1935, June 26, 1936, and October 19, 1938, Ridenour to Lawrence, undated; TVA file.

21. G. L. Ridenour to Una Roberts Lawrence, March 26 and June 25, 1936; Ridenour to Lawrence, July 22, 1935; TVA file.

22. *Baptist and Reflector*, March 23, 1933.

23. G. L. Ridenour to Una Roberts Lawrence, June 10, 1936, TVA file.

24. *Ibid.*

25. *Ibid.*

26. *Ibid*., and Ridenour to Lawrence, June 25, 1936, TVA file.

27. G. L. Ridenour to Una Roberts Lawrence, February 23, 1935, TVA file.

28. *Ibid*., and Ridenour to Lawrence, July 11, 1936, TVA file.

29. G. L. Ridenour to Una Roberts Lawrence, February 23, 1935, Ridenour to Lawrence, June 10, 1936, TVA file.

30. G. L. Ridenour to Una Roberts Lawrence, February 23, 1935, Ridenour to Lawrence, June 10, 1936, TVA file.

31. G. L. Ridenour to Una Roberts Lawrence, Feruary 23, 1935; Ridenour to Lawrence, undated, Ridenour to Lawrence, undated; TVA file.

32. G. L. Ridenour to Una Roberts Lawrence, June 10, 1935; Ridenour to Lawrence, November 6 and 23, 1935; Ridenour to Lawrence, August 26, 1935; Ridenour to Lawrence, March 26, 1936; TVA file.

33. G. L. Ridenour to Una Roberts Lawrence, February 23, 1935; Ridenour to Lawrence, August 26, 1935; TVA file.

34. G. L. Ridenour to Una Roberts Lawrence, undated; Ridenour to Lawrence, February 23, 1935; Ridenour to Lawrence, July 22, 1935; Ridenour to Lawrence, November 23, 1935; Ridenour to Lawrence, October 19, 1938; TVA file.

35. Agnes Whipple Ridenour to Una Roberts Lawrence, February 7, 1935; Agnes Ridenour to Arthur Morgan, April 11, 1935; TVA file.

Chapter 8

The text of this chapter originally appeared in a slightly different form as "Religion at the Polls: A Case Study of Twentieth-Century Politics and Religion in Florida," *The Florida Historical Quarterly*, LXXII (April 1994), 469–83.

1. Shawn Ryan, "Off the Record," *The Birmingham News*, March 2, 1990; Jerry Adler, Jennifer Foote, and Ray Sawhill, "The Rap Attitude," *Newsweek*, March 19, 1990, 57.

2. David R. Colburn and Richard K. Scher, *Florida's Gubernatorial Politics in the 20th Century* (Tallahassee: University Press of Florida, 1980), 35–39, 291.

3. Marie Marmo Mullaney, *Biographical Directory of the Governors of the United States, 1983–1988* (Westport, CT: Greenwood, 1989), 73–75.

4. Tom R. Wagy, *Governor LeRoy Collins of Florida: Spokesman of the New South* (Tuscaloosa: University of Alabama Press, 1985).

5. Albert J. Menendez, *Religion at the Polls* (Philadelphia: Westminster Press, 1977), 197–99.

6. *Ibid*., 203. For insight into the nature of Christian right political involvement see Matthew C. Moen, *The Christian Right and Congress* (Tuscaloosa: University of Alabama Press, 1989), and Moen, *The Transformation of the Christian Right* (Tuscaloosa: University of Alabama Press, 1992).

7. Albert J. Menendez, "Analysis: Clinton Won Most Religious Votes," *Baptists Today* 10 (November 26, 1992), 1; *The Alabama Report* 1 (November 1992), 2.

8. Menendez, *Religion at the Polls*, 207, 216.

9. US Bureau of the Census, *Religious Bodies: 1916* (Washington, 1919), pt. 1, 160–62.

10. US Bureau of the Census, *Religious Bodies: 1926*, 2 vols. (Washington, 1930), I, 44–45, 58, 162, 310.

11. Sidney J. Catts, *Birmingham Age-Herald* (Birmingham, AL), December 14, 1916.

12. *The Alabama Baptist*, March 26, 1891, June 22, 1893; *The Montgomery Advertiser*, April 9, 1904.

13. *Birmingham Age-Herald*, December 14, 1916.

14. *The Alabama Baptist* (Birmingham), August 2, 1894.

15. *Ibid.*, May 2, 1901; *Alabama Baptist State Convention, Report for 1904*, (n.p., 1904), 46; Hayneville *City-Examiner*, March 31, 1904.

16. Editorial, *The Alabama Baptist* (Birmingham), February 15, 1894.

17. *Ibid.*, February 1, 1900.

18. *Birmingham Age-Herald*, December 14, 1916.

19. Selected titles from *The Jeffersonian*, 1910–1916.

20. W. T. Cash, *History of the Democratic Party in Florida* (Tallahassee: Florida Democratic Historical Foundation, 1936), 123–24; Wayne Flynt, ed., "William V. Knott and the Gubernatorial Campaign of 1916," *Florida Historical Quarterly* 51 (April 1973), 423–30. The most complete account of the role of religious nativism in the 1916 Florida elections can be found in Wayne Flynt, *Cracker Messiah: Governor Sidney J. Catts of Florida* (Baton Rouge: Louisiana State University Press, 1977), 25–93.

21. M. F. Green to Park Trammell, May 12, 1916, Park Trammell Papers, reel 1, P. K. Yonge Library of Florida History, University of Florida (hereinafter, Trammell Papers).

22. William Collins to Trammell, May 15, 1916, S. G. Bartow to Trammell, May 15, 1916, R. C. Boulvar to Trammell, May 23, 1916, reel 1, Trammell Papers.

23. Fuller Warren, *How to Win in Politics* (Tallahassee: Peninsular Publishing Co., 1949), 175. For examples of the impact and spread of anti-Catholic nativism and bigotry during the 1920s see David P. Page, "Bishop Michael J. Curley and Anti-Catholic Nativism in Florida," *Florida Historical Quarterly* 45 (October 1966), 101–17; and Stephen R. Prescott, "White Robes and Crosses: Father John Conoley, The Ku Klux Klan, and the University of Florida," *Florida Historical Quarterly* 71 (July 1992), 18–40.

Chapter 9

The text of this chapter originally appeared in a slightly different form as "One in the Spirit, Many in the Flesh: Southern Evangelicals," Fourth Annual Hugo Black Symposium, University of Birmingham in Birmingham, 1979, *Varieties of Southern Evangelicalism*, edited by David E. Harrell, Jr., (Macon, GA: Mercer University Press, 1981), 23–44.

1. Walter B. Posey, *The Baptist Church in the Lower Mississippi Valley, 1776–1845* (Lexington: University of Kentucky Press, 1957), 2.

2. Bertram Wyatt-Brown, "The Antimission Movement in the Jacksonian South: A Study in Regional Folk Culture," *The Journal of Southern History* 36 (November 1970); 501–29; and Wyatt-Brown, "Religion and the Formation of Folk Culture: Poor Whites of the Old South," in *The Americanization of the Gulf Coast, 1803–1850*, Lucius F. Ellsworth, ed. (Pensacola: Historic Pensacola Preservation Board, 1972), 20–33.

3. Brooks Hays, "Reflections on the Role of Baptists in Politics and the Future of America," *Baptist History and Heritage* 11 (July 1976): 170.

4. *The Quarterly Review* 38 (July-August-September 1978): 10–11.

5. For discussions of what makes southern Evangelicals unique, I relied on many sources. For comparisons of southern and northern Evangelicals, see Martin E. Marty, *Righteous Empire: The Protestant Experience in America* (New York: Dial Press, 1970), especially 58–66. The best description of the homogeneous ideology of Presbyterians, Baptists, and Methodists which justifies the term "the Southern Church" is still Samuel S. Hill Jr., *Southern Churches in Crisis* (Boston: Beacon Press, 1968). Several works are especially useful for the early stages of southern folk religion: Steve McNeely, "Early Baptists in the South, the Formation of a 'Folk Religion,'" *The Quarterly Review* 35 (October-November-December 1974): 65–72; George Pullen Jackson, "Some Factors in the Diffusion of American Religious Folksongs," *Journal of American Folklore* 65 (October–December 1952): 365–69; Dickson D. Bruce Jr., *And They All Sang Hallelujah: Plain Folk Camp-Meeting Religion, 1800–1845* (Knoxville: University of Tennessee Press, 1974); John B. Boles, *The Great Revival, 1787–1805* (Lexington: University of Kentucky Press, 1972); and Donald G. Mathews, *Religion in the Old South* (Chicago: University of Chicago Press, 1977).

6. J. D. Grey, "Debate, Discussion for Decision, Not Division," *Baptist History and Heritage* 12 (October 1977): 231.

7. Ernest R. Sandeen, *The Roots of Fundamentalism: British and American Millenarianism, 1800–1930* (Chicago: University of Chicago Press, 1970), 73–75, 151–67, 240. Fundamentalist is used as an historic movement in western European theology which began in the reaction to the French Revolution.

8. Hoke S. Dickinson, ed., *The Cane Ridge Reader* (n.p., 1972).

9. Brooks Holifield, *The Gentlemen Theologians: American Theology in Southern Culture* (Durham: Duke University Press, 1978).

10. David M. Potter, *The South and the Sectional Conflict* (Baton Rouge: Louisiana State University Press, 1968), 3–16.

11. Mathews, *Religion in the Old South*, 12, 39–46; Bruce, *They All Sang Hallelujah*, 13–29, 114–15.

12. W. J. Cash, *The Mind of the South* (New York: Vintage Books, 1960), 297.

13. Timothy L. Smith, "Religion and Ethnicity in America," *The American Historical Review* 83 (December 1978): 1155–85. Not all of Smith's hypotheses about the relation between religion and ethnicity fit southern Evangelicals, but enough of them fit to provide a fascinating comparison.

14. Bruce, *They All Sang Hallelujah*, 100–104.

15. Robert Coles, "God and the Rural Poor," *Psychology Today* 5 (January 1972): 31–41.

16. Quoted in Frank D. Alexander, "Religion in a Rural Community of the South," *American Sociological Review* 6 (April 1941): 241–51.

17. Richard A. McLemore, "Tumult, Violence, Revolution and Migration," *Baptist History and Heritage* 9 (October 1974): 230–36.

18. See, for instance, Spencer Bidwell King Jr., "Baptist Leaders in Early Georgia Politics," *The Quarterly Review* 38 (October–November–December 1977): 76–79; David

Nelson Duke, "Henry Holcombe Tucker, Outspoken Baptist Journalist," *The Quarterly Review* 38 (October–November–December 1977): 67–76.

19. *Home Missions* 48 (October 1977): 5; *The Alabama Baptist*, July 27, 1978.

20. The best example of this kind of elitist analysis is Frederick A. Bode's *Protestantism and the New South: North Carolina Baptists and Methodists in Political Crisis, 1894–1903* (Charlottesville: University of Virginia Press, 1975). An excellent corrective to this view in Robert C. McMath, Jr., *Populist Vanguard: A History of the Southern Farmers' Alliance* (Chapel Hill: University of North Carolina Press, 1975). McMath writes that the idiom of agrarian protest was the language of evangelical Protestantism. Evangelical religion, concludes McMath, was as capable of supporting agrarian radicalism as of defending an unjust social order.

21. Carrollton *West Alabamian*, July 1, 1891.

22. *The Alabama Baptist*, March 24, 1892.

23. Editorial, *The Alabama Baptist* (Birmingham), July 21 and 28, 1892; December 10, 1891; July 5, 1894; August 10 and 24, 1893.

24. *Ibid.*, January 7 and July 21, 1892.

25. Victor I. Masters, *Country Church in the South* (Atlanta: Home Mission Board, 1916), 119.

26. *Ibid.*, 98.

27. Dr. J. W. Lester Papers, Auburn University Archives.

28. Masters, *Country Church*; Edmund des. Brunner, *Church Life in the Rural South* (NY: George H. Doran Company, 1923); L. G. Wilson, et al., "The Church and Landless Men," University of North Carolina *Bulletin*, 1 (March 1, 1922): 1–27.

29. Garin Burbank, *When Farmers Voted Red: The Gospel of Socialism in the Oklahoma Countryside, 1910–1924* (Westport, CT: Greenwood Press, 1976); and James R. Green, *Grass-Roots Socialism: Radical Movements in the Southwest, 1895–1943* (Baton Rouge: Louisiana State University Press, 1978), especially chapter four, "Propagating the Socialist Gospel," 126–75.

30. Quoted in Masters, *Country Church*, 40.

31. A sample of the newer scholarship which acknowledges the social conscience of southern Evangelicals includes: George B. Tindall, *The Emergence of the New South, 1913–1945* (Baton Rouge: Louisiana State University Press, 1967), especially 196–200; Kenneth K. Bailey, *Southern White Protestantism in the Twentieth Century* (New York: Harper and Row, 1964); John Lee Eighmy, "Religious Liberalism in the South During the Progressive Era," *Church History* 38 (September 1969): 359–72; Wayne Flynt, "Dissent in Zion: Alabama Baptists and Social Issues, 1900–1914," *The Journal of Southern History* 35 (November 1969): 523–42; Flynt, "Religion in the Urban South: The Divided Religious Mind of Birmingham, 1900–1930," *The Alabama Review* 30 (April 1977): 108–34; Flynt, "Alabama White Protestantism and Labor, 1900–1914," *The Alabama Review* 25 (July 1972): 192–217; Flynt, "Organized Labor, Reform, and Alabama Politics, 1920," *The Alabama Review* 23 (July 1970): 163–80; Billy Storms, "Southern Baptists and a Social Gospel: An Uneasy Alliance," unpublished seminar paper, Southern Baptist Theological Seminary, 1975, copy in author's possession.

32. Careful attention to the *Methodist Alabama Christian Advocate* between 1900

and 1914 reveals hundreds of articles on the settlement houses and urban problems in general.

33. Noreen Dunn Tatum, *A Crown of Service: A Story of Woman's Work in the Methodist Episcopal Church South, From 1878–1940* (Nashville: Parthenon Press, 1960), 241–81.

34. See *The Alabama Baptist*, June 18, 1913; February 13, 1907; and November 15, 1973 (for Wayne Flynt's essay "The Cry of the Children").

35. Quoted in Liston Pope, *Millhands and Preachers* (New Haven, CT: Yale University Press, 1942), 16–17.

36. For instance, see Jonathan O. Beasley, "The Reaction of the Southern Baptist Press to the Haymarket Incident of 1866," *The Quarterly Review* 33 (January–February–March 1973): 37–42.

37. Richard D. Lunt, *Law and Order vs. the Miners: West Virginia, 1907–1933* (Hamden, CT: Archon Books, 1979), 43, 134–35, 162.

38. Tom E. Terrill and Jerrold Hirsch, *Such As Us: Southern Voices of the Thirties* (Chapel Hill: University of North Carolina Press, 1978), 167–68. This entire oral history, entitled "There's Always a Judas," and the following one, "When a Man Believes," reveal the depth of social protest among evangelical textile workers.

Chapter 10

The text of this chapter originally appeared in a slightly different form as "Women, Society, and the Southern Church, 1900–1920," Religion in the South Conference, Birmingham-Southern College, 1985, *Religion in the South Conference Papers* (Alabama Humanities Foundation, 1986), 38–61.

1. *Southern Baptist Convention Annual*, June 12–14, 1984 (Executive Committee, Southern Baptist Convention), 65.

2. *Southern Baptist Advocate*, No. 5 (July/August 1985), 1.

3. Quoted in T. Scott Miyakawa, *Protestants and Pioneers: Individualism and Conformity on the American Frontier* (Chicago: University of Chicago Press, 1964), 129. For an example of historians who assume that Southern Protestants ignored the Social Gospel see Carl Degler, *Place Over Time: The Continuity of Southern Distinctiveness* (Baton Rouge: Louisiana State University Press, 1977), 23.

4. See Donald G. Mathews, *Religion in the Old South* (Chicago: University of Chicago Press, 1977), 97–124; and Anne Firor Scott, *The Southern Lady: From Pedestal to Politics, 1830–1930* (Chicago: University of Chicago Press, 1970), especially 134–63.

5. For a survey of women in the SBC, see H. Leon McBeth, "The Role of Women in Southern Baptist History," *Baptist History and Heritage*, XII (January 1977) 3–25.

6. *The Baptist World*, April 11, 1912.

7. Mary Elizabeth Massey, "The Making of a Feminist," *The Journal of Southern History*, XXXIX (February 1973), 20.

8. McBeth, "The Role of Women in Southern Baptist History," 10–11 and 24.

9. Lansing Burrows, "Woman's Position in the Church. Course on Woman's Work in the Church," Sermon ms. In Box 2, FF 55, Lansing Burrows Papers, Southern Baptist Archives, Nashville, Tennessee. Hereafter referred to as SBC Archives.

10. John A. Broadus, "Should Women Speak in Mixed Public Assemblies?" (Louisville, Kentucky: Baptist Book Concern, 1890), 1, 9–10, and 14. Copy in SBC Archives.

11. *The Alabama Baptist*, February 20, 1896.

12. T. T. Eaton, "The Bible on Women's Public Speaking" (Louisville, Kentucky: Baptist Book Concern, 1895), 24–25 and 33. Copy in SBC Archives.

13. *Alabama Baptist*, February 20, 1896; McBeth, "Women in Southern Baptist History," 10; and *Alabama Baptist*, April 2, 1896.

14. McBeth, "Women in Southern Baptist History," 8 and 11; and Broadus, "Should Women Speak in Mixed Public Assemblies?" 14.

15. Annie W. Armstrong, Letter to Dr. J. M. Frost, April 18, 1898, Folder 10a, Box 6, Frost-Bell Papers, SBC Archives.

16. For an excellent biography of Armstrong and her confrontation with Heck, see Bobbie Sorrill, *Annie Armstrong: Dreamer in Action* (Nashville, TN: Broadman Press, 1984), especially 111–16 and 161–69; see also correspondence in "Armstrong, Annie," Folder 6, Box 7, Frost-Bell Papers.

17. Annie W. Armstrong, Letter to J. M. Frost, December 29, 1902; and Armstrong, Letter to Frost, n.d. 1902; both in Folder 10a, Box 15, Frost-Bell Papers.

18. Annie W. Armstrong, Letter to J. M. Frost, October 6, 1902, Folder 10a, Box 15, Frost-Bell Papers.

19. For a discussion of this affair, see Sorrill, *Annie Armstrong*, 213–35. Sorrill found no specific evidence to link Armstrong to the notion that the Training School would become a matrimonial agency.

20. Annie W. Armstrong, Letter to Dr. R. J. Willingham, November 8, 1905, Folder 1a, Box 20, Frost-Bell Papers. For additional materials on the dispute see copies of articles from the *Christian Index*, Annie Armstrong, Letter to J. M. Frost, October 4 and November 8, 1905, and "History of Movement to Establish Woman's Missionary Training School."

21. Lee N. Allen, *The First 150 Years, 1829–1979: First Baptist Church, Montgomery, Alabama* (Montgomery: First Baptist Church, 1979), 124–27; and *The Baptist World*, June 7, 1917.

22. *The Baptist World*, June 7, 1917; and Maud McLure, Letter to Dr. J. M. Frost, April 15, 1911, Folder 8, Box 26, Frost-Bell Papers.

23. *The Baptist World*, December 12, 1912, January 18 and February 1 and 15, 1917.

24. *The Baptist World*, June 7, 1917.

25. Editorial, *The Alabama Baptist* (Birmingham), July 14, 1892 and September 19, 1895.

26. Professor H. H. Harris, *The Alabama Baptist* (Birmingham), March 5 and April 16, 1896.

27. *The Alabama Baptist* (Birmingham), October 29, 1896.

28. *The Baptist World*, July 29, 1909.

29. *The Baptist World*, August 1, 1912.

30. *The Baptist World*, July 1, 1909, October 19, 1911.

31. McBeth, "Women in Southern Baptist History," 12–14.

32. *The Baptist World*, May 26, 1910.

33. McBeth, "Women in Southern Baptist History," 14–15; and *Presbyterian Standard*, May 29, 1918.

34. Bill Sumners, "Southern Baptists and Women's Right to Vote, 1910–1920," *Baptist History and Heritage*, XII (January 1977) 46–48; and *The Baptist World*, April 7, 1910. Sumners argues that the SBC was deeply split over woman suffrage.

35. Sumners, "Southern Baptists and Women's Right to Vote," 49–50; and *The Baptist World*, February 1, 1912 and February 17, 1910.

36. *The Baptist World*, December 12, 1912.

37. *The Baptist World*, February 10 and May 19, 1910, and February 1, 1917; and Charles W. Deweese, "Deaconesses in Baptist History: A Preliminary Study," *Baptist History and Heritage*, XII (January 1977), 55.

38. McBeth, "Women in Southern Baptist History," 15–23.

39. *Folio*, 2 (Winter, 1985), 3.

Chapter 11

The text of this chapter originally appeared in a slightly different form as "'A Special Feeling of Closeness,' Mt. Hebron Baptist Church, Leeds, Alabama," *American Congregations, Volume I: Portraits of Twelve Religious Communities*, edited by James P. Wind and James W. Lewis (Chicago: University of Chicago Press, 1994), 103–58.

1. Clifford Geertz, *The Interpretation of Cultures: Selected Essays* (New York: Basic Books, 1973), 90–125, 140.

2. Donald Mathews, *Religion in the Old South* (Chicago: University of Chicago Press, 1977), 84–87.

3. Anne C. Loveland, *Southern Evangelicals and the Social Order, 1800–1860* (Baton Rouge: Louisiana State University Press, 1980), 161–62.

4. History Committee, Leeds Bicentennial Commission, Leeds, Alabama, *Leeds . . . Her Story* (Anniston, AL: Higginbotham, 1979), 45.

5. *Ibid.*, 56.

6. *Ibid.*, 60.

7. *Ibid.*, 7–8. Cahaba is spelled two ways in Alabama place-names: Cahaba and Cahawba.

8. Reid, *Baptists in Alabama*, 47–49; Davis C. Woolley, "Hosea Holcombe: Pioneer Alabama Baptist Historian," *Alabama Review* 14 (January 1961): 6–8.

9. Hosea Holcombe, *A History of the Rise and Progress of the Baptists in Alabama* (Philadelphia: King and Baird, 1840), 44.

10. Dickson D. Bruce Jr., *And They All Sang Hallelujah: Plain-Folk Campmeeting Religion, 1800–1845* (Knoxville: University of Tennessee Press, 1973), 4–93; John Boles, *The Great Revival, 1787–1805: The Origins of the Southern Evangelical Mind* (Lexington: University Press of Kentucky, 1972), 119–30, 169–81, 191, 195; William G. McLoughlin, *Revivals, Awakenings, and Reform* (Chicago: University of Chicago Press, 1978), 131–35.

11. Mt. Hebron Church Book and Minutes, 1819–1983, Alabama Baptist Historical Collection, Samford University Library, Birmingham, AL. Archivist Elizabeth Wells suggested this church because its minutes are nearly complete since its creation in 1819.

Such care with church records was not unusual among rural churches. Clerks obviously assumed their duties with an enormous sense of responsibility. As this essay makes clear, their task gained enhanced importance from the central role of kinship within the congregation. They preserved not just the records of a church but the history of kin across generations.

12. *Ibid.*

13. Mathews, *Religion in the Old South*, 42; Randy J. Sparks, "'A Wholesome, Godly Discipline': Race and Gender in Mississippi Evangelical Disciplinary Actions, 1806–1870," manuscript in possession of author. I am grateful to Professor Sparks for sharing his findings with me. Professor Larry James also presented a paper at the 1981 Southern Historical Convention entitled "Church Discipline in Antebellum Mississippi and Louisiana Baptist Churches" regarding the same topic.

14. Mt. Hebron Church Book and Minutes.

15. Dan Cloyd, "Prelude to Reform: Political, Economic, and Social Thought of Alabama Baptists, 1877–1890," *Alabama Review* 31 (January 1978): 48–64.

16. For insights on religious divisions within the southern church, 1870–1900, see: David Edwin Harrell Jr., "Religious Pluralism: Catholics, Jews, and Sectarians," in *Religion in the South*, ed. Charles Reagan Wilson (Jackson: University Press of Mississippi, 1985), 59–82; Wayne Flynt, "One in the Spirit, Many in the Flesh: Southern Evangelicals," in *Varieties of Southern Evangelicalism*, ed. David E. Harrell Jr. (Macon, GA: Mercer University Press, 1981), 23–44; Mickey Crews, "From the Back Alleys to Uptown: A History of the Church of God (Cleveland, Tennessee)," PhD diss., Auburn University, 1988, 24–52.

17. Herschel Edwin Campbell, "A Struggle for Life" (the story of Mt. Hebron Baptist Church), 9–10, unpublished church history, copy in Alabama Baptist Historical Collection, Samford University Library.

18. Mt. Hebron Church Book and Minutes.

19. John Boles, Introduction, *Masters and Slaves in the House of the Lord*, ed. John Boles (Lexington: University Press of Kentucky, 1988), 13–18. This important book challenges many traditional notions about the subservient role of slaves in antebellum southern churches and argues that the relationships were quite complex. In many churches black people had rights not available to them in secular society.

20. Larry M. James, "Biracial Fellowship in Antebellum Baptist Churches," in *ibid.*, 38–50; Randy Sparks, "Religion in Amite County," in *ibid.*, 62–72.

21. *Ibid.*, 37 and 78.

22. All descriptions of discipline come from Mt. Hebron Church Book and Minutes.

23. *Ibid.*

24. See Robert E. Praytor, "From Concern to Neglect: Alabama Baptists' Religious Relationship to the Negro, 1823–1870" (MA thesis, Samford University, 1971), 30–73.

25. Oral history with J. T. Poole and Margie Poole Martin, Leeds, Alabama, May 1, 1989, by Peter Branum. My thanks to Mr. Branum for his superb work as my research assistant.

26. Sparks, "A Wholesome, Godly Discipline," quoting Mathews, *Religion in the Old South*, 47–48; Rhys Isaac, *The Transformation of Virginia, 1740–1790* (Chapel Hill: Uni-

versity of North Carolina Press, 1982); and Bertram Wyatt-Brown, *Southern Honor: Ethics and Behavior in the Old South* (New York: Oxford University Press, 1982).

27. Mathews, *Religion in the Old South*, 101–24.

28. Mt. Hebron Church Book and Minutes.

29. Oral history with Margie Poole Martin.

30. This discrepancy is consistent with the pattern discovered by Randy Sparks in his investigation of 1,169 cases of church discipline in Mississippi between 1806 and 1870. White men were most frequently cited, and only about one-tenth of the charges involved white women, with dancing accounting for almost half (in Mt. Hebron, 20 of 58 disciplinary cases against white women involved the charge of dancing). See Sparks, "A Wholesome, Godly Discipline."

31. Examples abound. In December 1840 the church excluded Davidson McGuire for abuse of alcohol, and Sara McGuire requested a letter of dismissal in September 1841. In May 1882 the church excluded Jonathan D. Shugart for intoxication, and Alice Shugart requested her letter in July. They subsequently joined another denomination. In April 1891 the church lodged charges of drunkenness and profanity against J. H. Hudson, and in June excluded him from membership. His wife sought a letter of dismissal in April, but the church withheld her letter because charges were pending against her husband. In July he finally acknowledged his sins, was restored to fellowship, and both promptly requested and were granted letters of dismissal.

32. Church minutes during the second decade of the century are incomplete, so the church may have elected a female messenger somewhat earlier than this.

33. Reid, *Baptists in Alabama*, 48–49.

34. Campbell, "A Struggle for Life," appendices 3 and 4.

35. *Ibid.*, 7.

36. Mt. Hebron Church Book and Minutes, March 1843.

37. Interview with Dorothy Smith Flynt and Everett Smith, July 18 and 30, 1989; oral history with J. T. Poole and Margie Poole Martin.

38. "Christo-Centric," February 1935 and undated issue, copies in author's possession.

39. Oral history with Fred E. Maxey Jr., May 18, 1989, Leeds, Alabama, by Peter Branum. Maxey claims that his father became a Baptist after arriving in Alabama, but that his study of theology and his evangelistic efforts led him to Baptist doctrine.

40. *Ibid.*; Robin D. G. Kelley, *Hammer and Hoe: Alabama Communists During the Great Depression* (Chapel Hill: University of North Carolina Press, 1990), 196–97, 214.

41. Boles, *The Great Revival*, 183–203; Samuel S. Hill Jr., *Southern Churches in Crisis* (Boston: Beacon Press, 1967), 20–39.

42. Oral histories with J. T. Poole, Margie Poole Martin, Fred E. Maxey Jr.; T. C. West, April 30, 1989, Leeds, Alabama, by Peter Branum; Annabel Moore and Maggie Dee Wilkinson, April 18, 1989, Leeds, Alabama, by Peter Branum; Eloise Dison and Carla Dison Lawly, April 30, 1989, Leeds, Alabama, by Peter Branum.

43. Oral history with Annabel Moore and Maggie Dee Wilkinson.

44. History Committee, *Leeds . . . Her Story*, 168.

45. Oral history with Annabel Moore and Maggie Dee Wilkinson.

46. *Ibid.*

47. Oral histories with T. C. West, J. T. Poole, and Margie Poole Martin.

48. Mt. Hebron Church Book and Minutes.

49. Oral history with Fred Maxey Jr.

50. Oral histories with J. T. Poole, Margie Poole Martin, Fred E. Maxey Jr., T. C. West, Annabel Moore, and Maggie Dee Wilkinson.

51. Oral histories with J. T. Poole, Margie Poole Martin, T. C. West, Annabel Moore, Maggie Dee Wilkinson, Eloise Dison, and Carla Dison Lawly.

52. Oral history with T. C. West.

53. Oral histories with Annabel Moore, Maggie Dee Wilkinson, and T. C. West.

54. *Ibid.*, and oral history with Eloise Dison and Carla Dison Lawly.

55. Oral history with J. T. Poole and Margie Poole Martin.

56. *Ibid.*, and oral histories with Eloise Dison, Carla Dison Lawly, Annabel Moore, Maggie Dee Wilkinson, and T. C. West.

CHAPTER 12

The text of this chapter originally appeared in a slightly different form as "Religion for the Blues: Evangelicalism, Poor Whites, and the Great Depression," *Journal of Southern History*, LXXI (February 2005), 338). (Presidential address to the Southern Historical Association in Memphis, Tennessee, November 2004.)

1. May Jordan, *Where the Wild Animals Is Plentiful: Diary of an Alabama Fur Trader's Daughter, 1912–1914*, edited by Elisa Moore Baldwin (Tuscaloosa: University of Alabama Press, 1999), 3–4, 10, 15, 17, 24. I have consistently used the spelling and dialect of the poor rather than correct them.

2. *Ibid.*, 10.

3. *Ibid.*, 15.

4. *Ibid.*, 16.

5. *Ibid.*, 35.

6. *Ibid.*, 86 (first quotation, 96 (second quotation), 155 (third quotation), 159, 166, 179 (fourth quotation).

7. *Ibid.*, 180.

8. *Ibid.*, 23, 24, 77, 148 (first quotation), 180, 206 (second quotation).

9. See John B. Boles, *The Irony of Southern Religion* (New York, 1994).

10. Randy J. Sparks, "Religion in the Pre-Civil War South," and Paul Harvey, "Religion in the American South Since the Civil War," in John B. Boles, ed., *A Companion to the American South* (Malden, MA: Blackwell Publishers, 2002), 156–75, 387–406.

11. A sample of the rich published literature about the black church written since the early 1970s (arranged chronologically) includes John W. Blassingame, *The Slave Community: Plantation Life in the Antebellum South* (New York: Oxford University Press, 1972); Eugene D. Genovese, *Roll, Jordan Roll: The World the Slaves Made* (New York: Pantheon Books, 1974), especially 161–284; Milton C. Sernett, *Black Religion and American Evangelicalism: White Protestants, Plantation Missions, and the Flowering of Negro Christianity, 1787–1865* (Metuchen, NJ: Scarecrow Press, 1975); Lawrence W. Levine, *Black Culture*

and Black Consciousness: Afro-American Folk Thought from Slavery to Freedom (New York: Oxford University Press, 1977); Albert J. Raboteau, *Slave Religion: The "Invisible Institution" in the Antebellum South* (New York: Oxford University Press, 1978); Leon F. Litwack, *Been in the Storm So Long: The Aftermath of Slavery* (New York: Alfred A. Knopf, 1979), especially chap. 9; Charles Joyner, *Down by the Riverside: A South Carolina Slave Community* (Urbana: University of Illinois Press, 1984), especially chap. 5; James Melvin Washington, *Frustrated Fellowship: The Black Baptist Quest for Social Power* (Macon, GA: Mercer University Press, 1986); John B. Boles, ed., *Masters and Slaves in the House of the Lord: Race and Religion in the American South, 1740–1870* (Lexington: University Press of Kentucky, 1988); C. Eric Lincoln and Lawrence H. Mamiya, *The Black Church in the African American Experience* (Durham: Duke University Press, 1990); William E. Montgomery, *Under Their Own Vine and Fig Tree: The African-American Church in the South, 1865–1900* (Baton Rouge: Louisiana State University Press, 1993); Wilson Fallin Jr., *The African American Church in Birmingham, Alabama, 1815–1963: A Shelter in the Storm* (New York: Garland Publishing, 1997); Tracy Elaine K'Meyer, *Interracialism and Christian Community in the Postwar South: The Story of Koinonia Farm* (Charlottesville: University Press of Virginia, 1997); Milton C. Sernett, *Bound for the Promised Land: African American Religion and the Great Migration* (Durham: Duke University Press, 1997); Sylvia R. Frey and Betty Wood, *Come Shouting to Zion: African American Protestantism in the American South and British Caribbean to 1830* (Chapel Hill: University of North Carolina Press, 1998); Ward M. McAfee, *Religion, Race, and Reconstruction: The Public School in the Politics of the 1870s* (Albany: State University of New York Press, 1998); Christopher H. Owen, *The Sacred Flame of Love: Methodism and Society in Nineteenth-Century Georgia* (Athens: University of Georgia Press, 1998; Andrew Billingsley, *Mighty Like a River: The Black Church and Social Reform* (New York: Oxford University Press, 1999); and Larry Eugene Rivers and Canter Brown Jr., *Laborers in the Vineyard of the Lord: The Beginnings of the AME Church in Florida, 1865–1895* (Gainesville: University Press of Florida, 2001).

12. Liston Pope, *Millhands and Preachers: A Study of Gastonia* (New Haven, CT: Yale University Press, 1942), 122–24.

13. George L. Maddox and Joseph H. Fichter, "Religion and Social Change in the South," *Journal of Social issues*, 22 (January 1966), 44–58.

14. Erskine Caldwell, *Deep South: Memory and Observation* (New York, 1968), 12, 25–27 (first seven quotations), 39, 43–49, 53 (final two quotations).

15. For stereotypes and generalizations see Bryan Wilson, *Religious Sects: A Sociological Study* (New York: McGraw-Hill, 1970), 90–91; Barbara Hargrove, *The Sociology of Religion: Classical and Contemporary Approaches* (Arlington Heights, IL: AHM Publishing Corporation, 1979), 285–96; Robert Mapes Anderson, *Vision of the Disinherited: The Making of American Pentecostalism* (New York: Oxford University Press, 1979), 224–25, 238; George Barton Cutten, *Speaking with Tongues: Historically and Psychologically Considered* (New Haven, CT: Yale University Press, 1927), 4–5; James Lapsey and John Simpson, "Speaking in Tongues: Infantile Babble or Song of the Self? (Part II)," *Pastoral Psychology*, 15 (September 1964), 16–17; Virginia H. Hine, "Pentecostal Glossolalia: Toward a Functional Interpretation," *Journal for the Scientific Study of Religion*, 8

(Fall 1969), 214–15; and Frank Stagg, E. Glenn Hinson, and Wayne E. Oates, *Glossolalia: Tongue Speaking in Biblical, Historical, and Psychological Perspective* (Nashville: Abingdon Press, 1967), 96–97 (quotation on p. 97). I am indebted to Mickey Crews, whose 1981 seminar paper "Pentecostalism: Sociologically and Psychologically Interpreted" alerted me to many of these sources.

16. Clifford Geertz, *The Interpretation of Cultures: Selected Essays* (New York: Basic Books, 1973), 5 (sixth quotation), 90, 123 (first and second quotations), 125, 140 (third and fourth quotations), 250 (fifth quotation).

17. Wayne Flynt, "'A Special Feeling of Closeness': Mt. Hebron Baptist Church, Leeds, Alabama," in James P. Wind and James W. Lewis, eds., *American Congregations, Volume 1: Portraits of Twelve Religious Communities* (Chicago: University of Chicago Press, 1994), 103–58.

18. Quotations in the preceding two paragraphs are from oral history interviews conducted by Peter Branum with Annabel Moore, J. T. Poole, Margie Poole Martin, and T. C. West, April 18 and April 30, 1989, Samford University Oral History Collection (University Archives, Birmingham, AL; hereinafter cited as Samford University Oral History Collection). For a more detailed examination of Mt. Hebron, see Flynt, "'Special Feeling of Closeness,'" 103–58.

19. Robert Coles, "God and the Rural Poor," *Psychology Today*, 5 (January 1972), 31–41.

20. Robert Coles, *Children of Crisis, Volume II: Migrants, Sharecroppers, and Mountaineers* (Boston: Little, Brown and Company, 1967), 579 (first and second quotations), 587 (third quotation).

21. *Ibid.*, 593–95 (first four quotations, 605 (fifth quotation).

22. Works that explore religiously inspired poor-white radicalism include Garin Burbank, *When Farmers Voted Red: The Gospel of Socialism in the Oklahoma Countryside, 1910–1924* (Westport, CT: Greenwood Press, 1979); Lacy K. Ford Jr., *Origins of Southern Radicalism: The South Carolina Upcountry, 1800–1860* (New York: Oxford University Press, 1988); Robert H. Craig, *Religion and Radical Politics: An Alternative Christian Tradition in the United States* (Philadelphia: Temple University Press, 1992); Richard C. Goode, "The Godly Insurrection in Limestone County: Social Gospel, Populism, and Southern Culture in the Late Nineteenth Century," *Religion and American Culture: A Journal of Interpretation*, 3 (Summer 1993), 155–69; Wayne Flynt, *Alabama Baptists: Southern Baptists in the Heart of Dixie* (Tuscaloosa: University of Alabama Press, 1998), 205–50; Jim Bissett, *Agrarian Socialism in America: Marx, Jefferson, and Jesus in the Oklahoma Countryside, 1904–1920* (Norman: University of Oklahoma Press, 1999), and Jeanette Keith, "The Politics of Southern Draft Resistance, 1917–1918: Class, Race, and Conscription in the Rural South," *Journal of American History, 87* (March 2001), 1335–61.

23. For the role of evangelicalism in helping white people cope with modernization, see Robert C. McMath Jr., *Populist Vanguard: A History of the Southern Farmers' Alliance* (Chapel Hill: University of North Carolina Press, 1975), especially 64–76; Bruce Palmer, *"Man over Money": The Southern Populist Critique of American Capitalism* (Chapel Hill: University of North Carolina Press, 1980), 21–26, 126–37; Steven Hahn, *The Roots of Southern Populism: Yeoman Farmers and the Transformation of the Georgia Upcounty,*

1850–1890 (New York: Oxford University Press, 1983), 17; and Jeanette Keith, *Country People in the New South: Tennessee's Upper Cumberland* (Chapel Hill: University of North Carolina Press, 1995).

24. For two useful studies of Primitive or Old Regular Baptists see Howard Dorgan, *The Old Regular Baptists of Central Appalachia: Brothers and Sisters in Hope* (Knoxville: University of Tennessee Press, 1989) and John G. Crowley, *Primitive Baptists of the Wiregrass South: 1815 to the Present* (Gainesville: University Press of Florida, 1998).

25. Robert S. Weise, *Grasping at Independence: Debt, Male Authority, and Mineral Rights in Appalachian Kentucky, 1850–1915* (Knoxville: University of Tennessee Press, 2001), 56 (quotation), 60, 72–74.

26. Deborah Vansau McCauley, *Appalachian Mountain Religion: A History* (Urbana: University of Illinois Press, 1995), 221.

27. McCauley, *Appalachian Mountain Religion*, especially 7–12 (second quotation on p. 8), 212–27 (first quotation on p. 215). See also Bill J. Leonard, ed., *Christianity in Appalachia: Profiles in Regional Pluralism* (Knoxville: University of Tennessee Press, 1999).

28. David Edwin Harrell Jr., The South: Seedbed of Sectarianism," in Harrell, ed., *Varieties of Southern Evangelicalism* (Macon, GA: Mercer University Press, 1981), 46–48.

29. *Ibid.*, 46, 48, 50 (quotation).

30. *Ibid.*, 55–56. In *All Things Are Possible: The Healing Charismatic Revivals in Modern America* (Bloomington: Indiana University Press, 1975), Harrell describes the abject poverty from which many early southern pentecostal leaders came (William M. Branham, Oral Roberts, Jack Coe, T. L. Osborn, and A. A. Allen). See especially 27, 42, 58, 63, and 66–67 in *ibid.*

31. Anderson, *Vision of the Disinherited*; John B. Holt, "Holiness Religion: Cultural Shock and Social Reorganization," *American Sociological Review*, 5 (October 1940), 740–47; David L. Kimbrough, *Taking Up Serpents: Snake Handlers of Eastern Kentucky* (Chapel Hill: University of North Carolina Press, 1995), especially chap. 5, "Industrialization"; Charles Y. Glock, "The Role of Deprivation in the Origin and Evolution of Religious Groups," in Robert Lee and Martin E. Marty, ed., *Religion and Social Conflict* (New York: Oxford University Press, 1964), 24–36; Mickey Crews, *The Church of God*, especially chap. 1, "Populistic Religion: The Social Origins of the Church of God"; Paul K. Conkin, *American Originals: Homemade Varieties of Christianity* (Chapel Hill: University of North Carolina Press, 1997), 283, 302–10.

32. McCauley, *Appalachian Mountain Religion*, especially 7–9, 205–6, 306; Grant Wacker, *Heaven Below: Early Pentecostals and American Culture* (Cambridge, MA: Harvard University Press, 2001), especially 198–212; J. Lawrence Brasher, *The Sanctified South: John Lakin Brasher and the Holiness Movement* (Urbana: University of Illinois Press, 1994), 3–7, 143–44, 158.

33. See Crews, *Church of God*, 17–18, chap. 7 (quotation from chapter title); Brasher, *Sanctified South*, 157; Conkin, *American Originals*, 302, 311–12; and David Edwin Harrell Jr., *White Sects and Black Men in the Recent South* (Nashville: Vanderbilt University Press, 1971), particularly 94–95, 102, 108–9, 129. Scott Billingsley, "New Prophets for Emerging American Subcultures: The Rise of Women and African American Evangelists in the Independent Charismatic Movement, 1950–2000" (PhD diss., Auburn Uni-

versity, 2003) traces the resurgence of women in black pentecostal leadership during the late twentieth century.

34. Howard W. Odum, *Southern Regions of the United States* (Chapel Hill: University of North Carolina Press, 1936), 141, 143.

35. Harrell, "South," 50–51. In 1926 the South remained a Baptist-Methodist empire. The eleven former Confederate states plus Kentucky contained slightly more than three million Southern Baptists and over two million members of the Methodist Episcopal Church South, but there were only 292,000 members of the Churches of Christ; 18,000 members of the Church of God; 9,100 members of the Church of God, Anderson, Indiana; and fewer than 5,600 members of the Pentecostal Holiness Church. See Bureau of the Census, *Religious Bodies: 1926 Volume I—Summary and Detailed Tables* (Washington: United States Government Printing Office, 1930), 315–38. Between 1926 and 1950, national membership of the Southern Baptist Convention increased to 6,761,265, while membership figures for the Churches of Christ nearly doubled, for Pentecostal Holiness more than tripled, and for Church of God, Anderson, Indiana, nearly tripled. See Frank S. Mead, *Handbook of Denominations in the United States* (New York: Abingdon-Cokesbury Press, 1951), 185–89.

36. J. W. Jent, *The Challenge of the Country Church* (Nashville: Baptist Sunday School Board, 1924), 83–88, 107 (quotation), 133.

37. See L. G. Wilson, "The Church and Landless Men," *University of North Carolina Extension Bulletin*, 1 (March 1, 1922), 7–10; and Charles M. McConnell, "Farm Tenants and Sharecroppers," *Missionary Review of the World*, 60 (June 1937), 288. For similar conclusions about the correlation between high rates of white farm tenancy and low church attendance (a correlation that many rural sociologists did *not* find among black farm tenants), see Edmund de Schweinitz Brunner, *Church Life in the Rural South* (New York: G. H. Doran Company, 1923), especially 44–48, 80–92, and 102–5.

38. For the problem of tenants without appropriate Sunday clothes, see Melissa Walker, *All We Knew Was to Farm: Rural Women in the Upcountry South, 1919–1941* (Baltimore: Johns Hopkins University Press, 2000), 60–61; Federal Writers' Project, *These Are Our Lives* (Chapel Hill: University of North Carolina Press, 1939), 218; Rev. H. F. Carter to Franklin D. Roosevelt, October 7, 1935, PPF 21A, Georgia, Clergy Letters (Franklin D. Roosevelt Library and Archives, Hyde Park, NY).

39. Oral history with Kathleen Knight, by Daniel Knight, January 27, 1975; oral history with Lillie Mae Flynt Beason, by Wayne Flynt, January 3, 1976, both in Samford University Oral History Collection.

40. Oral history with Mrs. L. A. House, by Wayne Flynt, July 10, 1974, Samford University Oral History Collection. See also Federal Writers' Project, *These Are Our Lives*, 39, 60.

41. Flynt, *Alabama Baptists*, 376.

42. See Pope, *Millhands and Preachers*, 150–68; Jacquelyn Dowd Hall et al., *Like a Family: The Making of a Southern Cotton Mill World* (Chapel Hill: University of North Carolina Press, 1987), 124–26; and Crandall A. Shifflett, *Coal Towns: Life, Work, and Culture in Company Towns of Southern Appalachia, 1880–1960* (Knoxville: University of Tennessee Press, 1991), chap. 10 on "The Company Church," 190–98.

43. Oral history with Mrs. L. A. House; oral history with Luther V. Smith, by Benny Hendrix, November 27, 1974, Samford University Oral History Collection; oral history with Cecil Spencer, by Wayne Flynt and Everett Smith, December 20, 1977, in author's possession; oral histories with Lloyd Vick Minor, Pennington Gap, Va., August 20, 1974; L. F. Minor, Big Stone Gap, Va., August 20, 1974; and Glen Carter, Pennington Gap, Va., August 22, 1974, all three interviews by Wayne Flynt, Samford University Oral History Collection.

44. Michelle Brattain, *The Politics of Whiteness: Race, Workers, and Culture in the Modern South* (Princeton, NJ: Princeton University Press, 2001), 45; Hall et al., *Like a Family*, 20–21, 175–79 (quotation on p. 179).

45. Quotations from Hall et al., *Like a Family*, 193–94 (first quotation), 175 (second quotation).

46. Tom E. Terrill and Jerrold Hirsch, eds., *Such As Us: Southern Voices of the Thirties* (Chapel Hill: University of North Carolina Press, 1978), 157–69 (quotation on p. 167).

47. *Ibid.*, 12.

48. Margaret Jarman Hagood, *Mothers of the South: Portraiture of the White Tenant Farm Woman* (1939; reprint, New York: W. W. Norton, 1977), 23 (first quotation), 24 (second quotation).

49. *Ibid.*, 163 (quotations), 239.

50. James D. Ross Jr., "'I Ain't Got No Home In This World': The Rise and Fall of the Southern Tenant Farmers' Union in Arkansas" (PhD diss., Auburn University, 2004).

51. Elizabeth Anne Payne, "The Lady Was a Sharecropper: Myrtle Lawrence and the Southern Tenant Farmers' Union," *Southern Cultures*, 4 (Summer 1998) (quotation on p. 11), 15–18.

52. *Ibid.*, 8–10, 16–67.

53. *Ibid.*, 6.

54. *Ibid.*, 8, 19–21 (quotation on p. 21).

55. *Ibid.*, 22.

56. Marion Elias Lazenby, *History of Methodism in Alabama and West Florida: Being an Account of the Amazing March of Methodism through Alabama and West Florida* ([Nashville?], 1960), 655.

57. Herman Clarence Nixon, *Possum Trot: Rural Community, South* (Norman: University of Oklahoma Press, 1941), 55 (quotation); Nixon, *Lower Piedmont Country* (New York: Duell, Sloan & Pearce, 1946), 89–93.

58. Oral history with Ila Hendrix, by Ben Hendrix, May 1, 1976, Samford University Oral History Collection.

59. Jessie Mae Mills, "Red Hill—Churches of God, Perry County," Box 10791, Record Group 60 (Mississippi Department of Archives and History), cited in Lynn Price McWhorter, "The Piney Woods Church: The Here-and-Now and Otherworldly Functions of Poor White Religion," graduate seminar paper, Auburn University, 2002. See also Gary Don McElhaney, "Fire in the Pines: A History of the Assemblies of God in Mississippi, 1900–1936" (MA thesis, Mississippi State University, 1992).

60. James Seay Brown Jr., ed., *Up Before Daylight: Life Histories from the Alabama*

Writers' Project, 1938–1939 (Tuscaloosa: University of Alabama Press, 1982), 35–36 (third quotation on p. 36), 107–9 (first and second quotations on p. 108).

61. Gordon W. Blackwell, Lee M. Brooks, and S. H. Hobbs Jr., *Church and Community in the South: Report . . . for the Committee on Re-study of Religious Education of the Presbyterian Church in the United States* (Richmond, VA: John Knox Press, 1949), 17, 39, 260–61, 265 (first quotation), 387 (second quotation). For a similar analysis of 1930s class-based white churches, see Allison Davis, Burleigh B. Gardner, and Mary R. Gardner, *Deep South: A Social Anthropological Study of Caste and Class* (Chicago: University of Chicago Press, 1941) and John Dollard, *Caste and Class in a Southern Town* (New Haven, CT: Yale University Press, 1937), especially 220–49.

62. Interview with O. N. Andrews Jr., by Wayne Flynt, June 13, 2004.

63. Paul W. Terry and Verner M. Sims, *They Live on the Land: Life in an Open-Country Southern Community* (1940; reprint, Tuscaloosa: University of Alabama Press, 1993), 146–80.

64. *Ibid.*, 171 (first through fifth quotations), 180 (sixth through ninth quotations).

65. Bill C. Malone, "'Sing Me Back Home': Growing Up in the South and Writing the History of Its Music," in John B. Boles, ed., *Shapers of Southern History: Autobiographical Reflection* (Athens: University of Georgia Press, 2004), 91–100 (quotations on p. 99).

66. Thomas D. Norris, "Southern Baptists and the 'Okie' Migration: A Sectarian Rebirth in California, 1930s–1940s," *Locus*, 2 (Fall 1989), 35–47 (quotation on p. 39).

67. Oral history with Jim Hammitte, by Mary Thompson, December 3, 1974, Samford University Oral History Collection.

68. Monroe Billington, "The Alabama Clergy and the New Deal," *Alabama Review*, 32 (July 1979), 215–18 (quotation on p. 215).

69. G. F. Campbell to FDR, undated, PPF 21A, Alabama; W. B. Morgan to FDR, November 21, 1935, PPF 21A, Alabama; Rev. Robert Witty to FDR, September 26, 1935, PPF 21A, Florida; all in Clergy Letters. All remaining citations are to material from PPF 21A, Clergy Letters; hereinafter I will designate the state for each letter and will abbreviate the collection as CL.

70. J. L. Street to FDR, October 5, 1935, North Carolina, CL.

71. Rev. George F. Wolf to FDR, October 30, 1935, North Carolina, CL.

72. B. S. Drennan to FDR, September 25, 1935, South Carolina; A. M. Smith to FDR, September 28, 1935, South Carolina; J. K. Hall to FDR, September 26, 1935, North Carolina; all in CL.

73. Mrs. M. J. Tussenar to FDR, November 11, 1935, North Carolina, CL.

74. Rev. W. M. Worley to FDR, October 7, 1935, Tennessee. For similar letters, see Rev. J. W. Steward to FDR, October 15, 1935, Tennessee; Rev. J. L. Pike to FDR, October 15, 1935, Tennessee; Rev. Colno Farrow to FDR, September 25, 1935, North Carolina; Rev. S. L. Fulwood to FDR, December 23, 1935, North Carolina; B. S. Cooper to FDR, October 14, 1935, South Carolina; Rev. A. D. Smith to FDR, October 2, 1935, Mississippi; and Rev. J. W. James to FDR, November 9, 1935, Mississippi; all in CL.

75. J. B. Stephenson to FDR, October 12, 1935 (first quotation); R. H. Kelly to FDR,

September 26, 1935; W. D. Mobley to FDR, October 15, 1935; George W. Carroll to FDR, undated (second quotation); Rev. James Hill Couch to FDR, September 27, 1935 (third and fourth quotations); all in Georgia, CL.

76. W. T. Robbins to FDR, October 27, 1935; Kentucky; J. C. Humble to FDR, September 27, 1935, North Carolina; both in CL.

77. B. H. Coker to FDR, undated, Alabama; J. R. Tapp to FDR, November 11, 1935, Texas; both in CL.

78. J. N. Daugherty to FDR, October 1935, Florida; Rev. A. W. Hyche to FDR, September 29, 1935, Georgia; Rev. D. E. Newton to FDR, October 5, 1935, North Carolina; R. G. Joiner to FDR, October 10, 1935, Mississippi; Rev. J. Fraizer to FDR, October 23, 1935, South Carolina; W. J. Crowder to FDR, October 30, 1935, Tennessee; all in CL.

79. F. D. Coppin to FDR, October 14, 1935, Texas; Rev. Alton Pury to FDR, November 5, 1935, Tennessee; D. Taylor to FDR, October 10, 1935, Texas; all in CL.

80. Roosevelt Elliott to FDR, November 9, 1935, Kentucky, CL.

81. Rev. (Mrs.) Maggie L. Cheek to FDR, October 3, 1935, Virginia; Rev. Ida S. Lynch to FDR, October 1, 1935, Virginia; Anne M. Hunter to FDR, September 26, 1935, Florida; all in CL.

82. Mrs. Roy R. Keathley to FDR, October 9, 1935, Alabama; George Reynolds to FDR, October 2, 1935, Kentucky; Rev. John Hembree to FDR, October 7, 1935, Tennessee; all in CL.

83. Rev. J. H. Pope to FDR, October 1, 1935, South Carolina (first quotation); A. J. Goss to FDR, October 1, 1935, Georgia (second quotation); James R. Kincaid to FDR, October 24, 1935, Tennessee (third and fourth quotations); all in CL.

84. Howard S. Irvin to FDR, October 22, 1935, Virginia; A. B. Metcalf to FDR, October 9, 1935, Georgia; T. N. Kincaid to FDR, October 1, 1935, Arkansas; J. H. Walfenbarger to FDR, October 1, 1935, Tennessee; Rev. W. H. Hutson to FDR, October 1, 1935, Tennessee; Rev. John Wilson Lafferty to FDR, October 11, 1935, North Carolina; Rev. W. L. Hughes to FDR, October 3, 1935, North Carolina; Rev. J. E. Risner to FDR, November 20, 1935, Kentucky; Rev. Abner Mills to FDR, October 17, 1935, Kentucky; Rev. Williams Thomas Ida to FDR, October 8, 1935, Kentucky; Rev. P. R. Warren to FDR, September 25, 1935, Arkansas; Rev. R. E. Houston to FDR, October 10, 1935, Louisiana; Rev. J. H. Hooker to FDR, September 26, 1935, Georgia; all in CL.

85. Rev. J. J. Balentine to FDR, October 10, 1935, Arkansas; C. H. Gilliam to FDR, September 25, 1935, Arkansas; D. R. Gulledge to FDR, October 12, 1935, Tennessee; Bertha M. Knight to FDR, December 16, 1936 [1935?], Texas; N. H. Roberts to FDR, October 11, 1935, Mississippi; Rev. K. V. Judd to FDR, November 14, 1935, Kentucky; all in CL.

86. W. M. Ormon to FDR, October 14, 1935, Arkansas; C. F. Messer to FDR, November 1, 1935, Arkansas; Rev. M. C. McDonald to FDR, October 5, 1935, Arkansas; Rev. Garrett Marshalle to FDR, December 16, 1935, Kentucky; Rev. B. P. Coleman to FDR, October 8, 1935, Mississippi; Rev. N. J. Joyner to FDR, October 21, 1935, Tennessee; M. C. White to FDR, October 12, 1935, Georgia; all in CL.

87. E. Newberry to FDR, September 30, 1935, Florida; Lewis P. Kopp to FDR, October 1, 1935, Texas; Harris Gilliam to FDR, April 25, 1936, Tennessee; Rev. J. W. B. Pannell

to FDR, October 28, 1935, Alabama; Rev. J. Blanton to FDR, March 9, 1936, Alabama; Rev. A. C. Stevenson to FDR, October 9, 1935, Alabama; S. L. Loudermilk to FDR, October 2, 1935, Florida; Rev. W. P. Powell to FDR, October 8, 1935, North Carolina; Rev. Thomas A. Little to FDR, October 4, 1935, North Carolina; Rev. W. V. Brown to FDR, September 30, 1935, North Carolina; Rev. Ernest Eaton to FDR, October 1, 1935, Kentucky; D. P. Baker to FDR, October 5, 1935, South Carolina; D. D. Jones to FDR, October 2, 1935, South Carolina; H. P. Bennett to FDR, September 30, 1935, South Carolina; all in CL.

88. J. F. Brown to FDR, October 8, 1935, Georgia; Rev. J. W. Miller to FDR, October 1, 1935, Georgia; Andrew L. Stewart to FDR, September 30, 1935, Georgia; M. G. Cloer to FDR, October 14, 1935, North Carolina; Rev. J. N. Compton to FDR, October 11, 1935, South Carolina; all in CL.

89. Rev. J. P. Clevinger to FDR, October 4, 1935, Kentucky; T. S. Robins to FDR, October 12, 1935, Kentucky; Rev. L. D. Spears to FDR, October 1, 1935, Kentucky; G. S. Gibson to FDR, September 30, 1935, Tennessee; all in CL.

90. Rev. Orion S. Rowlett to FDR, December 3, 1935, Florida (first quotation); Rev. W. C. Portan to FDR, undated, Kentucky (second and third quotations); V. O. McSwain to FDR, October 1935, North Carolina (fourth quotation); C. L. Harris to FDR, September 28, 1935, North Carolina (fifth quotation); all in CL.

91. Rev. L. W. Burns to FDR, October 20, 1935, North Carolina (first and second quotations); Grant T. Mills to FDR, September 30, 1935, North Carolina (third quotation); Rev. J. N. Parker to FDR, September 27, 1935, Georgia; Rev. L. Parris to FDR, October 4, 1935, Georgia; Rev. H. R. Ross to FDR, October 9, 1935, Georgia; Rev. E. K. Ison to FDR, September 30, 1935, Kentucky; Rev. G. K. Fortinberry to FDR, October 4, 1935, Louisiana; all in CL.

Chapter 13

The text of this chapter originally appeared in a slightly different form as "Justice Hugo Black, Judge Roy Moore, the Ten Commandments, and Southern Identity: The Supreme Court and Southern Evangelicalism," Lecture to Baptist History and Heritage Society.

1. Bill J. Leonard, *Baptist Ways: A History* (Valley Forge, PA, Judson Press, 2003), 23–26.

2. *Ibid.*, 26.

3. William R. Estep, *Revolution Within the Revolution: The First Amendment in Historical Context, 1612–1789* (Grand Rapids, MI: William B Eerdmans Publishing Co., 1990, 105–19, 157–60.

4. Edwin S. Gaustad, *Liberty of Conscience: Roger Williams in America* (Grand Rapids, MI: William B. Eerdmans Publishing Co., 1991) 205.

5. Edwin S. Gaustad, *Neither King nor Prelate: Religion and the New Nation, 1776–1826* (Grand Rapids, MI: William B. Eerdmans Publishing Co., 1993), 41.

6. *Ibid.*, 156–58.

7. Edwin S. Gaustad, *Sworn on the Altar of God: A Religious Biography of Thomas Jefferson* (Grand Rapids, MI: William B. Eerdmans Publishing Co., 1996), 98–99.

8. *Ibid.*, 99–100.

9. Edwin S. Gaustad, "Thomas Jefferson, Danbury Baptists, and 'Eternal Hostility,'" *William and Mary Quarterly*, LVI: October 1999, 804.

10. Francis Wayland, *Notes on the Principles and Practices of Baptist Churches, 1856*, (New York: Arno Press Reprint Edition, 1980), 137.

11. *The Economist*, January 13, 2007, 32, attributes this insight to Jewish commentator Seymour Lipset.

12. For a brief discussion of the diverse views of Baptists and Baptist leaders on the issue of separation of church and state, see: "The Changing State of Church and State," *Baptist History and Heritage*, XXXIII: Winter 1998; and Edwin Scott Gaustad, "The Baptist Tradition of Religious Liberty in America," J. W. Dawson Institute of Church-State Studies, Baylor University, no date.

13. *United States Constitution and the Alabama Constitution of 1901, Ninetieth Anniversary Edition, 1991* (Charlottesville, VA: The Michie Company, 1991), 45–46.

14. Wayne Flynt, *Alabama Baptists: Southern Baptists in the Heart of Dixie* (Tuscaloosa: University of Alabama Press, 1998), 246, 250, 252–54, 261–62; quotation on p. 254.

15. *Ibid.*, 318.

16. Hugo Black, Jr. *My Father: A Remembrance* (New York: Random House, 1975), 172.

17. *Ibid.*, 172–74.

18. John Howard Burrows, "The Great Disturber: The Social Philosophy and Theology of Alfred James Dickinson," MA thesis, Samford University, 1970, 97–98.

19. Roger K. Newman, *Hugo Black: A Biography* (New York: Pantheon Books, 1994), 362–63. This is the finest of many biographies of Black and the one I have relied upon for most of my narrative.

20. *Ibid.*, 210–11.

21. Daniel G. Gibbens, "Are We a Christian Nation? The U.S. Supreme Court Response," in *International Perspectives on Church and State*, Manachem Mor, editor (Omaha, NE: Creighton University Press, 1993), 29.

22. Leonard, *Baptist Ways*, 35.

23. Newman, *Hugo Black*, 520–22; quotes from *Engle v. Vitale*, 370 U.S. 421, 82 S. Ct. 1261, 8L. Ed. 2d 601 (1962).

24. Newman, *Hugo Black*, 522–23.

25. Hugo and Elizabeth Black, *Mr. Justice and Mrs. Black: The Memoirs of Hugo L. Black and Elizabeth Black* (New York: Random House, 1986), 95.

26. Newman, *Hugo Black*, 523.

27. *Ibid.*, 524.

28. Hugo and Elizabeth Black, *Mr. Justice and Mrs. Black*, 95.

29. Flynt, *Alabama Baptists*, 489–90.

30. Newman, *Hugo Black*, quoted on 523–24.

31. For a thorough discussion of the Jones-Marsh cases, see Merlin Owen Newton, *Armed with the Constitution: Jehovah's Witnesses in Alabama and the U.S. Supreme Court, 1939–1946* (Tuscaloosa: University of Alabama Press, 1995).

32. Gaustad, *Neither King nor Prelate*, 38.

33. Gibbens, "Are We a Christian Nation?," 29.

34. Gaustad, *Liberty of Conscience*, 218.

35. Tony Freyer, *Hugo L. Black and the Dilemma of American Liberalism* (Glenview, Illinois: Scott, Forsman/Little, Brown Higher Education, 1990), 150. Gerald T. Dunne, *Hugo Black and the Judicial Revolution* (New York: Simon and Schuster, 1977), 370–71.

36. Harvey Cox, "The Warring Visions of the Religious Right," *The Atlantic Monthly* (November 1995), 59–69.

37. Neil A. Lewis, "At the Bar," *New York Times*, August 26, 1994.

38. Jeff Sharlet, "Through a Glass, Darkly," *Harper's Magazine* (May 2005): 33–43.

39. For a thoughtful, brief biography of David Barton, see Nate Blakeslee, "King of the Christocrats," *Texas Monthly* (September 2006): 174–75, 252–76.

40. *Birmingham News*, April 13, 1997.

41. Roy S. Moore, "Religion in the Public Square," *Cumberland Law Review*, 29 (1998–1999): 356–57.

42. *New York Times*, July 2, 2003.

43. "Religion and Government Survey," Capital Survey Research Center Poll, October 27, 2003.

44. *Mobile Register*, October 10, 2005.

45. *The Birmingham News*, January 1 and May 22, 2006.

46. *Ibid.*, May 21, 2006.

47. *Ibid.*, May 21, June 8, 2006.

48. *Ibid.*, February 4, 2007.

49. For Lippy's comprehensive study of religious pluralism, see Charles H. Lippy, *Pluralism Comes of Age* (Armonk, New York: M. E. Sharpe, 2000).

50. *Deep South Jewish Voice* (Birmingham, AL), January–February 2000.

51. *The Birmingham News*, January 14, 2000.

52. *The Mainstream Baptist* (Alabama), March 2007.

53. See, for instance, Mike Smith et al., "Separation of Church and State," in *Empowering Believers: Christian Citizenship Through the Culture Wars* (Nashville: Baptist Center for Ethics, 1996), 21–32.

54. *Birmingham Post-Herald*, April 22, 1998.

55. *Ibid.*, November 3, 1997.

56. *The Alabama Baptist*, October 7, 2004.

57. "Lexington: Shrinking Supremes," *The Economist*, December 16, 2006.

Chapter 14

The text of this chapter originally appeared in a slightly different form as "The South's Battle over God," Lecture at Lyon College, Batesville, Arkansas, November 2, 2006.

1. Walker Percy, *Lancelot* (New York: Farrar, Straus and Giroux, 1977), 176.

2. *Ibid.*, 219–22.

3. *Ibid.*, 219.

4. Harper Lee, *To Kill a Mockingbird* (New York: J. B. Lippincott Company, 1960), 45–46.

5. Eudora Welty, *The Optimist's Daughter* (New York: Random House, 1969, 1972), 108–9.

6. Quoted by Mark Silk, "Old-Time Religion Lives in New South," *Atlanta Constitution*, August 9, 1989.

7. William Faulkner, *Go Down, Moses* (New York: Vintage Books, 1973), 260.

8. *Baptist History and Heritage*, XXVIII (October 1993) 19.

9. *Deep South Jewish Voice*, January–February 2000.

10. *Ibid.*, October 1999. Recently, historians of southern religion have spent as much time describing this emerging pluralism as traditional homogeneity: Preston L. McKever-Ford, "Masks of the Sacred: Religious Pluralism in South Carolina," in Charles H. Lippy, editor, *Religion in South Carolina* (Columbia: University of South Carolina Press, 1993), 153–67; O. Hendall White Jr., and Daryl White, editors, *Religion in the Contemporary South: Diversity, Community, and Identity* (Athens: University of Georgia Press, 1993); Charles Reagan Wilson, *Judgment and Grace in Dixie: Southern Faith from Faulkner to Elvis* (Athens: University of Georgia Press, 1995); Charles H. Lippy, *Pluralism Comes of Age* (New York: M.E. Sharpe, 2000); Beth Barton Schweiger and Donald G. Mathews, editors, *Religion in the South: Protestants and Others in History and Culture* (Chapel Hill: University of North Carolina Press, 2004).

11. *The Alabama Baptist*, May 21, 1992.

12. *Ibid.*, May 13, 1999; *The Birmingham News*, April 26, 1999.

13. *The Birmingham News*, December 20, 2002.

14. *Ibid.*, September 12, 2006.

15. *Ibid.*, March 1, 1997.

16. *The Alabama Baptist*, June 5, 1997.

17. *Los Angeles Times*, March 19, 1994.

18. C. Kirk Hadaway, Penny Long Marler, and Mark Chaves, "What the Polls Don't Show: A Closer Look at U.S. Church Attendance," *American Sociological Review*, 58: December 1993.

19. *The Birmingham News*, May 20, 1990.

20. *The Birmingham News*, January 14, 2000.

21. *The Alabama Baptist*, October 5, 2006.

22. *The Birmingham News*, September 18, 1989 and July 25, 1992; *Baptists Today*, February 17, 1994.

23. *Birmingham Post-Herald*, June 13, 1995.

24. *Atlanta Journal-Constitution*, May 22, 1994; *Baptists Today*, July 14, 1994.

25. James Sellers, *The South and Christian Ethics* (New York: Associated Press, 1962), especially 47–51.

26. Bill J. Leonard, "Religion in the South: Profiles for the Future," mss. in possession of author.

27. *The Birmingham News*, August 23, 2006.

28. *Atlanta Journal-Constitution*, March 1, 1992.

29. *The Birmingham News*, April 14, 2004.

30. *New York Times*, March 4, 2003.

31. *Birmingham Post-Herald*, August 16, 2003).

32. E. O. Wilson, *Naturalist* (Washington, D.C.: Island Press/Shearwater Books, 1994), 33–46, 191–92; John M. Mulder, *Woodrow Wilson: The Years of Preparation* (Princeton, NJ: Princeton University Press, 1978), 1.

33. *The Economist*, March 18–24, 2006, 8.

34. Warren A. Nord, "Religious Literacy, Textbooks, and Religious Neutrality," *Religion & Education*, 16 (Winter 1989), 111–12.

35. Ira Berkow, "At Wit's End with 'We're No. 1,'" *New York Times*, January 7, 1984.

36. James Webb, "In Defense of Joe Six-Pack," *The Wall Street Journal*, June 5, 1995.

37. "Born Again! The Evangelicals," *Newsweek*, October 25, 1976; and "Born Again Politics," *Newsweek*, September 15, 1980.

38. Stetson Kennedy, "The Four Freedoms Down South," unpublished mss. in Stetson Kennedy Papers, Southern Labor Archives, Georgia State University, Atlanta, Georgia.

39. *The Birmingham News*, February 15, 2005.

40. *The Birmingham News*, May 9, 2005.

41. Wayne Flynt, *Alabama in the Twentieth Century*, (Tuscaloosa: University of Alabama Press, 2004), 187.

42. *The Birmingham News*, December 30, 1999.

43. *Ibid.*, November 12, 2003.

44. Sellers, *The South and Christian Ethics*, quotes on p. 115.

45. Quoted in Paul Harvey, *Redeeming the South: Religious Cultures and Racial Identities Among Southern Baptists, 1865–1925* (Chapel Hill: University of North Carolina Press, 1997) 191.

46. Shirley Ann Grau, *The Keepers of the House* (New York: Alfred A. Knopf, 1964), 143.

47. See Mark Newman, *Getting Right with God: Southern Baptists and Desegregation, 1945–1995* (Tuscaloosa: University of Alabama Press, 2001), 30.

48. For divisions within southern Methodists and Presbyterians emanating from conservative views on politics, theology, and race, see: Joel L. Alvis Jr., *Religion and Race: Southern Presbyterians, 1946–1983* (Tuscaloosa: University of Alabama Press, 1994); Peter C. Murray, *Methodists and the Crucible of Race, 1930–1975* (Colombia: University of Missouri Press, 2004); "'A Search for Life's Meaning': Religion and Civil Rights," in Randy J. Sparks, *Religion in Mississippi* (Jackson: University Press of Mississippi, 2001), 221–48; Donald E. Collins, *When The Church Bell Rang Racist* (Macon, GA: Mercer University Press, 1998); Merrill M. Hawkins Jr., *Will Campbell: Radical Prophet of the South* (Macon, GA: Mercer University Press, 1997). Many ministers penned memoirs of evangelical church anguish and division during the 1960s and 1970s. Two representative samples are: J. Herbert Gilmore Jr., *They Chose to Live: The Racial Agony of An American Church* (Birmingham First Baptist) (Grand Rapids: Eerdmans Publishing Co., 1972); W. J. Cunningham, *Agony at Galloway: One Church's Struggle with Social Change* (Galloway Memorial Methodist Church, Jackson, Mississippi) (Jackson: University Press of Mississippi, 1980).

Chapter 15

The text of this chapter originally appeared in a slightly different form as "God's Politics: Is Southern Religion Blue, Red, or Purple?," a lecture first presented at Lyon College in Batesville, Arkansas, then regularly updated and presented at The Southern Progressive Alliance for Exploring Religion (Birmingham), Baylor University (Texas), Mary Hardin Baylor University (Texas), and the Southern Regional Phi Alpha Theta Meeting (Auburn University, 2014).

1. For a full description of this incident, see *The Economist*, April 5–11, 2014, 29.

2. For excellent examples, see Brook Hays, *Politics is My Parish* (Baton Rouge: Louisiana State University Press, 1981); Oran P. Smith, *The Rise of Baptist Republicanism* (New York: New York University Press, 1997).

3. Christine Wicker, *The Fall of the Evangelical Nation* (New York: Harper One, 2008), ix.

4. *Ibid.*, 17–28.

5. *Ibid.*, 52–55.

6. *Ibid.*, 60–62.

7. *Ibid*, 86–92.

8. *Ibid.*, 99, 114–15, 118, 124–25, 135–36, 143, 196–98.

9. *The Economist*, October 9, 2010, 47–48.

10. Allan J. Lichtman, *White Protestant Nation: The Rise of the American Conservative Movement* (New York: Atlantic Monthly Press, 2008). Religion's place in American politics has become a flourishing cottage industry. For examples, see: David Barton, *The Jefferson Lies: Exposing the Myths You've Always Believed About Thomas Jefferson* (Nashville: Thomas Nelson, 2012); Warren Throckmorton and Michael Coulter, *Getting Jefferson Right: Fact Checking Claims About Our Third President* (Grove City, PA: Salem Grove Press, 2012); Patrick Hynes, *In Defense of the Religious Right* (Nashville: Nelson Current, 2006); Kathleen Kennedy Townsend, *Failing America's Faithful: How Today's Churches are Mixing God with Politics and Losing Their Way* ((New York: Warner Books, 2007); Senator John Danforth, *Faith and Politics: How the "Moral Values" Debate Divides America and How to Move Forward Together* (New York: Viking Press, 2006).

11. *New York Times*, September 30, 1986. *The New Republic* headlined a front page story, "America's Ayatollahs: The Fundamentalist Popular Four," September 29, 1986.

12. *The Birmingham News*, April 7, 2002. *New York Times*, November 2, 1998.

13. *The Alabama Baptist*, September 25, 1997.

14. Clyde Wilcox, "Religious Orientations and Political Attitudes: Variations Within the New Christian Right," *American Politic Quarterly* 15 (April 1987) 274–89; *Birmingham Post-Herald*, April 17, 1992; *The Birmingham News*, February 26, 1994; *New York Times*, May 30, 2004.

15. CBS News, September 24, 2004.

16. *Birmingham Post-Herald*, November 3, 1997.

17. *Boston Globe*, May 13, 2005; *The Birmingham News*, June 24 and August 24, 2005.

18. For white evangelical disillusion with the GOP, see David Kuo, *Tempting Faith: An Inside Story of Political Seduction* (New York: Free Press, 2006).

19. "Facing South," The Institute for Southern Studies, September 27, 2006.

20. Quoted in *The Birmingham News*, March 19, 1999.

21. *National Liberty Journal*, 35 (November 2006); *Birmingham News*, May 8, 2008; see also "The New Evangelicals," *USA Today*, October 6, 2008.

22. *Baptists Today*, February 2009.

23. "Politics in the Pulpit? Alabama Pastors Take a Stand," *AL.com*, October 25, 2012.

24. For comprehensive data, see "How the Faithful Voted: 2012 Preliminary Analysis," Pew Forum on Religion and Politics, November 7, 2012.

25. "113th Congress more religiously diverse, less Protestant," *Report from the Capital*, January 2013, Baptist Joint Committee for Religious Liberty.

Wayne Flynt's Works about Southern Religion Published in Books, Journals, and Anthologies from 1963 to 2011

"Reform Oratory in Alabama," *Southern Speech Journal*, XXIX (Winter 1963), 94–106.

"The Negro and Alabama Baptists During the Progressive Era," *Journal of the Alabama Academy of Science* 39 (April 1968), 163–67.

"Dissent in Zion: Alabama Baptists and Social Issues, 1900–1914." *Journal of Southern History*, XXXV (November 1969): 523–42. Reprinted in *Modern American Protestantism and Its World*, edited by Martin Marty. Reed Reference Publishing, 1993.

"The Ethics of Democratic Persuasion and the Birmingham Crisis," *Southern Speech Journal*, XXXV (Fall 1969), 40–53. Reprinted in *Ethics in Human Communication*, edited by Richard L. Johannesen. Columbus, OH: Charles E. Merrill Co., 1975; and in *Reader in Speech Communication*, edited by James W. Gibson. New York: McGraw-Hill Co., 1972.

"Organized Labor, Reform, and Alabama Politics, 1920," *Alabama Review*, XXIII (July 1970) 163–80.

"Alabama White Protestantism and Labor, 1900–1914," *Alabama Review*, XXV (July 1972), 107–28.

"Baptists and Reform," *Baptist History and Heritage* (October 1972), 211–22.

"Religion in the Land of Cotton," co-authored with Wallace M. Alston Jr., in *You Can't Eat Magnolias*, edited by Brandt Ayers. New York: McGraw-Hill, 1972.

"Religion in the Urban South: The Divided Religious Mind of Birmingham, 1900–1930," *Alabama Review*, XXX (April 1977), 108–34.

"Southern Baptists: Rural to Urban Transition," *Baptist History and Heritage*, XVI (January 1981), 24–34.

Essays on "Frank Willis Barnett" and "Sidney J. Catts," in *Encyclopedia of Southern Baptists*: III, 1608; IV, 2151: Broadman Press, 1971 and 1982.

"One in the Spirit, Many in the Flesh: Southern Evangelicalism," in *Varieties of Southern Evangelicalism*, edited by David E. Harrell Jr. Macon, GA: Mercer University Press, 1981.

"The Impact of Social Factors on Southern Baptist Expansion, 1800–1914," *Baptist History and Heritage*, XVII (July 1982), 20–31.

"Feeding the Hungry and Ministering to the Broken Hearted: The Presbyterian Church in the United States and the Social Gospel, 1900–1940," in *Religion in the South*, edited by Charles R. Wilson. Jackson: University of Mississippi Press, 1984.

"Alabama," *Encyclopedia of Religion in the South*, edited by Samuel S. Hill. Macon, GA: Mercer University Press, 1984, 8–22.

"Growing Up Baptist in Anniston, Alabama: The Legacy of the Reverend Charles R. Bell Jr., in *Clearings in the Thicket: An Alabama Humanities Reader*, edited by Jerry Elijah Brown. Macon, GA: Mercer University Press, 1985.

"Southern Baptists in Georgia," in *A Sourcebook for Teachers of Georgia History*, edited by James L. Hill. Columbus, GA: Brentwood University Press, for Georgia Humanities Foundation, 1986.

"Women, Society, and the Southern Church, 1900–1920," *Religion in the South: Conference Papers*: Alabama Humanities Foundation, 1986.

"Southern Protestantism and Reform, 1890–1930," in *Varieties of Southern Religious Experience*, edited by Samuel Hill. Baton Rouge, Louisiana State University Press, 1988.

"Southern Baptists and Appalachia: A Case Study of Modernization and Community," *Crossroads: A Journal of Southern Culture*, 2 (Fall 1993/Winter 1994), 59–76.

"Religion at the Polls: A Case Study of Twentieth Century Politics and Religion in Florida," *Florida Historical Quarterly*, LXXII, 4 (April 1994), 469–83.

"'A Special Feeling of Closeness': Mt. Hebron Baptist Church, Leeds, Alabama," in *American Congregations, Volume I: Portraits of Twelve Religious Communities*, edited by James P. Wind and James W. Lewis. Chicago: University of Chicago Press, 1994.

"The Baptists: Southern Religion and Emigres to Brazil, 1865–1885," in *The Confederados: Old South Immigrants to Brazil*, Cyrus B. Dawsey and James M. Dawsey, editors: University of Alabama Press, 1995.

"Southern Methodists and Social Reform," *International Social Science Review*, 74 (Issue 3/4 1999), 104–15.

"Alabama Baptists and the Second World War," *Baptist History and Heritage*, 36 (Summer/Fall 2001), 64–71.

"A Pilgrim's Progress Through Southern Christianity," in *Autobiographical Reflections on Southern Religious History*, edited by John B. Boles. Athens: University of Georgia Press, 2001.

"Not an Island unto Itself: Southern Baptists and the New Theological Trends (Liberalism, Ecumenism, and the Social Gospel) 1890–1940," *American Baptist Quarterly*, XXII (June 2003), 158–79.

"The Social Gospel and Richmond Baptists, 1900–1930," in *Profiles in Social Ministry*, edited by Fred Anderson. Richmond, VA: Center for Baptist Heritage and Studies, University of Richmond, 2004.

"Religion for the Blues: Evangelicalism, Poor Whites, and the Great Depression," *Journal of Southern History*, LXXI (February 2005), 3–28.

"The Persistence of Evangelical Denominationalism in the South and the Case for Denominational History," in *Religion in the Contemporary South: Changes, Continuities, and Contexts*, edited by Corrie E. Norman and Don S. Armentrout. Knoxville: University of Tennessee Press, 2005.

"Baptists in Black and White: Evangelical Diversity during the Montgomery, Alabama Bus Boycott," in *Baptist Identities: International Studies from the Seventeenth to the*

Twentieth Century, Volume 19, Studies in Baptist History and Thought, edited by Ian M. Randall, Toivo Pill, and Anthony R. Cross. Bletchley, UK: Paternostler, 2006.

"The Christian Scholar as Public Intellectual: The Struggle for Justice in Alabama," in *Thinking Christianly: Christian Higher Education and a Vigorous Life of the Mind: Essays in Memory of Thomas E. Corts*, edited by Paul R. Corts. Birmingham, AL: Sherman Oak Books of Samford University Press, 2011.

Books about Southern Religion by Wayne Flynt

Cracker Messiah: Governor Sidney J. Catts of Florida. Baton Rouge: Louisiana State University Press, 1977.

Taking Christianity to China: Alabama Missionaries in the Middle Kingdom. Tuscaloosa: University of Alabama Press, 1997. (Flynt was coauthor with Gerald W. Berkley.)

Alabama Baptists: Southern Baptists in the Heart of Dixie. Tuscaloosa: University of Alabama Press, 1998.

Index